Financial Markets
A Practicum

Elisabeth Oltheten
Kevin G. Waspi

Dedicated to the many students who, with good-natured humor, helped us correct the errors and omissions in the previous edition of the book. An to our colleagues who challenged us at every turn: Joe Finnerty, Matt Marcinkowski, David Sinow, and Theodore Sougiannis. With all this help it must be obvious that any remaining errors are our own fault.

greatriver
TECHNOLOGIES

Contents

Timeline

$\mathcal{A}$ study of financial markets and instruments requires a number of skills and abilities as building blocks. Like any structure, it is stronger if the foundation is well prepared. And, like any structure, the lack of foundation often goes unnoticed until the structure is under stress. Then the cracks begin to show.

If finance or financial markets is just a casual interest then the cracks don't really matter. But if finance is a profession then the cracks undermine the foundations of that profession and undermine you as a professional.

The dictionary provides several definitions for professional. Most of us prefer the Olympic games definition in that we all hope to make a considerable amount of money as professionals in finance. But there is a further definition. The *American Heritage Dictionary* states that a professional is someone with assured competence in a particular field or occupation. This definition is much more in line with the wisdom on the street which maintains that a professional is someone who pursues excellence for it's own sake.

Throughout your careers you will meet and compete with individuals who do exactly what is required; no more and no less. But the promotions and recognition will eventually go to those who go the extra mile: the true professionals. That touch of professionalism in your work tells your colleagues, your employers, your employees, your clients and—most importantly—yourself, that you are a respected expert in your field. It is a fact of life that a professional earns a degree of trust and credibility that nonprofessionals lack.

Nobody expects perfection; indeed the pursuit of perfection can lead to obsession rather than to professionalism. But we all expect the people with whom we associate to exhibit that degree of professionalism. We need to know that they have the degree of competence or expertise required to do the job, whether that job is managing a $500 million estate, governing a country, or returning a message.

Acquiring the degree of expertise required of a professional is not easy—if it were easy then everybody would do it—but it is worthwhile.

Chapter A   Math
Chapter B   Finance

F inance is communicated largely through numbers. This means that a degree of comfort with mathematics is absolutely essential. The level of mathematical expertise required at this introductory level is not high, but basic algebra is a necessity. Leaning to translate between English and math is a skill that requires practice. In many ways finance is one huge word problem. If you keep getting answers in gallons instead of miles, in assets instead of liabilities, then there is another Enron or Worldcom in the making.

A.1 - Mathematical Accuracy & Rounding

A portfolio with a published rate of return of 4.0% could have a rate of return anywhere between 3.950% and 4.049%, whereas a portfolio with a published rate of return of 4% could actually have a rate of return anywhere between 3.500% and 4.499%.

More numbers to the right of the decimal place implies more precision.

Example 1:

> An invitation to dinner for 6 pm allows you to arrive fashionably late. Anywhere to 6:30 is acceptable. At 6:31 you are closer to arriving at 7 pm rather than 6pm and, though late, it's no longer fashionable.

An invitation to a meeting at 6:03 pm means you better be there by 6:03 pm. The extra precision in the invitation communicates less tolerance for deviation.

Example 2:

> In February 1992, an American Patriot missile out of Dhahran, Saudi Arabia, failed to intercept an incoming Scud missile. The Scud hit an Army barracks killing 28. The General Accounting Office (GAO) attributed the failure to a rounding error in the guidance system.[1]

> *Calculator Techniques A-1:*
>
> Your calculator rounds according the number of decimal places specified. To change the specification use [2nd] [Format] choose the number of decimal places and [Enter].
>
> To specify a floating decimal use [2ND] [FORMAT] [9] [ENTER]. A floating decimal allows the calculator to show as many places to the right of the decimal as it needs.

---

1   The General Accounting Office B-247094, February 4, 1992 (www.fas.org/spp/starwars/gao/im92026.htm)

A.2 - Order of Operation

Mathematics is a precise language. An equation is solved left to right within the following hierarchy:

1. Parentheses
2. Exponents
3. Multiplication and Division
4. Addition and Subtraction

Example 3:

The price of a $100,000, 270 day T-bill quoted a bankers discount rate of 2.5% is given by

$$Price = \$100,000 \left[1 - 0.025 \frac{270}{360} \right] \qquad (Eq\ A\text{-}1)$$

Within the parentheses
...multiplication and division $\qquad Price = \$100,000 \left[1 - 0.01875 \right]$
...addition and subtraction $\qquad Price = \$100,000 \left[0.98125 \right]$
Outside the parentheses
...multiplication and division $\qquad Price = \$98,125$

If you forget the order of operations you erroneously calculate a price of $73,125.00; this $25,000 error can generate an F for Fired or a J for Jail time.

Multiplication and division associated with parentheses have added strength by association.

Example 4:

$$16 \div 2(2) \neq 16 \div 2 * 2$$

Parentheses $\qquad\qquad 16 \div 4 \neq 16 \div 2 * 2$

...multiplication and division $\qquad\qquad 4 \neq 16$

A.3 - Exponents

Exponents are shorthand for multiplication. Thus:

$$x * x = x^2$$

$$x^n * x^m = x^{n+m}$$

$$\left(x^n \right)^m = x^{n*m}$$

$$\sqrt[n]{x} = x^{1/n}$$

$$x^{-n} = \frac{1}{x^n}$$

Calculator Techniques A-2:

Although the calculator has [$\sqrt{n}$] and [x^2] buttons, more complicated exponents must all be done with the [y^x] button.

This means that to calculate $\sqrt[3]{125}$ we translate into $125^{1/3}$ and calculate
[1][2][5] [y^x] [( ] [3] [1/x] [ )] [=]

Example 5:

The rate of return on a portfolio for the first five months of the year is 6.0%.

The monthly time weighted rate of return is

$$\sqrt[5]{1.060} = 1.060^{1/5} = 1.060^{0.2} = 1.011721951 = 1 + 1.17\%$$

The annualized time weighted rate of return is

$$\left(\sqrt[5]{1.060} \right)^{12} = 1.060^{\frac{12}{5}} = 1.060^{2.4} = 1.150095957 = 1 + 15.01\%$$

Note that in this example we calculate the annualized rate of return from the 6.0% given, not from the 1.17% we calculated in the first equation. To do so would cause a rounding error; we would calculate a return of 14.98% rather than of 15.01%

Calculator Techniques A-3:

Your calculator has ten memory slots numbered 0 through 9. It is far easier to put a number in memory than to write it down and type it back into the calculator again.

To store a number in memory slot zero just use [STO][0]; to recall that number use [RCL][0].

A.4 - Dimensional Analysis

Dimensional analysis is a technical term for making sure the units come out right.

Example 6:

You have $3,500 and are heading for Amsterdam. The exchange rate is given as $1.24. You are not quite sure if that means that you have 4,340 euros or 2,822 euros and change. But now compare the two calculations:

$$\$3,500 * \frac{\$1.24}{€1} = \frac{\$}{€} \frac{\$\,4,340.00}{1}$$

$$\$3,500 * \frac{€1}{\$1.24} = \frac{\$\,€}{\$} \frac{3,500}{1.24} = €2,822.58$$

When we include units we can see that €2,822.58 makes a good deal more sense than $$4,340/€

Example 7:

In 1997 NASA lost a $125 million Mars Climate Orbiter because the calculations that determined the thrusters were based on pounds and feet rather than newtons and meters.[2]

A.5 - Simultaneous Equations

Simultaneous equations refers a set of equations that must be solved at the same time.

First, make sure that the set of equations are solvable: there must be one equation for each unknown. To solve for x, y, and z you need three separate equations. If there are only two equations, then one of the variables can only be solved in terms of the other two: z = x + y rather than z = 7.

Then solve the equations either by elimination or by substitution:

Example 8:

Your executive assistant brings coffee and doughnuts for your Monday morning strategy meetings. Last week he brought 2 cups of coffee and 3 doughnuts and submitted an expense of $2.80. This week he brought 4 cups of coffee and 1 doughnut and submitted an expense of $2.60. What is the per unit price of coffee and doughnuts?

---

2   "Math Error Equals Loss of Mars Orbiter", *Science News*, Vol. 156, no. 15 (October 9, 1999): 229.

Variables: We are asked to calculate the price of a cup of coffee (call it c) and the price of a doughnut (call it d).

Equations: $2c + 3d = \$2.80$ (Eq A-2)
                          $4c + d = \$2.60$ (Eq A-3)

Elimination: Multiply equation (A-2) by 2 and equation (A-3) by −1 then add.

$$4c + 6d = \$5.60$$
$$\underline{-4c - d = -\$2.60}$$
$$5d = \$3.00$$
$$d = \$0.60$$

Then substitute d = \$0.60 into either (A-2) or (A-3). If you don't get the same answer then you made a mistake somewhere.

$$2c + 3\,(\$0.60) = \$2.80 \qquad 4c + (\$0.60) = \$2.60$$
$$2c = \$1.00 \qquad\qquad 4c = \$2.00$$
$$c = \$0.50 \qquad\qquad c = \$0.50$$

Substitution: Solve (A-3) for one variable and then substitute into (A-2).

$$4c + d = \$2.60 \qquad (A\text{-}3)$$
$$d = \$2.60 - 4c$$

$$2c + 3d = \$2.80 \qquad (A\text{-}2)$$
$$2c + 3\,(\$2.60 - 4c) = \$2.80$$
$$2c + \$7.80 - 12c = \$2.80$$
$$10c = \$5.00$$
$$c = \$0.50$$

$$d = \$2.60 - 4(\$0.50) \qquad (A\text{-}3)$$
$$d = \$0.60$$

In either case coffee costs 50¢, and doughnuts cost 60¢.

A.6 - Summation Series

Summation series allow us to solve summations directly without summing a long series of numbers. The technique is to eliminate the series of unnumbered terms though subtraction. Essentially, the subtraction is engineered to let the middle terms cancel each other out, leaving us with the first term in the sum minus the last term in the sum.

The present value of a constant flow of payment C can be simplified from a summation to a simple formula.

$$P_n = \sum_{t=1}^{n} \frac{C_t}{(1+r)^t} \qquad \text{(Eq A-4)}$$

$$P_n = \frac{C_1}{(1+r)^1} + \frac{C_2}{(1+r)^2} + \frac{C_3}{(1+r)^3} + \ldots + \frac{C_n}{(1+r)^n}$$

$$\frac{P_n}{(1+r)} = \frac{C_1}{(1+r)^2} + \frac{C_2}{(1+r)^3} + \frac{C_3}{(1+r)^4} + \ldots + \frac{C_n}{(1+r)^{n+1}}$$

$$\text{If} \quad C_1 = C_2 = C_3 = \ldots = C_n \quad \text{then}$$

$$P_n - \frac{P_n}{(1+r)} = \frac{C}{(1+r)^1} - \frac{C}{(1+r)^{n+1}}$$

$$\frac{(1+r)P_n - P_n}{(1+r)} = \frac{C}{(1+r)}\left[1 - \frac{1}{(1+r)^n}\right]$$

$$rP_n = C\left[1 - \frac{1}{(1+r)^n}\right]$$

$$P_n = \frac{C}{r}\left[1 - \frac{1}{(1+r)^n}\right] \qquad \text{(Eq A-5)}$$

A.7 - Graphs

A graph is a picture of a mathematical sentence. A two-dimensional graph illustrates a relationship between two variables. Generally the independent variable is graphed on the horizontal (x) axis and the dependent variable is graphed on the vertical (y) axis.

Example 9:

The price of a $100,000 270 day T-bill depends on the Bankers' Discount Rate at which the T-bill is quoted.

$$\text{Price} = \$100,000\left[1 - \text{Rate} * \frac{270}{360}\right]$$

$$= \$100,000 - \$75,000 * \text{Rate}$$

There is a relationship between the Bankers Discount Rate (the independent variable on the x axis) and the price of the T-bill (the dependent variable on the y axis). For any rate we can calculate the price at that rate; for any price we can calculate the rate that generated that price. This relationship is graphed in Figure A-1.

Figure A-1: Price of a 270 day T-bill with respect to the Bankers' Discount Rate

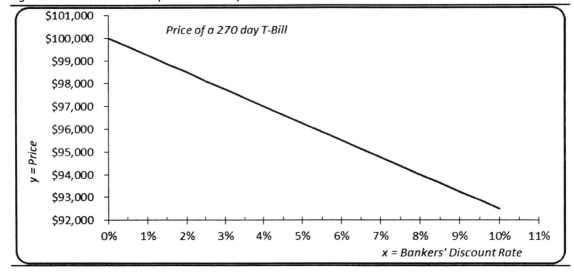

A.8 - Stock Price Charts

Stock graphs are a picture of the price of a stock over time. The independent variable is time and the dependent variable is the stock price.

A.8.1 - High-Low-Close Charts

A high-low-close chart shows the entire range of price movement for the relevant time period. In each time period a vertical line from the lowest to the highest price shows the price range; a horizontal tick marks show the closing price. A high-low-close graph thus has three dependent variables.

Figure A-2: Monthly High-Low-Close Chart of Google (GOOG) from August 2004 to May 2012

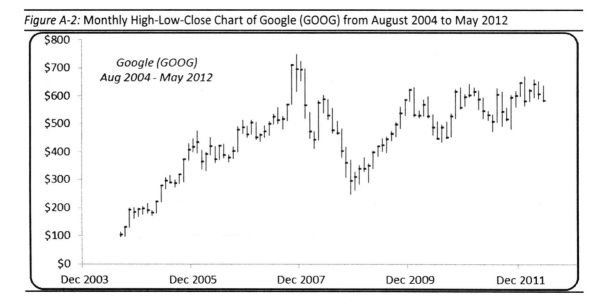

A.8.2 - Candlestick Chart

A candlestick chart also shows the entire range of price movement for the relevant time period. In each time period a vertical line from the lowest to the highest price shows the price range. This is the stick. A bar shows the open and closing price. If the closing price is higher than the open then the bar is white, indicating a positive rate of return. If the closing price is lower than the open then the bar is black, indicating a negative rate of return. There are infinite variations on the color combinations, but the light color indicates that the price is increasing; the dark color that it is decreasing.

A high-low-close graph thus has four dependent variables.

Figure A-3: Monthly Candlestick Chart of Google (GOOG) from August 2004 to May 2012

A.9 - Normal Distribution

Statistics tell us that if you have a large number of random events they will tend to distribute in a normal distribution. The normal distribution is a probability distribution with some convenient properties.

In a normal distribution with mean μ and standard deviation σ, observations will be

± one standard deviation of the mean 68.27% of the time,
± two standard deviations of the mean 95.45% of the time, and
± three standard deviations of the mean 99.73% of the time.

Actual distributions are rarely exactly symmetrical, especially stock prices, which cannot be negative. So the normal distribution represents an idealized form. However, many distributions are close enough to the normal that they can be treated as possessing normal characteristics.

Figure A-4: Standard Normal Distribution

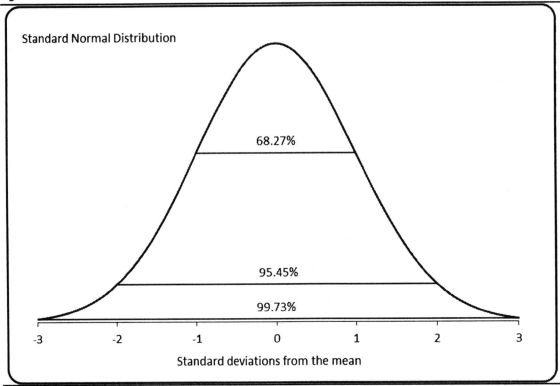

A.10 - *Variance & Standard Deviation*

Variance and standard deviation measure how far from the average individuals can be.

Example 10:

Consider the performance of an hypothetical stock fund. The average or expected return on the fund is 11% but, depending on the state of the economy, there will be a surprise or deviation from that expected return.

Table A-1: Calculating Standard Deviation

Scenario	prob-ability	Return R	Return^2 R^2	Deviation $(R - E[R])$		Deviation^2 $(R - E[R])^2$
Boom	1/3	+ 28.%	784	28% - 11% =	17%	17^2 = 289.
Normal	1/3	+ 12.%	144	12% - 11% =	1%	1^2 = 1.
Bust	1/3	-7.%	49	-7% - 11% =	- 18%	-18^2 = 324.
Sum:		33.%	977		0%	614.
Average:		$E[R]$ = 11.%	$E[R^2]$ = 325.667			σ^2 = 204.667

Technically, R^2 should technically be expressed as %%—but this makes no sense—so we leave it as a simple number. Note that 28^2 = 784 and 0.28^2 = 0.0784. Just remember to be consistent.

The expected return E[R] is 11%. When we don't see what we expect this is called the deviation. The deviation measures the surprise. The variance is the average squared surprise.

The variance and standard deviation can be calculated as

$$\sigma^2 = E[R^2] - E[R]^2$$
$$= 325.667 - 11^2$$
$$= 204.667$$
$$\sigma = 14.3062\%$$

(Eq A-6)

Calculator Techniques A-4:

Use [2ND][STAT] to obtain the statistics: [2ND] [ENTER] toggles the statistical rules between 1-V, LIN, Ln, EXP, and PWR. For one variable statistics we need 1-V.

We can now calculate the number of observations (n), mean (x), sample standard deviation (Sx), population standard deviation (σx), and sum of both X and X2.

DATA	enter	STAT	calculate
X01 =	28	1-V	
Y01 =		n =	3.0000
X02 =	12	x =	11.0000
Y02 =		Sx =	17.5214
X03 =	-7	σx =	14.3062
Y03 =		$\sum$X =	33.0000
		$\sum$X^2 =	977.0000

A.11 - Population versus Sample Statistics

If we are working with historical data rather than expectations or probabilities then we lose one degree of freedom. We now have an average rather than a true mean; a sample variance rather than a true variance.

❑ **Degrees of Freedom:** The number of independent components of a system minus the number of parameters or necessary relationships.

Degrees of freedom is the statistical equivalent of needing at least two points to define one line.

The variance on the first observation is 0 regardless of the variance of the population from which the observation is drawn. So the first observation tells us nothing. Thus when we sample a population we must adjust the measured variance for that first observation.

Population Variance $\quad \sigma^2 = \sum_i p_i (X_i - \mu)^2 \quad where \quad p_i \; is \; the \; probability \; of \; X_i$ (Eq A-7)

Sample Variance $\quad S^2 = \dfrac{n}{n-1} \dfrac{\sum_i (X_i - E[X])^2}{n}$ (Eq A-8)

Example 11:

We observe rates of change on the Dow Jones Industrial Average given in Table A-2.

Table A-2: Annual returns on the Dow Jones Industrial Average

Year	Return R	Return^2 R^2	Deviation (R - E[R])			Deviation^2 (R - E[R])^2
1999	25.221%	0.06361	25.221% - 3.481%	=	21.740%	0.04726
2000	-6.168%	0.00380	-6.168% - 3.481%	=	-9.649%	0.00931
2001	-7.104%	0.00505	-7.104% - 3.481%	=	-10.585%	0.01120
2002	-16.763%	0.02810	-16.763% - 3.481%	=	-20.244%	0.04098
2003	25.322%	0.06412	25.322% - 3.481%	=	21.841%	0.04770
2004	3.148%	0.00099	3.148% - 3.481%	=	-0.333%	0.00001
2005	-0.608%	0.00004	-0.608% - 3.481%	=	-4.089%	0.00167
2006	16.288%	0.02653	16.288% - 3.481%	=	12.807%	0.01640
2007	6.432%	0.00414	6.432% - 3.481%	=	2.951%	0.00087
2008	-33.837%	0.11449	-33.837% - 3.481%	=	-37.318%	0.13926
2009	18.819%	0.03542	18.819% - 3.481%	=	15.338%	0.02353
2010	11.023%	0.01215	11.023% - 3.481%	=	7.542%	0.00569
Sum:	41.773%	0.35844			0.000%	0.34389
Average:	3.481%	0.02987			0.000%	0.02866

We calculate the population and sample variance.

$$\sigma^2 : \quad E\,[R^2] - E\,[R]^2 \qquad = 0.02987 - 0.03481^2 \qquad = 0.02866$$

$$\sigma : \quad = 0.16929$$

$$s^2 : \quad \frac{n}{n-1}\left(E\,[R^2] - E\,[R]^2\right) \quad = \frac{12\left(0.02987 - 0.03481^2\right)}{11} \quad = 0.03126$$

$$s : \quad = 0.17681$$

The population standard deviation of 16.929% would be appropriate only if each year represented a possible scenario with the equal probability, but because we lose one degree of freedom in using sample data, the standard deviation is actually 17.681%

A.12 - Covariance

Covariance measures to what degree two variables move in tandem.

❑ **Procyclical:** An economic or financial measure that is positively correlated with the business cycle.

❑ **Countercyclical:** An economic or financial measure that is negatively correlated with the business cycle.

Thus gross domestic product (GDP), wages and salaries, and the price level tend to be procyclical. They increase during an upswing in the business cycle. Unemployment and education tend to increase during a downswing in the economy.

Example 12:

Consider the performance of the two hypothetical funds in Table A-3: a stock fund whose performance is procyclical, and a bond fund whose performance is countercyclical.

		Stock Fund		Bond Fund		
Scenario	Prob-ability	Return S	Deviation $S - \bar{S}$	Return B	Deviation $B - \bar{B}$	Co-Deviation $(S-\bar{S})(B-\bar{B})$
Boom	25%	+ 28%	+ 17%	- 3%	- 10%	- 170%
Normal	50%	+ 12%	+ 1%	+ 7%	0%	0%
Bust	25%	- 8%	- 19%	+ 17%	+ 10%	- 190%
Expected Value:		+ 11%	0%	+ 7%	0%	Cov = - 90%

Table A-3: Covariance of Hypothetical Stock and Bond Funds

The covariance of −90.0 tells us that there is an inverse relationship between the two funds; they move in opposite directions. The negative number results from the multiplication of a positive deviation and a negative deviation; if the deviations were both positive or both negative, then they would be moving in the same direction and the product of the two would be positive.

The variance of a number is the covariance with itself.

$$Cov_{x,y} = E\left[(X - E[X])(Y - E[Y]) \right]$$

$$Cov_{x,x} = E\left[(X - E[X])(X - E[X]) \right] = Var_x$$

(Eq A-9)

A.13 - Correlation

The magnitude of the covariance means very little except in relationship to the deviations of the variables themselves. To deal with this we calculate the correlation coefficient (rho).

$$\rho = \frac{Cov_{S,B}}{\sigma_S \, \sigma_B}$$

(Eq A-10)

$$\rho = \frac{-90.0}{12.7671 * 7.0711} = -0.9969$$

The correlation coefficient ρ can vary from +1 to −1.

ρ = −1 is a teeter-totter: when one end goes up the other must come down.
ρ = 0 is an ocean: the waves interact but their pattern appears to be completely random.
ρ = +1 is a scaffold: when one side does down the other side goes down by the same amount.

Calculator Techniques A-5:

Use [2ND][DATA] [2ND][CLR WORK] to clear old data

Use [2ND][DATA] to enter data.

Use [2ND][STAT] to obtain the statistics: [2ND] [ENTER] toggles the statistical rules between 1-V, LIN, Ln, EXP, and PWR. For two variable statistics we need LIN.

Note also that the calculator is designed to calculate from observations where each observation has a probability of 1/n. If we simply enter the numbers for boom, normal, and bust, each will be assigned a probability of 1/3.

In order to extract meaningful numbers from this calculation we enter the observations for normal economic growth twice. This way each of the four observations is assigned a probability of 1/4 with normal economic growth being assigned 1/4 probability twice.

DATA	enter	STAT	calculate	Translation
X01 =	28	LIN		
Y01 =	-3	n =	4.0000	number of observations
X02 =	12	x =	11.0000	mean of X
Y02 =	7	Sx =	14.7422	sample standard deviation of X
X03 =	12	σx =	12.7671	standard deviation of X
Y03 =	7	y =	7.0000	mean of Y
X04 =	-8	Sy	8.1650	sample standard deviation of Y
Y04 =	17	σy =	7.0711	standard deviation of Y
		a =	13.0736	alpha or Y intercept of linear regression
		b =	-0.5521	beta or slope of linear regression
		r =	-0.9969	correlation coefficient
		X' =	0.0000	predicted X value
		Y' =	0.0000	predicted Y value
		$\sum$X =	44.0000	sum of X
		$\sum$X^2 =	1,136.0000	sum of X^2
		$\sum$Y =	28.0000	sum of Y
		$\sum$Y^2 =	396.0000	sum of Y^2
		$\sum$XY =	-52.0000	sum of (X*Y)

A.14 - Regression Analysis

Regression is a technique whereby we try to discover the relationship between two variables from their observed values. If we have reason to believe that x and y are linearly related then we posit that relationship with the equation:

$$y = \alpha + \beta x \qquad \qquad \textit{(Eq A-11)}$$

We observe x and y. We use regression analysis to estimate the parameters α and β.

Suppose the relationship between x and y actually is $y = 3 + 2x$. We observe x and y without error.

❑ **Error:** An error is the difference between the observed, measured, or calculated value and its true value. An error is not a mistake; it's a deviation.

Figure A-5: Textbook regression

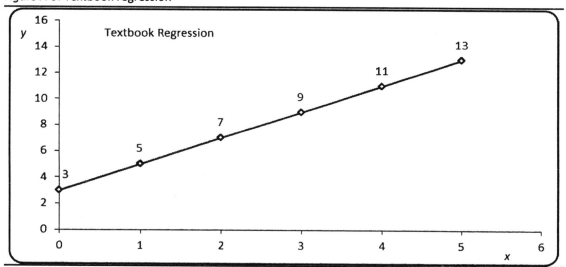

We can calculate beta and alpha in the regression equation $y = \alpha + \beta x$

$$\beta = \frac{n(\sum xy) - (\sum x)(\sum y)}{n(\sum x^2)-(\sum x)^2} = \frac{6(155) - (15)(48)}{6(55)-(15)^2} = 2 \qquad \textit{(Eq A-12)}$$

$$\alpha = \frac{\sum y-\beta\sum x}{n} = \frac{48 - 2*15}{6} = 3 \qquad \textit{(Eq A-13)}$$

or use our financial calculator to run the regression. In either case, we can estimate α and β, and deduce that the relationship between x and y is

$$y = 3 + 2 x$$

Calculator Techniques A-6:

Data	
x	*y*
0	3
1	5
2	7
3	9
4	11
5	13

If we run an ordinary least squares regression we find that the intercept (alpha) is 3 and the coefficient on *x* (beta) is 2.

We discover that $y = 3 + 2x$

This information allows us to estimate the relationship between the independent variable *x* and the dependent variable *y* as $y = 3 + 2x$.

The statistic $r = \rho = 1.00$ gives us an $R^2 = 1.00^2 = 1.00$. This means that 100% of the variation in the dependent variable *y* is systematic and is explained by the variation in the independent variable *x*.

We also can predict that for $x = 10$ $y = 3 + 2(10) = 23$. Enter 10 into X', go to Y', and compute.

DATA	enter	STAT	calculate
X01 =	0	LIN	
Y01 =	3	n =	6.0000
X02 =	1	x =	2.5000
Y02 =	5	Sx =	1.8708
X03 =	2	σx =	1.7078
Y03 =	7	y =	8.0000
X04 =	3	Sy	3.7417
Y04 =	9	σy =	3.4156
X05 =	4	a =	3.0000
Y05 =	11	b =	2.0000
X06 =	5	r =	1.0000
Y06 =	13	X' =	0.0000
		Y' =	0.0000
		∑X =	15.0000
		∑X² =	55.0000
		∑Y =	48.0000
		∑Y² =	454.0000
		∑XY =	155.0000

However, in real life we observe *y* with error. Note that we have built in the assumption that the errors are normally distributed with mean 0.

Figure A-6: Regression with normally distributed error

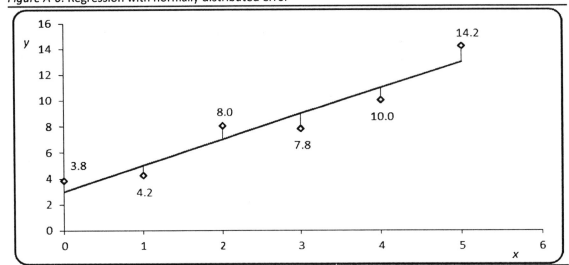

Calculator Techniques A-7:

Data		
x	y	e
0	3.8	0.8
1	4.2	-0.8
2	8.0	1.0
3	7.8	-1.2
4	10.0	-1.0
5	14.2	1.2

Now if we run an ordinary least squares regression we find that the intercept (alpha) is estimated as 3.057 and the coefficient on x (beta) is estimated as 1.977.

We therefore estimate the relationship between x and y as

$$y = 3.0571 + 1.9771x + e$$

which is fairly close to the real relationship of

$$y = 3 + 2x$$

but not exact.

DATA	enter	STAT	calculate
X01 =	0	LIN	
Y01 =	3.8	n =	6.0000
X02 =	1	x =	2.5000
Y02 =	4.2	Sx =	1.8708
X03 =	2	σx =	1.7078
Y03 =	8.0	y =	8.0000
X04 =	3	Sy	3.7417
Y04 =	7.8	σy =	3.4156
X05 =	4	a =	3.0000
Y05 =	10.0	b =	2.0000
X06 =	5	r =	1.0000
Y06 =	14.2	X' =	0.0000
		Y' =	0.0000
		$\sum X$ =	15.0000
		$\sum X^2$ =	55.0000
		$\sum Y$ =	48.0000
		$\sum Y^2$ =	454.0000
		$\sum XY$ =	155.0000

The statistic $r = 0.9579$ gives us an $R^2 = 0.9579^2 = 0.9175$.

This means that 91.75% of the variation in y is systematic and is explained by the variation in x. The remaining 8.25% is caused by something else.

R^2 is calculated as the ratio of the squared deviation from the mean of the predicted values of y to the squared deviations of the mean of the observed values of y.

$$R^2 = \frac{\sum (\hat{y} - \bar{y})^2}{\sum (y - \bar{y})^2} = \frac{11.4015}{12.4267} = 0.9175 \qquad \text{(Eq A-14)}$$

Deviations from the mean are calculated in Table A-4.

observed y	deviation from the mean $(y - \bar{y})^2$	predicted y	predicted y deviation from the mean $(\hat{y} - \bar{y})^2$
3.8	$(3.8 - 8.0)^2 =$ 17.64	3.057143	$(3.057143 - 8.0)^2 =$ 24.4
4.2	$(4.2 - 8.0)^2 =$ 14.44	5.034286	$(5.034286 - 8.0)^2 =$ 8.8
8.0	$(8.0 - 8.0)^2 =$ 0.00	7.011429	$(7.011429 - 8.0)^2 =$ 1.0
7.8	$(7.8 - 8.0)^2 =$ 0.04	8.988571	$(8.988571 - 8.0)^2 =$ 1.0
10.0	$(10.0 - 8.0)^2 =$ 4.00	10.965714	$(10.965714 - 8.0)^2 =$ 8.8
14.2	$(14.2 - 8.0)^2 =$ 38.44	12.942857	$(12.942857 - 8.0)^2 =$ 24.4
8.0	12.43	8.000000	11.4

Table A-4: Predicted deviations from the mean

In this example the difference between the true value of y and the observed value of y is fairly small. But look at what happens when the error with which we observe y increases.

Data		
x	y	e
0	5.5	2.5
1	7.0	2.0
2	4.6	-2.4
3	11.3	2.3
4	8.9	-2.1
5	10.7	-2.3

Now if we run an ordinary least squares regression we find that the intercept (alpha) is estimated as 5.2571 rather than the true value of 3, and the coefficient on x (beta) is estimated as 1.0971 rather than the true value of 2.

Therefore we estimate the relationship between x and y as

$$y = 5.2571 + 1.0971x + e$$

The R^2 is now 0.5573 This means that only 55.73% of the variation in y is systematic and is explained by the variation in x. The remaining 44.27% is unexplained by the model.

Figure A-7: Estimated relationship between x and y observed with error

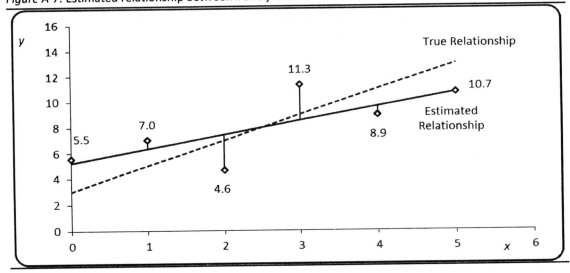

Chapter A - Questions and Problems

A-1:

Pi = 3.14159265358979323846264338327950288419716939937510...

A.   Round Pi to five decimal places.
B.   Round Pi to four decimal places.
C.   Round Pi to three decimal places.

A-2:

You calculate a portfolio rate of return of 7.349%

A.   Specify the rate of return to two decimal places.
B.   Specify the rate of return to one decimal place.

A-3:

The rates of return for the first three months of the year are 3.567% , 2.42%, and 3.5%

A.   Specify to four decimal places the smallest possible rate of return over the three-month period given the published rates of return.
B.   Specify to four decimal places the largest possible rate of return over the three-month period given the published return.
C.   Specify the total rate of return for the three-month period.

A-4:

Simplify

A. $-2x - [3 - (4 - 3x)] + 6x$

B. $-9 + \dfrac{9 + 20}{3(5)} - (-3)$

A-5:

A. $\sqrt[12]{1.20} =$

B. $\left[\sqrt[5]{1.07} * \sqrt[4]{1.05} * \sqrt[3]{1.10} \right]^{-12} =$

A-6:

Xavier has an income that is five-eighths that of Yasmine. However Xavier's expenses are one-half those of Yasmine, and Xavier saved 40% of his income. What percentage of her income does Yasmine save?

A-7:

Sam, a golden retriever, spies a rabbit in the midst of a clearing. The rabbit has a head start of 45 meters and jumps 2 meters every time Sam runs 3 meters. If the rabbit is smart, how close is he to the hedge?

A-8:

A tape player runs at a speed of 7.50 inches per second. How many hours of play will I get with an 1,800-foot-long tape ?

A-9:

Your company sells a nut mixture consisting of 1/3 pecans and 2/3 cashews. Pecans cost 3 times as much as cashews. You set the price at $4.40 per pound, which includes a 10% markup.

A.   What is the company's cost per pound of the mix?
B.   What is the company's cost per pound of cashews and pecans ?

A-10:

Nicholas and Alexander are 20 km from home with only one bicycle between them.

They decide that Nicholas will walk for a while and Alexander will take the bike, leaving it further along and walking the rest of the way. When Nicholas reaches the bike, he will bike home. Nicholas walks at 5 km/h and rides at 12 km/h. Alexander walks at 4 km/h and rides at 10 km/h.

A.   How far should Alexander ride the bike for both to arrive home at the same time?
B.   How long will it take for them to get home?
C.   When Nicholas reaches the bike, how far from home is Alexander?

A-11:

The average age at which the top people in your firm made partner is 40. If the average age at which the people who earned a CFA (Chartered Financial Analyst) designation made partner is 35 and the average age at which the people who did not earn a CFA designation made partner is 50 years, then what is the ratio of the number of partners who have earned a CFA designation?

A-12:

The accounting clerk at the Credit Union has lost track of the total original deposits made by five customers. All of the accounts earn simple annual interest. Luckily he can figure out who deposited what from the following clues.

A. Grace found a bank that pays 0.2% more than the account opened at the Credit Union. If Grace had used this other bank, Grace would have earned $40 more in simple annual interest.
B. Jennifer and John deposited a total of $21,500 into two accounts. One account is paying 5.88% and the other is paying 5.42% simple interest. In one year, the annual simple interest will be $1,236.60 for both accounts.
C. Michael's account, which pays 6.51%, will earn $524.55 more in simple interest than the simple interest earned in one year by Nathan's account. Nathan has an account that pays 6.18% annual interest. Michael and Nathan originally deposited $29,500 altogether.

A-13:

Dan, Mary, and Josh are all paid according to multiple times a company base salary determined on annual revenues plus a bonus based on the profitability of the number of houses they paint and the number of complaints filed against them. The company publishes salaries but without the names. The published list is

69 * Base + $3,790
96 * Base − $2,890
3 * Base + $14,140.

Can you help Dan figure out who earned what?

A. Dan earns 96x − 2890.
B. Mary earns $1,280 more than Dan
C. Josh makes the least amount of money.
D. Josh earns less than Dan. If Josh earned $16,270 more, Josh would earn more than Dan.
E. Dan earns more money than Josh and less money than Mary.

A-14:

This problem is attributed to Albert Einstein. He said that 98% of the people in the world cannot solve it.

There are 5 houses in 5 different colors. In each house lives a person with a different nationality These 5 owners drink a certain type of beverage, smoke a certain brand of cigar, and keep a certain pet. No owners have the same pet, smoke the same brand of cigar or drink the same drink.

Who owns the fish?

Clues:
A. The Brit lives in a red house
B. The Swede keeps dogs as pets
C. The Dane drinks tea
D. The green house is to the left of the white house
E. The green house owner drinks coffee
F. The person who smokes Pall Mall rears birds
G. The owner of the yellow house smokes Dunhill
H. The man living in the house right in the middle drinks milk
I. The Norwegian lives in the first house
J. The man who smokes Blend lives next door to the one who keeps cats.
K. The man who keeps horses lives next door to the man who smokes Dunhill
L. The owner who smokes Blue Master drinks beer
M. The German smokes Prince
N. The Norwegian lives next to the blue house
O. The man who smokes Blend has a neighbor who drinks water

There is only one solution that satisfies all 15 clues.

An extra challenge: Change clue D. to "The green house is to the left—but not directly to the left—of the white house". Now who owns the fish? Again, there is only one solution that satisfies all 15 clues, but the answer is different from the one you just calculated.

A-15:

Derive the formula for Net Future Value

$$FV = \frac{(1+r)}{r} C \left[(1+r)^t - 1 \right]$$

from

$$FV = \sum_{t=1}^{n} C_t (1+r)^t$$

A-16:

Assume the Bankers Discount Rate on Treasury bills is fixed at 3%. Thus the price of a $100,000 T-bill is given by

$$Price = \$100,000 \left[1 - 0.03 \ \frac{Days\ to\ Maturity}{360} \right]$$

A.   Identify the dependent and independent variables in this equation.
B.   What is the price of the T-bill at 120 days to maturity?
C.   What is the Price of the T-bill at 65 days to maturity?
D.   Can the price of the T-bill ever be more than $100,000?
E.   Graph the equation.

A-17:

Vincent owns 1000 shares of JP Morgan (JPM). The shares have a cost base of $40. The price of JP Morgan on any day in the coming year P $\sim N(\$50,\$100)$

A.   What does the notation $\sim N(\$50, \$100)$ mean?
B.   Draw the probability distribution indicating on the graph the probability of making a loss.
C.   What is the probability that Vincent makes a loss on this investment?

A-18:

On the toss of one die the possible outcomes are 1, 2, 3, 4, 5, 6.

A.   Calculate the expected value E[X].
B.   Calculate the expected value $E[X^2]$.
C.   Calculate the variance σ^2 and standard deviation σ using the formula $\sigma^2 = E[X^2] - E[X]^2$.
D.   Calculate the expected value E[X], variance σ^2, and standard deviation σ using your calculator.

A-19:

Show algebraically that the variance formula

$$\sigma^2 = E[X - E[X]]^2$$

is mathematically equal to the variance formula

$$\sigma^2 = E[X^2] - E[X]^2$$

$\mathcal{T}$he most fundamental and essential skill in finance is the ability to relate time and money: net present value. If you can map out a schedule of cash flows, positive and negative, understand the interest rate patterns along the applicable time line, and express the value of any or all of the schedule of cash flows in any given time segment along that time line, then you have a strong foundation in finance. If not, then you will never fully understand or be able to engineer even the most basic of financial concepts or instruments. And you will always be at the mercy of someone who can.

B.1 - Value & Time

The interest rate is defined as the cost of using money or the factor by which money today can be exchanged for money tomorrow. The short-term, risk-free, real rate of interest is determined by demand for, and supply of, short term risk-free loans.

❑ **basis point:** 1/100 of 1% ; if interest rates increase by 0.45% this is an increase of 45 basis points.

B.1.1 - Interest Rates

By Fisher's Law, the real rate of interest r, equals the nominal rate of interest i, adjusted for inflation p'.

❑ **Interest rate:** The interest rate is the percentage rate at which money must earn more money over time to compensate for the loss of its use.

❑ **Inflation:** Inflation is the rate at which the price level in the economy increases.

❑ **Deflation:** Deflation is the rate at which the price level in the economy decreases; the rate of inflation is negative

(Eq B-1)

$$(1+r) = \frac{(1+i)}{(1+p')}$$

$$r = \frac{i - p'}{1 + p'}$$

This relationship is often approximated by $r = i - p'$, which tends to be easier to use.

Example 1:

> You have your eye on a 1974 Pantera (silver, of course). In 2012 the Pantera is offered at $50,000. Instead of buying the Pantera, you put the $50,000 in a one year T-bill at 5%. One year later your T-bill matures at $52,500, and you buy the Pantera for the 2013 price of $51,000.

Nominal Interest is 5%	$i = \dfrac{\$52,500}{\$50,000} = 1.05$
Inflation is 2%	$p' = \dfrac{\$51,000}{\$50,000} = 1.02$
Real Interest Rate is 3%	$r = \dfrac{\$52,500}{\$51,000} = \dfrac{\$52,500\ /\ \$50,000}{\$51,000\ /\ \$50,000} = \dfrac{1.05}{1.02} = 1.0294$

Although the real rate of interest is 2.94118%, for most purposes 3% is close enough, since it is generally about as accurate as is the published inflation rate.

———————

B.1.2 - Compounding & Discounting

Virtually all financial decisions involve future cash flows, not just over one period, but over several.

Example 2:

In your portfolio you have three IOUs: one each for $100, £100., and ¥100. You would never consider just adding them together.

$100. £100. ¥100. M300.	M is the symbol for the generic term "Moneys." The very fact that there is no such thing as "Moneys" emphasizes our inability to add different currencies.

The amounts must be converted to a single denomination before they can be added.

If the exchange rates are given as 1.60 for pounds sterling and 100 for yen, then we calculate

$$\left[£100\ *\ \frac{\$1.60}{£1} = \$160.00 \right] \qquad \begin{array}{r} \underline{£100} \\ \$100 \\ +\$160.00 \\ \underline{+\ \$1.00} \\ \$261.00 \end{array} \qquad \left[¥100\ *\ \frac{\$1}{¥100} = \$1.00 \right]$$

Even though the exchange rates were not explicitly defined as $1.60/£ or ¥100/$ our knowledge of the relationships between these currencies allowed us to convert to a single currency.

———————

Example 3:

Similarly, if in your portfolio you have three IOUs: one each for $100 in year 1, $100 in year 2, and $100 in year 3, then the amounts must be converted to a single time period.

If the rates of rates of exchange between time periods are given as 3% and 4%, respectively, and we convert to year 2, we calculate

$100 $100 $100

$[\$100 * 1.03 = \$103.00]$

$100
+ $103.00
+ $96.15
$299.15

$\left[\dfrac{\$100}{1.04} = \$96.15 \right]$

B.1.3 - Time Lines

One of the most useful tools in finance is a time line. Although a time line is a graph in only one dimension, it has the same ability to clarify and illustrate as does the standard two-dimensional graph.

Figure B-1: Time line showing cash flows, interest rates, and semi-annual compounding

Dec 31, 2014	Dec 31, 2015	Dec 31, 2016	Dec 31, 2017	Dec 31, 2018
	3%	4%	5%	6%	
−$10,000	$500	$500	$500	$10,500

Note that graph clearly indicates the timing of the cash flows and the rates of interest in each time period. It also clearly indicates that although cash flows are annual, compounding is semi-annual.

B.1.4 - Future Value

The future value is the value of cash flows translated into future dollars.

Example 4:

Calculate the value of the cash flows in Figure B-1 on December 31, 2018.

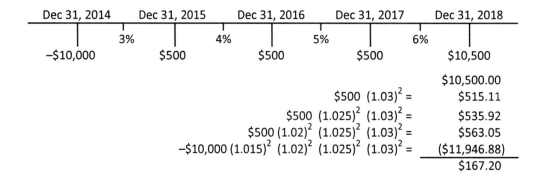

				Dec 31, 2018
				$10,500.00
			$500\ (1.03)^2 =$	$515.11
			$500\ (1.025)^2\ (1.03)^2 =$	$535.92
		$500\ (1.02)^2\ (1.025)^2\ (1.03)^2 =$		$563.05
	−$10,000\ (1.015)^2\ (1.02)^2\ (1.025)^2\ (1.03)^2 =$			($11,946.88)
				$167.20

❏ **Compounding:** Moving money forward in time: to the right along the time line.

B.1.5 - Present Value

The present value is the value of cash flows translated into current or present dollars.

Example 5:

Calculate the value of the cash flows in Figure B-1 on December 31, 2014.

Dec 31, 2014	Dec 31, 2015	Dec 31, 2016	Dec 31, 2017	Dec 31, 2018
	3%	4%	5%	6%
− $10,000	$500	$500	$500	$10,500

$$\$-10,000.00$$
$$\$485.33 \quad = \$500\ (1.03)^{-2}$$
$$\$466.48 \quad = \$500\ (1.025)^{-2}\ (1.03)^{-2} =$$
$$\$444.01 \quad = \$500\ (1.02)^{-2}\ (1.025)^{-2}\ (1.03)^{-2}$$
$$\$8,788.90 \quad = -\$10,000\ (1.015)^{-2}\ (1.02)^{-2}\ (1.025)^{-2}\ (1.03)^{-2} =$$
$$\$184.72$$

❏ **Discounting:** Moving money back in time: to the left along a time line.

B.2 - Currency & Exchange

❏ **Currency:** Currency is the unit in the medium of exchange. Thus the USA uses the US dollar ($, USD), the Euro Zone uses the euro (€, EUR) and Britain uses pounds sterling (£, GBP).

❏ **ISO codes:** The International Standard Organization for Standardization (ISO) provides a three-character code for each currency in use thereby, theoretically at least, reducing confusion between the numerous currencies called dollars but issued by different countries.

Table B-1: Currency information for select countries and regions

Country or Zone	Currency		ISO	Division	Authority
Canada	Dollar	C$	CAD	100 cents	Bank of Canada
China (PRC)	Yuan	$\overline{\pi}$	CNY	10 jiao 100 fen	People's Bank of China
Euro Zone	Euro	€	EUR	100 cents	European Central Bank
Great Britain	Pound Sterling	£	GBP	100 pence	Bank of England
India	Rupee	Rs	INR	100 paise	Reserve Bank of India
Japan	Yen	¥	JPY	none	Bank of Japan
USA	Dollar	$	USD	100 cents	Federal Reserve

❑ **Interest Rate Parity:** Under free markets there is a direct relationship between the rate of interest and the exchange rate of the currency in which the interest is earned. Interest rate parity assumes that the interest carries the same risk.

$$Exchange\ Rate\ X_{t+1} = X_t * \frac{\left(1 + i_{domestic} \right)}{\left(1 + i_{foreign} \right)} \qquad\qquad (Eq\ B\text{-}2)$$

Example 6:

I can earn 6% on US dollar deposit or 8% on a euro deposit. The current exchange rate is $1.25. I can calculate that the exchange rate will decline to $1.22685

If I put $100 in a US dollar deposit I will have $106.00 at the end of one year.

If I convert to euros at $1.25 and put €80.00 into a euro deposit I will have €86.40 at the end of one year.

$$\$100\ (1.06) = \$106.00 \qquad\qquad \$100\ \frac{€1}{\$1.25}\ (1.08) = €86.40$$

In order for the two results to be the same, the exchange rate one year from now must be $1.22685.

$$X = \$1.25\ \frac{1.06}{1.08} = \frac{\$106}{€86.40} = \$1.22685$$

Chapter B - Questions and Problems

B-1:

Claire deposits $10,000 in her bank account at 6% interest. How many years will it take to double her money?

B-2:

Simone wants to set up a bank account from which she can withdraw $5,000 in five years, $6,000 in six years, and $7,000 in seven years. The bank pays 6% interest annually. How much money must she deposit today to generate sufficient funds?

B-3:

You win the Investment Challenge and the prize is $1600: $100 in 2013, $200 in 2014, $300 in 2015, and $1000 in 2016. All prizes are paid out on May 1.

A. Calculate how much money the Investment Challenge Administration should have put aside on May 1, 2012 to pay these prizes. (Present Value)

B. Calculate how much money you would have in the bank on May 1, 2016, if you put each payment in the bank when you received it and the bank paid 3% interest. (Future Value)

C. Calculate the future and present value if the interest rates are 3% in 2012-13, 4% in 2013-14, 5% in 2014-15, and 6% in 2015-16 with interest rate valid from May 1 to May 1.

B-4:

When you entered the University of Illinois your Aunt Mabel made you a deal. She would put $1,000 into the Bank on the June 1 preceding each academic year in which you registered at the University of Illinois. The resulting balance you would get upon graduation (June 1). The interest is calculated and compounded annually.

A. You predict that the interest rate will be 4% during these four years. How much money should you receive from Aunt Mabel upon graduation?

The actual rate of interest is 5% in your freshman year, 6% in your sophomore year, 7% in your junior year, and 8% in your senior year.

B. You graduate on schedule after four years at the U of I. How much money does Aunt Mabel present you with upon graduation?

B-5:

Aunt Mabel promised to give you $1,000 when you successfully complete your freshman year at the University of Illinois; $2,000 when you successfully complete your sophomore year, $3,000 when you successfully complete your junior year, and $4,000 when you successfully complete your senior year. Aunt Mabel made this promise when you graduated from high school and let's assume you go directly to the U of I and graduate in four years.

A. How much money must Aunt Mabel set aside when you graduate from high school in order to keep this promise? Aunt Mabel assumes that the interest rate will remain at 4% all through your years at university and the bank where she keeps this money compound interest annually.

B. In your senior year interest rates increase to 12%. Thus after Aunt Mabel pays you your $4,000, how much money will be left in her bank account?

C. If Aunt Mabel had known that interest rates would increase to 12% in your senior year how much money would she have needed to set aside?

B-6:

Your bank offers a high-yield savings account that pays a nominal rate 6% per year and compounds quarterly. If this rate is guaranteed for the next five years, then how much would you need to deposit today to have $50,000 exactly five years from now?

B-7:

Your bank offers a high-yield savings account that pays a nominal rate 6% per year and compounds monthly. If this rate is guaranteed for the next five years, then how much would you need to deposit today to have $50,000 exactly five years from now?

Section I - Introduction to Financial Markets

$\mathcal{F}$inancial markets are an integral part of the economic system. Throughout this text, "the market" usually refers to U.S. markets for financial instruments, although financial markets throughout the world have many of the same characteristics. We will try to point out the differences where appropriate, but remind the reader that there are more similarities than differences in why financial markets exist globally.

Further, as you learn about the different markets and the instruments that trade in them, keep in mind that these instruments are proxies for the real assets of firms, governments, or households in the economy. Real assets are the property, equipment, people, and intellectual drivers in an economy. To a large extent, the efficient allocation of these real assets, and the achievement of a higher standard of living of all its participants, is dependent on the efficient function of financial markets. We tend to focus on financial assets but do not want to lose sight of the real assets they represent, and the beneficiaries of those assets, namely people. When financial markets function efficiently, society itself benefits.

Chapter 1   Financial Markets in the Economy

$\mathcal{T}$he function of financial markets is to transfer funds from those who have financial resources to those who can put it to better economic use. Without financial markets households would have no way to invest except in ventures to which they had direct access, and firms would have no access to capital they did not themselves generate.

1.1 - Circular Flow in the Economy

The circular flow diagram models economic activity at the most fundamental level. People live in units we call households and combine with others to form production units we call firms. Households and firms make the most fundamental economic decisions: what does the economy produce and who consumes it. They bring their decisions into the markets for both the factors of production and goods and services. These markets bring together supply and demand and match them through a price mechanism. The price then feeds back into households' and firms' decisions.

Figure 1-1: Circular Flow Diagram

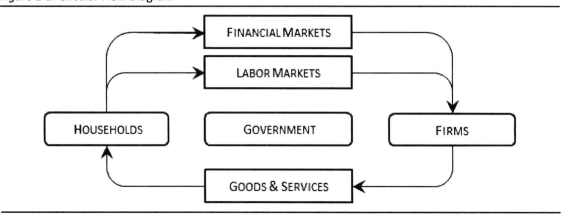

People also combine to govern themselves, so the circular flow diagram also includes government as a decision-making unit. The government affects households and firms directly, through regulation and taxation; and indirectly, through regulation, taxation, and participation in markets for both factors of production and for goods and services.

When markets function efficiently, decision making in both firms and households is optimal, labor and capital are fully employed, production is consumed, welfare is maximized, and the economy grows.

❑ **Utility:** In economic theory happiness and well-being are termed utility. Individuals are assumed to maximize utility just as firms are assumed to maximize profits.

❑ **Welfare:** In economic theory individuals and households have utility; a society has welfare. In a sense welfare is the aggregate utility of all the people in the economy.

❑ **Optimal:** Economic condition where one participant cannot be made better off without making someone else worse off.

1.2 - What Are Markets?

The focus of this text is markets for financial instruments, but markets are everywhere: from farmers' markets for produce to electronic markets such as eBay, markets form an everyday part of personal experience.

Markets can be global as well as local. From the Fulton Fish Market in New York City where fishermen sell their catch, to The Kashgar International Trade Market of Central and Western Asia (believed by some to be the world's oldest open-air marketplace), markets exist to bring prospective buyers and sellers together in hopes of completing a transaction.

With electronic markets like eBay, it is easy to see geography shrink to almost an insignificant factor. The click of your mouse on the "Buy It Now" button allows you to buy Italian shoes from a manufacturer thousands of miles away who you will never meet. In all of these examples we can see how markets are not confined to any one place or people. Markets truly are a global phenomenon.

1.2.1 - Primary Markets

The primary market is where new issues of equity or debt are sold.

When a corporation needs more capital to finance an expansion of its operations, it may offer shares of stock (the equity, or partial ownership of the corporation) or debt to investors. When a government needs capital to finance its activities and taxes do not generate sufficient receipts, it may borrow by selling bonds (evidence of indebtedness).

Investors have capital (money) on which they hope to earn a favorable rate of return, and the partial ownership in a corporation or holding a government bond may be a way for them to generate that return. If we buy shares directly from the corporation or bonds directly from the government, this is known as a "primary market" transaction.

In the circular flow diagram the primary market can be represented by an arrow from Households through the Financial Markets to Firms and Governments.

Figure 1-2: Primary Markets

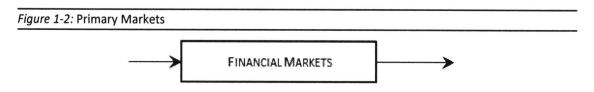

1.2.2 - Secondary Markets

The secondary market is the market for securities issued in the past.

In order to generate the rate of return the investor desires, he may need to sell the shares he purchased to someone else in the future. This is when a secondary market transaction will come into play.

Secondary markets are made up of transactions between buyers and sellers where neither has produced the traded items. In the case of shares of stock, investors who own it sell it to other investors who want it, and in the process, do not involve the corporation that issued the shares originally.

At first, it may seem that the primary and secondary markets are very separate and independent. The corporation generates funds when it sells its shares to an investor in the primary market, but it receives no funds when that investor turns around and sells those shares to someone else. But the price at which these shares are sold gives the corporation important information about its value.

In the circular flow diagram, the secondary market can be represented by an arrow from the Financial Market back to the Financial Market.

Figure 1-3: Secondary Markets

An important function of the secondary market is to provide liquidity to investors. Liquidity in a market provides the investor with potential buyers when he is ready to sell. Since a corporation has a right, but not an obligation, to buy back the shares of stock that it sold to public investors, the prospective investor needs to be able to sell his shares elsewhere. Without a well-developed secondary market for things like financial instruments, investors might be very reluctant to buy the shares in the first place.

Ownership rights must include a reasonable expectation of being able to sell the possession at some point in the future; secondary markets provide that opportunity. When we see trading activity on the floor of an organized security exchange such as the New York Stock Exchange (NYSE), we see the workings of a secondary market for shares of stock. We can quickly forget how that activity is intricately linked to the first sale of shares of stock to the public by the corporation years ago. Without the active secondary market, the original sale may never have taken place.

Example 1:

Google (GOOG) issued shares August 19, 2004, at $85 per share. When Susan speculator purchased 100 shares, her $8,500 went to Google. This was a primary market transaction.

One year later Susan sold her shares of Google to John Q. Investor at $283.58. John's $28,358.00 went to Susan, not to Google. This was a secondary market transaction.

When both the primary and the secondary markets function efficiently, they optimally allocate both capital and risk.

1.3 - The Returns Mechanism

Markets allocate goods and resources through the price mechanism. In the financial markets the price mechanism takes the form of a rate of change or returns mechanism.

Investors allocate their capital to securities that earn them the highest possible return on investment for the lowest possible risk. Firms seek funds that minimize their cost of capital and risk exposure. The market brings the demand for and the supply of funds together by adjusting the rate of return.

1.3.1 - Normal Return

We assume that all investors are risk averse. This means that investors will take on more risk only if they are compensated with a higher expected return. When an investor earns a return that exactly compensates him for risk he undertakes then this is called Normal Return.

If the prospect of a 7.1% rate of return on Google (GOOG) leaves you unwilling to invest, but the prospect of a 7.2% annual rate of return prompts you to buy shares, then the normal rate of return is 7.2%. This is the rate of return required to get you to part with your money.

When the market generates normal returns, financial capital is allocated optimally.

1.3.2 - Abnormal Return

Abnormal return is the difference between the actual return earned on an investment and the normal return.

$$\text{Abnormal Return} = \text{Actual Return} - \text{Normal Return} \qquad \textit{(Eq 1-1)}$$

If the normal return on Google (GOOG) is 7.2% and you actually get a 12.5% return, then the abnormal return is +5.3%.

The existence of consistent abnormal returns means that the market is not doing its job efficiently. When the market generates abnormal returns it distorts the flow of financial resources in the same way as does an inefficient price in the goods market or an inefficient wage in the labor market.

The abnormally high return on Google (GOOG) prompts you to put much more money into shares of Google (GOOG) the following year. This was an inefficient investment decision based on the abnormally high 12.5% return.

Figure 1-4: Normal Return

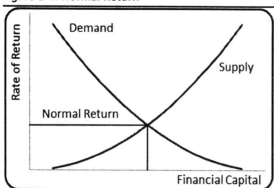

Figure 1-5: Abnormal Return

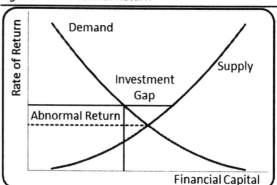

Example 2:

George Q. Farmer grows tomatoes on the back acre and sells his produce at $1 per pound. The price of tomatoes skyrocketed to $6/lb. George plowed under his beans, his squash, and his peppers and planted tomatoes—as did most of his neighbors.

The abnormal return on tomatoes lead to an inefficient decision. When George brings his tomatoes to market the oversupply has already dropped the price below $1/lb, and the shortage of beans, squash, and peppers created by these inefficient decisions leads to a sudden increase in their prices.

1.4 - Efficient Market Hypothesis

The role of financial markets in the economy is to optimally allocate financial resources and risk. It does so if it can generate normal returns through the market price mechanism.

We begin by assuming that investors are risk averse.

❑ **Risk Averse:** An investor will take on more risk if and only if he is compensated through the expectation of higher return.

❑ **Risk Neutral:** An investor will make investment decisions based on expected return without regard to the risk involved.

❑ **Risk Loving:** An investor will take on more risk for its own sake. Gambling reveals risk-loving behavior.

The Efficient Market Hypothesis states that a market is efficient if prices fully reflect all available relevant information. It relies on informed individual investors to bring this relevant information into the market through their buying and selling decisions.

Efficient markets mean that the expected returns implicit in the current price of the security reflect its risk: there are no abnormal returns. This means that the price of an asset reflects the information, expectations, and risk adjustment of all investors.

Under completely efficient markets no one can ever beat the market because the price of any security immediately reflects all information. On average, information moves so quickly that the market as a whole always knows more than any one individual investor.

Eugene Fama characterized three levels of informational efficiency: weak form, semistrong form, and strong form.[1]

1.4.1 - Weak Form Efficiency

Under weak form efficiency prices fully reflect all information conveyed by historical price and trading data. There is no systematic profit to be gained by analyzing price and trading information.

Tests against price and trading data on U.S. equity markets conclude that the market is weak form efficient, thus challenging the premise behind technical analysis or charting.

❑ **Technical Analysis:** Technical analysis is based on the idea that a pattern of stock prices reveals the pattern of demand and supply in the market. Technical analysis assumes that the information investors bring to the market can be charted, analyzed, and used to reveal the relative strength of demand and supply.

1.4.2 - Semistrong Form Efficiency

Under semistrong form efficiency prices fully reflect all publicly available information. There is no systematic profit to be gained by acting on fundamental analysis.

❑ **Fundamental Analysis:** Fundamental analysis is the evaluation of the economic and financial information relevant to the corporation's future earnings and growth with a view to determining the value or price that a share of the company should command.

Studies indicate that financial markets are semistrong efficient to some degree; it depends largely on the nature of the information studied.

Anomalies

Anomalies are defined as deviations from the norm or exceptions to a rule. Studies have identified anomalies in which the market fails the test of semistrong form efficiency under specific conditions.

❑ **Quarterly Earnings Reports Anomaly:** Several studies have shown that if you purchase stocks on the basis of strong quarterly earnings or quarterly earnings surprises and held these stocks for six months then the portfolio would earn positive abnormal profits. Since abnormal returns can be earned on the basis of public information, this result does not support the semistrong form of the efficient market hypothesis.

❑ **Value Line Anomaly:** Several studies have shown that if you buy and sell according to the Value Line recommendations then you can earn abnormal profits. Since abnormal returns can be earned on the

---

1   Eugene Fama , "Random Walks in Stock Market Prices", *Financial Analysts Journal*, Vol. 51, no. 1 (1995): 75-80.

basis of public information this result does not support the semistrong form of the efficient market hypothesis.

❏ **Small Firm Anomaly:** Several studies have shown that small firms systematically outperform larger firms with the same essential characteristics.

❏ **January Effect:** Studies have shown that the average return in January is systematical higher than the average return any other month. Further studies confirm that the size effect is greater in January and the January effect is greater for small firms than for large ones. This is an anomaly to the efficient markets hypothesis in the weak form since the January effect relies on calendar timing rather than publicly available information.

1.4.3 - Strong Form Efficiency

Under strong form efficiency prices fully reflect all information, whether publicly available or not. There is no systematic profit to be gained by trading on insider information.

Studies indicate that corporate insiders earn abnormal returns on trades based on insider information. These results constitute evidence against strong-form efficiency.

❏ **Insider Trading:** Insiders typically include major corporate officers, members of the board of directors, and significant shareholders—people who have access to confidential corporate information. These individuals are required to submit to the SEC monthly reports regarding their transactions in the stock of the firm. The SEC makes this information public about six weeks later. (The *Wall Street Journal* publishes a weekly column called "Insider Trading Spotlight" that discusses major insider transactions.)

Insider trading is illegal when it is based on material, nonpublic information. Criminal charges for willful violations of the insider trading laws are punishable by up to 20 years in prison and fines of up to $5 million for individuals/$25 million for corporations.[2]

❏ **Insider Trading Anomaly:** Further studies show that trading based on SEC announcements of insider trading also generates abnormal returns. These results constitute evidence against semistrong form efficiency because these abnormal profits are based on insider information after it becomes public.

1.4.4 - Characteristics of an Efficient Market

Efficient markets generally exhibit characteristics in common. When any of these characteristics are missing then this indicates an inefficient market: a market where abnormal profits can be found.

Essentially, in order for markets to be efficient investors must have access to information and then be able to trade on that information. This requires external (informational) efficiency, internal efficiency, and liquidity.

❏ **External or Informational Efficiency:** Informational efficiency requires that security prices fully reflect all available information. This requires three basic characteristics

---

2   Kevin Haynes, "Review of Insider Trading Case Law and Regulations", *University of North Carolina School of Law, ALI-ABA Business Law Course Materials Journal*, Vol. 29, no. 5 (2005): 5-16.

1]Timely and accurate information is available on past transactions and on current bids and asks.

2] A large enough number of investors actively participate in the market; that they analyze and value the securities for which they make buy and sell decisions.

3] Value-relevant information hits the market randomly (the nature and timing of one announcement is independent of the nature and timing of other announcements).

❑ **Internal Efficiency:** Internal efficiency requires that the cost of entering the market is low enough that investors can participate. Potential investors must have access to brokerage services and be able to buy and sell without facing prohibitive transaction costs.

❑ **Liquidity:** Liquidity in a market means that an asset can be bought or sold quickly at a price close to that of the previous transaction. We can detect liquidity through price continuity and depth

    ❑ **price continuity:** Prices change only marginally from one transaction to the next.

    ❑ **depth:** Numerous potential buyers and sellers are active in the relevant price and volume range.

1.5 - Markets: Investment or Gambling?

Is there a distinction between investment and gambling?

We hear comments like "Your great-grandfather lost all his money gambling in the stock market when it crashed", or "I wouldn't gamble on that stock". Are markets for financial instruments just another way to gamble?

If the corporation that issued the stock has no part in the flow of funds between investors in the secondary market trading of shares, aren't those investors in the secondary market just gambling on the future price of the shares? The answers to these questions could be yes, depending on the objectives that brought the participants to the marketplace.

It may be helpful to think of gambling as a form of entertainment that we willingly pay for, and investment as expecting a payment for the assumption of risk. Games of chance such as black jack, roulette, craps, et cetera are all well defined games of probability. If we throw two fair dice we know, with certainty, the probability of rolling each combination of numbers 2 through 12. We understand the payoffs made on the various bets possible, and therefore, we can see a process that has the favor (higher odds) on the side of the house.

The players at the table have a negative expected value to their activity of placing bets. The game is designed this way. The house has the advantage because that is their source of income. Understanding this, we realize that playing black jack, roulette, craps or any other casino game of chance is really the purchase of entertainment. Instead of going out to dinner and a movie, we use that money (and perhaps more) to buy the entertainment of the chance of winning more money than we lose.

The investment process differs in a subtle but important way. When we make an investment we enter into an economic transaction. There is uncertainty, and there is the expectation of payoff for accepting that uncertainty. But investment activities impact the marketplace and contribute to the efficient allocation of resources.

Example 3:

Your friend approaches you with a business opportunity. Your finance textbook sells for $10 more on the campus of a university just 50 miles away than it costs you on this campus. She has calculated the cost of round-trip travel between those two campuses and concludes that she can make $5 per book pure profit buying them here and selling them there at a lower price than present.

You are offered two opportunities to invest.

1] You can lend her your car and receive the fixed payment of $0.40 per mile (guaranteed by her parents), or

2] you can own one-half of the business entitling you to one-half of all profits so long as you pay one-half of all the expenses and do one-half of the work.

The expected return to either investment is positive, otherwise you wouldn't be interested at all. You might also get the sense that the potential return is higher with the partnership, but it also has more uncertainty.

This uncertainty derives from the competitive forces in the market for textbooks at the distant campus. At first, students there see the advantage to buying the book from your friend at the lower price. You earn a return on your investment in these transactions hoping to use a part of the profits to expand operations and earn even more.

But what about other students in your finance class? They see your profitable venture and set up similar partnerships. The supply of finance books on the other university campus increase and prices fall. Your potential profit is at risk.

And what about the original bookstore on that campus? They see your profitable venture and lower their price to undercut you. Your potential profit is at risk.

Absent regulation or artificial constraints, we would expect the book price to continue to fall to a market clearing price that generates a normal return to the sellers of the book at that campus, and makes it unprofitable for you to make a profit by transporting books from campus to campus. The market is at equilibrium.

However, your investment has a further effect: it has lowered the price of the book at the other campus. Students benefit from the price decline, and the booksellers make a rate of return that compensates them adequately for the risks they assume as booksellers. Unless conditions related to the cost of selling the books change (higher printing expenses, lower costs of transportation, etc.) or rates of return on alternative endeavors available to the booksellers change, given a steady demand, we expect this market to remain at equilibrium, and resources related to this marketplace to be allocated efficiently.

Chapter 1 - Questions and Problems

1-1:

Each of the following indicates a failure of which form of efficiency?

A. I use my computer and Internet link to chart the movement of all 30 Dow Jones Industrial stocks. I buy and sell according to my analysis of these price movements. If I can generate consistent abnormal returns in this manner then this is a failure of:

B. Charles is a member of the Board of Directors of the Royal Bank. If he can generate consistent abnormal returns in trading Royal Bank shares then this is a failure of:

C. Varya checks out all the Value Line publications and buys everything that Value Line recommends. If she can generate consistent abnormal returns then this is a failure of:

D. I watch *Wall Street Week* every week. Then when it's over I throw a dart at the *Wall Street Journal*. I buy whatever the dart hits. If I can generate consistent abnormal returns in this manner then this is a failure of:

E. John Q. Investor analyzes the quarterly earnings statements of some fifty obscure small-cap stocks. He then buys according to the earnings pattern disclosed. If he can generate consistent abnormal returns in this manner then this is a failure of:

F. George reads the financial pages every day. Whenever there is a report that the top insiders of a company are buying their company's stock he buys that company's stock; whenever there is a report that the top insiders of a company are selling their company's stock he sells that company's stock. If he can generate consistent abnormal returns in this manner then this is a failure of:

G. Thomas encounters the Wall Street rule of thumb which states "Sell in May and go away". He then makes sure that he sells everything at the end of April and buys it back again in August. If he can generate consistent abnormal returns in this manner then this is a failure of:

H. Sabrina's father is the limo driver to the President and CEO of RSG, an investment bank in New York. Sabrina buys RSG stock whenever her father overhears information indicating increased profits at RSG, and sells RSG stock whenever her father overhears information indicating decreased profits at RSG. If she can generate consistent abnormal returns in this manner then this is a failure of:

1-2:

Consider the quarterly Earnings Reports Anomaly. What characteristics of the informationally efficient market do you think might be violated?

1-3:

Peter L. Bernstein, in "Capital Ideas", relates the story of the Chicago university professor whose student spotted a $100 bill on the sidewalk. "The bill is not there, stated the professor. "If it were, the market is so efficient that someone would already have picked it up."[3]

What aspects of the Efficient Market Hypothesis does this story illustrate?

---

3   Peter L. Bernstein, *Capital Ideas: The Improbable Origins of Modern Wall Street*, New York: The Free Press, Simon & Schuster Inc, 1992, p211

Section II - Portfolio Theory

$\mathcal{P}$ortfolio theory derives the principles by which rational risk-averse investors select optimal portfolios. Portfolio theory dates from a 1952 paper entitled "Portfolio Selection"[1] The most striking feature of this work is not that it was written by a graduate student, but that it focused on the portfolio as a whole rather than on stocks selection as individual assets; an emphasis on teamwork rather than on individual stars.

Markowitz introduced the concept of an efficient or optimal portfolio. Efficiency is an economic term that describes maximum output for a minimum input. In the case of portfolio theory, this would mean maximizing expected return and minimizing risk of the portfolio as a whole. Markowitz pointed out that the risk of a portfolio depends not on the average riskiness of each separate investment in the portfolio but on the covariance of their returns; an emphasis on how each asset affects the riskiness of the portfolio rather than how risky it is on its own.

To design an efficient portfolio we must thus define and measure both the expected return and risk, explore the nature of diversification, and then bring these elements together into modern portfolio theory.

---

1   Harry M. Markowitz, "Portfolio Selection", *Journal of Finance*, Vol. 7, no. 1 (1952): 77-91

$\mathcal{W}$ hen we measure the rate of return on a portfolio of assets we are measuring the return on investment. We must devise techniques that allow us to measure not just the change in the value of a portfolio but the change in the value of the portfolio attributable to investment. This means we must adjust for changes in portfolio value that we do not want to measure, such as client deposits and withdrawals. We must also be able to measure and compare returns over different time periods.

2.1 - Holding Period Return

The total return from an investment, including all sources of income, for a given period of time. The period of time can be a year, a month, a day, or any combination thereof.

$$R = 1 + r = \frac{V_1}{V_0} \qquad \textit{(Eq 2-1)}$$

Example 1:

Your investment portfolio, initiated at $1,000,000 is valued at $1,200,000.00 at the end of the semester. The holding period return is calculated as:

$$R = 1 + r = \frac{\$1,200,000}{\$1,000,000} = 1.20 = 1 + 20\% \qquad r = +20\%$$

This means that for every $1.00 with which you began, you now have $1.20 . This means that you earned a return of +20%.

Example 2:

Your investment portfolio, initiated at $1,000,000 is valued at $800,000.00 at the end of the semester. The holding period return is calculated as:

$$R = 1 + r = \frac{\$800,000}{\$1,000,000} = 1.20 = 1 - 20\% \qquad r = -20\%$$

This means that for every $1.00 with which you began, you now have $0.80. This means that you earned a return of −20%.

2.2 - Cash Flows Adjusted Rate of Return

The cash flows adjusted rate of return is designed to calculate the rate of return accurately by adjusting for the timing of cash flows into and out of a portfolio. The CFA rate of return is designed to extract the return on investment by adjusting for any changes in the portfolio not directly attributable to the investment manager.

The Cash Flows Adjusted Rate of Return for any given period is given by:

$$R = 1 + r = \frac{\left[V_1 - \sum_{n=1}^{N} \left(\frac{D_n}{M} * CF_n \right) \right]}{\left[V_0 + \sum_{n=1}^{N} \left(\frac{M - D_n}{M} * CF_n \right) \right]}$$ (Eq 2-2)

where
   V_0 = the market value of the portfolio at the close of the previous period,
   V_1 = the market value of the portfolio at the close of the current period,
   M = the number of the days in the period. Cash flow adjusted returns are typically calculated over a one-month period so this would be the number of days in the month.
   CF_n = flows that are not attributable to the investment of the portfolio and so should not be included when we measure portfolio return, and
   D_n = the date on which cash flow$_n$ took place. Normally we don't know if the cash flow took place early enough to be invested for that day or not so, absent other information, we just use the date.

Example 3:

Three investment managers (Alice, Bob, & Carol) are each asked to manage a $1,000,000 portfolio. At the end of the month the value of their portfolios are $1,560,000, $1,540,000, and $1,500,000, respectively. In each case the client deposited to the portfolio an extra $300,000 during the month. This $300,000 represents an increase in the value of the portfolio that the investment manager did not generate and must be taken out of the calculation. But, given the difference in timing, who earned the best return?

Alice receives the extra funds before the market even opens on the 1st of the month, so Alice's portfolio really started at $1.30 million

$$R = \frac{\$1.56 - 0/30 * \$0.30}{\$1.00 + 30/30 * \$0.30} = \frac{\$1.56}{\$1.30} = 1.20$$ (Alice)

Bob receives the extra funds on the 10th, so Bob had the extra money to invest for the last 20 days of the month.

$$R = \frac{\$1.54 - 10/30 * \$0.30}{\$1.00 + 20/30 * \$0.30} = \frac{\$1.44}{\$1.20} = 1.20$$ (Bob)

Carol receives the extra funds on the 30th of the month after the markets close, so Carol's portfolio really managed her $1.0 million to $1.20 million and then received the extra funds.

$$R = \frac{\$1.50 - 30/30 * \$0.30}{\$1.00 + 0/30 * \$0.30} = \frac{\$1.20}{\$1.00} = 1.20$$ (Carol)

In each case we need to calculate the return for which the investment manager is responsible. We adjust out the cash flows not attributable to the way the portfolio is invested.

When there are many cash flows at various times of the month or when the cash flows are small compared to the overall value of the portfolio, we simplify by assuming that these cash flows occur at midmonth. This midmonth calculation is becoming less common as computers, databases, and automated accounting systems become more sophisticated.

$$\hat{R} = \frac{\left[V_1 - .5 * \sum_{n=1}^{N} CF_n \right]}{\left[V_0 + .5 * \sum_{n=1}^{N} CF_n \right]} \qquad \text{(Eq 2-3)}$$

Example 4:

The Investment Managers' Pension Plan shows the following activity for the Month of April

March 31	Market Value:	$12,380,000.00
April 6	Dividend Payment	4,340.00
April 12	Coupon Payment	60,000.00
April 15	Pension Contribution	92,000.00
April 21	Disbursement to Pension Pay system	−80,000.00
April 30	Market Value:	$12,400,000.00

We calculate the rate of return for April as

$$R = \frac{12,400,000.00 - \dfrac{15}{30}(92,000) - \dfrac{21}{30}(-80,000)}{12,380,000.00 + \dfrac{15}{30}(92,000) + \dfrac{9}{30}(-80,000)} = \frac{12,410,000}{12,402,000} = 1.000645457$$

$$= 1 + 0.0645\%$$

and estimate the rate of return under the midpoint assumption as

$$\hat{R} = \frac{12,400,000.00 - 0.5\,(12,000)}{12,380,000.00 + 0.5\,(12,000)} = \frac{12,394,000}{12,386,000} = 1.000646$$

$$= 1 + 0.0646\%$$

Holding period rates of return, appropriately adjusted for cash flows, are adequate for calculating returns over short periods of time. But for longer periods of time it is better to calculate the holding period return for each time period—usually one month—and to link the monthly rates of return together as needed.

2.3 - Statistical Rate of Return

If the rates of return on a portfolio are calculated monthly then we can also use statistical methods to calculate the total and average rate of return for the quarter, for the year, or for the decade.

❑   **Statistical Rate of Return:** The statistical rate of return assumes a constant investment at the beginning of every period. When you look at the return on an individual investment—without reference to when the investor bought, sold, or reinvested—or when you form expectations of future rates of return, then the statistical approach is the appropriate one to use.

To calculate the statistical rates of return we use the arithmetic total and average.

$$\overline{R_T} = \sum_{n=1}^{t} p_t \, R_t \qquad \qquad \textit{(Eq 2-4)}$$

where

p_t = the probability of observing R_t or $\dfrac{1}{n}$ where n is the number of observations

Example 5:

The rates of return for Bank of America Corporation (BAC) in the last three months of 2011 are given in Table 2-1.

Table 2-1: Bank of America (BAC)	
Month	Return
October	11.601%
November	- 20.205%
December	2.206%

The total rate of return for the quarter is –6.398%

$$\textit{Total Return} = 11.601\% - 20.205\% + 2.206\% = -6.398\%$$

The average rate of return for the quarter is –2.133% per month

$$\textit{Average Return} = \frac{11.601\% - 20.205\% + 2.206\%}{3} = \frac{-6.398\%}{3} = -2.133\%$$

The annualized rate of return is –25.592%. The annualized rate of return assumes that the three months used in the calculation are representative of returns for the entire year.

$$\textit{Annualized Return} = \left[\frac{11.601\% - 20.205\% + 2.206\%}{3} \right] * 12 = -25.592\%$$

The statistical rate of return or arithmetic average is the least biased estimate of the true mean μ of a population and is thus, by definition, equal to the expected value of the return E[R].

2.4 - Time-Weighted Rate of Return

If the rate of return on the portfolio is calculated monthly, we can use the time weighted rate of return to calculate the rate of return for the quarter, for the year, or for the decade.

❑ **Time Weighted Rate of Return:** The time weighted rate of return assumes that the portfolio is completely reinvested at the end of every period. When you look at the return on an investment when the investor bought, sold, and reinvested, the time weighted approach is the appropriate one to use.

To calculate the time weighted rates of return we use the geometric total and mean.

$$\overline{R}_T = \sqrt[T]{\prod_{t=1}^{T} R_t}$$

(Eq 2-5)

Example 6:

John Q. Investor put $1,000 into Bank of America shares at the close on September 31, 2011. The rates of return for Bank of America Corporation (BAC) in the last three months of 2011 were

Table 2-2: Bank of America (BAC)		
Month	Return	Portfolio Value
September		$1,000.00
October	11.601%	$1,116.01
November	-20.205%	$890.52
December	2.206%	$910.17

The total time-weighted rate of return on BAC for the quarter is – 8.983%

Total Return = (1 + 0.11601)(1 – 0.20205)(1 + 0.02206) = 0.91017 = 1 – 8.983%

The monthly rate of return on BAC for the quarter is – 3.089%

Average Return = $\sqrt[3]{1.11601 * 0.79795 * 1.02206}$ = 0.96911 = 1 – 3.089%

The annualized, time-weighted rate of return on BAC is – 31.375%

Annualized Return = $\left[\sqrt[3]{1.11601 * 0.79795 * 1.02206} \right]^{12}$ = 1 – 31.375%

2.4.1 - Statistical versus Time Weighted Rates of Return

Statistical rates of return are sample observations on a population—investment return— about which we need information. We use statistical returns to evaluate and predict risk and return in any other month drawn from the same population. Time weighted rates of return capture the reinvestment of one months gains or losses in subsequent months and are more appropriate in portfolio measurement.

Example 7:

John Q. Investor put $10,000 into the Sly Investment Fund at the beginning of the year. The rates of return for the first four months are given in Table 2-3.

Table 2-3: Sly Investment Funds Returns

Month	Return R		Rate of Return r	Portfolio Value
December				$10,000.00
January	1.5000	=>	50.0%	$15,000.00
February	0.5000	=>	-50.0%	$7,500.00
March	1.5000	=>	50.0%	$11,250.00
April	0.5000	=>	-50.0%	$5,625.00

The average rate of return for the four month period is 0.00%

$$R = \frac{1.50 + 0.50 + 1.50 + 0.50}{4} = 1.00 = 1 + 0.00\%$$

On average, the Sly Investment Fund earned 0.00% rate of return. Our expectation for the next month's return is thus 0%.

However, the monthly rate of return over the four month period is – 13.4%

$$R = \sqrt[4]{(1.50)\ (0.50)\ (1.50)\ (0.50)} = \sqrt[4]{0.5625} = 0.8660254 = 1 - 13.39746\%$$

JQ's $10,000 investment was worth $5,625.00 at the end of April not $10,000. His portfolio loses value overall because the gains and losses earned in each month were automatically reinvested in the following month.

When Sly lost 50% in February he lost 50% of JQ's original investment ($10,000 became $5,000). He also lost 50% of the gains he made in January ($5,000 became $2,500). Reinvesting all gains and losses this way means that over the four-month period he lost an average of 13.40% per month.

If we compare the value of the JQ's portfolio to one that loses 13.39746% of its value every month for four months, then we can see that the market value at the end of April is the same in both portfolios.

Table 2-4: Sly Investment Funds Returns

Month	Return r	Portfolio Value	Return r	Portfolio Value
December		$10,000.00		$10,000.00
January	-13.4%	$8,660.25	50.0%	$15,000.00
February	-13.4%	$7,500.00	-50.0%	$7,500.00
March	-13.4%	$6,495.19	50.0%	$11,250.00
April	-13.4%	$5,625.00	-50.0%	$5,625.00

2.5 - Internal Rate of Return

The internal rate of return is the rate that will make the net present value of all the cash flows to termination equal to zero.

$$0 = \sum_{t=o}^{T} \frac{CF_t}{\left(1 + \dfrac{rr}{n}\right)^t}$$ (Eq 2-6)

Consider the following time line showing an investment of $10,000 on December 31, 2012. The investment yields four cash flows over the life of the project as shown in Figure 2-1.

Figure 2-1: Time Line of Cash Flows from an Initial Investment of $10,000.

Dec 31, 2012	Dec 31, 2013	Dec 31, 2014	Dec 31, 2015	Dec 31, 2016
-$10,000	$510	$2,000	$4,500	$5,000

The internal rate of return on this investment is 6%.

At a discount rate of 6% the present value of the cash flows generated by the investment equals the $10,000 initial investment.

$$PV_{2012} = \frac{\$510}{(1.06)^1} + \frac{\$2,000}{(1.06)^2} + \frac{\$4,500}{(1.06)^3} + \frac{\$5,000}{(1.06)^4} = \$10,000$$

Therefore the Net Present Value of the entire investment equals zero.

$$NPV_{2012} = \frac{-\$10,000}{(1.06)^0} + \frac{\$510}{(1.06)^1} + \frac{\$2,000}{(1.06)^2} + \frac{\$4,500}{(1.06)^3} + \frac{\$5,000}{(1.06)^4} = \$0$$

If we evaluate the investment at the end of the time line, on December 31, 2016, then the Value of the investment is $12,624.58. This is also called the Future Value. But the Net Present Value of the investment is still $0.

$$PV_{2016} = -\$10,000(1.06)^4$$
$$= -\$12,624.58$$
$$PV_{2016} = \$510(1.06)^3 + \$2,000(1.06)^2 + \$4,500(1.06)^1 + \$5,000(1.06)^0$$
$$= \$12,624.58$$

$$NPV_{2016} = -\$10,000(1.06)^4 + \$510(1.06)^3 + \$2,000(1.06)^2 + \$4,500(1.06)^1 + \$5,000(1.06)^0$$
$$= \$0$$

Calculator Techniques 2-1:

Use the cash flow spreadsheet [CF] to specify the payment structure.

Then [IRR] [CPT] calculates the internal rate of return as 6.00%

DATA	Enter	Compute
CFo =	-10,000	
C01 =	510	
F01 =	1	
C02 =	2,000	
F02 =	1	
C03 =	4,500	
F03 =	1	
C04 =	5,000	
F04 =	1	
IRR		5.9996

Calculator Techniques 2-2:

Use the cash flow spreadsheet [CF] to specify the payment structure, but leave the initial investment unspecified.

Then use [NPV] to calculate the Present Value at any specified Rate I.

At I = 6.0% the present value is $9,999.88; at I = 8% the present value is only $9,434.29

DATA	Enter	Compute
CFo =	0	
C01 =	510	
F01 =	1	
C02 =	2,000	
F02 =	1	
C03 =	4,500	
F03 =	1	
C04 =	5,000	
F04 =	1	
NPV		
I =	6%	
NPV =		-9,999.88

Example 8:

You are given management of a trust of $100,000. $5,000 is paid to the trust beneficiary at the end of each year for three years. The trust is then terminated at a target value of $110,000 when the trust beneficiary reaches age 21.

Verify that you must earn a constant 8.1% return throughout the life of the trust to accommodate your client's requirements.

When in doubt use a time line.

Figure 2-2: Time Line of Cash Flows Required from the Trust

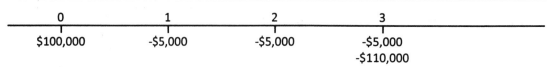

0	1	2	3
$100,000	-$5,000	-$5,000	-$5,000
			-$110,000

Mathematically:

$$\$100,000 \approx \frac{\$5,000}{1.081} + \frac{\$5,000}{1.081^2} + \frac{\$5,000}{1.081^3} + \frac{\$110,000}{1.081^3}$$

If we map out the investments and distributions of the trust, we can see that the 8.1% return generates the required $110,000 when the trust terminates.

Table 2-5: Investment Trust with an 8.1% IRR

Year	Invest	Return	Value	Distribute	Final Value
1	$100,000.00	8.10%	$108,100.00	$ -5,000.00	$ 103,100.00
2	$103,100.00	8.10%	$111,451.10	$ -5,000.00	$ 106,451.10
3	$106,451.10	8.10%	$115,073.64	$ -5,000.00	$ 110,073.64

The difficulty with the internal rate of return is that calculation is by trial and error. This is why calculators are essential.

Calculator Techniques 2-3:	DATA	Enter	Compute
Use the cash flow [CF] to specify the payment structure.	CFo =	-100,000	
	C01 =	-5,000	
	F01 =	2	
Note that the final payment is the sum of the last $5,000 annual payment and the terminal value of $110,000. If you separate them, then your calculator will calculate the rate of return as though the final payment were made in four years rather than three.	C02 =	-115,000	
	F02 =	1	
	IRR		8.0780

The internal rate of return (IRR) calculation is a familiar tool across all areas of finance: investment, wealth and risk management, and corporate finance. Best practice is to go beyond mere mathematical calculation and to appreciate its uses as well as to understand its assumptions and limitations. These themes will be examined in greater detail under fixed income markets where IRR forms the basis of various measures of yield.

Chapter 2 - Questions and Problems

2-1:

You begin the semester with $2,000,000.00. What would be the holding period rate of return if the market value of the portfolio at the end of the semester is

A. $2,124,770.00?

B. $1,843,748.00?

C. $2,000,000.00?

2-2:

The Union of Truck Drivers' Pension Plan shows the following activity for the month of January:

December 31	Market Value	$34,978,567.03
January 3	Bond Income	$14,400.00
January 15	Pension Contribution	$3,098.10
January 18	Bond Income	$600.00
January 21	Pension Payments	($9,879.20)
January 22	Dividend Received	$1,700.00
January 31	Pension Contribution	$3,098.10
January 31	Market Value	$34,993,897.09

A. Calculate the rate of return for January using the cash flow adjusted method.

B. Calculate the rate of return for January using the midmonth method. How does this compare with the exact method?

2-3:

John Q. Investor buys 1,000 shares of IBM at $57 per share. IBM pays a dividend of 30¢ per share, and at the end of the month IBM is trading at $56.75.

A. Is the dividend a cash flow in the rate of return calculation?

B. What is the rate of return for this investment?

2-4:

John Q. Investor purchased shares of Discovery Café on January 2nd at $25 per share. He earned a dividend of 25¢ on February 10th. John kept his dividend in cash (he did not reinvest it). The price of Discovery Café closed at

January	$28.
February	$30.
March	$29.

Ignoring brokerage commission, calculate

A.   The monthly return for each of January, February, and March

B.   The total time-weighted rate of return for the quarter

C.   The holding period return for the quarter

2-5:

Table 2-6 shows the market value for the Quark Investment Fund at the end of each month for six months and the corresponding rates of return.

Table 2-6: Quark Investment Fund

Date	Market Value	Return
December 31	$1,000,000.	
January 31	$500,000.	- 50%
February 28	$750,000.	+ 50%
March 31	$375,000.	- 50%
April 30	$562,500	+ 50%
May 31	$281,250.	- 50%
June 30	$421,875.	+50%

A.   Calculate the total and average rate of return for the six-month period. Would it be misleading for the Quark Investment Fund to quote these rate of return in a marketing brochure?

B.   Calculate the holding period return.

C.   Calculate the total and monthly time weighted rates of return. What do you notice?

2-6:

You purchased 1000 shares of Sun Microsystems (SUNW) in December 1995 at $2.50 per share. Sun Microsystems closed December 31, 2000, at $27.875. Sun does not pay dividends.

A.   What is the average monthly return on your investment in SUNW?

B.   What is the average annual return on your investment in SUNW?

2-7:

William Gates III gives me $1,000,000 to invest. At the end of the first year I must report to Mr. Gates a loss of 50% for the year. However, at the end of the second year I report a gain of 100% for the year.

A. What is the market value of Mr. Gates's portfolio at the end of the two-year period?

B. What is the average annual return on Mr. Gates's portfolio?

C. What is the expected annual return on the portfolio in year three?

2-8:

The rates of return on shares of Hypothetical Resources (HR) and Discovery Café (DVC) for the first four months of the year were

	Hypothetical Resources (HR)	Discovery Café (DVC)
January	3.6%	- 6.3%
February	23.5%	- 12.9%
March	- 12.9%	23.5%
April	-6.3%	3.6%

A. Susan Q. Speculator invested $1,000,000 in shares of each HR and DVC on December 31. Calculate the value of Susan's shares at the end of January, February, March, and April.

B. What is the holding period rate of return of Susan's investment over the four months? How does this compare to the time-weighted rate of return? To the statistical rate of return?

C. Why is Susan's four-month return on HR and DVC the same?

D. John Q. Investor invested $250,000 in shares of each HR and DVC on December 31, January 31, February 28, and March 31, leaving the uninvested portion of his $2,000,000 portfolio in cash. Calculate the value of John's shares at the end of January, February, March, and April.

E. What is the holding period rate of return on JQ's investment over the four months? How does this compare to the time-weighted rate of return? To the statistical rate of return?

F. Why is JQ's four-month return on HR different from the four-month return on DVC?

2-9:

You begin with a portfolio of $1 million on January 31. The market value of the portfolio is $1,020,000 at the end of February, $1,099,600 at the end of March, $1,074,750 at the end of April, and $1,730,000 at the end of May.

A.   What is the rate of return in each month?

B.   What is the holding period return?

C.   What is the average rate of return over the four-month period?

D.   What is the time weighted rate of return for the four-month period?

E.   What is the monthly time weighted rate of return?

F.   What was the annualized time weighted rate of return?

❑   **Accuracy Note:** All calculations should be taken to at least eight decimal places. This is crucial when you calculate the time weighted rate of return over several periods. The best way is to keep the monthly returns in the memory of your calculator rather than writing them down and reentering.

G.   Just as you go to publish your phenomenal results you remember that the client put an additional $500,000 into the account on May 1st. Go back and recalculate the rates of return.

2-10:

John Q. Investor purchased 1000 shares of Enron (ENRNQ) January 31, 2002, at $0.415. On February 28 Enron closed at $0.275

A.   What is the rate of return over the one-month period?

B.   What is the annualized time-weighted rate of return?

C.   What is the annualized statistical rate of return? Why does this number not make any sense?

2-11:

A trust is established with an initial cash balance of $100,000. You are required to pay $5,000 to the trust beneficiary at the end of each of the next three years. At the same time as the final $5,000 payment the $110,000 remaining in the trust will be paid out to the Hospital Foundation.

A.   What rate of return is being assumed in this trust structure?

B.   What rate of return would you require if the payment were only $4,000 per year and the terminal value of the trust was required to be $110,000?

C.   What if the payments were $6,000 per year with a terminal requirement of $100,000?

Chapter 2 - Financial Models

2.1 - Cash Flows Adjusted Rate of Return

Model 2.1 - Cash Flows Adjusted Rate of Return

Date	Description	Cash Flow	Market Value	Exclude	Calculations	
					Numerator	Denominator
March 31			$ 12,380,000.00			
April 6	Dividend Payment	$ 4,340.00				
April 12	Coupon Payment	$ 60,000.00				
April 15	Pension Contribution	$ 92,000.00		x		
April 21	Pension Disbursement	$ (80,000.00)		x		
April 30			$ 12,400,000.00			

Days in the month	
Rate of Return	
Ratio	
Rate of Return	

Rate of Return:

A. The template for Model 2.1 specifies the activity in an investment portfolio during the month of April. Cash flows that should not be measured as part of the investment rate of return are so indicated with an x in the Exclude column. User input is coded finance blue.

B. The unadjusted return is calculated from closing market value to closing market value. The denominator in I5 = E5, and the numerator in H13 = E13. Both market values are relayed into the calculation and so are coded finance green.

C. Make room for possible adjustments to the numerator and denominator by summing H14 = sum(H5:H13) and I14 = sum(I5:I13).

D. The Ratio in I19 = H14/I14 and the Rate of Return in I20 = I19-1. These are calculations so are coded black.

Cash flow adjustments:

E. To make the cash flow adjustments we need the number of days in the relevant month. I16 = DAY(B13).

F. To calculate the adjustment to the numerator we start with the first cash flow. Set H6 = IF($F6>"", -$D6*DAY($B6)/$I$16, 0). This is an =IF() statement that translates into: If there is a code in F6 then calculate the negative of the cash flow in D6, multiply by the days in the date in B6, divided by the total number of days in the month already calculated into I16. If not, then 0.

G. To calculate the adjustment to the denominator we use start with the first cash flow. Set H6 = IF($F6>"",$D6*($I$16 - DAY($B6))/$I$16,0). This is an =IF() statement that translates: If there is a code in F6 then calculate the cash flow in D6 times the remaining days in the date in B6 divided by the total number of days in the month. If not, then 0.

Cell Addresses and Locks

H. In both these cash flow adjustment formulae we use the locks on the cell address. The cell address is = \$D6 then the \$ locks the D but the 6 is unlocked. If we copy-drag this formula to another cell then the \$D6 will remain \$D6 even if we copy-drag to the right, but \$D6 will increase to\$D7, \$D8, \$D9, ... as we copy-drag down.

I.   The cell address \$I\$16 is locked in both column I and row 16. This way, as we copy-drag this formula we continue to use the number of days in the month calculated into cell I16.

J.   Shortcut: [F4] is a toggle that changes the lock on a cell formula. =D6 becomes =\$D\$6 becomes =D\$6 becomes =\$D6 becomes =D6. This way you can easily change the lock code as you build your formula into the cell.

K.   Copy-drag the formulae in H6:I6 down to H12:I12. The adjustments are now included in the rate of return.

L.   Test the model with the data from Example 2.4 and Question 2.2

Model 2.1 - Cash Flows Adjusted Rate of Return

Date	Description	Cash Flow	Market Value	Exclude		Calculations		
						Numerator		Denominator
March 31			\$ 12,380,000.00					\$ 12,380,000.00
April 6	Dividend Payment	\$ 4,340.00			\$	-	\$	-
April 12	Coupon Payment	\$ 60,000.00			\$	-	\$	-
April 15	Pension Contribution	\$ 92,000.00		x	\$	(46,000.00)	\$	46,000.00
April 21	Pension Disbursement	\$ (80,000.00)		x	\$	56,000.00	\$	(24,000.00)
					\$	-	\$	-
					\$	-	\$	-
					\$	-	\$	-
April 30			\$ 12,400,000.00		\$ 12,400,000.00			
					\$ 12,410,000.00		\$ 12,402,000.00	

Days in the month	30

Rate of Return	
Ratio	1.000645
Rate of Return	0.0645%

2.2 - Internal Rate of Return

Model 2.2 - Internal Rate of Return

Date		Cash Flow	IRR Calculations	
December 31, 2012	$	(10,000.00)	Total Payments	
December 31, 2013	$	510.00	Internal Rate of Return	
December 31, 2014	$	2,000.00		
December 31, 2015	$	4,500.00		
December 31, 2016	$	5,000.00		

A. User input consists of cash flows and the dates on which they occur.
B. Total payments are calculated as F4 = SUM(C$4:C$12). Note that $4 locks the cell address to row 4 and $12 locks the cell address to row 12.

Internal Rate of Return:
C. The internal rate of return is calculated as F5 = XIRR(C$4:C$12,B$4:B$12,5%) This translates as: calculate the internal rate of return from the cash flows in C$4:C$12 and the dates in B$4:B$12. Start the procedure at 5%.
D. Excel starts the procedure at 5%. The NPV at 5% is $300.55. This is too high, so try 6%. The NPV at 6% is – $0.12. This is too low, so try 5.9%. The NPV at 5.9% is $29.39. Excel continues this procedure until it calculates the IRR as 5.9974470734596200%
E. Test the model with the data from Example 2.8 and Question 2.11.

Model 2.2 - Internal Rate of Return

Date		Cash Flow	IRR Calculations		
December 31, 2012	$	(10,000.00)	Total Payments	$	2,010.00
December 31, 2013	$	510.00	Internal Rate of Return		6.00%
December 31, 2014	$	2,000.00			
December 31, 2015	$	4,500.00			
December 31, 2016	$	5,000.00			

$\mathcal{R}$isk is the measurable possibility of incurring a rate of return different from that which you expect. When we take a risk we know that the return can be higher or lower than we expect; the risk is that it is different from what we expect.

We measure risk in a number of different ways but uncertainty, by definition, cannot be measured.

3.1 - Risk and Uncertainty

If we throw a pair of dice then we can measure all possible outcomes and calculate the probability of each outcome.

In any one throw of the dice there is a probability that the result will be different from what we expect or want. We want a seven but throw a two. This is risk. Risk is measurable: The probability of throwing a seven is always 16.666667% no matter how lucky we think we are.

However, there is no uncertainty. We will never see a one; we will never see a thirteen; and we will never see a probability of throwing a seven at anything other than 16.666667%.

Table 3-1: Two Dice	
Outcome	Probability
2	1/36
3	2/36
4	3/36
5	4/36
6	5/36
7	6/36
8	5/36
9	4/36
10	3/36
11	2/36
12	1/36

In this case the experiment is designed so that there is no uncertainty; the introduction of uncertainty by adding a 13 or changing the probabilities by weighting the dice unequally is cheating and invalidates the game.

Neither natural nor financial phenomena are so accommodating. Insurance companies are hit with two "once every hundred years" storms in the same year and stock returns are totally outside the curve more frequently than possible if our risk measures were complete.

Eugene Fama[1] states "(Returns of) more than five standard deviations from the mean should be observed about once every 7,000 years. If fact such observations seem to occur about once every three to four years."

Similar observations on different markets suggest that no matter how sophisticated our measures of risk, there is still a significant degree of uncertainty that plays havoc with our models.

3.2 - Standard Deviation

Statistics tell us that if you have a large number of random events they will tend to distribute in the standard normal distribution. In a normal distribution, the mean is symmetrically surrounded by all the elements in its population. This is a very convenient and powerful property of normal distributions and allows us to describe the distribution with just two measures, the mean and the variance.

---

1   Eugene F. Fama, "The Behavior of Stock Market Prices", *Journal of Business* Vol. 38, (1965): 34-105.

If we could measure and record all the observations, the mean would be observable. But nature and markets are seldom so revealing. We must rely on the observable, measurable data and infer the true population mean and variance.

In a normal distribution with mean μ (mu) and standard deviation σ (sigma), observations will be

± one standard deviation of the mean 68.27% of the time,
± two standard deviations of the mean 95.45% of the time, and
± three standard deviations of the mean 99.73% of the time.

Figure 3-1: Normal Distribution

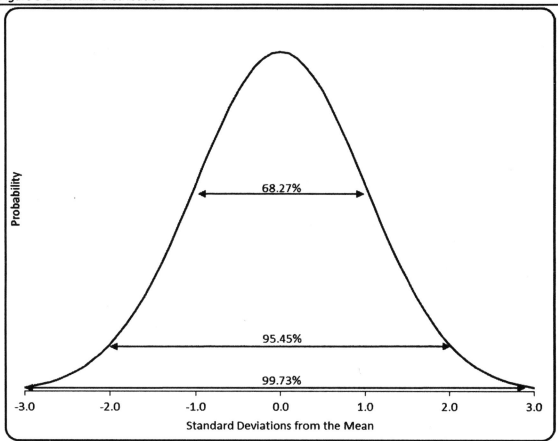

□ **Expected Value E[X]:** The expected value of a distribution is its arithmetic average or mean. The expected value of a distribution X is designated by E [X].

$$\mu: \quad \overline{X} = E\ [X] = \sum_{i=1}^{n} p_i\, X_i \qquad\qquad (Eq\ 3\text{-}1)$$

where the population mean μ is estimated by the sample mean $\overline{X}$ and p_i is the probability when you are working with predictions and $1/n$ when you are working with n pieces of historical data.

❑ **Variance (σ^2):** a measure of the dispersion of the observations around the mean. The variance is the average distance from the mean squared.

$$\sigma^2: \quad s^2 = E[X^2] - E[X]^2 \qquad\qquad \textit{(Eq 3-2)}$$

where the population standard deviation σ^2 is estimated by the sample variance s^2.

❑ **Standard deviation (σ):** a measure of the spread between the observed value and the expected value. The standard deviation equals the square root of the variance

$$\sigma: \quad s = \sqrt{E[X - E[X]]^2} \qquad\qquad \textit{(Eq 3-3)}$$

Standard deviation may be calculated on a single security or on a portfolio of investments. The standard deviation is calculated as follows

$$\sigma: \quad s = \sqrt{p_i * (X_i - E[X])^2}$$
$$= \sqrt{E[X - E[X]^2]}$$
$$= \sqrt{E[X^2] - E[X]^2}$$

where again p_i is the probability when you are working with predictions and $1/n$ when you are working with n pieces of historical data. $E[X]$ is the expected value or mean of X.

Example 1:

On the toss of one die the possible outcomes are 1, 2, 3, 4, 5, 6.

$$E[X] = \frac{1 + 2 + 3 + 4 + 5 + 6}{6} = \frac{21}{6}$$

$$E[X^2] = \frac{1^2 + 2^2 + 3^2 + 4^2 + 5^2 + 6^2}{6} = \frac{91}{6}$$

We calculate the variance and standard deviation as follows:

$$\sigma^2 = E[X^2] - E[X]^2 = \left(\frac{91}{6}\right) - \left(\frac{21}{6}\right)^2 = \frac{35}{12}$$

$$\sigma = \sqrt{\frac{35}{12}} = 1.707825$$

We tend to use σ rather than σ^2 because standard deviations are easier to visualize than variances.

Figure 3-2: Risk Visualization with Standard Deviation

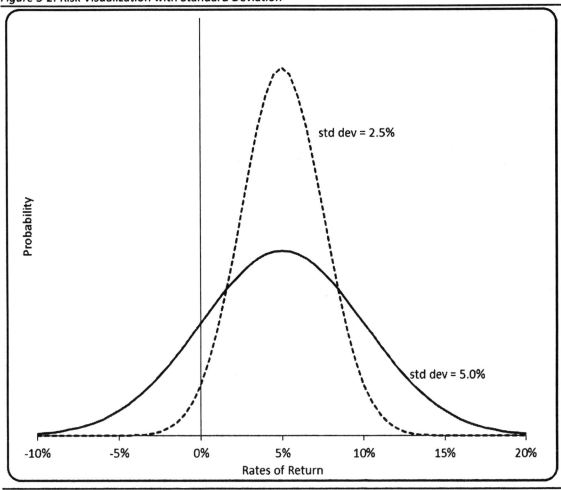

3.2.1 - Coefficient of Variation

The coefficient of variation (CV) is a standardized measure of dispersion about the expected value. It is generally regarded as a better measure of risk when the alternatives under consideration have widely different expected returns. The coefficient of variation is the ratio of risk to return and is given by

$$CV = \frac{\sigma}{E[R]} \qquad (Eq\ 3\text{-}4)$$

In Figure 3-3 it is difficult to see which investment is riskier. Although an investment with a standard deviation of 5% is riskier in absolute terms than one with a standard deviation of 2.5%, the real question is whether or not the added return is worth the added risk.

The coefficient of variation allows us to conclude that the added return does not compensate for the added risk because the CV increases from 0.5 to 0.625.

Figure 3-3: Coefficient of Variation

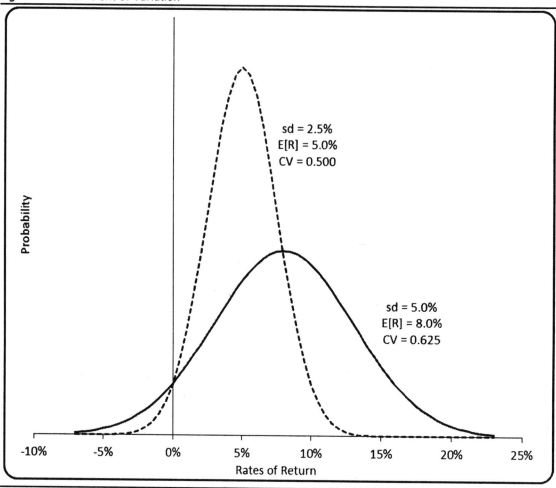

Example 2:

Over the ten-year period ending December 2011 shares of Apple (AAPL), Boeing (BA), Berkshire Hathaway B (BRK-B), and Caterpillar (CAT) generated returns as indicated in Table 3-2.

Table 3-2: Monthly Rates of Return January 2001 to December 2011				
	AAPL	BA	BRK-B	CAT
observations	120	120	120	120
Average Return	3.666%	1.044%	0.476%	1.252%
Standard Deviation	11.047%	8.115%	5.171%	10.869%
Variance	0.01220	0.00659	0.00267	0.01181
CV	0.333	0.631	0.562	0.944

From the standard deviations Apple appears to be a riskier investment than any of the others, but the coefficient of variation shows Caterpillar to be considerably more risky relative to expected returns than either Boeing or Apple.

Chapter 3 - Questions and Problems

3-1:

Show algebraically that the variance formula

$$\sigma^2 = E[\,X - E[\,X\,]]^2$$

is mathematically equal to the variance formula

$$\sigma^2 = E[\,X^2\,] - E[\,X\,]^2$$

3-2:

Using the data in Table 3-3 calculate the Variance and Coefficient of Variation. Which is the riskiest investment?

Table 3-3: Monthly Returns

	Procter&Gamble	Boeing	Google
	PG	BA	GOOG
Mean	1.07%	2.42%	6.24%
Std Dev	3.43%	3.58%	11.31%
Variance			
CV			

Chapter 3 - Financial Models

3.1 - Risk and Return

A. The template for model 3.1 specifies the Standard & Poor Index of the 500 largest, publicly traded American companies at the end of the calendar year for 26 years.

Model 3.1 - S&P Annual Rates of Return

	Sample Size	25	25	25	25
	Sum	209.708%	5.193	0.000%	75.740%
	Average	8.388%	1.068		
Sample	Variance	3.156%			3.156%
	Standard Deviation	17.765%			17.765%
Population	Variance	3.030%			3.030%
	Standard Deviation	17.406%			17.406%

Year End	S&P500	Return	1+r	Deviation	Deviation^2
2011	1,257.60	-0.003%	1.0000	-8.391%	0.704%
2010	1,257.64	12.783%	1.1278	4.394%	0.193%
2009	1,115.10	23.454%	1.2345	15.066%	2.270%
1988	277.72	12.401%	1.1240	4.013%	0.161%
1987	247.08	2.028%	1.0203	-6.361%	0.405%
1986	242.17				

Rates of Return:

B. Begin with 2011: D12 =C12/C13 − 1. Excel follows the rules of mathematics, so it calculates the ratio before subtracting the dollar with which you started.

C. Either hover the mouse over the bottom right corner of the cell until the cursor turns into a plus sign, then left click and drag the formula down the column or use the keyboard shortcut. The keyboard shortcuts minimize mousing time. Start in D12. Highlight range D12:D36 with Ctrl+Shift+ ↓. Then use Shift+Ctrl+D to copy the formula in D12 down the entire column to D36.

D. Sample Size: Use =COUNT(D12:D36) to verify that there are 25 rates of return

E. Sum: Use =SUM(D12:D36) to calculate the total rate of return. The =SUM() function adds together each element within the ().

F. Average: Use =D4/D3 to calculate the average annual rate of return

G. Sample variance and standard deviation: Use =VAR.S() and STDEV.S() to calculate sample statistics.

H. Population variance and standard deviation: Use =VAR.P() and STDEV.P() to calculate population statistics.

Time Weighted Rates of Return:

I. To calculate the time weighted rates of return we need to add the dollar with which we started, otherwise it won't get reinvested. So E12 is given by =C12/C13. Note that, in keeping with best practice, we calculate from the raw data in column C, rather than just adding 1 to the calculations in column D.

J. Sum: Use =PRODUCT() to calculate the total time weighted return. Just as the SUM(D12:D36) calculates D12+D13+ ... +D35+D36, PRODUCT(D12:D36) calculates D12xD13x ... xD35xD36

K. Average: Use =E4^(1/E3) to calculate the 25th root.

Variance and Standard Deviation:

L. Deviation: Calculate the deviation from the mean into column F. Use =D12-$D$5 and copy-drag the formula down the column. The $ in $D$5 keeps this exact number in the formula as you copy-drag; D12 changes to D13, D14, etc. The sum of the deviations should be zero. This confirms that the mean is in the middle (as it should be by definition).

M. Deviation^2: Calculate the squared deviation into column G. Use =F12^2 and calculate the sum.

N. Population Variance and Standard Deviation: The population variance is the average squared deviation. Use =G4/G3 for the variance and =SQRT(G8) for the standard deviation.

O.   Sample Variance and Standard Deviation: The sample variance is the average squared deviation. Use =G4/(G3-1) for the variance and =SQRT(G8) for the standard deviation.

Population and Sample Variances

The variances, both population and sample, as well as both measures of standard deviation were calculated using simple rates of return. The notion of an "average squared surprise" in variance becomes obvious from the calculations in D8 and G8. We get the same result from the Excel function as from the sum of the differences squared.

The population variance and standard deviation are calculated using the complete population. We assume that 25 observations we have are all that exist. We divide the sum by N to calculate the average.

The sample variance and standard deviation are calculated by dividing by N − 1 to account for the lost degree of freedom. The degrees of freedom are the number of observations we can use to calculate something.

For example, If we have one rate of return then we use it to calculate the mean. There is nothing left with which to calculate the standard deviation. If we have two rates of return we use both of them to calculate the mean. By definition they deviate from the mean by exactly the same amount. We only have one thing to measure.

The same statistics are calculated in column D using the VAR.S(), STDEV.S(), VAR.P(), and STDEV.P() functions built into Excel. While one of these cells is active, click the [fx] next to the formula bar at the top of the spreadsheet. A dialog box opens. It explains the formula and indicates over what range of cells the function calculates. Any preprogrammed function in Excel is nicely explained in this dialog box.

Excel Functions

To see all the functions in Excel, just open the function wizard. Click on the [fx] insert function button immediately to the right of the formula bar. If the active cell already has a function, then Excel will open the applet for that function. If the active cell does not already have a function, then Excel will open the Function Wizard. Use the drop-down list to sort through Excel's categories of functions, the function names to see Excel's selection of preprogrammed functions, and see a brief explanation of each one. For example, the Statistical category lists 98 different functions in alphabetical order. Variance functions are under V. Click on VAR.P() for population variance and VAR.S for sample variance. In each case you can click on "Help on this Function" for a more complete explanation as well as for the mathematical formula used in the calculation.

Some Interpretations

Your client asks: "If I invested in this market, what would I expect any single year's return to be?"

Assuming the returns were random and normally distributed, we could answer with the statistical average: 8.388%.

This answer is only part of the story though because we have not talked about the variability around that expectation. Using the past 25 years as a sample of what might be, we need to use the sample standard deviation of the returns to talk about the likelihood of expected returns: 17.406%

Now, using the properties of the normal distribution, we may be able to answer, "You could expect a random annual return in any year of 8.388% ± 17.406%, 68% of the time." In other words, 68% of the time, the return for any year should be between − 9.0% and 25.8%. If a higher certainty (confidence interval) were desired, then we could use two standard deviations above or below the mean for a 95% confidence, or three for 99%. Obviously, the more confident we are of the return, the wider the range of possible returns in that confidence interval. Does this guarantee that we cannot see a year when the returns fall outside these ranges? No, there is no guarantee with either statistics or investments.

We are trying to measure risk, and to that extent, we have a measure. To say that an observation COULD NOT fall outside the range, we would have to conclude that we have eliminated ALL uncertainty of the return.

In conclusion, our focus should be to understand what the statistics are telling us and how we can use them to make informed decisions. The task of memorizing formulas and computing statistics is an entirely mechanical process. The former are things for which people in finance should strive, the later represent things machines are designed to do quickly and accurately.

$\mathcal{D}$ iversification reduces risk exposure by establishing a portfolio of investments rather than investing in a single asset. Diversification reduces risk because stock prices and returns are imperfectly correlated. This is the theoretical equivalent of saying: "Don't put all your eggs in one basket."

The benefits of diversification were not always obvious. In a letter dated August 15, 1934, John Maynard Keynes wrote: "As time goes on, I become more convinced that the right method of investments is to put fairly large sums into enterprises which one thinks one knows something about and in management of which one thoroughly believes. It is a mistake to think that one limits one's risk by spreading too much between enterprises about which one knows little." Gerald Loeb[1] stated "Diversification is an admission of not knowing what to do and an effort to strike an average."

Modern portfolio theory and the theoretical underpinnings of diversification began with Harry Markowitz[2], who introduced the concepts of efficient portfolios and the benefits of diversification. Tobin[3] extended this concept by adding to the portfolio a risk-free asset, thus allowing investors to leverage their investments.

4.1 - How Diversification Reduces Risk

A portfolio is not a random collection of assets, but a combination of assets that together accomplish some specific objective. Diversification reduces risk because it combines assets whose deviation from their expected returns are sometimes in opposite directions.

Consider the performance of two hypothetical funds, a stock fund whose performance is procyclical, and a bond fund whose performance is countercyclical:

Table 4-1: Projected Returns on Stock and Bond Funds in Percentage Points

Scenario	Prob -ability	Stock Fund Return S	Stock Fund Deviation $(S-\bar{S})$	Bond Fund Return B	Bond Fund Deviation $(B-\bar{B})$	Portfolio Return $(S*B)$	Portfolio Deviation $(S-\bar{S})(B-\bar{B})$
Rapid Growth	25%	30.0	19.0	-2.0	-6.0	-60.0	-114.0
Balanced Growth	50%	12.0	1.0	5.0	1.0	60.0	1.0
Recession	25%	-10.0	-21.0	8.0	4.0	-80.0	-84.0
Expected Value	$E[X]$	11.0	0.0	4.0	0.0	-5.0	-49.0
	$E[X^2]$		2.010		0.135		
	σ		14.177		3.674		
	Covariance:			$COV_{B,S}$	-49.0		

The covariance of -49.0 tells us that there is an inverse relationship between the two funds; they move in opposite directions. The negative number results from the multiplication of a positive deviation and a negative deviation; if the deviations were both positive or both negative, then they would be moving in the same direction, and the product of the two would be positive.

---

1   Gerald Loeb, *The Battle for Investment Survival*, Wiley Investment Classic, 1935, 1996.
2   Harry M. Markowitz, "Portfolio Selection", *Journal of Finance*, Vol. 7 no.1 (1952): 77-91.
3   James Tobin, "Liquidity Preference as Behavior Towards Risk", *The Review of Economic Studies*, Vol. 25, (1958): 65-86.

We calculate the correlation coefficient ρ

$$\rho_{S,B} = \frac{Cov_{S,B}}{\sigma_S \ \sigma_B} = \frac{-49.0}{14.177 * 3.674} = -0.94066$$ *(Eq 4-1)*

Rearranging we can see that the covariance is calculated as

$$Cov_{S,B} = \rho_{S,B} \ \sigma_S \ \sigma_B$$ *(Eq 4-2)*

The correlation coefficient ρ = − 0.941 tells us that stock and bond returns in this case are almost perfectly negatively correlated.

If we put all our money into the stock fund, then we would expect the portfolio to suffer losses whenever the economy went into a recession. If we put all our money into the bond fund, then we would expect the portfolio to suffer losses whenever the economy went into a period of rapid growth. Rapid growth is often accompanied by higher inflation, higher yields on bonds, and thus falling prices for the bonds in our portfolio.

If we put both stock and bond funds into the portfolio, then when stocks are underperforming, the bond fund is generating higher than expected returns. If we balance our portfolio properly, then we can adjust the percentage of our portfolio in each fund to minimize our risk exposure for the expected return we generate. When we balance our portfolio this way we make it efficient.

4.2 - Efficient Portfolio Frontier

An efficient portfolio is one that is balanced such that it provides the maximum expected return for any given level of risk or the minimum level of risk for any given expected return.

❑   **Portfolio:** a group or collection of investments structured with the intention of achieving some objective (usually returns), subject to constraints (usually risk)

Example 1:

Suppose there are only two available investments

Tardis Intertemporal (TI) has an expected return of 21% with a standard deviation of 40%;
$$E[R_{TI}] = 0.15 \qquad \sigma_{TI} = 0.20 \qquad CV_{TI} = 1.33$$

Hypothetical Resources (HR) has an expected return of 15% with a standard deviation of 20%.
$$E[R_{HR}] = 0.21 \qquad \sigma_{HR} = 0.40 \qquad CV_{HR} = 1.905$$

Using only the coefficient of variation we might forego the opportunity to invest in Hypothetical Resources. It provides much more risk per unit of return than does Tardis Intertemporal. In so doing we would miss out on an important discovery in modern finance: that the relevant measure of risk is not the riskiness of the asset itself but how that risk contributes to the risk of the portfolio.

4.2.1 - Portfolio Return

The portfolio return is the weighted average of the expected returns of the components of the portfolio:

$$R_p = \sum_{j=1}^{N} (w_j \ R_j)$$ (Eq 4-3)

where w_j is the weight in the portfolio of asset j and R_j is the return on the asset

Example 2:

If we evaluate a portfolio of 67% Tardis Intertemporal (TI) and 33% Hypothetical Resources (HR), then we calculate the expected return of the portfolio as 17%

$$R = w_{TI} \ R_{TI} + w_{HR} \ R_{HR}$$

$$= 0.67 \ (0.15) + 0.33 \ (0.21) = 0.17$$

4.2.2 - Portfolio Variance

The variance and standard deviation of the returns on a portfolio reflects the covariance between the assets in the portfolio.

$$\sigma_p^2 = \begin{bmatrix} w_1 & \cdots & w_j & \cdots & w_n \end{bmatrix} \begin{bmatrix} \sigma_{1,1} & \cdots & \sigma_{1,j} & \cdots & \sigma_{1,n} \\ \vdots & & \vdots & & \vdots \\ \sigma_{j,1} & \cdots & \sigma_{j,j} & \cdots & \sigma_{j,n} \\ \vdots & & \vdots & & \vdots \\ \sigma_{n,1} & \cdots & \sigma_{n,j} & \cdots & \sigma_{n,n} \end{bmatrix} \begin{bmatrix} w_1 \\ \vdots \\ w_j \\ \vdots \\ w_n \end{bmatrix}$$ (Eq 4-4)

where w_j is the weight in the portfolio of asset j and σ_{ij} is the covariance between assets i and j.

If there are only two assets in the portfolio then this reduces to

$$\sigma^2 = (w_i^2 \ \sigma_i^2) + 2 \ (w_i \ COV_{i,j} \ w_j) + (w_j^2 \ \sigma_j^2)$$

$$= (w_i^2 \ \sigma_i^2) + 2 \ (w_i \ \sigma_i \ \rho_{i,j} \ w_j \ \sigma_j) + (w_j^2 \ \sigma_j^2)$$ (Eq 4-5)

Example 3:

If we evaluate a portfolio of 67% Tardis Intertemporal (TI) and 33% Hypothetical Resources (HR), then we calculate the standard deviation of the portfolio as 21.4%

$$\sigma^2 = (w_{TI}^2 \, \sigma_{TI}^2) + 2 \, (w_{TI} \, \sigma_{TI} \, \rho_{TI,HR} \, w_{HR} \, \sigma_{HR}) + (w_{HR}^2 \, \sigma_{HR}^2)$$

$$= 0.67^2 * 0.20^2 + 2(0.67 * 0.20 * 0.30 * 0.33 * 0.40) + 0.33^2 * 0.40^2$$

$$= 0.04599280$$

$$\sigma = 0.21445932$$

The Portfolio Effect

Note that although the expected return of the portfolio in the example is 33% of the way from the 15% expected return of Tardis Intertemporal to the 21% expected return of Hypothetical Resources, the standard deviation of the portfolio is much less than 33% of the way between 20% and 40%— in fact only a trifle more than the standard deviation Tardis Intertemporal alone.

Figure 4-1: Portfolio of 67% Tardis Intertemporal and 33% Hypothetical Resources

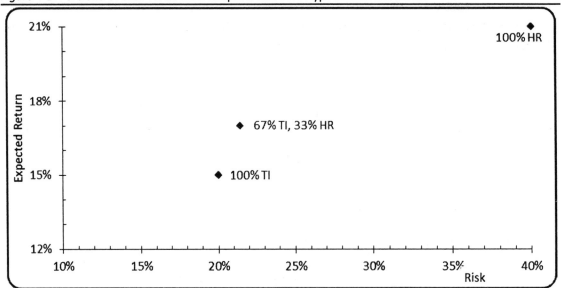

The pattern of risk and return over the full range of combinations of Tardis Intertemporal and Hypothetical Resources illustrates the diversification effect over the efficient portfolio.

❑ **Efficient Portfolio:** A portfolio is efficient if expected return cannot be increased without also increasing risk and conversely, risk cannot be decreased without also decreasing expected return.

The possible combinations of Tardis Intertemporal and Hypothetical Resources are shown in Figure 4-2. The part of this curve that is positively sloped (when return increases risk increases) represent efficient portfolios.

Figure 4-2: Efficient Portfolio Frontier

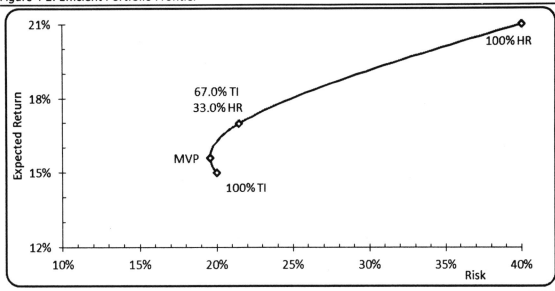

The portfolio with 100% Tardis Intertemporal (TI) is inefficient. No rational investor would choose this portfolio. From an undiversified portfolio of 100% Tardis Intertemporal we can both increase expected return from 15% to 15.6% and reduce risk exposure from 20% to 19.6% by rebalancing the portfolio to 90% Tardis Intertemporal and 10% Hypothetical Resources. The 90%/10% portfolio dominates.

❑ **Dominance Principle:** If two investments have the same expected return then the investment with the lower risk is preferred by all rational investors or dominates; if two investments have the same level of risk then the investment with the higher expected return is preferred by all rational investors or dominates.

Note that we start our portfolio with the least risky investment. Then, by adding a riskier stock to the portfolio, we can actually reduce portfolio risk. This is diversification. We continue to add the riskier stock until we get to the minimum variance portfolio.

❑ **Minimum Variance Portfolio:** is the portfolio on the efficient portfolio frontier with the lowest variance.

If we differentiate the portfolio variance σ^2 with respect to the weight in Tardis Intertemporal and set the result equal to zero, we can solve for the minimum variance portfolio weight w

$$\sigma^2 = (w^2\ \sigma_{TI}^2) + 2\ (w\ Cov_{TI,HR}\ (1-w)) + ((1-w)^2\ \sigma_{HR}^2)$$

$$\frac{\partial\sigma^2}{\partial w} = w\left(\sigma_{TI}^2 + \sigma_{HR}^2 - 2Cov_{TI,HR}\right) - \sigma_{HR} + Cov_{TI,HR} = 0$$

$$w = \frac{\sigma_{HR}^2 - Cov_{TI,HR}}{\sigma_{TI}^2 + \sigma_{HR}^2 - 2\ (Cov_{TI,HR})}$$

(Eq 4-6)

$$w = \frac{0.40^2 - 0.024}{0.20^2 + 0.40^2 - 2\ (0.024)} = .895$$

Thus at 89.5% Tardis Intertemporal the portfolio is balanced to minimize variance.

If we continue to increase the percentage of the portfolio invested in Hypothetical Resources then we can increase the expected returns but only by increasing the risk exposure. This upwardly sloping portfolio curve is called the efficient portfolio frontier. We can see from the efficient portfolio frontier that any diversified portfolio of HR and TI dominates a portfolio consisting of Tardis Intertemporal alone. However a portfolio consisting of Hypothetical Resources alone is efficient.

4.3 - Correlation and Diversification

The degree of correlation determines the degree of diversification.

❑ **$\rho = -1$:** Perfect negative correlation means that when returns are positive on Tardis then the returns on HR are negative. If you were placing a wager on a football game this would mean that you placed one bet on your team to win and another on your team to lose. Regardless of the outcome you will win one bet and lose the other.

❑ **$\rho = 1$:** Perfect positive correlation means that when the returns are positive on Tardis then the returns on HR are also positive. There is no diversification.

❑ **$\rho = 0$:** No correlation means that there is no systematic relationship between the returns on Tardis and the returns on HR. Sometimes they move in the same direction and sometimes they don't.

Figure 4-3 shows the efficient portfolio frontier assuming various different degrees of correlation between Tardis Intertemporal and Hypothetical Resources.

Figure 4-3: Efficient Portfolios of TI and HR where ρ= -1, 0, 0.3, and 1

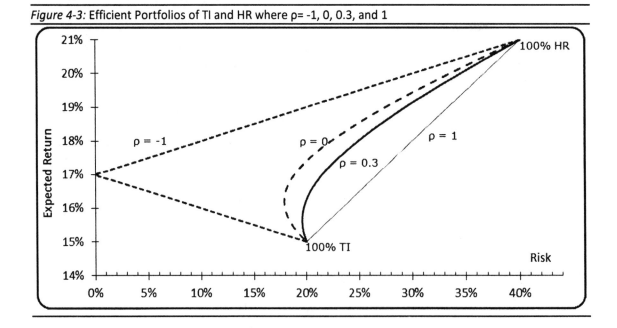

When ρ=1 there is no diversification effect at all. Mathematically the portfolio standard deviation reduces to:

$$\sigma^2 = (w_{TI}^2 \sigma_{TI}^2) + 2(w_{TI}\sigma_{HR} * 1.0 * w_{TI}\sigma_{HR}) + (w_{HR}^2 \sigma_{HR}^2)$$

$$= (w_{TI}\sigma_{TI})^2 + 2(w_{TI}\sigma_{HR})(w_{TI}\sigma_{HR}) + (w_{HR}\sigma_{HR})^2$$

$$\sigma = w_{TI}\sigma_{TI} + w_{HR}\sigma_{HR}$$

The standard deviation of the portfolio is equal to the weighted average of the standard deviations of the investments in the portfolio. Assuming that risk is directly proportional in this way is generally the first approach of a naive investor; it depends on the underlying assumption that the returns on all assets are perfectly correlated.

4.4 - The Risk-Free Asset and Leverage

When we are constrained to two risky assets, any portfolio on the efficient portfolio frontier is good choice. The best portfolio mix is purely a matter of individual risk aversion. However, when we add a risk-free asset to the portfolio we can narrow this down to a single optimal portfolio.

There is no correlation between the return on the risk-free asset and the returns of either of the risky assets. This means that when we combine any of the efficient portfolios with the risk-free asset we get a straight line. To see this, calculate the portfolio expected return and variance with $\rho_{P,rf} = 0$ and $\sigma_{rf} = 0$.

$$E[R] = w_P E[R_P] + w_{Rf} E[R_{Rf}]$$

$$\sigma^2 = (w_P^2 \sigma_P^2) + 2(w_P \sigma_{Rf} * 0.0 * w_P 0) + (w_{Rf}^2 0)$$

$$= (w_P \sigma_P)^2$$

$$\sigma = w_P \sigma_P$$

The standard deviation of the portfolio is the weighted average of the standard deviation of the weight in the risky portfolio: a straight line.

Example 4:

Assume that we can form a portfolio from risky assets Tardis Intertemporal (E[R] = 15%, σ = 20%) and Hypothetical Resources (E[R] = 21%, σ = 40%) between which there is a correlation coefficient of 0.3, and from a risk-free asset (E[R] = 10%, σ = 0%).

Now there is one optimal risky portfolio: the one that maximizes the marginal expected return. Combining the risk-free asset with any other portfolio would generate a portfolio allocation line with lower expected returns for every risk level.

Figure 4-4 shows the optimal portfolio [A] in this scenario. This portfolio consists of 62.6% TI and 37.4% HR. [B] shows the Minimum Variance Portfolio and [C] shows the efficient portfolio that generates the same expected return as [B] but with less risk.

Figure 4-4: Efficient Portfolio Frontier with the Portfolio Allocation Line

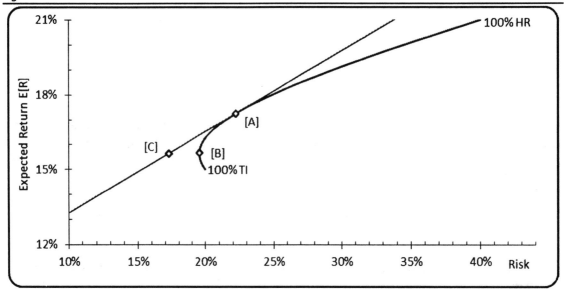

Table 4-2: Capital Allocation in Optimal and Minimum Variance Portfolios

	Return	Optimal Portfolio [A]	Min Var Portfolio [B]	Preferred Portfolio [C]	
Tardis Intertemporal (TI)	15%	62.6%	89.5%	77.7%	77.7% of 62.6% = 48.7%
Hypothetical Resources (HR)	21%	37.4%	10.5%		77.7% of 37.4% = 29.1%
Risk-free Asset	10%			22.3%	22.3%
Portfolio E[R]		17.24%	15.63%		15.63%
Portfolio σ		22.20%	19.57%		17.26%

Tobin[4] demonstrated that investors choose the optimal portfolio and then decide how much of their assets to allocate to that risky portfolio. This is known as the separation theorem.

❑ **Separation Theorem:** The separation theorem states that portfolio selection is separate from macro-asset allocation. This means that selection from among risky assets to form the optimal portfolio is completely separate from the decision of how much of the optimal portfolio to hold versus the risk-free asset.

---

4   James Tobin, "Liquidity Preference as a Behavior Towards Risk" *The Review of Economic Studies*, Vol. 25, (1958): 65-86.

4.5 - Limits To Diversification

In order to implement Markowitz's concept of diversification into a portfolio we would need to calculate the correlation coefficients and cross-correlation coefficients for every possible combination of over 10,000 stocks.

This task was simplified by Sharpe,[5] who pointed out that the correlations between the returns of any two stocks must come from the fact that these two stocks are each correlated with some basic underlying factor. This means that rather than calculate every possible correlation between every possible pair of stocks, we need calculate only the correlation between each stock and the one common underlying factor. This common underlying factor can be discovered as we explore the limits to diversification. William Sharpe was awarded the Nobel Prize in Economics in 1990 jointly with Harry Markowitz.

As we increase the number of securities in a portfolio, the portfolio variance approaches the average covariance between each pair of securities. If the average covariance were zero, it would be possible to eliminate all risk simply by holding a sufficient number of securities. However, most stocks are tied together in a web of positive covariances that set the limit to the benefits of diversification. This is the market portfolio or index that captures the common underlying factor with which all stocks correlate.

Thus a security's risk consists of systematic and unsystematic risk.

❏ **Systematic or market risk** : reflects economy or market wide forces which cannot be eliminated through diversification

❏ **Unsystematic, residual, or specific risk:** reflects industry or firm specific forces and can be eliminated through diversification

Figure 4-5: Portfolio Risk as the Number of Assets in the Portfolio Increases

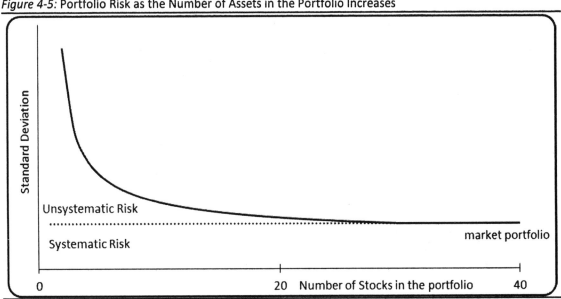

Studies indicate that the major benefits of diversification are achieved in portfolios of 12 to 18 stocks.

---

5   William F. Sharpe, "A Simplified Model for Portfolio Analysis", *Management Science*, Vol. 9, (1963): 277-293.

4.6 - The Market Model

The market model is the mathematical expression of this combination of systematic and unsystematic risk. It captures Sharpe's concept of the market as the common underlying factor.

$$R = \alpha + \beta R_M + e$$ (Eq 4-7)

where R is the return on the asset, R_M is the return on the market as a whole, and e is the error or residual which theoretically averages out to zero.

All other things equal we expect that if the market increases by 1% then

→if β = 0.4 then our stock will increase by 0.4%
→if β = 1.0 then our stock will increase by 1.0%
→if β = 1.6 then our stock will increase by 1.6%
→if β = -1.6 then our stock will decrease by 1.6%

❏ **Beta:** β is the index of market sensitivity.

❏ **Systematic Return:** βR_M is the systematic return. Because the market return is a theoretical concept, we use a broad-based stock market index as a proxy to represent the market.

❏ **Alpha:** α is the unsystematic return. Because the unsystematic return tends to be very volatile, we tend to factor out the stable portion of this return (the trend) and attribute this to α. The volatility we then attribute to the error, e.

Figure 4-6: The Characteristic Line: $\overline{R} = \alpha + \beta R_M$

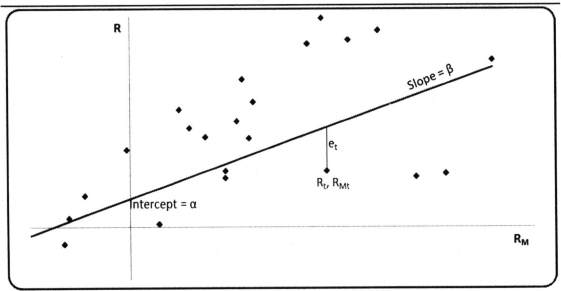

❑ **R^2**: is the statistical measure of how much of the variance in the security's return is due to the variance in the market return. Thus an $R^2 = 0.30$ means that 30% of the return to this security is due to market movement.

❑ **Regression Analysis:** Regression analysis is a statistical technique used to determine the degree of linear relationship between one or more independent variables (causes) and one dependent variable (effect).

❑ **Characteristic line:** A characteristic or regression line is the line representing the estimated linear relationship in a regression analysis.

4.7 - The Portfolio Beta

The portfolio beta reflects the relative volatility of the portfolio as a whole. The portfolio beta is calculated as the weighted sum of the individual security betas.

Example 5:

β (IBM) = 1.05
β (JNJ) = 0.25
β (INTC) = 1.90

If we put $30,000 in each of Johnson & Johnson and Intel and $40,000 in IBM the portfolio β is given by the weighted average:

$$\beta_P = \frac{(\$30 * 0.25) + (\$30 * 1.90) + (\$40 * 1.05)}{\$100} = 1.065$$

This is a good deal easier than calculating portfolio standard deviations.

Most stocks have betas in the range of 0.2 to 2.5. Occasionally we even find a negative beta, but this is extremely rare. A portfolio's beta gives some idea of the degree of risk exposure.

Table 4-3: Characterization of Beta

Portfolio	Beta	Expected Return	
Aggressive	$\beta > 1$		$E[R] > E[R_M]$
Index, Market, or Typical	$\beta = 1$		$E[R] = E[R_M]$
Defensive	$0 < \beta < 1$	$r_f <$	$E[R] < E[R_M]$
Un-correlated	$\beta = 0$	$r_f =$	$E[R]$
Hedge or Insurance	$\beta < 0$	$r_f >$	$E[R]$

Chapter 4 - Questions and Problems

4-1:

Warren Buffett stated, "If you are a know-something investor, able to understand business economics and to find five to ten sensibly-priced companies that possess important long-term competitive advantages, conventional diversification makes no sense for you. It is apt simply to hurt your results and increase your risk.[6]"

A. Does the quote actually argue the case against diversification? Why or why not?
B. How does this position compare to that of John Maynard Keynes and Gerald Loeb as quoted on the first page of this chapter?

4-2:

Consider the efficient portfolio frontier and the portfolio allocation line. What would happen to the Optimal Portfolio if the return on the risk-free asset increased? Decreased?

4-3:

The efficient portfolio frontier and portfolio allocation line suggest that all investors should hold the index fund and the risk-free asset, essentially foregoing stock picking. Is this a sustainable model?

4-4:

Table 4-4 gives the monthly returns for the Standard & Poor 500 Index, Minnesota Mining & Manufacturing (MMM), Bank of America (BAC), and Apple Inc (AAPL) during the fairly turbulent year 2011.

A. In how many of the twelve months are the returns all positive? In how many are they all negative?

B. Form a portfolio invested one-third in each of Minnesota Mining & Manufacturing (MMM), Bank of America (BAC), and Apple Inc (AAPL). Calculate the portfolio return for each month.

C. Calculate the standard deviation of the portfolio returns?

D. How does the risk exposure on this portfolio compare with the risk exposure on the individual stocks? With the S&P 500?

E. Use the normal distribution to show the risk involved in the portfolio versus the risk involved in each of the three individual stocks.

Hint: Use Financial Model 4-1.

---

6   Warren E. Buffet, "The Warren Buffet Business Factors (selected articles from the Letters of Warren E Buffett to the shareholders of Berkshire Hathaway Inc.)" Cesar Labitan Jr, MD Editor, Purdue University-Calumet.(2002) page 22.

Table 4-4: Monthly Rates of Return in 2011 on Selected Stocks

2001	S&P500	MMM	BAC	AAPL	Portfolio (1/3 in each stock)
January	2.265%	1.877%	2.924%	5.196%	
February	3.196%	5.528%	4.079%	4.093%	
March	-0.105%	1.377%	-6.648%	-1.331%	
April	2.850%	3.968%	-7.877%	0.465%	
May	-1.350%	-2.345%	-4.316%	-0.657%	
June	-1.826%	0.498%	-6.638%	-3.496%	
July	-2.147%	-8.129%	-11.405%	16.329%	
August	-5.679%	-4.143%	-15.757%	-1.447%	
September	-7.176%	-13.485%	-25.092%	-0.912%	
October	10.772%	10.071%	11.601%	6.152%	
November	-0.506%	3.252%	-20.205%	-5.578%	
December	0.853%	0.851%	2.206%	5.965%	

4-5:

Tardis Intertemporal (TI) has an expected return of 15% and standard deviation of 20%. Hypothetical Resources (HR) has an expected return of 21% and standard deviation of 40%. The correlation coefficient is 0.30

A. Calculate the expected return and standard deviation for a 50%/50% portfolio.

B. Calculate the standard deviation of the 50%/50% portfolio if there is no diversification ($\rho = 1.0$).

C. What is the impact on the risk exposure of the portfolio of the degree of correlation ($\rho = 0.30$ rather than $\rho = 1.0$)?

4-6:

A portfolio consists of Tardis Intertemporal (TI) (E[R]=15%, σ=20%) and Hypothetical Resources (HR) (E[R]=21%, σ=40%) . The correlation coefficient between TI and HR is 0.3.

Galifrey Educational Systems (GE) has an expected return of 17% and a standard deviation of 30%. Is a portfolio consisting entirely of Galifrey Educational efficient? Why or why not?

4-7:

A portfolio consists of Tardis Intertemporal (TI) (E[R] = 15%, σ = 20%) and Hypothetical Resources (HR) (E[R] = 21%, σ = 40%). The correlation coefficient between TI and HR is -1.0. The efficient portfolio frontier touches the zero risk axis with an expected return of 17%. How is this possible?

4-8:

You invest 92% of your portfolio in Fund A and 8% in Fund B

Stock Fund A	Stock Fund B	
$E[R_A] = 10\%$	$E[R_B] = 20\%$	Covariance of Returns = $Cov_{A,B} = 288$
$\sigma_A = 20\%$	$\sigma_B = 40\%$	

A. Calculate the correlation coefficient $\rho_{A,B}$

B. Calculate the expected return and standard deviation of your portfolio.

C. What would the expected return and standard deviation have been if there had been no benefits to diversification at all?

4-9:

You are assigned to invest a portfolio of $2,000,000. The current position of the portfolio is:

Table 4-5: Initial Portfolio Position

Shares	Issue	Price per share		Beta
100,000	Alliance Gaming	$	4.000	2.00
25,000	CSX Corp	$	35.000	0.92
25,000	Ameren Corp	$	25.000	0.71
	Cash	$	100,000.00	

A. What is the beta of the investment in cash? Why?

B. What is the portfolio beta?

C. How would you characterize this portfolio?

4-10:

You are hired by *Investments Unlimited* and assigned to manage a $2,000,000 portfolio.

The previous investment manager set up the portfolio so that $100,000 was invested in each of twenty different stocks. You calculate the portfolio beta and find that $\beta = .60$. You find this somewhat un-aggressive and propose selling off the Homestake Mining stock [$\beta = .35$] and buying Caterpillar [$\beta = 1.12$]. What will the portfolio beta be after you reposition the account?

Chapter 4 - Financial Models

4.1 - Portfolio Standard Deviation

Reference Question 4-4

Count:
A. We count the number of months in which the returns on all three stocks is positive with a =COUNTIF() function. Thus H5 =COUNTIF(D5:F5, ">0"). In January the model counts three observations >0. Copy-drag the formula down column H to December. In May, August, and September the model counts zero observations >0.
B. We use H20 =COUNTIF($H$5:$H$16, 3) to total the number of months in which all three companies generated a positive rate of return, H21 =COUNTIF($H$5:$H$16, 0) to total the number of months in which all three companies generated a negative rate of return, and H22 =COUNTIFS($H$5:$H$16, ">0", $H$5:$H$16, "<3") to total the number of months in which the number of positive returns was both greater than zero and less than 3. The =COUNTIFS() functions allows multiple conditions to be applied simultaneously.
C. We =SUM() the number of months in each category to make sure we didn't miss any of the 12 months.

Portfolio Return:
D. We calculate the portfolio return in each month with a weighted average. This assumes that we invested equally in each of the three companies.
E. We can use any one of several formulae. In increasing order of sophistication: =AVERAGE(D5:F5), =(D5+E5+F5)/3, =SUM(D5:F5)/3, and SUM(D5:F5)/COUNT(D5:F5). Each produces the same result to 16 decimal places.

Mean and Standard Deviation:
F. Calculate the average and sample standard deviation on the S&P500 into C17 and C18, respectively.
G. Copy-drag C17:C18 across to column G to calculate the same statistics on each asset and on the portfolio.

Probabilities under a Normal Distribution:
H. To generate the normal distribution we relay the ticker symbols to row 25 so we can use them as labels in the graph. Thus C25 =C4 and copy-drag across.
I. We begin with a fairly wide range of possible monthly returns: from – 50% to +50%. The fairly wide range is dictated by BAC , which has a standard deviation of just under 11%. Three standard deviations on either side of the mean requires a range of about 66%.
J. We use the NORM.DIST(X, M, SD, FALSE) function is Excel. This function calculates the probability density at X under the normal distribution with mean M and standard deviation SD. So under the S&P500, C26 =NORM.DIST($B26, C$17, C$18, FALSE). NORM.DIST(-50%, 0.096%, 4.611%, FALSE) calculates that, under a normal distribution with mean 0.096% and standard deviation 4.611%, there is a probability of 0.000000 of seeing a rate of return of – 50%.
K. We can copy-drag the formula across the row. The $ in $B26 keeps X = – 50%
L. We can copy-drag the formula down each column. The $ in C$17 and C$18 keeps the mean and standard deviation in rows 17 and 18, respectively.

Graph

M. To generate the graph highlight range B25:G36 and select [XY Scatter] from the Chart block in the Finance Ribbon.

N. Format the graph so that it looks professional. In each step select the component of the graph by using your mouse and the left button. A more reliable method is to click inside the chart so that the Chart ribbons show at the top of the spreadsheet. Select [Layout]. The first item in the ribbon is a drop-down list of all the components of the graph your have selected—even the ones you can't see. Select the item you want to change and then click on the [Format Selection] command directly under the drop-down box.

1. Delete the legend and horizontal gridlines. In each case select the offending item with your mouse and hit the delete button.

2. Format the vertical axis so that there are no axis labels or tickmarks. Use [Vertical Axis], [Format Selection]. Under [Axis Options] set [Tick Mark Type] and [Axis Labels] to None.

3. Format the chart area so that the border frames the chart area in your own color and style. Use [Chart Area], [Format Selection]. Under [Border Color] select [Solid Line] and select a color. Under [Border Styles] select a width—1.5px is usually sufficient—and click on [Rounded Corners] to give a smoother edge.

4. Use [Layout] [Chart Title] to add a title. Focus the mouse inside the Chart Title box. While your mouse is in the Chart Title box go to the formula bar and type =, then click your mouse in cell B24, and hit enter. This generates a dynamic chart title. Whatever you put in cell B24 will automatically relay to the chart title.

5. In each normal distribution curve, format the curve in your own color and style. Use [Series ...], [Format Selection]. Under [Line Color] select [Solid Line] and select a color. Under [Line Styles] select a width—1.5px is usually more than sufficient—and click on [Smoothed Line] to give a smoother, more natural appearance to the distribution.

6. To add the dynamic label select one point on the curve. If this is difficult, select the entire curve and use the left and right arrows to select a single observation. Then use [Layout], [Data Labels] [More Data Label Options]. De-click []Y value, and click []Series Name.

7. Use the Home Tab to format the label color to match the color of the curve. The color coordination allows you to easily identify which label belongs to which curve.

Model 4.1 - Diversification

2011	S&P500 (S&P)	Minnesota Mining & Manufacturing (MMM)	Bank of America (BAC)	Apple (AAPL)	Portfolio (1/3 in each company) Portfolio	+ve
January	2.265%	1.877%	2.924%	5.196%	3.332%	3
February	3.196%	5.528%	4.079%	4.093%	4.567%	3
March	-0.105%	1.377%	-6.648%	-1.331%	-2.201%	1
April	2.850%	3.968%	-7.877%	0.465%	-1.148%	2
May	-1.350%	-2.345%	-4.316%	-0.657%	-2.439%	0
June	-1.826%	0.498%	-6.638%	-3.496%	-3.212%	1
July	-2.147%	-8.129%	-11.405%	16.329%	-1.068%	1
August	-5.679%	-4.143%	-15.757%	-1.447%	-7.116%	0
September	-7.176%	-13.485%	-25.092%	-0.912%	-13.163%	0
October	10.772%	10.071%	11.601%	6.152%	9.275%	3
November	-0.506%	3.252%	-20.205%	-5.578%	-7.510%	1
December	0.853%	0.851%	2.206%	5.965%	3.007%	3
Mean	0.096%	-0.057%	-6.427%	2.065%	-1.473%	
St Dev	4.611%	6.290%	10.677%	5.888%	6.067%	

Months in which all returns positive	4
Months in which all returns negative	3
Months in which returns mixed	5
Total Months	12

Diversification and Risk Profiles

	(S&P)	(MMM)	(BAC)	(AAPL)	Portfolio
-50%	0.000000	0.000000	0.000904	0.000000	0.000000
-40%	0.000000	0.000000	0.026643	0.000000	0.000000
-30%	0.000000	0.000076	0.326626	0.000002	0.000104
-20%	0.000650	0.041636	1.665582	0.006044	0.062061
-10%	0.787524	1.818210	3.532945	0.830169	2.448935
0%	8.649629	6.341925	3.117191	6.371582	6.384901
10%	0.861605	1.766870	1.144052	2.732405	1.099886
20%	0.000778	0.039318	0.174656	0.065473	0.012519
30%	0.000000	0.000070	0.011091	0.000088	0.000009
40%	0.000000	0.000000	0.000293	0.000000	0.000000
50%	0.000000	0.000000	0.000003	0.000000	0.000000

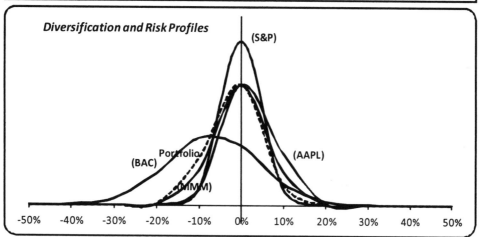

Diversification and Risk Profiles

4.2 - Model the Efficient Portfolio Frontier

Input:

A. The template for Model 4.2 specifies the data for Tardis Intertemporal (TI) and Hypothetical Resources (HR).

Model 4.2 - Efficient Portfolio Frontier			
	TI	**HR**	**Rho**
E[R]	15%	21%	30%
Sigma	20%	40%	

B. Set up the column for the percentage of the portfolio in TI. Enter 0% in C9. Then C10 = C9+.05 to increment the weight by 5% in each row. Copy-drag down the column to fill. You should now have a column that goes from 0% to 100% in 5% increments.

C. Set up the column for the percentage of the portfolio in HR. Because the portfolio must add up to 100% D9 = 1-C9. Copy-drag down the column to fill. You should now have a column that goes from 100% to 0% in 5% increments.

D. To restore the border highlight the range B7:F29, select the borders icon in the [Format] block of the Finance Ribbon. From the drop-down menu select Thick Box Border.

Portfolio E[R] = w_{TI} E[R_{TI}] + w_{HR} E[R_{HR}]:

E. Begin with the 100%-0% portfolio. E9 = ($C9*$C$4)+($D9*$D$4). Note how the cells are locked. Cell addresses in column C refer to Tardis Intertemporal; cell addresses in column D refer to Hypothetical Resources. As this formula is copied down the column, $C9 and $D9 will increment to $C10 and $D10. This allows the formula to calculate using the new portfolio weights. $C$4 and $D$4 will remain locked. This allows the formula to calculate using the same expected return data in each calculation.

F. Remember that [F4] toggles the locks in the formula bar. If your cursor is in a cell address [F4] will toggle that address. If you highlight multiple cell addresses in the formula [F4] will toggle all the cell addresses highlighted.

G. Copy-drag the formula down column E to E29.

Portfolio σ = $\sqrt{(w_{TI}^2\ \sigma_{TI}^2) + 2\ (w_{TI}\ \sigma_{TI}\ \rho_{TI,HR}\ w_{HR}\ \sigma_{HR}) + (w_{HR}^2\ \sigma_{HR}^2)}$

H. Don't try entering the entire formula at once; build it one step at a time, locking the cell addresses for σ and ρ as you go. This will minimize the probability that one typo will wipe out the entire formula. Type one part, hit enter, verify that you have it typed correctly, and return your cursor to the formula bar to continue.

1. F9 = (($C9 * $C$5)^2)
2. = . . . + 2*($C9 * $C$5 * $F$4 * $D9 * $D$5)
3. = . . . + (($D9 * $D$5)^2)
4. = SQRT(. . .)

The final formula should be = SQRT(($C9 * $C$5)^2) + 2*($C9 * $C$5 * $F$4 * $D9 * $D$5) + (($D9 * $D$5)^2)). Place your cursor in the formula bar. You will notice that the cell addresses are color coded, and that the cells referenced have matching color coded borders. This allows you to verify that you are referencing the correct cells.

I. Copy-drag the formula down column F to F29.

J. Check that the result in your spreadsheet for the 50%/50% portfolio matches your answers in Question 4-5 A.

Graph:

K. Graph the EPF with X = sigma and Y = E[R]. Excel will default X = E[R] so start with an empty XY scatter. In the Finance Ribbon select Scatter from the chart block. Select the "Scatter with Smooth Lines". This will generate a line without markers.

L. Use [Design] [Select Data] [Add] to specify Series Name as B7, X as F9:F29, and Y as E9:E29.

M. If you selected the incorrect form of the XY scatter then you can change this selection by formatting the series. Use [Series ...], [Format Selection] . Under [Marker Options] select None to remove the markers, under [Line Color] select [Solid Line] and select a color, and under [Line Style] a width— 1.5px is usually more than sufficient.

N. If the EPF looks jerky, format the Series. From the drop-down list in the top left corner choose Series: "Efficient Portfolio Frontier" and [Format Selection]. You can also use your cursor to [Format Data Series]. Under [Line Style] click [] smoothed line.

O. To add axis labels use [Layout] [Axis Titles][Add Primary Horizontal Axis Title] and [Add Primary Horizontal Axis Title].

P. To make the axis labels dynamic focus the mouse inside the Axis Title box. While your mouse is in the Axis Title box go to the formula bar and type =, then click your mouse in cell F8. This generates a dynamic axis title. Whatever you put in cell F8 will automatically relay to the axis title.

Test the Model:

Q. Test the model by changing the model data. Remember that you can only change the numbers that are coded blue as inputs.

R. The expected return, standard deviation, and EPF should change as you change the model data.

Model 4.2 - Efficient Portfolio Frontier			
	TI	HR	Rho
E[R]	15%	21%	30%
Sigma	20%	40%	

Efficient Portfolio Frontier				
Portfolio	TI	HR	E[R]	Sigma
	0%	100%	21.0%	40.0%
	5%	95%	20.7%	38.3%
	10%	90%	20.4%	36.6%
	15%	85%	20.1%	35.0%
	20%	80%	19.8%	33.4%
	25%	75%	19.5%	31.9%
	30%	70%	19.2%	30.3%
	35%	65%	18.9%	28.9%
	40%	60%	18.6%	27.5%
	45%	55%	18.3%	26.1%
	50%	50%	18.0%	24.9%
	55%	45%	17.7%	23.7%
	60%	40%	17.4%	22.7%
	65%	35%	17.1%	21.8%
	70%	30%	16.8%	21.0%
	75%	25%	16.5%	20.4%
	80%	20%	16.2%	19.9%
	85%	15%	15.9%	19.7%
	90%	10%	15.6%	19.6%
	95%	5%	15.3%	19.7%
	100%	0%	15.0%	20.0%

Efficient Portfolio Frontier

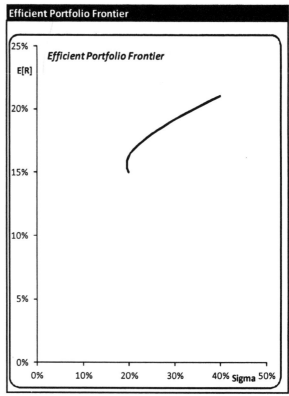

Efficient Portfolio Frontier

$\mathcal{M}$ odern portfolio theory marks the dominance of teamwork over the search for individual stars in investment. The risk and return of any particular asset should not be considered in isolation but in terms how it contributes to the risk and return of the portfolio as a whole.

The Capital Asset Pricing Model (CAPM), attributed to Sharpe,[1] Lintner,[2] and Treynor,[3] extends this concept by stating that the expected return of a portfolio, or any asset in a portfolio, depends on its systematic risk beta rather than on its total risk. Moreover, the super portfolio in Tobin's Separation Theorem is the market portfolio itself.

5.1 - Capital Asset Pricing Model

The principle behind the CAPM is that portfolios seeking higher returns must pay the price of higher risk. The CAPM seeks to quantify this relationship between increased risk and the returns necessary to compensate the investor for taking this increased risk. Essentially CAPM states that, in a competitive market,

❏ the market portfolio should earn a risk premium $[\ E[R_M] - r_f\ ]$ over and above the risk free rate.

❏ a stock's expected risk premium should vary in direct proportion to its beta β.

$$E[\ R_j\ ] = r_f + \beta_j \left[\ E[\ R_M\ ] - r_f\ \right]$$
(Eq 5-1)

where

$E[R_j]$ = the expected return on investment j
r_f = the risk free rate
β_j = the beta generated by the market model on investment j
$E[R_M]$ = the expected return on the market

The CAPM means that the expected returns that compensates the investor for the beta risk undertaken for all investments must plot along the security market line. For any portfolio, given its beta, we can predict the expected rate of return that compensates for the level of risk.

❏ **Risk Premium:** The risk premium of a security or portfolio is the expected return on the portfolio in excess of the risk free rate of return. This is the added return required to compensate the investor for the exposure to systematic risk.

---

1 William F. Sharpe, "Capital Asset Prices: A Theory of Market Equilibrium under Conditions of Risk", *Journal of Finance*, Vol. 19 no.3 (1964): 425-442.

2 John Lintner, "The Valuation of Risk Assets and the Selection of Risky Investments in Stock Portfolios and Capital Budgets", *Review of Economics and Statistics*, Vol. 47 (1965): 13-37.

3 Jack Treynor, "Towards a Theory of Market Value of Risky Assets", unpublished manuscript, 1961

5.2 - Indexing

According to modern portfolio theory, the market portfolio itself offers the highest rate of return per unit of risk. The most efficient portfolio is the market itself. We can generate a portfolio of beta = x by putting x% of our portfolio into a market index fund and the remainder into T-Bills.

The advantage of the index fund approach is that we have already diversified away unsystematic risk. Indexing is a passive or buy-and-hold investment strategy designed to replicate the performance of the market portfolio or stock market index.

Example 1:

We have $1,000,000 to invest. The risk-free rate is 1.0%, and the S&P 500 index fund returns an average of 6.3%. By adjusting the portfolio balance we can set the portfolio beta to any value we want.

β = 0.0		E[R] = 1.0% + 0.0 [6.3% - 1.0%] = 1.00%					
	100%	Risk Free:	$1,000,000.	@ 1.0%	=	$1,010,000.	
	0%	Index Fund:	$0.	@6.3%	=	$0.	
		Portfolio:	$1,000,000.			$1,010,000.	1.00%

β = 0.5		E[R] = 1.0% + 0.5 [6.3% - 1.0%] = 3.65%					
	50%	Risk Free:	$500,000.	@ 1.0%	=	$505,000.	
	50%	Index Fund:	$500,000.	@6.3%	=	$531,500.	
		Portfolio:	$1,000,000.			$1,036,500.	3.65%

β = 1.0		E[R] = 1.0% + 1.0 [6.3% - 1.0%] = 6.30%					
	0%	Risk Free:	$0.	@ 1.0%	=	$0.	
	100%	Index Fund:	$1,000,000.	@6.3%	=	$1,063,000.	
		Portfolio:	$1,000,000.			$1,063,000.	6.30%

β = 2.0		E[R] = 1.0% + 2.0 [6.3% - 1.0%] = 11.60%					
	-100%	Risk Free:	-$1,000,000.	@ 1.0%	=	- $1,010,000.	
	200%	Index Fund:	$2,000,000.	@6.3%	=	$2,126,000.	
		Portfolio:	$1,000,000.			$1,116,000.	11.6%

This example allows us to break down the CAPM and understand its component parts.

The 5.3% risk premium is the spread we earn when we borrow at 1.0% to invest at 6.3%. When β = 2.0 we borrow twice the value of our portfolio to invest in the market portfolio so we earn (on average) twice the 5.3% spread. We must add 1.0% because we borrow the first million from ourselves. Thus the expected return of this leveraged portfolio is 1.0% + 2 (5.4%) for the predicted return of 11.6%.

1900-2010: Market Risk Premium

Dimson, Marsh, and Staunton estimate the risk premium in markets around the world using data from 1900 to 2010. Over this 110-year period the real U.S. interest rate averaged 0.96% and the equity risk premium averaged 5.26%.[4]

If we set up a portfolio to duplicate the performance of an equity index then we need to manage the portfolio so that the weight of each company in our portfolio equals the weight of the same company in the index we are trying to track.

❑ **Bogey:** The bogey is the target index in an indexing strategy.

❑ **Tracking Error:** The tracking error is the difference between the performance of the portfolio and the bogey when the index is not perfectly duplicated. The tracking error can be eliminated by putting the whole portfolio in treasury bills and buying index futures.

❑ **Diamond:** The "Diamond" is a unit investment trust designed to track the Dow Jones Industrial Average.

❑ **SPDR:** Standard & Poor Depository Receipt called a "Spider" is a unit investment trust designed to track the S&P 500 index.

5.3 - The Security Market Line

The CAPM provides a relationship between systematic risk β and the normal rate of return that a security with a risk of β should generate. This relationship is graphed as the security market line. When markets are efficient and in equilibrium, all securities should generate a normal return defined by the CAPM:

$$E[R_j] = r_f + \beta_j \left[E[R_M] - r_f \right]$$

(Eq 5-1)

This relationship between β and expected return is graphed as the security market line (SML).

❑ **Security Market Line:** The security market line is the relationship described by the CAPM equation; it specifies the linear relationship between the level of systematic risk β and the normal return E[R].

---

4   E. Dimson, P. March, & M. Staunton, "Equity Premiums Around the World", in *Rethinking the Equity Risk Premium*, ed. P.B. Hammond, M.L. Leibowitz & L.B. Siegel, (Research Foundation of CFA Institute, 2011).

Figure 5-1: The Security Market Line where r_f = 1.0% and E[R_M] = 6.3%

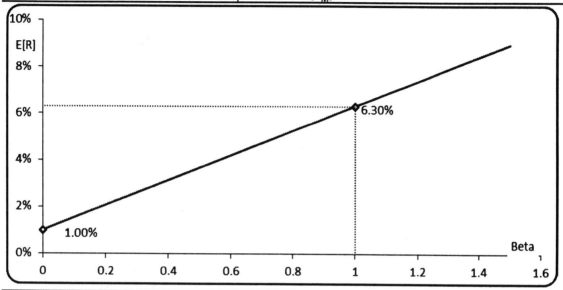

5.4 - Identifying Abnormal Returns

Because the CAPM describes the relationship between normal expected returns and beta risk, when a company generates returns inconsistent with the security market line this indicates abnormal returns.

Example 2:

Discovery Café has a β = 1.20. With a T-bill rate of 1.0% and a market rate of 6.3%, the normal return we should expect to generate on Discovery Café is given by

$$E\ [\ R_{DVC}\ ] = 1.0\% + 1.20\ \big[\ 6.3\% - 1.0\%\ \big]$$

$$= 7.36\%$$

If Discovery Café actually generates an average return of 9.56% then there is a difference between the expected return predicted by the statistical average and the expected return generated by the CAPM.

Statistical Average: E[R] = 9.56%

Abnormal Return: + 2.2%

CAPM: E[R] = 7.36%

The difference or abnormal return is +2.2%. This is also referred to as the Jensen's alpha of the stock. Stocks with positive alphas generate a higher return than warranted by their systematic risk. This is illustrated in Figure 5-2.

Figure 5-2: The Security Market Line with Discovery Café showing Abnormal Returns of +2.2%

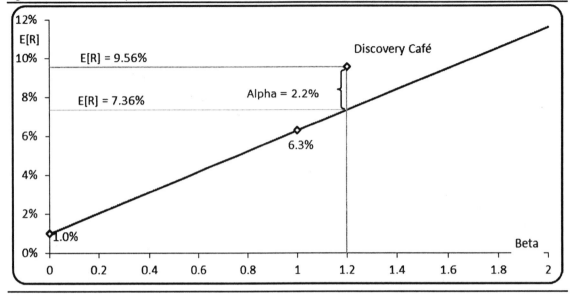

5.4.1 - Risk Adjusted Return

Modern portfolio theory suggests several risk adjusted rates of return. Essentially this allows a more straightforward comparison of portfolio returns earned under different market conditions. A 0% rate of return for a year when the market earned 10% overall is dreadful, whereas the same 0% earned when the market declined 10% is brilliant. Similarly, a portfolio earning 10% with minimal risk may be preferred to a portfolio earning 15% with a much higher risk

Jensen's Alpha

Jensen's alpha is a measure of the abnormal return as defined by the CAPM. Note that in the formula for Jensen's alpha we are measuring the return on the portfolio ex-post: realized returns rather than expectations.

$$\alpha = R_p - \left[r_f + \beta_p \left(R_M - r_f \right) \right] \qquad \text{(Eq 5-2)}$$

Sharpe and Treynor Ratios

Both Sharpe and Treynor measured the ratio of the return earned by the portfolio in excess of the risk free rate to risk. In this sense both are variations of the coefficient of variation.

Sharpe used the standard deviation of the returns of the portfolio, whereas Treynor used the beta of the portfolio. Although Treynor's ratio is used more frequently and is often called the return to volatility, it does require that we define a market proxy against which to calculate the beta. Sharpe's ratio requires no market proxy and can be calculated from the rates of return themselves.

$$\frac{1}{CV} = \frac{R_p}{\sigma_p} \qquad\qquad (Eq\ 5\text{-}3)$$

Sharpe ratio:
$$R_{Sharpe} = \frac{R_p - r_f}{\sigma_p} \qquad\qquad (Eq\ 5\text{-}4)$$

Treynor ratio:
$$R_{Treynor} = \frac{R_p - r_f}{\beta_p} \qquad\qquad (Eq\ 5\text{-}5)$$

5.4.2 - The Multifactor CAPM

The CAPM essentially assumes a single systematic factor that affects all portfolios assets to some degree or other. However there may be other factors beyond the return on the market portfolio to which portfolio assets respond: GDP growth rate, the price of oil, even the political party in power. CAPM thus extends to

$$E\ [\ R_p\ ] = \alpha_p + \beta_{p1}\ E\ [\ R_1] + \beta_{p2}\ E\ [\ R_2\ ] \qquad\qquad (Eq\ 5\text{-}6)$$

where

   $E[R_p]$ is the expected return on portfolio p,
   β_{p1} is sensitivity to the market portfolio based on one factor, and
   β_{p2} is sensitivity to a market portfolio based a second factor.

5.4.3 - Is Beta dead?

In June 1992 Fama & French[5] published a paper in which they report that their results indicate that β does not really seem to explain the cross-section of average stock returns. They suggest that a multifactor CAPM in which firm size and the ratio of book value to market value of common equity proxy the risk of the stock does more to explain returns. Fama and French recommend a three factor model of the form:

$$E\ [\ R_p] - r_f = \alpha + \beta_1\ E\ \left(\left[\ R_{Market}\right] - r_f\ \right) + \beta_2\ E\ \left[\ R_{Size}\right] + \beta_3\ E\ \left[\ R_{Book\ to\ Market}\right] \qquad (Eq\ 5\text{-}7)$$

Proponents of the "beta is dead" position point out that the basic assumptions of the CAPM

1. There are no taxes or transaction costs
2. All investors have identical investment horizons.
3. All investors have identical opinions about expected returns, volatilities and correlations of available investments.

are unrealistic and restrictive, and so CAPM is too limited to be of any practical use. However, so long as the CAPM is one of the many tools available to the investor rather than the single definitive indicator, it will continue to be useful.

---

5 Eugene Fama and Kenneth French, "The Cross-Section of Expected Stock Returns", *Journal of Finance*, Vol. 47, no. 2 (1992): 427-465.

Chapter 5 - Questions and Problems

5-1:

Explain the rationale behind the security market line (SML). In other words why does it make intuitive sense?

5-2:

Your research department gives you the following information based on the monthly data over the past ten years.

Investment	Annual Return	Standard Deviation	Beta
T-Bills	3.3%	0.0%	
Market Index Fund	12.3%	15.0%	
Discovery Café	14.8%	27.3%	0.8

A.   Specify the equation for the security market line

B.   Graph the security market line. Specify and label the intercept and slope of the SML.

C.   Calculate the normal return on Discovery Café as predicted by the CAPM

D.   Calculate the abnormal return for Discovery Café over the past ten years.

E.   Add Discovery Café to the SML.

F.   Calculate the Sharpe and Treynor ratio for each of the three possible investments. What do you notice?

Table 5-1: Data for Question 5-3

State of the Economy	Probability	Expected Rate of Return					
		T-Bills	Compu-lectrics	Gold Mines	American Rubber	Index Fund	Portfolio
Rapid Growth	0.1	8.0%	50.0%	-20.0%	30.0%	43.0%	
Above Average	0.2	8.0%	35.0%	-10.0%	45.0%	29.0%	
Average	0.4	8.0%	20.0%	0.0%	7.0%	15.0%	
Below Average	0.2	8.0%	-2.0%	14.7%	-10.0%	1.0%	
Recession	0.1	8.0%	-22.0%	28.0%	10.0%	-13.0%	
Beta		0.00	1.29	-0.86	0.68	1.00	

5-3:

You have just landed a job in the trust department at a large bank. Your first assignment is to invest $100,000 from an estate for which the bank is trustee. The trust is expected to terminate in one year and the terms of the trust restrict investment alternatives to T-bills, an index fund maintained by the bank, and the three stocks in which the original client had an interest: Compulectrics (an electronics firm), Gold Mines, and American Rubber (manufactures tires etc).

The bank's economic and forecasting staff developed probability estimates for each state of the economy, and the investment department has a guru and a sophisticated computer system that estimates the rate of return for each alternative for each state of the economy. You gather and compile from these sources the information in Table 5-1.

A. Why is the T-bill return independent of the state of the economy? Do T-bills constitute a completely risk-free return?

B. Why do Compulectrics returns move with the economy and Gold Mines returns move counter to the economy?

C. Calculate the expected rate of return for each alternative. If the trust specified risk neutral investment strategy, what should you invest in?

D. Eventually you realize that investing on a risk neutral basis might get your client upset. You are not sure which is the best risk measure, so you calculate the standard deviation and coefficient of variation for each alternative and compile the results.

E. Calculate the correlation coefficient between Compulectrics and Gold Mines. What would be the expected return, standard deviation, and coefficient of variation for a portfolio of $50,000 in each of Compulectrics and Gold Mines. How does the risk of the portfolio compare with that of the individual stocks?

F. Use the CAPM to calculate a required rate of return for each investment alternative. How do the expected rates of return compare with the required rates of return? What about the portfolio considered in question E?

G. Calculate the Sharpe and Treynor ratios for each investment alternative and the 50%/50% portfolio. What do these ratios tell you about each investment alternative?

H. Construct the security market line. Plot the expected rates of return for each investment alternative against its β. What pattern do you detect? (Where are the undervalued investments? The overvalued investments?)

I. Suppose investors raised their inflation expectations by 3% over current estimates. What effect would this have on required returns?

J. Suppose that investors' risk aversion increased enough to cause a 3% increase in the market risk premium. What effect would this have on the required returns of high and low risk stocks?

5-4:

Consider the following rates of return over a five-year period for the S&P 500 Index, Amerisource Bergen Corp (ABC), and Goldman Sachs (GS)

Year	Index	ABC	GS
2011	0.0%	10.3%	-45.4%
2010	12.8%	32.2%	0.4%
2009	23.5%	47.4%	101.9%
2008	-38.5%	-20.2%	-60.1%
2007	3.5%	0.1%	8.6%

A. If you invested $10,000 in each of ABC and GS at the beginning of 2007 what would be the value of each investment at the end of 2011?

B. Using your business calculator calculate for ABC the
    1. Expected annual return
    2. Population standard deviation
    3. Sample standard deviation
    4. Alpha
    5. Beta

C. Calculate the same statistics for GS.

D. Calculate the correlation coefficient between ABC and GS.

Chapter 5 - Financial Models

5.1 - Capital Asset Pricing Model

A. The template for Model 5.1 specifies rates of return for the S&P 500 Index, Amerisource Bergen Corp (ABC), and the three-month U.S. Treasury bill, for 36 months ending December 2011.

Descriptive Statistics:

B. Observations: Use = COUNT(C:C) to count the number of rates of return in column C. The function COUNT() will only count numbers. If we use COUNTA(C:C) we get 38 instead of 36 because it also counts the label "S&P 500" in C4 and the spacer in C2 that governs the width of column C. We use C:C rather than C5:C40 so that if we have fewer than or greater than 36 months, the model still works without having to change any of the formulae.

C. Use =AVERAGE(C:C), =VAR.P(C:C), and STDEV.P(C:C) to calculate the mean, variance, and standard deviation. Copy-drag to the right to calculate the same statistics for columns D and E.

Market Model:

D. We calculate the alpha and beta in the equation R_{ABC} = alpha + beta $R_{S\&P500}$ with =INTERCEPT(D:D,C:C) and =SLOPE(D:D,C:C). In these formulae the known Ys are always specified first, and the known Xs second: =FUNCTION(known Ys, known Xs)

E. Multiple R is given by =CORREL(D:D,C:C) and the Standard Error by =STEYX(D:D,C:C). The other regression statistics do not have the generic =FUNCTION(known Ys, known Xs) so we leave them blank for now.

F. We need to enter the number of independent variables in the regression, 2, manually. Note that, as an input to the model, it is coded blue.

G. R^2 = the Multiple R squared; =H17^2

H. Adjusted $R^2 = R^2 - ((k - 1)/(N - k)) * R^2$, where N is the number of observations and k is the number of independent variables. This translates into Excel as =H18-((H21-1)/(H5-H21))*(1-H18)

Amerisource Bergen Corp   ABC

Rates of Return

Month	S&P 500	ABC	T-Bills
Dec 2011	0.853%	0.108%	0.001%
Nov 2011	-0.506%	-8.627%	0.001%
Oct 2011	10.772%	9.471%	0.002%
Sep 2011	-7.176%	-5.836%	0.001%
Aug 2011	-5.679%	3.615%	0.002%
Jul 2011	-2.147%	-7.464%	0.003%
Jun 2011	-1.826%	0.437%	0.003%
May 2011	-1.350%	1.710%	0.003%
Apr 2011	2.850%	2.730%	0.005%
Mar 2011	-0.105%	4.352%	0.008%
Feb 2011	3.196%	5.996%	0.011%
Jan 2011	2.265%	5.100%	0.013%
Dec 2010	6.530%	10.600%	0.012%
Nov 2010	-0.229%	-5.726%	0.012%
Oct 2010	3.686%	7.078%	0.011%
Sep 2010	8.755%	12.390%	0.013%
Aug 2010	-4.745%	-8.709%	0.013%
Jul 2010	6.878%	-5.606%	0.013%
Jun 2010	-5.388%	1.503%	0.010%
May 2010	-8.198%	1.653%	0.013%
Apr 2010	1.476%	6.674%	0.013%
Mar 2010	5.880%	3.138%	0.013%
Feb 2010	2.851%	3.155%	0.009%
Jan 2010	-3.697%	4.565%	0.005%
Dec 2009	1.777%	5.589%	0.004%
Nov 2009	5.736%	11.828%	0.004%
Oct 2009	-1.976%	-1.028%	0.006%
Sep 2009	3.572%	5.021%	0.010%
Aug 2009	3.356%	8.367%	0.014%
Jul 2009	7.414%	11.161%	0.015%
Jun 2009	0.020%	-4.367%	0.015%
May 2009	5.308%	10.375%	0.015%
Apr 2009	9.393%	3.001%	0.013%
Mar 2009	8.540%	2.834%	0.018%
Feb 2009	-10.993%	-12.417%	0.025%
Jan 2009	-8.566%	1.851%	0.011%

Naming Cells:
I.   We have calculated alpha into Cell H13. If you focus in H13 you can see the name of the cell in the formula bar directly to the left of the gray function button fx. You can give the cell an alias by typing alpha into this name space. Now you can refer to this cell as either =H13 or =alpha. Rename H14 as beta in the same way.
J.   In the Finance ribbon, click on Name Manager. The Name Manager allows you to see, edit, or delete the names that have been created in the spreadsheet.

Characteristic Line:
K.   Graph the returns on the market on the *x*-axis and the returns on ABC on the *y*-axis using an XY scatter chart. To do this highlight the range C4:D40, making sure to include the labels in row 4. Use [XY Scatter] from the Chart block in the Finance Ribbon.
L.   Format the series so that it has markers but no line. To do this select the series and [Format Selection] from the Chart [Layout] ribbon. Under [Line Color] select [No Line]. Under [Marker Options] select [Built-in] and use the drop-down menu to select the particular style and size you prefer. [Marker Fill], [Marker Line Color], and [Marker Line Color] allow you to build various marker shapes, sizes, colors, and styles. Experiment to see what styles work best for you.
M.   Calculate the characteristic line between two endpoints. To do this find the minimum and maximum monthly return on the S&P 500. Use =MIN(C:C) and MAX(C:C). This gives us the X coordinates of the two endpoints.
N.   Calculate the predicted return on ABC for each endpoint using =alpha + beta*H25. Note that it is easier to understand the formula if we use named cells. =$H$13+$H$14*H25 works just as well but, if there is an error, it is harder to debug.
O.   Copy-drag down to I26.
P.   Click in the chart and use [Design] [Select Data][Add] to add this to the chart. Specify G23 as the Series Name, H25:H26 as the Series X Values and I15:I26 as the Series Y Values.
Q.   Format the series so that it has a line but no markers. To do this select the series and [Format Selection] from the Chart [Layout] ribbon. Under [Marker Options] select [None]. Under [Line Color] select [Solid Line] and select a color. Under [Line Styles] select a width.
R.   To remove the redundant 00s from the axis labels use select the axis from the [Layout] drop-down and [Format Selection]. Under [Number] select the appropriate style and change the number of decimals to 0. Do this for both the vertical and horizontal axis.

Capital Asset Pricing Model:
S.   The beta for T-bills and the market index. These assets were chosen because their betas are assumed to be 0 and 1, respectively. Type in 0 and 1. Use =beta for the beta of Amerisource Bergen Corp.
T.   The observed annual return on each asset is the average monthly return *12.
U.   The normal return is predicted by the CAPM. The risk free rate is in cell J31 (or you can name this cell rf); the expected market rate is in cell H31 (or you can name this cell Rm).
V.   The abnormal return can then be calculated as the observed minus the normal return.

CAPM:

W. Graph beta on the *x*-axis, and the observed annual return and the normal annual return on the *y*-axis, using an XY scatter chart. Start with an empty XY Scatter.

    1. Use [Design] [Select Data][Add] to add the observed Returns. Specify G31 as the Series Name, H30:J30 as the Series X Values and H31:J31 as the Series Y Values.

    2. Use [Add] again to add the Normal Returns. Specify G32 as the Series Name, H30:J30 as the Series X Values and H32:J32 as the Series Y Values.

X. Format the observed annual returns so that it has markers but no line and the normal annual returns so that it has a line but no markers.

Y. To get the drop lines representing the abnormal returns add error bars to the observed annual returns series. Click in the chart to select the series or use [Layout] and choose the correct series from the drop down menu on the far left of the ribbon.

Z. Use [Layout] [Error Bars] [More Error Bar Options] [Vertical Error Bars] [[Minus] [No cap] [Custom] and specify the Range H33:J33. This will add an error bar equal to the abnormal return. If excel also adds a bunch of horizontal error bars do not panic. Just select with your mouse and hit the delete button.

AA. To add labels select the series and use [Layout] [Data Labels]

AB. Spend some time formatting output and charts so that your model is clear, clean, and professional.

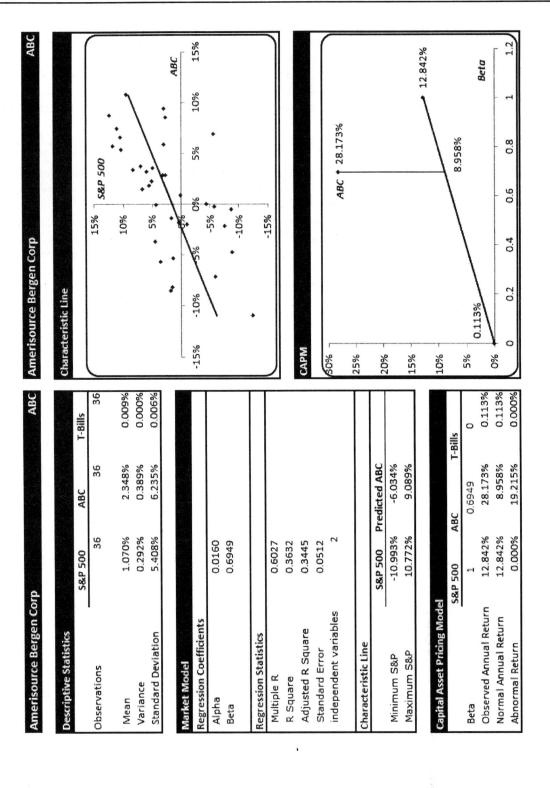

Amerisource Bergen Corp   ABC

Descriptive Statistics

	S&P 500	ABC	T-Bills
Observations	36	36	36
Mean	1.070%	2.348%	0.009%
Variance	0.292%	0.389%	0.000%
Standard Deviation	5.408%	6.235%	0.006%

Market Model

Regression Coefficients

Alpha	0.0160
Beta	0.6949

Regression Statistics

Multiple R	0.6027
R Square	0.3632
Adjusted R Square	0.3445
Standard Error	0.0512
independent variables	2

Characteristic Line

	S&P 500	Predicted ABC
Minimum S&P	-10.993%	-6.034%
Maximum S&P	10.772%	9.089%

Capital Asset Pricing Model

	S&P 500	ABC	T-Bills
Beta	1	0.6949	0
Observed Annual Return	12.842%	28.173%	0.113%
Normal Annual Return	12.842%	8.958%	0.113%
Abnormal Return	0.000%	19.215%	0.000%

Amerisource Bergen Corp   ABC

Characteristic Line

CAPM

$\mathcal{E}$ quity is defined as partial ownership. Shareholders are the owners of the firm. Initially they provide the equity capital to get the company started. As owners, shareholders are entitled to the after-tax earnings of the firm after the payment of prior claims such as bond interest and preferred share dividends, they are entitled to a voice in the management decisions of the company, and they are entitled to sell their ownership in the company.

$\mathcal{E}$ quity markets begin with a business.

We begin with the Discovery Café, a cyber-café in the Survey Building of the University of Illinois. The Discovery Café begins as a partnership: Elisabeth Entrepreneur and Joe W. Partner each put in $10,000 and each own one-half of the Discovery Café. Essentially we have created a company with two shares authorized and outstanding, each with a par value of $10,000.

❑ **Authorized Shares:** Authorized shares refers to the maximum number of shares the firm may issue under the terms of its charter.

❑ **Outstanding Shares:** Outstanding shares refers to those authorized shares issued and sold by the company.

6.1 - Private Equity Market

After two years of operation the Discovery Café seeks to expand to three new locations at the University of Illinois. This expansion requires a capital infusion beyond the ability of the Discovery Café to finance directly. The partners seek to bring in a venture capitalist. In doing so the Discovery Café is seeking funding through the private equity market.

❑ **Venture Capital:** Venture capital is funding provided by investors, or groups of investors, who take partnerships in start-up firms.

6.1.1 - Private Placements

Under private placement the entire issue is offered to accredited investors (generally institutional investors) rather than to the general public. Private placements are exempt from SEC registration. Relevant corporate and financial information is circulated through a private placement memorandum rather than through a prospectus.

❑ **Private Placement Memorandum:** The private placement memorandum is a financial report that outlines the current financial status of the company, the management team, and detailed plans for expansion. It outlines the structure of the firm and offers a part ownership in the company.

❑ **Accredited Investors:** Accredited investors are investors who are able to analyze the risk and return characteristics of the offering and have the financial resources to bear these risks.

Many firms issue bonds through private placement. This affords the firms a much quicker way to access capital without having to wait for regulatory approval. Most of these private placement bonds are then exchanged for identical bonds after the firm files a registration statement with the SEC so that accredited investors are able to sell the bonds to the public investment community, giving them the liquidity all public investors seek.

To enter the private equity market the Discovery Café puts together a private placement memorandum. After some negotiation the Discovery Café offers a 40% ownership in return for the $50,000 needed to expand across campus.

Essentially we have split the company into 100 shares authorized and outstanding. Of these 100 shares, 40 are sold to the venture capitalist for $50,000. Of the remaining 60 shares, 30 go to Elisabeth Entrepreneur and 30 to Joe W. Partner.

6.2 - Public Equity Market

The Discovery Café expands successfully to sites across the University of Illinois and then decides to expand to university campuses across the United States. The partners agree that expansion of this magnitude requires more funding than the company can raise in the private equity market. The Discovery Café decides to enter the public equity market.

The public equity market consists of individual investors. The Discovery Café offers the general public a chance to own a piece of the company for the first time. This is called an initial public offering (IPO) or going public.

Before we can sell shares of a company to the general public, we must register with the SEC.

❑ **Initial Public Offering:** An IPO is the first offer of partnership in a company to the general public.

2012: Facebook

In February 2004 Harvard undergraduate student Mark Zuckerberg, created thefacebook.com. In September he introduced the Facebook Wall, an electronic forum for users to post messages to their friends.

After breathtaking growth in the number of monthly active users (MAUs) and revenues from the sale of display advertisements to those MAUs, the company offered 421,233,615 shares of Class A Common stock to the public on May 17, 2012 at $38.00 per share.

Funding the growth of the company over this eight-year period, various investors, including Zuckerberg's father in 2004 and 2005, made loans and took ownership positions. At that time the company issued stock in the form of Class B common shares to principal insiders of the company. As many as five different series (designated A through E) of convertible preferred shares were issued to various external venture capital investors and private equity managers. Shares of the Class B stock are convertible into Class A shares at any time, but have 10 votes per share, compared to the one vote per share of Class A stock.

This is a familiar means by which company founders and early investors maintain control over the company, while holding a minority position in the capitalization of the company.

6.2.1 - The Securities and Exchange Commission

The Securities and Exchange Commission (SEC) is an independent, nonpartisan, quasi-judicial agency with responsibility for administering the federal securities laws. The purpose of these laws is to protect investors by ensuring that they have access to all material information concerning publicly traded securities, to regulate firms engaged in the purchase and sale of securities and to regulate the provision of investment advice and services.

Early efforts to regulate securities markets in the U.S., now known as Blue Sky Laws, were enacted by the States, not by the Federal Government. It is widely held that Kansas pioneered this initiative with the first comprehensive securities act, which was passed by the Kansas Legislature and became law on March 15 of 1911. Several states and Canadian provinces followed with enactment of similar laws, and 22 years later, the United States enacted the Federal Securities Act of 1933. Interestingly, unlike the Kansas law and many Blue Sky Laws, the federal securities laws do not include substantive merit requirements, but require only that securities offerings include full disclosure of all material facts in an offering of securities! "Buyer Beware" is the federal law of the land.

❑ **Blue Sky Laws:** Laws designed to protect investors from securities fraud at the state level. The term Blue Sky is thought to derive from the comments of Justice McKenna of the U.S. Supreme Court who referred to speculative ventures that have nothing more than so many feet of blue sky.

The Securities Act of 1933, together with the Securities Exchange Act of 1934 which created the SEC, was designed to restore investor confidence in U.S. capital markets by providing investors and the markets with more reliable information and clear rules of honest dealing. The guiding principles of these laws are quite simple: Companies publicly offering securities for investment dollars must tell the public the truth about their businesses, the securities they are selling, and the risks involved in investing. People who sell and trade securities—brokers, dealers, and exchanges—must treat investors fairly and honestly, putting investors' interests first.

These principles do not speak to the merit of an investment, only to the ability of potential investors access to information on the issuer and the securities it intends to sell.

The SEC is governed by five commissioners, one of which is designated chairman by the president of the United States. All commissioners are appointed by the president, with the advice and consent of the Senate, for a fixed term of five years. No more than three commissioners may be of the same political party. The terms are staggered so that one term expires June 5th of each year.

The SEC has its headquarters in Washington, D.C., and operates regional offices in eleven cities.

❑ **SEC Registration:** All corporate securities offered to the public in the United States must be registered with the SEC with the following exceptions:
     ❑ Issues offered only within the boundaries of one state
     ❑ Issues of $1 million or less
     ❑ Issues not offered to the public

❑ **Reporting Requirements:** Any company that offers shares to the public in the United States is required to file financial reports with the SEC. These financial reports must be prepared in accordance with Generally Accepted Accounting Principles (GAAP).

Financial reports, filed electronically with the SEC, are available through EDGAR

❑ **EDGAR:** The Electronic Data Gathering, Analysis, and Retrieval system, performs automated collection, validation, indexing, acceptance, and forwarding of submissions by companies and others who are required by law to file forms with the SEC. Its primary purpose is to increase the efficiency and fairness of the securities market for the benefit of investors, corporations, and the economy by accelerating the receipt, acceptance, dissemination, and analysis of time-sensitive corporate information filed with the agency.

6.3 - Initial Public Offering (IPO)

The initial public offering is put together by an investment bank or banks who underwrite the issue. The underwriter or underwriting syndicate buys the new shares from the company and sells them to the investing public. The underwriter also sells shares allocated to early investors—founders, venture capitalists, and private equity investors—so that they can realize profits.

❑ **Investment Bank:** An investment bank is a financial intermediary between companies and investors. Investment banks underwrite debt and equity issues and advise and negotiate mergers and acquisitions.

❑ **Underwriter:** An underwriter facilitates an offering of debt or equity by acting as the market maker of a new issue. The underwriter buys the issue from the company and undertakes to sell into the market.

The underwriters make their profit from the underwriting spread: the difference between the price paid to the company and the public offer price. Because, by definition, the underwriter takes on the risk of bringing shares of a company to the investing public, this covers only firm commitment offers. Best efforts are also referred to as underwriting, although this is technically incorrect.

❑ **Firm Commitment:** The underwriters purchase all shares of the initial public offering. Any shares not taken up by the investing public remain the property of the underwriters.

❑ **Best Effort:** The underwriters make a best effort to sell all the shares of an initial public offering to the public. Any shares not taken up by the investing public remain the property of the company. If less than a specified percentage of the shares are sold, the issue is canceled completely, and the underwriters forego the fee.

6.3.1 - Prospectus

The firm prepares a prospectus. This is a formal written offer to sell shares of the company. The prospectus must include all the information needed for an investor to make an informed investment decision: a description of the company's business, a history of financial statements certified by an independent public accountant, details of the company's plans including what it plans to do with the funds raised by selling shares, key provisions and features of the security being offered, company management and officers, and any pending litigation.

The prospectus is filed with the SEC.

❑ **Registration Statement:** The preliminary prospectus filed with the SEC for approval. Form S-3: Registration statement under Securites Act of 1933 requires basic information on the company and its intention to sell certain securities to the public. Much of the information at this point such as number of shares, price, and the details of how the offering will come to market are intentionally left blank because these aspects will be developed during the offering process.

❑ **Red Herring:** A preliminary prospectus, stating on the cover page in red ink that the Registration Statement is not yet effective, may be circulated during this approval period. The red herring was introduced by the rule-making authority of the SEC in 1952. Rule 132 was intended to get information into the hands of investors early enough to make an informed decision.

Figure 6-1: The first page of the Discovery Café Statutory Prospectus, or Offering Circular

---

Filed pursuant to Rule 424(B)4   Filed Pursuant to Rule 424(b)(4)

PROSPECTUS   4,000,000 Shares

Discovery Café

CLASS A COMMON STOCK

Discovery Café, Inc. is offering 3,000,000 shares of Class A common stock and the selling stockholders are offering 1,000,000 shares of Class A common stock. We will not receive any proceeds from the sale of shares by the selling stockholders. This is our initial public offering and no public market currently exists for our shares of common stock.

We have two classes of common stock, Class A common stock and Class B common stock. The rights of holders of Class A common stock and class B common stock are identical, except voting and conversion rights. Each share of Class A common stock is entitled to one vote. Each share of Class B common stock is entitled to two votes and is convertible at any time into one share of Class A common stock. The holders of our outstanding shares of Class B common stock will hold approximately 60.0% of the voting power of our outstanding capital stock following this offering, and each of our founders, Chairman and CEO, Elisabeth Entrepreneur, and CFO, Joe W. Partner will hold or have the ability to control approximately 27% of the voting power of our outstanding capital stock following this offering.

Our Class A common stock has been approved for listing on the NASDAQ Global Select Market under the symbol "CAFE".

We are a "controlled company" under the corporate governance rules for NASDAQ-listed companies, and our board of directors has determined not to have an independent nominating function and instead to have the full board of directors responsible for nominating members of our board.

Investing in our Class A common stock involves risk. See "Risk Factors" beginning on page 13.

PRICE $50.00 A SHARE

	Price to Public	Underwriting Discounts and Commissions	Proceeds to Discovery Café	Proceeds to Selling Shareholders
Per share	$50.00	$0.345	$49.655	$49.655
Total	$200,000,000	$1,380,000	$148,965,000	$49,655,000

We and the selling stockholders have granted the underwriters the right to purchase up to an additional 20,000 shares of Class A common stock to cover over-allotments.

The Securities and Exchange Commission and state regulators have not approved or disapproved of these securities, or determined if this prospectus is truthful or complete. Any representation to the contrary is a criminal offense.

The underwriters expect to deliver the shares of Class A common stock to purchasers on July 2, 2012.

MORGAN STANLEY   J.P. MORGAN   GOLDMAN SACHS & CO.
              BofA MERRILL LYNCH   WELLS FARGO SECURITIES
                                        BMO CAPITAL MARKETS
June 21, 2012

Once approval is received from the SEC, the underwriters set an initial public offer date and based on information gathered, set the offer price.

❑ **Statutory Prospectus:** The final copy of the prospectus is also called an offering circular.

❑ **Offer Price:** The offer price is the price the investor pays for the newly issued share. The offer price includes the underwriters' commission.

6.3.2 - The IPO

When you buy an IPO at the offer price from the underwriter this represents a transaction in the primary market. The shares are then bought and sold in the secondary market. If the IPO immediately begins trading in the secondary market at a price higher than the public offer price then it is a hot issue.

Figure 6-2: Red Hat Linux (RHAT) IPO

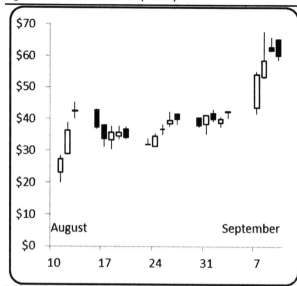

Red Hat Linux (RHAT) was the classic hot issue. It went public August 11, 1999, at an offer price of $28. On the same day it hit a high of $56¾, an increase of 102.7%. Four weeks later, September 8, shares reached a high of $135¼, an increase of 383.0% on the offer price.

(Adjusted for the 2:1 split the offer price was $14, the high on the issue date was $28⅜ and the high on September 8 was $67⅝)

The stock reached a high $302⅝ ($151^5/_{16}$ split adjusted) December 8, 1999 , split 2 for 1 January 10, 2000 and, by the end of March 2002 was trading just over $5 per share.

Figure 6-3: Red hat Linux (RHAT) Monthly Prices from August 1999 to August 2002.

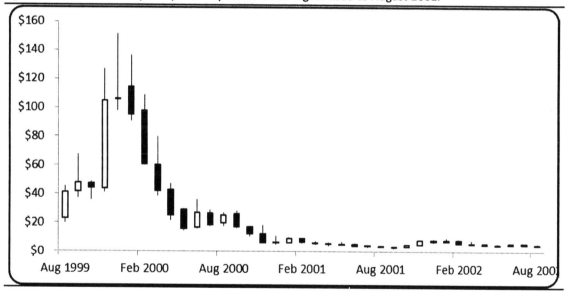

However, research shows that even hot IPOs tend to underperform comparable firms for the three-year period after the initial offer date.[1]

❑ **Flipping:** Buying IPOs at the offer price and selling them in the first day of trading, usually at a substantial profit. Flipping is usually associated with institutional investors because they get the bulk of the IPO allocations.

If a new issue is not taken up at the public offer price then the underwriters are left with unsold shares. If the underwriting contract is best effort rather than a firm commitment then the offer may be withdrawn. If the issue is withdrawn then investors must sell back their shares to the underwriters for the public offer price.

---

1   Jay Ritter, "The Long-Run Performance of Initial Public Offerings", *Journal of Finance* Vol. 46 (1991): 3-47.

Figure 6-4: Vonnage (VG) IPO

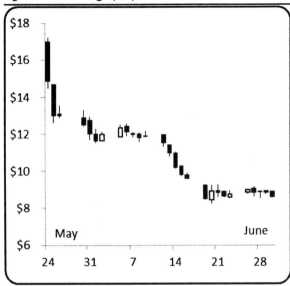

Vonage (VG) provides broadband telephone services that uses Voice Over Internet Protocol (VOIP). Vonage went public May 24, 2006, at an offer price of $17. It fell 13% before the close on the same day and was down 50% by the end of the first month of trading.

The Vonage IPO reserved 13.5% of the offered shares for its customers. On May 31 Vonage released a statement that the company would not buy back shares at the $17 offer price and that it would pursue customer-shareholders who did not pay for the shares they were allocated.

A class action lawsuit filed June 2 alleges that Vonage targeted customers because they knew that institutional investors who normally buy IPOs were reluctant to buy.

On June 19 Verizon filed suit charging Vonage with several patent infringements on technology used to transfer signals between VOIP and traditional phones, security, and enhanced phone service features.

2012: The Facebook IPO

Facebook appears to be closer to the case of Vonage than that of Red Hat. After pricing the issue at $38.00 after markets closed Thursday May 17, 2012, the stock was delayed in opening Friday on the NASDAQ market by technical problems plaguing the electronic order entry system and the companion communication network that confirmed orders, executions, and positions.

In hectic trading of 573,576,400 shares in that first, short day of trading, the stock opened at $42.05, traded as high as $45.00, and as low as $38.00. It closed on its first day of public trading at $38.23,

disappointing most observers based on the excitement leading up to the public offering. In three subsequent days of trading, the stock never regained its $38.00 initial pricing, and traded as low as $30.94.

Numerous lawsuits were filed against Facebook and its underwriters for possible violations of the federal securities laws related to disclosure of material information. Lawsuits were also filed against NASDAQ alleging negligence on the part of the stock exchange operator, which delayed the initial trading in Facebook due to technical issues causing delay of execution confirmations notifying customers of completed trades for several hours. All in all, quite a dubious distinction for a company's first week of public ownership.

Figure 6-5: Facebook (FB) IPO

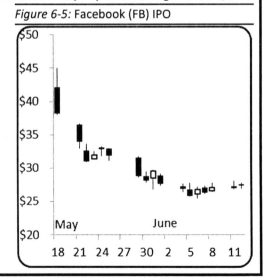

6.3.3 - Subscription Rights

A subscription right is a distribution to existing shareholders of a negotiable right to buy newly issued shares of the company at a specified subscription price. This subscription price is often below the offer price at which the stock is offered to the general public.

A right has a life of several weeks and, during this time, trades in the secondary market.

❑ **Standby Commitment:** The rights offering itself is usually handled by an investment bank under a standby commitment. This commitment obliges the investment bank to buy any shares not subscribed for under the rights offering.

Example 1:

Discovery Café has 300,000 shares issued and outstanding and is trading at $100 per share. The company issues 30,000 new shares with a subscription price of $80. Under the terms of the offering ten rights are required to subscribe to one new share, and each shareholder is issued one right for each share owned.

We can buy 10 shares at $100, receive 10 rights, and then subscribe for one additional share at $80. This gives us 11 shares for a total cost of $1080

We can also purchase 110 rights after the offering and then subscribe to 11 shares at $80. This also gives us 11 shares for a total cost of $880 + 110 times the price of the right.

The law of one price dictates that, in equilibrium, the two methods should yield the same cost basis for the same share of the company, so we can calculate the fair market value of each right as $1.82

$$\$1080 = \$880 + 110p$$
$$p = 1.8181 = \$1.82$$

6.3.4 - American Depository Receipts (ADRs) and Shares (ADSs)

Investing in a foreign company can be troublesome. If you want to buy shares of Siemans AG (Germany) you must first find a broker who has, or will find, a contact broker on the German Exchange in Frankfurt, exchange dollars for euros, decipher the German language and accounting standards, deal with dividends received in euros and, when you decide to sell, convert the proceeds back to American dollars.

American depository receipts (ADRs) and American depository shares (ADSs) were designed to make it easier for American investors to invest directly in foreign companies.

An intermediary, such as the Bank of New York, buys shares of Siemens. The bank keeps these shares on deposit, deciphers both the German language and accounting standards into English and GAAP and translates, at bankers' rates, euros into dollars. The bank then issues receipts to represent the shares on deposit.

❑ **American Depository Receipts (ADR):** An ADR is a negotiable receipt representing common stock of a foreign company held in trust by a U.S. bank. Holders of the ADR are entitled to dividends and capital gain. The issuing company is not involved in the creation of an ADR, and the US bank is registered as the owner of the shares in trust. The bank creating the ADR is responsible for translating the quarterly and annual reports of the company and for distributing dividends in American dollars. This is also called an unsponsored ADR.

Note that an ADR need not necessarily have a one-to-one correspondence with the underlying stock. ADRs are generally packaged to appeal to the American investor. If shares of a particular foreign stock trade at the equivalent of $5 per share, then the bank could package the ADR so that each ADR represents 10 shares and trades at $50.

Alternatively, the issuer (Seimens) deposits shares of the company in trust in a bank in Germany. It then registers the ADSs with the Securities and Exchange Commission (SEC) in the United States and with the securities dealers (Merrill Lynch) through which it decides to issue the ADSs. The ADS is then sold in the same way as any other share.

❑ **American Depository Shares (ADS):** An ADS is a negotiable receipt representing common stock of a foreign company held in trust by a foreign bank. Holders of the ADS are registered with the issuing firm as shareholders and are entitled to vote (including by proxy) the shares they own. The firm must provide the holders of the ADS with quarterly and annual reports in English and the foreign bank is responsible for distributing dividends in American dollars. (Also called a sponsored ADR.)

Siemens AG trades on the New York Stock Exchange under the ticker symbol SI. It is defined as a 1:1 ADR. This means that one share of SI in New York is equivalent to one share that trades on XTRA in Frankfurt. It is a unsponsored listing so defined as an American Depository Receipt.

6.3.5 - Terminology

❑ **Treasury Shares:** Shares the corporation has repurchased. Treasury shares carry no voting rights and do not earn dividends.

❑ **Par Value:** Common stock may have a par, stated, or face value. Initially, the par value represented the value of the corporate assets the share represented as held by the board of directors in trust for the owners (shareholders) of the company. However, the par value of a stock is now nothing more than an accounting device and par values are often set arbitrarily at some nominal amount.

❑ **Classified Stock:** Common stock may be separated into different classifications, generally labeled Class A, Class B, Class C, etc. The differences between classes are often voting rights, and each class has its own dividends, but each company has its own methods and must be investigated separately.

❑ **Market Capitalization:** The market capitalization of a firm is its total market value and equals the number of shares outstanding times the price per share.

Chapter 6 - Questions and Problems

6-1:

A venture capitalist puts $50,000 into the Discovery Café and acquires 40% of the company. Elisabeth Entrepreneur and Joe W. Partner each own 30%.

A.   What is the market value of Joe Partner's share of the company?

B.   What is the market capitalization of Discovery Café?

6-2:

The Discovery Café decides to issue 300,000 shares, 40% of which will be offered to the public. Of the remaining 60% the original partners Elisabeth Entrepreneur and Joe W. Partner, each retain 30% and the venture capitalist retains 40%. The shares are issued at $50 per share, of which the underwriters take 5%.

A.   What is the market capitalization of the firm?

B.   How many shares are offered to the public?

C.   How much money is raised through the initial public offering? How much capital does the Discovery Café realize through the IPO?

D.   Each of the original partners, Elisabeth Entrepreneur and Joe W. Partner initially put $10,000 into the business. What their share of the business worth after the IPO? What is the rate of return on their original investment?

E.   The venture capitalist put $50,000 into the business in the first round of financing. What is his share of the business worth after the IPO? What is the rate of return on his original investment?

6-3:

When a corporation holds treasury stock it can

A.   register the stock under any name it might deem appropriate.
B.   retire it.
C.   reissue the stock as debt securities.
D.   hold it without disclosure to the registrar.

6-4:

Discovery Café has 300,000 shares issued and outstanding and is trading at $100 per share. The company issues 100,000 new shares with a subscription price of $90. Under the terms of the offering, three rights are required to subscribe to one new share and each shareholder is issued one right for each share owned.

A.   If all the shares offered are taken up how much money will the Discovery Café raise?

B.   What should the market capitalization of the Discovery Café be after this cash infusion?

C.   What should the price per share be after the new shares are issued?

D.   What is the fair market value of each right?

6-5:

Treasury stock can be described by which of the following statements?

I   It has voting rights and is entitled to a dividend when declared.
II   It has no voting rights and no dividend entitlement.
III   It is authorized but unissued stock.
IV   It has been issued and repurchased by the corporation.

A.   I and III
B.   I and IV
C.   II and III
D.   II and IV

6-6:

A prospectus must include

I   the effective date of registration.
II   whether or not the underwriter intends to stabilize the price of the issue if necessary
III   a statement indicating that the SEC has not yet approved the issue
IV   disclosure of material information concerning the issuer's financial condition.

A.   I, II, and IV only
B.   I and IV only
C.   II and III only
D.   I, II, III, and IV

6-7:

Northstar Gold plans to offer 300,000 shares of its 2,000,000 common share offering to its own employees. How many shares must it register as publicly offered?

A. 300,000
B. 1,700,000
C. 2,000,000
D. 2,300,000

6-8:

Webstuffing Inc. will issue 1,000,000 new shares of common stock at offer price of $30/share. For each share sold, the managing underwriter receives $2.10 plus $0.30 for expenses and the selling group receives $1.80

I   How much is the total spread for the Webstuffing Inc offering?

    A. $1.80
    B. $2.10
    C. $2.40
    D. $4.20

II   How much money does the managing underwriter receive to cover all of its advertising and other miscellaneous expenses if all shares are sold under the offer?

    A. $300,000
    B. $1,800,000
    C. $2,100,000
    D. $2,400,000

III   How much money will Webstuffing receive from the offering?

    A. $2,400,000
    B. $27,600,000
    C. $27,900,000
    D. $28,200,000

In the primary market the company issues shares and raises capital by selling these shares to the general public. But once the shares are sold, they're gone. Anyone who wants shares must now convince an existing shareholder to sell. This buying and selling takes place in the secondary market.

Every organized secondary market faces the challenge of bringing buyers and sellers together efficiently; and every organization answers this challenge in a slightly different way. There are several organized secondary markets in equities, each of which claims superiority in bringing buyer and seller together efficiently.

2012: Facebook (FB)

A heated example of the rivalry between these exchanges is seen in the events surrounding the Facebook (FB) IPO. Facebook (FB) began trading on NASDAQ on Friday May 18th. Due to technical issues, execution confirmations notifying customers of completed trades were delayed for several hours.

Lawsuits were filed that alleged negligence on the part of NASDAQ OMX Group, the stock exchange operator that delayed the initial trading in Facebook (FB). Executing brokers, market making businesses that back retail order execution for brokers like Fidelity and TD Ameritrade, alleged losses of millions of dollars. The losses experienced came from honoring trades that were canceled or changed during a period of around two hours on that Friday.

Within the first week of public trading of the shares, rumors of Facebook officials contacting the NYSE about moving the listing to it from NASDAQ caused further controversy.

7.1 - The Stock Exchange

A stock exchange is an organized market where member brokers meet to buy and sell securities for themselves and their clients. An exchange can be a physical place where brokers meet like the floor of the New York Stock Exchange or a system of interlinking computers that match brokers' orders somewhat like a matchmaking system.

The exchange has traditionally been a closed society or club owned and regulated by its members. This is now giving way to an exchange as a publicly owned company that must compete in the business of providing a market in which shares can be bought and sold. Shares of the New York Stock Exchange trade on the New York Stock Exchange.

NYSE Euronext is the holding company and the first cross-border exchange group created by the combination of NYSE Group, Inc. and Euronext N.V., on April 4, 2007. The common stock of NYSE Euronext trades on the NYSE and other global exchanges under the ticker symbol NYX. In 2006, NASDAQ completed its separation from the National Association of Securities Dealers (NASD) and began to operate as a national securities exchange. The next year, NASDAQ combined with the Scandinavian exchange group OMX and officially became The NASDAQ OMX Group. The common stock of NASDAQ OMX Group trades on the NASDAQ Global Select Market and other global exchanges under the ticker symbol NDAQ.

To trade securities on the exchange the brokerage firm must be a member or sit on the exchange. This term derives from the early history of the New York Stock Exchange when brokers actually had a seat at a large table. The exchange establishes a fixed number of memberships or seats, which can then be bought and sold. The price of a seat is thus market determined.

❑ **Listing:** Only issues listed with the exchange may be traded. To have its shares listed, a company must satisfy specific listing requirements in terms of shares, shareholders, earnings, and volume of trades, as specified by the exchange.

7.1.1 - Market Concepts and Terminology

Different markets are organized in different ways. To understand in which ways trading differs we need to define key concepts.

Continuous Versus Call Markets

In a continuous market prices are determined continuously through the hours that the market is open. In a continuous market prices reflect the order flow as much as it reflects supply and demand.

❑ **Order Flow:** The order flow is the pattern of orders reaching the market.

In a call market orders are collected for the next auction. These auctions take place at regular intervals throughout the trading day. Each auction determines the market clearing price or fix.

❑ **Fix:** The fix is the market clearing price in an auction.

Example 1:

> The New York Stock Exchange is a continuous market from the opening bell at 9:30 am to the closing bell at 4:00 pm Eastern Time. The London Bullion Market Association comes to a morning (10:30 am) and an afternoon (3:00pm) gold price fix.[1]

Price-Driven versus Order-Driven Markets

In a price-driven market competing market makers are interposed between buying and selling brokers. In essence the market maker acts as a wholesaler for the stock. London and NASDAQ are major exchanges that operate on this system.

In an order-driven market brokers come together directly or input their orders into a computer, which matches the buy and sell orders. Canada, France and Germany operate on this system. American and Japanese markets use a similar approach but with the addition of market makers to ensure continuous markets.

---

1   The London Metal Exchange (LME) was founded as the Royal Exchange in 1571. The LME now trades contracts on base metals such as aluminum, copper, iron, lead, nickel, tin, and zinc. Gold and silver are traded by members of the London Bullion Market Association (LBMA), loosely overseen by the Bank of England. Five members of the LBMA meet electronically twice daily to "fix" the gold price in a process known as the London Gold Fix.

Some Terminology

❏ **Transparency:** Transparency refers to the absence of closed door deals. In a fully transparent market all transactions are open and visible so that all participants are fully and rapidly informed. The more rapid and widespread the dissemination of information the less likely that profit can be made through access to private information.

❏ **Execution Cost:** Execution costs refer to the difference between the execution price of a security and the price that would have existed in the absence of that trade.

❏ **Information Based Trade:** An information based trade is a trade made because an **informed trader** believes he has information not yet reflected in the price.

❏ **Informationless Trade:** An informationless trade is a trade made by a **liquidity trader** to reallocate his portfolio. The liquidity trader has no information not already reflected in the price.

❏ **Board Lot:** A Board or Round Lot refers to the trading unit defined by the exchange. Shares bought and sold in odd or broken lots carry a higher brokerage commission, or trade at a less advantageous price, than those sold in board lots.

Historically, exchanges defined the regular trading unit as 100 shares of stock. In September 2010 the NYSE eliminated the Exchange's separate odd lot execution system. Odd lots can now be traded on the existing NYSE Market Model. This change improved the efficiency and speed of execution for all client orders because odd lot and mixed lot orders fully interact against NYSE quoted liquidity. All orders trade at the Display Book regardless of size.

Most exchanges followed the NYSE example.

7.2 - Brokers, Dealers, Market Makers, and Specialists

A broker is an agent of an investing client; the broker takes no position in the securities he trades. A broker belongs to the club where buying and selling take place (the stock exchange) and can get the shares for you more efficiently than you can. The broker buys or sells the shares for you and charges you a commission.

A dealer maintains his own position in the securities he trades. This means that when you want to buy shares, rather than going out to find a seller, the dealer can sell you shares from his inventory. The dealer thus supplies immediacy.

❏ **Immediacy:** Immediacy is the ability to trade as soon as the order is received rather than to wait for the coincidence of buyers and sellers.

A market maker is a dealer who guarantees that he will always stand ready to buy and ready to sell shares in the stock in which he makes a market. This ensures that there is always a market for the issue. Whenever you want to buy, the market maker will sell; whenever you want to sell, the market maker will buy. The market maker thus provides a continuous auction market.

The market maker thus always has a bid (at which he will buy) and an ask (at which he will sell). He makes the market in which you can trade.

A specialist is the dealer designated by the exchange as the only market maker on the floor of the exchange for specifically assigned stocks. The specialist executes orders for other brokers, keeps the limit order book, and is required to maintain fair and orderly markets.

The specialist also opens the market: he examines the orders that have accumulated since the market close and sets the open price at which the market will clear at the opening bell. Note that this means that although the market is continuous from the opening bell to the closing bell ,it opens with a call market in which opening price is fixed.

Example 2:

> I decide to go into business for myself buying and selling copies of the course book *Financial Markets: A Practicum*.
>
> I buy a copy of the book for you, saving you the trip to the campus bookstore. I know both the authors and the publisher so I can get a better price than you can. For this service I charge you $25 for the book and $1 commission. In this instance I am a broker.
>
> I have a number of copies of the book in my office. If you come and buy a book from me, I sell it to you from inventory. If you want to sell a book to me, I will add it to my inventory. To make a profit I naturally buy at a lower price than I sell. On my office door I post the price at which I will buy (bid) and the price at which I will sell (ask). I also charge a markup instead of commission. In this instance I am a dealer.
>
> I promise that between the hours of 9:00 and 4:00 my office will always be open and I will always stand ready to buy or to sell books to anyone who comes. If my inventory of books dwindles to nothing, then I raise both my bid and ask. If my inventory threatens to spill over into the hallway then I lower both my bid and ask. In this instance I am a market maker.
>
> I am designated by the university as the only market maker on campus. Others may buy and sell, but no one else can make a market in this book. In this instance I am the specialist.
>
> As a specialist I post a bid of $40 and an ask of $44. If someone comes to my office to buy, he buys at $44. If another comes to my office to sell, he sells at $40. If they are both at my office door at the same time, then I introduce them and they trade with each other at $42.
>
> University policy prohibits professors from making money off their students in this way, so the provost immediately shuts down my book dealing operation.

Most European exchanges are matching markets where brokers match buy and sell orders on behalf of their clients. On the London Exchange (prior to 1986) there were firms that were exclusively market makers on the exchange floor. These stock jobbers bought and sold shares for their own account and dealt with brokers acting for the public. Some floor exchanges are a mix of the above. These include the NYSE, Amex,[2] and Tokyo, which are essentially broker exchanges but have specialists.

------

2   The NYSE completed its acquisition of the American Stock Exchange (Amex) in October 2008.

7.2.1 - Determinants of the Bid-Ask Spread

❑   **Bid:** The bid is the highest price per share the potential buyer is willing to pay.

❑   **Ask:** The ask or offer is the lowest price per share the potential seller is willing to take.

Example 3:

Trading begins in shares of Discovery Café. Potential buyers and sellers gather at the exchange and enter into the trade system the price at which they are prepared to trade:

Robert can immediately buy shares from Harriet at $49.60 per share, but there the trading stops.

The highest bid is now $49.50 (George) but no one is willing to sell at that price; the lowest ask is $49.70 (Anna) but no one is willing to buy at that price.

The inside quote is now $49.50 to $49.70

Table 7-1: Discovery Café

	Buyers' bid	Sellers' ask
$50.00		Emma
$49.90		Frank
$49.80		Elizabeth
$49.70		Anna
$49.60	Robert	Harriet
$49.50	George	
$49.40	John	
$49.30	Henry	
$49.20	Augusta	
$49.10		
$49.00		

❑   **Bid-ask spread:** The quoted bid-ask spread is the difference between the lowest ask price quoted and the highest bid quoted in a specified market. The bid is always lower than the ask. A narrow bid ask spread generally indicates a more efficient market.

Example 4:

If you wish to buy shares immediately then you must do so by meeting the best asking price: if you set your bid to $49.70, you can trade with Anna immediately.

A dealer, market maker, or specialist sets a bid and ask in this market. If the bid is too high then the dealer buys shares into inventory at a higher price than anyone else is willing to pay; if the bid is too low then he will buy no shares at all. If the ask is too low then the dealer sells shares from inventory at a lower price than anyone else; if he sets his ask too high then he doesn't sell at all.

Example 5:

If a market maker enters the market for Discovery Café then he can set his bid and ask anywhere between $49.50 and $49.70. In order to ensure that he sells before Anna does, he must set his ask below Anna's ask of $49.70 (if prices are in 10¢ increments). The bid-ask spread has now narrowed from 20¢ to 10¢. Now if you wish to buy immediately, you must do so by meeting the best asking price of $49.60. The narrower bid-ask spread lowers your cost of buying shares.

7.3 - The New York Stock Exchange:

The United States has the widest range of financial services and markets available of any of the developed economies. New York dominates with both the New York Stock Exchange (NYSE) and the American Stock Exchange (AMEX). There are also five regional exchanges: the Pacific Exchange in Los Angeles, the Chicago Exchange,[3] and smaller exchanges in Philadelphia, Boston, and Cincinnati.

The New York Stock Exchange began in 1792 when, faced with cut-rate competition from a group of powerful government bond merchants, twenty-four brokers signed the Buttonwood Tree Agreement. The agreement created a closed club in which members agreed to trade only with each other and to abide by a 0.25% commission rate. Buttonwood Tree Agreement was named after the huge Sycamore in front of 68 Wall Street under which brokers gathered to trade. Brokers gathered at the Tontine Coffee House, but unless the weather was particularly vile, trading itself still took place outdoors.

The New York Stock and Exchange Board was a call market. At 11:30 am the duly elected president of the Exchange called out each stock on the official list. As each stock was called, the brokers would call out their bids and asks. When trades were completed in one stock the president would call out the next. There were thirty listed stocks at that time. Trading was completed by about 1:00 pm. All trades were to be settled— stock certificates delivered and paid for—by 2:15 of the following business day.

By 1871 the system of calling out the stocks one by one gave way to a continuous market, and the NYSE marked the advent of the specialist. The specialist is the designated market maker for a number of stocks. He remains at his post throughout the trading day. In this way, brokers know that everyone interested in trading a particular stock will be gathered in front of the same specialist's post. The specialist is both a market maker and a referee among brokers. He is responsible for maintaining "fair and orderly markets" and, if he fails to do so, can lose his specialist designation.

On the NYSE today the market procedure works as follows: a broker who wishes to fill an order approaches a particular location or post on the floor of the exchange where the relevant stock is traded. Some fifteen such posts exist, and each is allocated around 100 stocks. The broker can get the current bid-ask spread from the specialist who has a permanent location at that post, he can negotiate with other brokers at the post, or wait for another broker to happen around with another order. A limit order can be left with the specialist who, for a commission known as floor brokerage, will process the order when possible.

On April 4, 2007, the NYSE Group, Inc. combined with Euronext N.V. to become the first cross-border exchange group. Euronext, based in Amsterdam, was itself a result of the merger of the Amsterdam, Brussels, and Paris Stock exchanges. Euronext had also acquired the Lisbon Exchange and the London International Futures and Options Exchange (LIFFE).

Now known as NYSE Euronext (NYX), the Company's exchanges are located in Europe and the United States and trade equities, futures, options, fixed-income, and exchange-traded products. With approximately 8,000 listed issues (excluding European Structured Products) from more than 55 countries, NYSE Euronext's equities markets—the New York Stock Exchange, NYSE Euronext, NYSE MKT, NYSE Alternext, and NYSE Arca— represent one-third of the world's equities trading.

---

3   The Chicago Exchange was founded in 1882. In 1949 the merger of the Chicago, St.Louis, Cleveland, and Minnesota/St. Paul to formed the Midwest Exchange. It changed its name back to the Chicago Exchange July 8, 1993.

The Specialist

The specialist system evolved because in a continuous market where brokers trade with each other there is no guarantee of a simultaneous coincidence of buyer and seller. Leaving a limit order with a specialist allows the broker to move on to another post. The role of specialist evolved so that some specialists started buying and selling on their own account, thus giving brokers the advantage of immediate execution of their orders. In 1934 the Securities and Exchange Act stated explicitly that specialists must maintain a fair and orderly market in the shares in which they specialize. On the NYSE there is one market maker or dealer per stock, hence the term *specialist*.

The specialist acquires information not readily available to other brokers. This knowledge is necessary in the role of specialist, but it also provides the opportunity to influence the price. To prevent such abuse the NYSE examines the details of all transactions for a one-week period approximately eight times per year. In addition specialists make a weekly report to the exchange on transactions made on their own account, and a computer surveillance system flags unusual price changes and allows the exchange to retrieve trade data.

This system has continued to evolve, and some terminology has changed with different NYSE Equities Membership Types. These include three key market participants: Designated Market Makers, Trading Floor Brokers, and Supplemental Liquidity Providers.

❏ **Designated Market Makers:** These are the specialists. They manage the auction process, combining the physical auction on the floor of the exchange with the electronic trade system that includes computer-generated orders. Designated market makers assume responsibility for maintaining fair and orderly markets.

❏ **Trading Floor Brokers:** Floor brokers trade for their clients and for other brokers. Floor brokers can execute trades in physical auction on the floor or route their orders through the electronic trade system.

❏ **Supplemental Liquidity Providers:** Supplemental Liquidity Providers are market makers. They trade only for their own proprietary accounts, not for clients, and undertake to maintain a bid and ask on each of the securities to which they are assigned.

The open outcry procedure seems somewhat peculiar in the era of instant global communications, but the NYSE defends this procedure as a way of preventing secret deals from taking place on the floor of the exchange.

Off Hours Trading

Trading hours for the NYSE are from 9:30 am to 4:00 pm Eastern Time. In June 1991 The NYSE introduced two after-hours crossing sessions, which have since been merged into one.

❏ **Crossing Session:** The crossing session allows program trades—baskets of at least 15 issues—entered into the electronic trade system. The crossing session is from 4:00 pm to 6:30 pm Eastern Time.

7.4 - The American Stock Exchange

The American Stock Exchange began as a split of brokers from the NYSE. Traders who remained in the street came to be called curbstone brokers. To differentiate themselves from the other brokers, these brokers specialized in the stocks of small, newly created enterprises. In 1911 the curbstone brokers grew to become the New York Curb Market, with a constitution that set higher brokerage and listing standards. In 1921 the New York Curb Market moved indoors to a new building on Greenwich Street in lower Manhattan. Even indoors, the new trading posts were topped by a globe that resembled the lampposts on the street. In 1953, the New York Curb Exchange changed its name to the American Stock Exchange (Amex).

Amex suffered from the rapid growth of the OTC market and the relatively easier listing requirements demanded by NASDAQ. The Exchange responded to these competitive pressures by trading securities other than equities, starting with listed stock options in the 1970s. AMEX dominated the trading in Exchange Traded Funds (ETFs) such as Spiders (based on the S&P indices) and Diamonds (based on the Dow Jones indices).

Amex merged with NASDAQ in November 1998, regained its independence in 2004, and was acquired by NYSE Euronex in October 2008. On December 1, 2008, the Curb Exchange building at 86 Trinity Place was closed, and the Amex Equities trading floor was moved to the NYSE Trading floor at 11 Wall Street and is now called NYSE Alternext.

7.5 - NASDAQ

The over-the-counter market emerged originally as a way of buying and selling the shares of companies not listed on any of the exchanges. This OTC market is supervised by the National Association of Securities Dealers (NASD). Now it is possible to buy listed shares, Treasury bonds and some foreign securities OTC. Over 90% of Treasury bonds, all municipal bonds, and a large proportion of corporate bonds are bought and sold OTC rather than through the exchanges.

The OTC market has never had a trading floor and, prior to the development of the electronic network that links dealers, the market was extremely fragmented. In 1971 the NASD introduced an Automated Quotation system that linked dealers nationwide by a screen-based system. This system is known as the National Association of Securities Dealers Automated Quotation or NASDAQ.

The NASD monitors the bid-ask spreads, and the computer system checks new data against representative and maximum allowable spreads. In addition, the SEC also scrutinizes price behavior.

In 1982 NASDAQ introduced the National Market System (NMS), which now includes over 2500 companies. NMS requires that price and trade data hit the system within 90 seconds of a completed transaction. In addition, there must be at least four market makers for an NMS stock as opposed to two for ordinary NASDAQ shares.

Small company shares that do not qualify for NMS listing trade in the Over-The-Counter (OTC) Bulletin Board, an electronic quotation service maintained by NASDAQ or in The Pink Sheets. The Pink Sheets get their name from the old pink sheet listing of dealers in small, less frequently traded securities published by the National Quotation Bureau Inc. This market has become more sophisticated and includes electronic price display of dealer quotes and is now known as Pink Sheets LLC.

❑ **Pink Sheets:** Pink Sheets are the quotes on issues that trade over-the-counter

In July 2006 NASDAQ introduced a third layer of traded securities for public companies that will have the highest initial listing standards in the world. Advertised as a Blue Chip market for blue chip stocks, the "NASDAQ Global Select Market" would have financial and liquidity requirements that are higher than those of any other market.

In 2000 the NASD voted to spin off NASDAQ into a separate publicly owned, for-profit corporation. NASDAQ began trading under the ticker symbol NDAQ on the NASDAQ electronic market on July 2, 2002. In 2007, NASDAQ combined with the Scandinavian exchange group OMX to become The NASDAQ OMX Group. Today, the NASDAQ OMX Group owns and operates 24 markets, 3 clearinghouses, and 5 central securities depositories, spanning six continents. This makes NASDAQ OMX the world's largest exchange company, with 18 markets trading equities 6 more trading options, derivatives, fixed income, and commodities.

Figure 7-1: Example of a NASDAQ Level II Screen

CAFÉ	DISCOVERY CAFÉ			TICKER	
L	54.28		6	+ 0.08	Last	Shares
B	54.27	A	54.29	12x10	54.25	2
O	54.20	L	54.20	H	54.28	54.25	4
					54.26	2
MLCO	54.27	3	CIBC	54.29	10	54.26	1
LAZA	54.27	2	FBCO	54.30	2	54.27	1
MSCO	54.27	12	AGED	55.30	3	54.26	1
VCAP	54.26	5	GSCO	56.30	2	54.27	4
BANC	54.26	6	HSBC	57.30	5	54.27	6
BEST	54.25	3	LEGG	58.30	9	54.28	2
JPMS	54.25	4	PWJC	54.31	12	54.27	1
SBSH	54.25	1	DJLP	54.32	1	54.28	1
ARCA	54.24	1	AGED	54.32	1	54.28	4
AANA	54.23	2	DAIN	54.33	3	54.28	6

Discovery Café last traded at $54.28. The inside bid is $54.27 for 300 shares from Merrill Lynch (MLCO). The inside offer (ask) is $54.29 for 1000 shares from the Canadian Imperial Bank of Commerce.

Today's lowest price was $54.20 and the highest price was $54.28

Market Efficiency

In 1996 several NASDAQ market makers were investigated for various practices, most particularly the practice of paying for order flow: client buys were executed at prices higher than the best bid and client sales were executed at lower than the best ask. In response the SEC imposed on NASDAQ market makers new "Order Handling Rules" in 1996, and spreads fell about 30% as a result.

Nonetheless, academic research showed that an auction market such as the NYSE resulted in better trades (in tighter ranges, less volatility, less difference in price between trades) and, in a report released January 8, 2001, the SEC concluded that the NASDAQ system of competing market makers still produces wider bid-ask spreads than the specialist supervised auction system of the NYSE.

In response to this criticism, NASDAQ introduced SuperMontage. SuperMontage combines information from market makers and electronic communication networks into one central order routing system. This combined the NASDAQ system of competing market makers with an automatic order matching system that brings buyers and sellers together without the dealer or market maker interposed between them.

1993: Order Flow Inducements

In "Market Integration and Price Execution for NYSE-Listed Securities" *Journal of Finance* 48; 1009-1038 (July 1993), Charles M.C. Lee stated that for NYSE-listed securities, the price execution of seemingly comparable orders differs systematically by location. These discrepancies exist despite the introduction of the Intermarket Trading System (ITS) that immediately disseminates trades and quote revisions to all trading locations.

Since 1988, NASD and regional specialists have paid brokers cash rebates—typically one cent per share—for directing customer orders to their trading center. These cash rebates are one of the many "order flow inducements" between brokers and dealers that may influence how brokers route their customers' orders. Such "inducements" compromise brokers' primary responsibility to their customers if the price execution differs by location. In general, executions at the Cincinnati, Chicago, & New York stock exchanges are the most favorable to the trade initiators, while executions at NASD are least favorable. The intermarket price differences depend on the size of the trade, with the smallest trades exhibiting the biggest per-share price difference.

7.6 - Electronic Communication Networks (ECNs)

Electronic communication networks provide computer-assisted trading in that they put buyers and sellers together by computer without going through the NYSE, AMEX, or NASDAQ. ECNs are computerized order routing systems. Buyers and sellers enter bids and asks into the system, and the computer matches buyer and seller whenever they enter the same price. Because the montage of bids and asks are visible this is essentially a silent auction with the computer as auctioneer.

The vast majority of ECN trades involve NASDAQ stocks traded during regular market hours. The SEC reported that by June 2000 ECNs accounted for approximately 30% of share volume and 40% of dollar volume of NASDAQ securities and approximately 3% of total share and dollar volume in listed securities.

Initially, ECNs made the market more fragmented as prices quoted on ECNs drifted away from those quoted by NASDAQ. In 1996 the SECs mandated "Order Handling Rules", which required market makers to integrate the best quotes they put on ECNs with the quotes they posted on NASDAQ. Essentially it prevented market makers from quoting one price on an ECN and another price on NASDAQ. As a result bid-ask spreads on NASDAQ narrowed by about 30%, and the market became much less fragmented.

In December 1998 the SEC enacted regulation ATS (Alternative Trading System) under which ECNs could either register as exchanges (with all the regulatory requirements) or remain registered as broker-dealers.

Initial reactions by major established exchanges to the threats posed by ECNs included building their own systems to compete. NASDAQ responded with the Super Montage system, basically the addition of an electronic order routing system to the traditional competing market makers. Other exchanges responded with similar systems, until the competition resolved itself through merger and acquisition. Instinet and Island, two of the larger ECNs, merged in 2002 to become Inet. Inet, in turn, was acquired by NASDAQ in 2005. Archipelago Exchange, the other of the largest ECNs, was acquired by the NYSE in the same year.

7.7 - Issues in the Secondary Markets

A number of issues and side topics are relevant to the secondary markets in the United States.

7.7.1 - Ticker Symbols

A ticker symbol is a character code that identifies a security. The ticker symbol is assigned by the primary exchange on which the security trades. Historically, issues that trade on the New York or American Stock Exchange carried a one-, two-, or three-character ticker symbol [such as AT&T (T), Alcoa (AA), & PepsiCo (PEP)]; issues that trade over NASDAQ carried a four character ticker symbol [such as Intel (INTC), Oracle (ORCL), & Microsoft (MSFT)]

In 2007 the SEC ruled that a company listed on the NYSE or AMEX could keep its three-character ticker when it moved its listing to NASDAQ. A year later, the rule was expanded to allow companies with two- and even one-character ticker symbols to keep their coveted symbol when moving from the NYSE or AMEX to NASDAQ. Now, even first-time listings on NASDAQ can have fewer than four-character ticker symbols.

In May 2012, Facebook began trading on NASDAQ with the ticker symbol FB.

Today, the number of letters making a ticker symbol follows less rigorous convention, but generally, a fifth character is a footnote character that imparts specific information. The Intermarket Symbol Reservation Authority (ISRA) has oversight of ticker symbols assignment in the United States.

Foreign company shares, either ADRs or ADSs, are indicated by the footnote character Y, such as Heineken (HINKY), Nestlé (NSRGY) and Lukoil (LUKOY). If the stock is an actual foreign share, not an ADR or ADS, the footnote character is F, such as Nestlé (NSRGF) and Lukoil (LUKOF). With Nestlé and Lukoil both the ADR and the foreign shares trade over the counter.

Example 6:

> After Enron (ENE) declared bankruptcy in December 2001 it was delisted from the NYSE and assigned the ticker ENRN. It then traded over the counter under the symbol ENRNQ; the Q meant that the company had already filed for bankruptcy.

7.7.2 - National Market System

The secondary market is fragmented. All orders are not traded the same way. In an unfragmented market all orders for a security would trade in the same way: on the floor, through the specialist. Now these orders can be traded on one of several exchanges, OTC, or routed upstairs to Instinet—a system that allows large institutional investors to trade directly with each other. The concern with fragmented markets is that, regardless of in which market the trade takes place, it should be made at the most favorable price.

To address this issue the Securities Act of 1975 directed the SEC to facilitate the establishment of a national market system for securities, the characteristics of which are

❏ **Centralized reporting of all transactions:** Centralized reporting requires a composite tape to report all transactions in a stock regardless of where that transaction took place. The NYSE now has a composite tape of all NYSE listed stocks.

❏ **Centralized quotation system:** Under this system a broker seeking to sell your 1000 shares of IBM could see the prevailing quotes on the NYSE as well as any regional exchanges on which IBM is listed, along with quotes from the various OTC market makers.

❏ **Centralized limit order book (CLOB):** The CLOB would contain all limit orders from all exchanges. Although the technology is available the NYSE opposes its development and use.

❏ **Competition among market makers :** Free and open competition has always existed OTC (where it has served to squeeze bid-ask spreads), but it was opposed by the NYSE.

The Securities and Exchange Commission (SEC) requires that each participant in an effective National Market System Plan (NMS Plan) ensure that a current and complete version of the NMS Plan is posted on a central web site. The Financial Industry Regulatory Authority (FINRA) is the largest independent regulator for all securities firms doing business in the United States, and as such, coordinates these different systems and disseminates information on their interaction.

There are currently three principal plans in operation in the U.S. They are

❏ National Market System Plan for the Selection and Reservation of Securities Symbols (the Intermarket Symbol Reservation Authority, or "ISRA" Plan)
❏ Consolidated Tape Association Plan/Consolidated Quotation Plan (CTA/CQ Plans)
❏ Joint Self-Regulatory Organization Plan Governing the Collection, Consolidation, and Dissemination of Quotation and Transaction Information for NASDAQ-Listed Securities Traded on Exchanges on an Unlisted Trading Privilege Basis (OTC UTP Plan)

Additional information and development news about these plans is available on the FINRA website at http://www.finra.org/Industry/Regulation/Guidance/NationalMarketSystemPlans/

A Rose by any other Name ... If you find it somewhat confusing that the term *National Market System* refers both to the U.S. Congress definition of the ideal capital market of the future and a subset of NASDAQ be not intimidated. The confusion was intentional. The NASD blatantly used the term as a marketing tool to suggest the superiority of the NMS over other exchanges.

7.7.3 - Subpennies and Ticks

A tick is the smallest increment in which prices can be quoted. Goods and services in the U.S. have price ticks of a penny; the next highest price after $10 is $10.01. House prices are quoted in ticks of $1000. The next higher price after $100,000 is $101,000., not $100,000.01

Stocks historically traded in ⅛ ths of a dollar (12.5¢). In 1997 this practice evolved to $^{1}/_{16}$ ths (6.25¢). In 2000 the U.S. Equity markets converted from quoting stock prices in eighths and sixteenths to quoting prices in dollars and cents.

Rather than following the example of other exchanges, such as Toronto, where prices are quoted in nickel ticks (the next highest price after $10.00 is $10.05) the NYSE went to penny ticks (the next highest price after

$10.00 is $10.01). NASDAQ took this one bizarre step further and went to subpennies or 1/100¢. The next highest price after $10.00 is $10.0001.

One of the affects of the tick change was to fragment execution. Under a nickel tick we can have 1000 shares bid at $10 and another 1000 at $10.05. Under a subpenny tick we can have 100 shares bid at $10., 100 shares bid at $10.0001, 100 shares at $10.0002, etcetera. Now to sell 1000 shares we need to make 10 separate transactions at 10 different prices rather than selling 1000 shares at one price.

One area of concern is Stepping Ahead. Specialists and market makers are required to yield to client orders at any price. If a client bids $10 and a market maker bids $10 then the client order gets executed first. If the market maker wants to get his bid in ahead of the client, he must bid a higher price. This is called stepping ahead of the client. When the tick was ⅛, this meant that stepping ahead added $12.50 to the cost of a 100-share board lot. At a penny tick the cost of stepping ahead is $1.00 At a subpenny tick a market maker can step ahead by $0.0001; the cost of stepping ahead of the client is now 1¢.

7.7.4 - Institutional Investors

Institutional investors are pension funds, insurance companies, mutual funds, and trusts. They are similar to deposit taking institutions in that they aggregate savings from a variety of sources and invest the proceeds. One of the most significant features of the past three decades has been the increase in the importance of these institutional investors.

❑ **Upstairs Market:** Institutional trades are generally executed through a network of trading desks in the upstairs offices of investment banks, institutional investors, brokers, and dealers; hence the term upstairs market. The upstairs market thus refers to trades that take place without using the stock exchange. These trades are also referred to as off exchange or off board (because the NYSE is referred to as The Big Board).

❑ **Block Trades:** Block trades are trades of more than 10,000 shares or more than $200,000. The block goes to the upstairs market where the trader matches it with another block trade. If any portion of the block cannot be traded upstairs then the brokerage firm can fill the order, in whole or in part, on its own account, or it can be executed through a competing market maker.

The increase in block trading put a significant strain on the existing specialist system.

  ❑ Capital: Specialists had trouble coming up with the capital needed to acquire large blocks of stock.
  ❑ Commitment: Even when specialists had the capital they were unwilling to assume the risks involved.
  ❑ Contacts: Rule 113 of the NYSE prohibits specialists from trading directly with nonbrokers. This means that they cannot contact the institutions that would normally take the opposite side of a block trade.

The specialists' lack of capital, commitment, and contacts lead to the development of block houses. Block houses are brokerage companies that specialize in executing block trades.

❑ **Program Trades:** Program or basket trades involve the buying and/or selling of a large number of issues simultaneously.

❑ **Frontrunning:** Frontrunning occurs when the broker uses his knowledge of an impending block or program trade to trade advantageously on his own account.

7.7.5 - Circuit Breakers

Circuit breakers refer to a set of rules that limit equities trading automatically when the circuit breaker is triggered. Although the rules apply directly to only the NYSE, other exchanges have agreed to halt trading whenever NYSE trading is halted. The circuit breakers, adopted in 1988 and amended in November 1997, are based on the net change in the Dow Jones Industrial Average from the previous day's close. Circuit-breaker points represent the thresholds at which trading is halted market-wide for single-day declines in the Dow Jones Industrial Average (DJIA). Circuit-breaker levels are set quarterly as 10, 20, and 30 percent of the DJIA average closing values of the previous month, rounded to the nearest 50 points

The first time the circuit breakers halted trading was Monday October 27, 1997. The Dow fell 350 points by early afternoon, and trading was stopped at 2:35 pm (New York) for 30 minutes. When the market reopened at 3:05 the accumulated backlog of sell orders caused the market to plunge 200 points in 25 minutes. This triggered the second trading halt, and the market closed at 3:30 with the Dow Jones down 554.26 points at 7161.15 Although the second circuit breaker halts the market for one hour, under the old rules, (amended November 1997) when the trigger came after 3 pm it effectively closed the market for the day.

In the second-quarter of 2012, the 10-, 20- and 30-percent decline levels, respectively, in the DJIA were:

❑ **Level 1 Halt:** A 1,300-point drop in the DJIA before 2 p.m. will halt trading for one hour; for 30 minutes if between 2 p.m. and 2:30 p.m.; and have no effect if at 2:30 p.m. or later unless there is a level 2 halt.

❑ **Level 2 Halt:** A 2,600-point drop in the DJIA before 1:00 p.m. will halt trading for two hours; for one hour if between 1:00 p.m. and 2:00 p.m.; and for the remainder of the day if at 2:00 p.m. or later.

❑ **Level 3 Halt:** A 3,900-point drop will halt trading for the remainder of the day regardless of when the decline occurs.

The concept of circuit breakers was expanded from entire markets into covering individual stocks, after the May 6, 2010, "Flash Crash".

Two years after the event, the debate of what caused it and whether another "Flash Crash" could occur rages on. Postmortem examinations of trades on that day challenge the findings of the SEC-CFTC report on the event. Even members of the commissions authoring the report are less than satisfied with it, or the changes made to the system to prevent another flash crash, including the regulation of "high-frequency traders".

❑ **High-Frequency Traders:** High-frequency traders are firms who use high-speed computers to execute thousands of in-and-out trades every millisecond of the trading day under the belief of providing liquidity to the market. This highly secretive style of market making and trading is still one aspect of public markets much in debate and unsettled by regulators.

May 6, 2010: Flash Crash

On May 6, 2010 the market was already nervous, with the Dow Jones Industrial Average down 161 points at 2 pm, two hours before the close. Shortly after 2:30 pm the decline began in earnest and, at 2:42 pm the Dow was down 422.28 from the previous close. In the next five minutes of trading the Dow dropped another 573.27 points to 9,872.57. The low for the day was 9,787.17, a decline from the previous close of 1,080.95 points.

The market recovered itself just as quickly, recovering 543 points in approximately a minute and a half. By 4 pm the market closed at 10,520.32, down 347.80, but compared to the thousand plus point drop at 2:47pm, down a mere 347.80 was a relief to all.

During the flash crash shares of individual stocks were executed at irrational prices. Shares of Exelon Corp (EXC) dropped from $40 to 41¢. Within minutes it was back to $40. Boston Beer (SAM) fell from $56 to 1¢. Within minutes it was back at $56. When the dust cleared the Exchanges negated trades made at prices more than 60% off their previous close. But it was a wild ride in any case.

The flash crash appeared to begin with the E-mini S&P 500 future. This is a futures contract defined as $50 times the S&P 500 index. A lack of liquidity was attributed to a huge sell order that absorbed all the available buys. As a result existing market sell orders hit stub quotes. Stub quotes are bids and asks generated by market makers (or the exchanges on their behalf) at levels far away from the current market in order to fulfill continuous two-sided bid-ask obligations even when a market maker has withdrawn from active trading. In effect, the stock market was trading blind and running on autopilot. In the 20 minute period between 2:40 pm and 3:00 pm, (Eastern Time), over 20,000 trades (many based on retail-customer orders) across more than 300 separate securities were executed at prices 60% or more away from their 2:40 pm prices and were later cancelled. Figures 7-2 and 7-3 show the price movement on the DJIA and on Exelon after these extreme trades were eliminated and trading ranges were made public.

Beginning in June 2010, the SEC instituted new rules. If any S&P 500 stock rises or falls 10% or more in a 5 minute period between 9:45 am and 3:35 pm ET. all U.S. stock exchanges must halt trading in that stock for 5 minutes.

Further reading:
  September 30, 2010, joint SEC-CFTC report to the Senate Banking Committee, and House Committee on Financial Services. http:/www.sec.gov/news/studies/2010/marketevents-report.pdf

Figure 7-2: DJIA May 3 to May 7, 2010

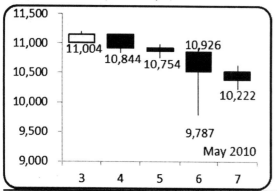

Figure 7-3: Exelon (EXC) May 3 to May 7, 2010

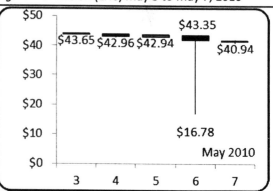

Chapter 7 - Questions and Problems

7-1:

You are a broker with *Investments Unlimited*. Your client phones you and places a buy order for 1,000 shares of Microsoft at the Market. You punch MSFT into your NASDAQ terminal and see the following information:

MICROSOFT(MSFT)	BID	ASK
Market Maker #1	122.1043	122.3081
Market Maker #2	122.1030	122.4070
Market Maker #3	122.0523	122.1032
Market Maker #4	122.0510	122.3010

You immediately phone market maker # _____

and execute the transaction at $_____ .

7-2:

The table at the right indicates that the quote for FLY is

A. 32.50 - 33
B. 32.65 - 33
C. 32.75 - 32.90
D. 32.80 - 32.85

7-3:

The table to the right indicates that the size of the market for FLY is

A. 100 by 100
B. 100 by 400
C. 200 by 400
D. 400 by 700

Buy	FLY	Sell
	33	100 BD G
	.95	200 BD F
	.90	100 BD D
		300 BD E
	.85	
	.80	
200 BD C	.75	
100 BD B	.70	
200 BD A	.65	
	.60	
	.55	
	.50	

7-4:

Trading in InterScam International (ISI) is stopped on the NYSE because of an influx of orders. What happens on the other exchanges?

A. All trading in ISI stops.

B. All trading in ISI stops on the regional exchanges but not on the American Stock Exchange.

C. Trading in ISI may continue on regional exchanges as well as on NASDAQ but it will not be reported on the tape until trading resumes on the NYSE.

D. Trading in ISI may continue on regional exchanges as well as on NASDAQ, and all trades are reported as they occur.

O wning and trading equities can be a career for some, a pastime for others, or a fundamental skill to many in financial planning and budgeting throughout their lives. For this reason, it is a good idea for everyone to have some knowledge of market traded equities.

Most of us, at some point in our working lives, will make active investment decisions involving stocks, bonds, or other assets as we choose how to allocate personal and retirement funds. Most employers who offer retirement plans require the employee to choose how funds are to be invested. These choices may not be as specific as individual equities, bonds, real estate, et cetera, but they will be choices of asset classes or mutual funds that have many of the attributes of the individual assets themselves.

Thus a basic understanding of the structure of secondary markets and the basics of owning and trading equities is not only required of finance professionals, but it has also become a fundamental component of basic financial literacy.

8.1 - Trade Orders

A trade order is an instruction conveyed to a broker, who then executes or fills the order. Because there is always some delay between the time the order is given and the time it can be executed, several types of orders have evolved to cope with the possible consequences of this delay.

Execution Priority

Orders are executed according to:

- ❏ Price. (A buy order at $50.01 is executed before a buy order at $50.00.)

- ❏ Time. (A buy order at $50.00 received at 10:00 am is executed before a buy order at $50.00 received at 10:01 am)

Preferential Trading Rules

Preferential trading rules state that where the order of a client competes at the same price with a nonclient order (an order of an account in which a partner, director, officer, shareholder, or employee of the Broker holds a direct or indirect interest) the client's order is given priority of execution over the nonclient order.

8.1.1 - At-the-Market Order

A market order is an instruction to buy or sell a security immediately at the best price available.

- ❏ **Buy 1000 DVC:** Buy 1000 shares of Discovery Café at the current market price.
- ❏ **Sell 1000 DVC:** Sell 1000 shares of Discovery Café at the current market price.

The disadvantage of a market order is that market conditions can change in the interval between the time the order is given and the time it is executed.

Example 1:

DVC trades at $92. You submit a market buy order for 100 shares. By the time your order reaches the floor, the stock has risen to $119. You just invested $11,900 rather than $9,200. If you submitted the buy order because you felt that Discovery Café should rise to $100, then buying at $119 is rather pointless.

8.1.2 - Limit Order

A limit order is an instruction to buy or sell at a specific price or better.

- ❑ **Buy 1000 DVC limit $90:** Buy 1000 shares of Discovery Café but pay no more than $90 per share.
- ❑ **Sell 1000 DVC limit $92:** Sell 1000 shares of Discovery Café but take no less than $92 per share.

All limit orders have an expiry date. If the order cannot be executed within the limit before the close of trading on the expiry date, then the order expires limit out. The disadvantage of a limit order is that the order may not be executed at all.

- ❑ **Limit Out:** A limit order that expires because the price per share in the market does not allow the order to be executed

Example 2:

DVC closes Thursday at $92. You submit a limit order to buy 100 shares limit $92. DVC opens at 92.01, increases throughout the day, and closes at $119. The order is limit out and is not executed at all. You just missed out on a $27 increase.

- ❑ **Limit Order Book:** The limit order book is the list of outstanding limit orders. These orders will be executed when and if market conditions allow.

8.1.3 - Stop Order

A stop order is an instruction to buy or sell that becomes a market order as soon as the market price of a board lot reaches a specified level. This type of order is designed to get an investor out of an existing position before any more damage is done. A stop sell order is designed to minimize losses when a stock in which you have a position starts to slide. A stop buy order is designed to minimize losses when the price of a stock you have sold short increases unexpectedly.

- ❑ **Sell 1000 DVC stop $70:** If Discovery Café decreases to $70 then put in a market sell for 1000 shares.
- ❑ **Buy 1000 DVC stop $110:** If Discovery Café increases to $110 put in a market buy for 1000 shares.

The disadvantage of a stop order is that it becomes a market order as soon as the stop price is reached. There is no certainty that it will be executed at that price.

Example 3:

> DVC starts to slide, triggering your stop loss order at $70. Your market order goes through at $59 as DVC slides to $50.

8.1.4 - Stop Limit Order

A stop limit order is an instruction to buy or sell that becomes a limit order as soon as the market price of a board lot reaches a specified level.

- ❑ **Sell 1000 DVC stop $70 limit $60:** If Discovery Café decreases to $70 then sell 1000 shares, but don't take less than $60 per share.
- ❑ **Buy 1000 DVC stop $110 limit $120 :** If Discovery Café increases to $110 then buy 1000 shares, but don't pay more than $120 per share.

The disadvantage of a stop limit order is that it becomes a limit order as soon as the stop price is reached. There is no certainty that the order will be executed.

Example 4:

> DVC starts to slide, triggering your stop loss order at $70. The market drops directly through to trade at $59. Your order is not executed because it became a limit order good only to $60. The following week DVC trades at $25.

8.1.5 - Other Orders

The market, limit, stop, and stop limit are the most commonly used orders. There are variations and conditions that are used less frequently.

Market if Touched Order

A market-if-touched (MIT) order is a stop order in reverse: it is designed to get an investor into a position rather than out of one.

- ❑ **Sell 1000 DVC MIT $110:** (market-if-touched sell). If Discovery Café increases to $110 then sell 1000 shares to lock in the profits on the shares I own
- ❑ **Buy 1000 DVC MIT $70:** (market-if-touched buy). If Discovery Café decreases to $70 then buy 1000 shares.

Good Through Order

A good through order is good for a specified number of days and then automatically canceled if not filled.

Open or Good-Til-Canceled Order

An open, or good-til-canceled (GTC), order stays on the books until executed or canceled by the client. To avoid an unwieldy build-up of open orders on the broker's trading books many firms put a limit (30, 60, or 90 days) and then ask the client if he wishes to renew the order. Most firms periodically remind clients of open orders still pending to avoid misunderstandings over "forgotten" open orders.

Other Orders

❏ **All-or-None Order:** An all-or-none order is an instruction that specifies a minimum number of shares that must be bought or sold before the client will accept the fill.

❏ **Any-Part-Order:** An any-part-order is the opposite of an all-or-none: the client will accept the order filled in bits and pieces, board, odd, or broken lots.

❏ **Fill-or-kill Order:** A fill-or-kill order specifies that the order should be filled immediately in full or canceled.

❏ **Switch Order:** A switch order is an instruction to sell one security and use the proceeds to buy another. The broker sells board lots of one security to purchase board lots of another until both sides of the order are completed.

1968: Back Office Crisis

Throughout the post war years stock market investment and trading increased. By 1954 the Dow Jones Industrial Average (DJIA) had regained its September 1929 high of 381.17, twenty-five years after the crash. By the end of 1967 the index was flirting with 1,000. Trading volume soared from five to fifteen million shares per day in less than three years.

The back office of brokerage firms was the home to a multi-step process that laboriously delivered and registered paper certificates. Attempts to computerize were costly and largely ineffective. The fun was in trading, not in back office accounting.

The number of fails increased to dangerous levels. A fail occurs when a delivery of the certificate fails to match up to a recorded trade. Either there is a certificate and no acknowledged trade or a there is a trade with no certificate. Discrepancies between recorded investments on client accounts and actual securities amounted to billions of dollars.

On June 12, 1968 securities markets were closed every Wednesday, just to let the back office catch up. It didn't work. By December 1969 fails peaked at just over $4 billion. On January 2, 1969, Wednesdays were restored to the trading calendar without really addressing the problem.

The back office crisis was ended by a bear market. From December 1968 to June 1970 the DJIA declined 28% and trading volume decreased by a third.

Further Reading:
John Brooks, *The Go-Go Years; the Drama and Crashing Finale of Wall Street's Bullish 60s*, Wiley Investment Classics, 1973.

8.2 - Dividends & Splits

Once you become an owner you can receive income from the firm in the form of dividends, and the shares themselves can divide or split.

8.2.1 - Dividends

A dividend is a distribution to shareholders. The distribution is generally in cash (10¢ per share) or, less frequently, in shares (1 share for each 10 shares). The dividend is determined by the board of directors. Most large companies pay regular quarterly dividends, but there is no legal obligation to do so.

❑ **Declaration Date:** The date on which the board of directors officially declares a dividend. The company announces the dividend amount, the record date, and the pay date.

❑ **Record Date:** The date on which you must be registered with the corporate trustee as the owner of shares in the company. Only registered shareholders are entitled to receive the declared dividend.

❑ **Ex-Dividend Date:** The date on which the stock trades without the declared dividend. The ex-dividend date or ex-date is set by the primary exchange on which the shares trade and is generally two business days prior to the record date. The assumption is that if you buy the stock prior to the ex-date your purchase will be registered by the record date.

❑ **Payable Date:** The date on which the dividend is actually paid.

Accrued Accounting

Under the rules of accrued accounting, we credit the dividend to the portfolio on the ex-date. Accrued accounting reflects the fact that the portfolio has earned the dividend and will receive the proceeds even if we sell the shares immediately.

Example 5:

> March 20 the Board of Directors of the Discovery Café declares a dividend of 30¢ to shareholders of record April 3, payable April 21. The NYSE sets the ex-date at April 1.

> Investors who buy shares before the opening bell April 1 buy the shares with the dividends still attached; investors who buy shares of Discovery Café after the opening bell April 1 buy the shares ex (without) dividend.

Figure 8-1: Discovery Café Dividend of 30¢ Ex April 1

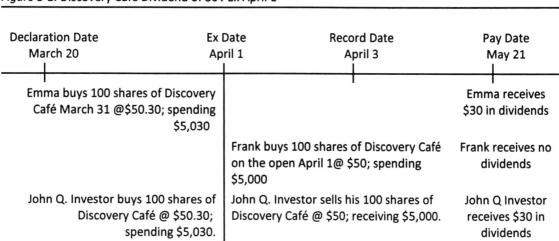

Declaration Date March 20	Ex Date April 1	Record Date April 3	Pay Date May 21
Emma buys 100 shares of Discovery Café March 31 @$50.30; spending $5,030			Emma receives $30 in dividends
	Frank buys 100 shares of Discovery Café on the open April 1@ $50; spending $5,000		Frank receives no dividends
John Q. Investor buys 100 shares of Discovery Café @ $50.30; spending $5,030.	John Q. Investor sells his 100 shares of Discovery Café @ $50; receiving $5,000.		John Q Investor receives $30 in dividends

8.2.2 - Stock Splits and Consolidations

A stock split or consolidation occurs when a company redefines its shares into smaller or larger units. The split has no effect of the company's net worth or the value of the shares outstanding: 2 million shares at $60 per share is worth the same as 4 million shares at $30 per share.

❑ **Stock Split:** A stock split occurs when a company redefines its shares into smaller units. Generally, corporations split their stock to lower the share prices and to broaden ownership.

Example 6:

In 1979 shares of IBM sold at about $350 per share. A board lot of 100 shares thus required an investment of $35,000. In 1979 IBM split 4:1 reducing the price per share to less than $100. The split made shares more popular with small investors and thus reduced the dominance of institutional trading.

Splits may also precede exchange listing. A corporation must have at least 1.1 million publicly traded shares, a per share price of at least $4, and at least 400 shareholders of 100 shares or more before its shares can be listed on the NYSE.

Example 7:

Discovery Café (DVC) has 400,000 shares trading at $150 per share. Market capitalization is thus $60m. The board of directors declares a three for one stock split for shareholders of record October 31. The NYSE then sets the ex-date at November 1. After the opening bell November 1 Discovery Café will have 1,200,000 shares trading at $50 per share for a total market capitalization of $60m.

Figure 8-2: Discovery Café Splits 3:1

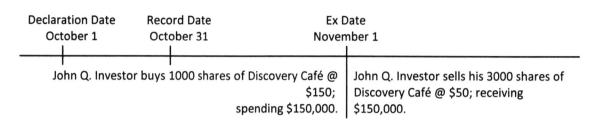

Declaration Date	Record Date	Ex Date
October 1	October 31	November 1

John Q. Investor buys 1000 shares of Discovery Café @ $150; spending $150,000.

John Q. Investor sells his 3000 shares of Discovery Café @ $50; receiving $150,000.

Berkshire Hathaway (BRK)

Berkshire Hathaway (BRK) was created in 1955 from the merger of Berkshire Cotton Manufacturing and Hathaway Manufacturing. The company was acquired in 1965 by Warren Buffet. With the textile industry in what appeared to be a permanent slump, Buffet used Berkshire Hathaway as a base from which to acquire a wide variety of companies in other industries. He began by buying the National Indemnity and the National Fire & Marine Insurance Companies, both of Omaha, Nebraska. Thereafter BRK acquired, or acquired a significant share of, companies such as See's Candy, Buffalo News, Blue Chip Stamps, Nebraska Furniture, Borsheim's, Fechheimer Brother's, Scot & Fetzer, H.H. Brown Shoe, Dexter Shoe, Wescoe Financial, The Washington Post, GEICO (Government Employees Insurance Company), Capital Cities/ABC, and Coca-Cola. BRK also held significant numbers of shares in Gillete, Wells Fargo, General Dynamics, and the Federal Home Loan Association.

Berkshire Hathaway has a zero tolerance policy on stock splits. Through all the years of growth and acquisition Berkshire Hathaway shares have never split. The shares traded at prices in excess of $93,000 per share during 2006. This price per share put it out of the reach of most investors.

Buffet was unwilling to abandon his no split policy, so he created a new class of shares instead. The original Berkshire Hathaway (BRK) became Berkshire Hathaway Class A shares (BRKa or BRK.A) and the company issued new Berkshire Hathaway Class B shares (BRKb or BRK.B) which trade at a prices roughly 1/30th of the class A shares.

This structure prevailed until January 2010. In February 2010, Berkshire Hathaway completed the purchase of the 77.4 percent of Burlington Northern that it did not already own. The cash-and-stock transaction was valued at $26.4 billion, or $100 per share, and valued all Burlington Northern at about $34 billion.

In January 2010, in preparation of Berkshire Hathaway's purchase of the Burlington Northern Santa Fe Railroad company, it conducted a 50-for-1 split of its Class B shares, which traded around $3,400, to let Burlington Northern shareholders do stock swaps rather than be forced to cash out and pay taxes. Higher-priced Class A shares were not split. The Class B shares then became 1/1,500 the price and 1/10,000 the voting rights of the Class A shares. Holders of class A stock are allowed to convert their stock to Class B, though not vice versa.

Figure 8-3: Berkshire Hathaway (BRK-A) January 1990 through June 2012

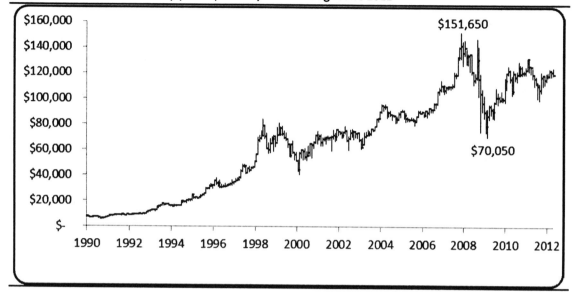

- ❑ **Reverse split / Consolidation :** A reverse split occurs when a company redefines its shares into larger units. In general, reverse splits are used to increase the price of the stock, moving it out of the speculative "pennies stock" and into the investment grade "dollars stock" range.

2011: Citigroup (C) Consolidation

For a decade Citigroup (C) shares traded in the $40 to $57 range, with a high of $57 in December 28, 2006. In October 2007, amid news of trouble with off-balance sheet structured investment vehicles (SIVs) the stock price began to slide. It broke through the $40 level on November 2, 2007, and closed the year at $29.69. On March 5, 2009, Citigroup (C) traded at a low of $0.97 before finally settling in the $3 to $4 range.

NYSE rules require that the 30-day average price of a listed stock remain above $1.

On May 9, 2011, Citigroup consolidated 1:10. The shares closed at $4.52 on Friday May 6 and opened at $44.89 on Monday May 9, 2011.

8.3 - Margin Transactions

A margin transaction occurs when the investor pays part of the cost of his investment in cash and borrows the remainder from his broker, using the investment itself as collateral. This leverage increases the risk of the transaction. Minimum margin requirements are set by the Federal Reserve and by the exchange on which the security is traded.

❏ **Margin:** The percentage of the value of the stock for which you must deposit money. If you buy stock on 25% margin you pay 25% of the cost and you borrow 75% from your broker. Buying on margin leverages your investment, increasing both the potential return (or loss) and the risk.

❏ **Leverage:** Leverage is defined as the amplification in the return earned on equity when the investment is financed, wholly or partially, through debt.

$$Leverage \; = \; \frac{1}{margin} \hspace{3cm} (Eq\ 8\text{-}1)$$

When you acquire stock or other investments on margin you are increasing the financial risk of the investment beyond the risk inherent in the security itself. You should increase your required rate of return accordingly.

❏ **Initial Margin:** Initial margin is the margin deposit the investor must make to make the purchase.

❏ **Maintenance Margin:** Maintenance margin is the minimum margin the investor must keep in the margin account when the stock price changes

❏ **Margin Call:** A margin call occurs when the minimum margin requirement is no longer met and the broker requires additional funds to be deposited. When you get a margin call you must bring your margin account up to the initial margin level.

When the margin is 50% leverage is 1/.50 = 2. This means that if the rate of return on the underlying investment is 10% the rate of return for the leveraged investor is 20%.

Example 8:

> You buy 1000 shares Discovery Café (DVC) at $50 for a total cost of $50,000. A 50% initial margin requirement allows you to borrow $25,000. Your equity is $25,000. This is illustrated in Figure 8-4.
>
> If Discovery Café increases to $70, the market value of your shares increase to $70,000, $25,000 of which you owe to your broker. Your equity is thus $45,000 or 64% (45,000/70,000).
>
> However, if Discovery Café decreases to $40 the market value of your shares decreases to $40,000, $25,000 of which you owe to your broker. Your equity is thus $15,000, or 37.5%.
>
> If the maintenance margin is 40% then you would have fallen below this level and triggered a margin call. The margin call requires you to increase your equity back to the original level of 50%. A deposit of $5,000 would reduce your debt to your broker to $20,000 and increase your equity to $20,000

Figure 8-4: Margin and Equity for Example 8 Margin Purchase of Discovery Café

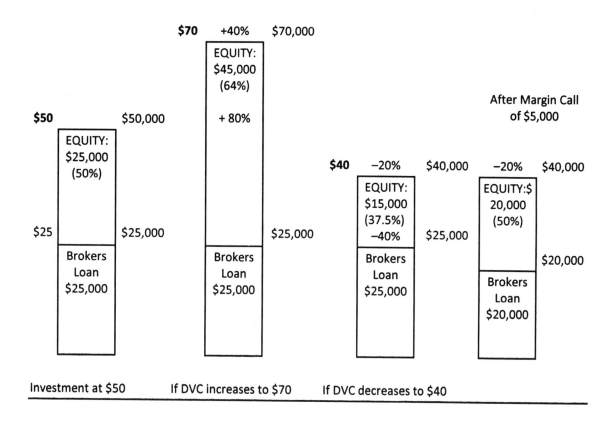

Investment at $50   If DVC increases to $70   If DVC decreases to $40

❑ **Regulation T:** Margin transactions are governed by Regulation T of the Federal Reserve. Under Regulation T the initial margin must be no less than 50% of the purchase price of the stock, and maintenance margin can be no less than 25% of the value of the position. House requirements, the margin requirements mandated by your broker, are frequently higher than the Regulation T minimums.

8.4 - *Short Sales*

Investors perpetually seek to buy low and sell high, but you can also make a profit by selling high and then buying low. This is called a short sale.

❑ **Short Sale:** A short sale is the sale of a security that the seller does not own. This is a speculative transaction done in the belief that the price of the security will fall. The seller will then be able to **cover** the sale by buying it back later at a lower price.

Example 9:

You short sell 1000 shares of Discovery Café (DVC), borrowing the shares from John Q. Investor's portfolio and selling them to Susan Speculator.

Table 8-1: Example 9 Short Sell of Discovery Café

October 2	Short sell 1000 shares Discovery Café at $98.	$	98,000.00
	broker borrows 1000 shares Discovery Café from JQ for delivery to Susan Speculator.		
	the proceeds of the short sale are left on account with the broker, and must always cover the short sale (equal the market price).		
December 12	Buy 1000 shares Discovery Café at $52.	$	-52,000.00
	broker delivers these 1000 shares to JQ to replace the shares borrowed.		
	Profit (before brokerage commission and borrowing fee)	$	46,000.00

8.4.1 - Tick Rules

Restrictions on short sales imposed by the exchange to prevent price destabilization have taken the form of Tick Rules. For nearly sixty-nine years a short sale could only be made at a price higher than the immediately preceding trade (a plus tick), or at a price equal to the last trade if it is higher than the last different price (a zero-plus tick). Not surprising, short sales of stocks bring about serious regulatory discussions during times of market stress and plunging prices and are considered unnecessary, perhaps even a nuisance during prolonged market advances.

❑   **Tick:** A tick is the smallest price increment, generally 1¢.

❑   **Uptick Trade Rule:** The uptick trade rule allows a short sale when the most recent trade is on an uptick: the price increases over the previous sale.

❑   **Zero Uptick Trade Rule:** The zero uptick rule allows a short sale when the most recent trade leaves the price unchanged but the trade before that was on a uptick.

In 1938, the U.S. Securities and Exchange Commission (SEC) adopted the uptick rule, more formally known as Rule 10a-1. This ruling was issued after SEC examination and public commentary following the market break of 1937. During the Great Depression, typically defined as the period beginning with the stock market crash in the U.S. on October 29, 1929, known as Black Tuesday, through the early 1940s, 1937 was particularly harsh. Called a recession within a depression by historians, economic activity and stock prices fell steeply from feeble recovery levels and brought more market regulation and intervention. The original rule was implemented when Joseph P. Kennedy, Sr. was SEC commissioner, and with few modifications, remained in effect until the SEC eliminated the uptick rule on July 6, 2007, just before the onset of the recession of 2008.

In 2008 exchanges began to impose modified versions of the uptick rule covering certain stocks (usually banks, insurance, and financial companies) and even banned outright the short selling of those companies.

On September 18, 2008, four days after Lehman Brothers filed for bankruptcy, the SEC issued emergency orders halting the short selling of 799 financial issues and requiring institutional money managers to report new short sales of other issues[1].

By 2010, the SEC adopted a short sale circuit breaker that, if triggered, imposes a restriction on the prices at which securities may be sold short. Rather than formal rules, these 334 pages of regulation, and the volumes of rules spawned by them, attempts to force exchanges to establish, maintain, and enforce written policies and procedures designed to prevent abusive short selling. Although complex, and replete with exceptions, the basic concept can be boiled down to a circuit breaker that would stop short selling completely once a stock has declined more than 10% from the previous close.[2]

For obvious reasons, calls to bring back the formal Tick Rules and their simplicity ring out loud when markets experience volatile sell-offs and complicated schemes seem ineffective.

8.4.2 - Dividends:

The short seller must pay any dividends due to the investor who lent the stock.

Example 10:

> Discovery Café pays a dividend of $0.20 per share November 9 (during the period of the short sale in the previous example). The 1000 shares of Discovery Café you borrowed from J.Q. Investor are now registered to Susan Speculator, and she gets the $200 from Discovery Café. However, J.Q. wants the dividend on the stock he leant you. Therefore, you must now pay the same amount ($200) to J.Q.'s account to cover the dividend he would have received had he not loaned the shares to you. This reduces the profit of the short sale (before brokerage etc.) from $46,000 to $45,800.

Table 8-2: Short Sell of Discovery Café with a Dividend Equivalent Payment

October 2	Short sell 1000 shares Discovery Café at $98.	$	98,000.00
	broker borrows 1000 shares Discovery Café from JQ for delivery to Susan Speculator		
November 9	Pay dividend equivalent to JQ	$	-200.00
December 12	Buy 1000 shares Discovery Café at $52.	$	-52,000.00
	broker delivers these 1000 shares to replace the shares borrowed.		
	Profit (before brokerage commission and borrowing fees)	$	45,800.00

---

1   The order and complete list of the 799 financial issues are available from the SEC at
    http://www.sec.gov/news/press/2008/2008-211.htm

2   Securities and Exchange Commission, *Amendments to Regulation SHO, February 26, 2010*
    http://www.sec.gov/rules/final/2010/34-61595.pdf

8.4.3 - Margin Requirements

Short sales, like all margin transactions, are governed by Regulation T of the Federal Reserve. Reg T requires a margin of 150% of the market value of the security on all short sales. This means that 100% of the proceeds of the short sale plus an additional 50% must be deposited to the margin account.

The value of the short position will change with the price of the stock. If the value of the margin account falls below 130% of the value of the short position then the investor will be issued a margin call.

Example 11:

When you sold 1000 shares of Discovery Café at $98 the $98,000 you received from the sale went right into your margin account. In addition you must deposit a further $49,000 to your margin account for a total of $147,000 (150% of $98,000).

After you pay $200 dividend equivalent to JQ you have $146,800 in your margin account. When you cover your short position at $52 per share the $52,000 required to pay for the shares comes out of your margin account. This leaves $45,800 when the trade is completed. This is your profit.

Table 8-3: Short Sell of Discovery Café with 150% Margin Requirement

October 2	Short sell 1000 shares Discovery Café at $98.	$	98,000.00
	Deposit to your brokerage account	$	49,000.00
	Broker transfers to your margin account	$	-147,000.00
November 9	Transfer from Margin Account	$	200.00
	Pay dividend equivalent to JQ	$	-200.00
December 12	Buy 1000 shares Discovery Café at $52.	$	-52,000.00
	Broker transfers from your margin account	$	146,800.00
	Withdraw original margin deposit from your brokerage account	$	-49,000.00
	Profit (before brokerage commission and borrowing fee)	$	45,800.00

8.4.4 - Borrowing Fees

Securities are often loaned flat. This means there is no fee to borrow the securities. Under some circumstances securities are loaned at a premium. This means that the lender charges a borrowing fee. The borrowing fee is generally computed on a basis of dollars per share per day.

Short sells are possible only if a loan of stock is available from a current shareholder. It is not uncommon for brokerage agreements to include a loan consent agreement that allows the broker to lend securities held in the customer's account. Institutional investors provide another source of securities loans. These securities loans provide these institutional investors with an additional source of return on the equities they hold.

8.4.5 - Short Interest

Short interest is the total number of shares of a company that have been sold short. Short interest is commonly expressed in shares but can also be expressed as the percent of total shares outstanding.

❑ **Short Interest:** Short interest is the total number of shares of a company that have been sold short.

$$\text{Short Interest} = \frac{\text{shares short}}{\text{shares outstanding}} \qquad \textit{(Eq 8-2)}$$

❑ **Days-to-Cover:** Days-to-cover is the number of days it would take the total short interest to cover its position based on the average shares traded per day.

$$\text{Days-to-Cover} = \frac{\text{shares short}}{\text{shares per day}} \qquad \textit{(Eq 8-3)}$$

Example 12:

The Discovery Café has 9,000,000 shares outstanding and trades an average of 100,000 shares per day. If the total of all short positions is 900,000 shares then the short interest is 900,000 shares or 10% and it would take 9 days to cover this position.

$$\text{Short Interest:} \quad \frac{900,000 \text{ shares short}}{9,000,000 \text{ shares outstanding}} = 0.10 = 10\%$$

$$\text{Days to Cover:} \quad \frac{900,000 \text{ shares short}}{100,000 \text{ shares per day}} = 9 \text{ days}$$

8.5 - Graphical Representation

Equity positions can be represented graphically. The horizontal axis shows the price per share of the equity position. The value line shows the market value of the portfolio at each underlying stock price. The profit line shows the profit on the portfolio at each underlying stock price. This distance between the value and profit lines is the initial investment.

Figure 8-5: Long Position of 100 Shares Discovery Café Purchased at $50 Per Share

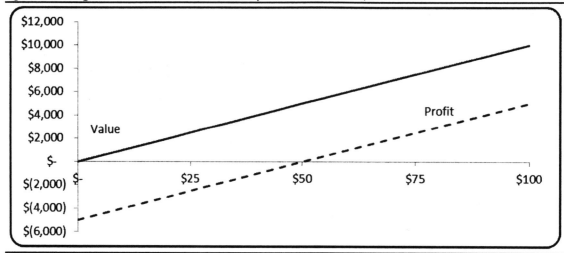

Figure 8-6: Short Position of 100 Shares Discovery Café Sold Short at $50 Per Share

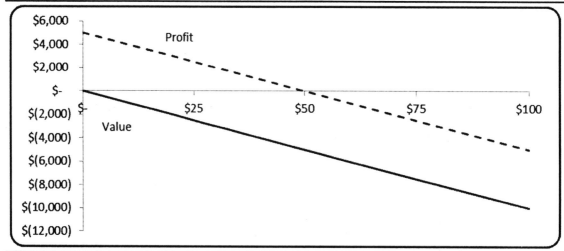

Figure 8-7: Probability Distribution Associated with the Price of Discovery Café

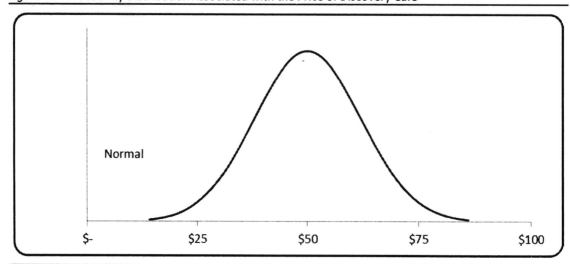

8.6 - Stock Market Indices

When someone asks, "How's the market today?" it's generally not a good idea to give a complete answer. There are over 10,000 issues listed on the NYSE, AMEX, and NASDAQ; a complete answer would involve considerable time and confusion. What we need is a simple statistic that captures an overall picture of the market; we need an index.

8.6.1 - Price-Weighted Indices

A price-weighted series is an arithmetic average of current prices.

$$Index_t = \frac{\sum_{i=1}^{N} P_{it}}{D_t} \qquad \text{(Eq 8-4)}$$

where P_{it} is the price of stock i on day t and D_t is the adjusted divisor (the divisor is adjusted for stock splits etc).

❑ **Dow Jones Industrial Average:** The Dow Jones Industrial Average is the longest running stock market index. In 1884 Charles Dow took the average of 11 stocks, 9 railroads and 2 industrials and set it to a base of 10. The average was published by Edward Jones in the paper that was to become the *Wall Street Journal*. By 1886 the list was refined to include only industrials, and by 1928 it was expanded to include 30 stocks. Today the Dow Jones is an index of 30 large, well-known industrial stocks that are generally the leaders in their respective industries.

❑ **Nikkei 225:** The Nikkei is an average of 225 stocks in the first section of the Tokyo Stock Exchange. The first section is the Tokyo equivalent of Blue chip stocks.

❑ **Blue Chip:** Blue Chip stocks are shares in large stable companies with a proven record of long-term growth.

8.6.2 - Value-Weighted Indices

A value-weighted series is based on the change in the total market value of the stocks in the sample. Lest ye forget, the market value is the number of shares outstanding times the share price.

$$Index_t = \frac{\sum_{i=1}^{N} P_{it}\, Q_{it}}{\sum_{i=1}^{N} P_{i\,(base)}\, Q_{i\,(base)}} * Index_{t-1} \qquad \text{(Eq 8-5)}$$

where Q_{it} is number of outstanding shares of stock i on day t and $Q_{i(base)}$ is the number of outstanding shares on the base day.

The disadvantage of a value-weighted index is that it is dominated by companies with large market values.

❑ **S&P500:** Standard & Poor's computes several indices, the most popular of which is the S&P 500. This includes 400 industrials, 40 utilities, 40 financial issues, and 20 transportation issues. The S&P 500 includes 86% of the market capitalization of the NYSE and 13% of NASDAQ.

❑ **S&P MidCap 400:** Standard & Poor's index of 400 U.S. companies with a market capitalization of between $1billion and $5 billion. To be included in the index the stock must be widely held and have sufficiently liquidity to ensure efficient pricing.

❑ **S&P SmallCap 600:** Standard & Poor's index of 600 U.S. companies with a market capitalization of between $300 and $400 million, although there are some companies with a market capitalization of up to $1 billion.

❑ **NASDAQ Composite:** The NASDAQ indices begins in February 1971 at a base value of 100. All common stocks listed on NASDAQ are included in the index, and new stocks are included when they are added to the system. Each stock is also assigned to a sector index.

❑ **NASDAQ 100:** Index of the 100 largest nonfinancial firms listed on NASDAQ's National Market. This index begins in 1985 at a base value of 100.

❑ **New York Stock Exchange Composite Index:** The NYSE composite begins in 1965 at a base value of 100 and includes all stocks listed on the NYSE. The NYSE also runs industrial, utilities, transportation, and financial sector indices.

❑ **Russell Indices:** The Frank Russell Company runs an index of the 3000 largest U.S. stocks in terms of market capitalization known as the **Russell 3000**. Of these 3000 companies the largest 1000 form the **Russell 1000** index of large cap stocks, and the remaining 2000 form the **Russell 2000** index of small cap stocks. The median market capitalization in the Russell 2000 was $474 million in 2012.

8.6.3 - Unweighted Indices

An unweighted or equally weighted index is a geometric or arithmetic average of the percentage changes in stock prices.

$$Geometric\ Index_t = \left[\prod_{i=1}^{N} \frac{P_{it}}{P_{i\,t-1}}\right]^{\frac{1}{N}} * Index_{t-1} \qquad (Eq\ 8\text{-}6)$$

$$Arithmetic\ Index_t = \frac{\sum_{i=1}^{N} \frac{P_{it}}{P_{i\,t-1}}}{N} * Index_{t-1} \qquad (Eq\ 8\text{-}7)$$

❑ **The Financial Times Ordinary Share Index:** Also known as the 30-share index, the FTOI is an unweighted index of 30 blue chip issues traded on the London Exchange. The FT30 includes oils and financial firms so it is not an industrial index like the Dow Jones.

❑ **FTSE 100:** The Financial Times Stock Exchange 100 share index, also called FTSE (Footsie), is an arithmetic average of the 100 largest stocks (market cap greater than £1 billion) on the London Stock Exchange.

❑ **Value Line Composite Index:** Also called the Value Line Geometric Index, the VLG is a geometric average of the return on the approximately 1700 stocks followed by Value Line. Value line also runs the Value Line Arithmetic index.

1973/74: Bear Market

On November 4, 1972, the Dow Jones Industrial Average closed above 1,000 for the first time in history. It had reached 1,000 on January 18, 1966, but failed to close above that mark. The year closed with the Dow at 1,020.02 on December 29, 1972.

In the following 24 months the Dow lost 40% of its value, closing December 31, 1974, at 616.24. The downturn was attributed to the end of Bretton Woods and the OPEC Oil crisis. But it was much worse in London than in New York, where the market index lost 73% of its value over the same period.

1987: Black Monday

October 1987 was a volatile month in the market. The Dow Jones Industrial Average touched a high of 2,662.37 on October 2, declined over the next two weeks, and closed Friday October 16 at 2,246.73.

On Monday, October 19, 1987, the market suffered its largest ever percentage decline, dropping 507.99 points to 1,738.74. This represented a one day return of – 22.6%.

In comparison, on Black Monday, October 28, 1929, the Dow dropped only 12.8% in a single day. The difference between 1929 and 1987 was that Black Monday 1929 was followed by Black Tuesday in which the Dow fell a further 11.7%, whereas Black Monday 1987 was followed by a Tuesday and Wednesday that saw the Dow back to 2,027.85: A two day gain of 16.6%.

Chapter 8 - Questions and Problems

8-1:

John Q. Investor calls his broker at 6:00 am and submits the following three orders:

> A market buy order for 2000 shares of DVC
> A limit sell order for 2000 shares of DVC at $90
> A stop loss order for 2000 shares of DVC at $80

During the day DVC opens at $88 and rises to $102. What happens to each of JQ's orders?

8-2:

Discovery Café is trading at $80 per share. John puts in a stop sell at $70, Joe puts in a market-if-touched sell at $90, and Kevin puts in a limit sell at $90. Explain what each order is designed to do.

8-3:

You buy 10,000 shares of Caterpillar (CAT) on January 10 at $80, sell 4,000 shares of Caterpillar on January 11 at $79.50, and sell the remaining 6,000 shares on January 17 at $82. Caterpillar paid a dividend of $0.50 with an ex-date of January 11 and a pay-date of February 12.

A.   How much in dividends do you receive?

B.   What is the holding period return on this investment (before commission)?

8-4:

You decide to buy 1,000 shares of Proctor & Gamble (PG) on 60% margin. PG is trading at $78 per share.

A.   How much must you pay to your broker? (Do not include commission)

B.   Graph the position

8-5:

When margin is 25% the leverage is 4.

A.   Use a purchase of 1000 shares of Discovery Café (DVC) at $50 to demonstrate that this relationship.

B.   Graph the position

8-6:

John Q. Investor purchased 1000 shares of Enron (ENE) at $49.10 on June 30, 2001, on a 50% margin. On December 31, 2001, Enron closed at $0.60

A. What is JQ's initial investment in this position?

B. What was the six-month rate of return on shares of Enron?

C. What was the leverage on JQ's investment?

D. How much money did JQ lose on this investment? What was his rate of return?

8-7:

Susan Speculator short sold 10,000 shares of Enron (ENE) at $49.10 on June 30, 2001, and covered December 31, 2001, at $0.60

A. How much money did Susan need to deposit to her margin account on June 30?

B. How much money did Susan make on this position? What was her rate of return?

8-8:

John Q. Investor takes a short position on 5,000 shares of IBM, selling at $75 per share on January 2, 2003. Annual dividends are estimated at $2.50. Dividends are paid quarterly and the last Ex date was December 28, 2002. JQ's broker charges him $100 for the loan of the shares every six months.

A. How much money must JQ deposit to his margin account.

B. To what price must IBM fall by July 1, for J.Q. to make a profit?

C. Graph this position as of July 1.

The price on IBM rises continually until mid August, then begins to fall. It closes December 31 at $70 per share. JQ covers January 2, 2004, at 69.

D. What is JQ's profit on this investment?

E. How much money can JQ withdraw from his margin account when this transaction is closed?

F. Graph the position as of January 2. Use the same graph as in C. What happens to the short position as time progresses?

G. What is JQ's holding period return on this investment?

8-9:

Your client purchased 100 shares of Intel (INTC) at $120. Intel rose to $150, and he would like to protect his unrealized profits. Which of the following orders should he use?

A. sell stop at $149
B. sell limit at $150
C. sell limit at $150.01
D. sell stop at $150.01

8-10:

Bill Q. Gates sold Apple (AAPL) short when it was trading at $19. Apple is now trading at $14, and Bill would like to protect his profit. Which of the following orders should he use?

A. sell stop at $13.99
B. sell limit at $14
C. buy limit at $14
D. buy stop at $14.50

8-11:

Bill Q Gates sold Apple (AAPL) short when it was trading at $19. He put in a buy stop order at $14. The order is activated when Apple

A. falls to $14 or below
B. falls below $14
C. rises to $14 or above
D. rises above $14

8-12:

Your client's margin account has the following positions:

Long Market Value:	$500,000.
Short Market Value	$270,000.
Debit Balance	$120,000.
Credit Balance	$220,000.

The total equity in her account is

A. $100,000.
B. $150,000.
C. $220,000.
D. $330,000.

8-13:

John Q. Investor deposits $10,000 into his margin account with an initial margin requirement of 50% and buys the maximum amount of Discovery Café permitted at $50 per share. The following day Discovery Café increased to $55.

A. How many shares of Discovery Café did JQ purchase?

B. What was JQ's profit?

C. What was JQ's rate of return on his investment?

D. To what extent was JQ's investment leveraged?

8-14:

It is Thursday February 7, 2013. The Microsoft Board of Directors has just declared a special dividend of $5.00 per share, payable Wednesday March 6, 2013, to shareholders of record, Wednesday, February 27. The only market holiday in February is Presidents' Day, Monday February 18.

A. The Declaration Date is?

B. The Pay Date is?

C. The Ex-dividend Date is?

D. The last day for you to buy the shares of Microsoft and still earn the dividend is?

E. You buy 100 shares of Microsoft on Tuesday, February 27, 2013. How much in dividends do you receive?

Chapter 8 - Financial Modeling

8.1 - Index Calculation

Model Data:

A. The template for this model includes the year end stock price and number of shares for each of the 30 companies included in the Dow Jones Industrial Average. Use the Finance Ribbon and shortcuts to format appropriately and line up decimal places. Remember your shortcuts:

1. Shift+Ctrl+T   = Titlebar
2. Ctrl+T   = subTitles
3. Shift+Ctrl+B   = Finance Blue
4. Shift+Ctrl+G   = Finance Green
5. Shift+Ctrl+B   = black with no background and no borders
6. Shift+Ctrl+1   = comma format to two decimal places
7. Shift+Ctrl+4   = currency format to two decimal places

B. We need to set each of the indices to our starting point of 100.00 to begin. This starting point is set for the price weighted index in cell D37. It is coded finance blue as an input. The value weighted and unweighted indices take the same starting point. This means that D38 and D39 are set to = D37 and are coded finance green; they are inputs for their own index models, but they are set as equal to the starting point for the first model.

We will calculate each index separately; the price-weighted in J37:N37; the value-weighted in P38:T38; and the equally-weighted in V39:Z39. We then relay these indices into D37:H39 so that it is easier for the user to see and compare and easier to graph.

Price-Weighted Index:

$$Index_t = \frac{\sum_{i=1}^{N} P_{it}}{D_t}$$

(Eq 8-4)

C. Begin by calculating the sum of prices. So use J35=Sum(). Copy-drag across so that you calculate the sum for each year.

D. Our base year is 2007, so the index is relayed from D37 to J37 as the starting point. Code it green.

E. We calculate the divisor D for 2007 as J36 = J35/J36.

F. In 2008 the sum of prices decreased from \$1,667.19 to \$1,169.69. The starting point of 1,667.19 is captured by the divisor D. So set K36=J36 for now. The index is then calculated as K37 = K35/K36.

G. Use Shift+Ctrl+4 to format the sum, Shift+Ctrl+1 and increase to 6 decimal places to format the Divisor, and Shift+Ctrl+1 and increase to 3 decimal places to format the index.

H. Copy-drag both the divisor and the index calculations to the right.

I. The index calculated for 2009 is now wrong because our calculations do not adjust for a 2:1 split in General Electric[3]. If GE had not split then its stock price would be \$30.26 instead of \$15.13. We can put \$30.26 into L12, calculate that the index should be 83.671, and then put the price back to \$15.13

---

3   There was no 2:1 stock split in GE. Very few companies split during a down market, and from December 2006 through December 2011 the DJIA declined by 2%. None of the component companies issued a stock split. The 2:1 split on GE was created artificially so that we could test the adjustment procedure.

J. We need to change the divisor. Simple algebra tells us that we need to make the divisor capable of dealing with a stock split, so

$$D_t = \frac{D_{t-1} \sum_{i=1}^{N} P_{it}}{\sum_{i=1}^{N} P_{it} + adj}$$

where adj represents the adjustments we would need to make to undo the effect of the split.

K. In 2009 the adjustment is the $15.13 we would need to add to the price of GE. So we enter $15.13 into L34.[4]

L. Code L34 blue as an input and re-calculate the divisor for 2009 as L36 = (K36*L35)/(L35+L34). We confirm that the resulting index calculates as 83.671

M. Copy-drag the divisor formula to the left to K36 and to the right to M36:N36 so that all years have the corrected version. Make sure you don't overwrite your initial divisor in J36.

N. Relay the indices calculated in K37:N37 to E37:H37 for graphing. Leave the numbers in E37:H37 black. Although these numbers are inputs into the graph, a graph is not a separate model so these numbers remain outputs of the index model not inputs to a derivative model or portion thereof.

Price-Weighted Index calculations

	2007	2008	2009	2010	2011
Adj:			$ 15.13		
Sum:	$ 1,667.19	$ 1,169.69	$ 1,379.82	$ 1,529.72	$ 1,614.30
Divisor:	16.671900	16.671900	16.491072	16.491072	16.491072
Index:	100.000	70.159	83.671	92.760	97.889

Value-Weighted Index:

$$Index_t = \frac{\sum_{i=1}^{N} P_{it} Q_{it}}{\sum_{i=1}^{N} P_{i\,(base)} Q_{i\,(base)}} * Index_{t-1} \qquad (Eq\ 8\text{-}5)$$

O. Begin by calculating the value of each company in each year. So P3 = D3*J3. Copy to all companies all years. To do this select P3. Keep the shift key depressed as you use the arrow key to highlight P3:T3. Release the Shift Key. Ctrl+R to copy right. Keep the shift key depressed as you use the arrow key to highlight P3:T32. Release the Shift Key. Ctrl+D to copy down.

P. Use P35=Sum(P3:P32) to sum the values of all companies in 2007. Copy-drag across so that you calculate the sum for each year.

Q. Our base year is 2007, so the index is relayed into P38 as the starting point. Code it green.

R. In 2008 the total market value of these 30 companies decreased from $4.4 trillion to $3.0 trillion. The index is then calculated as Q38 = P38*Q35/P35. Copy-drag to the right.

S. We don't need to make any adjustments for the split in GE. If we undo the effect of the split by adjusting the price from $15.13 to $30.26 then we would need to also adjust the number of shares outstanding from 10,647.495 to 5,323.7475 million shares. The market value of GE remains the same.

T. Relay the indices calculated in Q38:T38 to E38:H38 for graphing.

---

4 If a $60 stock splits 2:1 to $30 then we need to add $30; if a $60 stock splits 3:1 to $20 then we need to add $40; if a $60 stock splits 4:1 to $15 then we need to add $45, et cetera.

Value-Weighted Index calculations					
	2007	2008	2009	2010	2011
Sum:	$ 4,396,766.96	$ 3,006,360.21	$ 3,491,068.31	$ 3,656,626.22	$ 3,664,501.33
Index:	100.000	70.159	83.671	92.760	97.889

Equally-Weighted Index:

$$\text{Geometric Index}_t = \left[\prod_{i=1}^{N} \frac{P_{it}}{P_{i\,t-1}} \right]^{\frac{1}{N}} * \text{Index}_{t-1} \qquad \text{(Eq 8-6)}$$

U. Begin by calculating the return for each company in each year. Note that there is no return for 2007 because we would need data for 2006 to be able to calculate this. So we begin in 2008 with W3 = K3/J3. Copy to all companies in years 2009 through 2011.

V. In each year we need to calculate the geometric mean over all companies. Use W34 = Product(W3:W32)^(1/30) or W34 = Product(W3:W32)^(1/count(W3:W32)). Copy-drag across so that you calculate the product for each year.

W. Translate the each product into a rate of return number so that we can check that our index makes sense. So W36 = W35-1. Use Shift+Ctrl+5 and increase the number of decimal places.

X. Our base year is 2007, so the index is relayed into V39 as the starting point. Code it green.

Y. In 2008 the market lost about one third of its value. We can see that for every dollar at the end of 2007 we had only 66¢ by the end of 2008. The average rate of return of these 30 companies was 33.8%. The index is then calculated as W39 = V39*W35. Copy-drag to the right.

Z. The index calculated for 2009 is now wrong because our calculations do not adjust for a 2:1 split in General Electric. The easiest way to incorporate the split is to adjust the return formula for GE in 2009 in cell X12. Change the formula from X12 = L12/K12 to X12 = (2*L12)/K12. This can be coded red (Shift+Ctrl+R) to indicate a plug or forced fix.

AA. Relay the indices calculated in W39:Z39 to E39:H39 for graphing.

Equally-Weighted Index calculations					
	2007	2008	2009	2010	2011
Product:		0.6617	1.2112	1.0804	0.9861
Returns		-33.83%	21.12%	8.04%	-1.39%
Index:	100.000	66.167	80.139	86.585	85.382

Grouping:

AB. You can set the spreadsheet so that the graph appears closer to the top of the sheet by grouping. With your mouse select the numbered row indicators on the left side of the spreadsheet from 3 to 32. The entire sheet from row 3 to 32 will highlight. From the [Data] ribbon select [Group]. Excel will add a grey bar to the left with a line and 30 dots and a [-] at the bottom. When you click on the [-] Excel will hide your working numbers. When you click on the [+] Excel will show your working numbers again.

AC. You can group rows and columns. To remove grouping use [Ungroup] in the [Data] ribbon.

Graph:

AD. Select C36:H39 and create a Line Chart. Format according to your own style. Remember to attach floating labels. To do this select the last data point in the series, or select the entire series and use the forward arrow key to move from one point to the next until you get to the last one. From the [Chart Tools] [Layout] ribbon select [Data Labels] [More Data Label Options] and, under Label Options select Series Name and Value.

Index Calculations					
INDEX	**2007**	**2008**	**2009**	**2010**	**2011**
Price-Weighted	100.000	70.159	83.671	92.760	97.889
Value-Weighted	100.000	68.377	79.401	83.166	83.345
Equally-Weighted	100.000	66.167	80.139	86.585	85.382

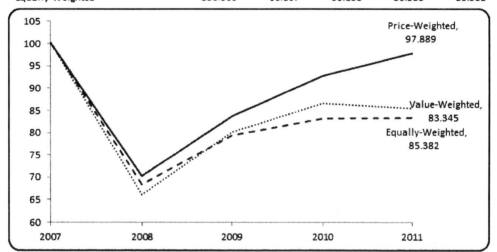

AE. Notice that exactly the same data creates three very different indices. In the price weighted index IBM at $183.88 carries the most weight: 11.39% of the total index. In the value weighted index IBM carries only 5.91% of the total index. If each company was 1/30th of the index it would be 3.33% so both indices are overweight in this stock.

AF. Similarly, At $84.76 Exxon Mobile represents 5.25% of the price weighted index, and 11.09% of the value weighted index. At $17.91 General Electric represents 1.11% of the price weighted index, but 5.16% of the value weighted index. This can create some very different indices. A split can also change the index by changing the weight of the company. If Exxon Mobile had executed a 10:1 split in 2006 then it would have a different effect on the price weighted index throughout the five years of data in this model.

Notes for Advanced Users:

AG. Type INDEX into cell C36. Now regenerate the graph. Note that Excel now numbers the observations 1 through 5 and treats the years 2007 through 2011 as a fourth dependent variable. To accommodate values of 2000 the indices are clustered down around the horizontal axis.

AH. If you take INDEX out of cell C36 and regenerate the graph excel once more assumes that the years 2007 through 2011 are meant to be labels for the horizontal axis rather than another dependent variable.

Dow Jones 30 Components		Shares Outstanding (in millions of shares)					Price (per share at year end)				
Ticker	Company Name	2007	2008	2009	2010	2011	2007	2008	2009	2010	2011
AA	Alcoa Inc.	848.148	800.317	974.378	1,021.442	1,064.304	$ 36.55	$ 11.26	$ 16.12	$ 15.39	$ 8.65
AXP	American Express Company	1,169.426	1,159.892	1,189.169	1,203.764	1,161.482	$ 52.02	$ 18.55	$ 40.52	$ 42.92	$ 47.17
BA	Boeing	744.063	704.834	697.599	733.580	743.234	$ 87.46	$ 42.67	$ 54.13	$ 65.26	$ 73.35
BAC	Bank of America Corporation	4,438.318	5,017.579	8,650.272	10,085.147	10,135.872	$ 41.26	$ 14.08	$ 15.06	$ 13.34	$ 5.56
CAT	Caterpillar, Inc.	635.960	603.234	622.728	634.703	646.620	$ 72.56	$ 44.67	$ 56.99	$ 93.66	$ 90.60
CSCO	Cisco Systems, Inc.	6,066.967	5,855.087	5,752.585	5,542.762	5,375.864	$ 27.07	$ 16.30	$ 23.94	$ 20.23	$ 18.08
CVX	Chevron Corporation	2,111.442	2,031.791	2,006.268	2,012.428	1,991.484	$ 93.33	$ 73.97	$ 76.99	$ 91.25	$ 106.40
DD	E.I. du Pont de Nemours	899.048	902.361	903.730	912.894	923.919	$ 44.09	$ 25.30	$ 33.67	$ 49.88	$ 45.78
DIS	Walt Disney Company	1,903.485	1,851.027	1,865.011	1,893.584	1,796.513	$ 32.28	$ 22.69	$ 32.25	$ 37.51	$ 37.50
GE	General Electric Company	5,053.105	5,261.093	10,647.495	10,654.718	10,557.351	$ 74.14	$ 32.40	$ 15.13	$ 18.29	$ 17.91
HD	Home Depot, Inc.	1,687.617	1,695.458	1,700.412	1,638.821	1,541.568	$ 26.94	$ 23.02	$ 28.93	$ 35.06	$ 42.04
HPQ	Hewlett-Packard Company	2,573.869	2,416.201	2,364.169	2,190.426	1,984.033	$ 50.48	$ 36.29	$ 51.51	$ 42.10	$ 25.76
IBM	International Business Machines	1,377.955	1,343.458	1,313.603	1,242.361	1,178.618	$ 108.10	$ 84.16	$ 130.90	$ 146.76	$ 183.88
INTC	Intel Corporation	5,847.000	5,562.000	5,522.000	5,578.000	5,092.000	$ 26.66	$ 14.66	$ 20.40	$ 21.03	$ 24.25
JNJ	Johnson & Johnson	2,861.750	2,774.568	2,759.100	2,746.254	2,730.849	$ 66.70	$ 59.83	$ 64.41	$ 61.85	$ 65.58
JPM	JP Morgan Chase & Co.	3,359.044	3,732.358	3,936.824	3,924.322	3,797.689	$ 43.65	$ 31.53	$ 41.67	$ 42.42	$ 33.25
KFT	Kraft Foods Inc.	1,547.195	1,469.128	1,477.157	1,746.774	1,766.749	$ 32.63	$ 26.85	$ 27.18	$ 31.51	$ 37.36
KO	Coca-Cola Company	2,310.977	2,313.555	2,317.181	2,322.034	2,271.232	$ 61.37	$ 45.27	$ 57.00	$ 65.77	$ 69.97
MCD	McDonald's Corporation	1,182.758	1,114.545	1,079.187	1,056.507	1,023.218	$ 58.91	$ 62.19	$ 62.44	$ 76.76	$ 100.33
MMM	Minnesota Mining & Manufacturing	713.229	692.955	707.958	714.859	700.845	$ 84.32	$ 57.54	$ 82.67	$ 86.30	$ 81.73
MRK	Merck & Company, Inc	2,176.567	2,114.186	3,054.476	3,080.881	3,047.921	$ 58.11	$ 30.40	$ 36.54	$ 36.04	$ 37.70
MSFT	Microsoft Corporation	9,355.439	8,895.573	8,879.121	8,555.523	8,412.182	$ 35.60	$ 19.44	$ 30.48	$ 27.91	$ 25.96
PFE	Pfizer, Inc.	6,829.805	6,742.935	8,069.536	8,009.951	7,686.967	$ 22.73	$ 17.71	$ 18.19	$ 17.51	$ 21.64
PG	Procter & Gamble Company	3,105.639	2,985.705	2,921.734	2,799.193	2,751.320	$ 73.42	$ 61.82	$ 60.63	$ 64.33	$ 66.71
T	AT&T Inc.	6,064.759	5,893.000	5,901.000	5,910.000	5,926.000	$ 41.56	$ 28.50	$ 28.03	$ 29.38	$ 30.24
TRV	The Travelers Companies, Inc.	644.950	584.523	546.373	459.044	401.392	$ 53.80	$ 45.20	$ 49.86	$ 55.71	$ 59.17
UTX	United Technologies Corporation	988.508	950.616	937.539	923.407	906.088	$ 76.54	$ 53.60	$ 69.41	$ 78.72	$ 73.09
VZ	Verizon Communications Inc.	2,890.327	2,840.484	2,840.648	2,826.783	2,831.091	$ 43.69	$ 33.90	$ 33.13	$ 35.78	$ 40.12
WMT	Wal-Mart Stores, Inc.	4,004.809	3,922.552	3,810.172	3,561.994	3,424.697	$ 47.53	$ 56.06	$ 53.45	$ 53.93	$ 59.76
XOM	Exxon Mobile	5,463.626	5,086.649	4,731.898	5,042.557	4,793.208	$ 93.69	$ 79.83	$ 68.19	$ 73.12	$ 84.76

*I*n chapter 1 we stated, "Financial markets are an integral part of the economic system." Furthermore, " ... financial markets throughout the world have many of the same characteristics." These two statements are nowhere more evident than in the various markets for equity capital. The fundamental elements seen in markets for U.S. equities are present in markets for equity across the globe because so many economies are market-based economies. Whether in London, New York, or Tokyo, public security markets thrive in ways that evolve into a single market for capital: true globalization of markets.

The evolution of global trading in goods into global trading of capital is natural. Fifty years ago, it was uncommon to see an automobile in the United States that was manufactured by a non-U.S. company. Today, it is difficult to tell which is a "domestic" or "foreign" car, the Ford (assembled in Mexico) or the Honda (assembled in Ohio). China and India are quickly becoming manufacturing giants in the global economy and, in the process, becoming more in need of investment capital to expand.

Absent artificial barriers, that capital is flowing from investors throughout the world, so long as the expectation of return compensates for the anticipated risks. Interestingly, three companion developments are occurring in these global markets for capital.

The first is the evolution of secondary markets themselves from "member-based organizations" to exchange traded public companies. We can now own shares in the business of the New York Stock Exchange (NYX), Nasdaq (NDAQ), the Chicago Mercantile Exchange (CME), and a number of European exchanges.

The second evolutionary development is the linking of exchanges into each other. NYSE Euronext is an amalgamation of physical trading floors and electronic networks of exchanges in Amsterdam, (the world's oldest formal exchange for stocks), Brussels, Lisbon, London, New York, and Paris. NASDAQ-OMX Group owns and operates 24 markets, 3 clearinghouses, and 5 central securities depositories, spanning six continents. Eighteen of the 24 markets trade equities. The other six trade options, derivatives, fixed income, and commodities and include the Philadelphia Stock Exchange (the oldest stock exchange in America, having been in operation since 1790).

The third avenue of evolution is that of regulations in capital markets. In the past, regulations have been very segregated geographically because exchanges and the participants in those markets were very homogeneous. With investor capital flowing across boarders almost seamlessly, the process of regulation becomes more interlinked and is moving more toward a single intention, if not a single entity eventually, regulating the public markets for capital.

The history of economic events, market milestones and regulatory changes of markets is as volatile as are markets themselves. An overview of these is best seen on a timeline, where the interactions of government, commerce, politics, and markets become inseparable. As you read through the long list of panics and upheavals in the market, you should be able to identify elements of recent history that have all, in one form or another, happened before. And if anyone tells you that this time is different, you'll know exactly why that's just not true.

9.1 - The Era Without Regulation: 1790–1932

To understand the evolution of regulatory efforts of securities markets requires some amount of historical familiarity with economic and market calamities prior to central regulation. The 18th, 19th, and early 20th centuries in America offer a wealth of perspective. For in-depth reading, see:

Charles Poor Kindleberger, *Manias, Panics and Crashes: A History of Financial Crisis*. 4e. John Wiley and Sons, 2000.

Carmen M. Reinhart and Kenneth S. Rogoff. *This Time Is Different: Eight Centuries of Financial Folly*. Princeton University Press, 2009.

❑ **1790:** The federal government of the United States issued $80 million in bonds to repay the Revolutionary War debt, marking the birth of the U.S. investment markets. The Philadelphia Stock Exchange, the oldest U.S. exchange market for securities, traces its roots to this year.

❑ **1792:** 24 stockbrokers signed the "Buttonwood Agreement", essentially establishing the NYSE.

❑ **Panic of 1819:** Triggered by a collapse in cotton prices, the panic of 1819 was the first major American depression. It was attributed to pressures created by the War of 1812, lasted two years, and hit the agricultural sector the hardest, resulting in farm foreclosures and bank collapses.

❑ **1830s:** Wall Street evolved with traders still doing business in the street. These "curbstone brokers" helped to build a raging U.S. economy by specializing in the stocks of small, newly created, and often very risky enterprises such as turnpikes, canals, and railroads. Investors were drawn to the dream of quick profits and speculative opportunities were everywhere. In 1837, Samuel Morse filed the U.S. Patent for the telegraph and, with his assistant Alfred Vail, developed the Morse code.

❑ **Panic of 1837:** The Panic of 1837 is an early example of global market contagion. The source of the panic was a combination of factors: years of building and defending an Empire generated problems in Britain, the wheat crop failed, cotton prices collapsed, speculation in land ran rampant, and the variety of currency in circulation in the U.S. generated financial problems. A number of brokerage firms in New York failed and at least one well-known New York City bank president was reported to have committed suicide. As the effect rippled across the nation, real estate prices collapsed, and a number of state-chartered banks failed. Early labor union movements were effectively stopped, and the price of labor plummeted. It is called the second-longest American depression, with effects lasting roughly six years, until 1843.

❑ **Panic of 1857:** The Panic of 1857 was short but savage. This was the first panic attributed to the financial markets rather than being blamed on agricultural or banking calamities. The Ohio Life Insurance and Trust Company, which actually engaged principally as a bank in New York City , had engaged in highly levered speculation in railroad stocks and bonds. The bank failed. New York's financial district became nearly riotous, as crowds of frantic investors clogged the streets around Wall Street. Stock prices plummeted, and more than 900 mercantile firms in New York were shut down. At year end, the American economy was a wreck. One victim was a future Civil War hero and U.S. president, Ulysses S. Grant. It was reported that he was bankrupt and pawned his gold watch to buy Christmas presents that year.

❑ **1859:** Petroleum was discovered in western Pennsylvania, and oil stocks quickly begin trading on the curb market, allowing the first of many "wildcatter" speculative bubbles.

❏ **1861–1865 Civil War:** More than 600,000 Americans died in the U.S. Civil War. Earlier experiments with various types of central banks and the regulation of privately owned banks left the federal government technically bankrupt at the start of the war. In his address to Congress on December 3, 1861, President Lincoln outlined his "American Plan", an economic policy meant to restore the federal government to financial health and break the stronghold of powerful private bankers supported by British interests.

Philadelphia banker Jay Cooke was employed by Treasury Secretary Chase to become the sole agent for the sale of Treasury bonds to finance the war. Cooke sold small government bonds to the average citizen. With 2,500 subcontracted agents, Cooke sold over $1.3 billion worth of bonds to citizens between 1862 and 1865. As Lincoln had argued in his Annual Address of 1861, the U.S. citizenry would finance the war, not powerful foreign interests.

Lincoln signed the National Currency Act on February 25, 1863, and the National Banking Act on June 3, 1864, establishing three basic principals: federal supervision of commercial banks, reserve requirements and capitalization minimums, and currency and the Greenback as the only legal tender. At that time currency was created by commercial banks based on their holdings of U.S. Treasury Bonds; Greenbacks were actually new U.S. Treasury issues used to finance the war and circulated as money. A great number of Coinage Acts and changes to the monetary structure of early America figure prominently in economic and market events.

❏ **1867:** The first stock ticker system using Morse Code was unveiled in New York City in 1867. These early systems provided the first mechanical means of conveying stock prices over long distances over telegraph wires.

❏ **1869:** The Universal Stock Ticker was developed by Thomas Edison in 1869. It used alphanumeric characters and allowed for security prices to be disseminated quickly over great distances.

❏ **Panic of 1873:** Sixteen short years after the last panic, railroads—or at least the rampant speculation in railroads—resulted in another financial collapse. Jay Cooke and Company went bankrupt in September 1873. The stock market collapsed, and again, many related businesses were forced into bankruptcy.

The Official Census of 1870 stated a population of 38,558,371 men, women, and children in the U.S., of which approximately 12 million were considered to be the nation's official workforce. Some 3 million lost their jobs. This level of unemployment lead to a populist movement known as the "Greenback Party". The U.S. Treasury effectively, though not officially, moved to a gold standard. The Fourth Coinage Act of 1873 embraced the gold standard and demonetized silver in an attempt to rein in inflationary pressures. The depression lasted from 1873 to 1878.

❏ **1890:** New technology was everywhere. In 1876 Alexander Graham Bell patented the telephone. By the 1880s, Edison's Ticker Tape machine was a common feature in offices of New York bankers and brokers. In 1890 exchange members created the New York Quotation Co. in order to consolidate the network and ensure accuracy of reporting of price and volume activity throughout the system.

❏ **Panic of 1893:** The panic of 1893 set another record as the most severe depression on record. And again the panic began in the financial markets.

In May 1893 the New York stock market began to slide. By late June the selling became panic selling and the stock market crashed. A severe credit crisis resulted. By the end of 1893 more than 16,000 businesses had failed. Among these failed businesses were 156 railroads and nearly 500 banks. Unemployment spread until one in six Americans had lost their jobs.

The first "Occupy Wall Street Movement" (circa 2011), known as "Coxey's Army," was actually a march on Washington D.C., of unemployed men. The protesters demanded that the government provide public works jobs. The leader, Jacob Coxey, was imprisoned for 20 days.

❑ **1895:** By the middle of the 1893 depression, the Federal Treasury was nearly out of gold; the many previous coinage acts had simply failed to provide a stable monetary system. A well-connected, wealthy, private banker, John Pierpont Morgan, offered President Grover Cleveland a plan whereby he and the Rothschilds would supply the U.S. Treasury with 3.5 million ounces of gold to restore the treasury surplus in exchange for a 30-year bond issue. The bond helped to recapitalize the U.S. Treasury with gold bullion, but it fanned the already bitter feelings against wealthy industrialists and bankers who controlled government finance and, hence, controlled government.

❑ **1896:** In 1896, at the Democratic National Convention in Chicago, a former Congressmen from Nebraska, William Jennings Bryan, won his party's presidential nomination with a now famous "Cross of Gold" speech. Americans were bitterly divided by the pseudo gold standard in effect since 1873. Bryan's speech advocated a plan where U.S. money would be backed by both gold and silver, much like the recommendation of Secretary of the Treasury Alexander Hamilton in 1791. Ironically, although Bryan became the Democratic party's presidential candidate over the incumbent Democratic President Grover Cleveland (who supported a gold standard), he lost the general election to William McKinley. The United States formally adopted the gold standard in 1900.

❑ **1900:** Congress passed the Gold Standard Act, formally placing the United States on the gold standard. The Great Galveston Hurricane struck Texas, leaving an estimated 8,000 dead and one of the largest gulf ports in the country destroyed.

❑ **1901:** John Pierpont Morgan expanded from railroads and banking into industrial sectors with the creation of U.S. Steel. U.S. Steel had an authorized capitalization of $1.4 billion, making it the first billion-dollar industrial company in the world.

❑ **1902:** By 1902, John D. Rockefeller built Standard Oil Company into one of the most dominant companies in the United States, controlling 90% of oil output and producing an annual income of $45 million. In 1902 the gross domestic product (GDP) of the US was estimated at $24 billion.

❑ **1905:** W. E. B. Du Bois and William Monroe Trotter started a black civil rights group known as the Niagara Movement. Although disbanded in 1908, these roots grew to become the NAACP.

❑ **1906 San Francisco Earthquake:** The Great San Francisco Earthquake struck on April 18, 1906, killing some 3,000 people out of a population of 410,000. Between 227,000 and 300,000 more were left homeless. The largest port of trade in the western US, and a critical center of commerce is devastated.

❑ **Panic of 1907:** Also known as the Bankers' Panic, the panic of 1907 had been building since the last great panic of 1893. With the industrialization of America and the resulting migration from the farm to urban workplaces, more members of the growing middle class were drawn to the prospect of wealth through investments. This generated rampant speculation in securities. The term "Bucket Shop" describes the offices where unregulated side bets on securities prices were placed by speculators who did not have enough money to buy the securities themselves.

The panic had many causes. Banks, which had lent freely on speculative investments (and made many directly), cut back on lending to protect their capital. Depositors, with the memory of losses suffered in bank collapses of 1893, withdrew deposits, exacerbating the liquidity crunch.

The panic was triggered October 16, 1907 by the news that F. Augustus Heinze's scheme to corner the stock of United Copper Company failed. The news revealed the vast network of interlocking relationships between banks, trust companies, and industrial companies and resulted in more banks coming under suspicion of being insolvent.

By October 21st, news that one major bank would stop clearing checks for the Knickerbocker Trust Company, the third largest trust in New York City, brought the panic to a fever pitch. That evening, John Pierpont Morgan organized a meeting of officials from top New York banks, but he decided not to back the trust companies. Two days later, Morgan reconvened the meeting and aid began to come from several other sources, including J. D. Rockefeller (who deposited $10 million with the Union Trust) and announced his support for Morgan. Secretary of the Treasury George Cortelyou and the major New York financiers discussed plans to combat the crisis. In an attempt to stem the outflow, Cortelyou deposited $25 million of the Treasury's funds in national banks the following morning.

One week later, the supply of "call money", overnight bank loans to brokers to finance securities purchases, was virtually non-existent. Bids for money with rates as high as 60% interest went without soliciting a response; no one was willing to lend. By Friday, financiers again went to Morgan, who was in control of most of the available funds. As bankers convened in Morgan's office, the call money rate on the exchange reached 100%, and another money pool was required, but this time with a modification. Morgan allowed the market to determine the call money rate, which remained at nearly 50% most of the day, generating an outcry against the bankers for profiteering at the expense of the marketplace. Bankers began to question their own wisdom and the National Banking Era itself, given the larger risks they were required to finance on a recurring basis.

The Panic of 1907 cements the end to the National Banking Era, which lasted from 1863 to 1914, and planted the seeds for the formation of the Federal Reserve System.

❏ **1908 Aldrich-Vreeland Act :** The Aldrich-Vreeland Act established the National Monetary Commission. In addition to modifications to national bank currency rules, it recommended a strong Central Bank of the Nation, ultimately resulting in the Federal Reserve Act of 1913.

❏ **1911:** The first comprehensive securities act was passed by the State of Kansas Legislature and became law on March 15. Known as the Kansas "Blue Sky" law, it included the merits of an investment in being offered to the public. The term Blue Sky refers grandiose claims made by promoters of securities that had no more tangible value than a few feet of blue sky. The saying would be immortalized in the Court's opinion written by Justice McKenna of the United States Supreme Court in *Hall vs. Geiger-Jones Co.*, 242 U.S. 539 (1917). The pattern of states writing similar laws grew, leading to the formation of the National Conference of Commissioners on Uniform State Laws. This amalgamation produced the Uniform Sale of Securities Act in October 1929, which was adopted in just five states, and abandoned in 1943.

❏ **1913 Federal Reserve Act:** One design idea from the National Monetary Commission in 1908 and its Aldrich Plan was to create a "Reserve Association", which would make emergency loans to member banks, print money, and act as the fiscal agent for the U.S. government. The Reserve Association was to be a consortium of large national banks that could act as a united "bank to banks", but strongly objected to due to distrust of the large private bankers. The Federal Reserve System addressed these concerns by including more public involvement and control. Previous attempts at creating a stable central bank of the nation lacked these public elements, leading to the demise of The First Bank of the United States (1791–1811), and The Second Bank of The United States (1816–1836).

The Federal Reserve would have the Federal Reserve Board, overseers appointed by the president, and confirmed by Congress, which would have control over policy decisions. Also, instead of the proposed currency being an obligation of the private banks, the new Federal Reserve note was to be an obligation of the U.S. Treasury. Finally, membership by nationally chartered banks was mandatory, not optional, thus generating a level of oversight previously not seen at the federal government level.

❑ **Revenue Act of 1913:** Along with the adoption of the 16th Amendment to the Constitution, the act lowered tariffs on imported goods (principally the main income source to the federal government of America up to this time) and reintroduced a federal tax on corporate and individual income. Previous income taxes had been declared unconstitutional after their imposition. The significance of the 16th Amendment is that from this point forward, income taxes would quickly grow to be the principal means of financing the federal government.

❑ **1914–1918 The Great War:** The First World War drew the economic and political titans across the globe into a horrible struggle mobilizing nearly 70 million in a battle between the Allies and Axis powers. The result was nearly 9 million killed; economic, political and, social upheaval; the end of some empires; and the birth of others. The cease-fire came into effect at the 11th hour of the 11th day of the 11th month; 11 am, November 11, 1918.

Despite all hope for lasting peace, the stage was set for more conflict in the future. Germany's Weimar Republic accepted blame for the war and agreed to pay punitive reparations. With exports decimated, Germany did so by borrowing from the United States. Runaway inflation in Germany during the 1920s contributed to the economic collapse of the Weimar Republic, adding to the stress in the global economic system.

❑ **Black Thursday 1929:** On Thursday October 24, 1929, the stock market lost 11% of its value at the opening bell. Debate continues, but often mentioned as a cause of this chaotic break in the six-year bull market that saw stock prices increase five fold, is the Congressional debate on the Smoot-Hawley Tariff Act. Just as in the panic of 1907, private bankers rushed to support prices in an effort to protect their risky positions. Large buy orders placed by a banking consortium throughout the day allowed the market to close with price levels roughly constant but, unlike the bankers' rescue efforts in 1907, the calm was short lived. News of the event spread across the globe over the weekend.

❑ **Black Monday 1929:** Markets opened Monday October 28 facing a tidal wave of sellers. On this Black Monday the stock market lost 13% of its value. The next day, Black Tuesday, saw a further 12% decline. The record trading volume of 16 million shares on Black Tuesday would stand unchallenged for nearly 40 years. Although it is believed that as little as 16% of the American population was invested in stocks, the severe impact on business confidence, and again bank capital, which forced banks to constrict lending, led to a crisis in confidence across the globe, which severely constricted consumer spending.

❑ **The Tariff Act of 1930:** The "Smoot-Hawley Tariff Act" was sponsored by Senator Reed Smoot and Representative Willis C. Hawley and signed into law on June 17, 1930. The roaring 20s was a period of great prosperity for industry and the growing workforce moved into the cities from farms, agriculture was in serious recession throughout this period. Political and economic pressures combined to support the passage of this act, which raised U.S. tariffs on over 20,000 imported goods to record levels. Not surprisingly, many other nations enacted retaliatory tariffs, and international trade in goods collapsed to one-half their activity.

9.2 - The Era of Federal Regulation: 1932–1999

If the 18th, 19th and early 20th centuries in America offer a wealth of perspective on an era absence of securities regulation, 1932 begins the effort to change that. By the end of the twentieth century securities regulation was a critical component of financial markets. Regulatory arbitrage, choosing the market in which to register and trade based on the prevailing regulatory environment, began to affect political and economic decisions around the world. Our focus in the timeline turns more toward federal regulatory efforts and omits many important economic and political events and concentrates on regulation in the US.

For an authoritative review of the most prominent laws and links to the actual text of each see:

> U.S. Securities and Exchange Commission, *The Laws that Govern the Securities Industry* , at
> http://www.sec.gov/about/laws.shtml

❑ **1932:** The Pecora Hearings, named for Ferdinand Pecora, who conducted the Congressional hearings on Wall Street, investigated the reasons for the crash and searched for means to prevent crashes in the future. On July 8, 1932 the Dow Jones Industrial Average closed at 41.22—its lowest level of the 20th century—down 89% from its peak of 381.17 on September 3, 1929.

❑ **Securities Act of 1933:** The Securities Act of 1933, also known as the "truth in securities" law, had two principal goals: First, the public must be able to access accurate information about the companies in which they invest. Second, the public must be protected from fraud.

Unless specifically exempted, securities offered to the public must be registered, and must include accurate, audited financial statements. Investors can claim for damages under the law if the information is inaccurate.

The Great Depression hit a bottom in 1933. Unemployment reached 25% of the workforce, loan defaults reached record levels, and more than 5,000 banks failed. Agriculture was ruined for years as bad farming practices and drought created the "Dust Bowl" across central U.S. and Canada.

❑ **The Banking Act of 1933:** Often called the Glass-Steagall Act, the Banking Act of 1933 established the Federal Deposit Insurance Corporation (FDIC) and imposed a number of banking reforms intended to control speculation. One such reform mandated the separation of commercial deposit and lending bank activity from that of investment baking and underwriting of securities, brokerage, trust, and insurance businesses. The act expanded the oversight powers of the Federal Reserve to member banking activities. The act took its name from its Congressional sponsors, Senator Carter Glass of Virginia, and Representative Henry B. Steagall of Alabama.

❑ **Securities Exchange Act of 1934:** The Securities Exchange Act of 1934 was the most sweeping federal regulation of its day. It established the Securities Exchange Commission (SEC) and gave the commission the authority to register, regulate, and monitor market participants including brokerage firms, transfer agents, and clearing agents. The law identified self-regulatory organizations (SROs) such as stock exchanges, and gave the commission broad authority to regulate them. The law defined and prohibited fraudulent schemes, and gave the SEC the authority to punish wrongdoers.

Finally, the 1934 act requires companies to file the quarterly and annual reports we now find on EDGAR.

❏ **Gold Reserve Act of 1934:** In an effort to rein in deflationary price pressures, the act required that all gold and gold certificates held by the Federal Reserve be surrendered and vested in the sole title of the United States Department of the Treasury. It outlawed most private possession of gold, forcing individuals to sell their gold to the Treasury in return for paper money. The gold was stored in the U.S. Bullion Depository known as Fort Knox in Kentucky. The act also changed the nominal price of gold from $20.67 to $35 per troy ounce .

❏ **Public Utility Holding Company Act of 1935:** The Public Utility Holding Company Act was designed to break apart large, usually overleveraged, public electric utilities, which were often used as a means to enter nonregulated and risky businesses. The act used the newly formed SEC to exercise oversight in the structure, businesses, and operational territories of public utility companies.

❏ **The Banking Act of 1935:** The Banking Act modified sections of the Banking Act of 1933 and further concentrated monetary policy control mechanisms in the hands of the Federal Reserve.

❏ **The Commodity Exchange Act of 1936:** In the Commodity Exchange Act of 1936 Congress tried to limit speculation in commodities by regulating traders as well as exchanges. It created the Commodity Exchange Authority (CEA) as a bureau of the U.S. Department of Agriculture.

❏ **The Maloney Act of 1938:** The Maloney Act amended the 1934 Securities Exchange Act, mandating a national association of brokers and dealers. Its purpose was to create and enforce disciplinary rules and promote ethical principles of trade. The SEC was granted power to review all disciplinary decisions and rules of the body. This lead to the formation of the National Association of Securities Dealers (NASD) as a Self-Regulatory Organization (SRO) in 1939.

❏ **Trust Indenture Act of 1939:** The Trust Indenture Act of 1939 addressed debt instruments such as notes and bonds, issued to the public. It did with bonds what the 1933 act did with stocks. The act requires a formal arrangement between the issuer (borrower) and investor (lender) known as the trust indenture. The trust indenture specifies a named trustee to maintain and enforce the investor protection specified in the contract. This document is fundamental to analyzing the investment merits of a bond.

❏ **Investment Company Act of 1940:** The Investment Company Act regulates financial intermediaries that pool investor money into trusts, mutual funds, and other entities designed to manage portfolios of financial assets. These trusts and funds are required to disclose investment objectives, practices, and structures of the investment pool. This act did with trusts and funds what the 1933 act did with equities and the 1934 act did with bonds. Again, the SEC is not required to rule on the merits of the investment; it just ensures that the information required to make an informed investment decision is accurate.

❏ **Investment Advisers Act of 1940:** The original act set rules for individuals and firms that charge fees for investment advice offered to the public. Advisors were required register with the SEC and follow regulations designed to protect the investing public. The act was significantly amended in 1996 and 2010, as individual states now play a larger role in this regulatory exercise.

❏ **NASD Uniform Practice Code of 1941:** The 1941 Code standardizes the listing and delivery process for U.S. securities.

❏ *SEC v. W.J. Howey*—**1946:** This landmark Supreme Court Case defined "security" under federal securities law. It provided the test for the existence of an "investment contract," one of the most important instruments listed in the statutory definition of a security, which provides authority for oversight to the SEC.

❑ **SEC v. Ralston Purina —1953:** Another important Supreme Court Case was critical in establishing tests for the availability of the "private offering" exemption under the 1933 act, which ended some abuse of the intent of the original act.

❑ **Uniform Securities Act of 1956:** The act made an attempt to balance the need to protect investors from fraud with the need of states and businesses to raise capital efficiently. The act was adopted by 37 states, entirely, or in part. One example of its simplifying effect is "registration by coordination", which allows securities registered at the federal level to escape further state regulatory hurdles.

❑ **Securities Act Release No. 4708—1964:** The "Come To Rest Abroad" release states that corporate offerings that are meant to be held by investors outside of the U.S. do not need to meet requirements of the 1933 Act. This statement opened up the growth of the euro markets. Euro markets is the name generically applied to U.S. issues outside U.S. jurisdiction.

❑ **The Williams Act of 1968:** The amendment to the 1934 act required holders of securities with intent to acquire a firm to file details of their offers with the SEC. It also required that all shareholders receive the same offer over the same period of time.

❑ **Securities Investor Protection Act of 1970:** The rapid expansion of investment, trading, and the number of brokerage firms, throughout the 1960s culminated in the "back office crisis" in 1968. As a result of antiquated systems and limited capital, many firms were merged with others, or closed their doors. In response to investor complaints, Congress created the Securities Investor Protection Corporation (SIPC) under this act. Much like the FDIC for banks, it established a fund, financed by fees from broker-dealers, which SIPC administered to protect customer accounts at failed brokerage firms.

❑ **NYSE Rules—1970:** The NYSE significantly reduced rules prohibiting investment banks from being publicly listed. This enhanced the ability to raise capital and allowed traditionally conservative partnerships to operate, assume positions in securities, and move into more aspects of markets than ever before. This is the genesis of the "Too Big To Fail" doctrine.

❑ **Commodity Futures Trading Act of 1974:** Congress granted authority to regulate trading of all commodities, including commodity-based options, forwards, and futures contracts, to the Commodity Futures Trading Commission (CFTC). The CFTC replaced the Commodity Exchange Authority (CEA) established in 1936.

❑ **ERISA 1974:** The Employee Retirement Income Security Act (ERISA) was not securities regulation, but it had significant implications for pension investment. ERISA sought to protect the interests of employee benefit plan participants and beneficiaries from the actions of plan sponsors and trustees by establishing minimum standards for pension plans in private industry.

❑ **Securities Act Amendments of 1975:** This sweeping change to the 1933 act covered many fronts. It charged the SEC with responsibility for creating a composite quotation system and for spearheading development of a national system for the efficient clearance and settlement of securities transactions. It broke down the NYSE rule that prohibited the trading of NYSE stocks in other markets and eliminated fixed commission rates charged on stock transactions.

❑ **The Municipal Securities Rule-making Board 1975:** The Municipal Securities Rule-making Board (MRSB) was established by Congress as a response to the crisis in New York City Municipal bonds in the same year. Panic selling of the bonds ultimately resulted in a federal government guarantee to stem investor fears. The purpose of the MSRB was to establish fair practices for underwriting and trading of municipal securities and assume responsibilities for monitoring and enforcing these standards among its members.

❑ **SEC Moratorium on Options Trading Expansion 1977:** The SEC expressed concern over the rapid expansion of listed stock options. It ordered a review of the market and temporarily halted new listings. The moratorium was lifted in 1980, when the SEC proposed slight changes to practice, but allowed new listings to begin again.

❑ **1878 MSRB Rule G-15:** Rule G-15 established standards that gave customers in municipal fixed-income instruments the ability to compare yields across alternative investments. Prior to G-15, almost all securities law revolved around the trading of stocks.

❑ **1979 CUSIP Rule:** In 1979 the MSRB required that all trade confirmations of municipal bonds contain the Committee on Uniform Security Identification Procedures (CUSIP) number. The practice spread throughout the industry, allowing for quick digital alphanumeric identification of securities for settlement and clearing procedures, as well as for price transparency.

❑ **Futures Trading Act of 1982:** The Futures Trading Act amended the Commodity Futures Trading Act of 1974. It legalized options trading on agricultural commodities and specified that the CFTC would regulate them.

❑ **The Tax Equity and Fiscal Responsibility Act of 1983:** Although TEFRA was a change in U.S. Tax Code, one element of the act eliminated bearer securities. The ban effectively forced electronic book-entry issuances, eliminating the use of paper certificates.

❑ **Insider Trading Sanctions Act of 1984:** The SEC receives authority to sue for damages up to three times the amount of profits gained (or losses avoided) from trading on inside information.

❑ **Revised Uniform Securities Act of 1985:** The 1985 modification to the 1956 Uniform Securities Act was controversial and resisted. Essentially, the modification weakened the states' rights to regulate securities as to their merit as "fair," "just," and "equitable", rather than on the basis of how their issuers met federal disclosure requirements.

❑ **1988 Rule 19c-4:** SEC Rule 19c-4 attempted to require corporations issue all classes of stock to follow the one-share, one-vote structure. This rule was subsequently struck down in a 1990 court ruling.

❑ **1989 Rule 15c2-12:** SEC Rule 15c2-12 increased regulation of municipal bond underwriters and disclosure requirements on municipalities who sell public debt. The rule was made in response to the $2 billion default of the Washington Public Power System in 1983. (Sometimes, regulation efforts move slowly)

❑ **Market Reform Act of 1990:** The SEC was authorized to take certain emergency actions in efforts to maintain (or restore) fair and orderly markets in periods of panic.

1986: The Big Bang

Wall Street dominated securities markets. The City of London, once the world's dominant financial center, was burdened with regulation and dominated by old school networks. It was more of a gentleman's club than a thriving financial market and in no position to compete in the new global environment.

On October 27, 1986, a deregulation package was implemented in one big bang. It abolished fixed commissions, changed the London Stock Exchange from open outcry to electronic screen based trading, and ended the forced divide between brokers, advisors, and stockjobbers (market makers).

Glass-Steagall was still in effect in the US, so London became the target of regulatory arbitrage: It was just easier to move the operation to London than to deal with the regulatory environment in New York. Businesses, people, and money moved into the City from all over the world, reinvigorating the market but also making it a great deal more volatile.

9.3 - The Era of Deregulation (1999–

Beginning in 1932, the previous era of lax regulation in the securities changed greatly with the Great Depression. Another great change occurred late in the 20th century, when efforts to deregulate markets gained traction. The wisdom of such will be debated for a long time.

❑ **The Gramm-Leach-Bliley Act (GLBA) of 1999:** Amazing as it may seem coming at a time of increasing instability in markets globally, this act effectively repealed the 1933 Glass-Steagall Act by removing the structural impediments of banks owning broker-dealers or engaging in securities activities. It gave the SEC authority to regulate banks in their securities business.

❑ **The Commodity Futures Modernization Act of 2000:** This 262-page deregulatory bill was tucked into an 11,000 page conference report for the Consolidated Appropriations Act of 2001 as a rider. It included provisions that effectively exempted swaps and their derivatives from regulation by either the CFTC or the SEC. It also included a special exemption for energy derivatives trading, which would later become known as the "Enron loophole".

❑ **Sarbanes-Oxley Act of 2002:** Fiercely debated to this day, Sarbanes-Oxley was one of the most far-reaching attempts to reform American business practices since the 1930s. It followed the bankruptcy of industry titans Enron (December 2, 2001) and WorldCom (July 21, 2002), and attempted to address the accounting fraud and lack of financial disclosure common to both firms. The act created the Public Company Accounting Oversight Board (PCAOB) to oversee the activities of the accounting and auditing profession.

❑ **Net Capitalization Rule Exemption of 2004:** This SEC action exempted the five largest investment houses: Bear Stearns, Goldman Sachs, Lehman Brothers, Merrill Lynch, and Morgan Stanley, from higher capital requirements created in the SEC's 1975 rule.

❑ **Emergency Economic Stabilization Act of 2008:** Enacted October 3, 2008, this sweeping legislation authorized the United States Treasury to spend up to US$700 billion to purchase distressed assets, especially mortgage-backed securities, and ultimately to invest directly in banks through the Troubled Asset Relief Program (TARP).

Events leading to this monumental marriage of public tax dollars with private concerns made economic panics of the past small in comparison. Early in the year Citigroup, the world's largest bank, reported a 4th quarter 2007 loss of $9.8 billion, the largest in the firm's 196 year history, and announced a $12.5 billion capital injection from investors in Kuwait, and Singapore. Much of the loss was due to an $18.1 billion write-down to the value of investments, predominantly sub-prime mortgage backed securities.

This type of financial result would be seen in financial institutions around the world, and the losses seemed to be growing in magnitude and frequency. Merrill Lynch reported a forth-quarter loss larger than any in its 96-year history.

By March 2008, Bear Stearns was partnered with JP Morgan Chase in a Federal Reserve engineered and financed deal. Along with Bear Stearns announcement, the Federal Reserve opened its discount window lending facility to investment banks, (as opposed to just member commercial banks), an action not taken since the depths of the 1930s depression. These early relief actions actually seemed to calm markets. The Dow Industrial Average rose from 11,951 on March 14 to just over 13,000 on May 19 2008.

The relief was short lived. By July, IndyMac Bank, a $32 billion "Federal Savings Bank" headquartered in Pasadena, California, was closed by the Office of Thrift Supervision (OTS) and the Federal Depositors Insurance Corporation (FDIC), making it the second largest bank failure in the US history. Daily swings of 300 to 400 points in the DJIA became common as markets for overnight loans between banks became almost nonfunctional with rumors of yet another large bank about to fail dominating news. Asian, European, and South American markets seemed to move in lockstep, eliminating any diversification benefit to the global investment community.

Safe haven stores of money such as short-term US Treasury bills had become the only place fund managers felt safe, driving the prices of T-bills higher and driving corresponding yields to zero. The yield even went negative at times. It was a flight to quality, signaling that investors preferred a known small loss over an uncertain but potentially larger loss. Investors were no longer risk averse; they had become risk intolerant.

Coordinated efforts by the world's central banks to inject liquidity into the global banking system did little to quell the fears. Over the weekend of September 13-14, Merrill Lynch was acquired by Bank of America but efforts to save Lehman Brothers failed. AIG, the world's largest insurance company, faced with the failure of close to $1 trillion worth of credit default swaps, was nationalized by the U.S. Treasury.

On Thursday September 16, the Reserve Primary Fund, a large money market mutual fund "broke the buck". Losses on their investment portfolio caused the $1.00 net asset value to fall to 97 cents. In the 37-year history of money market mutual funds, this was only the third fund to have broken the buck. But in 2008, at roughly $3.8 trillion, the industry was far larger than it was in 1978 and 1994. The next morning, the Federal Reserve and U.S. Treasury announced a temporary program that would, "insure the holdings of any publicly offered eligible money market mutual fund - both retail and institutional - that pays a fee to participate in the program.[1"]

Rumors began to spread that the Federal Reserve and U.S. Treasury were working on a huge plan to aid the financial markets, and domestic auto manufacturers were openly discussing with Congress a potential $50 billion loan guarantee program to stave off bankruptcy.

On September 25th the OTS seized Washington Mutual Bank from Washington Mutual, Inc. and placed it into receivership with the Federal Deposit Insurance Corporation (FDIC). This $327 billion institution, the sixth largest bank in the US, became the nation's largest bank failure on record, following withdrawal of $16.7 billion in deposits during a 9-day bank run. The next day, Washington Mutual Inc. filed for bankruptcy. The FDIC sold the banking subsidiaries to JP Morgan Chase for $1.9 billion.

By the end of September, with the modern world appearing to be spiraling out of control, Congress debated, rejected, amended, rejected, and on October 3, passed the Emergency Economic Stabilization Act of 2008. The U.S. Treasury provided capital to 707 financial institutions through the purchase of senior preferred shares of stock, which also included warrants for future Treasury purchases of common stock in each[2].

❑ **Dodd-Frank Wall Street Reform and Consumer Protection Act of 2010:** The title is testimony to the complexity and scope of this 848 page (single-spaced) law. It makes significant changes to most securities laws. Two years after its passage final rules and regulations were not yet completed. Dodd-Frank establishes a Financial Stability Oversight Council (FSOC) with broad authority over money and finance, and requires government regulatory agencies to write rules and regulations on almost every aspect of commerce.

---

1   US Department of the Treasury *Press Release hp-1147, 9/19/2008*
     http://www.treasury.gov/press-center/press-releases/Pages/hp1147.aspx)
2   US Department of the Treasury *Capital Purchase Program,*2008
     http://www.treasury.gov/initiatives/financial-stability/programs/investment-programs/cpp/Pages/capitalpurcha seprogram.aspx)

The Sarbanes-Oxley Act of 2002 as a Response to Corporate Scandals: Analysis, Criticism, and Implications for the International Market

Elisabeth Oltheten and Theodore Sougiannis
Οικονομια Ταχυδρομος
March 2004

The Sarbanes-Oxley Act (Sarbox), signed into law July 30, 2002, was specifically enacted to restore investor confidence in a financial system severely shaken by a series of scandals in the U.S. market. The Act includes a wide range of measures that form the basis of a legislation-based approach to effective corporate governance. These measures include standards for corporate audit committees, requirements for auditor independence and auditor oversight, certification of financial reports by the corporation's executive officers, prohibition of corporate loans to directors and executive officers, and requirements for improved corporate financial accounting and enhanced disclosures.

Sarbanes-Oxley, criticized as ineffective in the US environment for which it was designed, has been even more severely criticized for its impact internationally. Globalization means that regulation enacted in the US addresses the world. Ten percent of Securities and Exchange Commission (SEC) registrants are non-US companies. At the NYSE, 470 of 2800 listings represent non-US companies, with a combined global market cap of $4.6 trillion, or about 30% of the total exchange[1]. Lawrence A. Cunningham, Professor of Law and Business at Boston College points out that

> "By US standards, (Sarbanes-Oxley) is a codification, fitting easily if clumsily into the US corporate template, more nearly incremental tinkering than substantive reform. ... [However], for many non-US corporations, the fit is alien, superfluous or conflicting."[2]

Corporate audit committees

Sarbox mandates that firms have audit committees comprised solely of independent directors. It defines an independent director as someone who is not an "affiliate" of the firm, and does not accept compensatory fees from the firm beyond director's fees. However, it leaves open the definition of "directors' fees." The SEC is currently trying to decide whether such fees will include stock grants, stock options, or future retirement benefits.

Sarbanes-Oxley makes the audit committee "directly responsible" for the appointment, compensation, and oversight of the work done by the auditor pertaining to the company's external financial reporting. The audit committee is also "directly responsible" for resolving financial reporting disagreements between management and auditor and has the authority to hire independent counsel and other advisors as it sees fit. Thus, Sarbox grants rights to, and imposes obligations on, the audit committee that it did not have before. Research in the U.S. supports the view that firms with more independent directors have more transparent and more reliable financial reports, less evidence of earnings management, and less financial fraud. Firms with more independent audit committees engage auditors that act more independently of management and engage in less earnings management.

Independent audit committees are almost unheard of at many European and Asian companies. In Europe and Japan, outside auditors are chosen by shareholders, not the audit panel, as required by Sarbanes-Oxley. For example, in Germany supervisory board audit committees must include employee representatives that, by Sarbox definition, are not independent. Porsche CEO Wendelin Wiedeking cited this as the "crucial factor" in its decision to abandon its listing on the New York Stock Exchange.

However, many of the Sarbanes-Oxley provisions, although developed by Congress as a political response, are implemented by the SEC. And the SEC rules generated in response to Sarbanes-Oxley contain accommodations to address the incompatibility for non-US registrants. Thus SEC rules permit compliance with home-country requirements on the matter of auditor independence, including permitting non-management employees to serve on audit committees, allowing shareholder selection or ratification of auditors rather than the audit committees, and permitting alternative bodies such as a board of auditors to fulfill auditor oversight roles.

Auditor independence and auditor oversight

Sarbox limits the types of non-audit services that auditing firms can perform for their clients. It prohibits eight categories of non-audit services, leaving tax services as the primary non-audit service available to audit clients. It also requires the client's audit committee to pre-approve any and all non-audit services. Audit and non-audit fees paid to the auditor must be disclosed in the firm's proxy statements. The reason for these disclosures is that non-audit fees impair auditor independence. For example, large non-audit fees paid by Enron in 2000-2001 to Arthur Andersen, Enron's auditor, have been cited as a prime motivator behind Andersen's apparent complicity in allowing Enron to commit financial fraud. At this point research results are mixed on whether auditors sacrifice their independence by accepting non-audit engagements.

A key feature of Sarbox is the establishment of the Public Company Accounting Oversight Board (PCAOB). Prior to Sarbox, public accounting firms "policed" themselves by conducting peer reviews. Under that peer-review system, no big 8/6/5/4 auditing firm ever produced a negative peer review of its brethren. The PCAOB supplants that system by acting as an oversight mechanism. All public accounting firms must register with the PCAOB and any accounting firm regularly auditing more than 100 publicly traded companies is subject to an annual inspection by the PCAOB. Sarbox regulates both U.S. and non-U.S. public accounting firms operating in the US. It gives PCAOB a broad range of powers, including the ability to permanently revoke the operations of any audit firm or individual auditor for intentionally violating professional standards. Sarbox also requires the lead audit partner and the audit partner responsible for reviewing the audit to rotate of the audit every five years.

Financial Disclosure

In response to the Enron's debacle, Sarbox requires the SEC to issue final disclosure rules for all material off-balance-sheet transactions and to complete a study of special purpose entities (SPEs). Reports indicate that in fiscal year 2000 Enron had over 4,000 SPEs and that most of Enron's pretax earnings came from these SPEs, and not from its "regular" earnings. Many have argued that Enron's limited and opaque disclosures about SPEs in its financial statements contributed to the market's misunderstanding of Enron's true financial condition. Sarbox requires reconciling pro forma financial information with reported accounting numbers and providing more timely disclosures of material items for the company's financial condition.

Certification requirements

One of the most widely publicized provisions of Sarbanes-Oxley is the requirement that the principal executive officers must personally certify financial reports. Under the Securities and Exchange Act of 1934 companies are required to submit quarterly and annual reports, but under Sarbanes-Oxley, CEOs and CFOs must certify and personally attest that these reports fairly and accurately represents the financial condition and operations of the company.

The certification requirement is the result of lessons learned in attempts to assign responsibility for corporate wrongdoing. As an individual I am responsible for the consequences of my actions but as a corporate officer I can hide behind a corporate responsibility that is assignable to no one. To establish liability prior to Sarbox it was required to show not only that the executive had constructive knowledge of the false information but also that a "scheme or artifice" existed. Requiring proof of both knowledge and intent to defraud, the law tacitly encouraged incompetence or at least plausible deniability.

Stricter controls existed for government contractors. In the 1980s Congress responded to accusations of abuse by enacting the Weinberger Certificate, requiring senior executives of government contractors to certify that all indirect cost proposals were acceptable and accurate. The law thus assigned specific constructive knowledge to corporate officers based on the certification.

Sarbanes-Oxley applies the same certification standards to publicly traded companies. The CEO and CFO can no longer claim plausible deniability. A CEO or CFO who certifies an inaccurate report faces a fine of $1 million and/or a prison sentence of 10 years. Further, if it can be shown that the CEO or CFO had "knowledge" and acted "willfully" in certifying a report he could face a fine of $5 million and a prison sentence of 20 years. In effect Sarbox places the responsibility for financial fairness and accuracy directly on the shoulders of the CEO and CFO.

In order to give the CEO and CFO the confidence they need to verify their company's financial reports, Sarbox requires that all public companies implement a system of internal controls that ensures the completeness of financial reporting at every level of the corporation. Essentially, in the absence of plausible deniability, corporations must provide the guidance and support necessary for their employees to carry out their responsibilities. Many corporations have instituted a system of sub-certification — the result of which is that employees with primary knowledge certify that the information they disclose is fair and accurate. The CEO and CFO must also certify the implementation and evaluation of these internal controls. Thus Sarbox requires the CEO and CFO to certify that not only are the financial statements accurate but that they have taken steps to ensure that if they were inaccurate they would know about it.

An Example: HealthSouth

In the US the legislative system (Congress and the House of Representatives) makes the law, but the judicial system explains and interprets these laws. The first test of the Sarbanes-Oxley certification provision is the case against Richard Scrushy, CEO of HealthSouth. Scrushy was charged with directing a $2.7 billion accounting fraud and indicted on 85 counts of conspiracy, fraud, money laundering, and falsely certifying financial statements filed with the Securities and Exchange Commission.

Scrushy denied any knowledge of the manipulation of HealthSouth's books, blaming the conspiracy to defraud the government and HealthSouth investors on underlings: plausible deniability. Fifteen former HealthSouth executives, including all five past chief financial officers, have pleaded guilty to various fraud charges in connection with the accounting scandal and are expected to testify.

Scrushy is expected to challenge the constitutionality of the Sarbanes-Oxley certification. The result of the challenge will profoundly affect our ability to assign responsibility for financial wrongdoing to top management. The case comes to trial August 23, 2004.
[Richard Scrushy was found not guilty on all charges June 29, 2005]

Prohibition of Corporate Loans to Directors and Executive Officers.

One third of the largest corporations in the US have outstanding loans to directors and company executives. While the purpose of these loans often appear reasonable, such as loans for relocation, the benefit is often abused. All too often the loan becomes unreasonably large and is eventually forgiven. Tyco extended a $19 million no-interest loan to CEO L. Dennis Kozlowski that was later forgiven; Worldcom extended loans of $263 million to its CEO, and Enron extended a loan of $81 million to its CEO.

These loans are frequently undetected and undetectable. There is no category on the balance sheet for forgiven loans or loans that stay on the books without repayment.

Loans may also take the form of split-dollar life insurance. The corporation buys a life insurance policy and pays the premiums; the executive names the beneficiary. When the policy pays out the beneficiary reimburses the corporation in the amount of the premiums and the remainder goes to the beneficiary. Enron purchased a $12 million policy on its CEO requiring premiums of over $1 million. Estee Lauder paid out $26 million on a split dollar policy on its CEO and Comcast paid out $20 million over three years on a policy for its Chairman.[3]

Sarbanes-Oxley prohibits an executive officer or director from receiving direct or indirect loans or any form of personal financing for any reason from the corporation or any of its subsidiaries. Any personal financing is to be provided by third party lenders. However, Sarbox does not specify "personal loan" with sufficient clarity to include split-dollar life insurance and zero price or cash-less option prices. Failure to close this loophole has generated some discussion regarding the effectiveness of Sarbox and on the ability to legislate ethics.

Sarbanes-Oxley in Europe

Truth in financial statements is a European as well as an American issue. As recently as August 7, 2002, Goran Tidstrom, President of the Federation of European Accountants, stated that he believed accounting scandals in the United States would not spill over into Europe's financial markets because European companies use a different accounting philosophy from that in the U.S. European standards are based on principles rather than on rules. In other words, in the U.S. what is not specifically forbidden is allowed. In Europe, an accounting decision must be justified on the basis of sound business principles.

Yet in the past year Europe has been hit with a series of accounting scandals. In February Dutch retailer Royal Ahold uncovered an $856 million accounting hole at its U.S. Foodservice unit and another €73 million in accounting irregularities. In March British construction equipment rental firm Ashtead Group PLC revealed accounting errors at its U.S. Sunbelt Rentals business and said past profit had been inflated by about £11.5 million. In June French engineering company Alstom disclosed a charge of €51 million after understating losses on a railcar contract at its U.S. transport arm. In December, Italian food company Parmalat revealed a €4 billion discrepancy in its financial statements after the Bank of America accused Parmalat's Cayman Islands subsidiary with forging documents. Continuing investigations reveal a Byzantine network of subsidiaries to create assets, disguise losses, and misappropriate funds. On December 24 Parmalat filed for bankruptcy protection, two years after Enron.

That these European accounting scandals all have roots in the US is no coincidence. The intense scrutiny on accounting issues and corporate governance in the United States under Sarbanes-Oxley prompts auditors and companies to examine their books more carefully, bringing many of the problems to light. The International Herald Tribune comments:

> "The fact that Parmalat's auditors failed to detect a vast fraud over such a long period has left corporate governance specialists in Europe stupefied, as many in the United States were by Enron."[4]

A case in point is Swedish insurer Skandia. Skandia made news by complying with Sarbox audit committee requirements even though it does not trade in the US[5]. Skandia replaced its traditional audit committee of the company's Chairman and one other director with three independent, non-executive directors, at least one of who has a high level of financial expertise. On December 1, the company's Chairman, Bengt Braun, resigned amid allegations of financial fraud and misappropriation of funds. It would appear than an independent audit of the financial statements is more critical that the system on which those financial statements are based.

International Convergence or Rules versus Principles

Sarbanes-Oxley requires the SEC to study the financial accounting system to ascertain the extent to which it's "principles based" as opposed to "rules based" and to determine how long it will take to achieve a "principles based" system. It also requires financial accounting standard setters to adopt procedures assuring prompt consideration of new rules reflecting "international convergence on high quality accounting standards." The main difference between principles based and rules based accounting standards are that principles apply more broadly. They provide fewer exceptions or gray areas, and less interpretive and implementation guidance for applying the standards through these gray areas. Obviously this would increase the need to apply professional judgment; but whose professional judgment? For the principles based approach to work all financial market participants (regulators, accountants, managers, auditors, etc.) must be equally committed to changing procedures and processes to uphold the principles.

One consequence of applying accounting standards with fewer exceptions will be increased volatility in reported earnings. The argument is that an advantage of principles-based accounting standards would force the auditor to pass professional judgment on the economic substance of the transactions rather than engage in a search for legal loopholes. This obscures the real point: if management and auditors were competent and honest the financial statements would be accurate regardless of the accounting system. But what if management and the auditor are not competent and honest? We need a system based on principles but with sufficient rules to guide the accountant through certain cases of complex transactions. This is convergence in the accounting system: bringing together the principles based system that dominates Europe and the rules based system that dominates the US should address the problems of financial accuracy far more effectively than either system alone.

Evidence on the impact of Sarbox

There is already evidence that CEOs are increasing their involvement in the financial reporting processes and pursuing better technologies to leverage their existing systems to analyze and identify potential business and/or financial inconsistencies. CEOs are reinforcing the tone of high accountability, responsibility, and financial and business integrity across all levels of their organizations. CEOs and audit committees are becoming more engaged with their external auditors, including more extensive discussions about accounting, reporting, internal controls, and audit-related matters. Executive management has heightened its overall awareness and involvement in the design, implementation, and monitoring of internal controls over financial reporting. The external auditor and the audit committee are engaging in more open discussions and are having more substantive, active, and direct interaction. Both the frequency and length of audit committee meetings have increased. Auditors are being asked to provide more observations on the quality of financial statements, management, and the internal audit function. Audit committees are asking auditors to discuss in more detail their procedures for interim reviews of quarterly financial statements (quarterly financial statements are not audited). Audit committee members are expanding their knowledge of the company's financial management and

reporting and the role of the independent auditor, and have increased their time commitment and involvement in communicating and meeting with management and auditors. Companies and audit committees are recognizing that additional education and training on accounting and auditing matters may be necessary to ensure audit committee members' understanding of financial reporting issues.[6]

■

[1] www.nyse.com (January 8, 2004)

[2] Speech to the Federation of Securities Exchanges, June 12, 2003.

[3] Leblebici, L., (2003) Corporate Scandals and The Sarbanes-Oxley Act.

[4] International Herald Tribune, December 26, 2003.

[5] Tony McAuley, CFO Europe, September 22, 2003.

[6] Ernst & Young 2003.

$\mathcal{G}$overnments at all levels, government agencies, and corporations of all sizes borrow money in the financial markets. As evidence of the debt incurred, the borrower issues a security that specifies the terms under which the debt, principal and interest, is to be repaid.

❏ **Principal:** The principal is the amount borrowed and repaid. This is also called the face value of the debt.

❏ **Interest:** The interest is the fee charged by a lender as a percent of the principal.

❏ **Maturity:** The maturity is the date on which the principal of the loan is to be repaid.

Debt markets facilitate buying and selling of these instruments. At each transaction the buyer and seller of the debt security must agree on the price today of the remaining payments specified by the debt instrument.

Debt is structured in various forms, generally categorized by the way in which interest is paid. The great majority of debt instruments fall into one of four categories.

❏ **Interest-at-Maturity:** The principal portion of the loan plus interest is paid at maturity.

❏ **Discount Paper:** The debt is specified with a given principal to be paid at maturity. The note is then purchased at less than the face value. The difference between the price and the value at maturity constitutes the interest.

❏ **Coupon:** The principal portion of the loan is repaid at maturity. Interest is specified at a percent of the principal and paid periodically.

❏ **Amortized:** The principal and interest are repaid in equal instalments over the life of the loan. As the principal decreases from payment to payment, the interest portion of the constant payment decreases and the principal portion increases with every payment.

In this section we consider Money Markets.

Chapter 10   Money Markets
Chapter 11   Money Market Instruments

$\mathcal{M}$ oney markets trade debt with a term to maturity at issue of one year or less. Because periodic interest payments over a such a short time horizon is impractical, money market debt is predominantly issued as interest-to-maturity or as discount paper. In each case the interest is prorated for the number of days over which the instrument is held, but interest-at-maturity calculates the interest from the initial amount, whereas discount paper calculates the interest from the maturity amount.

10.1 - Discount Paper

Discount paper is specified with a given principal to be paid at maturity. The note is then purchased at less than the face value. The difference between the price and the value at maturity constitutes the interest.

Discount paper is quoted on a bankers' discount rate.

❑ **Bankers' Discount:** The rate at which a value is discounted. The banker's part of the bankers' discount rate is based on a 360-day year.

$$P_{Market} = Principal \left[1 - Rate \frac{days}{360}\right] \qquad (Eq\ 10\text{-}1)$$

Example 1:

We purchase a $1,000,000 note maturing in 60 days at a discount of 3%. The purchase price is $995,000.00

$$P_{Market} = \$1,000,000 \left[1 - 0.03 \frac{60}{360}\right]$$
$$P_{Market} = \$995,000.00 \qquad (Eq\ 10\text{-}2)$$

Figure 10-1: Discount Paper

This IOU is defined by the principal amount of $1,000,000 and the maturity date June 30.

The price at which it trades in the market reflects the present value of the $1,000,000 on the settlement date.

> *IOU*
> *$1,000,000.*
> *Discovery Café*
> *June 30*

We buy the $1,000,000 note on May 1 for $995,000.00. On June 30, 60 days later, the note matures, and we receive the principal value of $1,000,000. The difference between the purchase price and the principal, $5000.00, is our interest over the 60 days we hold the note.

We can place this on a time line:

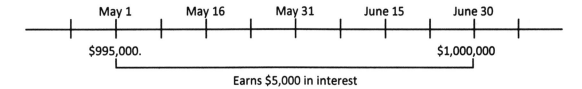

Earns $5,000 in interest

10.1.1 - Money Market Yield

The money market yield is the return on investment, prorated to a 360-day year. Yields are normally quoted on an annual basis so that we can compare yields on investments of different maturities. Money market yield or CD equivalent yield makes the yield on money market instruments directly comparable.

$$Yield_{MM} = \frac{Interest}{Investment} * \frac{360}{days}$$ (Eq 10-3)

Example 2:

We paid $995,000 for the $1,000,000 note maturing in 60 days. We thus earned $5,000 on an investment of $995,000 over 60 days. Factored up to a 360-day year we calculate a money market yield of 3.015%

$$Yield_{MM} = \frac{\$5,000.00}{\$995,000.00} * \frac{360}{60}$$

$$= 0.0050251 * \frac{360}{60}$$

$$= 3.015\%$$

10.1.2 - Straight Yield

On a simple interest or straight yield basis we revert back to a 365-day year (or 366 if a leap year).

❑ **Simple Interest:** Simple interest means that interest is paid once at the end of the year. Simple interest is the same as compounding annually.

$$Yield_s = \frac{Interest}{Investment} * \frac{365}{days}$$ (Eq 10-4)

Example 3:

We paid $995,000 for the $1,000,000 note maturing in 60 days. We thus earned $5,000 on an investment of $995,000 over 60 days. Factored up to a 365-day year we calculate a straight yield of 3.057%

$$Yield_S = \frac{\$5,000.00}{\$995,000.00} * \frac{365}{60}$$

$$= 0.0050251 * \frac{365}{60}$$

$$= 3.057\%$$

10.1.3 - Ask Yield

Dealers' quote sheets and other bond quotes restate the bank discount rate to the bond equivalent yield or ask yield. The ask yield is the bond equivalent yield on the investment. It derives its name from the assumption that investors buy at the dealer's ask rate. The ask yield is calculated so that we can compare the yield on a money market instrument quoted on a bankers' discount basis, to the yield on a coupon-bearing bond quoted at twice the semi-annual yield.

The ask yield on a money market instrument with 182 days to maturity or less is equal to the straight yield.

$$Yield_{Ask} = \frac{Interest}{Investment} * \frac{365}{days} \qquad where \ days \le 182 \qquad (Eq\ 10\text{-}5)$$

The ask yield on a money market instrument with 183 days to maturity or more is adjusted for the semi-annual compounding.

$$\frac{P_{Face}}{P_{Market}} = \left(1 + \frac{Y_{Ask}}{2}\right)\left(1 + \frac{(days - 182.5)\ Y_{ASK}}{365}\right) \qquad where \ days \ge 183 \qquad (Eq\ 10\text{-}6)$$

which simplifies to

$$Y_{Ask} = \frac{-\ days \pm \sqrt{days^2 + 730\ (days - 182.5)\ \dfrac{Interest}{Investment}}}{(days - 182.5)} \qquad (Eq\ 10\text{-}7)$$

The quadratic equation (Eq 10-7) has the familiar form $\dfrac{-b \pm \sqrt{b^2 - 4ac}}{2a}$, but only one result has any real meaning in finance.

Example 4:

We purchase the $1,000,000 note discounted at 3% over 270 days for $977,500.00, earning $22,500 interest. The return on investment is calculated over the 270-day investment as we calculate a money market yield of 3.069% and an ask yield of 3.096%

$$Yield_{HoldingPeriod} = \frac{\$22,500.00}{\$977,500.00} = 2.302\%$$

$$Yield_{MoneyMarket} = \frac{\$22,500.00}{\$977,500.00} * \frac{360}{270} = 3.069\%$$

$$Yield_{Straight} = \frac{\$22,500.00}{\$977,500.00} * \frac{365}{270} = 3.112\%$$

$$Yield_{Ask} = \frac{-270 \pm \sqrt{270^2 + 730\,(270-182.5)\frac{\$22,500.00}{\$977,500.00}}}{(270 - 182.5)}$$

$$= \frac{-270 \pm 272.7091281}{87.5} = -620.239\%, \quad 3.096\%$$

In this example −620.239% is mathematically correct, but it makes no sense. Earning $22,500 on an initial investment of $977,500 does not reflect a yield on investment of −620%. An investment yield of 3.096% does make sense.

Because years come in 365 and 366 days, the formula must be adjusted when the money market instrument extends over February 29.

$$Y_{ASK} = \frac{-days \pm \sqrt{days^2 + 730\,(days - 182.5)\frac{Interest}{Investment}}}{(days - 182.5)} \quad 365-day\ year$$

$$= \frac{-days \pm \sqrt{days^2 + 732\,(days - 183)\frac{Interest}{Investment}}}{(days - 183)} \quad 366-day\ year$$

10.2 - Interest-at-Maturity

Interest-at-maturity paper is quoted on a yield over a 360-day year. The maturity is then calculated as principal plus interest.

❏ **Interest-at-Maturity:** The rate at which interest accrues based on a 360-day year.

$$P_{Maturity} = Principal \left| 1 + Rate \frac{days}{360} \right|$$
(Eq 10-8)

Example 5:

We purchase a $1,000,000 note maturing in 60 days at a yield of 3%. The purchase price is $1,000,000.00 and the note matures at $1,005,000.00

$$P_{Maturity} = \$1,000,000 \left[1 + 0.03 \frac{60}{360} \right]$$

$$P_{Maturity} = \$1,005,000.00$$
(Eq 10-9)

Figure 10-2: Interest-at-Maturity

This IOU is defined by the principal amount of $1,000,000 borrowed today, and the maturity date June 30.

The value at which it matures reflects the future value of the $1,000,000 borrowed on the maturity date.

> *IOU*
> *$1,000,000.*
> *Discovery Café*
> *June 30*

We buy the $1,000,000 note on May 1 for $1,000,000. On June 30, 60 days later, the note matures, and we receive $1,005,000. The difference between the purchase price and the principal, $5000.00, is our interest over the 60 days we hold the note.

We can place this on a time line:

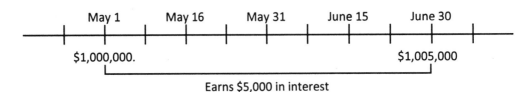

10.2.1 - Yields

Money market, straight, and ask or bond equivalent yields for interest-at-maturity paper are calculated in the same way as for discount paper

Example 6:

We purchase a 270-day $1,000,000 note at 3%, earning $22,500 over 270 days. The return on investment is calculated over the 270-day investment as we calculate a money market yield of 3.000% and an ask yield of 3.027%

$$Yield_{HoldingPeriod} = \frac{\$22,500.00}{\$1,000,000.00} = 2.250\%$$

$$Yield_{MoneyMarket} = \frac{\$22,500.00}{\$1,000,000.00} * \frac{360}{270} = 3.000\%$$

$$Yield_{Straight} = \frac{\$22,500.00}{\$1,000,000.00} * \frac{365}{270} = 3.042\%$$

$$Yield_{Ask} = \frac{-270 \pm \sqrt{270^2 + 730(270-182.5)\frac{\$22,500.00}{\$1,000,000.00}}}{(270 - 182.5)}$$

$$= \frac{-270 \pm 272.6484687}{87.5} = 3.027\%$$

In examples 4 and 6 we calculate the interest in the same way.

$$Interest = \$1,000,000 \left[0.03 \frac{60}{360} \right] = \$5000.00$$

But with interest-at-maturity paper the interest is added to the principal—so the initial investment is greater. Consequently the yield on that investment is lower.

Table 10-1: Table of Yields on $1m at 4.0% for 90 days

	Discount Paper	Interest-at-Maturity
Price	$990,000.00	$1,000,000.00
Interest	$10,000.00	$10,000.00
Maturity	$1,000,000.00	$1,010,000.00
Yield $_{Holding\ Period}$	1.010%	1.000%
Yield $_{Money\ Market}$	4.040%	4.000%
Yield $_{Ask}$	4.097%	4.056%

Chapter 10 - Questions and Problems

10-1:

A 300 day money market instrument has a face value of $1,000,000. It trades at 6%. Calculate the interest from discount paper and interest-at-maturity formulae. How do they compare?

10-2:

A $3,000,000 discount note maturing in 364 days is discounted at 4%. What is the market value?

10-3:

A $2,000,000 discount note maturing in 72 days sells for $1,986,000.00 What is the discount rate?

10-4:

A $1,000,000 note is discounted at a rate of 3% and sells for $984,000. In how many days does the note mature?

10-5:

The money market yield on a 90-day discount note is 3%. What is the discount rate?

10-6:

You are offered a $1,000,000 364-day T-bill at 6% and a $1,000,000 364-day CD at 6%. The T-bill is discount paper and the CD is interest-at-maturity. Use the money market yield to decide which is the better investment.

10-7:

You have $1,000,000 to invest over 180 days. You can put it in a CD at 5% or take a T-bill of any denomination. The T-bill is discount paper and the CD is interest-at-maturity. At what discount rate are you indifferent between the two investments?

$\mathcal{M}$ oney market instruments are a subset of tradable fixed-income debt instruments. The maturity dates are within one year of the issue date, making money market instruments short-term by design. Tradable refers to the ability an investor has to transfer ownership of the contract prior to the end of its term.

In contrast, retail time deposits at a savings bank are nonnegotiable; I cannot sell my six-month certificate of deposit to you. If I need the money prior to maturity, I need to ask the bank to break the CD, which they will usually do subject to certain monetary penalties.

The term *debt* refers to the fact that one entity (government, business, financial intermediary, etc.) is borrowing money from another entity (investor). This is not a form of partial ownership of the entity by the investor, as is equity.

Table 11-1: The Distinguishing Characteristics of Key Money Market Instruments

Instrument	Pricing	Issuer	Distinguishing Characteristic
Treasury Bills	Discount Paper	U.S. Treasury	Backed by the "Full Faith and Credit" of the U.S. Government
Commercial Paper		Corporations	Short Term Corporate Debt
Bankers' Acceptances		Banks	Finances self-liquidating transaction involving non-U.S. entity
Certificates of Deposit	Interest at Maturity		Borrowing by banks from investors
Federal Funds			Borrowing by banks from other banks
Repurchase Agreements		Money Market Dealers	Borrowing with financial assets as collateral to lend or invest at a higher rate

11.1 - Treasury Bills

Treasury bills are issued by the Department of the Treasury of the U.S. government. They represent debt of the government and are issued and traded on a bankers' discount basis.

Table 11-2: Treasury Bills

Maturity	Days to Mat	Bid	Ask	Chg	Ask Yld
May 8, 2014	7	4.48	4.47	-0.01	4.54
May 15, 2014	14	4.55	4.54	-0.01	4.61
May 22, 2014	21	4.54	4.53	0.01	4.61
May 29, 2014	28	4.60	4.59	-0.02	4.67
June 5, 2014	35	4.66	4.65	...	4.74
June 12, 2014	42	4.67	4.66	-0.01	4.75
Jul 31, 2014	91	4.76	4.75	...	4.87
Aug 7, 2014	98	4.77	4.76	...	4.89
Oct 16, 2014	168	4.81	4.80	0.01	4.98
Oct 23, 2014	175	4.82	4.81	0.01	4.99
Oct 30, 2014	182	4.83	4.82	0.01	
Apr 30, 2015	364	4.98	4.96	...	5.02

Financial Pages, May 1, 2014

Example 1:

The $100,000 T-bill maturing August 7, 2014, is bid at 4.77% and asked at 4.76%. The bid and ask are taken from the sample T-bill quote in Table 11-3

$$P_{Bid} = \$100,000 \left(1 - 0.0477 \, \frac{98}{360} \right) = \$98,701.50$$

$$P_{Ask} = \$100,000 \left(1 - 0.0476 \, \frac{98}{360} \right) = \$98,704.22$$

A dealer will buy from you at $98,701.50 (low) and sell to at $98,704.22 (high).

Note also that if you buy this T-bill and then change your mind then you will buy at $98,704.22 (high) and sell at $98,701.50 (low) losing $2.72 plus commission.

How to make a fool of yourself

When putting together a previous version of this text I pulled a T-bill quote out of *the Wall Street Journal* for the current year, 1996. I worked out the example and, after several attempts and one change in calculator, I had to admit to myself that I could not verify the ask yield quoted in *the Wall Street Journal*. I tried other bills. I even tried using the previous day's *Wall Street Journal*. I simply could not verify the ask yield.

Naturally I set up a spreadsheet program designed to calculate the ask yield and put an entire day's T-bill quote into it. The difference between the published ask yield and the ask yield I calculated was systematic: it started out small with the short-term T-bills and increased as the term to maturity increased.

I checked with my university colleagues. They verified my results. The *Wall Street Journal* was publishing ask yields we could none of us verify.

I called Kirk Robinson, our friendly regional *Wall Street Journal* representative. Kirk, quite understandably, disclaimed any responsibility for the calculation in question, but he did give us the name of someone in New York... who gave us the name of someone else... who gave us the name of someone else. Finally we got in touch with someone down in Arizona who could help us.

In a tone of voice that clearly said, "And you people teach this stuff?!" he pointed out that 1996 was a leap year. Try multiplying by 366.

I returned to my spreadsheet and replaced the 365 day year with a 366 day year and, sure enough, all our ask yields matched the numbers in the *Wall Street Journal*.

The moral of this embarrassing story is : Yes, leap years count.   E.O.

The rules for Leap years are:

1]   Every four years is a leap year (1904, 1908, 1912, . . . 1992, 1996 ...)

2]   Every 100 years we skip a leap year. (1700, 1800, and 1900 were not leap years)

3]   Every 400 years we skip a skipped leap year (1600 and 2000 are leap years.)

Correctly programmed calendars will have 2000 as a leap year, as will calendar programs that ignore rules 2] and 3]. However, those calendars programmed with rules 1] and 2] but not 3] will skip the leap year in 2000.

So be warned.

11.1.1 - Primary Market

Treasury securities are issued on an auction basis: 4-week (28-day) T-bills are auctioned on Tuesdays for Thursday issue; 13-week (91-day) and 26-week (182-day) T-bills are auctioned on Mondays for Thursday issue; 52-week (364-day) bills are auctioned every four weeks on Tuesday for Thursday issue. The Treasury also issues cash management bills to cover temporary shortfalls, with the term to maturity determined by how long the Treasury expects the shortfall to last. As a result, Treasury bills mature on Thursdays.

❑ **Book Entry:** Treasury bills are book entry. This means that there are no physical securities issued. The Treasury bill is paperless, an entry in the database at the Bureau of the Public Debt.

The Treasury accepts competitive bids and noncompetitive or quantity bids.

❑ **Competitive Bid:** A competitive bid is quoted on a bank yield basis. Competitive bids are limited to 35% of any one issue at auction. Bids are submitted through the Treasury Automated Auction Processing System (TAAPS) for banks, registered brokers, and other institutional investors.

❑ **NonCompetitive Bid:** A noncompetitive or quantity bid is submitted with a quantity, up to $5 million in principal value, but no yield. Quantity bids are always filled in full at the rate established by the auction. Non-competitive bids for amounts from $100 to $5 million can be submitted through TreasuryDirect.

Once the bids are all in, the Treasury fills the bid from the Federal Reserve, the non-competitive bids, and the competitive bids in reverse order by yield. The established discount rate is then the weighted average yield on all successful competitive bids.

Single Price Auctions

Prior to 1992, competitive bids were filled at the actual yield in each successful bid. Bid too low and, though guaranteed all the Treasuries for which you bid, the resulting price would be too high to make a required profit. Bid to high and, although you would pay a low price, you risk not getting any securities at all.

❑ **Winner's Curse:** The curse of the winner in any auction procedure is that, because the price paid was the highest price bid, it was higher than the consensus value of the article purchased.

From 1992 through 1998 Treasury auctions were converted to a single price auction in which all successful bids are filled at the weighted average on all successful competitive bids. The single price auction removes the fear of bidding too low a yield. This would tend to exert a downward bias on the yields bid, increasing prices. On the other hand, a single price auction would tend to diminish the incentive to collude in the bidding process. This would tend to remove a downward bias on the yields bid, decreasing prices.

Call Market

Note that this market, like any auction market, is a call not a continuous market. All the bids are collected and then matched. A call market does not experience the problems of order flow, bids waiting for an ask to show up or asks waiting for a bid to show up. On the other hand, a call market does not allow participants to derive information from the continuous action. You can't look at an outcome and revise your own bid to take advantage of this new information.

11.1.2 - Secondary Market

The secondary market for Treasury securities is an OTC market where a group of securities dealers provide continuous bids and offers on specific outstanding Treasuries.

❏ **On-the-Run:** The most recently auctioned Treasury issue of any given maturity is on-the-run. These issues are generally more liquid, and their bid-ask spreads are smaller than off-the-run issues.

❏ **Off-the-Run:** A Treasury issue with a given maturity is off-the-run if there is a more recent auction and issue for the same term to maturity.

11.2 - Commercial Paper

Commercial paper is a short-term promissory note with a fixed maturity. It represents the debt of the issuer, generally a corporation.

The use of commercial paper developed in response to the limitations imposed by the unique characteristics of the U.S. banking system. In other systems, demands for credit in one part of the country could be offset by surpluses in other parts of the country. In the U.S., where banks were restricted to a single state or to a single location, this was much more difficult. Thus firms in credit-scarce, high-interest-rate areas began selling commercial paper in the capital markets.

Commercial paper rates are quoted on a discount basis. When an issuer sells interest-bearing paper he converts the rate paid from a discount rate to an equivalent simple interest rate so that the investor gets the same rate of return whether he buys discount or interest-bearing paper. The interest-bearing paper makes it easier for those who wish to invest a fixed dollar sum ($1m).

Commercial paper is divided roughly into traditional financial and nonfinancial paper, and asset-backed paper.

❏ **Traditional Commercial Paper:** Commercial paper is unsecured. There is no specific collateral; it is secured on the issuing company's ability to generate sufficient revenue to pay its debt.

❏ **Asset-Backed Commercial Paper:** Commercial paper secured with specific collateral. This can be a bank line of credit, accounts receivable, or specific assets of the firm. Most asset-backed commercial paper is issued through special-purpose vehicles (SPV). SPVs are separate entities created to buy the collateral assets from the parent company and borrow the money to pay for these assets.

The Federal Reserve reports that at the end of April 2012 there is just over $1 trillion in commercial paper outstanding.

Figure 11-1 shows Commercial Paper outstanding in the U.S. from 2001 through to the end of April 2012. The market peaked in July 2007 at just under $2.2 trillion. At that time the market was 55% asset-backed, 36% financial, and 9% nonfinancial commercial paper.

By the end of April 2012 asset-backed fell to 38%, and financial and nonfinancial commercial paper increased to 43% and 19%, respectively.

Figure 11-1: Commercial Paper Outstanding

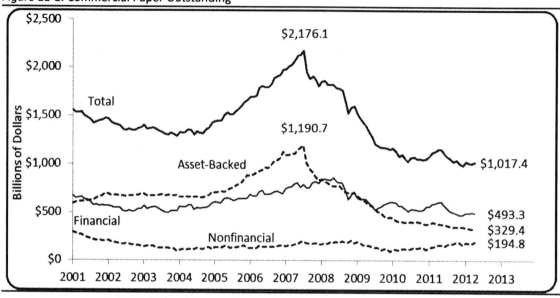

Public offerings of commercial paper are exempt from SEC registration and prospectus requirements if the issuer uses the proceeds to finance current transactions, and the paper matures within 270 days. Most commercial paper matures in less than 30 days because issuers are able to borrow at the base of the yield curve, usually the lowest interest cost available.

The Federal Reserve Board (FRB) reports commercial paper rates and issued and outstanding data. In December 2011, 68.3% of the commercial paper issued in the U.S. was issued with 1 to 4 days to maturity. Even with historically low interest rates, the rate is still lowest at the base of the yield curve.

Figure 11-2: Composition of U.S. Commercial Paper

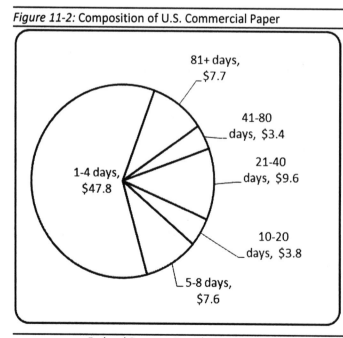

Table 11-3: Rates on AA rated paper

Term in Days	non financial	Financial	Asset-backed
1 day	0.05%	0.04%	0.61%
7 day	0.07%	0.04%	0.59%
15 day	0.08%	0.04%	0.47%
30 day	0.10%	0.06%	0.33%
60 day	0.11%	0.10%	0.31%
90 day	0.14%	0.18%	0.32%

The smooth yield curve we see on AA-rated financials and non-financials is not repeated in asset-backed commercial paper. Rates on asset-backed commercial paper reflect higher risk of default as well as decreased transparency.

11.2.1 - Ratings

Prior to 1970 commercial paper was largely unrated. In June 1970 the Penn Central Railroad defaulted on its commercial paper. As a result, it became common practice for firms to rate their commercial paper and to arrange for bank lines of credit.

1970: The Wreck of the Penn Central Railroad

When the market first developed, Commercial Paper was nothing more than a corporate IOU: unrated and unsecured. This changed with the bankruptcy of the Penn Central railroad.

On February 1, 1968 the New York Central and Pennsylvania railroads were joined in the greatest merger in U.S. railroad history. The cost of running the railroad was enormous. In August 1968 Penn Central sold $35 million in commercial paper. It was the first time a railroad had ventured into this market. In December of the same year the ICC (Interstate Commerce Commission) gave the Penn Central permission to issue up to $100 million in commercial paper. This was increased to $150 million in May 1969 and to $200 million by October. At this time the ICC warned that commercial paper was designed to meet short-term borrowing requirements and not appropriate for long-term financing of capital expenditures or for the refinancing of maturing long-term debt. The statement that using short-term commercial paper to fulfill long-term financial needs could expose the company to serious risk goes into the category of famous last words.

By the end of 1969 the Penn Central was spending $260,000 per day on interest payments alone. By May 1970 there was a run on Penn Central's commercial paper. When the railroad filed for bankruptcy on June 21, 1970, it still had $82 million in commercial paper outstanding.

Further reading: Daughen & Binzen, *The Wreck of the Penn Central*, Signet, 1971.
                                Stigum, *The Money Market*, Dow-Jones Irwin, 1990.

❑ **Rating:** an evaluation of the firm's credit-worthiness by a professional outside service such as Moody's, Standard & Poor's, and Duff & Phelps. Although each rating company has its own variation, in general an A rating (AAA, AA, A) indicates the highest quality debt, a B rating (BBB, BB, B) indicates medium to low-grade debt, a C rating (CCC, CC, C) indicates highly speculative and risky, and a D (DDD, DD, D) indicates that the company is already in default.

Commercial Paper ratings are slightly different from bond ratings in scale and meaning. Because the commercial Paper is of such a short term, the primary focus of the rating is the likelihood, not the severity, of default. Investors in commercial paper hold the short-term unsecured debt of the issuer, and in bankruptcy proceedings stand a small chance of recovery.

For example, Moody's uses Prime 1, Prime 2, Prime 3, and Not Prime as the four rating possibilities. When issued, the vast majority of commercial paper in the U.S. is rated either Prime 1 (the highest which roughly corresponds to long-term debt ratings of AAA to A3 in range) or Prime 2 (the next highest rating which roughly corresponds to long-term debt ratings of A2 to Baa2 in range).

❑ **Bank Lines of Credit:** To eliminate the risk that an issuer will be unable to sell new paper, issuers back commercial paper with bank lines of credit, which states that the bank will pay off the issue when it comes due if the issuer fails to do so. Bank lines are essentially insurance against default.

❑ **Rolling:** The majority of commercial paper is paid off by rolling: the issuer sells new paper to generate funds to pay off the maturing paper.

❑ **Run:** A run on commercial paper occurs when a corporation can no longer pay off its maturing paper because it is unable to sell its new issue or to persuade creditors to take the new issue in place of the maturing paper.

11.2.2 - Primary Market

The primary market on commercial paper consists of directly and dealer placed paper.

❑ **Directly Placed Paper:** Directly placed paper is sold directly from the issuer to the investor. The issuer is usually a finance company. The investor is usually a large institutional investor (investment companies, money market funds, pension funds, and insurance companies).

❑ **Dealer Placed Paper:** Dealer-placed paper is underwritten by a securities firm, which then sells it in the market.

11.2.3 - Secondary Market

There is no active secondary market in commercial paper in the U.S. The failure of such a market to develop is due to the heterogeneity of the paper and the lack of demand. The short term to maturity means that most investors hold the paper until it matures.

❑ **Buy back:** a purchase of commercial paper by the corporation (or its underwriter) of the corporation's own paper. Generally dealers who sell commercial paper will buy it back at the going market rate plus ⅛. Buy backs have been estimated at 1 to 1½ percent of dealer placed paper.

11.2.4 - Market Failure

The commercial paper market is particularly sensitivity to issues in investor confidence. Commercial paper is very short term. If a firm rolls four-day paper then it must convince investors of the firm's ability to repay its debt every four days. If a firm fails to keep investors confident, it will be faced with a demand to pay its debt in full within four days. This was the case with Countrywide Financial.

2007: Countrywide Financial

In 2007 Countrywide Financial was the largest home mortgage lender in the U.S. But house prices were falling, and Countrywide was holding mortgages worth more than the houses on which these mortgages were written. The collateral could no longer support the debt.

In July 2007 Countrywide announced a 33% drop in second quarter profits. Investors lost confidence: If homeowners could no longer pay off the full amount of the debt they owed to Countrywide Financial, then how could Countrywide Financial be able to repay its debt to investors.

The commercial paper market began to shrink. In one month the asset-backed CP market declined by 14.8%. The entire U.S. commercial paper market declined 10.2%, losing $222.9 billion in about four weeks.

In August 2007, Countrywide Financial, unable to borrow the funds it needed in the commercial paper market, announced that it would tap the $11.5 billion in lines of credit from the company's various banks. It wasn't enough. Third quarter losses totaled $1.2 billion, and in January 2008 Countrywide Financial was sold to Bank of America for $4 billion in stock, a drop from $43 to $7.16 per share in one year.

The commercial paper market, particularly asset-backed paper, continued to contract. In September 2008 the commercial paper market suffered a crisis in confidence so severe that it triggered intervention by the Federal Reserve in the form of the Commercial Paper Funding Facility.

2008: Commercial Paper Funding Facility

The Commercial Paper Funding Facility (CPFF) was created by the Federal Reserve Bank of New York in October 2008.

On September 15, 2008, Lehman Brothers, the fourth-largest investment bank in the U.S., filed for bankruptcy. Three days later AIG required a $182.5 billion bailout.

Investors no longer had confidence that commercial paper could be repaid. There was a run on the commercial paper market. Firms everywhere were not only unable to borrow funds, but they were also faced with the prospect of being forced to pay off all their short-term debt within days, or file for bankruptcy protection.

The CPFF was a special-purpose vehicle (SPV) funded by the Federal Reserve. The money was used to buy the commercial paper that investors would no longer finance. The CPFF invested $780 billion in commercial paper issued by both domestic and foreign firms. The facility was closed in April 2010 when the last issue was repaid in full and the funds repaid to the Federal Reserve.

11.2.5 - Foreign Borrowing

An increasing number of non-U.S. companies and governments issue commercial paper in the U.S. money market. Foreign borrowing now accounts for some 20% of the U.S. commercial paper market. Most foreign issuers of commercial paper borrow dollars in the U.S. money market and swap them for their own currency. This reduces their cost of borrowing by some 50 to 150 basis points.

11.2.6 - Euro-Commercial Paper

Euro-Commercial Paper (ECP) is commercial paper issued through dealers in London. Most ECP is issued in U.S. dollars, but ECP is also available in Euros, Yen (Euroyen paper), Guilders, Australian (Aussie dollar), New Zealand (Kiwi dollar), Hong Kong dollars, and Pounds Sterling. (Because this is London, the Euro sterling paper is actually domestic paper as well as part of the global ECP market.)

There are five major differences between the Euro-commercial paper and the U.S. commercial paper markets.

❏ The maturity of Euro-commercial paper is generally longer. The average maturity is close to 90 days compared to 35 days in the U.S. commercial paper market.

❏ U.S. commercial paper must be backed by unused bank lines of credit; there is no such restriction in the EuroCP market.

❏ U.S. commercial paper may be directly or dealer placed; EuroCP is generally dealer placed.

❏ The U.S. market is dominated by a few dealers; the Euro-market has many participating dealers.

❏ The U.S. secondary market is thin and illiquid; it is principally a primary market where most investors hold the commercial paper until maturity. Largely due to the longer maturities, the secondary EuroCP market is well developed and active.

11.2.7 - Commercial Paper in the International Capital Market

Canada has had a commercial paper market for many years. Commercial paper markets have also been established in Britain, Sweden, France, Japan, and Australia. Most are based on the commercial paper market in the U.S. Due to the globalization of the capital markets any investor, issuer, or dealer can start in any market, in any number of currencies, and swap himself back to any other currency. This creates an opportunity for arbitrage.

11.3 - Bankers Acceptances

Bankers' acceptances or bills of exchange are financial instruments that date back to the 12th century when early forms of these bills were used to finance international trade. Now most of the BAs outstanding are third country acceptances. The prominence of third-country financing in the U.S. acceptance market reflects the fact that the U.S. market is the only world financial center in which there is a wide market for dollar denominated BAs. A large proportion of BAs finance grains, cotton, and oil.

BAs are defined by the Federal Reserve as paper used to finance a specified set of self-liquidating, commercial transactions not to provide working capital.

Example 2:

Computer Imports Inc. of New York contracts with *Cambridge Instruments U.K.* for the delivery of 10 super computers. The agreed price is $4m to be paid 60 days after the date of shipment.

❑ Computer Imports arranges with its bank (JP Morgan Chase) to issue a letter of credit sent to *Cambridge Instruments'* bank (Barclays), which guarantees that payment will be made. *Cambridge Instruments* is informed by its bank that payment is guaranteed, and they ship the computers.

❑ Cambridge Instruments presents the shipping documents to Barclays as evidence that the computers have been shipped as required. *Cambridge instruments* receives from Barclays the payment of $3.98m. ($4m * (1 – .03(60/360) assuming 3% bankers' discount rate).

❑ JP Morgan Chase accepts the transaction when Barclays proves that the computers have been shipped and the money paid out to *Cambridge Instruments* in accordance with the agreement. This creates the Bankers' Acceptance. The BA is now essentially an IOU for $4m payable in 60 days. Barclays "bought" it for $3.98m. The BA is backed by the shipping documents to the computers.

❑ Barclays sells the BA back to the issuer (JP Morgan Chase) for $3.98m (Barclays Bank is very efficient and does this all in one day.)

❑ If JP Morgan Chase holds the BA in its investment portfolio it is recorded on its balance sheet as an investment. JP Morgan Chase can also sell the BA in the money market, either directly to an investor or through a dealer.

❑ If JPM sells the BA into the money market then 60 days later the holder of the BA presents it to JP Morgan Chase bank for its face value of $4m, which JP Morgan Chase recovers from *Computer Imports Inc.*

11.4 - Certificates of Deposit

Certificates of deposit (CDs) are debt instruments issued by banks. The money market CD is not the same as the small denomination CD offered to the public. The small denomination CD is evidence of a time deposit at a fixed rate of interest for a fixed time period and is nonnegotiable (you cannot resell your CD to someone else).

Although available in $100,000 denominations, CDs are generally sold in $1 million lots and are quoted on an interest-bearing basis.

❑ **Nonnegotiable CD:** Nonnegotiable CDs must be held to maturity and are subject to monetary penalties if the underlying deposit is withdrawn prior to the maturity date.

❑ **Negotiable CD:** Negotiable CDs may be sold in the secondary market.

❑ **Money Market CD:** CDs with maturities of less than one year pay interest upon maturity.

❑ **Term CD:** Term CDs have a term to maturity of more than one year generally pay interest semi-annually. Because we are still in the money market a year has 360 days.

❑ **Variable Rate CD:** The two most prevalent type of variable rate or floating rate CDs are the 6-month CD with a 30-day roll and the 1-year CD with a 90-day roll. On each roll date, accrued interest is paid and a new coupon rate is set, usually at a specified spread above some index.

Most CDs are issued at 30 to 90 days. The market is very thin at maturities over 6 months. There are two reasons for this.

❑ Many investors buying CDs are corporations funding tax and dividend dates that are at most 90 days in the future. These investors need liquidity and prefer shorter paper rather than having to resell paper of longer maturity.

❑ On a normally shaped yield curve it is cheaper to buy long money by rolling 90 day CDs.

The market for CDs with a maturity of more than 6 months is referred to as a professional investors' market.

11.4.1 - Primary Market

Most banks issuing CDs prefer to place as many as possible directly with customers. One disadvantage of issuing CDs through dealers is that these same CDs may end up in the market at just the time the bank wants to borrow additional funds, thereby creating a situation in which it must compete with itself to write CDs. Many banks have their own dealer departments and market their own CDs. Finally, most of the demand for CDs is generated by money market funds.

CDs are generally sold in million dollar lots. However, dealers who have branch networks have made a big business out of selling both CDs and BAs to retail accounts for smaller denominations.

11.4.2 - Secondary Market

Dealers operate in two markets:

❏ **Retail Market:** The retail market in which dealers do business with customers, and the

❏ **Inside Market:** The inside market in which dealers trade with each other.

Although liquidity in the CD market, measured in terms of bid-ask spreads, is fairly good when interest rates are stable, the CD market reacts more violently to a change in rates than does the T-bill market. One reason for this is that banks respond to rising interest rates by writing more CDs. Therefore the supply becomes uncertain.

11.4.3 - Euro CDs

Euro CDs are CDs issued outside the U.S., generally in London. Though traditionally issued only in American dollars, there is now a growing market for CDs issued in Japanese Yen. Euro CDs can be issued by American as well as by foreign banks. Euro CDs trade at a higher yield than domestic CDs for two reasons.

   ❏ Euro CDs are less liquid

   ❏ Investors view Euro CDs as a riskier investment. This view is largely illusionary. Any Euro CD issued by the London branch of an American bank is a direct obligation of the parent company.

   ❏ Sovereign risk, the risk that Britain might suspend payment on EuroCDs might be negligible, but the risk that Greece suspends payments is not.

❏ **Sovereign Risk:** Sovereign risk is the risk that changes in the social, political, and economic environment in a foreign country affects the market instrument. For example, if Greece leaves the Eurozone, payment on EuroCDs issued by Greek Banks might be suspended.

❏ **Lock-up CD:** Lock-up CDs are issued in London with the understanding that they will not be traded in the secondary market.

11.4.4 - Yankee CDs

Yankee CDs are American dollar CDs issued in the U.S. by branches of foreign banks. Foreign banks generally sell CDs in the American market through dealers. The dealer is instrumental in overcoming the lack-of-familiarity hurdle that foreign banks face in the U.S. As a result of this lack of familiarity some Yankee CDs must pay substantially more than domestic issuers until the name of the issuer gains acceptability in the market.

Yankee CDs also tend to be less liquid than domestic CDs. In down markets dealers are often unwilling to take a position in Yankee CDs.

11.5 - Federal Funds

All banks and depository institutions (including savings & loans, credit unions, and branches of foreign banks) are members of the Federal Reserve System and are required to keep reserves on deposit at their district Federal Reserve Bank. (There are twelve Federal Reserve Banks.) A commercial bank's reserve account is just like any non-interest-bearing account except that each member bank is required by law to maintain a minimum average balance in its reserve account over the two-week reserve period. The size of this minimum average balance or required reserve depends on the size and composition of the bank's deposits. Reserve ratios are higher for transactions (demand) deposits than nontransaction (savings and term account) deposits. Thus the funds a bank can lend out or otherwise invest is equal to the deposits it takes in less the reserves it is required to maintain.

Banks temporarily short on their reserve requirements can borrow short-term funds

- ❑ Borrow directly from the Federal Reserve at the Discount Window
- ❑ Borrow from other banks in the Federal Reserve System that have excess reserves (trading either directly or through New York brokers), and/or
- ❑ Enter into repurchase agreements

- ❑ **Discount Window:** The Federal Reserve maintains a discount window where member banks can borrow funds at the discount rate, provided the bank puts up acceptable collateral. Bank borrowing at the Fed is limited despite the fact that the discount rate is generally lower than other sources of temporary funding. This is because the Fed views borrowing at the discount window as a privilege to be used only to meet short-term liquidity needs. Frequent use of the discount window triggers the stage one informational call to find out why the bank needs to borrow so often and the stage two administrative counseling call to advise a restructuring of the banks' borrowing practices.

Member banks can also borrow and lend to each other in the federal Funds market at the federal funds rate. Because the nation's largest corporations tend to concentrate their borrowing in big money market banks in New York and other large financial centers, the loans and investments these banks must fund often exceed the deposits they receive. Many smaller regional banks often take in more in deposits than they can lend (profitably) locally. Since large banks must meet their reserve requirements and since excess reserves yield no return to the smaller banks, the federal funds market developed wherein they could lend and borrow to maintain or optimize their reserve accounts.

Some transactions are made directly between banks, others are made through New York brokers. Despite the fact that federal fund transactions are loans, lending is referred to as a sale of federal funds, and borrowing is referred to as purchase of federal funds.

The operation of the federal funds market and related activities requires tens of thousands of transfers daily among thousands of banks and other depository institutions. This happens over the Fed Wire System. Under this system a bank's computer is linked by wire to the computer at its district Federal Reserve Bank, which is linked in turn to the fed's central computer in Culpepper, Virginia.

The bulk of the money sold in the federal funds market is overnight money. The federal funds rate is quoted on a 360-day year.

Example 3:

If the overnight rate is 3%, then $10 million overnight could be purchased for

$$\$10,000,000 \left(0.0300 \ \frac{1}{360} \right) = \$833.34$$

You would borrow $10 million today and repay $10,000,833.34 tomorrow.

_____

❑ **LIBOR:** (LYE-bor) the London Inter Bank Offered Rate is the rate that the most creditworthy international banks charge each other on large Eurodollar loans. Eurodollars are deposits of U.S. dollars in banks outside the United States and are frequently used in settling international accounts. LIBOR is generally the base rate, to which a risk is added, for other Eurodollar loans to less creditworthy corporate and government borrowers.

❑ **Eurodollars:** Eurodollars are dollar deposits held in banks outside the jurisdiction of the Federal Reserve. The Euro in Eurodollars derives from the history of these deposits, which were generally held in Europe. But today Eurodollars are dollars held anywhere outside the United States; EuroYen are yen held anywhere outside Japan; and—at least theoretically—EuroEuros would be euros held outside the jurisdiction of the European Central Bank.

_____

11.6 - *Repurchase Agreements*

A repurchase agreement is the simultaneous sale and repurchase of a security. The repo market works just like a pawn shop for securities; a repo agreement is essentially a loan with the underlying security as collateral.

The element that makes repurchase agreements a favorite form of short-term financing is the technical nature of the agreement. From the perspective of a bank, it has the use of someone else's funds and agrees to return them. This sounds like a deposit, but since it is not, there are no reserve requirements. Banks frequently hold large investments in marketable securities like U.S. Treasury issues. These issues are very easy to use in repurchase agreements.

From the perspective of a securities dealer, a repurchase agreement is very lucrative way to finance inventory; in effect owning financial assets with borrowed money. Since the Federal Reserve regulates how much of the value of securities can be borrowed (margin requirements under Regulation T and U as applicable to borrowers), securities dealers can finance huge amounts of inventory in securities through repurchase agreements, thereby avoiding the more stringent margin regulations on loans.

The overnight repo rate is generally less than the federal funds rate. Many nonbank investors who have funds to invest very short term and who do not want to incur any price risk have nowhere to go but the repo market because they cannot participate in the federal funds market. Also, lending money through a repo transaction is safer than selling fed funds because a sale of fed funds is an unsecured loan.

The repo market generates almost as many buzzwords as money. The buzzwords are defined in the following example of a repurchase agreement.

Example 4:

> A dealer needs to borrow $10 million. He enters into a repurchase agreement with the city of Urbana. The dealer offers as collateral Treasury bills valued at $10.1 million.
>
> The dealer does a repo or sells collateral, reversing out his $10.1 million Treasury bills as security. The margin or haircut is the difference between the value of the collateral and the $10 million loan.
>
> Urbana reverses the repo or buys collateral, reversing in securities. As the lender, Urbana protects itself from credit risk by taking a margin.

❑ **Margin or "Haircut":** The margin protects the lender against simultaneous default and a decrease in the value of the collateral security below the value of the loan. The margin is set according to the term of the repo and the price volatility of the security.

The borrower also faces a credit risk. To protect itself against simultaneous default by Urbana and an increase in the value of the T-bill, the dealer could reduce his risk by asking for a reverse margin, although this is less common.

❑ **Open Repo:** Under an open repo or continuing contract the term of the repurchase is unspecified. Either side can terminate the contract, and the borrower has the right of substitution: he can pull the security and substitute other collateral of equal or greater value.

❑ **Specific Issues Market:** In the specific issues market an investor is looking to reverse in a specific security, frequently to cover a short position. He covers the short position by lending in the repo market to cover the short and then buying the security later to cover the repo.

Major dealers in government securities run books in repo and reverse; they take in collateral on one side and hang it out on the other, earning a profit by charging a lending rate slightly higher than the rate at which they borrow.

❑ **Matched Book:** If a dealer repurchases securities out for the same period that he reverses them in, then he is running a matched book. Essentially the book matches the time period over which money is borrowed and lent. Spreads on these transactions are narrow, but the volume is enormous.

❑ **Mismatched Book:** Dealers who anticipate a decrease in interest rates lend for longer terms (repo long) and borrow for shorter terms (reverse short), and vice versa. This is a mismatched book. Both the profits and the risks are higher.

Example 5:

> David Q. Dealer wants to buy the $4m, 60 day, JP Morgan Chase Bankers Acceptance created in example 2. David has $4.1m in 87-day Treasury bills, currently quoted at 1.10. Another dealer will take the T-bills on a 60-day Repurchase Agreement at 2.6% with a haircut of 1%.
>
> David separates this potential investment into its components to see if the deal makes sense. The bankers acceptance will generate $20,000 in interest over the 60-day period. To borrow the $3.98m on the repo he will be charged interest of $17,246.67

$$\$3{,}980{,}000 \left(0.0260 \; \frac{60}{360} \right) = \$17{,}246.67$$

Essentially David will pay \$17,246.67 in interest to earn \$20,000.00 in interest: a profit of \$2,753.33

Table 11-4: Bankers Acceptance & Repurchase Agreement breakdown

Instrument	Day 0	Day 60	Net
Bankers Acceptance	(\$3,980,000.00)	\$4,000,000.00	\$20,000.00
Repurchase Agreement	\$3,980,000.00	\$3,997,246.67	\$17,246.67
T-bills	securities out	securities in	
Net		\$2,753.33	\$2,753.33

The deal will go forward so long as David can make collateral of 101% of the \$3.98m borrowed: \$4,019,800.

$$\$3{,}980{,}000 \; (1 + 0.01) = \$4{,}019{,}800.00$$

David's T-bills are valued at \$4,089,100.83 and are thus accepted as collateral.

$$\$4{,}100{,}000 \left(1 - 0.0110 \; \frac{87}{360} \right) = \$4{,}089{,}100.83$$

David agrees that he is extraordinarily lucky to do a repo for 60 days. In general he would do serial repos one, two, or three days at a time. In each repo he would be working with the repo rate on that particular day, so he would be exposed to interest rate risk.

Chapter 11 - Questions and Problems

11-1:

Royal Dutch Petroleum has just signed agreement with Saudi Oil to buy 2,000,000 barrels of oil at $60.00 per barrel, delivery to be made in Rotterdam, and payment to be made in American dollars, 60 days from now. A quick check with the Bank of America (with whom Royal Dutch has a long-term financial relationship) reveals that the discount rate is 3¼%. Saudi Oil accepts this rate, the deal is signed, faxed to all concerned, and Saudi Oil starts loading.

A. Saudi Oil presents the loading papers to the Bank of Arabia, proving that they have fulfilled their obligation to ship the oil. How much money does the Bank of Arabia credit to Saudi Oil's account?

B. The Bank of Arabia presents the shipping documents to the Bank of America, and the Bank of America wires how much to the Bank of Arabia?

C. The Bank of America puts the bankers' acceptance on the market, selling directly to you at *Investments Unlimited*. The BA looks like a good investment but you do not have the necessary cash in your investment account, but you do have a number of 150-day Treasury bills. The repo rate is 3⅛%. You borrow how much on a repo.

D. The lender (another dealer with offices in the same Wall Street Office Building) requires a haircut of ¼%, so you reverse out Treasuries worth how much? Why does the dealer reversing in securities require a haircut?

E. T-bills come in denominations of $100,000 so you reverse out how many T-bills worth how much? (Use the quote provided below.)

F. Sixty days later the Bank of America pays off the bankers' acceptance, and you repay the loan on repo. What was your profit on this transaction?

Table 11-5: Treasury Bill Quote

Days to Maturity	Bankers' Discount rate quoted on	
	Day 0: day BA is accepted	Day 60: day BA matures
30	3.26	2.70
60	3.37	2.74
90	3.41	2.77
120	3.45	2.79
150	3.50	2.81

11-2:

Commercial paper is issued with a term to maturity ranging from 1 day to

A. 7 days.
B. 90 days.
C. 270 days.
D. 364 days.

11-3:

Which of the following are characteristics of commercial paper?

    I.   Backed by money-market deposits
    II. Negotiated maturities and yields
    III. Issued by commercial banks
    IV. Not registered as securities

A. I and II
B. I, II, and III
C. II and IV
D. III and IV

11-4:

Which of the following finances imports and exports?

A. Eurodollars
B. Banker's Acceptances
C. ADRs
D. Commercial Paper

11-5:

Which of the following describes the prime rate?

A. The base rate on corporate loans at large U.S. money center commercial banks.
B. Reserves traded among commercial banks for overnight use in amounts of $1 million or more
C. The charge on loans to depository institutions by the New York Federal Reserve Bank
D. The charge on loans to brokers on stock exchange collateral.

11-6:

Which of the following describes the federal funds rate?

A.   The base rate on corporate loans at large U.S. money center commercial banks.
B.   Reserves traded among commercial banks for overnight use in amounts of $1 million or more
C.   The charge on loans to depository institutions by the New York Federal Reserve Bank
D.   The charge on loans to brokers on stock exchange collateral.

11-7:

Which of the following describes the discount rate?

A.   The base rate on corporate loans at large U.S. money center commercial banks.
B.   Reserves traded among commercial banks for overnight use in amounts of $1 million or more
C.   The charge on loans to depository institutions by the New York Federal Reserve Bank
D.   The charge on loans to brokers on stock exchange collateral.

11-8:

Which of the following describes the call money rate?

A.   The base rate on corporate loans at large U.S. money center commercial banks.
B.   Reserves traded among commercial banks for overnight use in amounts of $1 million or more
C.   The charge on loans to depository institutions by the New York Federal Reserve Bank
D.   The charge on loans to brokers on stock exchange collateral.

*C*orporations, governments at all levels, and government agencies borrow money in the financial markets. As evidence of the debt incurred the borrower issues a security that specifies the terms under which the debt, principal and interest, is to be repaid.

❑ **Principal:** The principal is the amount borrowed and repaid. This is also called the face value of the debt.

❑ **Interest:** The Interest is the fee charged by a lender as a percent of the principal.

❑ **Maturity:** The maturity is the date on which the principal of the loan is to be repaid.

Debt markets facilitate buying and selling of these debt instruments. At each transaction the buyer and seller of the debt security must agree on the price today of the remaining payments specified by the debt instrument.

Public markets for debt allow borrowers and lenders to more efficiently find each other. In the primary market of debt, borrowers (issuers) secure capital from investors (lenders) in the form of a loan. As with equities, secondary markets provide liquidity. Few investors would lend in the debt market if they were unable to sell the debt on to other investors.

Unlike the market for equity, however, the investor has no ownership stake in the borrowing entity. Instead there is a contractual relationship that requires the borrower to repay the bond holder as it would repay a bank loan.

The advantage of the debt market is that it offers more lenders and more liquidity than can the market for bank loans alone. Banks have limited amounts of capital and need to diversify their loan portfolios. Obviously banks cannot supply the entire demand for borrowed funds. Thus the existence of the public debt markets lowers the cost of borrowing across the economy.

There is no better example of this than the U.S. government and its needs to finance its operations. With over $15 trillion of debt outstanding in 2012, the federal government's appetite for borrowed funds is larger than the capitalization of the twelve largest commercial banks in the world.[1]

---

1   A table appearing in the article "The World's Biggest Banks" in the June 30, 2011 issue of *The Economist* shows tier-one capital for year-end 2010 in $billions for the twelve largest banks in the world. The largest, Bank of America, has approximately $160 billion. Only the top seven exceed $100 billion. Obviously all ten combined could provide a total of tier-one capital of less than $2 trillion.

$\mathcal{D}$ ebt is structured in various forms, generally categorized by the way in which interest is paid. The great majority of debt instruments fall into one of four categories.

❑ **Interest-at-Maturity:** The principal portion of the loan plus interest is paid at maturity.

❑ **Discount Paper:** A note is specified with a given principal to be paid at maturity. The note is then purchased at less than the face value. The difference between the price and the value at maturity constitutes the interest.

❑ **Coupon:** The principal portion of the loan is repaid at maturity. Interest is specified at a percent of the principal and paid periodically.

❑ **Amortized:** The principal and interest are repaid in equal installments over the life of the loan. As the principal decreases from payment to payment, the interest portion of the constant payment decreases and the principal portion increases with every payment.

12.1 - Structure of a Bond

A bond is essentially a contract to pay a series of cash flows specified by the principal and coupon and effective until maturity.

❑ **Coupon:** The rate of interest is called the coupon rate because bonds were originally issued in bearer form, and each bond carried a series of coupons, which the owner would clip off as the payment came due and send it to the issuer's paying agent. Now most bonds are registered, and the coupon is simply a monetary transfer sent directly to the registered owner.

❑ **Principal:** The principal payment is the amount of the loan on which the interest is calculated. Often referred to as the face value, the principal is most commonly repaid at then end of the loan payment on the maturity date.

❑ **Maturity Date:** The date at which the final principal payment is made and the contract expires.

The coupon rate, principal value, and maturity date are specified in the contract between borrower and lender, and engraved on the bond—and thus never change through the life of that bond.

Example 1:

Discovery Café borrows $1,000,000 on August 15, 2012, for four years at 6%. It issues a legal contract that legally obliges Discovery Café to

1]   repay to the contract holder the principle amount of $1,000,000 on August 15, 2016.
2]   to pay to the contract holder $30,000 (½ of 6% of $1,000,000) interest semi-annually. Because the maturity date is August 15, 2016, the semi-annual payments occur February 15 and August 15. The $30,000 paid February 15 pays the interest on the debt from August 15 to February 15, and the $30,000 paid August 15 pays the interest on the debt from February 15 to August 15.

Figure 12-1: This hypothetical Discovery Café Bond specifies a contractual obligation to repay principal of $1,000,000 on August 15, 2016, and to pay semi-annual interest at the rate of 6%

Discovery Café
Subordinated Debenture 6.0%
due August 15, 2016

Discovery Café Incorporated, a corporation of the state of Illinois (hereinafter called the Company) for value received hereby promises to pay the registered holder hereof, on August 15, 2016, the principal sum of
One Million Dollars.
$1,000,000.

Interest to be paid on the 15th day of February and August at the rate of 6% per annum et cetera, etcetera, etcetera...
Issued August 15, 2012

Figure 12-2: The 4-year 6% Discovery Café bond is essentially a contract of nine promissory notes, each of which is due or matures on a different date.

Discovery Café

Principal Value $1,000,000.00
August 15, 2016

$30,000 August 15, 2013	$30,000 August 15, 2014	$30,000 August 15, 2015	$30,000 August 15, 2016
$30,000 February 15, 2013	$30,000 February 15, 2014	$30,000 February 15, 2015	$30,000 February 15, 2016

The time line shows the payments promised under the contract. The semi-annual interest is paid at the end of each relevant six-month period so the final coupon is paid with the principal, when the bond matures

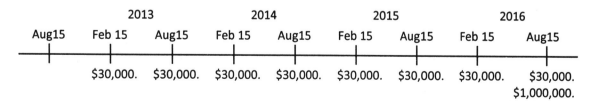

12.2 - Price Yield Determination

Bonds are negotiable, which means that the bond contracts can be bought and sold in a secondary market. When you buy a bond you are buying the remaining interest and principal payments specified in the contract.

The price of a bond reflects the value of the payments remaining in the contract. The yield is the internal rate of return on the investment or price paid.

❏ **Prices:** The price of a bond is the percentage of principal value of the bond agreed to by the buyer and seller. Expressing the price as a percentage eliminates the need to specify separate prices for bonds of different denominations.

❏ **Yield:** The yield on a bond is the internal rate of return on investment. Because the remaining payments on the bond are fixed by contract, the more you pay for the bond, the lower the internal rate of return on investment.

When a bond trades, price and yield are jointly determined in the market. The relationship between price and yield is given by the present value of the payments specified by the bond contract.

$$Price = \sum_{t=1}^{2n} \frac{Coupon_t}{\left(1+\frac{Yld}{2}\right)^t} + \frac{Principal}{\left(1+\frac{Yld}{2}\right)^{2n}} \qquad (Eq\ 12\text{-}1)$$

$$Price = \frac{Coupon}{\left(\frac{Yld}{2}\right)} \left[1 - \frac{1}{\left(1+\frac{Yld}{2}\right)^{2n}}\right] + \frac{Principal}{\left(1+\frac{Yld}{2}\right)^{2n}}$$

The price-yield equation—one equation in two unknowns—emphasizes the interdependency of price and yield

❏ **Price → Yield:** If we know the price then we can calculate the yield. Conversely, we cannot calculate the return on investment if we don't know the amount of the investment.

❏ **Yield → Price:** If we know the yield then we can calculate the price. Conversely, we cannot calculate the price we are willing to pay for a bond if we don't know the yield we require on our investment.

Both price and yield change every time the bond changes hands, but coupon, principal, and maturity are fixed during the life of the bond.

Example 2:

Discovery Café issues a $1,000,000 6% semi-annual coupon bond maturing August 15, 2016. When it issues the bond August 15, 2012, investors demand an internal rate of return of 8% so Discovery Café must issue its bond at $932,672.55 rather than $1,000,000.00

$$P = \frac{Coupon}{\frac{Yd}{2}} * \left[1 - \frac{1}{\left(1 + \frac{Yd}{2} \right)^{2n}} \right] + \frac{Principal}{\left(1 + \frac{Yd}{2} \right)^{2n}}$$

$$= \frac{\$30,000}{0.04} \left[1 - \frac{1}{(1.04)^8} \right] + \frac{\$1,000,000}{(1.04)^8}$$

$$= \$201,982.3462 + \$730,690.205$$

$$= \$932,672.55$$

Example 3:

John Q. Investor can buy one of three bonds. Each is issued by Discovery Café; each has a principal amount of $1,000,000; and each matures August 15, 2016. But each carries a different coupon rate: 4%, 6%, and 8%.

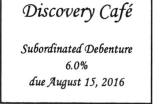

Discovery Café	*Discovery Café*	*Discovery Café*
Subordinated Debenture 4.0% *due August 15, 2016*	*Subordinated Debenture* 6.0% *due August 15, 2016*	*Subordinated Debenture* 8.0% *due August 15, 2016*

12.2.1 - Bonds at Par

If John Q. Investor buys the 6% bond at par he pays face value, $1,000,000. The 6% coupon bond yields 6% internal rate of return because the payments promised by the bond are 6% of the par value of the bond.

The cash flows are the same if John puts the $1,000,000 in a bank account that pays 6% interest, and then withdraws all the interest every six months.

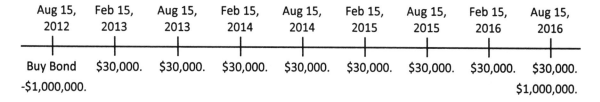

Aug 15, 2012	Feb 15, 2013	Aug 15, 2013	Feb 15, 2014	Aug 15, 2014	Feb 15, 2015	Aug 15, 2015	Feb 15, 2016	Aug 15, 2016
Buy Bond -$1,000,000.	$30,000.	$30,000.	$30,000.	$30,000.	$30,000.	$30,000.	$30,000.	$30,000. $1,000,000.

❑ **At Par:** When a bond sells for precisely its face value then it sells at par. If you buy a bond at par and hold it to maturity then it will generate an internal rate of return on investment equal to its coupon rate.

12.2.2 - Bonds at a Discount

The 4% coupon bond pays interest of $20,000 instead of $30,000 every six months. The only way John Q. Investor will be persuaded to buy this bond is if we make him an offer he can't refuse. If we allow him to buy the bond for $929,803.08 then his investment yields a 6% internal rate of return. This discount in the purchase price makes the 4% bond competitive with the 6% bond purchased at par.

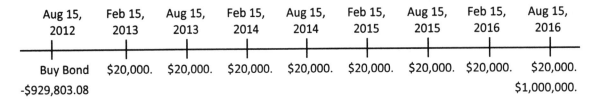

Aug 15, 2012	Feb 15, 2013	Aug 15, 2013	Feb 15, 2014	Aug 15, 2014	Feb 15, 2015	Aug 15, 2015	Feb 15, 2016	Aug 15, 2016
Buy Bond	$20,000.	$20,000.	$20,000.	$20,000.	$20,000.	$20,000.	$20,000.	$20,000.
-$929,803.08								$1,000,000.

❑ **Discount:** When a bond sells at less than its face value it sells at a discount. If you buy a bond at a discount and hold it to maturity then it will generate an internal rate of return on investment higher than its coupon rate.

12.2.3 - Bonds at a Premium

The 8% coupon bond pays interest of $40,000 instead of $30,000 every six months. John Q. Investor finds this the most attractive bond of the three until he finds that he must compete with other buyers who find it equally attractive. Competitive bidding in the market pushes the price up to $1,070,196.92. John refuses to bid any higher than this because he can always get a 6% return on his investment by purchasing the 6% coupon bond at par or the 4% coupon bond at $929,803.08. If he purchases the 8% coupon bond at $1,070,196.92 he will also earn a 6% internal rate of return, but paying more than $1,070,196.92 would make no sense.

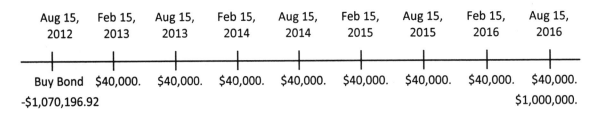

Aug 15, 2012	Feb 15, 2013	Aug 15, 2013	Feb 15, 2014	Aug 15, 2014	Feb 15, 2015	Aug 15, 2015	Feb 15, 2016	Aug 15, 2016
Buy Bond	$40,000.	$40,000.	$40,000.	$40,000.	$40,000.	$40,000.	$40,000.	$40,000.
-$1,070,196.92								$1,000,000.

❑ **Premium:** When a bond sells for more than its face value it sells at a premium. If you buy a bond at a premium and hold it to maturity then it will generate an internal rate of return on investment lower than its coupon rate.

When John purchases his bond he considers the price of the bond, the yield on investment that price will generate, and what yields are available in competing investments, before he buys. When John buys his bond, price and yield are thus jointly determined in the market.

Calculator Techniques 12-1:

Bond Information:

1. The Settlement Date (SDT) is the date we value bond. (mm.ddyy)

2. The coupon (CPN) is the specified coupon rate (%).
3. The Redemption Date (RDT) is the date we redeem the contract and get our investment back
4. The Redemption Value (RV) is the amount we get back expressed in percent of face value (%)

BOND	Enter	Compute
SDT =	8.15.12	
CPN =	6.000	
RDT =	8.15.16	
RV =	100.000	
ACT		
2/Y		
YLD =		6.000
PRI =	100.000	
AI =		0.000

Market Conditions:

❏ ACT means calculate this based on actual days in the year, and 360 means calculate this based on 360 days in the year. Use [2ND][SET] to toggle these values. U.S. corporate and municipal bonds use 360 and U.S. Treasury notes and bonds use actual.

❏ 2/Y means 2 coupon payment per year. 1/Y means one coupon payment per year. Use [2ND][SET] to toggle these values.

Market Information:

Yield (YLD) and Price (PRI) are determined in the market. You must enter one in order to calculate the other. In this example we enter the yield and calculate the price; we can also enter the price to calculate the yield.

❏ The Price (PRI) is the percent of face value paid for the bond (%).
❏ The Yield (YLD) is the internal rate of return (%).
❏ Accrued Interest (AI) is used to adjust for bonds purchased between coupon dates and is expressed in percent of face value (%).

Calculator Techniques 12-2:

The Business Calculator is automatically set to default formats. To reset [2ND][FORMAT] and toggle [2ND][SET] between alternates.

Use Dec = 9 for floating decimals

FORMAT	Enter	Compute
DEC =	9	Set Decimals
DEG		/RAD
US 12-31-1990		EUR 31-12-1990
US 1,000.00		EUR 1.000,00
Chn		/AOS

Chn (chain) means that calculation are made as you enter them. AOS (Algebraic Operating System) means that calculations are made according to algebraic rule as in most scientific calculators.

12.3 - Price Yield Curve

The bond price yield formula

$$Price \quad = f\left(\; Yield \; \right)$$

$$Price \quad = \sum_{t=1}^{2n} \frac{C_t}{\left(1 \; + \; \dfrac{Yd}{2} \right)^t} \quad + \quad \frac{P}{\left(1 \; + \; \dfrac{Yd}{2} \right)^{2n}}$$

represents the continuum of price and yield combinations that can result when the bond trades in the market. The graph of these price yield combinations is called the Price Yield Curve.

Figure 12-3: The Price Yield Curve for the Discovery Café 4 year, 6% Semi-Annual Coupon Bond

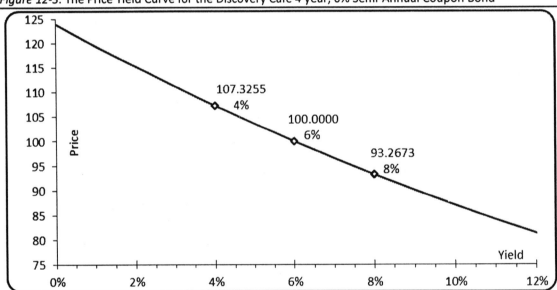

12.4 - Yields

The yield on a bond is the rate of return on an investment under specific assumptions. Thus the precise definition of yield depends on the context in which the term is used.

12.4.1 - Nominal Yield

The nominal yield is the coupon rate. A bond with a 6% coupon rate has a nominal yield of 6%. This means that the coupons pay 6% of the face value every year.

12.4.2 - Current or Income Yield

The current or income yield is the annual income as a percentage of its price.

$$Income\ Yield = \frac{Coupon\ Rate}{Price}$$

(Eq 12-2)

Example 4:

If the 6% August 15, 2016, bond prices to yield 8% (Price = 107.325481), then the current yield is given by

$$Income\ Yield = \frac{6.000\%}{107.325481\%}$$

$$= 5.590\%$$

This means that 5.590% of the invested amount comes back to the investor in income flow every year.

12.4.3 - Promised Yield to Maturity

The promised yield to maturity is the internal rate of return over the life of the bond if all payments under the contract are paid as promised.

The promised yield to maturity is the fully compounded rate of return on a bond bought at the current market price and held to maturity. This is the internal rate of return on the bond and thus uses the net present value calculation.

$$Price = \sum_{t=1}^{2n} \frac{C_t}{\left(1 + \frac{YTM}{2}\right)^t} + \frac{P}{\left(1 + \frac{YTM}{2}\right)^{2n}}$$

There are two assumptions built into the yield-to-maturity calculation:

1) the investor holds the bond to maturity and
2) all coupon payments are reinvested at the computed yield.

Without these assumptions well in mind an investor can succumb to yield illusion.

❑ **Yield illusion:** Yield illusion is the erroneous expectation that a bond will provide its stated yield to maturity without recognizing the reinvestment assumption. During periods of very high interest rates investor "lock in" high yields by buying long bonds. These investors are suffering from yield illusion because they will not get the promised yield to maturity unless they can reinvest the coupon payments at the same high rates.

❑ **Interest-on-Interest:** The income earned on the reinvestment of the coupon payments.

Example 5:

A $1,000 25-year bond with a coupon rate of 8% is purchased at par ($1,000). If you invest $1,000 at 8%, consistently reinvesting all coupon payments again at 8%, for 25 years, you would have $7,106.68. This $7106.68 consists of

❑ $1,000 principal repayment,

❑ $2,000 in coupon repayments ($40 twice a year for 25 years), and

❑ $4,106.68 on interest earned on the coupon payments reinvested at 8%.

$$C\left[\frac{(1+r)^{2n} - 1}{r}\right] \;=\; \$40\left[\frac{(1.04)^{50} - 1}{0.04}\right] \;=\; \$6,106.68$$

If you never reinvest these payment then you finish the 25 years with $3000 rather than $7106.68, and your return on investment is slightly less than 4.444% rather than 8%

$$\$1,000 \;=\; \frac{\$3,000}{\left(1 + \dfrac{0.04443}{2}\right)^{50}} \;=\; \frac{\$7,106.68}{\left(1 + \dfrac{0.08}{2}\right)^{50}}$$

If you reinvest the coupon payments, but at less than 8% then your actual yield on this investment is somewhere between 4.444% and 8%.

12.4.4 - Realized Yield

The realized yield is the holding period yield of a bond that is sold or redeemed before it matures. It is calculated the same way as the yield to maturity but with the holding period rather than the number of years to maturity and with the sale price or redemption price of the bond rather than its par value.

$$P_{market} \;=\; \sum_{t=1}^{2hp} \frac{C_t}{\left(1 + \dfrac{Yld_{hp}}{2}\right)^t} \;+\; \frac{P_{selling}}{\left(1 + \dfrac{Yld_{hp}}{2}\right)^{2hp}}$$

12.4.5 - Effective Annual Rate

The Effective annual rate is the annualized return on an investment.

If *m* is the number of times per year that the interest is compounded and *r* is the nominal rate, then

$$Effective\ annual\ rate = \left(1 + \frac{r}{m}\right)^m - 1 \qquad (Eq\ 12\text{-}3)$$

Example 6:

A $1,000 bond with a 10% coupon or nominal rate will pay out $100 per year; $50 every six months. The effective annual rate is 10.25%

$$\left(1 + \frac{0.10}{2}\right)^2 = 1.1025 = 1 + 10.25\%$$

If interest is continuously compounded ($m \rightarrow \infty$) and *r* is the nominal rate, then

$$Effective\ annual\ rate = e^{rt} - 1 \qquad (Eq\ 12\text{-}4)$$

Example 7:

A $1,000 bank account with a 10% annual interest rate compounded continuously will actually pay out $105.17 per year. The effective annual rate is 10.517%

$$e^{0.10} - 1 = 0.105170918 = 10.517\%$$

❑ **Effective Annual Rate:** Most bonds pay out half the annual rate semi-annually. The effective annual rate is the rate of interest, which provides an identical dollar future value under annual compounding.

❑ **Bond Equivalent Rate:** Restatement of the rate of interest as twice the semi-annual interest rate. This is called the bond equivalent because most U.S. bonds pay out half the stated annual rate every six months.

Chapter 12 - Questions and Problems

12-1:

John Q. Investor has $1,000,000 to invest and is considering two possible investments to be held over a term of four years. The first is a bank account offering interest at 6% per annum, the second is the Discovery Café four-year 6% bond.

A. If John leaves all his funds in the bank account, what will his balance be at the end of four years? Draw the time line for this strategy.

B. If John withdraws $30,000 at the end of each six-month period, what will his balance be at the end of four years? Draw the time line for this strategy. How does this compare to the time line for the Discovery Café bond?

C. If John purchases the Discovery Café bond and deposits each payment from the bond in the bank account, what will his balance be at the end of four years? Draw the time line for this strategy.

12-2:

The price yield equation is given by

$$Price = \sum_{t=1}^{2n} \frac{C_t}{\left(1 + \dfrac{Yld}{2}\right)^t} + \frac{P}{\left(1 + \dfrac{Yld}{2}\right)^{2n}}$$

A. Adjust the price yield equation for a bond with quarterly coupon payments.

B. Adjust the price yield equation for a bond with monthly coupon payments

12-3:

Calculate the price of a 6% August 2016 bond if, when it was issued in August 2012,

A. the prevailing yield was 7%.

B. the prevailing was 5%.

12-4:

You have 6% $1,000,000 bond issued June 1, 2012, and maturing June 1, 2024.

A. John Q. Investor purchased this bond at issue when yields were at 6%. Calculate the price of the bond at that time.

B. Yields increased to 8% by June 2014 when John sold his bond to Warren Buffet. At what price should the bond have changed hands?

C. Yields fell to 4% by June 2018 when Warren sold the bond to you. What price did you pay for the bond?

12-5:

Calculate and draw the price yield curve for an 8%, 20 year bond.

12-6:

John Q. Investor has $1000 to invest. He can either

A. buy a $1000 5% semi-annual coupon bond with 4 years to maturity at par or
B. place the $1000 in a long-term savings account for 4 years at 5% compounded semi-annually.

Draw the timeline for each alternative. In what way do these investments differ?

12-7:

You purchase a 10-year 10% bond at par for $1,000. Directly after you bought the bond the yields fell to 5% and remained at 5% for five years. At this time

A. What is the interest earned on the bond to date?

B. What is the interest-on-interest earned to date?

C. What is the capital gain or loss has accrued to date?

D. What is the yield on this bond?

E. Explain the interaction of price risk and reinvestment risk.

12-8:

A $100 12% bond maturing March 1, 2024, is purchased September 1, 2011 at $147.99. It is sold March 1, 2011, for $118.85

A. What is the yield to maturity on the date of purchase?

B. What is the yield to maturity on the date of sale?

C. What is the realized or holding period yield?

12-9:

John Q. Investor purchases a $10,000 8% bond maturing January 15, 2040, at par on January 15, 2005. John sells the bond July 15, 2012, to Susan Speculator at 98.875, who turns around and sells it to Tyrone Trader six months later at 101.000. Tyrone holds the bond for 10 years and then sells it to the Bears Players Pension Plan at par.

A. What is John's realized yield on this investment?

B. What is Susan's realized yield on this investment?

C. What is Tyrone's realized yield on this investment?

D. What is the Bears Pension Plan realized yield on this investment if the investment manager holds the bond to maturity?

12-10:

You purchase a 12% bond (the nominal rate is 12%).

A. What is the effective annual rate of interest if the bond pays coupon annually?

B. What if the bond pays semi-annually?

C. What if the bond pays quarterly?

D. What if the bond pays monthly?

E. What if interest is compounded continuously?

F. Because the bond remains a 12% bond under all these scenarios, why does the effective annual rate increase with the payment frequency?

$\mathcal{B}$ onds are negotiable. This means that, once issued, they can trade in the secondary market. The primary consideration when a bond trades is the negotiated price and the interest earned since the last payment date. The amount of interest earned will depend on principal, coupon rate, and the exact date on which ownership of the bond officially transfers from seller to buyer.

13.1 - Settlement Date

A trade settles when the buyer and seller fulfill their obligations. The seller delivers the securities, and the buyer pays the price. Different markets settle according to their own practice, often determined by the length of time it takes for the paperwork to catch up to the trade. Equities in the United States settle in three business days. Foreign Exchange market trades settle in two business days.

Treasury Securities are registered book entry, which means that registration changes required when the securities change hands are a simple matter of changing the records. Thus Treasury securities settle on the next business day. Corporate bonds settle through registrations through corporate trustees. This takes longer. Thus corporate securities—equities and debt—settle in three business days.

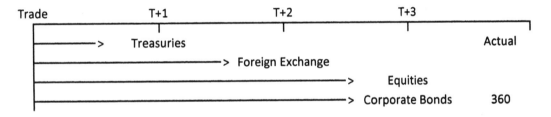

13.2 - Accrued Interest

Coupons are paid in arrears to the registered owner on the coupon date. Thus when the bond trades between coupon dates, the coupon payment must be divided between buyer and seller. How to do so equitably depends on whether the bond trades actual or 360. Treasury securities trade based on actual days in the year; corporate and municipal bonds trade based on 360 days in the year.

Example 1:

John Q. Investor purchases a 6% $1,000,000 two-year bond maturing August 15, 2014, at Issue August 15, 2012. Interest begins to accumulate immediately. Six months later the accumulated interest is paid to the registered owner of the bond.

John receives the first coupon payment of $30,000 February 15, 2012, and begins accumulating interest again on February 16.

John sells the bond at 98.75 for settlement June 13, 2012. The base price of the bond is thus $987,500.00 However, John has accumulated interest from February 16 through to June 13. This accumulated interest will eventually be paid to the registered bond holder as part of the coupon payment due August 15. To compensate John for the interest he earned, the total price of the bond is increased to include compensation for this accrued interest.

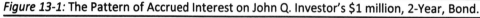

Figure 13-1: The Pattern of Accrued Interest on John Q. Investor's $1 million, 2-Year, Bond.

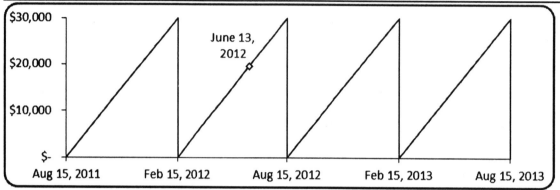

❑ **Base Price:** The base price is the quoted price of the bond. If John sells his bond at the quoted price of 98.75 then the base price of John's million dollar bond is $987,500.00

❑ **Accrued Interest:** Accrued interest is interest earned since the last coupon payment.

❑ **Invoice Price:** The invoice price is the total price of the bond consisting of the base price and accrued interest.

Different markets calculate accrued interest in slightly different ways.

13.3 - Accrued Interest (Actual)

Treasury bond markets trade on actual days in the year basis. If the bond John sells is a Treasury bond we calculate the accrued interest as follows

The coupon period from February 15 to August 15, 2012 is calculated as 182 days. 2012 is a leap year so we include February 29, 2012, in the coupon period

Feb 15 to Aug 15 :

(29-15) + 31 + 30 + 31 + 30 + 31 + 15 = 182 days

John Q. Investor owned the bond, earning interest, for first 119 days.

Feb 15 to June 13:

(29-15) + 31 + 30 +31 + 13 = 119 days

The buyer will hold the bond for 63 days.

June 13 to Aug 15:

(30-13) + 31 +15 = 63 days

The coupon payment is divided accordingly.

Month	Days
January	31
February	28/29
March	31
April	30
May	31
June	30
July	31
August	31
September	30
October	31
November	30
December	31

$$\$30,000 * \frac{63}{182} = \$10,384.62 \qquad \text{buyer's earned interest}$$

$$\$30,000 * \frac{119}{182} = \$19,615.38 \qquad \text{John's earned interest}$$

The invoice price of the bond is the base price of the bond plus accrued interest. Thus in this example the invoice price of the bond is $1,007,115.38

$987,500.00	base price
$19,615.38	accrued interest
1,007,115.38	invoice price

13.3.1 - Calculator Techniques (Actual)

Calculator Techniques 13-1:

The Business Calculator automatically accounts for accrued interest. Thus for the August 15, 2013, $1,000,000 bond, accrued interest (AI) is given as 1.961538% of face value.

1.96153846%* $1,000,000 = $19,615.38

Unfortunately, the bond spreadsheet does not give the number of days in the coupon period (182), nor the number of days used (63) to calculate this accrued income.

BOND	Enter	Compute
SDT =	6.13.12	
CPN =	6.000	
RDT =	8.15.13	
RV =	100.000	
ACT		
2/Y		
YLD =		7.11877943
PRI =	98.750	
AI =		1.96153846

Calculator Techniques 13-2:

For the days calculation we use the date spreadsheet.

Use [2ND] [DATE] to open the date spreadsheet. Enter the beginning and ending dates for the period you wish to calculate. Make sure that the calculation is set to ACT (for actual days) and compute DBD (days between dates).

The calculator confirms the 63 days between the settlement date and the next coupon date.

DATE	Enter	Compute
DT1 =	6.13.12	
DT2 =	8.15.12	
DBD =		63
ACT		
2/Y		
DT1 =		WED =
DT2 =		WED =

If you now return to the two dates you entered and hit compute, the calculator will tell you that the settlement date was a Wednesday.

13.3.2 - Yield-to-Maturity Calculations (Actual)

The calculation of the yield to maturity is also affected because we now hold the bond for a partial period to the first coupon payment, rather than for the whole six months.

	Aug 15, 2012	Feb 15, 2013	Aug 15, 2013
	$30,000.	$30,000.	$1,030,000.

June 13, 2012

← 63 days
← 63 days + 1 semi-annual period
← 63 days + 2 semi-annual periods

The calculator gives a yield to maturity of 7.11877943%. Calculating the present value of the bond using a semi-annual rate of 3.55938971 gives us:

$$= \frac{\$30,000}{1.0355938971^{\left(\frac{63}{182}\right)}} + \frac{\$30,000}{1.0355938971^{\left(1 + \frac{63}{182}\right)}} + \frac{\$1,030,000}{1.0355938971^{\left(2 + \frac{63}{182}\right)}}$$

$$= \quad \$29,638.987 \quad + \quad \$28,620.280 \quad + \quad \$948,856.118$$

$$= \quad \$1,007,115.38 \qquad\qquad Q.E.D.$$

Note that in each term $\left(1 + \frac{Yld}{2}\right)^{t}$ in the price calculation, t includes the 63 days as $\frac{63}{182}$ of a semi-annual period.

13.4 - Accrued Interest (30/360)

Corporate bonds trade on a 30/360 basis. This means that we assume 30 days in every month and 360 days in every year. This tends to confuse the general population, which collectively scratches its head over a convention that pays interest every February 29 and 30 but refuses to pay interest for January 31.

If the 6% August 13 bond purchased from John Q. Investor is a corporate bond then the actual trade took place June 10, 2012, for settlement June 13, 2012.

Feb 15, 2012	Aug 15, 2012	Feb 15, 2013	Aug 15, 2013
$30,000.	$30,000.	$30,000.	$1,030,000.
118 days –	– 62 days		
June 13, 2012			

By convention, every month has 30 days, every coupon period has 180 days, and every year has 360 days.

The coupon period from February 15 to August 15, 2012 is calculated as 180 days. The leap year issue is immaterial because February enters the calculation with 30 days.

Feb 15 to Aug 15 :
(30-15) + 30 + 30 + 30 + 30 + 30 + 15 = 180 days

John Q. Investor owned the bond, earning interest, for first 118 days.

Feb 15 to June 13:
(30-15) + 30 + 30 +30 + 13 = 118 days

The buyer will hold the bond for 62 days.

June 13 to Aug 15:
(30-13) + 30 +15 = 62 days

Month	Days
January	30
February	30
March	30
April	30
May	30
June	30
July	30
August	30
September	30
October	30
November	30
December	30

The coupon payment is divided accordingly.

$$\$30,000 * \frac{62}{180} = \$10,333.33 \qquad \text{buyer's earned interest}$$

$$\$30,000 * \frac{118}{180} = \$19,666.67 \qquad \text{John's earned interest}$$

The invoice price of the bond is the base price of the bond plus accrued interest. Thus in this example the invoice price of the bond is $1,007,166.67

$987,500.00	base price
$19,666.67	accrued interest
$1,007,166.67	invoice price

13.4.1 - Calculator Techniques (30/360)

<table>
<tr><td colspan="3">Calculator Techniques 13-3:</td><td>BOND</td><td>Enter</td><td>Compute</td></tr>
</table>

	BOND	Enter	Compute
	SDT =	6.13.12	
	CPN =	6.000	
	RDT =	8.15.13	
	RV =	100.000	
	360		
	2/Y		
	YLD =		7.11959316
	PRI =	98.750	
	AI =		1.96666667

Calculator Techniques 13-3:

The Business Calculator automatically accounts for accrued interest. Note that the calculator is set for a 360-day rather than an actual year.

For the August 15, 2013, $1,000,000 bond, accrued interest (AI) is given as 1.96666667% of face value.

$$1.96666667\% * \$1,000,000 = \$19,666.67$$

The invoice price is thus
$$\$987,500.00 + \$19,666.67 = \$1,007,166.67$$

And the yield to maturity is 7.11959316%

Calculator Techniques 13-4:

The date spreadsheet confirms 62 days to the next coupon payment. Note that there is no leap year problem. February has neither 28 nor 29 days; it has 30 days, regardless of the year.

If you now return to the two dates you entered and hit compute the calculator will tell you that the settlement date was a Wednesday.

DATE	Enter	Compute
DT1 =	6.13.12	
DT2 =	8.15.12	
DBD =		63
ACT		
2/Y		
DT1 =		WED =
DT2 =		WED =

13.4.2 - Yield-to-Maturity Calculations (30/360)

Again, the calculation of the yield to maturity is also affected because we now hold the bond for a partial period to the first coupon payment, rather than for the whole six months.

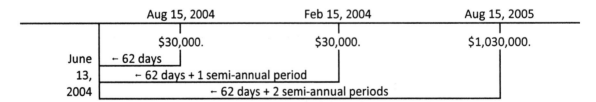

We calculate the net present value of the bond using a semi-annual rate of 3.559797 (7.11959316%/2)

$$= \frac{\$30,000}{1.03559797^{\left(\frac{62}{180}\right)}} + \frac{\$30,000}{1.03559797^{\left(1 + \frac{62}{180}\right)}} + \frac{\$1,030,000}{1.03559797^{\left(2 + \frac{62}{180}\right)}}$$

$$= \quad \$29,640.719 \quad + \quad \$28,621.840 \quad + \quad \$948,904.099$$

$$= \quad \$1,007,166.67 \qquad\qquad Q.E.D.$$

13.4.3 - The 31st of the Month (30/360)

The assumption of 30 days per month and 360 days per year raises the issue of what to do on the 31st of the month.

In the United States the 31st of the month is considered to be the 1st of the following month. Thus a bond that settles on May 31 is calculated as though it were June 1.

In Europe the 31st of the month is considered to be the 30th of the month. Thus a bond that settles on May 31 is calculated as though it were May 30.

Example 2:

John Q. Investor purchases a $10,000 Discovery Café 6% August 15, 2024, bond at 99½ to settle at the end of May 2012.

This is a U.S. corporate bond.

Calculator Techniques 13-5:	BOND	Enter	Compute
	SDT =	5.31.12	
Using our business calculator we calculate accrued interest on	CPN =	6.000	
	RDT =	8.15.24	
May 30, 2012: AI = 1.7500% * $10,000 => $175.00	RV =	100.000	
May 31, 2012: AI = 1.7667% * $10,000 => $176.67	360		
June 1, 2012: AI = 1.7667% * $10,000 => $176.67	2/Y		
	YLD =		6.05727776
Settlement on May 31 generates the same results as	PRI =	99.500	
settlement on June 1.	AI =		1.76666667

Example 3:

John Q. Investor purchases a $10,000 Café Découverte 6% August 15, 2024, bond at 99½ to settle at the end of May 2012.

This is a European corporate bond.

Calculator Techniques 13-6:	BOND	Enter	Compute
	SDT =	31.05.12	
If we had a European business calculator we could calculate accrued interest on	CPN =	6.000	
	RDT =	15.08.24	
May 30, 2012: AI = 1.7500% * $10,000 => $175.00	RV =	100.000	
May 31, 2012: AI = 1.7500% * $10,000 => $175.00	360		
June 1, 2012: AI = 1.7667% * $10,000 => $176.67	2/Y		
	YLD =		6.05726392
Settlement on May 31 generates the same results as settlement on May 30.	PRI =	99.500	
	AI =		1.75000000

Note that your Texas Instruments BA II Plus calculates according to U.S. corporate bond convention, even if you set it to display dates and numbers in European format. However Excel will calculate bonds according to either U.S. corporate (basis = 0) or European corporate (basis = 4) convention.

Chapter 13 - Questions and Problems

13-1:

You put in an order for a $1,000,000. 12 ⅜% May 15, 2025, bond at 132.75. It settles June 13, 2018. If this is a U.S. Treasury bond

A. What is the trade date?

B. What is the purchase price of this bond before accrued interest?

C. Accrued interest for how many days adds how much to the price of the bond?

D. What is the total invoice price of the bond?

E. When will you receive your first coupon?

F. How much will you receive on this first coupon payment date?

G. On the first coupon payment date you will have earned how much in interest over how many days?

H. What is the yield to maturity?

I. Set up the net present value / yield to maturity calculation.

J. How do the answers to each of these questions change if this is a corporate bond?

13-2:

You put in an order for a $1,000,000. 9% June 1, 2019, bond. It settles May 30, 2018, priced to yield 7% If this is a U.S. Treasury bond:

A. What is the trade date?

B. What is the purchase price of this bond before accrued interest?

C. Accrued Interest for how many days adds how much to the price of the bond?

D. What is the total invoice price of the bond?

E. When will you receive your first coupon?

F. How much will you receive on this first coupon payment date?

G. On the first coupon payment date you will have earned how much in interest over how many days?

H. What is the yield to maturity?

I. Set up the net present value / yield to maturity calculation.

J. How do the answers to each of these questions change if this is a corporate bond?

Chapter 13 - Financial Models

13.1 - Bond Calculator

Objective:
To profile a bond, given a market yield, and generate the price yield curve.

Formats:
A. Begin by formatting the template[1].
B. Set the Titlebars. Select B1:D1 and either click Title in the Finance Ribbon or use the shortcut Shift+Ctrl+T. Do the same for B11:D11, B17:E17, F1:G1, I1:J1, and B25:J25.
C. Set the inputs to Finance Blue. Select D3:D8 and either click on [Finance Fonts][Blue] in the Finance Ribbon or use the shortcut Shift+Ctrl+B. Do the same for D13:D14.
D. Set the formats for the input.
    I.   Principal is in dollars and cents so click on the $ in the Finance Ribbon or use the shortcut Shift+Ctrl+$.
    II.   Coupon and Yield are both in percent so click on the % in the Finance Ribbon or use the shortcut Shift+Ctrl+%. Increase the number of decimal places by clicking on the ←0.0 in the Finance Ribbon.
    III. Maturity and Settlement are both dates so use Ctrl+1 to open the Format Applet. From the menu on the left choose Date. Select the appropriate date format from the right hand side.
E. Hide the spacers in A1, E1, H1, and K1 by setting the font to white-on-white. Either click on [Finance Fonts] [White] in the Finance Ribbon or use the shortcut Shift+Ctrl+W.

Drop-Down Boxes:
F. A drop-down box allows the user to select from a specific set of inputs. To create the drop-down box begin in D7.
    I.   Click on [Data Validation] in the Finance Ribbon.
    II.   In the Data Validation applet, under [Allow], select list. This triggers the checkbox [In-Cell dropdown], checked by default.
    III. Under [Source], select range $D$18:$D20.
    IV.   [OK]
G. Create another drop-down box in D8 restricted to the data in $D$22:$D$23

Hidden Codes:
H. Set a hidden code in C7 with a Vertical Lookup. C7=VLOOKUP(D7,$D$18:$E$20,2,0) matches the user input in D7 with the first column of $D$18:$E$20 and returns the matching value in column 2. The 0 forces Excel to respond only to an exact match.
I. Test this parameter by selecting the type of bond with the drop-down box in D7. Verify that C7 shows the correct code in every instance.
J. Hide the code by setting the color of the type to white.
K. Set a hidden code in C8 with a VLOOKUP() to $D$22:$E$23

---

1   The guidelines assume that you are running the Finance Ribbon designed for Financial Markets: A Practicum.

Name Cells:

L.   Name cells in column D according to the naming conventions in our Business Calculator. The names are specified in column C. So the principal in D3 is named P, the Coupon rate in D4 is named CPN, et cetera. By naming these cells now, it makes our formulae easier to compose.

M.   To check or edit names use the Name Manager in the Finance Ribbon.

Calculate Bond Price:

N.   Calculate the bond price quote into D15 using Price(): D15= Price(SDT,RDT,CPN,YLD,100,$B$8,$B$7). Format to at least four decimal places. Even though this is a percent of face value there is no % in the price.

Bond Calculator:

O.   Excel provides a number of built-in excel functions. They are constructed in the same way as the =Price() function.

    I.   G8 =COUPPCD() Date of the previous coupon payment.

    II.   G9 =COUPNCD() Date of the next coupon payment.

    III.   G10 =COUPNUM() The number of coupon payments remaining to maturity.

    IV.   G12 =COUPDAYBS() Number of days from the previous coupon payment to the settlement date.

    V.   G13 =COUPDAYSNC() Number of days from the settlement date to the next coupon payment.

    VI.   G14 =COUPDAYS() Number of days in the semi-annual period. The accrued interest is calculated from the coupon, the days to accrue, and the days in the semi-annual period.

P.   Verify that the answers given by your excel calculator are the same as those given by your business calculator.

Q.   Calculate the Coupon in G7 as = P*CPN/$C$8.

R.   Calculate the Base Price in G3 as = P*PRI/100.

S.   Calculate Accrued Interest in G4 as = Coupon * Days to Accrue / days in Semi-Annual Period

T.   Calculate the Invoice price in G5 as the sum of the base price and accrued interest.

U.   Format appropriately. Remember to add top borders to G5 and G14 to indicate that these numbers are totals.

Yields:

V.   Calculate Nominal Yield as =CPN.

W.   Calculate Income Yield as =100*CPN/PRI.

X.   Calculate Yield to Maturity as = YLD.

Y.   Calculate Capital Gain as $= Frequency * \left(\sqrt[Coupons\ Remaining]{\dfrac{Principal}{Invoice\ Price}} - 1 \right).$

So for our current example this is $2 \left(\sqrt[97]{\dfrac{10{,}000.00}{\$13{,}438.45}} - 1 \right) = 2 \left(\dfrac{10{,}000.00}{\$13{,}438.45}^{1/97} - 1 \right).$

This translates into XL as =$C$8*(((P/G5)^(1/$G$10))-1)

Price Yield Curve:

Z.   Format the yields in column I to percent, so click on the % in the Finance Ribbon or use the shortcut Shift+Ctrl+%.

AA.   Price the bond to yield 0%, so J3 =PRICE(SDT,RDT,CPN,I3,100,$C$8,$C$7). Note that C7 and C8 are locked so that the formula consistently points to the frequency and basis.

AB.   Format to four decimal places.

AC. Copy-drag the formula down the column or highlight J3:J23 and use the shortcut Ctrl+D to copy down.

AD. Pick a market yield at random and verify your model's results with your business calculator.

Price Yield Curve Chart:

AE. Highlight the price yield curve data I3:J23 and click on the [XY Scatter Charts (with smooth lines)] in the Finance Ribbon.

AF. Format by removing the legend (select with your mouse and hit the delete button).

AG. Format the prices in the Y axis to eliminate the unnecessary zeros.

AH. Format the Horizontal Gridlines so that they blend into the background. To do this use [Chart Layout] and select [Vertical (Value) Axis Major Gridlines] from the drop-down list at the left. [Format selection]. Set Line Color and Line Style to suit.

AI. Format the data series by setting the [Marker Options] to none, the [Line Color] to a color of your choice, and the [Line Style] to 1.0 or 1.5 points and smoothed line.

AJ. Add the current price and yield to the chart. To do this click on the chart. Under [Chart Design] [Select Data] [Add]. Specify the Series X values as $D$14 and the Series Y values as $D$15. Nothing will show on the graph, but the second series is there.

AK. Format the second series. To do this use [Chart Layout] and select [Series 2] from the drop-down menu on the left hand side. [Format selection]. Set the [Marker Options] to Built-in, [Marker Fill] to solid fill and choose a color, [Marker Line Color] to Solid Line and choose a color, and [Marker Line Style] and set the width (1.5pt should do it).

AL. Add the label. Select the marker you created in the previous step and use [Chart Layout] [Data labels] [More Data Label Options] and, under [Label Options], click on both X value and Y value. Keep in mind that the label will reflect the format in the cells to which the label is linked. If you change the market yield in D14, then the model will recalculate, and the label will move to reflect the new market yield and price. However, if you click in the label box and change the format directly, then XL breaks the link and, though the label will move, it will no longer reflect the recalculated data.

AM. In the View Ribbon de-click Gridlines or use the shortcut Alt+WVG

Bond Information				Bond Calculator			Yield	Price
Principal	P	$	10,000	Base Price:	$	18,512.52	0%	485.000
Coupon	CPN		8.000%	Accrued Interest:	$	300.00	1%	366.872
Maturity	RDT		May 31, 2061	Invoice Price:	$	18,812.52	2%	284.866
							3%	226.897
		US Corporate		Coupon:	$	400.00	4%	185.125
		Semi-Annual		Last Coupon Date:		November 30, 2012	5%	154.419
				Next Coupon Date:		May 31, 2013	6%	131.384
				Coupons Remaining:		97	7%	113.752
Market Information							8%	99.985
				Days to Accrue:		135	9%	89.033
Settlement	SDT		April 15, 2013	Days to Next Coupon:		45	10%	80.164
Yield	YLD		4.000%	Days in Semi-Annual Period:		180	11%	72.865
Price	PRI		185.1252				12%	66.767
				Nominal Yield:		8.000%	13%	61.604
Excel Function Codes				Income Yield:		4.321%	14%	57.181
		Treasury	1	Yield to Maturity:		4.000%	15%	53.350
		US Corporate	0	Capital Gain:		-1.299%	16%	50.001
		European Corporate	4				17%	47.049
							18%	44.426
		Annual	1				19%	42.080
		Semi-Annual	2				20%	39.970

Price Yield Curve

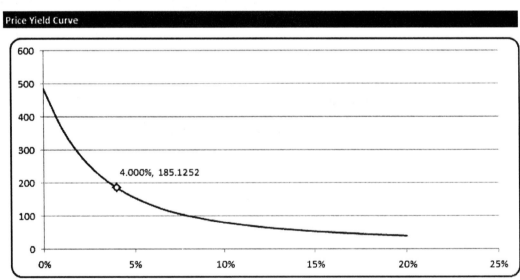

4.000%, 185.1252

$\mathcal{A}$ bond specifies the details of how debt, principal and interest, is to be repaid over time. Therefore, in order to value a bond, in terms of either price or yield on investment, we must first have a fundamental understanding of the relationship between interest rates and time.

14.1 - The Yield Structure

Six primary attributes are significant in determining the yield of a bond:

- ❑ **Term to maturity:** The life of the bond contract,
- ❑ **Coupon rate:** The interest specified by the bond contract,
- ❑ **Call provisions:** The contractual provisions whereby the bond can be paid off early,
- ❑ **Liquidity:** The ability to buy or sell quickly without affecting the price,
- ❑ **Risk of default:** The risk that the issuer will not pay coupon and/or principal when it is due, and
- ❑ **Tax status:** How income and capital gain are treated under the tax law.

Think of the yield structure as a six-dimensional diagram. Because we have trouble with six-dimensional diagrams, we generally hold five attributes constant and examine the sixth. Thus the yield structure for Treasury issues examines the relationship between yield and term to maturity for a zero-coupon bond, with no call provisions, high liquidity, no credit risk, and a zero tax rate.

- ❑ **Term Structure:** The term structure of interest rates is the relationship between the term to maturity and the yield to maturity for a sample of comparable instruments. By holding the other five determinants of yield constant, we ensure that the difference in yield between two bonds is due to the difference in their terms to maturity and not to a difference in coupon or risk.

- ❑ **Yield Curve:** The yield curve is the graphic representation of the term structure.

14.2 - Interest Rates Under Certainty

The relationship between interest rates over time is such that for any rate r over T periods

$$1 + r_T = \sqrt[T]{\prod_{t=0}^{T-1} (1 + r_t)} \qquad \text{(Eq 14-1)}$$

- ❑ **Spot Rate:** The spot rate is the year rate of interest now: r_0.

- ❑ **Forward Rate:** The forward rate is the interest rate contractually guaranteed for some future date: r_t, $t \neq 0$

  - ❑ r_1: The one-year rate, one year forward, is the one-year rate that will be in effect one year from now:
  - ❑ r_2: The one-year rate, two years forward, is the one-year rate that will be in effect two years from now:

Figure 14-1: Timeline for Interest Rates where t=0 on January 1, 2014

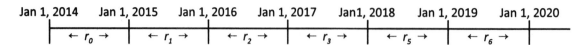

Example 1:

The Bank of Champaign has a series of retail certificates of deposit (CDs). The rates were set today. The one-year rate is set at 3.0% and the two-year rate is set at 4.0%. If John Q. Investor puts $1,000 in a two-year CD for two years he will get

$$\$1,000.(1.04)^2 = \$1,081.60$$

John's crystal ball tells him that one year from now the one-year rate will be set at 5%. If he puts $1,000 in a rolling one-year CD for two years he will get

$$\$1,000.00 \ (1.03)(1.05) = \$1,081.50$$

John is better off with the two-year guaranteed rate. He can also calculate that he is better off with the two-year rate so long as the one-year forward rate remains below 5.0097%

$$(1.04)^2 = (1.03)(1.050097)$$

The crystal ball allows us to predict the forward rates with certainty.

Example 2:

Assume again that the rate on the one-year CD is 3%. My crystal ball tells me that the one-year rates for the next four years will be 5%, 6%, 4%, and 2%, respectively.

Figure 14-2: Time line generated from my crystal ball

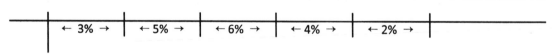

I can now calculate the spot rates:

1-year rate	3%		=	3.000%	=	3.0%
2-year rate	$\sqrt[2]{(1.03 * 1.05)} = 1.039952$		=	3.995%	=	4.0%
3-year rate	$\sqrt[3]{(1.03 * 1.05 * 1.06)} = 1.046592$		=	4.659%	=	4.7%
4-year rate	$\sqrt[4]{(1.03 * 1.05 * 1.06 * 1.04)} = 1.044940$		=	4.494%	=	4.5%
5-year rate	$\sqrt[5]{(1.03 * 1.05 * 1.06 * 1.04 * 1.02)} = 1.039904$		=	3.990%	=	4.0%

Note that the spot rate is a geometric average of the forward rates over the relevant time period. Thus when the forward rate is higher than the spot rate then the spot rate increases; when the forward rate is lower than the spot rate then the spot rate decreases.

Figure 14-3: Calculating Spot Rates from Future Rates in Example 2

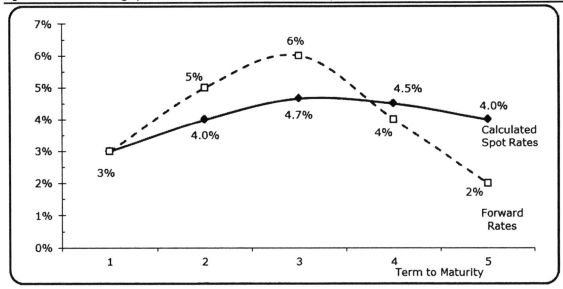

14.3 - Interest Rates Under Uncertainty

We derive the term structure of interest rates under certainty only because a textbook crystal ball predicts interest rates with certainty. In reality there are no crystal balls, and the expected one-year rate is not observable. But the two-year rate is observable.

$$\left(1 + r_{T\ year} \right)^T \left(1 + E[r_T] \right) = \left(1 + r_{year\ T+1} \right)^{T+1} \qquad \textit{(Eq 14-2)}$$

Example 3:

If we observe a one-year rate of 2.0% and a two-year rate of 2.6%, we can calculate that the market expects the one-year rate in one-year to be 3.204%.

$$1.020 * (1 + E[r_1]) = 1.026^2$$

$$1 + E[r_1] = 1.03203529$$

$$E[r_1] = 3.204\%$$

Example 4:

If we observe a four-year rate of 3.4% and a five-year rate of 3.5%, we can calculate that the market expects the one-year rate four years from now to be 3.901%.

$$(1.034)^4 (1 + E[r_4]) = (1.035)^5$$

$$E[r_4] = 0.03900968 = 3.901\%$$

Example 5:

Observed interest rates are 2.0%, 2.6%, 3.1%, 3.4%, and 3.5% for one-, two-, three-, four-, and five-year terms. We calculate the market-implied expectations of the one-year rates for the next four years

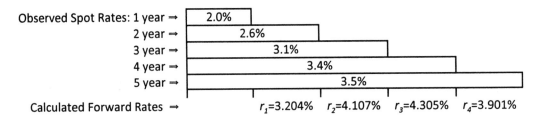

Figure 14-4: Calculating Future Rates from Spot Rates in Example 5

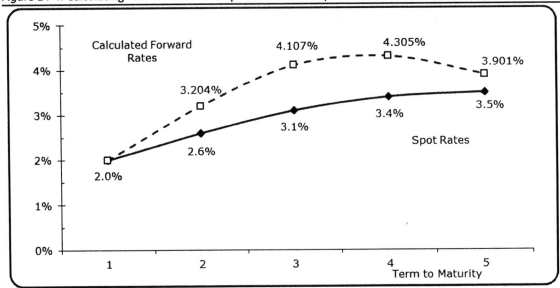

14.4 - Partial Periods and Compounding

The same pattern of interest rates prevails when interest rates span, and are compounded, over uneven or different time periods.

Example 6:

> John Q. Investor deposits $5,000 into a super-saver account with his local bank on December 1. The bank calculates and credits interest at the end of every calendar quarter on an actual day basis and resets the rate for the following quarter. John withdraws the entire balance on January 27.

Figure 14-5: Timeline for Interest Rates in JQ's Account

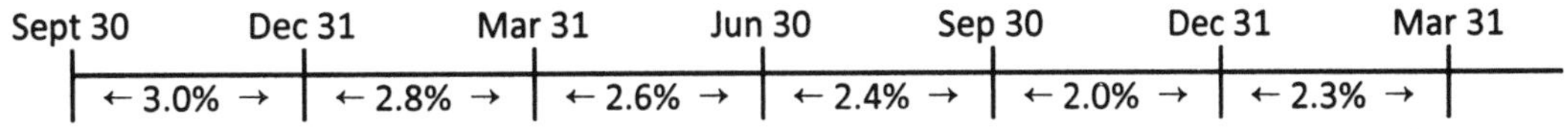

Sept 30	Dec 31	Mar 31	Jun 30	Sep 30	Dec 31	Mar 31
← 3.0% →	← 2.8% →	← 2.6% →	← 2.4% →	← 2.0% →	← 2.3% →	

John calculates his interest rate for the 16-month period as 2.48%. His calculations include the 30 days in December out of a 92-day quarter, 4 full quarters, and 27 days in January out of a 90-day quarter.

$$\left(1+\frac{\bar{r}}{4}\right)^{5\ 72/115} = \left(1+\frac{0.030}{4}\right)^{30/92}\left(1+\frac{0.028}{4}\right)\left(1+\frac{0.026}{4}\right)\left(1+\frac{0.024}{4}\right)\left(1+\frac{0.020}{4}\right)\left(1+\frac{0.023}{4}\right)^{27/90}$$

$$\frac{\bar{r}}{4} = \sqrt[5\ 72/115]{1.02899313} - 1$$

$$\bar{r} = 2.4789\%$$

14.5 - Deriving the Term Structure from Coupon Bonds

Our objective is to construct the yield curve. To do this we need a series of bonds, each with a different term to maturity, so we can measure and chart their yields. If the bonds are identical in every other respect (ceteris paribus) then any differences in yield must be due to term to maturity.

❑ **Ceteris Paribus:** Ceteris Paribus is Latin for all other things held constant.

To accomplish this we use Treasury securities. Treasury securities are negotiable securities representing U.S. government debt. Treasuries are considered free of credit risk because they are backed by the "full faith and credit" of the U.S. government. Income from Treasury securities are tax-exempt at the state and local level but taxable at the federal level.

If we construct our yield curve with Treasury securities then we know the bonds are identical in tax status, call provisions, liquidity, and default risk. However, the coupon rate will be a factor in our calculations.

14.5.1 - Direct Observations

We research Treasury rates and find the following information on U.S. Treasury bills. Because Treasury bills are money market instruments with no periodic coupon payments, the observed yields can be mapped directly into our zero-coupon yield curve.

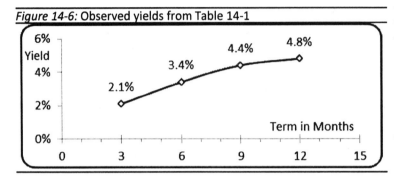

Figure 14-6: Observed yields from Table 14-1

Table 14-1:	Treasury Bill Rates
Term	Yield
3m	2.10%
6m	3.40%
9m	4.40%
12m	4.80%
15m	?
18m	?

14.5.2 - Calculating the Zero Coupon Yield : 15 months

There are no T-bills with a term to maturity of more than twelve months. However we find a 5.00% Treasury note with fifteen months left to maturity yielding 5.25%. The note matures August 15, 2014, and is priced at 99.6922 to settle May 15, 2013. Essentially we repeat example 5, but under real-world conditions.

Figure 14-7: 5% Treasury Note with Fifteen Months to Maturity

August 15, 2014	*Department of the Treasury*
	The principal sum of $10,000.[00]
	with interest calculated at 5.0%
	$250.[00] $250.[00]

We calculate the invoice price of the $10,000 note at $10,092.15

Table 14-2:	Treasury Bond Price Calculation		
		Quote	$10,000 Note
Base Price		99.692200	$9,969.22
89/181 days Accrued Interest		1.229282	$122.90
Invoice Price		100.921482	$10,092.15
Yield to Maturity		5.2500%	

Figure 14-8: Timeline for the 15-month Treasury Bond

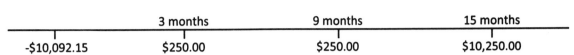

	3 months	9 months	15 months
-$10,092.15	$250.00	$250.00	$10,250.00

To calculate the 15 month, zero-coupon rate we use the fact that a Treasury Note with 15 months to maturity can theoretically be broken down into three components:

❑ a 3-month bill that we can value at the 3 month rate,
❑ a 9-month bill that we can value at the 9 month rate, and
❑ a 15-month bill that we can use to calculate the 15 month rate

This is the same as saying that a Treasury note that generates $250, $250, and $10,250 over the next 3-, 9-, and 15- month periods, respectively, must have the same price and yield as a portfolio of three zero coupon Treasury bills that generate $250, $250, and $10,250 over the next 3-,9-,and 15- month periods, respectively.

The price of $10,092.15 must reflect the 3-month rate on the first coupon payment, the 9-month rate on the second coupon payment, and the 15-month rate on the final coupon and principal payment. Therefore we calculate the present value of the first coupon at the 3-month rate of 2.1% and the second coupon at the 9-month rate of 4.4%.

Figure 14-9: Timeline for the 15-month Treasury Bond Separated Components

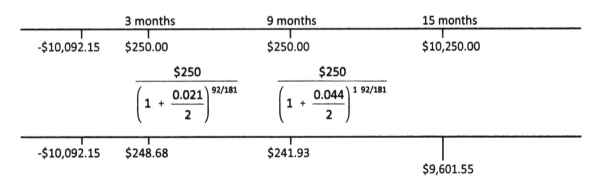

	3 months	9 months	15 months
-$10,092.15	$250.00	$250.00	$10,250.00

$$\frac{\$250}{\left(1 + \dfrac{0.021}{2}\right)^{92/181}} \qquad \frac{\$250}{\left(1 + \dfrac{0.044}{2}\right)^{1\ 92/181}}$$

	3 months	9 months	15 months
-$10,092.15	$248.68	$241.93	
			$9,601.55

The remaining value of the bond, $9,601.55, must come from the final payment due in 15 months. We should then be able to calculate the 15 month rate:

$$\$9,601.55 = \frac{\$10,250}{\left(1 + \dfrac{Yld}{2}\right)^{2\ 92/181}}$$

$$Yld = 2\left[\sqrt[2\ 92/181]{\frac{\$10,250}{\$9,601.55}} - 1\right]$$

$$Yld = 0.05279$$

Figure 14-10: Zero-Coupon Treasury Yield Curve to 15 Months

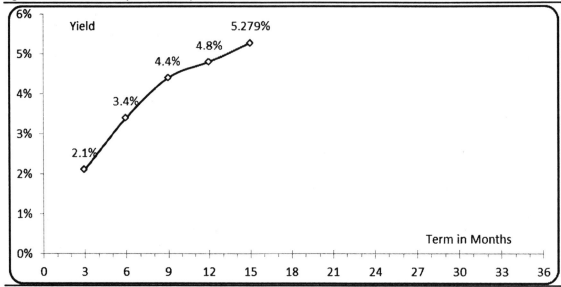

14.5.3 - Calculating the Zero-Coupon Yield : 18 months

We find a 4.50% Treasury note with eighteen months left to maturity yielding 5.30%. The note matures November 15, 2014, and is priced at 98.8609 to settle May 15, 2013.

Again, we repeat example 5, but under real-world conditions.

Figure 14-11: 4.5% Treasury Note with Eighteen Months to Maturity

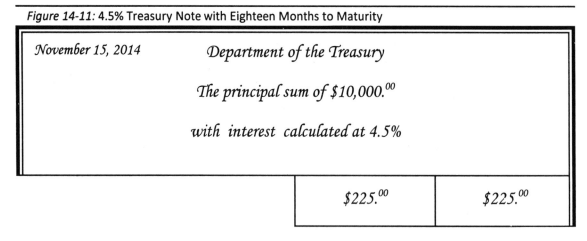

We calculate the invoice price of the $10,000 note at $10,092.15

Table 14-3: Treasury Bond Price Calculation

	Quote	$10,000 Note
Base Price	98.860900	$9,886.09
89/181 days Accrued Interest	0.000000	$0.00
Invoice Price	98.860900	$9,886.09
Yield to Maturity	5.3000%	

Figure 14-12: Timeline for the 18-month Treasury Bond

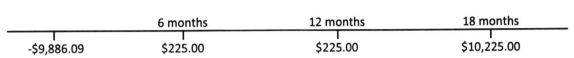

	6 months	12 months	18 months
-$9,886.09	$225.00	$225.00	$10,225.00

To calculate the 18-month, zero-coupon rate we use the fact that a Treasury note with 18 months to maturity can theoretically be broken down into three components:

- ❑ a 6-month bill that we can value at the 6-month rate,
- ❑ a 12-month bill that we can value at the 12-month rate, and
- ❑ a 18-month bill that we can use to calculate the 18-month rate

This is the same as saying that a Treasury note that generates $225, $225, and $10,225 over the next 6-, 12-, and 18- month periods, respectively, must have the same price and yield as a portfolio of three zero coupon Treasury bills that generate $225, $225, and $10,225 over the next 6-,12-,and 18- month periods, respectively.

The price of $9,886.09 must reflect the 6-month rate on the first coupon payment, the 12-month rate on the second coupon payment, and the 18-month rate on the final coupon and principal payment. Therefore we calculate the present value of the first coupon at the 6-month rate of 3.4% and the second coupon at the 12-month rate of 4.8%.

Figure 14-13: Timeline for the 18-month Treasury Bond Separated Components

	6 months	12 months	18 months
-$9,886.09	$225.00	$225.00	$10,225.00
	$\dfrac{\$225}{\left(1 + \dfrac{0.034}{2}\right)^1}$	$\dfrac{\$225}{\left(1 + \dfrac{0.048}{2}\right)^2}$	
-$9,886.09	$221.24	$214.58	
			$9,450.27

The remaining value of the bond, $9,450.27, must come from the final payment due in 18 months. We should then be able to calculate the 18 month rate:

$$\$9,450.27 = \frac{\$10,250}{\left(1 + \dfrac{Yld}{2}\right)^3}$$

$$Yld = 2\left[\sqrt[3]{\frac{\$10,250}{\$9,450.27}} - 1\right]$$

$$Yld = 0.05322$$

Figure 14-14: Zero-Coupon Treasury Yield Curve to 18 Months

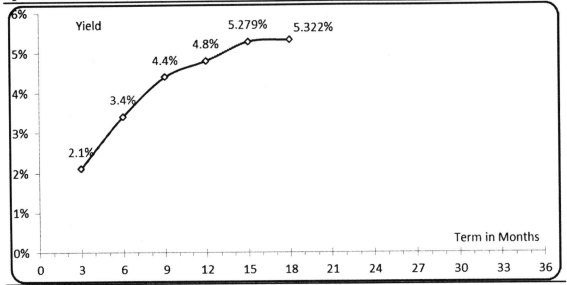

❑ **Bootstrapping:** Continuing this process in 3-month increments is known as bootstrapping rates from coupon securities. If we did this out to a 360-month term, we would have extracted the term structure of interest rates across a 30-year time horizon.

14.5.4 - The Shape of the Yield Curve

Three theories attempt to explain the shape of the yield curve.

❑ **Expectations Hypothesis:** Under the expectations hypothesis the yield curve reflects the short period yields expected in the future. (This is what we used in the example.) Thus an inverted yield curve results when interest rates are expected to fall. Investors lock in higher yields by investing in long-term bonds. They bid up the prices of long-term issues (forcing yields to decline) and avoid short-term issues (making yields rise).

❑ **Liquidity Preference Hypothesis:** Under the liquidity preference theory investors require higher yields on longer term issues to compensate them for the higher price volatility. Because volatility increases as we try to predict interest rates and inflation further and further into the future, the longer the term to maturity, the higher the risk premium.

The liquidity preference hypothesis does not imply that we should expect to see yield curves that are only upward sloping, or normal. It does remind us that even when we see a downward-sloping (inverted) yield curve, the risk premium in longer term securities is keeping the curve from being even more downward sloping than it might be without liquidity preference.

The yield curve shows a definite upward bias suggesting that the expectations and liquidity preference theory together more accurately explain the shape of the yield curve than either theory alone.

❑ **Segmented Market Hypothesis:** The segmented market hypothesis, also known as the preferred habitat theory, institutional theory, or hedging pressure theory, states that large (especially institutional) investors structure their investment policies to suit their tax liabilities, the types and maturity structures of liabilities in general, and the specific requirement of their clients or depositors. Thus the shape of the yield curve reflects the supply and demand for funds within each maturity segment of the market.

The preferred habitat theory is more flexible than the market segmentation theory. Preferred habitat recognizes that although a specific maturity range is preferred, the investor is willing to adjust provided the payoff is high enough.

Experience indicates that the yield curve is formed by the behaviors outlined in all three hypotheses.

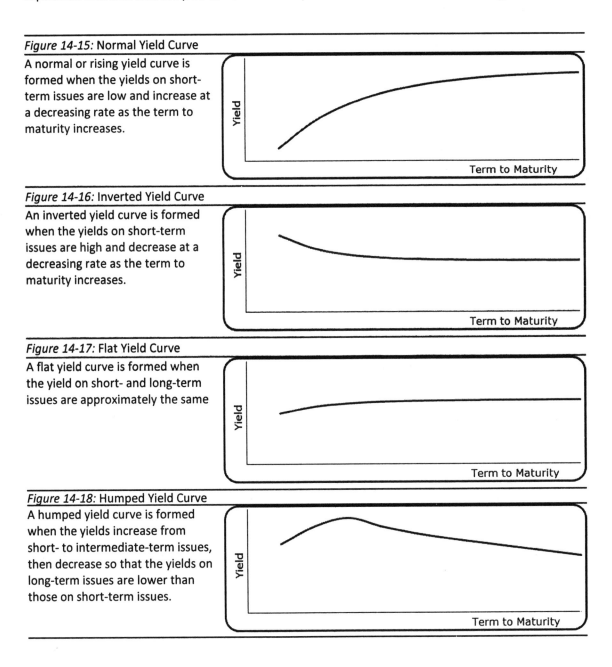

Figure 14-15: Normal Yield Curve

A normal or rising yield curve is formed when the yields on short-term issues are low and increase at a decreasing rate as the term to maturity increases.

Figure 14-16: Inverted Yield Curve

An inverted yield curve is formed when the yields on short-term issues are high and decrease at a decreasing rate as the term to maturity increases.

Figure 14-17: Flat Yield Curve

A flat yield curve is formed when the yield on short- and long-term issues are approximately the same

Figure 14-18: Humped Yield Curve

A humped yield curve is formed when the yields increase from short- to intermediate-term issues, then decrease so that the yields on long-term issues are lower than those on short-term issues.

1997: Asian Contagion

The last decade of the 20th Century was one of dramatic global economic growth. The period was dominated by the spread of technology, freedom of trade, free flow of capital, and investment opportunities. Few regions grew more dramatically than Southeast Asia.

Thailand, Malaysia, Indonesia, Singapore, and South Korea experienced growth rates of 8 to 12%, and attracted massive inflows of foreign capital seeking high rates of return. The IMF and World Bank proclaimed an Asian Economic Miracle. However, this miracle was built on the two fragile elements of inflows of foreign capital, and growth of Asian exports to mature economies, rather than on fundamental growth in economic productivity and domestic demand.

Thailand's economy developed into a bubble fueled by hot money. Hot money is highly speculative and can change almost without warning. Thailand required more and more hot money as the size of the bubble grew. Foreign debt-to-GDP ratios rose from 100% to 167% in the four largest Southeast Asian Nations economies in 1993-96, and went beyond 180% as the bubble broke. The countries became addicted to export growth. As the exports to GDP ratio rose from 35% in 1996, to over 55% in 1998, little domestic demand was developed.

Complications set in when the US tightened monetary policy in response to a quick recovery from a slump in 1990. Rising U.S. interest rates and a rising U.S. dollar had serious implications in Asian economies. Many of the smaller "Asian Tiger" economies pegged the value of their currencies to the value of the U.S. dollar. A stronger dollar meant the central banks of the Asian economies had a tough decision to make: raise interest rates and spend precious central bank reserve assets to maintain the fixed (pegged) exchange rate, or let the value of their currencies depreciate versus the dollar. If local currencies such as the Thai Bhat, Malaysian Ringgit, Indonesian Rupiah, and South Korean Won were devalued, foreign investors would face losses. This would jeopardizing the flow of hot money.

Despite efforts by Asian central banks and the IMF policies to maintain higher interest rates, the outflows of foreign capital had begun. Worse, these higher interest rates put more stress on already weak local banks and corporations. Asian economies crumbled, and the situation rapidly degenerated into a full-fledged panic and classic run on the banks of Asia.

Global financial markets reacted. On October 27, 1997 the Dow Jones Industrial Average dropped 554.26 (-7.18%) to 7,161.15. This was the 12th biggest percentage loss and 3rd biggest point loss on record at this time.

The Thai Bhat, historically pegged at 25 to the dollar, was allowed to float in July 1997, and reached its low of 56 to the dollar in January 1998. The Thai stock market had fallen 75%. Indonesia experienced a greater shock with an exchange rate of 2,600 rupiah to the dollar in mid 1997, becoming more than 14,000 to the dollar during January 1998. The stage was set for more dramatic events, and 1998 did not disappoint.

Chapter 14 - Questions and Problems

14-1:

My Bloomberg Terminal gives me the following simple interest rates

one year	3.0%
two year	4.0%
three year	4.6%
four year	5.0%
five year	5.2%

A. If the yield curve is formed solely from expectations, what does the market expect the one-year rate to be in one, two, three, and four years?

B. Plot the yield curve and the forward rates.

14-2:

My crystal ball tells me that the one-year interest rates over the next five years will be 3%, 5%, 7%, 8%, and 9%

A. Plot the yield curve

B. Calculate and plot the market-implied forward rates.

14-3:

Our Bloomberg quotes a 3% T-bond with 21 months to maturity at a yield of 5.8%. The bond matures February 15, 2014, and is priced at 95.3878 to settle May 15, 2013.

A. Using the rates in the box to the right calculate the 21 month zero-coupon rate.

B. Graph the yield curve

Table 14-4: Quote for Question 14-3

Term to Maturity	Yield
3m	2.100%
6m	3.400%
9m	4.400%
12m	4.800%
15m	5.279%
18m	5.322%
21m	
24m	

$\mathcal{D}$uration is the average, weighted by present value, term to maturity of a schedule of payments. Because bonds are, by definition, a structure of payments, duration applies easily to bonds. But any structure of payments, including assets and liabilities, has a duration. Economically, duration is equal to the negative interest rate elasticity of net present value.

Duration captures the structure of a schedule of payments, which payments come where in the schedule. Thus duration is a relevant measure when we look at the timing of cash flows, the assessment of risk, and the management of fixed income portfolios.

15.1 - Duration, Income, and Capital Gain

John Q. Investor is considering two bonds. Both bonds were issued by Discovery Café. Both are $1,000 bonds that mature in exactly five years, both are annual coupon bonds, and both are priced to yield 7% on investment. The only difference between the two bonds is that they have different coupon rates: one is a 5% coupon bond, and the other is a 9% coupon bond. This difference is critical because it shifts the return on investment between capital gain and income.

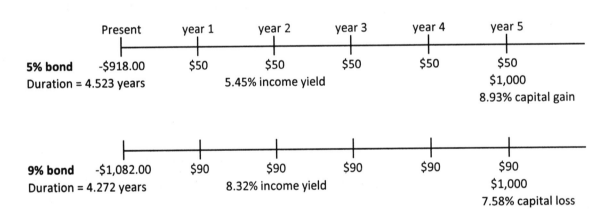

By choosing the 5% bond John chooses a lower income yield to get a capital gain, shifting his return on investment to the end of the five-year period. The weighted average term to maturity of this bond is 4.523 years.

By choosing the 9% John chooses to take a capital loss to generate a higher income yield, shifting his return on investment to earlier years. The weighted average term to maturity is 4.272 years, a bit shorter than the 5% bond.

This difference in the timing of payments, hence the duration, also captures the different risk exposures of the two bonds.

Figure 15-1: Price Yield Curves for the 5% and 9%, 5-year, Annual-Coupon Bonds

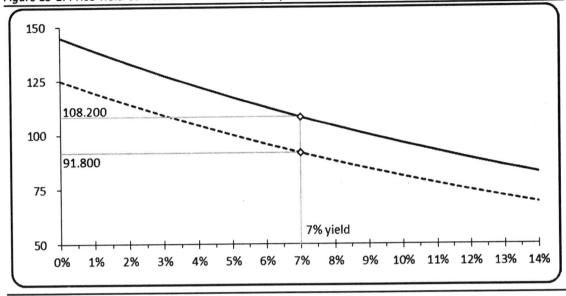

Note that either John is not subject to tax on capital gains or income or, if he is, the rate at which each is taxed is identical. Suffice to say that we are purposely keeping tax implications out of our discussion at this point, but acknowledge that tax treatment is one of the six determinants of interest rates in the marketplace.

15.1.1 - Duration and Risk

Every bond is sensitive to changes in the market rate of interest.

❑ **Reinvestment Risk:** Reinvestment risk is the risk that coupon payments paid out of the bond cannot be reinvested at the same yield.

❑ **Price Risk:** Price risk is the risk that the price of the bond will fall.

When yields go up all bond prices go down, but not all prices go down by the same amount. The degree to which prices change in response to a change in market yields is the volatility.

15.2 - Price Volatility

When we do sensitivity analysis, duration is one of our most useful measures.

John considers the 5% coupon and 9% coupon annual coupon bonds. Both bonds are priced to yield 7%, but John is concerned about price volatility.

❑ **Price Volatility:** The sensitivity of price to a change in yield. The 1% price volatility at any yield y% is the percentage change in price from y − ½% to y + ½%. Price volatility is thus the estimate of the slope of the price yield curve.

$$Volatility_y = \frac{\Delta P}{P} = \frac{P_{y+\%} - P_{y-\%}}{\left(\dfrac{P_{y+\%} + P_{y-\%}}{2}\right)} \qquad\qquad \text{(Eq 15-1)}$$

Example 1:

The 5% and 9%, 5-year, annual-coupon bonds are priced to yield 7%. We can calculate the 1% price volatility as the change in price in a 1% change in yield centered at 7%: from 6½% to 7½%

5% annual coupon bond	9% annual coupon bond
$V_{7\%} = \left[\dfrac{89.885 - 93.766}{91.800}\right]$	$V_{7\%} = \left[\dfrac{110.389 - 106.069}{108.200}\right]$
$= 0.0423$	$= 0.0399$
$= 4.23\%$	$= 3.99\%$

Figure 15-2: 1% Price Volatility for the 5% and 9%, 5-year, Annual-Coupon Bonds

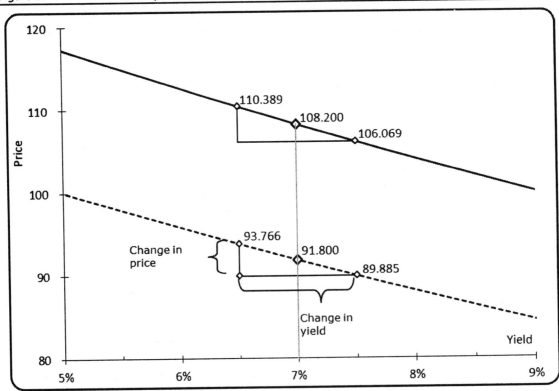

Both bonds have a term to maturity of five years, annual coupon payments, the same principal repayment, and experience the same change in yield, so why should the price of the 5% bond be more volatile than the price of the 9% bond?

The difference in the change in price comes from the timing of the cash flows. The 5% bond has more of its payments, including the capital gain, at the end of the five-year period, where the impact of a change in interest rate is greater. The 9% bond shifts the payments forward along the time line where the impact of a change in interest rates is lower.

15.3 - Calculating Duration I

Duration is the average, weighted-by-present value, term to maturity. Thus we can calculate the duration of the 5% bond as 4.523 years and the duration of the 9% bond as 4.272 years.

$$
Duration_y = \frac{\sum_{t=1}^{T} t \dfrac{C_t}{\left(1+\dfrac{y}{n}\right)^t}}{\sum_{t=1}^{T} \dfrac{C_t}{\left(1+\dfrac{y}{n}\right)^t}} = \sum_{t=1}^{T} t \frac{NPV_{yt}}{P_y} \qquad (Eq\ 15\text{-}2)
$$

Table 15-1: Duration and Convexity Calculation for the 5-year 5%, Annual-Coupon Bond

Time	Payment	NPV	% of Investment	Duration	Convexity
years	C_t	$NPV_{7\%\ t}$	$\dfrac{NPV_{7\%\ t}}{P_{7\%}}$	$t\ \dfrac{NPV_{7\%\ t}}{P_{7\%}}$	$t\ (t+1)\dfrac{NPV_{7\%\ t}}{P_{7\%}}$
1	50	46.7290	0.050903	0.050903	0.101806
2	50	43.6719	0.047573	0.095146	0.285437
3	50	40.8149	0.044461	0.133382	0.533528
4	50	38.1448	0.041552	0.166208	0.831041
5	1050	748.6355	0.815511	4.077535	24.465212
	$P_{7\%}$ = $918.00		1.000000	4.523 yrs	26.217 yrs^2

Table 15-2: Duration and Convexity Calculation for the 5-year 9%, Annual-Coupon Bond

Time	Payment	NPV	% of Investment	Duration	Convexity
years	C_t	$NPV_{7\%\ t}$	$\dfrac{NPV_{7\%\ t}}{P_{7\%}}$	$t\ \dfrac{NPV_{7\%\ t}}{P_{7\%}}$	$t\ (t+1)\dfrac{NPV_{7\%\ t}}{P_{7\%}}$
1	90	84.1121	0.077738	0.077738	0.155475
2	90	78.6095	0.072652	0.145304	0.435912
3	90	73.4668	0.067899	0.203697	0.814789
4	90	68.6606	0.063457	0.253828	1.269142
5	1090	777.1549	0.718258	3.591289	21.547734
	$P_{7\%}$ = $1082.00		1.000000	4.272 yrs	24.223 yrs^2

The 9% bond has the same term to maturity as the 5% bond, but less of the bond's value is payable in the fifth year. In this sense the 9% is a shorter bond than the 5%: The duration is only 4.272 years. The convexity calculation will be used later. It is simply more convenient to calculate duration and convexity at the same time.

Figure 15-3: Weighted by Present Value Term to Maturity on the 5% and 9% Annual-Coupon Bonds

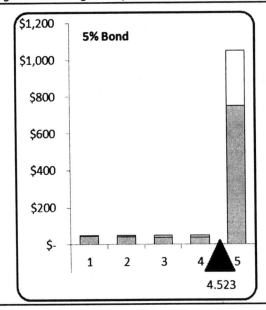 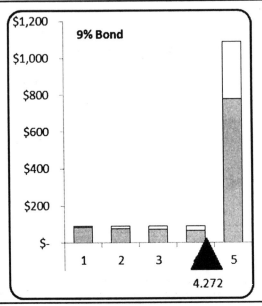

Figure 15-3 shows the nominal payments of the 5% and 9% annual coupon bonds. The only part that has weight is the present value of those payments when discounted at 7%. Assume these present values are sitting on a teeter-totter. The fulcrum must sit at exactly 4.523 and 4.272 years for the weights to balance.

15.4 - Calculating Duration II

Duration measures the weighted-by-present-value average time to maturity. When interest is compounded annually then we can calculate duration directly in years. However, when interest is compounded semi-annually we calculate duration in semi-annual periods and convert to years. Similarly, when interest is compounded monthly we calculate duration in months and convert to years.

Example 2:

The Discovery Café December 31, 2017, 6% semi-annual coupon bond is quoted at 102.500 to settle March 2, 2014. To calculate duration and convexity we use a $10,000. bond. The denomination makes no difference to the result, but we want a large enough bond to generate enough decimal places in our calculations.

Table 15-3: Discovery Café Bond Price Calculation

	Quote	$10,000 Bond
Base Price	102.000000	$102,000.00
89/181 days Accrued Interest	1.033333	$103.33
Invoice Price	103.033333	$10,303.33
Yield to Maturity	5.41186%	

Table 15-4: Duration and Convexity Calculation for the Discovery Café Bond[1]

Time	Payment	NPV	% of Investment	Duration	Convexity
$^{118}/_{180}$	$300	$294.79	0.028612	0.018756	0.031052
$1\,^{118}/_{180}$	$300	$287.03	0.027858	0.046120	0.122474
$2\,^{118}/_{180}$	$300	$279.47	0.027124	0.072029	0.263305
$3\,^{118}/_{180}$	$300	$272.10	0.026409	0.096540	0.449449
$4\,^{118}/_{180}$	$300	$264.93	0.025713	0.119710	0.677028
$5\,^{118}/_{180}$	$300	$257.95	0.025036	0.141592	0.942375
$6\,^{118}/_{180}$	$300	$251.16	0.024376	0.162238	1.242024
$7\,^{118}/_{180}$	$10,300	$8,395.90	0.814872	6.238297	53.995923
		P = $10,303,33	1.000000	6.895283	57.723632

Time is measured in semi-annual periods. The first payment of $300 is 118 days out of a 180-day semi-annual period away. The present value of this payment is calculated as

$$PV = \frac{\$300}{\left(1 + \dfrac{0.0541186}{2}\right)^{\frac{118}{180}}} = \$294.79$$

and the duration and convexity are calculated as

$$D_s = \frac{\$294.79}{\$10,303.33}\left(\frac{118}{180}\right) \qquad C_s = \frac{\$294.79}{\$10,303.33}\left(\frac{118}{180}\right)\left(1 + \frac{118}{180}\right)$$

We calculate duration and convexity in semi-annual periods. The duration of 6.895283 semi-annual periods converts to 3.4476 years, and the convexity of 57.723632 semi-annual periods[2] converts to 14.4309 years[2.]

$$D = \frac{6.895283\ semis}{\dfrac{2\ semis}{years}} = 3.4476\ years \qquad C = \frac{57.723632\ semis^2}{\left(\dfrac{2\ semis}{year}\right)^2} = 14.4309\ years^2$$

---

1 The calculations in this example were taken from the model developed at the end of this chapter. If you find that your hand calculated numbers are slightly different from those presented in Table 15-4, then this is most likely due to the effect of rounding.

Figure 15-4: Weighted by Present Value Term to Maturity on the Discovery Café Bond

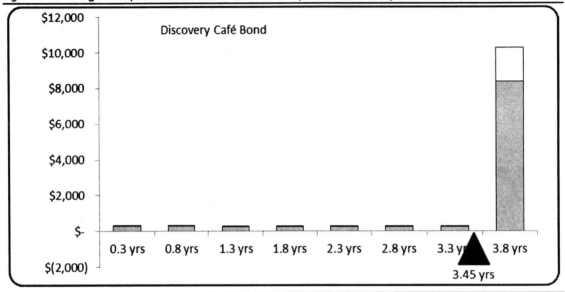

Figure 15-4 shows the nominal payments of the $10,000 Discovery Café semi-annual coupon bond. Again, if the only part that has weight is the present value then the balance point is the duration.

Any schedule of payments under any compounding structure has a duration.

Example 3:

We calculate the duration and modified duration of a schedule of monthly payments as specified in the table. The required return on the investment is 6%.

Table 15-5: Duration and Convexity Calculation of a Structured Monthly Payment Schedule

Time	Payment	PV @ 6%	% of Investment	Duration	Convexity
1	$100	99.50249	12.814%	0.128142	0.256285
2	$80	79.20596	10.200%	0.204008	0.612023
3	$60	59.10893	7.612%	0.228367	0.913467
4	$40	39.20990	5.050%	0.201983	1.009914
5	$20	19.50741	2.512%	0.125611	0.753667
6	$0	0.00000	0.000%	0.000000	0.000000
7	$100	96.56896	12.436%	0.870551	6.964407
8	$200	192.17704	24.749%	1.979931	17.819378
9	$200	191.22094	24.626%	2.216341	22.163405
				5.954920	50.492439
	P = $776.50		100.000%	/12	/144
				= 0.496 yrs	= 0.351 yrs^2

Note that because we calculated duration and convexity in months the duration is 5.9 months or 0.496 years and the convexity is 50 months^2 or 0.351 years^2.

15.5 - Volatility & Modified Duration

Volatility can be estimated directly from duration. Volatility is the change in the price due to a change in yield. Thus bond price volatility and duration are directly related. This relationship is direct, but inverse, so as rates rise, we expect to see prices fall, and vice versa.

$$Volatility = \frac{\Delta\ Price}{Price} = -\frac{Duration}{\left(1 + \frac{y}{n}\right)} * \Delta y$$

$$= -\ Modified\ Duration * \Delta y \qquad (Eq\ 15\text{-}3)$$

Table 15-6: Volatility Calculation for the 5% and 9%, 5-year, Annual-Coupon Bonds

---

5% bond: $\qquad Volatility = -\frac{4.523\ yrs}{1.07} * 1\% = -4.23\%$

9% bond: $\qquad Volatility = -\frac{4.272\ yrs}{1.07} * 1\% = -3.99\%$

The volatility in response to a 1% change in required yields is such a convenient measure that we call it the modified duration. Thus the duration of the 5-year 5% bond is 4.523 years and the modified duration is 4.227 years and the duration of the 5-year 9% bond is 4.272 years and the modified duration is 3.993 years.

❑ **Modified Duration:** The modified duration is the slope of the price yield curve. Modified Duration thus gives us the price volatility in response to a 1% change in yield.

$$Modified\ Duration = \frac{Duration}{\left(1 + \frac{y}{n}\right)} \qquad (Eq\ 15\text{-}4)$$

Example 4:

The Discovery Café December 31, 2017, 6% semi-annual coupon bond, quoted at 102.500 to settle March 2, 2014, invoices at 102.0333 percent of face value. The duration is 3.4476 years and the convexity is 14.4309 years^2. We calculate the modified duration using equation 15-4 where n = 2, to reflect semi-annual compounding

$$Modified\ Duration = -\frac{3.4476\ yrs}{\left(1 + \frac{5.41186\%}{2}\right)} = -3.3568\ yrs$$

Thus when interest rates increase by 1% the price of the bond should decrease by 3.3568%; when interest rates decrease by 1% the price of the bond should increase by 3.3568%

15.5.1 - Volatility & Convexity

Convexity is an approximate measure of the curvature of the price-yield relationship. The concept of convexity is important because the duration and volatility measures are essentially linear approximations of a convex price-yield curve. The modified duration is tangent to the price-yield curve at a specific yield. The more convex the curve the more serious the miss-estimation of volatility.

Figure 15-5: Price Yield Curve of a 10-year 10% Semi-Annual Coupon Bond (Convexity: 130 yrs^2)

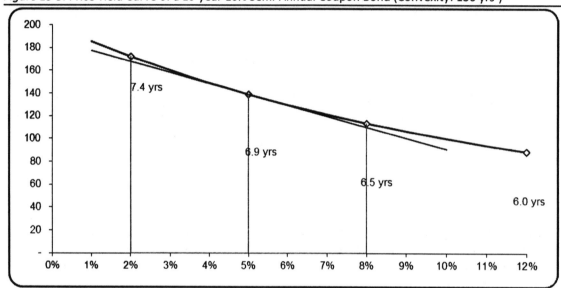

Figure 15-5 shows the price yield curve of a 10-year 10% semi-annual coupon bond, priced to yield 5%. The modified duration is 6.9 years and is represented by the straight line tangent to the price yield curve at the 5% yield at which the bond is currently priced.

The convexity of the bond at 5% is calculated as 130 yr^2. We can see that the duration of 6.9 years, relevant when the bond is priced to yield 5%, becomes less accurate as we move away from the 5% valuation, but not seriously so.

Figure 15-6 shows the price yield curve of a 50-year 10% semi-annual coupon bond, priced to yield 5%. The modified duration is 17.0 years and is represented by the straight line tangent to the price yield curve at the 5% yield at which the bond is currently priced.

The convexity of the bond at 5% is calculated as 1,021 yr^2. We can see that the duration of 17.0 years, relevant when the bond is priced to yield 5%, becomes increasingly irrelevant as we move away from the 5% valuation, from 12.1 years at 8% to 24.0 yrs at 8%.

Figure 15-6: Price Yield Curve of a 50-year 5% Semi-Annual Coupon Bond (Convexity: 1,021 yrs^2)

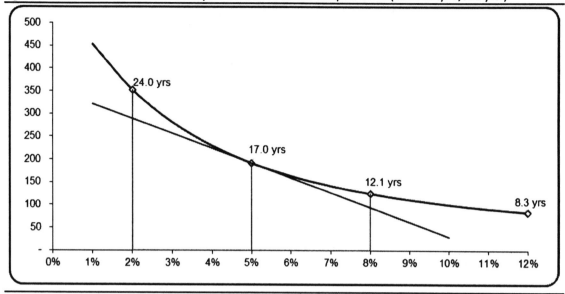

Thus we require a convexity correction of the bond price estimated by modified duration alone.

Note that the actual price of the bond is always higher than the estimate from the modified duration indicates. Note also that Convexity increases with

- ❑ Lower coupon rates
- ❑ Longer maturity
- ❑ Lower yield (the curve is more convex in the lower-yield (upper left) segment.

15.5.2 - The Convexity Correction

The modified duration is the slope of the tangent to the price yield curve at the current yield to maturity. Modified duration gives us an estimate of volatility: How sensitive is the price of the bond to a change in yield?

To increase the accuracy of our estimate we add the convexity correction to the duration estimate.

Recall the Taylor expansion.

- ❑ **Taylor Expansion:** The Taylor expansion is a mathematical technique that allows us to approximate the value of a function (a price yield curve at some yield near 5%) when it is near a value we already know (the price when yield is 5%)
.

When we apply the Taylor expansion to the price yield curve the numerators begin to look suspiciously like the duration and convexity we calculated earlier.

$$\frac{\Delta P}{P} = - \frac{\sum_{t=1}^{T} t \dfrac{NPV_{yt}}{P_y}}{\left(1+\dfrac{y}{n}\right)} \Delta y + \frac{1}{2} \frac{\sum_{t=1}^{T} t\,(t+1) \dfrac{NPV_{yt}}{P_y}}{\left(1+\dfrac{y}{n}\right)^2} \Delta y^2 \qquad (Eq\ 15\text{-}5)$$

$$\frac{\Delta P}{P} = - \frac{Duration}{\left(1+\dfrac{y}{n}\right)} \Delta y + \frac{1}{2} \frac{Convexity}{\left(1+\dfrac{y}{n}\right)^2} \Delta y^2 \qquad (Eq\ 15\text{-}6)$$

$$\frac{\Delta P}{P} = - \ Modified\ Duration\ \Delta y + \frac{1}{2}\ Modified\ Convexity\ \Delta y^2 \qquad (Eq\ 15\text{-}7)$$

Applying the Convexity correction to our original estimates on the 5 year 5% annual coupon bonds we get a more accurate estimate of the price volatility.

Table 15-7: Price Response, with Convexity Correction, to a 1% Increase in Yield

% change in price using Duration	+	Convexity Correction		=	Estimated price change
- $\dfrac{4.523}{(1.07)}$ (+0.01)	+	$\dfrac{1}{2}\ \dfrac{26.217}{(1.07)^2}$	$(+0.01)^2$	=	
- 4.23 (+0.01)	+	11.449	$(+0.01)^2$	=	
- 0.042271028	+	0.001144947		=	- 0.041126081
- 4.23%	+	0.11%			- 4.113 %

The actual decrease in price is 4.115% (from $918 to $880.22) rather than the estimated 4.113%, but this is closer than the duration only estimate of 4.23%.

Table 15-8: Price Response, with Convexity Correction, to a 1% Decrease in Yield

% change in price using Duration	+	Convexity Correction		=	Estimated price change
- $\dfrac{4.523}{(1.07)}$ (-0.01)	+	$\dfrac{1}{2}\ \dfrac{26.217}{(1.07)^2}$	$(-0.01)^2$	=	
- 4.23 (-0.01)	+	11.449	$(-0.01)^2$	=	
+ 0.042271028	+	0.001144947		=	0.043415975
+ 4.23%	+	0.11%			+ 4.342%

The actual increase in price is 4.344% (from $918 to $957.88) rather than the estimated 4.342%, but this is closer than the duration only estimate of 4.23%.

❑ **One final note:** Duration and convexity start with the bond valuation equation. This equation assumes a flat yield curve (all the coupon payments were discounted at the same rate regardless of the term). The calculations we have been playing with assume that this flat yield curve shifts up and down. The price change estimations get more crude as the yield curve deviates from this flat line.

15.6 - Portfolio Duration

A portfolio of bonds has a duration equal to the weighted average of the durations of the individual bonds in the portfolio.

Example 5:

John Q. Investor has a portfolio consisting of the following assets:

Table 15-9: John Q's Portfolio of Assets

Principal	Coupon	Term	Yield	Duration	Market Value
$10,000.00	6%	12 yrs	@8%	8.3970	$8,475.30
$10,000.00	12%	6 yrs	@8%	4.5858	$11,877.01
$1,000.00				0.0000	$1,000.00
					$21,352.31

Note that the duration of cash is 0. John calculates the duration of the assets in his portfolio as 5.884 years

$$Duration_{Assets} = \frac{\$8,475.30 \ (8.397 \ yrs) \ + \ \$11,877.01 \ (4.5858 \ yrs) \ + \ \$1,000.00 \ (0.0 \ yrs)}{\$21,352.31}$$

$$= \quad 5.884 \ yrs$$

Chapter 15 - Questions and Problems

15-1:

Yields on five-year annual-coupon Treasury securities rise ½% to 8.75%. The price on this security drops 2 points to 96.5. Estimate the duration.

15-2:

John Q. Investor purchased a semi-annual coupon-bearing Treasury at par. The duration was 9 years. Yields then rose 1% to 8.5% Calculate the price of the Treasury after the rate increase.

15-3:

Calculate the duration and convexity of a 270-day $1,000,000 T-bill.

15-4:

Calculate the percentage price change on a 4.0% corporate bond maturing 30 November 2020 to a 1½% increase in yield. The bond is quoted at 102.500 to settle 15 April 2013. The duration is calculated as 6.9685 yrs and the convexity at 57.2141 yrs².

15-5:

Calculate the percentage price change on a 4.0% corporate bond maturing 30 November 2050 to a 1½% increase in yield. The bond is quoted at 102.500 to settle 15 April 2013. The duration is calculated as 20.4014 yrs and the convexity at 605.7037 yrs².

Chapter 15 - Financial Models

15.1 - Duration and Convexity

Objective:

To calculate the duration and convexity for the bond profiled in the financial model developed in Chapter 13.

Formats:

A. Begin either with the model developed in Chapter 13 or begin with the template and rebuild the bond calculator. It's best if you can do this now without referring to the detailed instructions.

B. Make sure that the price of the bond is an input. Go to D15. Enter the price quote of the bond and use Shift+Ctrl+B to render the input Finance Blue.

C. Set the Titlebars. Select M1:S1 and either click Title in the Finance Ribbon or use the shortcut Shift+Ctrl+T.

D. Set the sub-Titles: Select M5:S5 and either click sub-Title in the Finance Ribbon or use the shortcut Ctrl+T.

E. Hide the spacers in A1, E1, H1, and K1 by setting the font to white-on white. Either click on [Finance Fonts] [White] in the Finance Ribbon or use the shortcut Shift+Ctrl+W.

Payment Number:

F. Begin with the # column. This is designed to count the number of payments left on the bond contract. Enter 1 into M6.

G. Use Fill to count automatically.
   1. Click in cell M6. This establishes the starting point as 1.
   2. Click on Fill in the Data Manipulation and Analysis section of the Finance Ribbon
   3. Choose [Series in Columns]
   4. Specify Step Value as 1 and Stop Value as 100
   5. OK

H. Column M now counts from 0 to 100 in increments of 1. Use Ctrl+↓ to jump to M105, which should contain the number 100. Use Ctrl+↑ to jump back to M5.

Time:

I. M6 represents the first partial period. Use the days already calculated in the bond profile, so M6=$G$13/$G$14

J. XL will automatically format to a floating decimal. Set the format to fraction. Use Ctrl+1 to open the format Cell applet. Click on the Number Tab. Use [Fraction]/ [Up to three digits (312/943)]. XL will automatically reduce the fraction so a 90-day present value period out of 180 days will show as ½ rather than 90/180, but this is the only format that will allow for both corporate bonds (where the denominator is 180) and Treasury bonds (where the denominator can be 181, 182, 183, or 184).

K. We continue with column M, adding a semi-annual period to the partial period for every semi-annual payment under the contract. We know how many such payments there are because we calculated the coupons remaining into G10.

L. So N7 =IF($M7>$G$10,"",1+$N6). This translates as IF (the bond payments have ended) THEN = "" ELSE = 1 + the value in the cell above)

M. Copy-drag to N105.

Date:

N. The dates of the payments are calculated from the maturity date backward one semi-annual period at a time.

O. So O6 =IF($M6>$G$10,"",EDATE(RDT,-6*($G$10-$M6))) This translates as IF (the bond payments have ended) THEN = "", ELSE Calculate the date(from the redemption date RDT, backward six months at a time, for the number of periods between this and the last payment).

P. Copy-drag to O105

Payment:

Q. Calculate the cash flow from the bond data. To make sure that we catch the final principal repayment use en embedded if() statement.

R. So P6 =IF($M6>$G$10,"",P*(IF($M6=$G$10,1,0)+(CPN/2))) This translates as IF (the bond payments have ended) THEN ="", ELSE Principal Value of the Bond * (X + CPN/2)). Where X is determined by another IF. IF(this is the last bond payment THEN X=1, ELSE 0).

S. Copy-drag to P105.

T. To test this change the bond data and make sure that the cash flow changes accordingly.

Present Value:

U. Calculate the present value of each payment.

V. So Q6 =IFERROR(P6/((1+YLD/2)^$N6),""). Note that we use the YLD in cell D14 and the IFERROR() to put the "" into the cell if there is no payment from which to calculate the present value.

W. Copy-drag to Q105.

X. Sum the present values into Q3. So Q3=SUM(Q$6:Q$105).

Y. Verify that the sum of the present value equals the invoice price of the bond.

Calculate Yield

Z. Yield is calculated, so use Shift+Ctrl+K to render the font black.

AA. If you want to calculate yield by function you can do so with   D14 =YIELD(SDT,RDT,CPN,PRI,100,$C$8,$C$7), OR

AB. If you want to calculate yield by forcing the sum of the present values to equal the invoice price then you can do so with Goal Seek. First make sure that the yield in D14 is a value (4%) not a formula (=YIELD(...)

    1. Click on Goal Seek in the Data Manipulation and Analysis section of the Finance Ribbon.

    2. Set cell Q3.

    3. Type in the invoice price.

    4. By changing cell D14.

    5. [OK]

Percent of Bond Price:

AC. Calculate the percent of the bond price which each payment represents. So R6=IFERROR($Q6/$Q$3,"").

AD. Copy-drag down to R105.

AE. Copy-drag the sum in Q3 to R3 and verify that you have 100% of the bond price accounted for in the total.

Duration:

AF. Calculate the duration of each payment. So S6=IFERROR($R6*$N6,"")

AG. Copy-drag down to S105.

AH. Copy-drag the sum in R3 to S3.

AI. Calculate the Duration into G21. So G21 =S3/$C$8.

Convexity:

AJ. Calculate the convexity of each payment. So T6=IFERROR($R6*$N6*(1+$N6),"").

AK. Copy-drag down to T105

AL. Copy-drag the sum in S3 to T3.

AM. Calculate the duration into G23. So G23 =S3/($C$8^2).

AN. If necessary, add labels to cells F21 and F23.

Test:

AO. Double check your model against the problem sets at the back of this chapter.

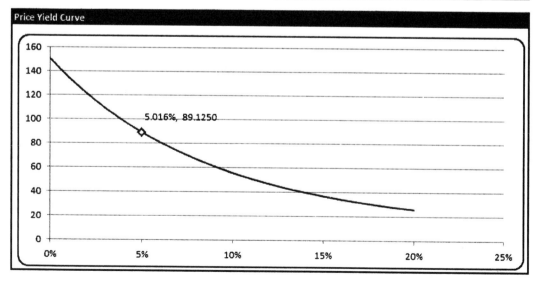

Bond Information			Bond Calculator			Yield	Price	MD
Principal	P	$ 3,000	Base Price:	$	2,673.75	0%	150.859	
Coupon	CPN	3.875%	Accrued Interest:	$	43.59	1%	135.280	
Maturity	RDT	May 31, 2026	Invoice Price:	$	2,717.34	2%	121.549	
						3%	109.433	
	US Corporate		Coupon:	$	58.13	4%	98.730	
	Semi-Annual		Last Coupon Date:		November 30, 2012	5%	89.263	
			Next Coupon Date:		May 31, 2013	6%	80.880	
			Coupons Remaining:		27	7%	73.446	
Market Information						8%	66.847	
			Days to Accrue:		135	9%	60.980	
Settlement	SDT	April 15, 2013	Days to Next Coupon:		45	10%	55.758	
Yield	YLD	5.016%	Days in Semi-Annual Period:		180	11%	51.104	
Price	PRI	89.1250				12%	46.949	
			Nominal Yield:		3.875%	13%	43.235	
Excel Function Codes			Income Yield:		4.348%	14%	39.911	
	Treasury	1	Yield to Maturity:		5.016%	15%	36.931	
	US Corporate	0	Capital Gain:		0.734%	16%	34.255	
	European Corporate	4				17%	31.849	
			Duration:		10.0546	18%	29.683	
	Annual	1	Convexity:		125.2283	19%	27.729	
	Semi-Annual	2				20%	25.963	

Price Yield Curve

5.016%, 89.1250

Duration & Convexity Calculation							
#	Time		Date	Payment	PV	%	Duration	Convexity
					$ 2,717.34	100.0%	20.1093	500.9132

#	Time		Date	Payment	PV	%	Duration	Convexity
1		1/4	May 31, 2013	$58.13	$ 57.77	2.1258%	0.0053	0.0066
2	1	1/4	November 30, 2013	$58.13	$ 56.35	2.0738%	0.0259	0.0583
3	2	1/4	May 31, 2014	$58.13	$ 54.97	2.0231%	0.0455	0.1479
4	3	1/4	November 30, 2014	$58.13	$ 53.63	1.9736%	0.0641	0.2726
5	4	1/4	May 31, 2015	$58.13	$ 52.32	1.9253%	0.0818	0.4296
6	5	1/4	November 30, 2015	$58.13	$ 51.04	1.8782%	0.0986	0.6163
7	6	1/4	May 31, 2016	$58.13	$ 49.79	1.8323%	0.1145	0.8302
8	7	1/4	November 30, 2016	$58.13	$ 48.57	1.7874%	0.1296	1.0691
9	8	1/4	May 31, 2017	$58.13	$ 47.38	1.7437%	0.1439	1.3307
10	9	1/4	November 30, 2017	$58.13	$ 46.22	1.7011%	0.1573	1.6128
11	10	1/4	May 31, 2018	$58.13	$ 45.09	1.6594%	0.1701	1.9135
12	11	1/4	November 30, 2018	$58.13	$ 43.99	1.6188%	0.1821	2.2310
13	12	1/4	May 31, 2019	$58.13	$ 42.91	1.5792%	0.1935	2.5633
14	13	1/4	November 30, 2019	$58.13	$ 41.86	1.5406%	0.2041	2.9089
15	14	1/4	May 31, 2020	$58.13	$ 40.84	1.5029%	0.2142	3.2660
16	15	1/4	November 30, 2020	$58.13	$ 39.84	1.4661%	0.2236	3.6333
17	16	1/4	May 31, 2021	$58.13	$ 38.87	1.4303%	0.2324	4.0093
18	17	1/4	November 30, 2021	$58.13	$ 37.91	1.3953%	0.2407	4.3926
19	18	1/4	May 31, 2022	$58.13	$ 36.99	1.3612%	0.2484	4.7819
20	19	1/4	November 30, 2022	$58.13	$ 36.08	1.3279%	0.2556	5.1762
21	20	1/4	May 31, 2023	$58.13	$ 35.20	1.2954%	0.2623	5.5742
22	21	1/4	November 30, 2023	$58.13	$ 34.34	1.2637%	0.2685	5.9749
23	22	1/4	May 31, 2024	$58.13	$ 33.50	1.2328%	0.2743	6.3773
24	23	1/4	November 30, 2024	$58.13	$ 32.68	1.2026%	0.2796	6.7805
25	24	1/4	May 31, 2025	$58.13	$ 31.88	1.1732%	0.2845	7.1836
26	25	1/4	November 30, 2025	$58.13	$ 31.10	1.1445%	0.2890	7.5858
27	26	1/4	May 31, 2026	$3,058.13	$ 1,596.21	58.7417%	15.4197	420.1869
28								
29								
30								
31								
96								
97								
98								
99								
100								

15.2 - Modified Duration

Objective:

To calculate the tangent to the price yield curve using the duration

Modified Duration

A. Calculate modified duration into G22. So G22 =G21/(1+YLD/2)
B. To estimate the price at each yield we need first to manipulate the volatility equation 15-3.

$$Volatility = \frac{\Delta\ Price}{Price} = -\frac{Duration}{\left(1 + \dfrac{y}{n}\right)} * \Delta y$$

(Eq 15-3)

to get

$$\frac{\hat{P} - P}{P} = -\frac{Duration}{\left(1 + \dfrac{y}{n}\right)} * (\hat{y} - y)$$

$$\hat{P} = P\left[\ 1 - Modified\ Duration\ * (\hat{y} - y)\ \right]$$

C. Translate the equation into an Excel formula. So K3 = PRI*(1-$G$22*($I3-YLD)).
D. Copy-drag to K23.

Graph:

E. Add the modified duration calculated prices in column K to the graph.
  1. Click in the Graph.
  2. From the Chart Tools Ribbon use [Design] [Select Data] and [add].
  3. Specify the series name as =K1.
  4. Specify the series X values as the yields in I3:I23.
  5. Specify the series Y values as the price estimates in K3:K23.
F. Format the series to fit your own professional style.
G. The modified duration line extends into negative prices at high yields. To prevent these negative price from showing in your chart you can restrict the Y axis. To do this use [Chart Tools] [Layout] and select [Vertical (Value) Axis] and [Format selection]. Under [Axis Options] click on Fixed for the minimum, and specify the minimum as 0. Leave all other options on auto.

Bond Information				Bond Calculator			Yield	Price	MD
Principal	P	$	3,000	Base Price:	$	3,086.25	0%	131.484	127.296
Coupon	CPN		3.875%	Accrued Interest:	$	43.59	1%	122.381	120.249
Maturity	RDT		May 31, 2021	Invoice Price:	$	3,129.84	2%	113.995	113.202
							3%	106.265	106.156
		US Corporate		Coupon:	$	58.13	4%	99.137	99.109
		Semi-Annual		Last Coupon Date:	November 30, 2012		5%	92.559	92.062
				Next Coupon Date:		May 31, 2013	6%	86.486	85.015
				Coupons Remaining:		17	7%	80.876	77.968
Market Information							8%	75.691	70.922
				Days to Accrue:		135	9%	70.897	63.875
Settlement	SDT		April 15, 2013	Days to Next Coupon:		45	10%	66.460	56.828
Yield	YLD		3.466%	Days in Semi-Annual Period:		180	11%	62.353	49.781
Price	PRI		102.8750				12%	58.549	42.734
				Nominal Yield:		3.875%	13%	55.023	35.688
Excel Function Codes				M		3.767%	14%	51.753	28.641
		Treasury	1	Yield to Maturity:		3.466%	15%	48.719	21.594
		US Corporate	0	Capital Gain:		-0.498%	16%	45.903	14.547
		European Corporate	4				17%	43.287	7.501
				Duration:		6.9685	18%	40.856	0.454
		Annual	1	Modified Duration:		6.8499	19%	38.595	(6.593)
		Semi-Annual	2	Convexity:		57.2141	20%	36.491	(13.640)

Price Yield Curve

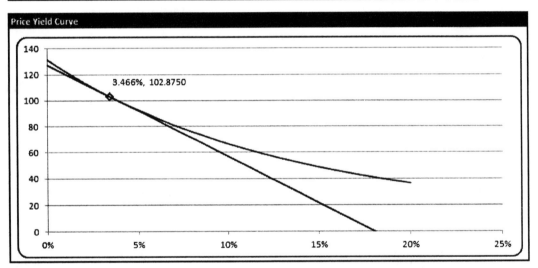

Immunization is a bond portfolio management technique of matching durations to eliminate, or at least minimize, interest rate risk.

❑ **Interest Rate Risk:** Interest rate risk consists of price risk and reinvestment risk.

❑ **Price Risk:** Price risk is the risk that the price of the bond will decrease and the bond is sold before maturity.

❑ **Reinvestment Risk:** Reinvestment risk is the risk that coupon payments cannot be reinvested at the promised yield to maturity.

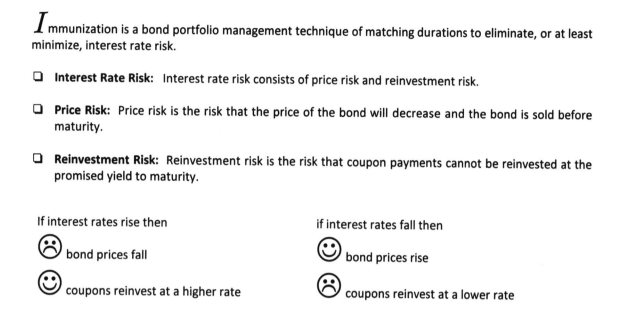

If interest rates rise then

☹ bond prices fall

☺ coupons reinvest at a higher rate

if interest rates fall then

☺ bond prices rise

☹ coupons reinvest at a lower rate

16.1 - Immunizing a Bond Portfolio

Price and reinvestment risk move in opposite directions. In 1971 Fisher & Weil[1] showed that the modified duration gives the time period when these two risks exactly offset each other.

A portfolio of bonds is immunized from interest rate risk if the modified duration of the portfolio always equals the remaining investment horizon. If the duration is too long then you are not immunized against an increase in interest rates (the drop in bond prices is too large to be offset by increased reinvestment rates) and if the duration is too short then you are not immunized against a decrease in interest rates (the increase in bond prices is insufficient to offset lower reinvestment rates).

Thus to immunize a portfolio of bonds balance the portfolio such that:

$$Duration_{Assets} = Duration_{Liabilities}$$ (Eq 16-1)

16.2 - The Failure to Immunize

To illustrate how and why immunization works we can examine the outcome of a simplified fixed-income portfolio problem

---

1   Fisher & Weil "Coping with the Risk of Interest Rate Fluctuations: Returns to Bondholders from Naive and Optimal Strategies" *Journal of Business*, Vol. 44 (October 1971):408–431

Example 1:

John Q. Investor is a assigned the management of a trust that must generate $1,000,000 in two years. The client is somewhat eccentric and limits the trust to annual coupon bonds. There are two companies that issue such bonds:

❏   Tardis Intertemporal has a series of 8% annual-coupon bonds with three years left to maturity.
❏   Hyothetical Resources issues one-year 7% annual coupon bonds every year

Both bonds are issued in $1,000 lots and both are trading to yield 10%. Using 10% compounded annually we calculate the present value of the liability as $826,446.28 and the price the bonds at 95.027 and 97.273, respectively.

Table 16-1: Time line for the Assets and Liabilities in Example 1

	t = 0	t = 1	t = 2	t = 3
LIABILITY:	$826,446.28		$1,000,000	
ASSETS:				
TI 8% Bond	$950.26	$80	$80	$1080
HR 7% Bond	$972.73	$1,070		

John suffers from yield illusion. He thinks that if he puts the entire portfolio into three-year bonds that he will lock in a yield of 10% for three years. So John plans to put the entire portfolio into three-year 8% Tardis Intertemporal bonds.

$$\frac{\left[\dfrac{\$1,000,000}{1.10^2}\right]}{\$950.26} = 869.7 \twoheadrightarrow 870 \ bonds$$

$$870 * \$950.26 = \$826,726.20$$

❏   At t = 0 purchase $870,000 in TI 8% three-year bonds for a total of $826,726.20.

❏   At t = 1 the trust earns 870 * $80 in coupon payments for a total of $69,600. The $69,600 is reinvested at the prevailing interest rate. Because there is only one year until the trust matures John puts the entire amount in a money market fund that gives us the market rate.

❏   At t = 2 the trust earns 870 * $80 in coupon payments for a total of $69,600 and then liquidates the trust and turns it over to the client. At t = 2 the three-year bond Tardis Intertemporal bond has one year remaining to maturity.

John, mindful of interest rate risk, sets up the following table, mapping out the consequences to the trust should yields fall to 9%, remain at 10%, or rise to 11%.

Table 16-2: Failure to Immunize Alternate Scenarios

	Yields change to		
	9%	10%	11%
t = 1:			
coupons from the 870 8% TI bonds	$69,600.00	$69,600.00	$69,600.00
t = 2:			
coupon received at t = 1 reinvested at the market rate	$75,864.00	$76,560.00	$77,256.00
coupons from the 870 8% TI bonds	$69,600.00	$69,600.00	$69,600.00
Sale of 870 8% TI bonds	870 * $990.83 = $862,022.10	870 * $981.82 = $854,183.40	870 * $972.97 = $846,483.90
TOTAL PORTFOLIO	$1,007,486.10	$1,000,343.40	$ 993,339.90
Net after $1,000,000 disbursement	$7,486.10	$343.40	($6,660.10)

John realizes that the price risk is much greater than the reinvestment risk. Using the differences method to analyze the impact of financial decisions John sees that although there is a positive reinvestment effect from an increase in yields, it is not nearly large enough to offset the price effect.

Table 16-3: Failure to Immunize summary of Alternate Scenarios

Differences	Yields change to		
	9%	10%	11%
Reinvestment Effect	- $696.00	0.00	+ $696.00
Price Effect	+ $7,838.70	0.00	- $7,699.50
Net	$7,142.70	0.00	-$7,003.50

If John immunizes the portfolio he balances the assets so that the reinvestment and price risks are equalized. This balance requires that the assets in the portfolio mature at just the right time. Too early and the reinvestment effect is too big; too late and the price effect is too big. In this portfolio the assets matured too late.

16.3 - Immunizing the Portfolio

Immunization is an investment technique that balances the reinvestment and price effects so that they offset each other. To ensure that the assets mature when the liabilities come due, the portfolio is balanced such that:

$$Duration_{Assets} = Duration_{Liabilities}$$

Example 2:

John Q. Investor reconsiders the investment policy for his client. He calculates the duration of each of the annual coupon bonds as well as the duration of the liability.

Table 16-4: Duration Calculations of the Liability and of the 7% and 8% bonds

Duration of the Liability

year	Cash Flow	PV	PV/P	PV/P * t
t = 1	$0.00	$0.00	0.00000	0.00
t = 2	$1,000,000.00	$826,446.28	1.00000	2.00
	Present Value = $826,446.28		1.00000	2.00 yrs

Duration of the 7% 2003 bond

year	Cash Flow	PV	PV/P	PV/P * t
t = 1	$1,070.00	$972.73	1.00000	1.00
	Price = $ 972.73		1.00000	1.00 yrs

Duration of 8% 2005 bond

year	Cash Flow	PV	PV/P	PV/P * t
t = 1	$80.00	$72.73	0.07654	0.08
t = 2	$80.00	$66.12	0.06958	0.14
t = 3	$1,080.00	$811.42	0.85388	2.56
	Price = $ 950.26		1.00000	2.78 yrs

To immunize the portfolio we need to set the duration of the assets in the portfolio to the duration of the liability. To do this let W_7 and W_8 represent the weights (or proportions) of the portfolio's funds to be invested in the 7% and 8% bonds, respectively. Then solve the following system of equations:

$W_7 + W_8 = 1$ (The sum of the weights must equal 1 or 100% of the portfolio.)

$(1.00\ W_7) + (2.78\ W_8) = 2$ (The duration of the portfolio is the weighted average of the duration of the individual bonds.)

$W_7 = .4382 \rightarrow$ Invest 43.82% in 7% Hypothetical Resource bonds, and

$W_8 = .5618 \rightarrow$ Invest 56.18% in 8% Tardis Intertemporal bonds.

Thus John must buy 372 7% bonds maturing in one year and 489 8% bonds maturing in three years, for a total of $826,537.59. Note that we will require more funds to set up the trust than we originally estimated. This is because we must buy the bonds in $1000 lots and rounding up gives us a safety net.

$$\frac{0.4382 * \$826,446.48}{972.73} = 372.3 \Rightarrow 372\ 7\%\ \text{HR bonds}$$

$$\frac{0.5618 * \$826,446.48}{950.27} = 488.7 \Rightarrow 489\ 8\%\ \text{TI bonds}$$

We must begin the trust with AT LEAST $826,446.28 or we will fall short of our $1,000,000 obligation to the client. 372 7% HR bonds and 489 8% TI bonds gives us $826,537.59 as the initial portfolio value.

16.3.1 - Duration versus Modified Duration

It makes absolutely no difference whether you use duration or modified duration, so long as you remain consistent. To see this recalculate the weights using duration and modified duration.

$$1.00W_7 + 2.78W_8 = 2 \quad \textit{versus} \quad \frac{1.00}{1.10^7}W_7 + \frac{2.78}{1.10^8}W_8 = \frac{2}{1.10}$$

16.3.2 - Buying and Selling Bonds

The second change John will make in the portfolio is that he will reinvest in the bond market rather than looking for a money market account. This means that when the first set of coupons are paid into the portfolio the proceeds will be used to buy a new round of one-year 7% Hypothetical Resource bonds. Only residual cash will be invested in a money market or simple interest bearing account.

If yields decrease and the price of the bond goes up then we can buy fewer bonds than we originally planned; if yields increase and the price goes down then we can buy more bonds than we originally planned.

Table 16-5: Immunization: Alternate Scenarios

	Yields change to		
	9%	10%	11%
t = 1:			
Coupon from the 489 8% Ti bonds	$39,120.00	$39,120.00	$39,120.00
Coupon from the 372 7% HR bonds	$26,040.00	$26,040.00	$26,040.00
372 7% HR bonds mature	$372,000.00	$372,000.00	$372,000.00
Total cash received in 2003	$437,160.00	$437,160.00	$437,160.00
Purchase X 7% 04 bonds	445 * $981.65 = ($436,834.25)	449 * $972.73 = ($436,755.77)	453 * $963.96 = ($436,673.88)
Residual Cash	$325.75	$404.23	$486.12
t = 2:			
Coupon from the X 7% HR bonds	$31,150.00	$31,430.00	$31,710.00
X 7% HR bonds mature	$445,000.00	$449,000.00	$453,000.00
Coupon from the 489 8% TI bonds	$39,120.00	$39,120.00	$39,120.00
Sale of 489 8% TI bonds	489 * $990.83 = $484,515.87	489 * $981.82 = $480,109.98	489 * $972.97 = $475,782.33
Residual Cash	$355.07	$444.65	$539.59
Total Portfolio Value	$1,000,140.94	$1,000,104.63	$1,000,151.92

Again, using the differences method to analyze the impact of financial decisions, John sees a balance between the value of the portfolio at risk through reinvestment and through price.

Table 16-6: Summary of Alternate Immunization Scenarios

Differences	Yields change to		
	9%	10%	11%
Coupon from the X 7% HR bonds	- $280.00	0.00	+ $280.00
X 7% HR bonds mature	- $4,000.00	0.00	+ $4,000.00
Interest on Residual Cash	- $89.58	0.00	+ $94.94
Reinvestment Effect	- $4,369.58	0.00	+ $4,374.94
Sale of 489 8% bonds	+ $4,405.89	0.00	- $4,327.65
Price Effect	+ $4,405.89	0.00	- $4,327.65
Net	+ $36.31	0.00	+ $47.29

16.4 - *Immunization in Practice*

Just as bonds do not come with conveniently timed annual coupons on the dates your client wishes to resolve the trust, so portfolios are generally not managed with convenient algebraic formulae. In practice, immunization is a moving target. Every time there is a cash flow from or to the fund we reimmunize, buying and selling the bonds according to several criteria, of which immunization is one.

Example 3:

Ivan Investor manages a trust fund for the benefit of several beneficiaries. Under the terms of the trust, the fund is paid out to the beneficiaries in 8.6 years. The portfolio now holds the following assets:

Table 16-7: Summary of Portfolio Assets at market close January 12, 2013

				Price	Market Value	Duration
$20,000	Discovery Café	6.875%	5/7/27	102.0445	$20,657.17	9.28
$50,000	Tardis Intertemporal	3.500%	3/15/20	80.7580	$40,947.73	6.21
$25,000	Galifre Educational	4.000%	5/9/27	75.7542	$19,113.56	10.36
$20,000	Hypothetical Resources	2.000%	10/10/15	88.5043	$17,803.07	2.66
$50,000	U.S. Treasury	2.000%	5/15/18	97.2691	$48,794.78	5.07
$50,000	U.S. Treasury	2.500%	8/15/23	93.1517	$47,085.35	9.22
$50,000	U.S. Treasury	3.000%	12/15/33	85.5309	$42,880.82	15.14
	Cash				$22,783.95	0.00
	Portfolio Total				$260,066.43	

Ivan's spreadsheet calculates the market value, including accrued interest to date, and the duration of each bond. The duration of the portfolio equals the weighted-by-market-value duration of the assets.

$$D = \sum_{i=1}^{n} w_i R_i$$

$$= \frac{\$20,657.17 \ (9.28) \ + \ \$40,947.73 \ (6.21) \ + \ ... \ + \ \$22,783.95 \ (0.00)}{\$260,066.44} = 7.78 \ years$$

The duration of the assets is short of the target of 8.6 years, so Ivan purchases $20,000 of a twenty- to thirty-year bond to increase the duration of the portfolio.

Chapter 16 - Questions and Problems

16-1:

John Q. Investor is a assigned the management of a trust that must generate $1,000,000 in three years. The client is somewhat eccentric and limits the trust to annual coupon bonds. There are two companies that issue such bonds. Tardis Intertemporal has a series of 8% annual coupon bonds with three years left to maturity. The bond is priced to yield 10% and has a duration of 2.78 years. Hypothetical Resources issues one-year 7% annual coupon bonds every year. The bond is priced to yield 10% and has a duration of 1 year.

A. John points out that he cannot immunize the portfolio under these restrictions. How does John know that he has been given an impossible task?

B. Demonstrate that, given a 1% variation in yield, the trust cannot be immunized. Calculate the value of the portfolio at risk if the yields decrease to 9% or increase to 11% if John puts everything into the 8% bond, reinvests by buying more 8% bonds, and puts residual cash into a money market or simple interest-bearing account.

16-2:

You are hired as an Investment Manager for *Investments Unlimited* and are given a bond portfolio to manage. You examine the Trust Agreement and find that *Investments Unlimited* is obliged to pay out $1 million in three years and $2 million in five years. The portfolio holds a number of bonds and a large cash balance.

Calculate the duration of the liability assuming yields of 7.00% Use the table to show your work and remember to use semi-annual periods.

A. What is the present value and duration of the liability?

B. You calculate the duration of the assets of the portfolio as 5.45 years. What kind of bonds would you add to the portfolio?

16-3:

You are hired as an investment manager for *Investments Unlimited* and given a $1,000,000 bond portfolio to manage. You calculate the duration of the liability to be 5.0 years. The client specifies that you are restricted to two bond issues. IBM has a 6%, 10-year bond, with a duration of 7.56 years, and is quoted at 92.894. GE has an 11%, 5-year bond, with a duration of 4.00 years, and is quoted at 116.633. Both bonds come in denominations of $1,000.

A. Calculate that the percentage of the portfolio you should invest in GE and in IBM bonds in order to immunize the portfolio.

B. How many GE and IBM bonds should you buy?

C. What is the prevailing yield?

16-4:

You are the portfolio manager for a trust, the terms of which provide **ten** scholarships to the Department of Finance at the University of Illinois. Each scholarship is to be paid in four equal installments of $25,000 each over the four years of undergraduate study starting at the end of next year. **Thus the fund must generate $250,000 in one year, $250,000 in two years, $250,000 in three years, and $250,000 in four years.**

A.   Assume an interest rate of 4%. What is the duration of the trust obligation? (Remember that we are now dealing with semi-annual coupon bonds again so you need to calculate the duration of the trust obligation in semi-annual periods.)

B.   Approximately how much money will we require to set up the trust as specified?

You are restricted to two different bond issues. The first issue is a 6% bond that has seven years left to maturity and the second issue is a 3% bond that has two years left to maturity. The computer system you set up as soon as you graduated (it's tied right to the firm's trading desk and the bond data is updated every three minutes) gives you the following information: the 6% bond is trading at 112.106 and its duration is 5.90 years and the 3% bond is trading at 98.096 and its duration is 1.96 years.

C.   Why is the 6% bond trading at a premium and the 3% bond at a discount?

D.   If each bond has a par value of $1,000, how many of each bond issue must you buy to immunize the portfolio? Set up the stewardship report that reflects the value of the trust at the outset.

E.   Six months have gone by. You receive on behalf of the trust the first coupon payments. How much money is paid into the trust?

F.   The trust is now one year old. The money you received six months ago was reinvested in a cash account at 3%, and another set of coupon payments have come in. What is the **cash** position of the trust?

The 6% bond now has six years to maturity, and the 3% bond has one year to maturity. Your trusty computer system tells you that the 6% bond is trading at 110.575, and its duration is now 5.18 years and the 3% bond is trading at 99.029, and its duration is now 0.9926 years.

G.   Set up a stewardship report showing the assets of the trust prior to payment of the first installment of the scholarship. What is the rate of return on the portfolio?

H.   You must now pay out the first installment of the scholarship. How are you going to do this? Why?

The Instruments that trade in the debt markets fall generally into four main categories:

❑ **Government Bonds:** Government bonds represent the debt of the federal government. U.S. Treasuries are backed by the "full faith and credit" of the U.S. government and so are considered credit risk free. The United States Department of the Treasury is the largest single issuer of debt in the world. Treasury securities (represented by more than 30 T-bill issues and over 180 different T-note and T-bond issues) account for some $8.9 trillion in marketable securities.

❑ **Municipal Bonds:** Municipal bonds represent debt of the various state and local governments and authorities from general revenue bonds issued a state to a revenue-backed issue from a local school board. Interest on municipal bonds are tax exempt at the federal level and often and the state and local level as well. The U.S. municipal bond market accounts for approximately $2.9 trillion in debt with millions of issues from over 70,000 separate issuers.

❑ **Corporate Bonds:** Corporate bonds represent debt of corporations large and small. The terms of the debt are governed by contract and so these bonds tend to have more features and conditions than Treasuries. They also carry more risk. The U.S. corporate bond market accounts for approximately $7.5 trillion with over 10,000 different issues.

❑ **Asset-backed Securities:** Asset-backed securities are based on an underlying portfolios of debt— anything from mortgages to credit-card debt—that is pooled and passed on to investors. Asset-backed securities represented approximately $11.1 trillion in debt securities in 2010.

Securities Outstanding			in billions ($1,000,000,000) of dollars		
	1990	1995	2000	2005	2010
U.S. Treasury Securities	2,196	3,307	2,952	4,166	8,853
Federal Agency Debt	422	924	1,854	2,616	2,728
Municipal Debt	1,179	1,267	1,481	2,226	2,925
Mortgage-Backed Securities	1,278	2,353	3,566	7,213	8,912
Asset-Backed Securities	76	256	1,052	1,950	2,150
Money Market Instruments	1,157	1,177	2,663	3,434	2,865
Corporate Debt	1,350	1,951	3,358	4,965	7,536
TOTAL	$7,658	$11,235	$16,926	$26,570	$35,969

Statistical Abstract of the United States: 2012 Table 1199

$\mathcal{T}$he United States Department of the Treasury is the largest single issuer of debt in the world. This market has been fueled by the massive government deficits that have characterized U.S. public finances. The federal debt, which stood at some $530 billion in 1975, grew to $8.853 trillion with a further $2.728 trillion in contingent liabilities where the government acts as guarantor to the debt issued by various federal agencies by the end of 2010. By the end of June 2012 the federal public debt outstanding totaled $15.8 trillion.[1]

Treasury securities trade actual and settle T+1. This means that accrued interest is calculated based on the actual days in the month and year. The settlement date is one business day after the trade.

17.1 - Treasury Securities

Treasury securities consist of bills, notes, bonds, and inflation indexed securities.

Treasury bills are issued at auction with less than one year to maturity and trade as discount paper in the money market. Treasury notes and bonds are semi-annual coupon-bearing bonds. Notes are issued with 2 to 10 years to maturity. Bonds are issued with more than 10 years to maturity.

Treasury Inflation Protected Securities (TIPS) are issued with a fixed interest rate but a principal amount that is adjusted with inflation. The semi-annual coupon payments are thus based on the inflation-adjusted principal at the time the coupon is paid.

17.1.1 - Primary Market

The primary market consists of approximately 20 primary or recognized dealers.

❑ **Primary Dealers:** Primary dealers are banks or brokers recognized by the Federal Reserve as market makers in Treasury bills, notes, and bonds

Most primary houses are American, but foreign houses have also established a presence. This market is regulated by the Federal Reserve, which sets trading standards and imposes capital requirements. Recognition by the Federal Reserve as a primary dealer confers both prestige and profitable position from which to deal bonds. In exchange, primary dealers are required to bid in all Treasury auctions and to make a market in Treasury securities.

Notes and bonds are issued on a yield auction on a regular basis. These auctions operate on the same basis as do the T-bill auctions.

---

1   TreasuryDirect reports the national debt to the penny on a continuous basis.
     http://www.treasurydirect.gov/NP/BPDLogin?application=np

17.1.2 - Secondary Market

The secondary market is largely an over-the-counter market, where dealers trade over computer and telephone lines. It consists of several submarket sectors.

17.1.3 - When-Issued Market

In the when-issued market an investor buys a security from another investor (usually a primary bond house) after the announcement of a bond issue but before the bond is actually issued by the Treasury. The seller undertakes to obtain and deliver the bond to the purchaser as soon as it is issued.

Inside Market

The inside market refers to the market where treasury dealers trade with each other through interdealer or government brokers.

❑ **Interdealer Brokers:** Interdealer Brokers are brokers who do not trade on their own account but rather provide brokerage services to bond dealers so that these dealers can trade anonymously. This anonymity is crucial to the dealer because he does not wish to convey too much information about the position of the firm's book to other dealers.

This inside market is not accessible to nondealers in Treasury securities. Even attempts to disseminate information to large institutional traders has met with considerable resistance.

Outside Market

Dealers also trade with investors and other brokers on the outside or retail market.

17.1.4 - Dealers' Profit

Dealers' profits are made from three sources.

❑ **Bid-Ask Spread:** Dealers buy at a lower price than they sell the same issue at the same time. (Review the determinants of the bid-ask spread in the equity section.)

❑ **Profit on Book:** This is the appreciation of the portfolio (book) the dealer holds in inventory.

❑ **Carry:** Few dealers have the upfront capital needed to run a primary dealer book. Thus inventory holdings of treasury securities are financed largely through repurchase agreements. The difference between the interest earned on securities in inventory and the cost of financing that inventory is called the carry. Because the notes and bonds thus financed have a longer term to maturity than the repo, the carry depends on the shape of the yield curve. Steep normal yield curves magnify the carry, whereas inverted yield curves can make the carry negative.

17.2 - Pricing Treasury Notes & Bonds

Treasury notes and bonds are quoted on a price rather than a yield basis.

❑ **Treasury Bond Prices:** Treasury note and bond prices are specified on a percent of face value basis or dollars per $100 face value to 32nds. Notes and bonds are denominated in multiples of $1,000.

	Table 17-1:	Treasury Notes and Bonds Quote			
	Issue		Bid	Ask	Chg	AskYld
6¼	2/15/13	n	104:09	104:10	-1	0.14%
3¼	8/15/13	n	103:18	103:19	-1	0.26%
4¼	1/15/16	i	114:00	114:01	-2	0.35%
4⅜	11/15/18		120:27	120:29	-2	1.02%
3⅛	5/15/20		115:26	115:28	-4	1.04%
2⅞	11/15/24		114:01	114:03	-4	1.62%
2½	2/15/40		96:03	96:04	-2	2.70%

Financial Pages, June 2, 2012

❑ **Issue:** The issue specifies the coupon rate and maturity.

❑ **n:** The n indicates a note. The 6.25% February 15, 2013, and 3.25% August 15, 2013 are both notes.

❑ **i:** The i indicates an inflation indexed issue (TIPS)

❑ **Bid/Ask:** The quote of 96:03 to 96:04 refers to a bid of $96^3/_{32}$ % and an ask of $96^4/_{32}$ %. Since these quotes are for transactions of $1 million lots, this means you can buy the $1 million bond for $961,250.

❑ **64ths:** On occasion you will see a + after the quote. A quote of 96:04+ means that the price is 96 and 4/32 plus 1/64. The million dollar note will now cost you $961,406.25 (the + just cost you $156.25).

17.2.1 - Stripped Treasuries

A Treasury note or bond pays the principal upon maturity and a semi-annual coupon. The process of separating off the coupons and selling them separately from the principal is called stripping. This process of stripping breaks down the original bond into a number of zero-coupon bonds each maturing at a different date.

❑ **STRIPS:** STRIPS is an acronym for Separate Trading of Registered Interest and Principal Securities. The yield on STRIPS conforms closely to the theoretical spot rates calculated from the principal and interest components of Treasuries. STRIPS are essentially zero-coupon bonds and sell at a discount to their face value. The opportunity to arbitrage between T-notes and STRIPS ensures that the yields on STRIPS never deviate significantly from the theoretical spot rates.

17.3 - Federal Agencies

A federal agency is essentially a middleman, borrowing in the financial market in the name of the U.S. government at an advantageous rate and making loans to specifically targeted entities.

Each federal agency establishes a fiscal agent through which it offers its securities. These are then sold through a syndicate of dealers, who distribute the agency's securities to investors and participate in making a secondary market for these securities.

Because agency securities are issued under the authority of Congress, they are exempt from registration with the SEC.

17.3.1 - Federally Sponsored Agency Securities

Federally sponsored agencies are privately owned entities that borrow funds and use them to make various types of loans to specific classes of borrowers. Congress takes the position that, for some groups of borrowers, the available supply of credit was too limited, too variable, or too expensive. Congress then sets up an agency to provide a dependable source of credit at the lowest cost possible to these disadvantaged borrowers.

Most federal agencies are supposed to set their lending rates so that they at least cover costs, and there was considerable support for allowing these agencies to borrow directly through the Treasury. However, if all the federal agencies borrowed through the Treasury it would increase the Treasury's outstanding debt by over $2.7 trillion. Also the nature of the agency debt differs: most Treasury debt is the result of government deficits, a true national debt; agency debt is incurred to make loans to creditworthy borrowers.

Although sponsored by the federal government, only Farm Credit Financial is backed by the federal government. Thus the debt of these agencies will show a higher yield than T-notes and bonds. This yield spread reflects higher credit risk and lower liquidity.

17.3.2 - Federal Financing Bank

As federal agencies proliferated, their borrowing caused a number of problems. Agency issues compete with each other and with Treasury issues for funds. An uneven flow of issues to the market could result in interest rate fluctuations from one week to the next. To avoid this, the Treasury schedules the timing and the size of both its own and agency issues to ensure a smooth flow of federal issues to the market. As agencies proliferated, this timing became more and more difficult. Also, many smaller agencies were not well known to investors and were thus obliged to pay relatively high borrowing rates.

To deal with these problems, in 1973 Congress set up the Federal Financing Bank, a government institution supervised by the Secretary of the Treasury, from which these federally related institutions could obtain their financing.

The Federal Financing Bank financial statements show loans of $57.1 billion at the end of fiscal year 2011. These loans are federally guaranteed. Included in the statements are loans to the Rural Utilities Service in the Department of Agriculture, the U.S. Postal Service, the Credit Liquidity Fund in the National Credit Union Administration, the Department of Energy, General Services Administration, Historically Black Colleges and

Universities in the Department of Education, Foreign Military Sales in the Department of Defense, Veterans Administration Transitional Housing Program, Small Business Administration, and the Federal Railroad Administration in the Department of Transportation.

All are federally guaranteed loans, borrowed through the Department of the Treasury.

17.4 - International Government Bonds

Most national governments issue debt. There are two broad categories of such bonds: internal and external. Internal bonds are issued in the country's domestic currency and are issued primarily within their own borders to their own citizens. External bonds are issued in another currency, often U.S. dollars or euros. These are referred to as dollar bonds or euro bonds.

Debt issues of historically stable governments, U.S. Treasuries, United Kingdom Gilts, and Government of Canada Bonds, are commonly considered risk-free of default because they have never failed to make a payment as promised.

But not all governments are crated equal, nor are all government bonds credit-risk free. Governments can, and some do, default on their debt. Unlike corporations, governments cannot simply default, enter a courtroom, and agree to the terms negotiated with creditors. With corporations, the most frequent result is the lenders exit the bankruptcy proceedings owning the corporation, as their debt is converted to equity through the bankruptcy process. For this reason, the International Monetary Fund has power to intervene and, in effect, act as the bankruptcy judge. The IMF hopes to come to agreeable terms to each the borrower and the lenders, but no "ownership" issues are possible. IMF terms to the bankrupt country may include austerity programs and other politically unpalatable measures. In summary, no two cases are ever alike. However, we can become more knowledgeable and possibly make better investment decisions with a brief review of two well studied country defaults.

1998: Russian Default

On August 18, 1998, the Russian government defaulted on $30.9 billion in ruble-denominated short-term debt. At the time of the default the Russian government was also in default of interest payment on some $60 billion in direct foreign debt, and debt in the private sector was trading at close to 8-10¢ on the dollar.

On August 23 the IMF reported that it was looking into reports that some $10 billion of bailout funds had been diverted through New York to private holdings.

However, Russia never defaulted on its Eurobonds and in 2001 repaid over $1 billion in debt, and its bonds were once more trading at par.

2001: Argentinian Default

On December 23, 2001, Argentina defaulted.

After several years of recession, and under a fixed exchange regime, the economic crisis resulted in a run on the banks in Argentina. Fearing an eventual devaluation, individuals and corporations withdrew vast amounts of money, converted it to dollars under the fixed exchange rate, and sent the money out of the country. Unable to pay its debts, Argentina declared a moratorium on $155 billion in foreign currency debt making it, at the time, the biggest default in history.

2012: Greek Default

On March 9, 2012 Greece restructured €173 billion in debt, making it the biggest default in history.

This was not the first time Greece defaulted on its debt. The Greek War of Independence from the Ottoman Empire 1821–1832 was financed partly through Independence Loans. Greece defaulted on these loans in 1826. As a result Greece was shut out of the international debt market until 1879.

Greece did manage to borrow money through the auspices of the great powers: Britain, France, and Russia. It defaulted on these loans in 1843 and again in 1860. Greece defaulted again in 1893 and in 1931.

Further reading:
Carmen H. Reinhart and Kenneth S. Rogoff *This Time is Different: Eight Centuries of Financial Folly*, Princeton, NJ: Princeton University Press, 2009.

Chapter 17 - Questions and Problems

17-1:

Which of the following represents a Treasury note quote?

A. 8:20 - 8:00
B. 8.5%
C. 85:24 - 85:30
D. 85½ - 85 ⅝

17-2:

Which of the following represents a Treasury bill quote?

A. 8:20 - 8:00
B. 8.5%
C. 85:24 - 85:30
D. 85½ - 85 ⅝

17-3:

The holder of which of the following receives no interest?

A. Treasury STRIPS
B. Treasury notes
C. Treasury bonds
D. Treasury stock

$\mathcal{M}$ unicipal Bonds represent debt of states and subdivisions of states such as Counties, Cities, Municipalities, School Districts, and any number of governing bodies that have the ability to borrow included in their charter of authority. As with the debt of the Federal Government, repayment of the principal and interest is usually, but not always, through the collection of taxes by the entity on its constituents.

The 2012 Statistical Abstract of the U.S. showed that there were[1]

50	states
3,033	counties
19,492	municipalities
16,519	townships
13,051	school districts
35,381	special districts
89,526	governmental units

many of which borrow money by issuing municipal bonds. Note that only the federal government issues "government securities"; all other governments issue "municipal securities" or "muni's".

Many, but not all municipal bonds are referred to as "tax-free" bonds, which is really a misnomer. The mission of this text is to familiarize you with important elements of finance, not to educate on U.S. tax law, but some detail on tax law is warranted here for a full understanding of municipal bonds. The term "tax-free" refers to the treatment of the income (interest) component only, meaning that if the investor holding the bond is subject to U.S. federal Income taxes, they may exclude,[2] subject to limitations, the interest received on the bond in the calculation of taxable income. This ability to exclude interest income received on other types of debt, even the debt of the federal government, is not permitted. It is taxed at ordinary income tax rates.

Some municipal bonds are also referred to as "double tax-exempts" or even "triple tax-exempts".

Example 1:

Susan Q. Speculator lives and works on Wall Street. She also owns several bonds issued by the City of New York. New York City actually has an income tax of its own. So Susan pays income tax to city of New York City, to the state of New York, and to the U.S. Federal government.

It is possible, but by no means certain, that Susan could exclude the interest on her municipal bonds from her taxable income at all three levels of taxation.

---

1   *Statistical Abstract of the United States 2012*, Table 428 Number of Governmental Units by Type: 1952 to 2007

2   The U.S. tax code is too cumbersome for us to explore in this text. Nevertheless, no full discussion of municipal bonds as investments should ignore some of the fundamental elements of the code. Suffice to say that since the passage of the Tax Reform Act of 1986 (which created taxable municipal bonds and countless regulations defining and governing them), and the inclusion of the Alternative Minimum Tax Law in the Code (which may prohibit certain investors from excluding municipal bond interest from income, depending on a limitless number of circumstances), for purposes of this text, we treat all municipal bonds as if they afford the investor the ability to receive the income free of U.S. federal income tax. We also know enough about taxes to conclude the following: First, they are too complicated. Second, because of the first conclusion, you should always seek good tax counsel.

This allows governments to borrow at a lower interest rate because investors subject to high tax rates are focused on the after-tax rate of return. This search for after-tax return is a part of why the U.S. municipal bond market accounts for approximately $2.9 trillion in debt with literally millions of different issues outstanding from more than 70,000 separate issuers.

18.1 - Types of Municipal Bonds

In 2010 new issues of municipal bonds totaled $434.5 billion, of which $283.9 billion were revenue bonds and $150.9 billion were general obligation bonds.[3] California, New York, Texas, Florida, and Illinois issue the most debt.

18.1.1 - General Obligation Bonds

General obligation bonds are backed by the "full faith and credit" of the issuing agency. This means that the bonds are backed by the ability of the governmental unit to levy taxes. GOs are occasionally limited to the amount or type of tax that can be levied to pay off the bond issue, or extended to lay claim to specified fees or grants.

18.1.2 - Revenue Bonds

Revenue bonds are backed by the revenues of a specific project. These bonds are as creditworthy as the project they finance.

Industrial Development Bonds

IDBs are used to finance the purchase or construction of industrial facilities that are to be leased to firms at favorable rates. Essentially, IDBs provide low rate financing incentives to businesses who locate in a specified location or area.

Municipal Notes

By their very nature most municipal bonds are long-term. Municipal securities that are issued with three years to maturity or less are classified as notes. Most muni notes are interest bearing with interest paid at maturity. Notes that are issued to borrow against funds already in the pipeline are called anticipation notes.

❏ **Anticipation Notes:** Municipal notes issued as gap funding.

There are tax anticipation notes (TANs), revenue anticipation notes (RANs), tax and revenue anticipation notes (TRANs), project notes (PNs), construction loan notes (CLNs), et cetera.

---

3   *Statistical Abstract of the United States 2012*, Table 440 New Security Issues, State and Local Governments: 1990 to 2010.

Example 2:

> Winter City borrows money to pay for snow clearance in February but will receive the property tax revenue to pay for it on May 1. To bridge this gap Winter City issues anticipation notes, borrowing money in February, paying for snow crews, and repaying the debt with property tax receipts in May.

_____

❏ **Tax-exempt Commercial Paper:** Tax-exempt commercial paper is similar to corporate commercial paper. The interest rate is fixed at issuance based on a 360-day year and a maturity of less than 270 days. Most of municipal corporate paper is backed by bank lines of credit.

❏ **7-day demand notes:** Demand notes are private placement securities which might have a maturity on issuance of as long as forty years. It pays a floating rate usually linked to the prime rate and allows either the issuer to call, or the buyer to put, the bond on a five-business-day notice. Most 7-day demand notes are backed by a binding commitment from a major bank to provide interim financing if the issuer is faced with a large put. Seven-day demand notes allow issuers to borrow at the base of the yield curve. To the buyer, these bonds count as seven-day paper in the calculation of their average term to maturity, thus allowing funds to offset the longer term of other investments.

18.2 - Issuing Agencies

18.2.1 - States

General obligation bonds are generally considered free of credit risk, just as are government bonds. States will generally do whatever is necessary to see that its general obligations are met, if only because failure to do so would seriously reduce its ability to issue further debt. However, states cannot be sued without their own consent, which means that bondholders have little legal recourse if a state does default. Therefore, state-issued revenue or industrial development bonds may involve considerable risk.

18.2.2 - Local Governments

Local governments can be sued against their will; bondholders can thus enforce their claims through the courts, forcing local officials to collect or divert the funds needed to meet the specified debt requirements. With revenue bonds, the ability to force repayment of the bond issue extends only to the revenues specified by the bond issue.

Some local governments have defaulted (Cleveland, 1978–1979) and others have restructured their debt, calling in outstanding bonds and exchanging them for bonds with lower (or deferred) rates of interest and longer maturities (New York City, 1975).

2012: Stockton, California

In February 2012 Stockton, California, missed some $2million in payments due on a $332 million revenue bond issue. The September 2014 revenue bond was issued in June 2004 to cover parking structures.

In March Wells Fargo Bank filed a suit against the Stockton Public Finance Authority in its capacity as indenture trustee for the bonds. In April the courts awarded possession of the parking garages to Wells Fargo.

Stockton may be left no choice but to file for Chapter 9 bankruptcy.

❏ **Chapter 9 Bankruptcy:** Chapter 9 of the Bankruptcy code covers municipalities. The code allows municipalities to renegotiate collective bargaining agreements, pension provisions, and other benefits. The largest Chapter 9 bankruptcies to date were Jefferson County, Alabama, in November 2011 with over $4 billion in debt and Orange County, California, in 1994 with $1.7 in debt.

An investor concerned about the possible default of a municipal bond can buy default insurance. Often muni's are insured by the issuer, and the cost of insurance is offset by the lower interest on insured bonds.

18.2.3 - Special Districts and Authorities

Special districts and authorities such as school districts, airports, etc. are created by state charter. They may be granted monopoly power (like airports) as well as the rights to collect specific types of fees and taxes. The primary source of funds to repay debt for these districts and authorities are property taxes. Because property taxes support a multitude of entities (schools, libraries, sewers, etc.) the risk of the bonds that are backed by these taxes depend on any other debt based on the same property, as well as the value of the property itself.

18.3 - Tax Treatment

Through a reciprocal agreement with the federal government, interest on state and local government securities are exempt from federal taxes, and interest of federal securities are exempt from state and local taxation. Further, most states exempt their own issues from taxation. Therefore if you buy a bond issued by the state of Illinois then the income earned on the bond may be exempt from the State of Illinois income tax. But if you take the bond with you when you move to Wall Street then the income on the bond is subject to the income tax by both the state and the city of New York.

Note that the tax exemption applies to the interest paid on the security or, in the case of a discount note, on the discount *at issue*. However, if the price of the security changes after it is issued, the capital gain is treated as taxable investment income.

The tax exemption means that a municipal bond can be issued at a lower yield than the equivalent treasury security, thereby reducing the cost of borrowing and creating an attractive investment for investors with a higher-than-average marginal tax.

$$Yield_{Municipal} = \left(1 - Tax_{Marginal} \right) * Yield \qquad\qquad (Eq\ 18\text{-}1)$$

Example 3:

If 20-year Treasuries are currently yielding 6% and the marginal tax rate of target investors is 33%, then the state of Illinois can issue 20-year bonds at 4%.

$$Yield_{Municipal} = (1 - 0.33) * 0.06 = 0.0402$$

In addition to other risks, municipal bonds are subject to tax risk.

❑ **Tax Risk:** Tax risk refers to the possibility that the nature or extent of the tax exemption might change. This might happen because the investor's marginal tax rate changes (either through tax changes or through changes that affect only the investor) or the tax exempt status of a specific issue is questioned.

Both Moody's and Standard & Poor's rate municipal bonds, but the information required to rate the thousands of issues, often for obscure projects, makes reliable information very difficult to obtain.

18.4 - Municipal Bond Markets

Municipals are marketed through underwriters (dealers, investment banks, or a consortium of investors) or through competitive bidding. The secondary market is over-the-counter.

Municipal bonds do not come under the regulation of the SEC. However, the Securities Act Amendment of 1975 set up the Municipal Securities Rulemaking Board (MSRB) under the SEC specifically to develop rules for the municipal securities market.

❑ **Municipal Securities Rulemaking Board:** The MSRB is responsible for investor protection and regulation of municipal securities dealers. Its Web site allows investors to search for information and to file complaints.

❑ **Electronic Municipal Market Access:** EMMA provides free on line database system for municipal disclosures and trade data. The MSRB offers public education, statistical summaries, and market statistics.

Chapter 18 - Questions and Problems

18-1:

John Q. Investor is considering the following investments:

A. A 2.50% 12/15/32 Treasury bond priced at 68:04
B. A 1.25% 3/15/27 Treasury bond priced at 62:23
C. A 1.00% 9/1/27 Municipal bond priced at 75.667
D. A 3.2% 5/1/25 Municipal bond priced at 97.921

Both municipal bonds are rated AAA and are tax exempt in his state. Municipal bonds trade 360. It is June 1, 2012, and JQ's marginal tax rate is 27%. Which investment yields JQ the best after-tax return on investment?

18-2:

John Q. Investor is considering the following investments:

A. A 2.50% 12/15/32 Treasury bond priced at 68:04
B. A 1.25% 3/15/27 Treasury bond priced at 62:23
C. A 1.00% 9/1/27 Municipal bond priced at 75.667
D. A 3.2% 5/1/25 Municipal bond priced at 97.921

Both municipal bonds are rated AAA and are tax exempt in his state. Municipal bonds trade 360. It is June 1, 2012, and JQ's marginal tax rate is 33%. Which investment yields JQ the best after-tax return on investment?

Corporate bonds are fixed-income securities that represent debt of a corporation. Corporate debt comprises approximately 20% of the U.S. debt market. Most corporate bonds have semi-annual interest payments and a single maturity date. Corporate notes, with maturities of less than 10 years are generally non-callable. Notes are generally more popular during periods of higher interest rates when issuing firms want to avoid long-term obligations.

Corporate bonds trade 30/360 and settle T+3. This means that accrued interest is calculated based on the assumption that there are 30 days in every month and 360 days in every year. The settlement date is three business days after the trade.

19.1 - Corporate Bond Indenture

The Trust Indenture Act of 1939 requires that all corporate bonds and debt securities be issued under a contract called an indenture or trust deed. The indenture must be approved by the SEC and must provide for the appointment of an independent and qualified trustee The indenture is a legal contract between the borrower (corporation) and lender (investors) and specifies the terms of the debt, terms of repayment, and protective covenants. The trustee's responsibility is to protect and enforce the rights and represent the interests of investors (lenders) in the contract.

❑ **Protective Covenants:** Protective or restrictive covenants are conditions specified in the indenture. These covenants are designed to protect the investors' interests.

One common protective covenant is that all the direct or indirect wholly owned subsidiaries of the borrower guarantee the debt. The intent is to keep the assets of the entire firm in place for the benefit of the lenders, as opposed to having the firm sell assets (subsidiaries) away from creditors. This protection is important, but does not guarantee that any of the subsidiaries will remain profitable and able to make good on their guarantee.

Additional covenants may be restrictive in nature, and prohibit the subsidiary firms from additional borrowing beyond present debt levels, or require that any additional borrowing by the firm is subordinated (lower in priority of payments) to the bond at hand.

If the bond is a mortgage bond (it pledges specific real property as collateral for the bond), it may specify minimum insurance coverage, maintenance guarantees, periodic inspections, etcetera. Other bonds may specify that working capital, debt-equity ratios, or dividend levels must remain at certain levels to safeguard the ability of the borrower to make payments to investors in the bonds.

❑ **Sinking Fund Provisions:** A sinking fund is a reserve account set up to accumulate funds needed to pay the principal on the bond issue when it comes due or, in many cases, sooner. This ensures that the firm is actually putting aside sufficient funds to repay the principal on the bond. If the firm is unable to meet sinking-fund requirements, the bondholders can demand that the issue be redeemed.

This optional redemption provision generally requires the firm to deposit a fixed percentage of the principal amount outstanding into an account with the bond's trustee. The trustee is then given discretion on how the funds are used to retire a portion of the debt for the benefit of the borrower. If the bonds are trading at a discount to their face value, the trustee can simply purchase bonds in the open market with the funds and give them to the issuer, who then cancels this principal amount from the outstanding principal owed.

Another form of repayment under a sinking fund provision looks more like a call feature imbedded in the bond, and would be used if the bonds are trading at a premium to their face value. In this instance, the sinking fund allows the trustee to issue a call for the purpose of sinking fund redemption. This is basically a notice to the bondholders that a portion of their investment is being retired for which they will be paid par. Partial retirement can be done on a pro rata or by lot basis. Pro rata means that all investors in the bond have a fixed portion of their investment retired. By lot is more common. It means that a random draw determines which bondholders have their holdings retired. To the bondholder it is the same as having their bond called for early redemption under a call provision, but receiving no premium for early repayment as is common with a formal callable bond. Remaining bondholders are more secured in receiving their payments from a less indebted firm, but investors being refunded may be annoyed.

19.1.1 - Maturity

Whereas Treasury notes and bonds mature on either the 15th or the last day of the month—keeping the date constant makes it easier to manage the huge debt of the U.S. Government—Corporate Bonds can and do mature on any date from the first to the thirty-first. Each bond is different. Bond investors quickly discover that terms, conditions and conventions in corporate debt issues are much less structured than in government bonds. Details of each bond are limited only by the imagination of investment bankers and attorneys at the time the bond is created. This can require analysts of corporate bonds approach the task with the skills of Sherlock Holmes in their reading of the bond contract.

❑ **Serial Bonds:** Serial bonds are issues arranged such that the principal comes due on a series of specified dates rather than all at the end.

❑ **Bullet Maturity Bonds:** Bullet maturity bonds are issued such that the entire principal comes due at maturity.

19.1.2 - Ownership

The indenture also specifies how ownership of the bond is recorded and transferred.

❑ **Registered Bonds:** The company's registrar or trustee records the ownership of each bond. Interest and principal are paid directly to the registered owner.

❑ **Registered with Coupons:** Ownership is registered but interest is not paid automatically; the bondholder must claim each interest payment by detaching the coupon and presenting it to the company.

❑ **Bearer Bonds:** The certificate itself constitutes evidence of ownership. The owner must present the coupons to claim interest payments and the certificate itself to claim the principal. Because the ownership of these bonds cannot be traced, provisions in the Tax Equity and Fiscal Responsibility Act of 1982, (TEFRA) effectively ended the issuance of any new bearer form of debt in the U.S.

19.1.3 - Security

Security refers to specific assets offered by a company as collateral to secure the value of the loan. Contract language for securing a loan often uses the word lien.

❑ **Lien:** A lien is a mortgage, pledge, security interest, charge, or other any other kind of encumbrance that attaches specific property to the debt for eventual repayment.

In general, any form of security the issuer builds into a bond contract lowers the borrowing cost to them because investors are willing to accept lower returns for less risky investments.

Unsecured Debt:

Unsecured debt is backed by the ability of the company to generate revenues; it is not backed by a specific asset as collateral. In general, the less security attached to a bond, the more expensive it is for the company to borrow money because investors demand higher yields to compensate for the additional risk.

❑ **Debenture:** Longer term unsecured issues are generally called debentures. (This leads to some international misunderstandings; in the UK a debenture usually signifies a bond that has a prior claim on the firm's assets.) Debenture bondholders have a claim on the firm's unsecured assets and can, if the company fails to make a scheduled interest or principal repayment, force the firm into bankruptcy and claim its assets to pay off the bond.

❑ **Subordinated Debentures:** Subordinated debenture bondholders have a claim on the firm's assets after secured debt and debenture bondholders.

Secured Debt:

Most issues by utility and transportation companies are secured by specific assets. This means that if the company defaults on the debt, the trustee or bondholder may take possession of the relevant assets. If these are insufficient to satisfy the claim, the remaining debt has a general claim alongside any other unsecured debt against the other assets of the firm.

When debt issues utilize techniques to make them more secure, the firm loses flexibility, but lowers its borrowing cost. Investors are willing to accept lower returns for the lower risk in securitized debt.

❑ **Mortgage Bonds:** Mortgage bonds grant the bondholder a first-mortgage lien on specified property. Because this lien gives bondholders the legal right to seize and sell the property if the issuer defaults on the bond it provides greater security to the bondholder and a lower interest rate for the issuing corporation. Some of the mortgages are closed so that no more bonds may be issued against the mortgage. However, usually there is no specific limit to the amount of debt that may be secured (open mortgage), or there is a limit, but that limit has not yet been reached (open end mortgage). First mortgage bonds have a senior claim to second mortgage bonds. Mortgaged assets cannot be sold to raise funds without the consent of the mortgage bondholders.

The indenture generally obliges the issuer of the bond to insure the property against which the mortgage is secured and keep it in good repair.

Ford Motor Company

The Ford Motor Company Blue Oval is the logo first seen on the 1928 Ford Model A, and used by the company to this day.

By 2006, Ford Motor Company's future was in question. Its profits had turned into huge losses, and cost control measures—including elimination of the common stock dividend—were not enough to sustain the company's viability. Ford needed a large amount of cash to modernize its facilities.

Through a combination of bond offerings and bank consortiums of loans, Ford raised more than $23 billion, but at the cost of pledging everything owned. Stipulations in the borrowing agreements to banks included a novel mortgage: a claim on the intellectual property of the company. This included even the use of their copyrighted Blue Oval Ford trademark. Ford's real assets were either already pledged, or considered of little or no value. This mortgage was to remain in place so long as the rating on the publicly traded debt of the company was below investment grade.

In May 2012, Ford's debt was upgraded to a level deemed investment grade, and the company regained the right (without encumbrance) to these assets. Ford's Blue Oval was back home.

❑ **Collateral Trust Bonds:** Collateral trust bonds are secured by stocks, bonds, or notes placed with a trustee. Generally these bonds are issued by holding companies: firms whose assets consist of the common stock of their subsidiaries. The problem with collateral trust bonds is that this common stock represents a claim on the subsidiary that is junior to all other claims of the assets of the subsidiaries. Therefore the indenture to collateral trust bonds will generally place restrictions on any other debt or preferred shares the subsidiary issues.

Large bank holding companies commonly issue collateral trust bonds using the preferred stock issuances of their many subsidiary banks as the collateral for the loan. This is a complicated mechanism that allows the bank holding company to raise capital to meet regulatory capital requirements.

❑ **Equipment Trust Certificates:** Equipment trust certificates are secured by equipment. These are generally issued by transportation companies (railroads, airlines, trucking firms, etc.) who use the funds raised by the bond issue to purchase equipment (rolling stock, airplanes, trucks, etc.), which is in turn used as collateral for the bond issue. Equipment trust certificates are generally issued as serial bonds; the serial maturities reflect the nature of the collateral, which is subject to substantial wear and tear and tends to deteriorate rapidly. Equipment trust certificates appeal to investors because of their attractive yields and low default records. Bond rating agencies generally rate equipment trust certificates one grade higher than the firm's regular debt.

Equipment trust certificate bonds are often structured as pass-through certificates. Pass-through certificates bundle individual equipment trusts which hold title to the assets, and may have been financed initially by manufacturers of the equipment, or short-term bank loans.

American Airlines

The indenture for an ETC provides detail about the equipment, and can make for some intriguing reading.

An ETC issue of AMR Corp., the parent of American Airlines, contains descriptions like; aircraft type (make, model and configuration), registration number, the airplane's "N-number" (mandated by FAA rules to be visible on every airplane's tail), manufacturer's serial number, month of delivery, original principal amount (cost), and current appraised value.

One advantage of this type of secured debt is greater protection to the investor. When AMR Corp. filed for bankruptcy November 29, 2011, it listed $24.7 billion in assets and $29.6 billion in debt in Chapter 11 papers filed in U.S. Bankruptcy Court in Manhattan.[1]

The filing further stated that AMR had approximately $2.0 billion of enhanced equipment trust certificates (EETCs) outstanding, with maturities through 2021. $73 million of these certificates were secured by spare engines, and the remainder was listed as secured by American Airlines aircraft. The publicly traded unsecured debt of the company was trading as low as 30 cents on the dollar, while the secured debt traded at substantially higher prices.

❑ **Income Bond:** An income bond is an issue where coupon payments are contingent on earnings. If earnings are insufficient to make the payment then the bondholders cannot force the company into bankruptcy. The coupon is declared in arrears and paid when, and if, the company generates further earnings. Income bonds trade flat.

❑ **Flat:** Flat means without accrued interest. Income bonds (because the amount of the interest payment is uncertain) and bonds already in default (because the interest payment may not be paid at all) generally trade flat.

19.1.4 - Special Provisions

Bonds sometimes include special provisions such as puts and calls.

❑ **Put Bond:** A put bond includes a provision whereby investors can sell the bond back to the corporate bond issuer at a specified amount on specified dates before maturity.

The put creates a price floor on the bond. If market interest rates rise, rather than experience the customary decline in price, the put bond should trade no lower than the put price. The law of one price would allow riskless profit by purchasing put bonds below the put price and immediately selling them to the issuer at the put price. Obviously this protection to the investor has great value in a rising rate environment. Investors pay for this protection by accepting a lower yield on the bond than the yield on an otherwise identical, plain vanilla bond. The lower borrowing cost to the issuer is paid for when the firm is forced to redeem the bonds at a fixed price regardless of market forces.

---

1   *United States Bankruptcy Court Southern District of New York In re AMR Corporation, et al., Debtors.*
     http://www.amrcaseinfo.com/pdflib/4_15463.pdf

❑ **Poison Put:** The poison put is a provision that allows investors to redeem the bond at par in the event of a hostile takeover or the purchase of a large block of shares. A poison put is used to prevent hostile takeovers because huge redemptions of the putable bonds can create such a large cash obligation that the target company loses its appeal. In general, investors should not rely on this as a mechanism designed for their protection; the poison put is meant to protect the firm from unwanted takeover offers.

❑ **Callable Bond:** A call is a provision that allows the corporation to pay off the bond early.

19.2 - Call Provisions

A call provision allows the issuer to redeem all or part of the issue prior to maturity. The terms of the call provision vary, but they typically provide that the issuer can call the bond at par value plus a declining premium. Many callable bonds are restricted in the first few years after the issue. Some are noncallable, and some are noncallable for refunding. If a bond is noncallable for refunding then the firm can not pay off one bond issue by issuing another, although it can be called if it paid off using internally generated funds or a stock issue.

Note that an explicit call provision is different from a sinking fund agreement. The call is a right in favor of the issuer, to repay the debt early; a sinking fund is an obligation on the issuer to repay all or a part of the debt early.

The call provision on a corporate bond affects both the issuer and the investor.

19.2.1 - The Issuer

Call provisions provide corporate financial management with additional flexibility in financing corporate debt. In return for this flexibility, there is an additional cost to the borrower in the form of a higher yield to the investor, over an otherwise identical, but noncallable bond.

Issue:

In June 2010 the Discovery Café issues a $10 million, 7% bond maturing June 30, 2040. This constitutes a contract to pay the bondholder 3.5% every six months for thirty years and, if the issue was at par, the Discovery Café raised $10,000,000.

The issue is callable after ten years with a call price of par plus 10%. The call premium declines ½% for each year thereafter. Thus the schedule of call prices would be

2020:	110.00			
2021:	109.50			
2022:	109.00	2038:	101.00	
2023:	108.50 ...	2039:	100.50	
		2040:	100.00	which conveniently brings us to par at maturity.

Call

In June 2020 the required yield for equivalent bonds is 5%. Without the call feature these bonds would sell for 125.103. According to the terms of the indenture the Discovery Café can call the bond at par plus 10% penalty.

❑ **Call Price:** The call price is the price the company must pay if it calls the bond. The call price is par plus the call premium. In the case of the Discovery Café bond the call price is par plus 10%, thus 110.00

Discovery Café can refinance the corporate debt with a 5% bond issue also maturing June 30, 2040. Essentially the Discovery Café is borrowing money at 5% to pay off a loan at 7%.

The call replaces the entire bond issue, but at a lower coupon rate:

Call $10,000,000 in 7% 2040 bonds at 110.00	$	-11,000,000.00
Issue $11,000,000 in 5% 2040 bonds at 100.00	$	11,000,000.00
	$	0.00

To finance the call premium the debt load increases from $10m to $11m:

Principal payment in 2040 under the 7% bond	$	10,000,000.00
Principal payment in 2040 under the 5% bond	$	-11,000,000.00
	$	-1,000,000.00

The coupon payment is at a lower rate but on a higher debt:

7% semi-annual coupon on $10m debt	$	350,000.00
5% semi-annual coupon on $11m debt	$	-275,000.00
	$	75,000.00

The change in payments due to the call are given in the time line. Essentially the Discovery Café must decide if the decrease in semi-annual coupon payments is worth the increase in debt load.

June 20	Dec 20	Jun 21	Dec 21		Dec 2040	Jun 2040
$0	$75,000	$75,000	$75,000		$75,000	$75,000
						$-1,000,000

The present value of the change in payments is

$$PV = \sum_{t=1}^{40} \frac{-\$75,000}{(1.025)^t} + \frac{\$1,000,000}{(1.025)^{40}}$$

$$= \frac{-\$75,000}{0.025}\left[1 - \frac{1}{(1.025)^{40}}\right] + \frac{\$1,000,000}{(1.025)^{40}}$$

$$= -\$1,882,708.13 + \$372,430.62$$

$$= -\$1,510,277.51$$

The Discovery Café reduces the present value of its bond payments by $1,510,277.51 if it calls the 7% 2030 bond and replaces it with the 5% 2030 bond.

19.2.2 - The Investor

Although corporate management rather likes the flexibility afforded by call provisions, investors hold quite a different view. In theory the issuer's right to call a bond at par prevents the price of the bond from ever rising over the call price. A completely callable bond is a classic case of heads you win, tails I lose. This is one reason why many bonds include a call premium (like in the Discovery Café) or may preclude a call, or preclude a refunding call, for a specified number of years.

The effects of the call provisions must be taken into account when the investor buys the bond. Essentially the investor will buy a callable bond only if he is compensated for the effects of the call with a higher yield.

Promised Yield to Maturity

John Q. Investor purchased ten $1000 Discovery Café 7% 30-year bonds at par in 2010 when they were issued. He calculates his yield to maturity as 7%

$$P_M = \$10,000 = \sum_{n=1}^{60} \frac{\$350}{\left(1 + \frac{Yld_M}{2}\right)^n} + \frac{\$10,000}{\left(1 + \frac{Yld_M}{2}\right)^{60}}$$

$$Yld_M = 0.07$$

Yield to Maturity = 7.00%

Holding Period Yield

John Q. Investor— having fallen asleep in financial markets class—is totally unaware that the bond is callable. In 2020, John observes that yields have fallen to 5%. He calculates that the price of the Discovery Café 2040 7% bond should be 125.102775 and calculates his holding period yield as 8.63%

Calculator Techniques 19-1:	BOND	Enter	Compute
	SDT =	6.30.20	
Calculate the price of the Discovery Café bond in 2020 to be 125.102775	CPN =	7.000	
	RDT =	6.30.40	
	RV =	100.000	
	360		
	2/Y		
	YLD =	5.000	
	PRI =		125.102775
	AI =		0.000000

The holding period yield comes from the same bond price equation but JQ no longer holds the bond to maturity. He holds the bond for 20 semi-annual periods and then sells it (or so he thinks) for 125.102775.

$$P_M \;=\; \$10,000 \;=\; \sum_{n=1}^{20} \frac{\$350}{\left(1 + \dfrac{Yld_{HP}}{2}\right)^n} + \frac{\$12,510.28}{\left(1 + \dfrac{Yld_{HP}}{2}\right)^{20}}$$

$$Yld_H \;=\; 0.0863$$

Holding Period Yield = 8.63%

Using a redemption value of 125.102775 we see that if the bond were not callable and JQ sold it in a 5% market, his bond would yield a holding period return of 8.631490% The increased yield reflects the capital gain of $2,510.28 over 20 semi-annual periods.

Yield to Call

JQ's bonds are called at 110.00. When JQ purchased the bond he should have calculated both the yield to maturity and the yield to call.

In calculating the yield to call, remember an important characteristic of the bond call provision: It is a right, not an obligation. Even if interest rates have fallen from the time of the original issue, the firm still needs the capital required to repay the bonds early.

If the bond is refundable (the company can issue new bonds to raise capital needed to pay off the old bonds) access to the capital market is still required. Access to the capital market is not guaranteed, particularly if the borrower's financial condition has deteriorated. This became very apparent in the years after 2008 when interest rates fell to record lows, but many firms did not have access to new funds to retire outstanding, higher cost debt.

If the bond is nonrefundable, the firm must have other financial means: either accumulated profits, or the issuance of stock (a secondary offering). Again, in the years after 2008 accumulated profits and new stock issues were very scarce resources.

Calculator Techniques 19-3:

Calculate the yield-to-first call on the Discovery Café Bond using the first call date of 2020.

The call price 110.00 is entered as the redemption value of the bond.

Note that the yield-to-first call (7.68%) is less than the yield if the bond is not called (8.63%) because our capital gain is $1,000 rather than $2,510.28

BOND	Enter	Compute
SDT =	6.30.10	
CPN =	7.000	
RDT =	6.30.20	
RV =	110.000	
360		
2/Y		
YLD =		7.682763
PRI =	100.000	
AI =		0.000000

The Yield-to-Call is the yield calculated to the first call date rather than to the maturity date. The Yield-to-Call (or to be more specific the yield-to-first-call) is given by:

$$P_M \;=\; \$10,000 \;=\; \sum_{n=1}^{20} \frac{\$350}{\left(1 + \dfrac{Yld_c}{2}\right)^n} \;+\; \frac{\$11,000}{\left(1 + \dfrac{Yld_c}{2}\right)^{20}}$$

$$Yld_c = 0.0768$$

Yield to Call = 8.68%

JQ can calculate the yield to call for each call date in the schedule. The lowest of these is the yield-to-worst.

❑   **Yield-to-Worst:** The yield-to-worst is the lowest yield-to-call in the call schedule.

Realized Yield to Maturity

J.Q. uses the entire proceeds of the call ($11,000) to purchase DVC 5% bonds.

The yield to maturity over the originally planned 30-year period is no longer 7%, but 6.44% This is the realized yield-to-maturity or realized return on the bond. Note that the realized yield is between the old yield of 7% and the new yield of 5%. If you calculate something outside this range, you have made a mistake.

Realized yield must cover the period from purchase to maturity. This means that the original called bond must be exactly replaced with a replacement or equivalent bond issue. Make sure that no money changes hands at the call. In this case $11,000 redemption value exactly exchanges for $11,000 in replacement bonds. If John Q. Investor is required to change the amount of money tied up in this investment then the yield calculation on that investment will be contaminated.

$$P_M = \$10,000 = \sum_{n=1}^{20} \frac{10 * \$35}{\left(1 + \dfrac{Yld_R}{2}\right)^n}$$

$$+ \sum_{n=21}^{60} \frac{11 * \$25}{\left(1 + \dfrac{Yld_R}{2}\right)^n} + \frac{11 * \$1,000}{\left(1 + \dfrac{Yld_R}{2}\right)^{60}}$$

$$Yld_R = 0.0644$$

Realized Yield-to-Maturity = 6.44%

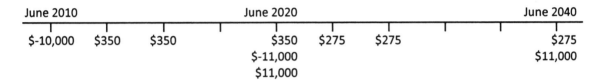

June 2010				June 2020					June 2040
$-10,000	$350	$350		$350	$275	$275			$275
				$-11,000					$11,000
				$11,000					

To calculate the realized yield we use the Cash Flow (CF) method. The bond spreadsheet assumes a constant coupon rate over the life of the bond. This is no longer appropriate. The cash flow method allows us to specify different payments through the life of a single investment.

Calculator Techniques 19-4:		DATA	Enter	Compute
The last coupon payment is added to the principal repayment cash flow because it takes place at the same time.		CFo =	-10,000	
		C01 =	350	
		F01 =	20	
The yield (IRR) is expressed in terms of semi-annual periods. To get the realized yield to maturity we must multiply be 2 to get 6.440884%		C02 =	275	
		F02 =	39	
		C03 =	11,275	
		F03 =	1	
		IRR		3.220442

Note that it makes no difference whether you have your calculator set to actual or 360; the results are the same. This is because we are doing all our calculations on the coupon date. The yield is the same, and the accrued interest is $0 no matter how you calculate it.

Table 19-1: Summary of Yields calculated on the Discovery Café Bond

Promised Yield to Maturity on 2010 issue	7.00%
Yield to First Call (2010 to 2020)	7.68%
Holding Period Yield (2010 to 2020) if bond had not been callable	8.63%
Holding Period or Realized Yield (2010 to 2040)	6.44%
Promised Yield to Maturity on 2020 issue	5.00%

19.3 - The Risk Structure

Six primary attributes are significant in determining the yield of a bond:

- ❑ **Term to maturity:** The life of the bond contract,
- ❑ **Coupon rate:** The interest specified by the bond contract,
- ❑ **Call provisions:** The contractual provisions whereby the bond can be paid off early,
- ❑ **Liquidity:** The ability to buy or sell quickly without affecting the price,
- ❑ **Risk of default:** The risk that the issuer will not pay coupon and/or principal when it is due, and
- ❑ **Tax status:** How income and capital gain are treated under the tax law.

The yield structure is the overall pattern of yields that reflect these six attributes. Because we have trouble with six-dimensional analysis, we generally hold five attributes constant and examine the sixth. Two of the most common views of the yield structure are the term to maturity and risk of default.

- ❑ **Term Structure:** The pattern of yields for bonds with similar coupon, call, liquidity, risk, and tax status, but different terms-to-maturity is called the term structure of yields. The term structure generates the yield curve.

- ❑ **Risk Structure:** The pattern of yields for bonds with similar term, coupon, call, liquidity risk , and tax status, but with different default risks is called the risk structure of yields.

19.3.1 - Default Risk

The difference in the yield of a liquid corporate issue and the Treasury issue of similar coupon and maturity reflects the risk of default and is called the yield spread. The yield spread generally increases over the term to maturity.

- ❑ **Spread:** The difference in return to investment is a spread. If stocks yield a return on investment of 11.2% and Treasuries yield 3.2%, then the spread on equities over treasuries is 8.0%. This is the equity risk premium underlying the CAPM.

Example 1:

Consider the following 20 year bonds:

6% FLY	Fly-By-Night	2032	YTM = 9.00%	The yield spread is 3% or 300 basis points.
6% DVC	Discovery Café	2032	YTM = 7.50%	The yield spread is 1½% or 150 basis points.
6% T-Bond	U.S. Treasury	2032	YTM = 6.00%	

The higher yield-to-maturity promised under the Fly-By-Night bond reflects the higher risk of default. Investors must be compensated for the greater degree of risk in holding Fly-By-Night bonds.

If Fly-By-Night carries the same degree of risk as Discovery Café then investors would sell their DVC and buy FLY because the bond structure and payments are identical, the risk is the same, but the Discovery Café bond is trading at 84.5868 and the Fly-By-Night bond is trading at 72.3976. This buying and selling would continue until both bonds traded at the same price to yield the same return on investment.

The yield to maturity on a bond is calculated on the assumption that all payments contractually specified by the bond will actually be paid. However, there is always a risk that the company will fail to make payments when they are due. Whenever the risk of default is greater than zero there is a difference between the yield to maturity promised under the contract and yield to maturity actually expected by the investor.

❑ **Promised Yield to Maturity:** The YTM calculated on the assumption that coupon and principal payments will be paid in full on the dates specified by the bond.

❑ **Expected Yield to Maturity:** The YTM adjusted for the probability that not all coupon and principal payments will be paid in full on the dates specified by the bond.

$$E[YTM] = Probability * Yield\ to\ Maturity_{PROMISED} \qquad (Eq\ 19\text{-}1)$$

When bond markets are in equilibrium, the expected yield to maturity of each bond must equal the expected yield to maturity of other bonds in the market. This equilibrium rate is the expected market yield.

❑ **Expected Market Yield:** The expected yield-to-maturity is thus the YTM of a fully diversified portfolio of all possible bonds with the same term, coupon, call, liquidity risk, and tax status.

19.3.2 - Default and Risk Premia

The spread on any yield to any bond over the comparable treasury can be broken down into two components: the risk premium and the default premium.

❑ **Risk Premium:** The difference between the expected yield-to-maturity and the yield-to-maturity of the risk-free bond is called the risk premium. The risk premium arises out of economy-wide or market-wide risk and thus reflects systematic risk. The risk premium is thus the added yield demanded by the investor as a return to taking the risk of moving from Treasuries to corporate bonds

❑ **Default Premium:** The difference between the expected yield-to-maturity and the promised Yield-to-Maturity is called the default premium. The default premium is company specific: greater the risk of default the greater the default premium.

Example 2:

We estimate a 4% probability that Discovery Café will default on its bonds. Thus the expected yield-to-maturity of the 6% DVC 2026 currently yielding 7.50% is 7.20%

0.04	*	0.00%	
0.96	*	7.50%	
		7.20%	Expected Yield-to-Maturity

Thus the risk premium is 120 basis points (7.20% − 6.00% = 1.20%) and the default premium is 30 basis points. (7.50% − 7.20% = 0.30%) where 6.00% is the yield on the comparable Treasury.

Example 3:

> We estimate a 20% probability that Fly-by-Night Resources will default on its bonds. Thus the expected Yield-to-Maturity of the 6% Fly-by-Night 2026 currently yielding 9.00% is also 7.20%
>
> $$
> \begin{array}{ccc}
> 0.20 & * & 0.00\% \\
> 0.80 & * & 9.00\% \\
> \hline
> & & 7.20\% \quad \text{Expected Yield-to-Maturity}
> \end{array}
> $$
>
> Thus the risk premium is 120 basis points (7.20% − 6.00% = 1.20%) and the default premium is 180 basis points. (9.00% − 7.20% = 1.80%) where 6.00% is the yield on the comparable Treasury.

Note that the calculation itself is grossly oversimplified. To be accurate we should estimate the probability that the bond defaults and pays 1¢ on the dollar, 2¢ on the dollar, etcetera, so that we have a complete map of the possible outcomes on this investment and the payout for each possibility. Because the time that the bond defaults, the eventual settlement of the defaulted bond, and the time of the settlement of the defaulted bond, are all variables, this calculation is extremely complex.

In actual defaults, the return to bondholders is highly uncertain and can run between total loss and extraordinary profits, based on the individual circumstances of the case. Sophisticated statistical modeling of possible returns in event of default is beyond the scope of this text, but is an intriguing engagement in finance. Examples of "vulture investors", those who purposely seek to own defaulted debt in an attempt to reap enormous returns, abound in financial history.

19.3.3 - Corporate Bond Ratings

Bonds are rated to provide investors with information regarding default risk. Ratings are based on current information provided by the issuer. A summary of the ratings issued by the three dominant bond ratings services: Moody's, Standard & Poor's, and Duff & Phelps is given in Table 19-2.

Although each rating service has its own proprietary methodology, basic measures of the firm's financial condition are commonly known to influence the rating assigned. A fitting analogy is the grade point average (GPA) that any student earns during a given semester or quarter. Each class grade is an element in the calculation of a grade for the term. Similarly, bond ratings are comprised of key measures of financial achievement by the borrower. One class may measure how well the firm's earnings cover its interest expense; another may measure the rate of return on invested capital. Obviously, the higher each of these measures, the higher the overall debt rating (GPA). Conversely, a measure of total indebtedness of the firm, like total debt to capital, works in reverse. A larger burden of borrowed capital makes for a riskier firm, hence a downward impact to its credit rating. Further, some measures are weighted more in their determination of the overall credit rating (some classes carry more credit hours than others). Rating services keep these methodologies very secretive.

Rating services issue overall ratings on corporations, as well as a rating on individual debt issued by the firm. The rating on the issue is further defined using the various covenants in the bond indenture agreement and takes into account the protections afforded lenders related to the specific contract terms. A first mortgage bond will often have a higher rating than an unsecured debenture of the same borrower. The unsecured borrowing may have the same rating as the firm's overall debt rating because it is a general obligation of the borrower, with no pledge of specific assets.

Table 19-2: Corporate Bond Ratings

Grade	Moody's	Standard & Poor's	Duff & Phelps	Explanation
Investment Grade	Aaa	AAA	AAA	Strongest possible capacity to pay interest and principal.
	Aa	AA	AA	Very strong capacity to pay interest and principal.
	A	A	A	Strong capacity to pay interest and principal. More susceptible to changes in economic conditions.
	Baa	BBB	BBB	Adequate capacity to pay interest and principal although the firm is susceptible to changing economic conditions.
Speculative Grade	Ba	BB	BB	The firm faces exposure to adverse business conditions or the debt is subordinated to senior debt assigned a Baa/BBB rating.
	B	B	B	The firm faces exposure to adverse business conditions which is likely to affect ability to pay interest or principal, or the debt is subordinated to senior debt assigned a Ba/BB rating.
	Caa Ca	CCC CC C	CCC CC C	Currently identifiable vulnerability to default or the debt is subordinated to senior debt assigned a higher rating.
	C	D	D	In default.
	NR	NR	NR	Not Rated. (Bonds are not rated either because no request has been made or there is insufficient data to rate the issue.)

* Moody's adds subcategories of 1, 2, 3; where A1 is higher than A2, but A1 is still lower than Aa3.
** Standard & Poor's adds subcategories + and – and appends an f to the rating (Aaf) when it rates a bond fund.

Note the classification of investment grade and speculative grade bonds.

❑   **Investment Grade Bonds:** Investment grade bonds are bonds that have been assigned to one of the top four ratings groups. Several classes of institutional investors (pension and insurance funds in particular) are restricted to investment grade bonds so maintaining this rating is important.

❑   **Speculative Grade Bonds:** The polite terminology for junk bonds is speculative grade bonds; the extremely polite terminology for junk bonds is high-yield bonds. These are bonds that have been assigned a lower rating or have no rating at all.

❑   **Fallen Angel:** A fallen angel is a bond that loses its investment grade rating.

Research tends to confirm that high yield bonds include a default premium more or less consistent with the added risk exposure.

When a rating service changes the rating on an outstanding bond, it is a significant event to both bondholders and the issuing firm. A rating upgrade signals lower risk in the debt, hence a lower required return to the investors, which is seen as a rise in price in the bonds. This corresponds to a lower (future) cost of borrowing to the firm. Conversely, if the rating on an outstanding credit is reduced, this signals an increase in risk, resulting in a higher required return to investors, which is seen as a fall in price of the bond. This corresponds to a higher (future) cost of borrowing to the firm. It is little wonder that a significant area of focus by bond portfolio managers is the continual monitoring of financial condition measures of firms. If changes in the conditions of firm's financial conditions can successfully predict a bond rating change, the portfolio manager could produce handsome returns by purchasing bonds prior to an upgrade, and selling (or shorting) bonds with impending (but yet unknown) downgrades.

2001: Enron

On December 2, 2001, Enron (ENE), a major trader of electricity and natural gas filed for bankruptcy. Officials from Enron's accounting firm, Arthur Andersen, testified in U.S. Senate hearings that Enron engaged in "possibly illegal acts" in establishing private partnerships that allowed Enron to move millions of dollars of debt off its balance sheet, while Enron maintained it fully cooperated with its auditors.

On October 15, 2001 the Enron 6.5% August 1, 2002, bond traded at 102.4134. The stock had dropped to $33.17 from a high of more than $90 in late 2000.

On October 24 Andrew Fastow, the CFO, resigned and fifteen days later Enron announced that it had overstated earnings by half a billion dollars over the previous five years. On this date the bonds were still rated investment grade, earning a BBB+ from S&P and Baa1 from Moody's. Enron was rated investment grade until November 28, when both Moody's and S&P issued a downgrade to speculative (junk). Enron declared bankruptcy December 2. The price of the Enron 6.5% August 1, 2002 bond declined to 17.7177 by December 14, 2001. The shares were trading at 63¢.

Figure 19-1: Enron 6.5% August 1,2002 Bond Price and Promised YTM October-December 31, 2001

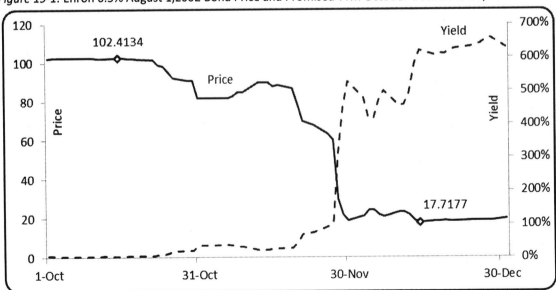

19.4 - Convertible Bonds

A convertible bond is a corporate bond (usually a subordinated debenture) that can, at the investor's discretion, be exchanged for shares of common stock of the issuer.

This feature can dramatically lower the cost of borrowing to the firm because the bond includes an embedded call option on the firm's stock. In other words, the investor (lender) has the right, but not the obligation, to exchange the bond for a fixed amount of stock in the company. Although the bond can specify number of shares or price per share, the conversion effectively fixes the price to the bondholder of the stock.
If the firm is profitable and growing, we may expect the price of the firm's publicly traded stock to increase over time, which makes the convertible bond more valuable. This upside price potential allows investors to accept very low interest rates on the bond because their return potential is limited only by the upside price potential of the stock, perhaps over a long time period if the bond has many years to maturity.

From the firm's perspective, a convertible bond allows it to (potentially) retire the debt without using cash, by printing its own "currency" in the form of new shares of its common stock.

Most convertible debt is also callable. This allows firms to force the conversion by calling the bond when the call price would result in the bondholder receiving less value than if they convert the bond into common stock. In addition, the reduction to the cost of borrowing from convertibility is usually much greater than the addition to cost of borrowing due to the bond being callable. This may cause one to wonder why all corporate bonds are not issued as convertible and callable given the apparent benefits to the firm. The investment community is not naïve and understands that convertible debt also dilutes the ownership interest of all shareholders when conversion occurs. The optimal capital structure of a firm is a very interesting academic topic in the study of finance, as well as a very rewarding career pursuit. Last, these characteristics of convertible bonds mean that prudent investors in convertible debt need to analyze the firm from the perspective of both a lender, as well as a potential owner. All investors should take this approach, for most bankruptcy cases are settled by the trustee ruling that common stockholders have no claim of value on the firm, and debt claims are settled by granting ownership of the remaining assets of the firm.

❏ **Investment Value:** The investment value of a bond is the estimate of the market value of the bond if it were not convertible.

❏ **Conversion Price:** The conversion price is the price per share of common stock if it is paid for with a bond. It is customary for the conversion terms to be expressed as a price per share (subject to adjustments necessary in the event of stock splits or stock dividends) in a convertible bond. This allows investors a direct comparison of the bond's worth in terms of stock to the market price of the stock at any time.

❏ **Conversion Ratio:** The conversion ratio is number of shares received in exchange for one $1,000 bond. The conversion ratio is either specified by the indenture or calculated by dividing the par value of the bond by the conversion price.

$$Conversion\ Ratio = \frac{Face\ Value\ of\ the\ bond}{Conversion\ Price} = \#\ of\ shares\ received\ in\ exchange \qquad (Eq\ 19\text{-}2)$$

❏ **Conversion Value:** The conversion value is the market value of the bond if it were converted to common shares and sold at the current market value.

$$\text{Conversion Value} = \frac{\text{Par Value of the Bond}}{\text{Conversion Price}} * \text{Market Price of the Stock} \qquad \text{(Eq 19-3)}$$

❑ **Parity:** Parity is the market price of a convertible bond at which conversion yields exactly zero profit. Parity exists when the market is in equilibrium

$$\text{Market Price of the Bond} = \text{Conversion Value} \qquad \text{(Eq 19-4)}$$

Example 4:

The indenture specifies that the Discovery Café bond is convertible to shares of common stock at $50 per share. The current market value of the stock is $55 per share.

The conversion ratio is 20: one $1,000 bond can be exchanged for 20 shares since $1,000/$50 = 20

The conversion value of the bond is $1,100.00 because 20 shares at $55 per share yields $1,100.00. If the market price of the bond is $1,100.00 then buying the bond, converting to shares, and selling the shares at market, yields a profit of zero.

$$\$1,100 = \frac{\$1,000}{\$50} * \$55$$

19.5 - Trading in Corporate Bonds

We tend to take as givens some of the benefits of the age of information we live in. Due in large part to the Internet, there are countless portals to information on trading of stocks throughout the world. Free Internet sites from Yahoo, MSN Money, Reuters, or other providers allow us to see deeply in to the secondary market trading of stocks on exchanges from New York to New Zealand. The same is not true in public markets for bonds.

Most of the trading in corporate bonds takes place over-the-counter. Although many corporate bonds are listed on the NYSE and some on the AMEX, these bonds are generally listed to satisfy the requirements of institutional investors that are prohibited from investing in unlisted securities. Poor liquidity means that bonds may not trade on a regular basis, and pricing information can be difficult to obtain.

In July 2002 the NASD introduced the Trade Reporting and Compliance Engine (TRACE). The TRACE system was designed to provide information on corporate bond transactions in the past 365 days.

In 2007, an SEC created the Financial Industry Regulatory Authority, Inc., or FINRA, as the successor to the National Association of Securities Dealers (NASD) and certain regulatory functions of the New York Stock Exchange (NYSE). The TRACE system of reporting bond transactions was one of the functions absorbed by FINRA.

FINRA continues to evolve, capturing more reporting of trades in a greater variety of bonds, yet competitive forces in secondary market bond trading bring more evolution. In mid 2012, Goldman Sachs announced it would introduce an electronic platform to cross customer trades of corporate bonds. The system would also have Goldman step in to fill orders that could not be matched or offset between customers, bringing more liquidity and transparency to the corporate bond market.

❏ **CUSIP:** The CUSIP (Committee on Uniform Security Identification Procedures) number is a unique number that identifies each security. CUSIP Numbers are assigned by the CUSIP Service Bureau at Standard & Poor's.

❏ **Plain Vanilla:** Wall Street speak for as simple as it gets, no added complications.

Figure 19-2: Hypothetical FINRA Sheet for a Discovery Café bond

DVC.CF / CUSIP: 467820DC4
Last: 105.027   Yield: 0.374%

Security Category:	Corporate		
Issue Description:	Note		
Issuer Name:	Discovery Café		
Coupon Rate:	2.100%		
Coupon Type:	Fixed		
Maturity Date:	05/06/15		

Item Description

Bond Type:		Industry:	Services
Last Price:		Industry Sub-Sector	Specialty Eateries
Yield:		Tax Status:	
Callable:		Insurance:	
Moody's Rating:	Aa3(5/22/2009)	Redemption Type:	
S&P Rating:	AA-(5/29/2009)	Pre-refund:	No
Fitch Rating	A+(6/22/2011)		
Pay Frequency:	Semi-annual		
First Coupon Date	05/06/2010		

Original Issue Information:

Offer Price:	99.919	Offer Size*:	$3,000.00
Yield to Maturity:	2.116%	Amount Outstanding*:	$3,000.00
Offer Date:	11/03/2009	* in thousands	
Settlement Date:	11/06/2009		

Call Schedule Information		**Put Schedule Information**	
Next Call Date:	11/06/2012	Next Put Date:	-
Call Price:	101.000	Put Price:	0.000
Call Frequency:	annual	Put Frequency:	-

Composite Trade Information

Last Sale		Daily Trade Summary	
Date:	06/01/2012	High Price / Equivalent Yield	105.027/0.374
Price:	105.027	Low Price / Equivalent Yield	105.000/0.383
Yield:	0.374%	Net Change (Price)	0.391

19.6 - Bond Market Indices

The creation and computation of a bond-market index is more complicated that the creation and computation of an equity-market index.

- ❑ Bonds are more diverse than stocks; there are thousands of issues, each with different terms, coupons, and call features, ranging from U.S. Treasuries to bonds in default.
- ❑ Bond maturities change over time, so the selection of bonds in the index must also change over time.
- ❑ The volatility of bond prices depends on the duration of the bonds in the index, and so is also constantly changing.

Most bond indices are value weighted using current prices and the par value of the issue currently held by the public. The indices include the price of each bond in the index portfolio, accrued interest, and coupon reinvestment.

- ❑ **B of A Merrill Lynch Bond Indices:** These began as the Merrill Lynch Indices. They track more than 5,000 bond issues. The series includes several corporate and U.S. Treasury master indices as well as over 150 sub-indices that segment the bond market by maturity, coupon, industry, and ratings quality. All bonds in the sample are taxable, nonconvertible, and have maturities of more than one year.

  On September 14, 2008, Bank of America announced its intention to buy Merrill Lynch, ending a 94 year history of independence for Wall Street's third largest investment bank. The purchase was concluded in January 2009, and now the indices are known as the Bank of America Merrill Lynch Indices

- ❑ **Lehman Brothers Indices:** These indices track over 4,000 bond issues. All bonds in the sample must have a minimum outstanding principal of $25 million and maturities of more than one year. Most issues are priced by traders, but prices on smaller less liquid issues are set using a proprietary (top-secret) computer algorithm

  With the failure of Lehman Brothers in September 2008, Barclays Capital took over the index business of the firm and maintains most of the indices previously constructed by Lehman.

- ❑ **B of A Merrill Lynch Convertible Securities Indices:** track between 550 and 600 convertible securities in three sectors: U.S. domestic convertible bonds, U.S. domestic convertible preferred stocks, and U.S. corporate Eurodollar convertible bonds.

- ❑ **B of A Merrill Lynch International Bond Indices:** includes a Eurobond Master Index and sub-indices for eleven Eurobond markets. These monthly indices measure total returns in both local currency and U.S. dollars.

19.7 - Medium Term Notes

A medium term note is an interest-bearing security that pays on a corporate bond basis. It is offered continuously, rather than being underwritten and issued at one point in time. General Motors Acceptance Corporation (GMAC) pioneered the medium term note by selling directly to investors in 1972. However, the market was thin, and investors demanded a relatively high yield.

The market for medium term notes received its biggest boost in March 1982 when the SEC adopted the Shelf Registration Rule (415). Corporate debt with a maturity of more than 270 days must be registered with the SEC. The shelf registration rule allowed a corporation to file current and historical financial statements and a schedule of the notes it plans to issue with the SEC. The issue is rated and then placed on the shelf (figuratively not literally) and sold when the corporation needs financing. Although the corporation may leave the issue, or portions thereof, on the shelf indefinitely, if it wants to sell more securities that it initially filed for, then it must amend the SEC registration and rerate the issue.

The shelf-registration rule is very convenient for corporations because it allows the company to go through one filing for the entire issue and then sell parts of the issue when it needs the financing.

Much of the liquidity in MTNs is due to Merrill Lynch, which gambled that there would be an active market in MTNs and committed itself to developing and maintaining an active secondary market. It set up a trading desk specifically for MTNs and earmarked a significant portion of its capital to taking positions in and to making markets in medium term notes. The MTN market mushroomed.

Originally medium term notes had maturities from 171 days to two or three years. Now MTNs are issued with maturities as far out as 30 to 40 years. Most MTNs are fixed rate, but floating rate MTNs are available. The floating rate MTNs are generally set at a spread to the Treasury rate of a comparable maturity or LIBOR and may be reset weekly, monthly, quarterly, or semi-annually.

In March 1988 the Depository Trust Company (DTC) created a book-entry system for MTNs. (Clearance of a physical security costs $25 to $30 per trade; book-entry clearance cost $1.50 per trade.) With the advent of this book-entry, or electronic form of registration and transfer, both the primary and secondary markets for MTN's mushroomed again. Institutional investors dominate this marketplace, as the convention for MTN registration is a minimum principal amount of $100,000 and multiples of $100,000.

19.7.1 - Medium Term Notes versus Corporate Bonds

Originally, medium term notes were essentially longer term commercial paper: short, straightforward, and unsecured. The MTN market was thus separate from the bond market where corporation offered sizeable debt issues underwritten by a dealer or syndicate of dealers. As the market evolved, MTNs acquired almost all the features of corporate bonds: maturities of up to 40 years, call provisions, and collateralization. Some MTNs are issued in foreign currencies. As the distinction between MTNs and corporate bonds is blurred the MTN market is displacing the short end of the corporate bond market.

The only real remaining distinction is that a corporate bond is underwritten and MTN is sold by a dealer on an agency basis. Thus a bond issue will net the issuing corporation a significant sum of money at a fixed rate whereas the issue of a medium term note will net the corporation a flexible flow of funds at whatever the market rate when the note is sold.

19.8 - Preferred Stock

Preferred stock is a hybrid of equity and debt. Technically it is a fixed-income security because the dividend is usually fixed at either a percentage of par value (like a coupon) or a stated dollar amount ($5 pfd). Preferred stock is a perpetuity because there is no maturity date, although almost all preferred stock is issued with a sinking fund provision.

Some issues of preferred stock have floating rate dividends, mimicking bonds offered with variable interest rates. Many issues of preferred stock are also callable, some are convertible, again characteristics normally associated with bonds. As one would expect, these features can drastically alter the investment risk and return associated with the issue.

Payments are technically dividends (and are treated as such in the tax code); therefore the directors may elect not to pay the preferred dividend without putting the company in default. In case of bankruptcy, preferred stockholders have priority over common stockholders in the distribution of assets. Priority in distribution of income (dividends) is also a feature of preferred stock. A company cannot pay a dividend on its common stock if it has omitted payment of dividend on its preferred stock. If the preferred stock is also cumulative, other benefits to preferred shareholders exist.

The yield on preferred stock is given by

$$Y_{Pfd} = \frac{Dividend}{Price_{Market}}$$

(Eq 19-5)

Example 5:

Mellon Bank Pfd B pays an annual dividend of $1.69 and, on October 7, 1993, sold for $27¾. The yield is 6.1%

$$Y_{Pfd} = \frac{\$1.69}{\$27.750} = 6.09009$$

❑ **Cumulative Preferred Stock:** Cumulative preferred stock is senior to noncumulative preferred stock. If the issuer is unable to pay dividends for some time and then recovers, cumulative preferred stockholders are entitled to arrears, noncumulative preferred stockholders are not. Before the company can begin paying dividends to its common stockholders, any and all dividends in arrears on cumulative preferred shares must be made current. This feature has handsomely rewarded investors in distressed firms where turnarounds have occurred.

❑ **Convertible Preferred Stock:** CP stock is convertible to common shares.

❑ **Adjustable-rate Preferred Stock:** ARP stock has a dividend rate that is reset periodically, either as a set spread over the Treasury bond rate or competitively (through an auction or remarketing process).

❑ **Perpetuity:** A perpetuity is a constant stream of cash flows with no specified maturity or end date.

19.9 - *Warrants*

Warrants are generally issued with the bond as an added feature to increase the value and marketability of the issue and are then detached from the bond and traded separately.

Very similar to a right, a warrant grants the right to purchase common stock at a specified subscription price from the issuer of the bond. The subscription price is generally higher than the market price of the stock. To exercise the warrant the investor may use the bond, valued at par, that was attached to the warrant in the first place to pay for the stock.

Although warrants are similar to rights, rights generally have a subscription price lower than the current market price of the stock, are issued to existing shareholders, and expire in a matter of weeks.

❑   **Bond Sweetener:** A bond sweetener is the use of a warrant as an addition to a bond as a reward for the buyers of a new issue bond offering. Buyers of the bond receive warrants that can be detached from the bond and traded separately in a secondary market which quickly develops.

In structuring a new bond issue to include these sweetener warrants, firms can lower the cost of the borrowing as compared to a bond issue that does not include the warrants, while not having to issue a convertible bond, which may dilute the equity of the firm. Investment bankers are really just frustrated cooks or alchemists, continually adding, subtracting, and substituting elements in the creation of securities, with predictable change to the final product.

19.10 - Foreign Bonds

By definition the international financial markets are more extensive than the market for any specific country. Debt issued by U.S. companies in the U.S. and marketed to U.S. investors are subject to regulation and SEC oversight. But corporations can issue bonds, and investors can buy and trade bonds, outside the United States in other currencies. Foreign bonds are bonds issued in a country and currency by a foreign issuer.

Yankee Bonds

Yankee bonds are bonds in which principal and interest are paid in U.S. dollars in the United States by non-U.S. governments or corporations.

Eurobonds

Eurobonds are bonds in which principal and interest are paid in a currency foreign to the market in which the bond is issued. Thus Eurodollar bonds are issued in U.S. dollars outside the United States; Euroyen Bonds are issued in Yen outside Japan, and EuroEuro bonds are issued in Euros outside the Eurozone.

Since the adoption of the euro as the single currency in the Eurozone the term Eurobonds has come to designate bonds issued by corporations and governments within the Euromarket. Because the Eurozone involves seventeen different countries, each with their own regulatory system, the Eurozone itself is largely unregulated. Issues and transactions are not subject to any particular nation's regulations. Bonds are issued in bearer form, can be denominated in any one of a number of currencies, and often pay annual coupons. Thus the Eurobond market is both a domestic market for Eurozone companies and an international market for others.

Most foreign bonds have designations designed to communicate only to insiders in the market. Thus Rembrants are bonds issued by foreign companies in the Netherlands, Matadors are issued in Spain, (both in euros), Bulldogs are issued by non-British companies in Britain in sterling, Matildas are issued in Australia in Australian dollars, and Samurai are issued by non-Japanese companies in Japan in yen. Dragon bonds however, are issued in U.S. dollars in the Pacific Rim.

Chapter 19 - Questions and Problems

19-1:

In 2000 Proctor & Gamble issues at par $10,000,000 in 7% bonds maturing October 2, 2030. The bond is callable after 10 years with a call premium of 10%, declining 1/2% per year after that.

A.   What was the yield to maturity?

B.   What was the yield to call?

Assume that in 2010 the market yield for the P&G 7% 2030 bond was 7%.

C.   What was the call price of the bond?

D.   What would be the price of the bond have been if it were not callable?

E.   Would P&G have called the bond? Why?

F.   If John Q. Investor purchased $10,000 in P&G bonds at par in 2000 and sells the bond in 2010 at this price, what is his holding period yield?

Assume that in 2015 the required yield for the P&G 7% 2030 bond is 5%.

G.   What is the call price of the bond?

H.   What would be the price of the bond be if it were not callable?

I.   If P&G calls the issue and finances the recall with a new 15 year bond issue at 5% how much does P&G save on its semi-annual coupon payment and principal repayment.

J.   What is the net present value of this saving?

K.   If John Q. Investor purchased $10,000 in P&G bonds at par in 2000 and uses the proceeds from the called bonds to buy the new P&G 5% 2030 bonds, what is his realized yield-to-maturity on the original bond purchase?

19-2:

Hypothetical Resources issues 12% semi-annual bonds with a term to maturity of 15 years. There is a call provision such that HR can call the bond in 6 years at a 20% call premium. The call premium declines 2% per year thereafter. The offer on the bond is currently 90.00.

A.   What is the yield to first call?

B.   What is the expected yield to maturity?

19-3:

The price of the Enron 6.5% August 1, 2002 bond declined from 102.4134 on October 15, 2001 to 17.7177 December 14, 2001. Over the same time period the price on Enron shares declined from $33.17 on October 15 to 63¢ on December 14.

A.   What was the promised yield-to-maturity on Enron 6.5% Aug 02 on October 15, 2001?

B.   If you had purchased $1,000,000 of Enron 6.5% Aug 02 on this date, how much would you have paid for the bond? (Use October 15 as the settlement date).

C.   What was the promised yield-to-maturity on Enron 6.5% Aug 02 on December 14, 2001?

D.   If you sold your $1,000,000 Enron 6.5% 08/02 bond on this date, how much would you receive for the bond? (use December 14 as the settlement date).

E.   What is your holding period rate of return on this investment?

F.   How does this compare to the holding period rate of return you would have earned had you bought Enron equity instead of debt?

19-4:

Assume Enron had a 6% semi-annual coupon bond maturing December 30, 2013. You purchased a $1000 bond at par December 30 1998. When Enron (ENE) filed for bankruptcy December 2, 2001, all coupon payments were suspended. Assume further that no more coupon payments are made and that, as part of the liquidation of Enron, these bonds pay 12¢ on the dollar on December 30, 2006.

A.   What is the promised yield to maturity at the time of purchase?

B.   Assume your crystal ball predicted the collapse of Enron with complete accuracy. What is the expected yield to maturity on the Enron bond?

C.   If the expected yield on equivalent bonds at the time of purchase had been 6%, what should you have paid for the $1000 Enron bond?

19-5:

6% 2013 Treasuries yield 6%; the 6% IBM 2013 with a 4% probability of default yields 7.50%; and the 6% Hypothetical Resources 2013 with a 10% probability of default yields 7.90%. Should you buy the IBM or the HR bond?

19-6:

Table 19-3: Bond Market Yields		
Bond	Promised YTM	Probability of Default
Alcoa 10% 2025	7.00%	8%
Hypothetical Resources 10% 2025	8.05%	20%
Treasury 10% 2025	5.24%	0%

A. The promised yield to maturity for the Alcoa bond includes a risk premium of how many basis points and a default premium of how many basis points?

B. The promised yield to maturity for the Hypothetical Resources bond includes a risk premium of how many basis points?

C. The promised yield to maturity for the Hypothetical Resources bond includes a default premium of how many basis points?

D. Speculative Issues Incorporated has a 40% probability of default. What yield to maturity must it promise in this market? This promised yield to maturity includes how many basis points default premium and how many basis points risk premium?

19-7:

The Tardis Intertemporal Bond is priced to yield a respectable 8.00%. Moody's and Standard & Poor's drop the rating on this bond announcing that the risk of default is approximately twice their original estimates. The yield shoots up to 12.00%. What is the new estimate of the probability of default?

19-8:

From your experience as an investment manager for *Investments Unlimited* you know that normally the yield spread between Baa and Aaa rated 20-year corporates is 40 basis points, and the yield spread between Aaa rated 20-year corporates and 20-year Treasury bonds is 80 basis points.

This morning your computer tells you that 20 year bonds are trading at the following yields.

6.80 %   T-Bonds
7.35 %   Aaa/AAA rated corporate bonds
7.90 %   Baa/BBB rated corporate bonds

You immediately jump into action. What do you do?

19-9:

Your client's astrologer recommends the Tardis Intertemporal Bonds, and your client swears his astrologer is never wrong. (Unfortunately a brief check reveals that the astrologer is a multimillionaire. Either he is never wrong or he has very rich and gullible clients). Tardis Intertemporal offers a 10% semi-annual coupon bond maturing in ten years.

A.   What is the price of a $1,000 bond if the market yield is 8%?

In a spirit of grim determination, you call your broker with an order for 100 $1,000 bonds. Your broker mutters something about one born every day and informs you that the bond is callable after five years at a call premium of 5%.

B.   What is the yield-to-call if you buy the bond at the market price you just calculated?

C.   What is the maximum price you would pay for the Tardis Intertemporal bonds if you knew with certainty that TI would call the bonds?

D.   What is the investment value (the maximum price you would pay for the bonds)?

The broker explains further that Tardis Intertemporal is a convertible bond: each $1000 bond is convertible to common shares of Tardis Intertemporal at $40/share. Your trusty computer tells you that common shares of Tardis are currently trading at $44.

E.   What is the conversion value of the bond (the maximum price you would pay for the TI bonds if you were buying them for conversion)?

F.   How will you invest your client's account?

G.   How do your answers change if the market yield is 12%?

Table 19-4: Work area for Q19-9

Prevailing Yield	Market Price (No Call) (A.)	Yield-to-Call (B.)	Maximum Price (Guaranteed Call) (C.)	Investment Value (D.)	Conversion Value (E.)
8%					
12%					

19-10:

Fly-By-Night Resources has three stock issues

Table 19-5: Work area for Q19-10

Stock Issue		Dividend per share	Total dividend paid
1,000,000. shares	common stock		
100,000. shares	$2 preferred		
100,000. shares	$2 cumulative preferred		
		Total	

After paying regular annual dividends once a year for twenty years, the board of directors was forced to suspend dividend payments entirely for the past two years. Now (in the third year) Fly-By-Night has generated a healthy profit, and the board of directors has earmarked $1,200,000 for dividend payments. Indicate the dividend payment for each stock issue and the total payout in Table 19-5.

19-11:

Minbari InterCaste issues a senior mortgage bond with a coupon rate of 8⅞%. The issue is priced at 93.353. A $1,000 bond pays an annual interest of

A. $85.00.
B. $85.51.
C. $88.75.
D. $96.35.

19-12:

When a mortgage bond goes into default, the bondholders have a claim against

A. the principal amount of the loan but not the interest.
B. the property pledged as collateral.
C. the issuer's assets.
D. the issuer's assets and any assets of subsidiaries or parent companies.

19-13:

Centari Prime Wigs and Costumers Inc. has $20 million 8% convertible debentures outstanding. The bonds are convertible at $25 per common share. The trust indenture has a provision that prevents dilution of the bondholders' potential ownership of the company. Centari declares a 10% stock dividend. How will the company comply with the dilution covenant of the indenture?

A. Adjust the conversion price to $16 per common share
B. Adjust the conversion price to $16.67 per common share
C. Adjust the conversion price to $22.73 per common share
D. Affer bondholders the choice of receiving 10 shares of stock or $40 cash per $1,000 bond.

19-14:

Friday June 13 Narn Financial stock closed at $56.50. Narn Financial 6% convertible debenture closed at 115.50. After the closing bell Narn announced that the debenture will be called at 102.25. The debenture is convertible into common stock at $59.25 per share. What should you do?

A. Sell the bond at 115.50.
B. Convert the debenture and sell the shares.
C. Short sell the shares
D. Allow the debenture to be called.

Asset-backed securities are based on an underlying portfolio of assets. The portfolios are then divided into units, which can be bought and sold in the financial markets just like any other negotiable security. Asset-backed securities fall into two broad categories: investment companies and securitized assets.

Investment companies take the form of unitized investment trusts, closed end funds, and mutual funds. The focus is on the investor. The structures are designed to take investment assets already in the market, pool them, and divide them up to make them accessible to individual investors who might otherwise not have the wealth and sophistication required to make this kind of investment. Mutual funds are a prime example of this.

Securitized assets take the form of mortgage or other debt-backed securities. The focus is on the creation of a secondary market where none existed before. For example mortgages are extended through banks. This is a primary market function. Securitization puts mortgages into a portfolio, divides the portfolio into units, and sells them to individual investors. This creates a secondary market where none existed before.

Some asset-backed securities, such as real estate investment trusts, fall into both categories.

20.1 - Investment Companies

Rather than buying securities directly, investors can invest in an investment company, which in turn owns securities. The advantages of buying into an investment company over buying individual investment securities arise from

❑ Access to securities that trade in large minimum denominations, which may be inaccessible to smaller investors

❑ Economies of scale such as diversification and lower transactions costs including search, evaluation, and commission rates.

❑ Professional management.

The Investment Company Act of 1940 classifies investment companies into

❑ **Unit Investment Trust:** An investment company that owns a fixed set of assets and often terminates on a specific prespecified date.

❑ **Closed-End Investment Company:** An investment company with a fixed number of shares. These shares are traded in the secondary market at a price determined by supply and demand.

❑ **Open-End Investment Company (Mutual Fund):** An investment company that creates shares or units whenever required by new investment and retires shares or units whenever redeemed. The price is determined by the underlying value of the assets of the company.

20.2 - Unit Investment Trusts

A unit investment trust is an investment company that owns a fixed set of securities (there is no trading except in very unusual circumstances) and the trust terminates on a specific predetermined date. The majority unit trusts invest in fixed income securities and carry a load.

❑ **Load:** The load on a fund is the additional fee levied on the purchase or sale of units in the fund.

❑ **Net Asset Value (NAV):** The NAV is the market value of the fund per unit into which the fund is divided.

Example 1:

The UIUC unit trust is established by buying $25,000,000 worth of Treasury securities of varying maturities and issuing 1,000,000 units. The trust terminates on December 31, 2024. Each unit is offered to the public at $25.875. When all the units are sold UIUC receives $25.875 * 1,000,000 = $25,875,000. This covers the cost of the bonds plus $875,000 for selling expenses (including financing charges while we were setting up the trust) and profit.

The Net Asset Value (NAV) of this trust is $25.00 and the load is $0.875 or 3.5%.

$$NAV = \frac{\$25,000,000}{1,000,000 \ units} = \$25.00 \ \ per \ unit$$

$$Load = \frac{\$25.875 - \$25.000}{\$25.000} = 0.035 \ (3.5\%)$$

Load charges range from 1% for short-term trusts to 3.5% for long-term trusts.

Investors in unit trusts may sell units through the trust dealer who runs a bid and ask on units of the trust. Alternatively the trust itself buys back the units at the Net Asset Value and sells sufficient bonds from the trust to make the redemption.

20.2.1 - Exchange Traded Funds

Exchange traded funds (ETFs) are investment trusts based on an index.

Most ETFs are designed with a "creation and redemption" feature. This allows authorized participants (usually very large institutional investors) to deposit an acceptable basket of securities and cash into the fund, and be issued shares of the ETF in exchange. Redemption is the same, but in reverse. Liquidity in both the ETF units and the underlying assets is enhanced with this feature. In addition, it allows for arbitrage, which tends to keep the value of the ETF shares very close to the value of the basket of securities it is meant to track.

The following ETFs are offered by the American Stock Exchange (AMEX). For more information on these unit investment trusts go to https://etp.nyx.com.

❑ **SPDR:** Standard & Poor's Depository Receipt, called a "spider", is a unit investment trust designed to track the S&P500 index. There are SPDRs (SPY), Mid Cap SPDRs (MDY), and several sector SPDRs

XLB	Basic Industries	XLY	Cyclical/Transportation	XLI	Industrial
XLV	Consumer Services	XLE	Energy	XLK	Technology
XLP	Consumer Staples	XLF	Financial	XLU	Utilities

❑ **Diamonds:** Diamonds (DIA) are units in the investment trust designed to track the Dow Jones Industrial Average. Again, there are several sector Diamonds

❑ **International ETFs:** The American Stock Exchange also offers Exchange Traded Funds based on the Morgan Stanley Capital International (MSCI) and Standard & Poor's Indices.

EWA	Australia	EWM	Malaysia	IEV	S&P Europe 350
EWO	Austria	EWW	Mexico	ILF	S&P Latin America 40
EWK	Belgium	EWN	Netherlands	ITF	S&P/TOPIX 150
EWZ	Brazil	EPP	Pacific Ex-Japan	IKC	S&P/TSE 60
EWC	Canada	EWS	Singapore		
EFA	EAFE Index	EWY	South Korea		
EZU	EMU Index	EWP	Spain		
EWQ	France	EWD	Sweden		
EWG	Germany	EWL	Switzerland		
EWH	Hong Kong	EWT	Taiwan		
EWI	Italy	EWU	United Kingdom		
EWJ	Japan				

20.3 - Open-End Investment Companies (Mutual Funds)

Unlike Unit trusts, managed companies are structured as corporations. They have a board of directors elected by the shareholders. The board of directors then hires an investment manager or management firm to invest the corporation's assets. Often the investment management firm is the subsidiary of the brokerage firm that set up the investment company.

The investment company must pay investment management fees (from ¼% to 1% of market value annually) as well as administrative and custodial expenses (usually ½% of market value annually).

Investment companies that continuously offer new shares, and repurchase outstanding shares, at or near their net asset value are called open-end investment companies or mutual funds. The term derives from the fact that their capitalization is open: the number of shares outstanding can change on a daily basis.

Example 2:

We decide to establish the UIUC Mutual Fund. The price is set arbitrarily at $100 per unit. One hundred fifty students each buy 1 unit of the fund thus generating $15,000. We purchase $15,000 in equities.

Growth:

The asset value of the portfolio increases by 2%: from $15,000 to $15,300. The NAV is thus recalculated to $102 per unit.

Now 5 more students want to buy units. They must do so at the new price of $102. We create 5 new units; these new units are supported by the $510 going into portfolio. We now have 155 units at $102 for a total portfolio value of $15,810.

Crash:

The asset value of the portfolio decreases by 40%: from $15,810 to $9,486. The NAV is recalculated to $61.20

The stock market panic spreads to the student population and 55 students redeem their units. To redeem these units we must pay out $3,366: 55 units at $61.20 per unit. This means that I must sell assets from the portfolio to generate enough cash to make redemptions.

We now have 100 units at $61.20 for a total portfolio value of $6,120.

Table 20-1: Accounting Summary for the UIUC Mutual Fund

	Units	NAV	Market Value
Open	+ 150	$100.00	+ $15,000.
Growth:	150	$102.00	$15,300.
Market value increases to $15,300	+ 5		+ 510.
Sell 5 more units @ $102	= 155		= $15,810.
Crash:	155	$61.20	$ 9,486
Market value decreases to $9,486.	- 55		- 3,366.
Redeem 55 units @ $61.20	= 100		= $6,120.

❑ **No load funds:** No load funds sell their shares at the NAV.

❑ **Loaded funds:** Loaded funds sell their shares at a premium, adding a load charge to the NAV. The load charge is limited by law to a maximum of 8.5% of the amount invested. Funds with a load charge of 3.5% or less are referred to as low-load funds.

❑ **Back-end load funds:** Back-end load funds charge the load when the shares are sold. The back-end load (also called redemption fees, exit fees, or contingent deferred sales charges) often decreases with the length of time the shareholder holds the shares, with the load as high as 6% of NAV if you hold the shares for less than six months, declining to 0% after five or six years.

❑ **12b-1 funds:** 12b-1 funds take out a load of up to 1¼% of market value per year to cover marketing the shares. The term 12b-1 comes from SEC Rule 12b-1, which allows open-end funds to cover selling costs in this way. These are sometimes referred to as hidden-load funds.

The load on mutual funds is calculated as a percentage of the invested amount rather than as a percentage of the net asset value.

$$NAV \ = \ \frac{\$25,000,000}{1,000,000 \ \text{shares}} \ = \$25.00 \ \ \text{per share}$$

$$Load \ = \ \frac{\$25.907 \ - \ \$25.000}{\$25.907} \ = 0.035 \ (3.5\%)$$

This difference allows Mutual Funds to sell units of $25.00 for $25.907, whereas the investment trusts with the same net asset value can sell for no more than $25.875. Both are at the maximum load of 3.5%

The IRS allows an investment company to avoid corporate income tax if it qualified under Subchapter M of the tax code as a regulated investment company by meeting diversification standards and by paying out at least 90% of its net income, exclusive of capital gains, each year. If capital gains are retained rather than distributed, the company must pay capital gains tax. Thus most investment companies make both income distributions and capital gains distributions, so that the investors can pay the taxes.

20.4 - Closed-end Investment Companies

Closed-end Investment companies have a fixed number of shares that trade on an exchange in the same way as any other publically held company.

Example 3:

> We decide to establish the UIUC Closed-End Fund. We create 150 units and set the price arbitrarily at $100 per unit. 150 students each buy 1 unit of the fund thus generating $15,000. We purchase $15,000 in equities.
>
> **Growth:**
> The asset value of the portfolio increases by 2%: from $15,000 to $15,300. The NAV is thus recalculated to $102 per unit.
>
> Now 5 more students want to buy units. However the capitalization of the fund is closed. If they wish to buy units they must persuade one of the existing unit holders to sell. They do this on the secondary market. Both the buyer and the seller know the published NAV of $102 per unit. Their negotiations can begin from there. Five units change hands. We still have 150 units at $102 for a total portfolio value of $15,300.
>
> **Crash:**
> The asset value of the portfolio decreases by 40%: from $15,300 to $9,180. The NAV is recalculated to $61.20
>
> The stock market panic spreads to the student population and 55 students seek to sell their units. Both sellers and buyers know the published NAV of $61.20 per unit. Their negotiations can begin from there. Fifty-five units change hands at various prices. However, no units are redeemed, so we are not forced to sell assets.
>
> We still have 150 units at $61.20 for a total portfolio value of $9,180.

Table 20-2: Accounting Summary for the UIUC Closed End Fund

	Units	NAV	Market Value
Open	+ 150	$100.00	+ $15,000.
Growth: Market value increases to $15,300.	150	$102.00	$15,300.
Crash: Market value decreases to $9,180.	150	$61.20	$9,180.

Because the fund trades on an exchange the price is determined by the demand and supply of the shares of the fund. This means that some funds may trade a price above their NAV (they trade at a premium) and others will trade at a price lower then their NAV (they trade at a discount). Typically, closed-end funds trade at a premium of roughly 10% of the NAV when they are initially offered. Then, within 120 days, the price falls to a discount of roughly 10% of NAV. Then the size of this discount fluctuates widely over time. Thus the closed-end investment fund carries two sources of risk: first the risk to the value of the underlying assets and second, the risk to the premium or discount at which the fund will trade.

Because these shares trade in an active secondary market, often exchange listed, if shares are available for loan, it is possible to short sell the stock. In theory, this should keep the premium or discount from becoming too large. Unlike exchange traded funds, closed-end company shares do not offer the creation and redemption feature. Exercising arbitrage opportunities with closed-end funds is therefore much more cumbersome and allows the premium or discount to be much larger than the very small tracking error present in ETFs.

20.5 - Mortgage Backed Securities

A mortgage is a debt secured by property, typically real estate. It is an amortized loan, which means that principal and interest are paid back in constant periodic (usually monthly) payments, and the loan principal decreases over time.

$$Monthly \ payment \ = \ Principal \ * \ \left[\frac{r \ (1+r)^{\ m}}{(1+r)^{\ m} \ - \ 1} \right] \qquad (Eq \ 20\text{-}1)$$

Where the monthly rate of interest is the mortgage rate divided by 12 and m is the number of months. This means that the first payment is predominantly interest and the last payment is predominantly principal.

Example 4:

Hermione Q. Homeowner takes out a $300,000 , 30-year, 3.5% fixed-rate mortgage on her house. Her monthly mortgage payment is $1,347.13

$$Monthly \ payment \ = \ \$300,000. \ \left[\frac{\dfrac{0.035}{12} \left(1 + \dfrac{0.035}{12} \right)^{\ 360}}{\left(1 + \dfrac{0.035}{12} \right)^{\ 360} \ - \ 1} \right] = \$1,347.13$$

Figure 20-1: Mortgage Payment Structure on the $300,000., 30-year, 3.5% Mortgage in Example 4

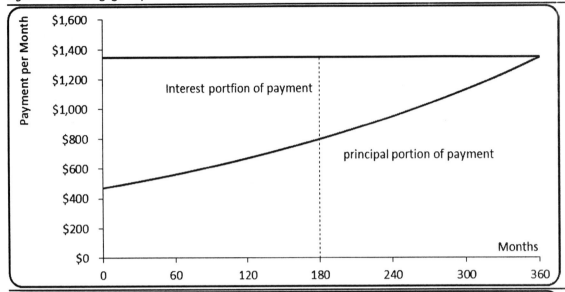

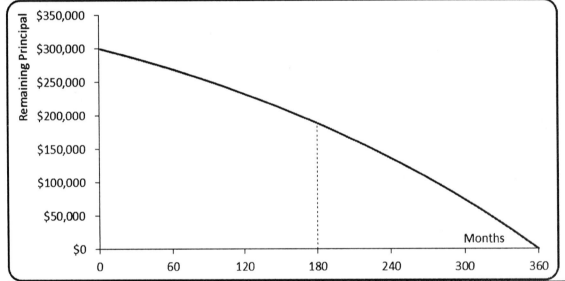

Calculator Techniques 20-1:	Enter	Display	
	[2ND] [CLR TVM]		
The loan parameter of 12 payment per year is set first. Then [2ND] [QUIT] returns the calculator to TVM mode.			
	[2ND] [P/Y] 12 [ENTER]	P/Y=	12.
	[2ND] [QUIT]		0.
Enter the term, principal, and interest rate. The principal is positive so the payments come out as negative.	30 2nd [xP/Y] [N]	N=	360.
	3.5 [I/Y]	I/Y=	3.5
	300000 [PV]	PV=	300,000.
	[CPT] [PMT]	PMT=	-1,347.13

Calculator Techniques 20-2:

Use the amortization schedule ([2ND] [AMORT]) to see the status after the payment for month 180 has been made. We calculate that the remaining principal balance, the principal and interest paid to date. As with other spreadsheets, use the [↑] and [↓] to navigate through the spreadsheet.

The principal paid and remaining sum to $299,999.81 rather than $300,000 so there is a rounding issue in the calculation.

DATA	Enter	Compute
P1 =	1	
P2 =	180	
BAL =		188,441.13
PRN =		(111,558.68)
INT =		(130,925.45)

If the mortgagor fails to make a payment on either interest or principal, then the mortgagee has the right to foreclose on the mortgage: selling the property pledged under the mortgage to pay off the debt.

❏ **Mortgagor:** The mortgagor is the individual or institution borrowing the money under a mortgage with real estate as collateral.

❏ **Mortgagee:** The mortgagee is the individual or institution lending money with real estate as collateral.

❏ **Foreclose:** Foreclosure is the legal process by which the mortgagee takes possession of the real estate used as collateral after the terms of the mortgage have not been met by the mortgagor.

20.5.1 - The Primary Market

Mortgages are generally originated by commercial banks, mortgage banks, credit agencies, insurance companies, and pension funds.

20.5.2 - The Secondary Market

Originators of loans, particularly long-term, fixed-rate loans like mortgages, seldom want to retain the interest rate risks associated with them. Selling the loan allows the bank to recycle the funds into new loans and begin the process of lending anew. Liquidity is enhanced in the primary market for loans, benefitting consumers with lower rates of interest. The buyer of the loans is an intermediary that pools the mortgages, then sells shares or participation certificates in the pool to sophisticated investors looking for monthly cash flows. This process is known as asset securitization.

20.6 - Securitization

The originator creates a pool of mortgages and sells shares or participation certificates in the pool through a broker. The process of pooling assets and selling participation certificates in the pool is known as asset securitization because it turns an asset into a negotiable security.

A variety of securities are created through this process. Many of their characteristics follow the characteristics of the loans that are being securitized. The two most common are residential mortgage-backed securities

(RMBS) and commercial mortgage-backed securities (CMBS). Most CMBS securities are created from a handful of large denomination loans on real property like commercial office buildings, large retail shopping centers, or even large apartment complexes. Frequently, these large loans have much shorter term to repayment of principal and seldom have monthly payments. In contrast, RMBS securities are created from a rather large number of smaller denomination loans on real property to homeowners. These loans typically require monthly payments of interest and principal and can have final maturities as long as 30 years.

Pass-through securities are a refinement of the securitization process. With many pass-through securities, the intermediary guarantees timely payment of interest and principal to investors in the pass-through certificates will continue, even if the underlying loans default. This is a key feature, and a very politically charged topic of debate when discussing agencies of the federal government that securitize loans.

20.6.1 - Ginnie Maes

The most common participation certificate of this type are the GNMA Modified Pass-Through Securities issued by the Government National Mortgage Association (GNMA), known as Ginnie Maes. The GNMA is a part of the Department of Housing and Urban Development (HUD). Therefore GNMAs are guaranteed by the full faith and credit of the U.S. government.

GNMAs are participation certificates in pools of residential mortgages. Each mortgage in the pool must be guaranteed by either the Federal Housing Administration, Veterans Administration, or Farmers Home Administration, thereby eliminating the credit risk, and each pool must have a principal amount of at least $1 million. The bank (or mortgage originator) applies to the GNMA for a guarantee that each participation certificate represents $25,000 worth of principal. Once the application is approved, the bank can sell the GNMAs in the secondary market. The interest paid on these securities is .5% less than the interest paid on the mortgages in the pool, with .1% going to the GNMA and .4% going to the institution that created the pool.

The owner of a participation certificate is entitled to the monthly prorated return of principal and interest on the underlying mortgages in the pool.

Example 5:

John Q. Investor purchases four $25,000 Ginnie Maes from a $1 million pool of 30-year mortgages. The mortgage rate for the mortgages in this pool is 12.5%, so the Ginnie Maes carry a stated interest rate of 12%.

J.Q. owns 10% of each mortgage in the pool. Each month J.Q. receives 10% of the aggregate net interest and principal paid by the mortgagees. These payment pass through the pool to the hands of the security holders.

There is no credit risk. If payment is late or the homeowner defaults, GNMA will use its own funds or borrow from the Treasury to make the payment until the mortgage is foreclosed and the property sold.[1]

---

1   For a more complete overview of the operation and requirements for participation under the Government National Mortgage Association, see http://www.ginniemae.gov/guide/guidtoc.asp

20.6.2 - Freddie Macs and Fannie Maes

Similar participation certificates are issued through the Federal Home Loan Mortgage Corporation (FHLMC). These certificates are issued in denominations of $100,000 or more, and are referred to as Freddie Mac. The Federal National Mortgage Association issues Fannie Maes. These institutions were federally sponsored but not federally guaranteed, so their certificates were not guaranteed by the full faith and credit of the U.S. government. This changed on September 7, 2008, when the Federal Housing Finance Agency (FHFA) placed Freddie Mac and Fannie Mae into a federal conservatorship.

2008: Fannie & Freddie

Prior to 2008, Fannie Mae and Freddie Mac had substantial lines of credit to the U.S. Treasury even though they were publicly-held companies. The combination of an implicit government guarantee in a company owned by its shareholders meant that they could be managed to generate profits for its shareholders during the fat years while counting on the U.S. Treasury to back-stop losses during the lean years. By July 2008, Fannie and Freddie either held or guaranteed $5.2 trillion of the U.S. $12 trillion mortgage market[2]. Fannie and Freddie were both too big to fail and too big to rescue.

In July the Treasury announced a line of credit to back both GSEs. But in a government bailout the shareholders rarely come out whole; share prices on both Fannie and Freddie declined sharply.

On September 7, 2008, the US Department of the Treasury placed both Fannie and Freddie into conservatorship. In exchange for capital support of $100 billion in each GSE, the Treasury was issued $1billion 10% preferred stock and warrants representing 79.9% ownership[3].

20.6.3 - Private-Label Pass-Throughs

Throughout the 1990s and into 2007, a growing number of banks began to offer their own pass-through mortgage certificates. Some of these certificates are backed by private insurance companies rather than by the federal government, while others are not guaranteed at all.

There are pools for commercial or industrial mortgages (CMBS) as well as for mortgages on conventional residential property (RMBS). These private-label pass-through securities are rated and must be registered with the SEC, unlike those created by the Government Agencies like GNMA, FNMA, and FHLMC, which are exempt from registration requirements. In addition, capital requirements imposed on the government sponsored mortgage entities were much lower than those imposed on banks. This difference in capital requirements and the fierce competition between private-label mortgage poolers and the agencies was a critical component in the eventual failure of the industry in 2008.

Another factor was the 1977 Community Reinvestment Act (CRA). It requires all banking institutions that

---

2   "The muddle-through approach: America's government tries a quick fix for the intractable problems of Fannie Mae and Freddie Mac", *The Economist*, July 14, 2008.

3   "Suffering a seizure: America's government takes control of Freddie Mac and Fannie Mae", *The Economist*, Sept 8, 2008.

receive Federal Deposit Insurance Corporation (FDIC) insurance offer credit in all the communities in which they are chartered to do business, particularly in low- and moderate-income neighborhoods. Compliance with this rule could be a problem. Lower-income or lower-collateral mortgage loans carry greater risk to the bank. Moreover, these high- risk loans rarely met the underwriting standards required to sell them to Government Agencies for securitization.

These underwriting standards were relaxed in 1990 as part of the Cranston-Gonzalez National Affordable Housing Act. The Act enshrined the principal that every American family should be able to afford a decent home in a suitable environment. Nowhere did it enshrine the principal that you had to be able to pay for it.

Common practices fell by the wayside. Equity requirements of 20% of the purchase price of the house gave way to 100% mortgage loans. Verification of income and employment gave way to "liars' loans" where nothing was verified. Essentially homeowners were buying houses on a 0% margin. In an environment of historically low interest rates, these subprime mortgages helped fuel a classic bubble in the US housing market. House prices rose more rapidly than the income that could support these prices.

Bubbles collapse. Reports from the Mortgage Bankers Association showed that in the first quarter of 2010, the delinquency rate (loans more than 30 days past due, but not in foreclosure) peaked at 10.1 percent of all mortgages surveyed. Delinquency and default rates for subprime and the category between sub-prime and investment grade known as "Alt- A" mortgage loans were much higher[4].

20.7 - Prepayment Risk

In the United States homeowners are allowed to prepay their mortgages at any time without penalty. This is similar to a call provision on a bond. In this sense prepayment or contraction risk is similar to call risk. (In Canada a mortgage may be prepaid without penalty only if the property is sold—this is similar to a call provision on a bond where there is a pre-specified call premium only if the bond is recalled for refunding.)

❑　**Prepayment Risk:** The risk that mortgagors pay off the loan early. This is similar to a call risk in bonds because the mortgagor has an incentive to pay early when mortgage rates decrease.

Investors in a pass-through mortgage pool receive a prorated share of the interest and principal payments made on the underlying mortgages. Therefore, every month the amount of the investment declines in size as the investor receive regularly scheduled principal payments. If a mortgage in the pool repays, then the investor receives the prorated share of the prepayment, the amount of the investment declines accordingly, and the prepaid mortgage no longer generates interest.

Prior to 2008, prepayment risk was considered the most important risk in mortgage-backed securities. In periods of falling interest rates, investors experienced quicker payments of principal and, hence, faced higher reinvestment risk. This characteristic also put a damper on price elasticity of the security, effectively creating a cap on market value, as few buyers would want to pay premiums for repayments of principal at par, now occurring faster and in larger amounts. Alternatively, when interest rates rise, mortgage holders have no incentive to pay any more than the fixed, monthly amount specified in the contract. This effectively causes the "average maturity" and, hence, duration of the mortgage pass-through certificate to grow longer, making the market price now more elastic as interest rates rise.

4　　Mortgage Bankers Association, *MBA's Quarterly National Delinquency Survey,*
　　　http://www.mortgagebankers.org/ResearchandForecasts/ProductsandSurveys/NationalDelinquencySurvey.htm.

Yields

Prepayment risk is reflected in higher yields than comparable treasury securities.

Systematic prepayment risk is reduced with pools of adjustable rate mortgages (ARM) since the rates are tied to an index. The interest rate on the mortgages in the pool are reset periodically (from every month to every six years) to an appropriate benchmark plus 1 or 2%. The variable rate reduces the incentive to prepay a mortgage when interest rates decline, but increases the incentive when interest rates rise.

Although most countries use a form of floating rate debt for financing private housing, the United States did not allow ARMs until the Garn-St. Germain Depository Institutions Act of 1982. Inflation and interest rates began to rise dramatically in the 1970s. This lead to a deregulation of the interest rates banks and savings & loans institutions were allowed to pay on deposits and charge on loans.

❏ **Savings & Loans:** Deposit taking institutions that were restricted to writing mortgage loans.

With fewer fixed-rate loans finding favor, or affordability, in the marketplace, ARMs grew in popularity. With modifications in the early 21st Century, creative variants began to appear in the marketplace.

❏ **Hybrid ARMs:** Hybrid ARMs set a fixed rate for a certain time, then floating to an index.
❏ **Option ARMs:** Option ARMs offered a choice of payment plans, including the payment of only the interest component.
❏ **Pay Option ARMs:** Pay Option ARMs allowed for payments smaller than the interest expense, or even the option to forego payment of any amount for fixed periods of time.

These schemes result in a negative amortization.

❏ **Negative Amortization:** Loan repayment in which accruing interest forces the loan balance to increase over time, rather than decrease, as amortizing loans are intended.

❏ **Underwater:** A homeowner is underwater when the outstanding balance on the mortgage—or mortgages—is greater than the value of the house collateralizing the mortgage.

Falling housing prices aggravate negative amortization, leaving borrowers underwater. With U.S. house prices falling by nearly 25% since peak in 2007, estimates showed nearly 16 million U.S. homeowners, or 31.4% of all homeowners with a mortgage, were underwater in 2012. These underwater homeowners owed some $1.2 trillion more than the value of their houses. These loans have experienced some of the highest rates of delinquency and default in the U.S.

20.8 - Collateralized Mortgage Obligations

Collateralized mortgage obligations (CMOs) were developed to overcome the major disadvantage of pass-through mortgage pools: the monthly payments and actual term to maturity are variable and uncertain. CMOs are serial bonds collateralized by a pool of mortgages or by a portfolio of mortgage-backed securities, designed to regularize the allocation and disbursement of principal and interest payments among investors. This is done by dividing the bond issue into tranches, typically classes A, B, C, ... Z. Each tranche is issued with a specific proportion of the total principal value of the mortgage pool.

❏ **Tranche:** A tranche in a collateralized obligation is similar to a class of equity; it allows dissimilar characteristics to be assigned to pieces of one investment.

The tranches are then retired sequentially. Initially all principal payments are allocated to tranche A and disbursed. The remaining tranches are allocated only interest payments. Payments may be made and allocated monthly, but more often CMOs disburse to investors quarterly or semi-annually.

When the tranche A bonds have all been paid off, principal payments are allocated to Tranche B and disbursed. The remaining tranches are allocated only interest payments. The Z or accrual tranche disburses neither interest nor principal until all other tranches have been paid off. Tranche Z accrues interest as additions to principal making it a payment in kind (PIK) bond in its initial stages. When the other tranches have all been retired then all the principal and interest payments go to the Z tranche. Thus, the Z tranche bonds are similar to a zero-coupon bond in all but the final stage of the CMO.

Yields on CMO tranches reflect this reallocation of prepayment risk, with the lowest yields on tranche A CMOs and the highest on tranche Z. However, although the prepayment risk can be reallocated among tranches, it cannot be reduced. If mortgage rates fall and the underlying mortgages are all paid off, then all tranches will be retired.

CMOs are rated according to the quality of the underlying mortgages and on the way the cash flows are structured. Cash flows must be sufficient to meet all obligations under any prepayment scenario, and the reinvestment rate on undistributed funds must be conservative.

20.8.1 - Inventive CMO structures

There are a number of inventive collateralized mortgage obligations; anything that finds a willing investor. A floating rate CMO is a tranche of a CMO for which the interest rate varies with a given index such as the T-bill rate or the London Inter-Bank Offered Rate (LIBOR). An inverse floater is a tranche of a CMO in which the given interest rate varies inversely with a given index.

It is a popular misconception that CMOs eliminate or reduce prepayment risk; they can't. All a CMO can do is rearrange the prepayment risk so that some participants shuffle risk off to other participants. There is nothing wrong with this so long as all participants are aware of the risk they face and are able to assess and evaluate it.

Commercial mortgage-backed securities (CMBS) are often structured with CMO-like characteristics such as different tranches. Because many commercial loans have prepayment penalties and repayment terms shorter than conventional residential mortgage loans, the CMO model seems to fit quite well. CMBS structures often use a real estate mortgage investment conduit (REMIC) for purposes of pooling and securitizing the individual loans because the tax law allows the trust to be a pass-through entity, which is not subject to tax at the trust level.

20.9 - Other Securitized Assets

Asset-backed securities have been issued on a variety of collateral: car loans, consumer credit (credit card loans), computer leases, and even non-performing loans. In general, securitized assets facilitate the reallocation of both financial capital and risk. However, this reallocation is optimal only if the participants in the market are fully aware of their risk exposure.

There is no substitute for the quality of the underlying asset (and its market value) in any of these imaginative securities. Caveat Emptor, Let the buyer beware, are two very important Latin words that apply quite reasonably to these securities. The principle of Caveat Emptor has been the property law doctrine on investments throughout modern times.

For an in depth review of the evolution, regulation, and explosion of what became the world's largest public debt market (U.S. Mortgage Backed Securities) see the book "Reckless Endangerment"

Further Reading:

Gretchen Morgenson and Joshua Rosner. *Reckles$ Endangerment: How Outsized Ambition, Greed, and Corruption Led to Economic Armageddon*, Times / Henry Holt, 2011

2008: *Collapse of Bear Stearns*

Bear Stearns was formed as an equity trading house in 1923. By 2008, it had become a publicly-owned, NYSE-listed, global investment banking company, specializing in asset-backed securities, particularly residential mortgage-backed securities (RMBS).

Early warning signs of serious problems include the failure of two in-house hedge funds that specialized in sub-prime mortgage-backed securities in July 2007. Not only were the funds themselves highly levered, the parent firm's pledge of over $3 billion bailout funds to them a month earlier, just stretched the parent company's balance sheet even further. With economic strains mounting and more housing-related debt defaulting throughout the remainder of 2007, the firm was quickly being pressured by its trading partners who knew the desperate condition of Bear. By March 2008, collateral requirements placed on the firm by its trading partners jeopardized its ability to continue business.

On March 16, fearful of an institutional run on Bear which could spread throughout the weakened investment banking sector, the Federal Reserve Bank of New York engineered a merger. As an incentive, the Federal Reserve would issue a $29 billion non-recourse loan to JP Morgan Chase (JPM) using Bear Stearns's assets, and JPM would pay $2/share to acquire Bear. Bear stock had traded as high as $170/share in early 2007. Shareholders were appalled at the price and several class-action lawsuits were filed. The price was raised to $10/share. On May 29, Bear Stearns shareholders approved the sale to JPMorgan Chase.

The Federal Reserve was sharply criticized by some and praised by others for their part in the transaction. The strongest criticism was that the Fed's actions created a moral hazard. Moral hazard is an incentive to take risks because the decision-maker is protected from the consequences of his decision. The Fed's actions encouraged other banks to believe that they too would be rescued if needed. Further criticism was that the Fed overstepped its legal authority in effectively financing the sale and backstopping losses to the buyer. Praise came from the investment community, regulators, and others, who saw a combined "public-private resolution" in averting a systemic threat to the entire global banking sector.

Informed observers recognized the irony of JPM, the bank, working with the central bank of the US to avert a banking crisis 101 years after John Pierpont Morgan, the banker, worked with other private banks to avert the 1907 Bankers' Panic. Often attributed to Samuel Clemens (Mark Twain), history does not repeat itself, but it does rhyme.

Chapter 20 - Questions and Problems

20-1:

You take out a 30-year $300,000 mortgage at 4.25%.

A. What is your monthly mortgage payment?

B. Of your first monthly payment, how much is interest and how much is principal repayment?

C. After your first monthly payment, what is the new principal amount?

D. At the end of the first year, what is your outstanding principal?

E. At the end of year ten, what is your outstanding principal?

20-2:

All of the following issue collateralized mortgage obligations except

A. Fannie Mae.
B. Ginnie Mae.
C. Sallie Mae.
D. Freddie Mac.

$\mathcal{T}$he markets for equities, money equivalents, and debt are all markets for financial securities. The security is negotiable and represents some claim on a government institution or corporation. Settlement—payment and delivery—occurs as immediately as the infrastructure allows. When these markets function efficiently they optimally allocate financial resources.

Forwards, futures, and options are contracts designed to allocate risk. Forward contracts, whereby payment and delivery are scheduled for a specified future date, have been found in cuneiform tablets as far back as the second millennium BC. Futures, standardized forwards that can trade in organized markets, owe their development to Antwerp and Amsterdam in the sixteenth and seventeenth centuries. Gelderblom and Jonker point out that historically, trade in futures and options have been equated with straight bets or gaming, activities with absolutely no redeeming economic value, rather than as markets that allocate, and provide the ability to manage, risk.[1]

Our focus on forwards, futures, and options—the fastest-growing area in securities markets over the past decades— will be on the redeeming economic value and management of risk potential they embody. We will also see, as with any financial instrument, how these can be used speculatively, even unknowingly, in ways that make casino gambling look like child's play.

The purpose and application of any financial instrument is the crucial element in judging the results. This class of securities just makes it obvious.   Only with a firm understanding of the of the fundamental elements of these instruments is the prudent use of them possible.

Chapter 21   *Futures Contracts and Clearing*
Chapter 22   *Hedges, Speculation, and Arbitrage*
Chapter 23   *Financial Futures*

---

1   Oscar Gelderblom and Joost Jonker, "Amsterdam as the Cradle of Modern Futures and Options Trading, 1550-1650"
     in *The Origins of Value* William N. Goetzmann and Geert Rouwenhorst editors, (New York: Oxford University Press,
     2005), p189-191.

$\mathcal{F}$orward and future contracts are legal agreements for the delivery of goods, services, or assets at a specified price, under specified conditions, where the specified date of delivery and payment is sometime in the future.

❏ **Spot Contract:** A spot contract is a contract for the delivery of goods, services, or assets at a specified price for immediate delivery and payment.

❏ **Forward Contract:** The terms of a forward contract reflect the specific needs of the buyer and seller and exposes both parties to default risk. The secondary market is almost nonexistent. Forward contracts are generally delivered.

❏ **Futures Contract:** Futures contracts are standardized as to quantity, quality, and delivery date. Futures trade through the exchange or clearinghouse on which they are listed, and there is no default risk in the contract.

The development of futures contracts, the exchanges on which they trade, and the clearinghouse to guarantee against the risk of default, provides financial markets with a mechanism whereby participants can manage price risk.

21.1 - Forward Contracts

A forward contract specifies payment and delivery at some future date.

Example 1:

George Q. Farmer enters into a contract with Archer Daniels Midland (ADM) to deliver 50,000 bushels of soybeans October 1 for $4.31 per bushel.

This forward contract allows George to manage the price risk associated with farming soybeans and ADM to manage the price risk associated with buying, processing, and selling agricultural products. However, this forward contract involves several sources of difficulty.

❏ **Coincidence of Needs:** Specific two-party contracts requires a coincidence of wants. George needs to find a buyer that needs 50,000 bushels of soybeans on October 1. Like a barter system, this relies on buyer and seller both needing to trade the same quantity on the same delivery date.

❏ **Risk of Default:** Unless the price remains fairly stable one or the other party will have an incentive to default on the contract. If the price of soybeans rises by October 1 then George would prefer to sell his soybeans elsewhere; if the price of soybeans falls by October 1 then ADM would prefer to buy soybeans in the spot market.

❏ **Alternative to Delivery:** There is no graceful way out of the two-party contract. If ADM decides it has overbought soybeans then it can negotiate with George (or George's lawyer) to cancel the contract, or wait until October, take delivery of the soybeans, and then sell them on the spot market. ADM could also try to find someone else who wanted to buy 50,000 bushels of soybeans on October 1 and deliver the soybeans it doesn't want in fulfillment of this contract.

The development of standardized futures contracts, organized markets in which to trade them, and clearing facilities to guarantee delivery, addresses each of these issues.

21.2 - Futures Contracts

Futures are forward contracts standardized as to quantity, quality, and delivery date so that they can trade in an organized market. The futures contract is a two-sided contract. An investor can take the buy side or the sell side. This differs from an equity or bond in that the claim exists because the issuer authorized it and the market allows it to change hands.

The standardized elements of the contract, everything except the price per unit, is determined by the exchange on which the contract trades. The exchange creates contracts for which there is a sufficient number of buyers and sellers to make a market.

Figure 21-1: Example Soybean Futures Contract

Soybean Contract	Soybean Contract
I promise to BUY *5,000 bushels #2 yellow soybeans with a* *minimum of 14% moisture for delivery* *November 2013* at ____431____ ¢ *per bushel* *Susan Speculator*	*I promise to SELL* *5,000 bushels #2 yellow soybeans with a* *minimum of 14% moisture for delivery* *November 2013* at ____431____ ¢ *per bushel* *George Q. Farmer*

When we enter into a soybean futures contract, we are committing to a transaction at a future date, at a specified price for a specific quantity of a known commodity.

In this example Susan Speculator commits to buy 5,000 bushels of #2 yellow soybeans at $4.31 per bushel on November 15, 2013.	In this example George Q. Farmer commits to sell 5,000 bushels of #2 yellow soybeans at $4.31 per bushel on November 15, 2013.

Note that we do not "buy a futures contract" or "sell a futures contract". Although it may be common vernacular to tell your broker to "Buy 10 November bean contracts at the market", the true action undertaken is to establish a long position in 10 contracts of soybeans for delivery in November. This obligates the investor to buy 50,000 bushels in November, with the expectation that he will take possession and pay for the goods at time of purchase. Establishing the long position now is not a transaction in soybeans now and there is no need to pay for them now.

The reverse is true for the investor who enters the order, "Sell 10 November bean contracts at the market". Nothing is sold, no money is paid the investor, and in reality, he has established a short position in 10 contracts of soybeans for delivery in November. This obligates him to sell 50,000 bushels in November, with the expectation that he will deliver the goods and accept payment at that time.

This is crucial to understanding how exchange traded futures (and forward contracts) actually work. It is also important to note at this point that establishing a short position in the futures market involves no borrowing of securities to sell, as does a short sale of stock, bonds, or other financial instruments.

21.3 - Futures Trading

Each contract is defined by the exchange on which it trades. The quote in Table 21-1 gives a small sample of the possible contracts that trade on the various exchanges.

It states that futures on soybeans are traded on the Chicago Board of Trade (CBOT), that each contract is for 5,000 bushels, and that prices are quoted in cents per bushel. There are numerous futures contracts for soybeans, each one for the same quantity of the same quality soybeans, but each for a different delivery date. Only five are included in the quote.

Gold trades on the New York Mercantile Exchange (NYMEX) on its Commodities Exchange (COMEX). Each contract is for 100 troy ounces of gold, and prices are quoted in dollars per ounce.

Both the CBOT and NYMEX are owned and operated by the CME Group.

❏ **Open, Hi, Low:** The quote shows that the July soybean contract opened at $13.82½ per bushel. During the day's trading the July contracts hit a high of $13.82¾ and a low of $13.51¼. Note that the quote format is in eighths. So '2 is 2/8.

The quote does not show that soybean prices, at just under $14/bushel, are close to the historical highs of almost $16/bushel set in July 2008. Over the past 20 years the price of soybeans have fluctuated between $4 and $16 per bushel.

❏ **Settle:** The settle or settlement price is the representative price over the closing period designated by the exchange. For example, the average of all trades executed in the last two minutes of trading. The settlement price on the July contract is down 19¾¢ from the previous day's settle of $13.82¼ per bushel.

In markets where liquidity is low the last trade may not reflect the closing value of the future. In these markets the settle is calculated from a specific formula based on the spot price of the underlying asset.

❏ **Open Interest:** Open interest is the number of contracts outstanding as at the close of trading. The open interest generally increases until a month before the contract matures and then declines rapidly as investors reverse their positions. Few investors really want 5,000 bushels of soybeans delivered to their Wall Street offices.

The soybean quotes show that at the time of this quote there was an open interest of 269,115 contracts on July soybeans. If this were the last day of trading then 1.35 billion (269,115 * 5,000) bushels of soybeans would actually be delivered.

❏ **Contango:** Pricing pattern where futures prices increase as the delivery dates get further out on the time line. In Table 21-1 gold futures prices form a contango. In a contango either the spot price must increase or the futures price must decrease because, at delivery, the spot and futures price must be the same.

❏ **Backwardation:** Pricing pattern where futures prices decrease as the delivery dates get further out on the time line. In Table 21-1 soybean futures prices form a Backwardation. In a backwardation either the spot price must decrease or the futures price must increase because, at delivery, the spot and futures price must be the same.

Table 21-1: Futures Price Quote

	Open	High	Low	Settle	Chg	Volume	Open Interest
AGRICULTURAL FUTURES							
Corn (CBOT) 5,000 bu; cents per bu							
Sept 2012	527'6	531'4	517'6	529'0	+3'0	26,665	169,111
Dec 2012	524'2	526'6	513'6	523'0	+1'0	63,616	378,842
Soybeans (CBOT) 5,000 bu; cents per bushel							
July 2012	1382'4	1382'6	1351'2	1362'4	-19'6	113,675	269,115
Sept 2012	1313'0	1315'4	1287'4	1295'0	-19'6	4,281	21,016
Nov 2012	1281'0	1282'0	1251'2	1255'6	-24'4	61,776	242,132
Nov 2013	1164'4	1164'4	1141'4	1145'4	-18'4	1,543	17,438
Nov 2014	1136'4	1136'4	1136'4	1136'4	-18'4	6	502
Orange Juice (NYBOT) 15,000 lbs; cents per pound							
Jul 2012	108.90	108.90	99.70	103.10	-5.50	565	15,212
Nov 2012	110.85	111.00	104.70	107.55	-5.20	26	4,203
METAL & PETROLEUM FUTURES							
Gold (COMEX) 100 troy oz; $ per troy oz							
June 2012	1567.4	1568.5	1532.8	1548.4	-28.2	227,194	150,173
Aug 2012	1570.0	1570.4	1535.0	1550.6	-28.2	26,873	129,222
Dec 2012	1573.5	1573.5	1539.8	1554.7	-28.2	17,737	49,158
Crude Oil, Light Sweet (NYMEX) 1,000 bbls; $ per bbl;							
July 2012	91.54	91.72	89.29	89.90	-1.95	251,509	311,078
Dec 2012	92.80	92.80	90.63	91.25	-1.83	42,531	179,421
INTEREST RATE FUTURES							
Treasury Bonds 30yr (CBOT) $100,000; pts 32nds of 100%							
June 2012	147:13	147:24	147:13	147:23	+0:07	658,984	622,475
Sept 2012	146:29	147:04	146:29	147:04	+0:07	178,775	299,373
Treasury Notes 2yr (CBOT) $100,000; pts 32nds of 100%							
Jun 2012	110:06	110:07½	110:06	110:08	+0:00½	377,115	760,530
Sept 2012	110:03½	110:04½	110:03	110:03½	+0:01	333,779	1,217,851
CURRENCY FUTURES							
British Pound (CME) £62,500; $ per £							
June 2012	1.5762	1.5770	1.5666	1.5703	-0.0070	126,034	183,896
Sept 2012	1.5749	1.5750	1.5674	1.5686	-0.0079	212	1,544
Euro (CME) €125,000; $ per €							
June 2012	1.2680	1.2689	1.2546	1.2574	-0.0146	388,094	372,728
Sept 2012	1.2694	1.2694	1.2559	1.2585	-0.0146	1,185	3,657
INDEX FUTURES							
DJ industrial Average (CBT) $10 * index							
June 2012	12393	12470	12290	12466	-11	3,092	16,231
Sept 2012	12245	12395	12245	12395	-10	150	5,450
S&P 500 Index (CME) $250 * index							
June 2012	1306.70	1318.80	1294.20	1315.70	+0.90	16,561	259,289
Sept 2012	1293.50	1311.90	1290.00	1309.20	+0.80	718	6,355

Financial Pages; May 2012

21.3.1 - Contract Definition

The exchange defines in detail the terms of each contract and the conditions under which it trades.

The objective is to specify a contract for which there is sufficient demand and supply to create an efficient market. If there is insufficient participation, then the exchange has not addressed the problem of coincidence of need. Volumes will be low, prices will not be efficient, and the exchange will not generate enough in the way of brokerage commissions for its members to warrant support of the contract it created.

Example 2:

The soybeans futures contract is 5,000 bushels of U.S. No. 2 yellow soybeans with a maximum of 14% moisture. If you deliver U.S. No. 1 soybeans with a maximum of 13% moisture you get 6¢ per bushel over the contract price. No. 3 fetches 6¢ per bushel under the contract price.

Table 21-2: Soybean Futures Contract Specifications (CBOT)	
Trading Unit	5,000 bu
Deliverable Grades	No.2 Yellow at par and substitutions at differentials established by the exchange
Price Quote	Cents and quarter-cents/bu
Tick Size	1/4 cents/bu ($12.50/contract)
Daily Price Limit	45 cents/bu ($2,500/contract) above or below previous day's settlement price. No limit in the spot month (limits are lifted two business days before the spot month begins).
Contract Months	Sep, Nov, Jan, Mar, May, Jul, Aug
Contract Year	Sep to Aug
Last Trading Day	The business day prior to the 15th calendar day of the contract month.
Last Delivery Day	Second business day following the last trading day of the delivery month.
Trading Hours	Open Auction: 9:30 am – 2:00 pm Central Time, Mon–Fri. Electronic: 5:00 pm – 2:00 pm. Central Time, Sun–Fri. Trading in expiring contracts closes at noon on the last trading day.
Ticker Symbol	Open Auction: S Electronic: ZS

CME Group Agricultural Contract Specifications

21.3.2 - Hybrid Trading

Note that soybean futures trade both open outcry and electronic.

Open outcry transactions are traded on the floor of the exchange from 9:30 to 1:15 Chicago time Mondays through Fridays. Investors can place market, limit, or stop orders. The order is transmitted to the exchange floor, and is taken to the designated pit for execution by a member of the exchange. The pit is a circular, square, or octagonal area with a set of descending steps on which members stand. The trading pit makes it easier to see and communicate.

Floor or pit brokers are members that execute client orders. They each keep their own record of client limit or stop orders that cannot be executed immediately. Floor traders, also known as locals or scalpers, trade on their own accounts. Floor traders are similar to market makers in that they hold an inventory of futures contracts, but they are not obligated to make a market in a specific contract.

Orders are announced in the pit by open outcry. The method of open outcry ensures that the order is exposed to everyone in the pit, thereby leading to the best possible execution price. At 2:00pm trading closes and the settlement price is established for the day.

At 5:00 pm the electronic markets open and computerized trading continues until 2:00 pm This is counted as part of the following day's trading. So Monday begins Sunday at 5pm and continues through 2 pm on Monday. The electronic trading day includes the 9:30 am to 2:00 pm open outcry session. This around-the-clock trading schedule allows traders from all over the world to participate even when the floor of the exchange is closed.

	<- Open Outcry ->	<-- Electronic -->
Chicago:	9:30 am – 2:00 pm	5:00 pm – 2:00 pm
San Francisco:	7:30 am – 12:00 pm	3:00 pm – 12:00 pm
Tokyo:	11:30 pm – 4:00 am	7:00 am – 4:00 am
Singapore:	10:30 pm – 3:00 am	6:00 am – 3:00 am
London:	3:30 pm – 8:00 pm	11:00 pm – 8:00 pm
New York:	10:30 am – 3:00 pm	6:00 pm – 3:00 pm

Trading takes place up to the last business day prior to the 15th of the month in which the futures deliver: essentially the 14th of the month unless the 14th falls on a weekend, in which case it is the Friday before. On the last day of trading the closing bell is rung at noon for that month's delivery contracts.

Delivery is two business days later.

These conditions are specific to soybeans. The CME Group web page provides particulars for each contract traded on exchanges it owns and operates. Specifications for contracts traded on other exchanges are generally available on the exchanges' Web sites.

21.4 - Futures Exchanges

In the United States futures trading is dominated by four exchanges. All are regulated by the Commodity Futures Trading Commission, an independent agency of the United States government.

21.4.1 - Chicago Board of Trade (CBOT)

The Chicago Board of Trade was founded in 1848. It created "to-arrive" contracts, which permitted farmers to sell their grain for later delivery. This allowed the farmer to store the grain either on the farm or at a storage facility nearby and deliver it to Chicago months later. It soon became apparent that the sale and delivery of the grain itself was not nearly as important as the ability to transfer the associated price risk.

The grain could always be sold and delivered anywhere else at any time.

In 1865 the CBOT formalized standardized exchange-tradeable futures contracts on grains. It also began the practice of requiring performance bonds called "margin" to be posted by buyers and sellers in its grain markets. In 1926, with the establishment of the Chicago Board of Trade Clearing Corporation to guarantee contracts, the elements of modern futures markets were in place.

The 1871 Chicago Fire destroyed the CBOT's first building and all its records. Two weeks later the Exchange reopened at its new emergency location: a 90-ft by 90-ft, wigwam at Washington and Market streets. The Exchange built new facilities at LaSalle & Jackson in 1885 and again in 1930. On each occasion the new building was the tallest in Chicago.

In 1975 Interest rate futures began trading in Chicago. By 1998 the CBOT introduced hybrid trading, combining open-outcry with electronic. In October 2005 the CBOT became a publically traded company listed on the NYSE (BOT).

In July 2007 the Chicago Board of Trade merged with the Chicago Mercantile Exchange to form the CME Group.

21.4.2 - Chicago Mercantile Exchange (CME)

The CME was founded in 1898 as the Chicago Butter and Egg Board. It became the Chicago Mercantile Exchange in 1919. The CME introduced currency futures in 1972, making it the first exchange to trade financial futures. The phenomenal growth of the CME makes it the second largest futures market in the world after Euronext.LIFFE.

In May 2001 the Chicago Mercantile Exchange and the Chicago Board Options Exchange (CBOE) established OneChicago, a joint venture exchange to introduce single stock futures. After several delays trading opened November 8, 2002. To date, volume is fairly thin.

In December 2002 the Chicago Mercantile Exchange became a publically traded company listed on the NYSE (CME). In July 2007 the Chicago Board of Trade merged with the Chicago Mercantile Exchange to form the CME Group.

21.4.3 - New York Mercantile Exchange (NYMEX)

The New York Mercantile Exchange (NYMEX, pronounced Nigh-Mex) includes the original New York Mercantile Exchange and the New York Commodities Exchange (COMEX). Comex itself was the creation of a 1933 merger of the National Metal Exchange, the Rubber Exchange of New York, the National Raw Silk Exchange, and the New York Hide Exchange.

NYMEX has facilities in the World Financial Center, where it trades a wide variety of metals and energy products. Trading is a combination of open outcry from 10 am to 2:30 pm—although different markets are open at slightly different times—and electronic trading from 3:15 pm to 9:50 am.

NYMEX Europe, the European subsidiary of the New York Mercantile Exchange, closed its open-outcry trading floor in London in favor of an all-electronic system in June 2006. Competition from the all-electronic ICE Futures, the former International Petroleum Exchange, meant that volumes were too low to maintain an open outcry system.

In November 2006 NYMEX became a publically traded company listed on the NYSE (NMX). In August 2008 both NYMEX and COMEX were acquired by the CME Group.

21.4.4 - New York Board of Trade (NYBOT)

The New York Board of Trade (NYBOT) derives from the merger of New York Cotton Exchange and the Coffee, Sugar and Cocoa Exchange.

The New York Cotton Exchange (NYCE) was created in 1870 to trade cotton. Although it kept the name for over a century the Cotton Exchange also traded other commodities, such as frozen concentrated orange juice, propane & heating oil, metals and mineral, and currency and index Futures. In 1994 the NYCE opened a trading facility in Dublin.

The Coffee Exchange was created in 1882, added Sugar in 1914, and Cocoa in 1925 to become the New York Coffee, Sugar, and Cocoa Exchange. Options were added in 1982. The two exchanges formed the Board of Trade of the City of New York in 1998 the New York Board of Trade (NYBOT) in June 2004.

The trading floor and headquarters of the New York Board of Trade in the World Trade Center were destroyed on September 11, 2001. Trading was moved to the emergency backup facility on Long Island. In February 2003, the NYBOT moved its World Financial Center headquarters and trading facility into the NYMEX Building in World Financial Center. In September 2007 it was renamed ICE Futures U.S., a wholly owned subsidiary of Intercontinental Exchange (ICE)

21.4.5 - London International Financial Futures Exchange (LIFFE)

The London International Financial Futures Exchange (LIFFE pronounced life) was founded in 1982, after Britain removed its currency controls. It began by trading interest rates futures. It merged with the London Traded Options Market (LTOM) in 1992 and with the London Commodity Exchange (LCE) in 1996. In January 2002 LIFFE was itself acquired by Euronext NV, which operates exchanges in Amsterdam, Brussels, Lisbon, and Paris, becoming Euronext.LIFFE.

21.5 - The Clearinghouse

The exchange takes on the responsibility of bringing buyer and seller together. The clearinghouse takes on the responsibility of ensuring that every contract traded on the exchange is honored and that existing positions can be reversed without default.

To ensure that no buyer or seller ever defaults on his contract, the clearinghouse takes the opposite side of every contract.
Example 3:

Susan Q. Speculator places an order to buy ten November soybean contracts. George Q. Farmer places an order to sell 10 November soybean contracts. Their brokers trade at 431. The contract specifies that George Q. Farmer will sell to Susan Q. Speculator 10 * 5,000 bushels of soybeans in November and that she will pay him $4.31 * 50,000 or $215,500. The open interest increases by 10 contracts.

Although it looks very much as though Susan Q. Speculator has a contract with George Q, Farmer, she actually has a contract with the clearinghouse. The clearinghouse splits the contract in two such that George and

Susan each have a contract with the CBOT.

Figure 21-2: The Clearinghouse Interposed Between Two Halves of a Contract

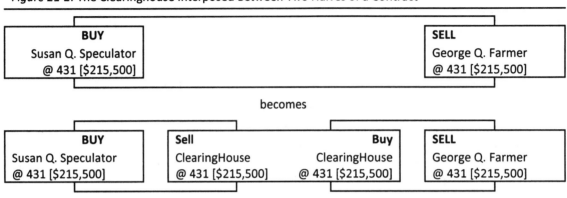

Note that the clearinghouse position is market neutral. This means that the clearinghouse makes no profits or losses, regardless of the price of soybeans.

Example 4:

Suppose that by November the price of soybeans drops to $4.00 per bushel. The futures contract obliges Susan to pay $4.31 per bushel. This constitutes a loss of $15,500. Payment is made at delivery so Susan decides to renege on the contract.

Because futures contracts are with the clearinghouse, George Q. Farmer is unaffected by Susan's unethical behavior; the clearinghouse honors its contract with George on Susan's behalf by selling soybeans on the spot market at $4.00 per bushel and taking the $15,500 loss. The clearinghouse would then take legal action against Susan.

Example 5:

On the other hand, suppose that by November the price of soybeans increases to $5.00 per bushel. Since George is obliged to sell at $4.31 per bushel, this constitutes a loss of $34,500. George decides to renege on the contract.

Because Susan's contract is with the clearinghouse, she is unaffected. The clearinghouse buys the soybeans on the spot market at $5.00 per bushel and sells them to Susan at the contracted price of $4.31, taking a loss of $34,500. The clearinghouse would then take legal action against George.

In either case the futures exchange, or the clearinghouse, becomes a center for legal action rather than an element in a functioning market. In order to avoid potential losses, the clearinghouse takes three measures designed to make sure that every market participant has more to lose by defaulting on their contract than by honoring it:

❑   It imposes **initial margin** requirements on both buyers and sellers.

❑   It **marks to market** at the close of business on each trading day.

❑   It imposes daily **maintenance margins** on both buyers and sellers.

21.5.1 - Initial Margin

Whenever a futures contract is traded, both the buyer and the seller are required to make security deposits. This initial or performance margin is intended to guarantee that the obligations under the contract will be fulfilled. The minimum margin is set by the exchange, though the margins required by the broker may be higher. Generally, higher margins are set on futures contracts with a greater price volatility since the clearinghouse faces larger losses on more volatile assets.

Example 6:

The minimum initial margin on soybeans is $810 per contract: both Susan and George must deposit $8,100 in cash, cash equivalents (such as a Treasury Bond), or a bank line of credit.

_____

The margins are reset periodically. An initial margin of $810/contract makes sense when Soybeans are trading at $4/bushel. But when Soybeans were trading at $13/bushel the initial margin was $3,375.

Note that $8,100 would not cover the loss under either of the preceding scenarios. This is where marking to market comes in.

21.5.2 - Marking to Market

The initial margin represents your equity. Equity is your initial margin adjusted for mark to market gains and losses, as well as any subsequent deposits or withdrawals of cash. Adjusting the equity to reflect the settlement price at the end of every trading day is referred to as marking to market. Essentially, marking-to-market is equivalent to unwinding your position at the closing price and reopening your position at that same closing price, at the end of every trading day.

❑   **Equity:** The equity in your account represents what your broker would return to you if your position was unwound at the closing price.

Equity can be calculated in two ways (both should give you the same answer)

1)   Calculate the market value of the futures contract as if the position would be closed out at the settlement price. Equity is then the total deposits to margin plus cumulative profit (loss).

2)   Calculate the change in the market value of the futures contract for the trading day. Equity is then the previous day's equity plus the day's profit (loss).

Example 7:

Assume that on the day following the initial trade, the price of soybeans increases to 441. All contracts are marked to market.

Susan Q. Speculator has a futures contract to buy November soybeans at 431. If Susan had closed out her position by selling November soybeans at the closing price of 441 then this transaction would give her a profit of $5,000 [50,000 * ($4.41 - $4.31)]. Susan's broker could return her margin deposit of $8,100 (since the broker would no longer need it to ensure her good behavior) plus her profit of $5,000. Thus Susan's equity is calculated at $13,100.

If on the following day the settlement price on November soybean contracts were 442 then Susan's equity would increase by another $500 to $13,600. If Susan had closed out her position by selling November soybeans at the closing price of 442 then this transaction would give her a profit of $5,500 [50,000 * ($4.42 - $4.31)]. Susan's broker could return her margin deposit of $8,100 plus her profit of $5,500. Thus Susan's equity is calculated at $13,600.

On the other hand, George would have lost $5000 as the price of soybeans increased to 441and another $500 as the price of soybeans increased to 442. His equity would decrease to $2,600. ($8,100 - $5,500). Now the clearinghouse might get a bit nervous. This is where the maintenance margin comes in.

Note an important function of futures markets in this example. With each increase in price, Susan's gain is exactly George's loss. Similarly, with each decrease in price, Susan's loss is exactly George's gain. In aggregate, futures markets are a zero-sum game.

This is an example of a perfect risk-transference mechanism.

Susan Q. Speculator has no intention of buying or selling soybeans, she has risk capital that she brings to a market that would otherwise be of no interest to her. She hopes to earn an acceptable rate of return because she is accepting the price risk against which George Q. Farmer would like to insure. Exchange-traded futures thus provide a mechanism by which speculators bring depth and liquidity to the market, further enhancing the benefits that producers and users of goods would find if the speculators weren't there.

21.5.3 - Maintenance Margin

The equity in an account must be maintained above a prescribed minimum. When the equity falls below this minimum the investor must bring his equity back up to the initial margin requirement: he receives a margin call from the broker.

❑ **Margin Call:** a margin call or variation margin is a notification that the money and assets you have deposited with your broker in your margin account is no longer enough to satisfy minimum or variation margin requirements.

Margin call must be met with a cash deposit; no other assets are acceptable on margin calls. The rules of a variation margin call state that the deposit of cash is in an amount such that the equity is reestablished to the initial margin required to enter the trade.

If the investor cannot make the margin call then the broker will close out the position by entering a reversing trade in the investor's account. If the trade results in a loss then the investor must compensate the broker for the loss, or legal action is taken.

❑ **Hypothecation:** Hypothecation occurs when an investor pledges securities as collateral on a loan. If securities are used to cover a margin obligation then the securities are hypothecated so that the broker can sell the securities if required to cover the position.

❑ **Rehypothecation:** Rehypothecation occurs when the broker borrows money and uses as collateral on the loan the hypothecated securities in customer accounts. Rehypothecation of client securities is limited (sic) to 140% of the debit balance on the client account.

Example 8:

Think of placing a bet that the Fighting Illini win the next football game. The bet is $10 per point difference.

If I win then you might become hard to find; if you win then I might become hard to find. So we pick a stakeholder. We each give him $200 to hold until the game is over. The stakeholder plays the role of the clearing house—he's not a party to the bet—but an impartial judge and banker. The $200 is our margin.

If the final score is Illini 21, Wolverines 7, then I win the bet by 14 points or $140. The stakeholder gives me my $200 back plus my $140 winnings for a total of $340. The stakeholder gives you back your $200 less $140, so you get back $60. This $60 equity is what keeps you from skipping town after the game.

If the score at halftime is 27 – 0 at halftime then you might be tempted to leave the game early. Honoring your bet involves a $270 loss, defaulting involves a $200 loss. To avoid this the stakeholder calculates the potential loss (marks to market) and intercepts you at the gate, extracting an additional $150 (margin call), to see the bet through to the end of the game.

———————

Example 9:

Susan Q. Speculator buys 10 soybean contracts at 431. She is long soybean futures. George Q. Farmer sells 10 soybean contracts at 431. He is short soybean futures.

The initial margin on soybeans is $810 per contract. The minimum maintenance margin is $600 per contract.

Over the next five days the price of soybean futures settles at 431, 441, 442, 430, and 436 cents per bushel. Table 21-2 shows the activity in two accounts calculated at the settle price of each trading day. Figure 21-3 shows this same information graphically.

———————

❑ **Day 1:** Trade at 431

■ **Susan Q. Speculator** buys 10 soybean contracts at 431. The contracts specify that she will buy 50,000 bushels soybeans at 431 per bushel for a total of $215,500. To guarantee performance she deposits $8,100 to her margin account.

Equity = $8,100.

■ **George Q. Farmer** sells 10 soybean contracts at 431. The contracts specify that he will sell 50,000 bushels soybeans at 431 per bushel for a total of $215,500. To guarantee performance he deposits $8,100 to his margin account.

Equity = $8,100.

❑ **Day 2:** Settlement price = 441

■ **Susan Q. Speculator** bought soybeans and watched the price go up 10¢ per bushel. On 50,000 bushels this means that she made an unrealized or paper profit of $5,000 today. Her equity increases to $13,100.

Equity = $8,100 + $5,000 = $13,100.

■ **George Q. Farmer** sold soybeans and watched the price go up 10¢ per bushel. On 50,000 bushels this means that he has lost $5,000 today. His equity decreases to $3,100. This equity of $3,100 is below the maintenance margin of $6,000 ($600 per contract) so George is issued a margin call. In order to keep the contract he must deposit a further $5,000 to his margin account, thereby bringing his equity back up to the initial margin requirement of $8,100.

Equity = $8,100 - $5,000 = $3,100.
+ $5,000 = $8,100.

❑ **Day 3:** Settlement price = 442

■ **Susan Q. Speculator** watched the price go up another 1¢ per bushel. On 50,000 bushels this means that she made a profit of $500 today. Her equity increases to $13,600.

Equity = $13,100 + $500 = $13,600.

The contract she bought at 431 for a total of $215,500 is now worth 442 for a total of $221,000. Susan's total profit to date is $5,500. So her total equity is $13,600.

Equity = $8,100 + $5,500 = $13,600.

■ **George Q. Farmer** watched the price go up another 1¢ per bushel. On 50,000 bushels this means that he has lost $500 today. His equity decreases to $7,600. This is above the maintenance margin of $6,000 ($600 per contract) so George receives no margin call today.

Equity = $8,100 - $500 = $7,600.

The contract he sold at 431 for a total of $215,500 is now worth 442 for a total of $221,000. George's total loss to date is $5,500. So his total equity is $7,600.

Equity = $8,100 + $5,000 (margin call) - $5,500 = $7,600.

❑ **Day 4:** Settlement price = 430

■ **Susan Q. Speculator** watched the price of soybeans drop 12¢ today. On 50,000 bushels this means she lost $6,000 in one day. Her equity drops to $7,600.

$$\text{Equity} = \$13,600 - \$6,000 = \$7,600.$$

The contract she bought at 431 for a total of $215,500 is now worth 430 for a total of $215,000. Susan's total loss to date is $500. So her total equity is $7,600. This is above the maintenance margin of $6,000, so Susan receives no margin call.

$$\text{Equity} = \$8,100 - \$500 = \$7,600.$$

■ **George Q. Farmer** watched the price of soybeans drop 12¢ today. On 50,000 bushels this means he made a profit of $6,000 in one day. His equity increases to $13,600.

$$\text{Equity} = \$7,600 + \$6,000 = \$13,600.$$

The contract he sold at 431 for a total of $215,500 is now worth 430 for a total of $215,000. George's total profit to date is $500. So his total equity is $13,600.

$$\text{Equity} = \$8,100 + \$5,000 \text{ (margin call)} + \$500 = \$13,600.$$

❑ **Day 5:** Settlement price = 436

■ **Susan Q. Speculator** watched the price of soybeans increase 6¢ today. On 50,000 bushels this means she made a profit of $3,000 today. Her equity increases to $10,600.

$$\text{Equity} = \$7,600 + \$3,000 = \$10,600.$$

The contract she bought at 431 for a total of $215,500 is now worth 436 for a total of $218,000. Susan's total profit to date is $2,500.

$$\text{Equity} = \$8,100 + \$2,500 = \$10,600.$$

■ **George Q. Farmer** watched the price of soybeans increase 6¢ today. On 50,000 bushels this means he lost $3,000 today. His equity decreases to $10,600. He would like to withdraw some of this money from his margin account. He cannot bring his equity below the initial margin, so George withdraws $2,500.

$$\text{Equity} = \$13,600 - \$3,000 \text{ (loss)} - \$2,500 \text{ (withdrawal)} = \$8,100.$$

The contract he sold at 431 for a total of $215,500 is now worth 436 for a total of $218,000. George's total profit to date is a loss of $2,500. So his total equity is $8,100.

$$\text{Equity} = \$8,100 + \$5,000 \text{ (margin call)} - \$2,500 \text{ (withdrawal)} - \$2,500 \text{ (loss)} = \$8,100.$$

This example simplifies the mechanics of trading somewhat. Actually only members of the clearinghouse have accounts that are marked to market at the end of every trading day. In turn each brokerage house acts as a clearinghouse for its own clients.

Table 21-3: Summary of Transactions Detailed in Example 9

Day	Settlement Price [Value]	Susan Q. Speculator (long soybean futures)					George Q. Farmer (short soybean futures)				
		Action	Profit Daily	Profit Cum	Deposit to Margin A/C	Equity	Action	Profit Daily	Profit Cum	Deposit to Margin A/C	Equity
1	431 [$215,500]	Buy 10 contracts@431 Initial Margin			$8,100.	$8,100.	Sell 10 contracts @431: Initial Margin			$8,100.	$8,100.
2	441 [$220,500]	Mark to Market	$5,000.	$5,000.		$13,100.	Mark to Market Margin Call	-$5,000.	-$5,000.	$5,000.	$3,100. $8,100.
3	442 [$221,000]	Mark to Market	$500.	$5,500.		$13,600.	Mark to Market	-$500.	-$5,500.		$7,600.
4	430 [$215,000]	Mark to Market	-$6,000.	-$500.		$7,600.	Mark to Market	$6,000.	$500.		$13,600.
5	436 [$218,000]	Mark to Market	$3,000.	$2,500.		$10,600.	Mark to Market Withdrawal	-$3,000.	-$2,500.	-$2,500.	$10,600. $8,100.
6	436 [$218,000]	Sell 10 contracts @ 436 to close		$2,500.	-$10,600.	$0.	Mark to Market	$0.	-$2,500.	-$2,500.	$8,100.

Figure 21-3: Graph of Susan's and George's Equity

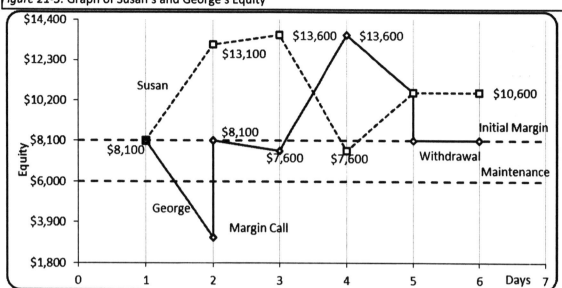

21.6 - Unwinding a Futures Position

Susan decides that she has speculated enough and decides to unwind or reverse her position. However, George does not want to reverse his side of the contract.

The only way out is for Susan to sell 10 November soybean contracts to someone else—John Q. Investor, for example. This closes out or unwinds Susan's position in November soybeans.

This is where the second function of the clearinghouse can be seen. Without the benefit of the clearinghouse Susan Q. Speculator would be obliged to wait until November, take delivery of 50,000 bushels of soybeans from George Q. Farmer and pay him $215,500; then deliver these soybeans to John Q. Investor in return for $218,000. Susan would therefore get her profit of $2,500 in November.

However, the clearinghouse automatically cancels offsetting positions. Susan's offsetting positions in November soybeans are immediately canceled. More importantly, Susan does not have to wait until November to take her $2,500 profit. As soon as the offsetting trade is executed she can withdraw the amount of her outstanding equity, so she get her profit immediately.

Figure 21-4: The Clearinghouse Cancels Offsetting Trades

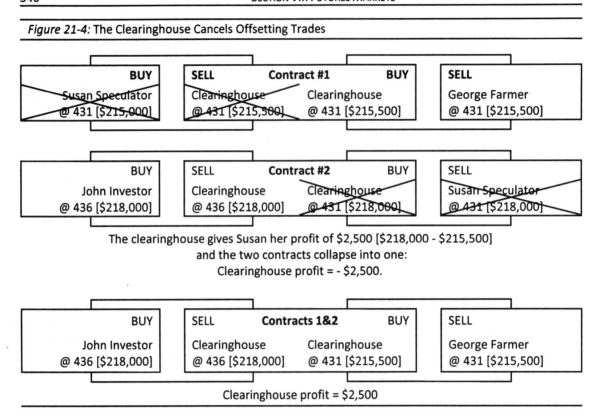

The clearinghouse gives Susan her profit of $2,500 [$218,000 - $215,500]
and the two contracts collapse into one:
Clearinghouse profit = - $2,500.

Clearinghouse profit = $2,500

21.7 - *Price Limits*

Price limits are set by the futures exchange subject to approval by the Commodity Futures Trading Commission.

❏ **Commodity Futures Trading Commission:** The CFTC was created by Congress in 1974 to regulate commodity futures and options markets. The mandate of the CFTC is to ensure market efficiency, to protect against fraud and manipulation, and to ensure the integrity of the clearing system.

The CBT price limit on soybeans (when the price is in the $/bushel range) is 45¢. This means that if November soybeans closed at 436 on the previous day then November contracts for less than 391¢ or more than 481¢ are not permitted to trade on the exchange. If a major news item hits (Hurricane Elisabeth wipes out the entire Illinois soybean crop) and investors think that 600¢ is a perfectly reasonable price for soybeans, then investors can do one of two things: trade off exchange, foregoing the advantages of dealing through a clearinghouse, or wait until the next day when the price limits would be 436¢ to 526¢ (481¢ ±45¢).

❏ **Limit Move:** A limit move occurs when trading stops because the price limit is reached. The settle reflects the price limit so that positions can be marked to market.

One result of the limit move to 481¢ is that there are days when nothing trades at all because all investors are unwilling to sell soybeans for less than 481¢. There can be limit moves for a number of successive days, with no trading taking place until the series of limit moves places the relevant price within reach.

Futures exchanges impose price limits in the belief that both clients and dealers overreact to new information, and that price limits reduce the price volatility of futures contracts.

2011: MF Global

MF Global was a clearing member of the Chicago Mercantile Exchange. A clearing member is an agent or conduit for the clearinghouse. An individual client may trade through a broker, the broker trades through a clearing firm, and the clearing firm trades through the central clearinghouse. Transactions cost are minimized because margin payments are calculated at the close of business every day and only net amounts actually transferred at every level.

MF Global filed for bankruptcy protection on October 31, 2011. At the time of the filing MF Global admitted to a shortfall of $891 million in customer accounts, $700 million of which was transferred to the London office to cover a highly leveraged $6.3 billion trade on European sovereign debt.

Customer accounts were frozen. The accounts themselves were transferred to other clearing members, but the margin these customers had deposited to MF Global as a clearing agent was not. The collateral posted by clients had been rehypothecated and was now gone. Clients were left with unsupported positions they could not trade or were forced to repost margin.

Rehypothecation is illegal in Canada. Canadian customers were able to recover their funds which were held by custodian Harris Bank. U.S. customers, whose funds were held by custodian JP Morgan, were left sitting on losses estimated at $1.6 billion.

Clients and brokers alike assumed that the system of initial margin, mark-to-market, and maintenance margin meant that no position was ever allowed to accumulate losses that might threaten the integrity of the contract. This assumption is valid only if client margin accounts are kept separate from the clearing firm's proprietary trading accounts. At MF Global segregated accounts were not kept segregated and the legal requirement to reimburse client accounts for securities rehypothecated by the clearing firm carries no weight if the clearing firm is under bankruptcy protection.

Chapter 21 - Questions and Problems

21-1:

In April George sold 10 November soybean contracts at 431. Since then he has deposited to his margin account a total of $10,600 in initial and maintenance margin. If November soybeans settle at 436 on the last day of trading,

A.   What is George's final position if he delivers on his contracts?

B.   What is George's final position if he unwinds his futures position on the last day of trading at 436?

21-2:

In April George sold 10 November soybean contracts at 431. Since then he has deposited to his margin account a total of $10,600 in initial and maintenance margin. In May John Q. Investor bought 10 November soybean contracts at 436 and deposited to his margin account a total of $8,100. On August 1 November soybeans settle at 436.

A.   On August 2 Hurricane Elisabeth destroys the entire Illinois soybean crop, and nobody is willing to sell soybean futures for less than 600. With a 45¢ daily price limit, how many days will pass before trading resumes?

B.   Assuming that the broker marks to market at the theoretical limit on each day, calculate the daily and cumulative paper profit, deposit to margin, and equity position for George Q. Farmer from day to day until trading resumes at 600¢.

C.   Assuming that the broker marks to market at the theoretical limit on each day, calculate the daily and cumulative paper profit, deposit to margin, and equity position for John Q. Investor from day to day until trading resumes at 600¢.

D.   How much can John withdraw from his margin account and still maintain his long position in soybeans?

$\mathcal{T}$he principal function of futures markets is to allow participants to manage risk deriving from adverse price movements.

❑ **Hedgers:** Hedgers buy and sell futures to offset an otherwise risky position in the spot or cash market. Even hedgers often unwind their positions without ever taking delivery of the underlying asset.

Example 1:

George Q. Farmer uses a short hedge. He knows that if the price at which he sells his soybeans is lower after the harvest then his income will decline accordingly. Therefore he sells soybean futures now. If the price of soybeans falls, then the profit on his futures position will offset the loss when he sells his soybeans in the spot market.

Example 2:

Exxon Mobil uses a long hedge. If the hurricane season is a severe one then Exxon will be forced to buy crude oil at higher prices. If it buys crude oil futures now, then if the price goes up the long futures position will generate enough profit to pay for the higher priced crude oil. Exxon also avoids the cost of storing the crude for later use.

❑ **Speculators:** Speculators buy and sell futures as financial investments, taking on risk to generate return.

Example 3:

Susan Speculator believes that the price of soybeans will go up. Buying five thousand bushels of soybeans now in the hope that the price will increase would present Susan with a cumbersome storage problem. Instead Susan buys soybean futures, waits until the price increases, then unwinds the position before delivery.

❑ **Arbitrageurs:** Arbitrageurs profit by the simultaneous buying and selling of closely related securities designed to take advantage of different prices of essentially the same asset.

Example 4:

John Q. Investor sees that the price of gold futures is high compared to the price of gold itself. He buys gold in the spot market now, sells the futures, and delivers the gold on contract. The profit on this transaction is the difference between the buy price spot and the sell price on the futures contract, less expenses.

22.1 - Basis

The basis is the difference between the spot or cash market price and the futures price. The basis is an essential tool in constructing a hedge.

$$Basis = P_{Spot} - P_{Futures}$$ (Eq 22-1)

Example 5:

If the futures price for soybeans is 431¢ and the spot price is $4.20 per bushel, then

$$Basis = \$4.20 - \$4.31$$
$$= -\$0.11$$

❑ **Convergence:** Typically the basis narrows over time until it equals zero on the delivery date. This is known as convergence.

22.2 - Constructing a Hedge

A Hedge is constructed by setting up a portfolio that is opposite and equal to the risk in the spot market. Essentially we take a long position in one asset and a short position in a similar asset; the gains in one position should offset the losses in the other position.

Example 6:

George Q. Farmer expects to harvest 50,000 bushels of soybeans in October. It is now April and the spot price for soybeans is $4.20/bushel. George has a long position in soybeans and therefore faces a price risk - he will lose money if the spot price of soybeans goes down by October. This is the risk he wishes to hedge.

Figure 22-1: George Q. Farmer's Timeline from Planting to Harvest.

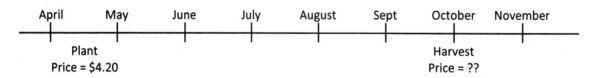

George's time line from planting to harvest is like an investment where you buy potential soybeans at $4.20 in land, seed, fertilizer, and labor, and then hope that the actual soybeans in October are worth at least your investment.

The uncertain situation that George faces in October is reflected in figure 22-2.

Figure 22-2: George Q. Farmer faces a Price Risk on the Soybeans that he Grows

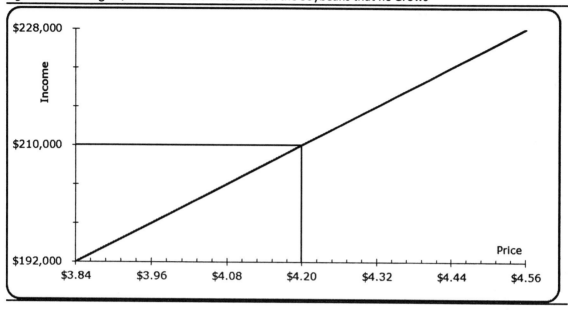

The key to setting up a hedge is to counteract the long position (soybeans growing in the field) with a short position in an investment whose price will move in the same direction.

Figure 22-3: Outline of a Short Hedge Strategy

Initial Risk Exposure: Long (Soybeans growing in the field)		Hedge Short (Futures Contracts)		Total Portfolio long spot & short hedge	
IF spot prices increase	🙂	futures price increase	☹️	Together:	😐
IF spot prices decrease	☹️	futures price decrease	🙂	Together:	😐

George sets the hedge by selling 10 November soybean contracts: 10 contracts because he estimates his harvest will be 50,000 bushels and the CBOT contract covers 5,000 bushels; November because George wants his hedge to last at least as long as his spot price risk, and he anticipates an October harvest.

22.3 - Textbook Hedge

A perfect or textbook hedge results when the basis remains unchanged.

When George is ready to harvest his soybeans in October, the spot price for soybeans has fallen from $4.20 to $4.00 per bushel (this is exactly the risk against which George set the hedge), and the futures price has fallen from 431 to 411.

George can now lift the hedge by buying 10 November soybean contracts at the current price of 411. The buy and sell cancel each other out, and George receives his equity of $18,100. The equity consists of the $8,100 initial margin plus the $10,000 profit earned on his short position.

With his futures contract negated George is now free to sell his soybeans on the spot market at $4.00 per bushel.

Table 22-1: George Q. Farmer: A Textbook Hedge			
April: (Hedge is set)	Sell November Futures: → 10 contracts at 431 [$215,500]	Margin:	- $8,100.
October: (Hedge is lifted)	Buy November Futures: → 10 contracts at 411 [$205,500]	Profit: Margin:	+ $10,000. + $8,100.
	Sell soybeans on the spot market at $4.00		+ $200,000.
		Net Position:	+ $210,000.
		Effective price per bushel:	$4.20

The effective price is George's net position per bushel of soybeans. It equals the spot price when we set the hedge. When the effective price exactly equals the initial spot price (the spot price when the hedge was set) we have a textbook hedge.

Initial Risk Exposure: Long (Soybeans growing in the field)		Hedge Short (Futures Contracts)		Total Portfolio long spot & short hedge
Spot price decreases $4.20 to $4.00	☹ 20¢ unhappy	Futures price decreases 431 to 411	☺ 20¢ happy	☺ completely neutral

The textbook hedge derives because the change in the spot price was matched exactly by the change in the futures price. In other words, the basis remained unchanged. When George set the hedge the basis was -11¢; when George lifted the hedge the basis was still -11¢.

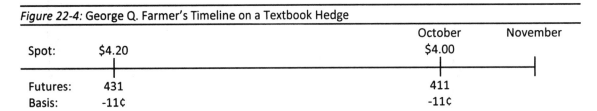

Figure 22-4: George Q. Farmer's Timeline on a Textbook Hedge

		October	November
Spot:	$4.20	$4.00	
Futures:	431	411	
Basis:	-11¢	-11¢	

George does have an alternative to unwinding the hedge and selling in the spot market in October, realizing a price of $4.20/bushel. He could harvest his crop in October, store the soybeans until November, and receive the contracted price of $4.31/bushel by delivering the beans under the terms of the contract.

However, storing the beans for a month is not cost free. He could pay a grain elevator to store his beans; they are in the business of doing this and gladly quote a price per bushel per day for their services. What if he has on-farm storage? Those bins, agitators, fans, dryers, and machinery necessary to move the grain, were put in place with the cost of capital to build and maintain the infrastructure.

Beyond storage costs, there is the potential problem with perishables like soybeans of shrinkage, decay, etc.

Finally, there is the more obvious cost of money. Receiving payment in October, rather than waiting until November, allows George to invest the payment to earn a rate of return for a month. Alternatively, an October sale lets him pay off his lenders a month earlier, the seed dealer, fertilizer, and fuel supplier he owes (and are charging interest on the balance) the costs of planting the crop.

22.4 - Basis Risk

Not all hedges are perfect. Suppose that in October, when George harvests his soybeans, the spot price for soybeans is $5.00 and the November futures price is 508.

George lifts the hedge by buying 10 November soybean contracts at the current price of 508. Because George is losing money on his futures position, he will have dealt with a number of margin calls over the past few months. When his equity is returned to him, George will realize a $38,500 loss on his futures position.

With his futures contract negated, George is now free to sell his soybeans on the spot market at $5.00 per bushel.

Table 22-2: George Q. Farmer: Hedge Position

April: (Hedge is set)	Sell November Futures: → 10 contracts at 431 [$215,500]	Margin:	- $8,100.
October: (Hedge is lifted)	Buy November Futures: → 10 contracts at 508 [$254,000]	Profit: Margin:	- $38,500. + $8,100.
	Sell soybeans on the spot market at $5.00		+ $250,000.
		Net Position:	+ $211,500.
		Effective price per bushel:	$4.23

The effective price of $4.23 per bushel is 3¢ higher than the $4.20 spot price when we set the hedge. This is no longer a textbook hedge.

Initial Risk Exposure: Long (Soybeans growing in the field)	Hedge Short (Futures Contracts)	Total Portfolio long spot & short hedge
Spot price increases $4.20 to $5.00 ☺ 80¢ happy	Futures price increases 431 to 508 ☹ 77¢ unhappy	☺ 3¢ happy

The effective price increases by 3¢ because the basis changes by 3¢. When George set the hedge the basis was -11¢; when George lifted the hedge the basis had narrowed to -8¢.

Figure 22-5: George Q. Farmer's Timeline on a Short Hedge where the Basis Narrows

			October	November
Spot:	$4.20		$5.00	
Futures:	431		508	
Basis:	-11¢		-8¢	

When George hedges his soybeans, he is trading a price risk for a basis risk. It is immaterial to George whether the price of soybeans is $1 or $10; it matters only whether the basis narrows, remains the same, or widens.

❑ **Long hedge:** A long hedge is the buy of a futures contract to hedge against an increase in the price of the asset that exposes you to a risk.

❑ **Short hedge:** A short hedge is the sale of a futures contract to hedge against a decrease in the price of the asset that exposes you to a risk.

Some may look at this example, where the spot market price rises to $5.00 in October, and wonder why George has gone through all the complications of this hedge. He still faces basis risk, and in the process of hedging, misses out on the opportunity to realize a selling price of $5.00/bushel in the spot market in October.

At the time the hedge was set in April, George anticipated that if he harvested an average crop yield of 50,000 bushels this season, given the known costs of raising the crop, the rate of return at a selling price of $4.20/bushel (plus or minus any basis risk he predicted) would adequately compensate him with a fair rate of return on his operation.

In April George knew that, in shielding himself from the risk of extraordinary losses due to a lower-than-expected price in October, he was depriving himself of the opportunity of extraordinary profits due to a higher-than-expected price in October. George was unwilling to accept the price risk. No doubt the unpredictability of weather, pestilence, and other factors affecting harvest yield has created enough uncertainty for him.

George Q. Farmer's position is illustrated in Figures 22-6, 22-7, and 22-8.

Figure 22-6 shows George's initial risky position. Soybean prices are projected to go to $4.31 by November, but prices are uncertain, and George assesses his risk accordingly. The normal distribution curve shows that George's best guess for soybean prices is a forecast of $4.31 with a standard deviation of 12¢ per bushel.

Figure 22-7 shows George's short position in soybean futures. George profits if soybean prices decrease. His best guess for soybean prices is still $4.31 with a standard deviation of 12¢ per bushel, but if he waits until the November delivery date then George is guaranteed $4.31 per bushel. The standard deviation on the normal distribution curve decreases until it reaches 0¢ per bushel at delivery.

Figure 22-8 shows George's net position. If George delivers on his futures contracts at $4.31 then the basis will go, with certainty, to 0. If George lifts his hedge before delivery then the outcome will depend on the basis. The price of soybeans, measured on the horizontal axis, is no longer a factor in George's position.

Figure 22-6: The Value of George's Soybean Harvest (Long) is at Risk Because George faces a Price Risk

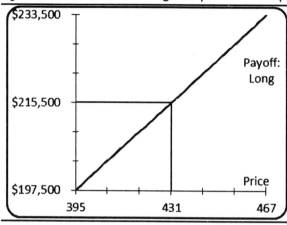

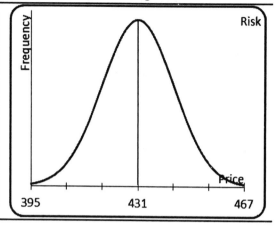

Figure 22-7: George's Short Futures Position Guarantees a Sale Price of 431 at Delivery

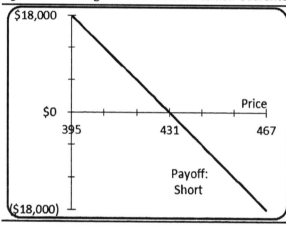

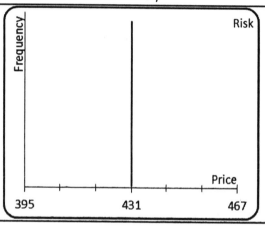

Figure 22-8: George's Hedged Position; If George Lifts the Hedge before Delivery he faces a Basis Risk

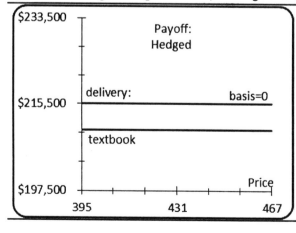

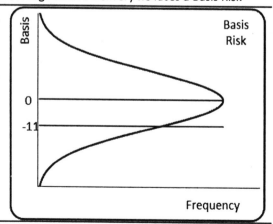

22.5 - Spreads and Cross Hedges

Spreads are differences between similar but not identical instruments (soybeans and soybean oil or July and August soybeans). Investors who hedge on a spread eliminate the risk associated with general price movements (as they do with a basis hedge) and face the risk associated with the change in the differences between the two similar investments.

When the future contract used to construct a hedge is on a related, but not identical, asset then we construct a cross hedge. For a cross hedge to work the price movements of the underlying commodities must be similar.

Example 7:

> George Q. Farmer produces squash: about 5,000 bushels per year, which he intends to sell to Kankakee Canning Corporation in October. George was so impressed with the hedge that you advised on his soybeans that he now asks you to construct a hedge for his October squash.
>
> However, there are no squash futures. George solemnly assures you that squash trades at 120% of the price of soybeans. Sure enough, squash is currently at $5.04 (120% of the $4.20 spot price in soybeans). There is no October contract on soybeans but there is a November contract.
>
> The current spot price for soybeans is $4.20, and the price for November soybeans is 431. We set up a cross hedge by selling one November soybean contract. Initial margin is $810. per contract.

22.5.1 - Textbook Cross Hedge

In October the spot price is $4.00 for soybeans and $4.84 for squash. When we lift his hedge the November futures price is 411.

Table 22-3: Initial Squash Price Risk and Cross-Hedge Position for George Q. Farmer

Hedge is set	Sell November Futures: → 1 contract at 431 ($21,550)	Margin:	- $810.
October (Hedge is lifted)	Buy November Futures: → 1 contract at 411 ($20,550)	Margin: Profit:	+ $810. + $1,000.
	Sell squash on the spot market at $4.84		+ $24,200.
		Net Position:	+ $25,200.
		Effective price per bushel:	$5.04

The effective price per bushel is equal to the $5.04 spot price we sought to lock in. However, in addition to basis risk, George also faces a cross hedge risk.

22.5.2 - Cross Hedge Risk

In October the spot price is $4.00 for soybeans and $4.85 for squash. When we lift his hedge the November futures price is 411.

Table 22-4: Initial Squash Price Risk and Cross Hedge Position for George Q. Farmer

Hedge is set	Sell November Futures: → 1 contract at 431 ($21,550)	Margin:	- $810.
October (Hedge is lifted)	Buy November Futures: → 1 contract at 411 ($20,550)	Margin: Profit:	+ $810. + $1,000.
	Sell squash on the spot market at $4.85		+ $24,250.
		Net Position:	+ $25,250.
		Effective price per bushel	$5.05

In this case, although the basis remained at -11¢, the price of squash is now $0.85 higher than the price of soybeans rather than $0.84 higher as before. A textbook cross hedge results only if the both the basis and the spot price difference remain the same.

Table 22-5: Summary of Cross Hedge Positions and Results

George	Textbook Hedge				NonTexbook Hedge			
	Set	Lift	Price Change	Profit/ (Loss)	Set	Lift	Price Change	Profit/ (Loss)
Spot Price (Squash)	$5.04	$4.84	- 0.20	- $1,000.	$5.04	$4.85	- 0.19	- $950.
Spot Price (Soybeans)	$4.20	$4.00	- 0.20		$4.20	$4.00	- 0.20	
Futures Price	$4.31	$4.11	- 0.20	$1,000.	$4.31	$4.11	- 0.20	$1,000.
Basis	- 0.11	- 0.11	0.00		- 0.11	- 0.11	0.00	
Spot Price Spread	0.84	0.84	0.00		0.84	0.85	- 0.01	
Net:			0.00	$0.			- 0.01	$50.

Note than in a cross hedge delivery is not an option. Holding the crop of squash harvested in October is unacceptable for delivery against the short contract for soybeans in November.

22.6 - Speculation

Futures provide scope and leverage not available in the underlying spot market.

Example 8:

John Q. Investor believes that frozen concentrated orange juice (FCOJ) is underpriced. He buys one contract for 15,000 pounds of FCOJ at $1.50/lb and makes a profit when the price increases by 10%.

Table 22-6: Long Futures Speculation in Frozen Concentrated Orange Juice

June	Buy September Future:		
	→ 1 contract at 150 ($22,500)	Margin:	- $1,000.
September	Sell September Futures:	Margin:	+ $1,000.
	→ 1 contract at 165 ($24,750)	Profit:	+ $2,250.
		NET POSITION:	+ $2,250.
		Rate of Return:	225%

John's rate of return is calculated as 225%. When an investor earns a rate of return of 225% on an investment that returns 10% the investors leverage is 22.5

$$\frac{\$2,250}{\$1,000} = 2.25 = 225\%$$

$$Leverage = \frac{225\%}{10\%} = 22.5$$

If John makes a similar investment in FCOJ directly his return would actually be less than 10% because he would need to pay to store 15,000 lbs of concentrate for the three months. Of course this leverage works when John's predictions are less accurate as well.

Example 9:

John predicts that the price of FCOJ will return to historical levels of $1.50 per pound so sells 1 contract. If John holds on to this investment after repeated margin calls then he loses $2,475

Table 22-7: Short Futures Speculation in Frozen Concentrated Orange Juice

September	Sell December Future:		
	→ 1 contract at 165 ($24,750)	Margin:	- $1,000.
December	Buy December Futures:	Margin:	+ $1,000.
	→ 1 contract at 181.5 ($27,225)	Profit:	- $2,475.
		NET POSITION:	- $2,475.
		Rate of Return:	- 247.5%

Note that in example 9 the market for futures allows John to take a short position in FCOJ without going through the procedure of borrowing 15,000 lbs of concentrate to sell. Thus futures markets facilitate speculation. This is the part of futures markets that cause the discussions of futures markets as gaming. However, speculators are an integral part of this market and perform an essential service; they willingly take on risk hedgers bring to the market. The price of any commodity is determined by demand and supply in the spot market. At delivery, the futures price reflect the price in the spot regardless of what speculation may have occurred during the life of the contract. But the speculation itself provides liquidity and gives hedgers a market in which to reduce risk that might otherwise reduce production and consumption.

22.7 - Spot-Futures Arbitrage

Arbitrage is the simultaneous buying and selling of closely related securities designed to take advantage of different prices of essentially the same asset.

Example 10:

> Discovery Café (DVC) is trading at $100 per share on the New York Stock Exchange. Trading on the NYSE is active and the price efficient. Discovery Café also trades on a small regional exchange in Urbana-Champaign Illinois. Trading is irregular and thin, and DVC is trading at $110.
>
> I calculate that I can make a risk-free profit by simultaneously buying shares on the NYSE at $100 and selling them in Urbana-Champaign at $110. I calculate further that brokerage costs are about $1.50 per share. I will continue to arbitrage until the share price in Urbana-Champaign declines to $101.50.
>
> Because I can arbitrage both ways the arbitrage free price P_{UC} in Urbana-Champaign is

arbitrage	arbitrage free price	arbitrage
Buy in Urbana-Champaign	$98.50 $\leq$ P_{UC} $\leq$ $101.50	Buy in New York
&		&
Sell in New York		Sell in Urbana-Champaign

> Thus the price in Urbana-Champaign can be efficient through arbitrage with a market that is efficient, even though the Urbana-Champaign market itself is not.

Spot-futures arbitrage means that the price of any futures contract is anchored by the underlying spot price. If the futures price is too low then arbitrageurs buy the futures and sell in the spot market, increasing the price of futures. If the futures price is too high then arbitrageurs sell the futures and buy in the spot market, decreasing the price of the futures. Thus arbitrage means that the futures price must reflect the spot price of the underlying asset plus the carrying charges necessary to carry the underlying asset to delivery.

As with the Discovery Café example we find the upper and lower bounds on the futures price by finding out at what futures price arbitrage profits go to zero. The essential difference is that we now arbitrage over markets separated, not by distance, but by time. The nature of the arbitrage as well as the cost of carry is asymmetric.

22.7.1 - Cash and Carry Arbitrage

Cash and carry arbitrage is a long position in an asset together with a short position in the corresponding futures contract. In cash and carry arbitrage we buy low in the spot market, carry it to the future, and sell high in the futures market.

Example 11:

In January 2013 the spot price of gold is $1,340 and twelve-month gold futures are trading at $1,420. The risk-free rate of interest is 5%. Storage and insurance costs are $2.40 per ounce per year.

Gold futures trade on the CBOT. One contract is 100 troy ounces. The initial margin is $3,600 per contract.

The arbitrage opportunity we explore is based on buying low at $1,340 and selling high at $1,420. We anticipate a gross profit (before carrying costs) of $80/ounce.

Table 22-8: Cash and Carry Arbitrage in Gold

January 2013		Cash Flow
→ Buy 100 troy ounces of gold on the spot market @ $1,340		- $134,000.
→ Storage and insurance		- $240.
→ Sell 1 Jan '14 gold futures contract @ $1,420		
	Initial margin	- $3,600.
→ Borrow at 5% for 12 months		+ $137,840.
Initial Investment		$0.

Note that the initial investment is forced to zero. This is done to ensure that we incorporate the time value of money into our calculations. One year later we realize our arbitrage profit.

Table 22-9: Cash and Carry Arbitrage in Gold at Delivery

January 2014		
→ Deliver gold at futures price of $1,420		+ $142,000.
→ Withdraw margin		+ $3,600.
→ Pay off debt	principle:	- $137,840.
	interest:	- $6,892.
Profit		+ $868.

We generate a profit of $8.68 rather than the $80 we anticipated. The $71.32 difference is the cost of carry: $2.40 storage and insurance and $68.92 interest. We can then calculate that successful arbitrage requires that the futures price must be greater than or equal to the spot price plus the carrying charges necessary to carry the gold to delivery.

$$P_{Future} = P_{Spot} + [Cost\ of\ Carry\ ]$$

$$P_{Future} = \$1,340 + [2.40 + 68.92]$$

$$P_{Future} = \$1,411.32$$

Ceteris paribus, as soon as the futures price increases to more than $1,411.32 we can make money through cash and carry arbitrage: buying spot low and selling futures high.

22.7.2 - Reverse Cash and Carry Arbitrage

Reverse cash and carry arbitrage is a short position in an asset together with a long position in the corresponding futures contract. In reverse cash and carry arbitrage we buy low in the futures market, carry it in reverse through time, and sell high in the spot market.

Example 12:

In January 2013 the spot price of gold is $1,340, and twelve-month gold futures are trading at $1,280. The risk-free rate of interest is 5%. Our broker charges $10,000 to borrow 100 ounces of gold for the 12-month period.

Gold futures trade on the CBOT. One contract is 100 troy ounces. The initial margin is $3,600 per contract.

The arbitrage opportunity we explore is based on buying low at $1,280 and selling high at $1,340. We anticipate a gross profit (before carrying costs) of $60/ounce.

Table 22-10: Reverse Cash and Carry Arbitrage in Gold

January 2013		Cash Flow
→ Short sell 100 troy ounces of gold on the spot market @ $1,340		+ $134,000.
→ Borrowing fee		- $10,000.
→ Buy 1 Jan '14 gold futures contract @ $1,280		
	Initial margin	- $3,600.
→ Invest and deposit on margin at 5% for 12 months		- $120,400.
Initial Investment		0.

Again the initial investment is forced to zero to ensure that we incorporate the time value of money into our calculations. One year later we realize our arbitrage profit.

Table 22-11: Reverse cash and Carry Arbitrage in Gold at Delivery

January 2014		
→ Take delivery of gold at futures price of $1,280		- $128,000.
→ Withdraw Margin		+ $3,600.
→ Cancel short position by delivering gold to our broker		
→ Cash in investment from margin account	principle:	+ $120,400.
	interest:	+ $6,020.
Profit		+ $2,020.

We generate a profit of $20.20 rather than the $60 we anticipated. The $39.80 difference is the cost of carry: $100.00 borrowing fee less the $60.20 interest earned on the interest bearing securities we placed in our margin account.

We can then calculate that successful arbitrage requires that the futures price must be less than or equal to the spot price less the carrying charges necessary to carry the gold to delivery. Note that in reverse cash and carry we buy at the futures price and carry it to the spot market.

$$P_{Future} + [Cost \ of \ Carry \ ] \ = \ P_{Spot}$$

$$P_{Future} \ = \ \$1{,}340 \ - \ [100.00 \ - \ 60.20]$$

$$P_{Future} \ = \ \$1{,}300.20$$

Ceteris paribus, as soon as the futures price decreases to less than $1,300.20 we can make money through reverse cash and carry arbitrage: buying futures low and selling spot high.

___

22.7.3 - Arbitrage Free Range

The arbitrage free range is the price range in which neither cash and carry nor reverse cash and carry arbitrage are profitable.

In examples 10 and 11 we derived the breakeven price of $1,411.32 for cash and carry arbitrage and the breakeven price of $1,300.20 for reverse cash and carry arbitrage. Between these two breakeven prices we are unable to make any arbitrage profit unless the cost of carry changes.

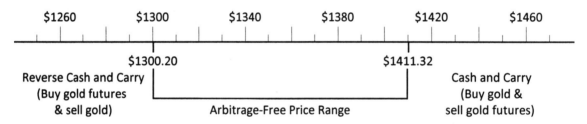

2008: Collapse of Lehman Brothers

Lehman Brothers traces its roots to the dry-goods store begun by three German brothers in 1850 in Montgomery, Alabama. Lehman Brothers began accepting payment in cotton from farmers for the purchase of goods. This lead to the formation of a second company, dedicated to cotton trading. When cotton trading moved to New York City, the Lehman brothers followed, and were instrumental in founding the New York Cotton Exchange in 1870. The NYCE is now part of the new Intercontinantal Exchange (ICE).

Lehman Brothers expanded into other markets and by the early 1900s was underwriting stock issues in concert with other investment banks. After a number of purchases and combinations with other broker/dealers and investment houses throughout the 1970s and '80's, Lehman Brothers Holdings became a publicly owned investment bank in 1994.

Chairman and CEO Richard S. Fuld, Jr. started his career with the firm in 1969 as a commercial paper trader. Fuld was credited for saving Lehman Brothers when he turned a loss of more than $100 million in 1993 into a profit of more than $4 billion in 2007.

By 2008, Lehman Brothers was the fourth largest investment bank in the US. However, huge profits came at a cost. Much of the growth in profitability was owed to two things which would become fatal in combination: mortgages and leverage. The firm rode the wave of private residential and commercial mortgage-backed securities creation, and did so with ever more borrowed funds. Measures of the firm's leverage vary, but common measures cited from annual reports show that it increased from 24:1 in 2003 to 31:1 by 2007. Lehman was effectively risking the total book value of itself on as small as a 4% decline in the value of its assets.

2008 was not the year to be over-exposed to sub-prime mortgages. When sub-prime mortgage loans began to unravel in early 2008 it forced firms like Bear Stearns to seek rescue by the Federal Reserve and JP Morgan Chase. Lehman failed to take the hint, and maintained its over-exposure. Some cite the March 2008 Bear-JPM deal as having bolstered the confidence of Lehman, an example of the moral hazard argument.

In the next five months Lehman made several attempts to sell itself to a variety of interested parties. It failed. As the situation became precarious the New York Federal Reserve brokered a deal for Lehman to sell itself to Barclays. The deal was reportedly vetoed by the Bank of England and Britain's Financial Services Authority in the 11th hour. Lehman filed for bankruptcy protection on September 15, 2008.

News sent the Dow Industrial Average to close more than 500 points lower that day, setting the stage for bigger losses in coming days. Markets for most assets from stocks to asset-backed securities to commercial paper were in complete chaos as interconnected brokers, dealers, clearing firms, insurance companies, and investors tried to sell any asset that could find a bid. From a high of almost $85/share early in 2007, Lehman stock was now worthless.

Further reading:
  Roger Lowenstein, *The End of Wall Street*, New York: Penguin Press, 2010
  Andrew Ross Sorkin, *Too Big To Fail*, New York: New York: Viking Penguin, 2009

Chapter 22 - Questions and Problems

22-1:

Tofu Inc. plans to buy 50,000 bushels of soybeans in October. Tofu Inc would like to hedge its price risk exposure on soybeans but there are no October futures in soybeans.

The current spot price for soybeans is $4.20, and the price for November soybeans is 431. Initial margin is $810, and maintenance is $600 per contract.

A. Construct a hedge strategy for Tofu Inc.

B. In October the spot price for soybeans is $4.00 and the November futures price is 411. What is the basis on November soybeans? What is the net position and effective price per bushel for Tofu Inc?

C. In October the spot price for soybeans is $5.00 and the November futures price is 508. What is the basis? What is the net position and effective price per bushel for Tofu Inc? Why is there a difference between this situation and the one in part B.

D. In October the spot price for soybeans is $1.00 and the November futures price is 111. What is the basis on November soybeans? What is the net position and effective price per bushel for Tofu Inc?

22-2:

The Kankakee Canning Corporation plans to purchase 5,000 bushels of squash in October. You are hired to construct a hedge. However, there are no squash futures. Your client assures you that squash trades at 120% of the price of soybeans. Sure enough, squash is currently at $5.04 (120% of the $4.20 spot price in soybeans). There is no October contract on soybeans but there is a November contract.

The current spot price for soybeans is $4.20, and the price for November soybeans is 431. Initial margin is $810, per contract.

A. Construct a cross hedge for the Kankakee Canning Corp.

B. In October the spot price is $4.00 for soybeans and $4.84 for squash. The November futures price is 411. How does the Kankakee Canning Corp. make out? How would they have made out had they had not hedged?

C. In October the spot price is $4.00 for soybeans and $4.85 for squash. The November futures price is 411. Now how does the Kankakee Canning Corp. make out? Why is there a difference between this situation and the one in part B?

22-3:

You are asked to provide a hedge strategy for Nescafé (world wide producers of Coffee) Nescafé will buy 3,750,000 pounds of coffee in early August. The spot price today is $2.50/lb. Use the futures quote below.

Construct a hedge portfolio for Nescafé. Use September futures. Make sure the hedge covers the entire planned purchase in August.

A. To set up the hedge we should (**buy / sell**) _____ September contracts.

In August, when Nescafé is ready to purchase its coffee the spot price is $4.00 per pound and the September futures contract is trading at 360.00

B. The basis on September futures has (**widened / narrowed**) by _____¢/lb (from _____ ¢/lb. to _____ ¢/lb).

C. Calculate the cash flows when the hedge is set in May and the hedge is lifted in August.

D. The effective price Nescafé must pay for its coffee is $ _____ /lb.

Table 22-12:	Futures Prices					
	Open	Hi	Low	Settle	Change	Open Interest
Coffee (CSCE) 37,500 lbs; cents per lb.					Initial Margin: $1,000/c	
May	244.00	246.00	239.00	240.00	-5.65	804
July	210.00	219.50	209.50	216.90	+5.50	15,119
Sept	190.50	196.25	189.50	194.50	+3.15	7,042
Dec	171.00	174.00	169.00	173.10	+1.80	4.742
Mar	158.50	160.00	157.00	160.00	+1.00	1,924
May	151.00	152.50	151.00	152.50	+.50	283
July	146.00	147.00	146.00	146.50	+.50	127
Est vol 7,623; vol Wed 9,527; open int 30,082, -79.						*Financial Pages*

22-4:

You are asked to provide a hedge strategy for Droste (worldwide producers of those lovely chocolate oranges). Droste will buy 60,000 pounds of frozen concentrated orange juice in early February. The spot price today is $1.10/lb. Initial margin is $500 /contract. Use the futures quote below.

A. If all the currently outstanding March futures are delivered then how many pounds of FCOJ will be delivered?

B. What is the basis on March futures?

C. What happened to the July, September, and November futures?

D. Construct a hedge portfolio for Droste. Make sure the hedge covers the entire planned purchase in February.

In February, when Droste is ready to purchase its FCOJ, the spot price is $1.20 per pound and the March futures contract is trading at 126.20

E. What happened to the basis on March futures? Is this is a textbook hedge?

F. Calculate the cash flows when the hedge is set today and the hedge is lifted in February.

G. What is the effective price Droste must pay for its FCOJ? How does this differ from the spot price when we set the hedge? Why?

Table 22-13: Futures Prices

	Open	Hi	Low	Settle	Change	Open Interest
Frozen Concentrated Orange Juice (CTN) 15,000 lbs; cents per lb.						
Jan	118.25	118.60	116.50	116.60	-.95	12,193
Mar	120.25	121.00	118.25	118.55	-1.00	6,706
May	122.60	122.60	121.50	120.55	-.85	1,697
July				122.55	-.85	1,535
Sept				122.55	-.65	208
Nov				122.55	-.65	554
Est vol 1,8503; open int 23,081, -981.						*Financial Pages*

22-5:

Nymex introduces a new mini copper contract defined as 10,000 pounds. The initial margin is $600 per contract. The spot price of copper is $3.70/lb. Copper storage and insurance is $10 per 10,000 pounds per month. Your broker will lend you copper for $300 per 10,000 pounds per month. You may borrow or lend at 5% per annum.

A.   What is the arbitrage free price range for 12-month copper futures (at what prices do the arbitrage opportunities disappear) if the interest rate at which you can borrow or lend is 5%?

B.   What is the arbitrage free price range for 12-month copper futures if the interest rate increases to 15%?

C.   What is the arbitrage free price range for 6-month copper futures if the interest rate is 15%?

D.   What is the arbitrage free price range for 3-month copper futures if the interest rate is 15%?

E.   What is the expected arbitrage free price range for copper futures if the interest rate is 15% and the delivery date is tomorrow?

22-6:

Platinum is trading in the spot market at $1200/ounce but your Bloomberg terminal shows that one-year platinum futures are trading at $1280/ounce.

You check up on the platinum contract and find that:
- ❑ Platinum futures trade on NYMEX.
- ❑ One contract is defined as 50 ounces.
- ❑ Initial margin is $3000 per contract.
- ❑ maintenance margin is $2500 per contract.

You check with your commodities brokers and find that:
- ❑ Storage and insurance is $5 per ounce for the year.
- ❑ Your brokers would charge you $200/ounce to lend you platinum for a year.
- ❑ Your brokers will also borrow or lend at 5% simple interest per year.

A.   Would you be able to profit by arbitraging between the two markets?

B.   Set up the arbitrage transaction and calculate your profit.

C.   Is this a cash and carry or a reverse cash and carry arbitrage?

22-7:

It is February. Tardis Intertemporal is trading at $50. Tardis Intertemporal May futures are trading at $45. The carry is estimated at 5% of the spot price.

A. What is the expected range of the futures price?

B. Set up an arbitrage trade strategy using ten futures contracts. One contract is for 1000 shares. Initial margin is $1,000 per contract, and your broker reminds you that Regulation T requires that you deposit margin of 150% on a short sale. You may borrow money at 10% per annum simple interest.

C. Is this a cash and carry or a reverse cash and carry arbitrage?

By April the price of Tardis Intertemporal has fallen to $20. The May future is now trading at $20.50.

D. If you close your position now instead of waiting for May, what would be the profit on your arbitrage trades?

By the May delivery date Tardis Intertemporal has risen to $72, and the May futures close at $72 as well.

E. What is the profit on your arbitrage trade?

F. Should I have aborted the arbitrage in April?

G. Why is this type of transaction virtually risk free?

Financial futures are futures contracts where the underlying asset itself is a financial instrument. Financial futures thus fall into the category of derivative instruments.

❑ **Derivatives:** Derivative instruments are financial instruments whose value is derived from another financial instrument.

A soybean future is a financial instrument because it derives its value from soybeans. An equity mutual fund is a derivative instrument because it derives its value from the financial instruments in the portfolio. The financial instruments in the portfolio derive their value from the companies the portfolio owns, but the investors who own mutual fund units own derivatives.

The Chicago Mercantile Exchange created the first modern financial future in May 1972 with currency futures on Canadian dollars, pounds sterling, yen, and Swiss francs. This set off a competition between the two Chicago Futures Exchanges in the creation of viable financial futures.

The CBOT created the first interest rate futures contract, on mortgage-backed securities in October 1975, but the contract was eventually pulled. The CME responded by introducing Treasury bill futures in January 1976. The CBOT introduced 20-year T-bond futures in August 1977 and followed with the creation of 10-, 5- and 2-year Treasury-note contracts over the next five years.

Index futures were first created by the Kansas City Board of Trade in October 1977. But various legal and regulatory delays meant that the Value Line Index contract began trading in February 1982. The CME followed with contracts based on the S&P 500 in April, and the NYSE Composite Index began trading on the New York Futures Exchange (NYFE) in May.

The CBOT held out for the Dow Jones Industrial Average with no success. In July 1984 the CBOT followed with the Major Market Index (MMI) contract based on the AMEX index of 20 stocks. The two indices were very closely related but not closely enough. Despite the fact that he MMI was the only U.S. Equity instrument that did not close during the 1987 crash, the volume was never high, and the contract has since been abandoned. The CBOT finally persuaded Dow Jones to license its index, and the DJIA Index futures began trading October 6, 1997.

Thus within a relatively short time period the market's ability to optimally allocate risk spread from commodity price risk to currency risk, interest rate risk, and equity market risk.

23.1 - Hedging with Interest Rate Futures

Futures on fixed-income securities such as Treasuries are referred to as interest rate futures.

For example, the CBOT specifies the long-term T-note future as a future on a $1,000,000 ten-year U.S. Treasury note with an 8% semi-annual coupon. The deliverable is a portfolio of equivalent T-notes that have an actual remaining term to maturity of not less than 6½ years and not more than 10 years. All notes delivered against a futures contract must be of the same issue, and the issue is then priced to yield 6%. However, most T-note futures are unwound prior to delivery.

Interest rate futures are used to hedge adverse movements in the interest rate in the same way soybean futures are used to hedge adverse movements in the price of soybeans.

Table 23-1: Interest Rate Futures

	Open	Hi	Low	Settle	Chg	Volume	Open Interest
Treasury Bonds (CBOT) $100,000 pts 32nds of 100%							
June 2012	147:13	147:24	147:13	147:23	+0:07	658,984	522,475
Sept 2012	146:29	147:04	146:29	147:04	+0:07	178,775	199,373
Dec 2012	147:18	147:26	147:18	147:26	+0:08	113	1,307
2-Year Treasury Notes (CBOT) $100,000 pts 32nds of 100%							
Jun 2012	110:06	110:07½	110:06	110:08	+0:00½	377,115	760,530
Sept 2012	110:03½	110:04½	110:03	110:03½	+0:01	333,779	1,217,851

Financial Pages; May 2012

Quotes on Treasury note and bonds futures are in points and 32nds of a point. For example 147:16 equals $147 \, {}^{16}/_{32}$ or 147.500% of face value.

23.1.1 - Short hedge

A short hedge is the sale of a financial futures contract to hedge against a increase in interest rates (a decrease in the price of the asset).

Example 1:

John Q. Investor owns a $1m 15-year 5.0% T-Bond which is now trading at 90:06. It thus yields 6.001%.

JQ strongly suspects that interest rates will rise in the next three months, causing the value of the bond to drop. He constructs the hedge in much the same way as we did for George Q. Farmer. (You should be able to verify the bond prices and yields; the futures prices are given in the market and reflect the increase in yields)

Table 23-2: Short Hedge

Set Hedge	$1m 5.0% 15 year T-bond @ 90:06	$901,875.00
	Sell 10 bond futures @ 91:19	- margin
	[$915,937.50]	
	basis = 1:13 ($1.406250)	

If yields now increase to 7%, then the hedge offsets the decrease in the market value of the bond.

Table 23-3: Short Hedge after Three Months and an Increase in Yields

Lift Hedge	$1m 5.0% 14¾ year T-bond @ 81:25 + 1.25 AI	$817,812.50
	(Decrease of $71,562.50)	$12,500.00
	Buy 10 bond futures @ 83:03	+ margin
	[$830,937.5]	π = 85,000.00
	basis = 1:10 ($1.3125)	
	Market Value of Portfolio:	$915,312.50
	Change in Market Value:	$13,437.50

In example 1 the loss on the bond was more than offset by the profit on the futures. This discrepancy derives from two sources.

First, the fair value of the bond includes accrued interest of $12,500.00. The futures hedge has no accrued interest. The deliverable on the contract is a hypothetical 6%, 20-year bond. This means that the 20 years to maturity is measured from the delivery date. Until the hypothetical bond is delivered we can accrue no interest. Thus interest rate futures are priced constant maturity or flat; there is no accrued interest in the price. JQ uses interest rate futures to hedge against interest rate risk. The price of the bond is at risk, the rate at which the bond accrues interest over the three-month period is not. So a textbook hedge would offset the change in the base price of the bond only, and would leave the portfolio with an increase in value of $12,500.00 over the three-month period.

Second, the basis narrowed by 3/32 (from 1:13 to 1:10). The futures hedge generated a profit of $85,000.00, whereas the base price of the bond decreased by only $84,062.50. This increases the portfolio value by 3/32% of $1million: $937.50.

The asset JQ owns is 15-year 5% T-bond and that the futures contract is for a 20-year 6% T-bond. So the impact of an increase in yield will not be exactly the same on both bond structures. This makes a textbook interest rate hedge very unlikely.

23.1.2 - Long hedge

A long hedge is the purchase of a financial futures contract to hedge against a decrease in interest rates (an increase in the price of the asset).

Example 2:

> John Q. Investor is the investment manager of a pension fund. He knows that a pension contribution of somewhere in excess of $1m will be deposited to the fund in three months. He plans to buy a $1m 5.25% 15-year T-Bond that now trades at 92:21. It thus yields 6%.
>
> JQ strongly suspects that interest rates will fall, making the planned investment in the targeted T-bond that much more expensive. He constructs the long hedge in much the same way as he did for Tofu Inc. and Kankakee Canning. (You should be able to verify the bond prices and yields; the futures prices are given in the market and reflect the decrease in yields.)

Table 23-4: Long Hedge		
	$1m 5.25% 15 year T-bond @ 92:21 [$926,562.50]	
Set Hedge	Buy 10 bond futures @ 91:19 [$915,937.50] basis = 1:02 ($1.06250)	- margin

If yields now decrease to 5% then the hedge offsets the increase in the purchase price of the Bond.

Table 23-5:	Long Hedge after three months and a decrease in yields	
	$1m 5.25% 15 year T-bond @ 102:20 (Increase of $99,687.50)	$1,026,250.00
Lift Hedge	Sell 10 bond futures @ 101:25 [$1,017,812.50] basis = 0:27 ($0.84375)	+ margin π = $101,875.00
	Net Purchase Price of the T-bond:	$924,375.00
	Change in Purchase Price:	- $2,187.50

The basis narrowed by 7/32 so the purchase price of the bond decreased by 7/32% of $1 million: $2,187.50.

Example 2 includes a number of assumptions.

First, we assume that when JQ targets a 15-year bond for purchase he buys Treasury bonds with 15 years to maturity from the date of purchase. So we are assuming that the invoice price includes no accrued interest.

Second, we assume that the 15-year Treasury on the date of purchase has a coupon rate of 5.25%. A different coupon rate would change the price that JQ must pay for the bond.

Third, we assume a number of things about the consensus opinion on interest rates. The futures price when the hedge is set reflects a market prediction that yields will increase to 6.77% by delivery date. The futures price when the long hedge is lifted reflects a market prediction that yields will decrease to 5.85% by delivery date. In a changing interest rate environment the prices on interest rate futures can be very volatile.

In both hedge examples we have conveniently ignored the $3,000 initial margin requirement on each futures contract. The cost of carrying the margin must be worked into the hedge.

23.2 - Speculating with Interest Rate Futures

Speculation on interest rates is easier in the futures market than in the spot market. It is as easy to sell as to buy futures, so the problem of borrowing T-bonds to sell short doesn't arise. And because we trade on margin, speculators derive all the benefits and risks of substantial leverage.

Long-term interest rates are at 6.00%. Susan Q. Speculator expects rates to decline to 5% within six months. She explores the possibility of speculating on T-bonds directly (Strategy A) and on speculating with interest rate futures (Strategy B)

The asymmetric rates of return derive largely because Susan gets the $30,000 coupon in both scenarios. She also has the opportunity to extend the speculation over additional months, taking the chance that her prediction of lower interest rates will simply take longer than we thought.

With strategy B Susan buys six-month T-bond futures at 100:00. The initial margin of $2,500 per contract means that she can buy 400 T-bond contracts for a total initial margin of $1,000,000. Note that the futures price implies that the market expects no decrease in rates. If the market expected the decrease in rates then futures would already be trading at a premium.

Susan is now long T-bond futures with a face value of $40m; a leverage of 40:1. She must unwind her position prior to the delivery date because if she goes to delivery she will be required to purchase a portfolio of T-bonds for which she must pay $40 million. When Susan speculates with futures she must not only be right about the decline in interest rates, she must also be right within a fairly short period of time.

Table 23-7: Strategy B: Buy 400 T-Bond Futures

Jan	Buy 400 July T-Bond Futures @ 100:00			
	[-$40,000,000.]	margin:	- $1,000,000.	- $1,000,000.
July	If interest rates are:		5%	7%
	sell 400 July T-bond futures at 112:12			
	[π = $44,950,000 - $40,000,000]		+ $4,950,000.	
	broker returns margin:		+ $1,000,000.	
	sell 400 July T-bond futures at 89:14			
	[π = $35,775,000 - $40,000,000]			- $4,225,000
	broker returns margin:			+ $1,000,000
	Profit		+ $4,950,000	- $4,225,000
	Rate of Return (semi-annual)		+ 495.0 %	- 422.5 %

Not all Susan's profit/loss would be realized on the date of the final trade. If her interest rate predictions were right then she could withdraw from her margin account whenever the equity was above $1m, and if her predictions were wrong then she would have had to meet margin call from time to time or close her position.

23.3 - *Speculation with Index Futures*

Index Futures are based on an underlying index rather than on underlying assets. Therefore delivery is not of a financial instrument (or, CME forbid, a whole basket of shares in the 500 issues that make up the S&P 500) but as a cash settlement.

Table 23-8: Index Futures

	Open	Hi	Low	Settle	Chg	Volume	Open Interest
Dow Jones Industrial Average (CBOT) $10 times index							
Jun 2012	12500	12503	12400	12429	-107	1,426	17,526
Sept 2012	12420	12420	12358	12358	-106	2	12
Dow Jones Industrial Average Mini (CBOT) $5 times index							
Jun 2012	12538	12586	12401	12429	-107	135,469	101,289
Sept 2012	12486	12497	12335	12358	-106	243	2,735
S&P 500 Index (CME) $250 times index							
June 2012	1319.00	1322.70	1312.00	1315.00	-8	11,280	261,379
Sept 2012	1312.50	1315.10	1306.10	1308.50	-8	278	6,906
Dec 2012	1299.60	1302.60	1299.60	1302.00	-8	160	7,626

Financial Pages, May 2012

Example 3:

Susan Speculator purchases one September S&P 500 future at 1308.50. On September 15 the S&P 500 closes at 1400.00

Table 23-9: Speculating with S&P500 Index Futures

May 2012	Buy 1 Sept S&P500 future	
	[$250 *1308.50 = - $302,125.00]	- $20,000.
September 2012	Take delivery in cash equivalent	+ $20,000.
	[$250 * 1400.00 = + $350,000.00]	π = + $47,875.00

Susan's investment is leveraged 34:1. Her investment in futures returned 239.375% on a market return of 6.99%.

Example 4:

Susan Speculator sells one September Dow Mini future at 12358. On September 15 the Dow Jones Industrial Average closes at 13,222.17

Table 23-10: Speculating with Dow Mini Index Futures

May 2012	Sell 1 Sept Dow future	
	[$5 *12358. = + $61,790.00]	- $3,125.
September 2012	Deliver in cash equivalent	+ $3,125.
	[$5 * 13,222.17 = - $66,110.85]	π = - $4,320.85

Again, Susan's investment is leveraged. She is using a smaller contract so leverage is only 20:1. Nonetheless, her investment in futures generated a loss of 138.267% on a market return of -6.99%.

Stock Index Futures provide relatively inexpensive and highly liquid positions similar to those obtained with diversified stock portfolios.

Example 5:

Terrence Q. Trustee has $1.1m to invest. Rather than investing in 500 separate stocks in order to track the S&P 500, he buys a $1m Treasury bill and uses the Treasury bill itself to fulfill margin requirements on the purchase of S&P 500 futures. The initial margin on S&P 500s is $20,000 per contract.

As a best case/worst case scenario, Terrence assumes that the S&P 500 can either increase or decrease by 10% from the projected value of 1302.00 in the seven-month period to delivery.

Terrence is a trustee for other peoples' money, not a speculator; he does not want to leverage the account. So he buys 4 contracts.

Table 23-11:	Indexing with S&P 500 Futures			
May	Buy 4 Dec S&P 500 futures @ 1202.00			
	[-$1,202,000.00] margin:		- $80,000.	- $80,000.
	Buy 214 day T-bill @ 3%		- $982,166.67	- $982,166.67
	Total Purchases		$1,062,166.67	$1,062,166.67
December	Scenario		+10%	-10%
	S&P 500		1,322.20	1,081.80
	sell 4 Dec S&P500 futures @ 1322.20			
	[π = $1,322,200 - $1,202,000]		+ $120,200.	
	broker returns margin:		+ $80,000.	
	sell 4 Dec S&P futures @ 1081.80			
	[π = $1,081,800 - $1,202,000]			- $120,200.
	broker returns margin:			+ $80,000.
	T-bill matures		$1,000,000.	$1,000,000.
	Market Value		$1,200,200.	$959,800.
	Holding Period Return		+ 13.00%	- 9.64%

Terrence could have a generated a portfolio diversified across all 500 issues in the S&P 500 index by investing in S&P 500 Depository Receipts. By using S&P 500 index futures he can gain the same return on the market and also gain interest on the Treasury bill he uses as margin. The slight leverage on the futures contracts renders a ±10% return on the market as a holding period return of ±11.316%. The $37,833.33 interest on the T-bill contributes 3.562% to the holding period rate of return regardless of what the market does.

23.3.1 - Hedging with Index Futures

We can alter the volatility (aggressiveness) of your portfolio by putting part of a portfolio in index futures thereby hedging a portion of the market risk. Because the market portfolio has a $\beta = 1$, buying stock index futures increases the portfolio's β and selling stock index futures decreases the portfolio's β.

Index futures can be used to create a $\beta = 0$ portfolio. This means that its return is totally uncorrelated with the market. This does not mean that there is no risk; it means that there is no systematic risk. Portfolio returns depend on the unsystematic risk exposure.

Hedge Ratios

The number of futures contracts required to hedge an equity portfolio is given by:

$$\text{Number of Futures Contracts} = \left[\frac{\text{Portfolio Market Value}}{\$\text{multiplier} * \text{Futures Value}} \right] * \left(\beta_{Portfolio} - \beta_{Target} \right) \qquad (Eq\ 23\text{-}1)$$

Example 6:

We have an equity portfolio with a market value of $4,200,000. The portfolio beta is 1.5 The S&P500 futures contract is defined as $250 times the index and is currently trading at 1120 per contract. To reduce the portfolio beta from 1.5 to 0.3 would require 18 contracts.

$$\left[\frac{\$4,200,000}{\$250 * \$1120} \right] * \left(1.5 - 0.3 \right) = 18 \ contracts$$

Table 23-12: Hedging with Index Futures

Set Hedge	Sell 18 S&P500 contracts @ 1120	- margin
	[18 * 250 * 1120 = $5,040,000]	
	Portfolio of equities	$4,200,000.00

If the market now declines by 10% then the futures price should decrease to 1008, and the portfolio of equities should decline by 15% to $3,570,000.

Table 23-13: Hedging with Index Futures

Lift Hedge	Buy 18 S&P500 contracts @1008	+ margin
	[18 * 250 * 1008 = $4,536,000] π=	$504,000.00
	Portfolio of equities market value	$3,570,000.00
	Portfolio Market Value:	$4,074,000.00
	Rate of Return:	-3.00%

If we generate a portfolio return of -3% on a market return of -10% then we calculate the portfolio beta as $\beta = \dfrac{-3\%}{-10\%} = 0.3$.

23.4 - Arbitrage with Index Futures

Index arbitrage is the simultaneous sale of an overpriced index future and purchase of the underlying stock, with a view to reversing the transactions when the future is no longer overpriced, or vice versa.

Institutional Investors and market professionals have computer systems that continuously monitor the differences between index futures and the underlying index. Whenever it detects a significant variation (greater than the carry) the computer immediately issues market orders to the stock and futures exchanges to lock in nearly riskless returns.

❑ **High-Frequency Trading:** High-frequency trading is the use of a series of quick trades to capitalize on even the smallest price movement or discrepancy.

❑ **Algorithmic Trading:** An algorithm is a step-by-step procedure or rule. Algorithmic trading is a set of instructions programmed into a computer, which then issues trade orders according to the procedure.

Although well-programmed and carefully monitored programs can generate arbitrage profits far more efficiently than traditional trades, an unwarranted assumption (house prices will always rise) or a glitch in the program can create havoc just as quickly.

The flash crash May 6, 2010 was likely triggered by a large sale of index futures, which rapidly migrated into a sell-off across related markets as algorithmic trades responded to sudden moves and the absence of buy orders in the market. Equally worrying is that with anywhere from 50% to 70% of trading volume in futures contracts generated by algorithmic trading, shutting down the programs creates a liquidity vacuum into which stub bids can trade at unwarranted prices.

23.5 - Hedging with Weather Futures

In February 1999 the Chicago Mercantile Exchange announced that it intended to trade futures contracts based on the weather in Chicago and seven other major U.S. cities. The contract would be based on indices of heating degree days and cooling degree days. By 2012 these weather-based contracts had expanded to cover cities all over the world as well as frost, snowfall, rainfall, and hurricane futures.

The cooling or heating degree day contracts are defined as $20 times the cooling or heating degree days for the specific city.

❑ **Cooling/Heating Degree Days:** Cooling degree days (CDD) measure the energy required to cool a building or area; heating degree days (HDD) measure the energy required to heat a building or area.

$$CDD = \sum_{i=1}^{T} Max\left(0, T_i - 65°F\right) \tag{Eq 23-2}$$

$$HDD = \sum_{i=1}^{T} Max\left(0, 65°F - T_i\right) \tag{Eq 23-3}$$

Example 7:

On August 1, the temperature in Chicago reaches a high of 93° and a low of 69°. The average temperature for August 1 was thus 81°. This is 16° higher than the 65° target, so August starts with CDD = 16.

On August 2 the average temperature is 78.5°, so August now has 29.5 cooling degree days: 16 for August 1 and 13.5 for August 2.

If the month of August accumulates 288.0 cooling degree days then the August contract for Chicago will deliver at $20 * 288.0 = $5,760.00.

Example 8:

The Savoy Chicago is a luxury hotel. When the summer is very hot and humid, the entire hotel runs its air-conditioning systems full blast, day and night. This tends to get expensive.

To hedge against additional cooling costs the Savoy's financial manager buys 5 weather futures. The Chicago August contract is defined as $20 times cooling degree days, and that the current settlement price is 300.

Scenario one: The summer is very hot and humid. At delivery the official index of cooling degree days is at 412. The hotel makes a profit of $11,200. This profit goes to offset the higher costs of cooling the rooms in the hotel.

$$5 \text{ contracts } \frac{\$20}{\text{contract}} (412 - 300) \ CDD = \$11,200.00$$

Scenario two: The summer is rather cool and rainy. At delivery the official index of cooling degree days is at 220. The hotel makes a loss on the weather future of $8,000. This loss comes out of the air-conditioning budget, which we can afford because we didn't use it to cool the rooms in the hotel.

$$5 \text{ contracts } \frac{\$20}{\text{contract}} (220 - 300) \ CDD = - \$8,000.00$$

23.5.1 - Finance GPA Futures

Futures can be constructed on almost anything; anything except onions. On almost anything else, all you really need is a robust contract built on a measurable outcome and enough buyers and sellers to generate a fair market.

The University of Illinois begins trading Finance GPA futures contracts. Each contract is defined as $1,000 times the final GPA of the graduating class. Obviously the outcome must be between 0.0 and 4.0 so the initial margin is set at $4,000. This is the maximum that can be lost on this contract so there is no need to bother with marking to market or margin calls.

Contracts are traded every weekday from noon until 1 pm in the Business Quad. Contracts are cleared through the dean's office.

Example 9:

One sunny afternoon in March we observe two students, Kevin and Joe, trading 1 Finance GPA contract at 3.00.

Figure 23-1: Finance GPA Futures Trade

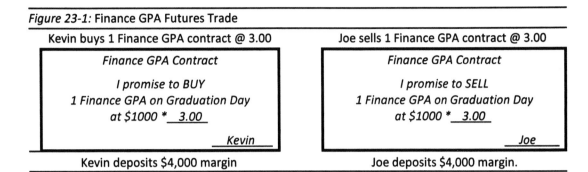

Kevin buys 1 Finance GPA contract @ 3.00	Joe sells 1 Finance GPA contract @ 3.00
Finance GPA Contract *I promise to BUY* *1 Finance GPA on Graduation Day* *at $1000 * ___3.00___* ___Kevin___	*Finance GPA Contract* *I promise to SELL* *1 Finance GPA on Graduation Day* *at $1000 * ___3.00___* ___Joe___
Kevin deposits $4,000 margin	Joe deposits $4,000 margin.

The dean's office collects $8,000 in initial margin and the open interest is one.

The final GPA is announced on graduation day by the dean. This year it comes in at 3.41 The contracts come to delivery.

Table 23-14: Results of the Finance GPA Futures trade

Kevin buys at GPA worth 3.41 at 3.00 so he makes a profit of $410.			Joe sells a GPA worth 3.41 at 3.00 so he makes a loss of $410.		
Buy:	$1000 * 3.00 =	- $3,000.	Sell:	$1000 * 3.00 =	$3,000.
a GPA worth	$1000 * 3.41 =	$3,410.	a GPA worth	$1000 * 3.41 =	- $3,410.
	Profit	$410.		Profit	- $410.
Kevin collects his equity of $4,410 from the dean's office. The $4,410 consists of his $4000 initial margin plus his $410 profit.			Joe also goes to the dean's office to collect his equity of $3,590. The $3,590 consists of his $4000 initial margin less his $410 loss.		

The dean's office collected $8,000 (2*$4,000) in initial margin when Kevin and Joe entered into this contract and the dean's office paid out $8,000 ($4,410 + $3,590) when the contract delivered.

23.6 - Futures Regulation

Exchange traded futures date back to the founding of the Chicago Board of Trade in 1848. Prior to 1974 federal regulation focused on dealing with price manipulation in agricultural markets.

❑ **Grain Futures Act:** The Grain Futures Act of 1922 required agricultural futures contracts to be traded on recognized futures exchange.

❑ **Commodity Exchange Act:** The Commodity Exchange Act of 1936 established regulatory authority over agricultural markets under the Department of Agriculture. It allowed the Commodity Exchange Authority to limit the size of speculative positions.

Neither the CEA nor the many amendments to it were ever really effective in eliminating speculative abuse or price manipulation.

1958: The Onion Futures Act

In 1955 Sam Seigal and Vincent Kosuga cornered the market in onions. It was a good market to corner; onion futures represented some 20% of all trades on the Chicago Mercantile Exchange.

Seigel and Kosuga began by buying all the onions on offer. It was estimated that by the end of 1955 they controlled 98% of the onions available in Chicago. Millions of pounds of onions were shipped to Chicago to cover their purchases. The price for a 50-pound bag of onions rose to $2.75

Then Seigel and Kosuga began taking short positions. The onions in storage were shipped out of Chicago to be cleaned, reconditioned, and shipped back. All the onions arriving in Chicago created the illusion of a bumper crop. The price began to fall, and Seigel and Kosuga began selling into a falling market. By August 1956 they had driven the price of a bag of onions down to 10¢, less than the price of an empty bag.

Congressional Representative (later President) Gerald Ford sponsored the Onions Futures Act, which banned trading in onions futures completely. The CME sued to have the act declared unconstitutional on the grounds that it unfairly restricted trade. But the law still stands. Which is why we trade futures contracts in corn, soybeans, pork bellies, orange juice, and heating degree days, but no onions.

❑ **Commodity Futures Trading Commission Act:** The Commodity Futures Trading Commission Act of 1974 created the CFTC to regulate commodity futures and options markets. The mandate of the CFTC is to ensure market efficiency, protect against fraud and manipulation, and ensure the integrity of the clearing system.

The CFTC regulated a market where futures contracts had expanded from agricultural products to non-agricultural commodities like gold, silver, and oil, to financial futures like currencies, Treasury bonds and stock market Indices. The CFTC also regulates commodity trading advisors and commodity pool operators who must pass the Series 3 Exam (equivalent to the Series 7 Exam in equities) and register with the National Futures Association.

❑ **National Futures Association:** The National Futures Association (NFA) is a self-regulatory organization, based in Chicago, created by the futures industry under the auspices of the CFTC ACT.

Registered members are required to make sure that their customers are aware of the risks involved in trading futures. They are also required to keep their own funds separate from those of their customers and to mark-to-market on each customer account at the end of every trading date. Information on members, including record of complaints, is available through the National Futures Association BASIC system.

❑ **BASIC:** The Background Affiliation Status Information Center (BASIC) tracks the records of the CFTC on members, including historical information and any disciplinary actions.

Increased regulation did not eliminate price manipulation. In 1980 the Hunt Brothers cornered the market in silver. In 1995 Yasuo Hamanaka of Sumitomo Corporation, a trading company based in Japan, attempted to corner the copper market. The company absorbed estimated losses of $2.6 billion it attributed to unauthorized trades. In 2006 Brian Hunter of Amaranth Advisors in the United States attempted to corner the market in natural gas. The fund faced losses estimated at $6.5 billion and was liquidated.

1980: Silver Thursday

In 1980 Nelson and William Hunt cornered the market in silver. The corner collapsed on March 27, 1980, Silver Thursday.

In 1970 the price of silver was less than $2/oz. But the 1970s was a decade of inflation. In 1974 the general price level increased by 12%. The price of silver rose as well, reaching $6 in 1974. The price declined slightly, but then moved up to $6 again in 1978.

In 1979 the Hunt brothers started buying silver contracts until, in January 1980, they controlled an estimated 192 million ounces of silver, about one third of the non-monetary silver in the world. The price rose from $6 to $48.70/oz. Investors cried foul. COMEX responded by adopting Silver Rule 7. Silver Rule 7 specified that no individual could carry more than 50 contracts for any given delivery month and no more than 2000 contracts in total. If COMEX had been the only exchange it might have worked, but the Hunts practiced what came to be known as regulatory arbitrage. They took delivery of the actual silver and moved their futures purchases to the London Metal Exchange where there was no Silver Rule 7. Moreover, they found that it was more effective to arbitrage by becoming insiders: the Hunts purchased 5% of their brokerage firm Bache Halsey Stuart Shields.

But even as insiders, the Hunt fortune was insufficient to maintain a corner in the silver market for very long, and by this time the Hunt brothers were significantly overextended. Even a small decline in the price of silver would put them at risk, and no price rises forever. The shorts began to accumulate sell contracts.

As the price began to fall the Hunts were issued a margin call of $100 million. Rumors began to spread that they would be unable to make margin, and the selling started in earnest. The price of silver collapsed, and financial markets faced panic. The Hunts were left facing a potential loss of $1.7 billion.

A consortium of banks provided a $1.1 billion line of credit, staving off panic. The Hunts were eventually forced into bankruptcy in 1988, reputedly one of the biggest bankruptcy in Texas.

The trend toward tighter regulation was reversed with the Commodity Futures Modernization Act.

❏ **Commodity Futures Modernization Act:** The Commodity Futures Modernization Act of 2000 deregulated contracts between sophisticated investors by defining these contracts as neither securities (which would place them under the SEC), nor futures (which would place them under the CFTC).

It can be argued that several aspects of the CFMA contributed to subsequent failures. It prohibited the regulation of energy markets, to which the collapse of Enron is attributed. It prohibited the regulation of credit default swaps, to which the $700 billion bailout of AIG is attributed. It legalized rehypothecation to which the collapse of MF Global is attributed.

Chapter 23 - Questions and Problems

23-1:

After attending a dinner party at which Ben Bernanke was also a guest, you become convinced that interest rates are going up in the near future. You decide to sell 100 September 20 year T-bond futures.

The sale is executed at 101:18. Margin requirements are $2,500 initial and $2,000 maintenance per contract. Each contract is defined as $100,000.

A.   Your futures contracts require you to sell how much in T-bonds at delivery? For what total amount?

B.   How much are you required to deposit in initial margin?

At the end of the following three days T-bond futures settle at 101:00, 102:02, and 102:12

C.   Calculate your profit and equity on each date. Do you receive a margin call? If so, for how much?

Bernanke is discovered to have thousands of outstanding futures contracts. He is impeached and replaced. The market goes into a tailspin, and rates plummet. You phone your broker in a panic. Your broker closes you out at 109:31

D.   What is your total loss on this investment?

23-2:

Assume that in September, a 270-day T-bill is quoted at 3.00%. You can borrow or lend at 3.00% What is the price range of a March future on 90 day T-Bills?

Margin is $1,200 per contract. One contract is defined as $1m, and your broker charges you $200 borrowing fee to short sell his $1m T-bill. (HINT: By March the 270 day T-bill will be a 90 day T-bill.)

23-3:

You have a portfolio of $2,000,000 to invest. You select a number of stocks based on their individual firm-specific characteristics, but you calculate the portfolio's beta at 1.9 To reduce the beta of the portfolio you decide to sell ten S&P futures contracts at 1120. The S&P 500 contract is defined as $250 times index and carries an initial margin of $2000 per contract.

A.   You calculate that the 10 contract hedge will reduce the portfolio beta to what value?

B.   Let the S&P 500 decrease by 10%. and then see what happens to the market value of your portfolio. What is the beta of the hedged portfolio?

C.   Why is there a difference between the betas you calculated in A and in B?

23-4:

You speculate that the market will crash before December. Use 100 S&P 500 December contracts to set up this speculation.

A. The market ends the year at exactly the same value as it was on November 28. What is your profit or loss on this speculation?

B. If the market had crashed and the S&P500 had lost 30% of its November 28 value by delivery date, what would have been your profit on this speculation?

Table 23-15: Futures prices

	Open	Hi	Low	Settle	Chg	Volume	Open Interest
S&P 500 Index (CME) $250 times index							
Dec	115550	116480	114070	115050	-470	9,390	464,524
March	115300	116600	114300	115230	-480	2,100	81,574
Est vol 135,008; Index: 1,149.50 -7.92					*Financial Pages*, November 28		

23-5:

You enter into a contract with Ferari to Import 100 top-of-the-line sports cars. Payment of 12m euros is to be made February 15. Using the information in the table below, set up a hedge against possible revaluation of the euro.

A. Suppose that on February 15 the euro is trading at 0.8750 and the March futures contract is trading at 0.8715. What happens to the basis? What is the result of the hedge?

B. Suppose that on February 15 the euro is trading at 0.9275 and the March futures contract is trading at 0.9240. What happens to the basis? What is the result of the hedge?

Table 23-16: Futures Prices

	Open	Hi	Low	Settle	Change	Volume	Open Interest
Euro Fx (CME) Euro 125,000; $ per Euro							
Dec	.8797	.8832	.8763	.8816	+.0019	.9632	108,588
March	.8786	.8820	.8751	.8789	+.0018	.9640	2,744
Est vol 14,673; Spot Price € = 0.8834					*Financial Pages*, November 28		

23-6:

We enter into a contract to buy 10 supercomputers for which we agree to pay £10,000,000 in 90 days, which would bring us to the end of July. The current exchange rate is $1.5942. We decide to buy 160 September futures contracts at 1.5934

A. What is the basis on this contract? Use the currency futures quote above.

On July 30 the future is trading at 1.7100 and the spot rate on sterling is $1.7106

B. What is the basis now?

C. How much does it cost us to buy our supercomputers.

The interest rate on U.S. dollars is 5.0% and on sterling is 4.84%. The 90-day forward rate on sterling is $1.5948.

D. Would it be better to use the 90-day forward contract or the September futures contract to hedge our position?

Options have been used in the history of commerce for almost as long as forward contracts.

Thales (624 – 547 BC), a philosopher from the Greek city of Miletus, may have been one of the first people to get rich by trading options. According to Aristotle:

> "There is an anecdote of Thales the Milesian and his financial device, which involves a principle of universal application, but which is attributable to him on account of his reputation for wisdom. He was reproached for his poverty, which was supposed to show that philosophy was no use. According to the story, he knew by his skill in the stars while it was yet winter that there would be a great harvest of olives in the coming year, so, having little money, he gave deposits for the use of all the olive presses in Chios and Miletus, which he hired at a low price because no one bid against him. When the harvest time came, and many wanted them all at once and of a sudden, he let them out at any rate which he pleased, and made a quantity of money. Thus, he showed the world that philosophers can easily be rich if they like."[1]

The opportunity to design a contract to fit a need is only limited by the imaginations of the parties to it. In the case of Thales he took an option on the use of the olive presses, reserving them for his own use should he need them.

Today we see options on almost everything imaginable; we are as familiar with options as we are with things like manufacturers' coupons in the voluminous advertising supplements filling our Sunday newspaper. In the purchase and sale of real property, an option to buy a piece of farmland, a commercial building, or a house for personal residence, gives the prospective buyer time to get financing in order and assures the seller that there is a serious intent to complete the transaction. Without it, the seller is reluctant to reserve the house from the marketplace for fear of missing the opportunity to sell to someone else.

Unlike forward contracts and exchange traded futures contracts, options convey rights, not obligations, to buy or sell. This may seem like a subtle difference, but is a fundamental reason why options exist. If forwards and futures accomplished the same purpose, then there would be little demand for, or supply of, options.

As you learn about the numerous option features, functions, and strategies that follow in these pages, imagine almost any asset as the underlying asset in the contract. You may find that by doing so, it becomes intriguing and potentially very rewarding for the inventor of options yet to be created.

---

1   Aristotle, *The Politics*, Chapter 11, Book 1

O ptions, like futures, are contracts under which settlement—payment and delivery—take place at some specified future date. However, options, unlike futures, give the buyer of the contract the right to default. This means that we need two options contracts, one where the buyer has the right to default (call) and one where the seller has the right to default (put).

24.1 - Options Concepts

An option is a contract in which the writer of the contract grants the buyer the right, but not the obligation to buy from, or to sell to, the writer a specific asset at a specific strike or exercise price, within a specified period of time. The simplest example of an option is a store coupon. The store writes a coupon that gives the bearer the right, but not the obligation, to buy the item at the special price quoted.

Figure 24-1: Call Option Disguised as a Coupon

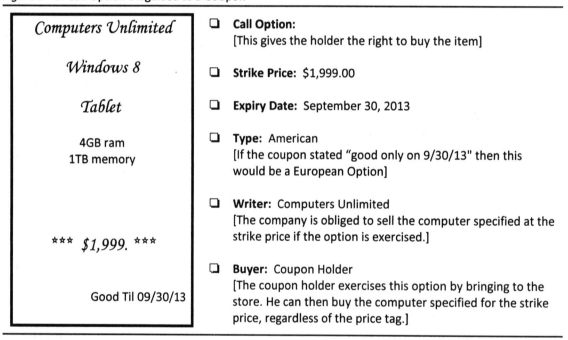

| *Computers Unlimited* | ❏ | **Call Option:** [This gives the holder the right to buy the item] |

❏ **Call Option:**
[This gives the holder the right to buy the item]

❏ **Strike Price:** $1,999.00

❏ **Expiry Date:** September 30, 2013

❏ **Type:** American
[If the coupon stated "good only on 9/30/13" then this would be a European Option]

❏ **Writer:** Computers Unlimited
[The company is obliged to sell the computer specified at the strike price if the option is exercised.]

❏ **Buyer:** Coupon Holder
[The coupon holder exercises this option by bringing to the store. He can then buy the computer specified for the strike price, regardless of the price tag.]

The value of the coupon depends on the price of the underlying item. The option can be in-, at-, or out-of-, the-money.

❏ **Out-of-the-Money:** An option is out-of-the-money whenever the option has an unfavorable strike price with respect to the market price.

❏ **Expire:** An option expires worthless when the buyer of the option chooses not to exercise it.

Example 1:

> If the Tablet PC specified in the option is priced at $1,799 then the option is worthless. We purchase the Tablet PC at $1,799 and let the option expire. In this case the option is Out-of-the-Money; it has a value of $0.

❑ **Deep Out-of-the-Money:** An option that is very much out-of-the-money can be referred to as deep out-of-the-money, often referred to by its acronym DOOM.

❑ **At-the-money:** An option is at-the-money whenever the strike price is roughly equal to the market price. There are variations on the at-the-money-option: near-the-money if the price is fairly close, or right-on-the-money if the exercise price is exactly equal to the price of the underlying item.

Example 2:

> If the Tablet PC specified in the option is priced at $1,999, then the option is still worthless. We purchase the Tablet PC at $1,999 but we let the option expire anyway. In this case the option is at-the-money but even so has a value of $0.

❑ **In-the-Money:** An option is in-the-money whenever the option has an favorable strike price with respect to the market price.

❑ **Exercise:** An option is exercised when the buyer of the option chooses to make use of the right to buy or sell at the strike price as specified in the contract.

Example 3:

> If the Tablet PC specified in the option is priced at $2,199, then we could exercise the option and buy it at $1,999. In this case the option is in-the-money and has a value of $200.

❑ **Deep In-the-Money:** An option that is very much in-the-money can be referred to as deep-in-the-money.

This relationship between the value of the option and the price of the underlying item is most commonly presented as a payout graph.

❑ At prices at or below the strike price $1,999 the option expires with a value of $0.
❑ At prices greater than the strike price $1,999 the value of the option is the difference between the price of the underlying item and the strike price. (Price - $1,999).

Thus the value of the option is given by the equation

$$\text{Value} = \text{Max} (0, \text{Price} - \$1,999)$$

which basically states that an option is just like a future but when the value becomes negative we have the right to throw it away.

Figure 24-2: Payout Graph of the Tablet PC Option

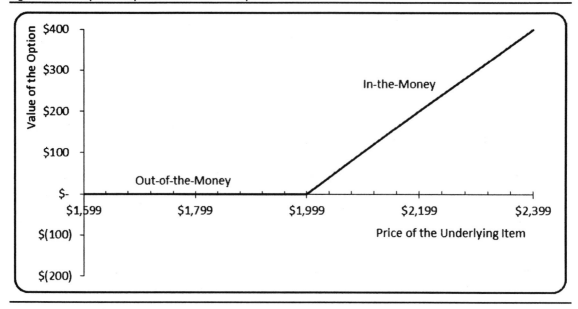

24.2 - Stock Options

A stock option is a contract in which the writer of the contract grants the buyer the right, but not the obligation, to buy from, or to sell to, the writer shares of stock at specific strike or exercise price, within a specified period of time.

❏ **Call Option:** A call option is a contract that grants the buyer the right to BUY the specified stock at the strike price on or before the expiry date.

❏ **Put Option:** A put option is a contract that grants the buyer the right to SELL the specified stock at the strike price on or before the expiry date.

❏ **Premium:** The price of an option is called a premium. The premium is paid by the buyer of the option to the writer and compensates the writer for complying with the buyer's exercise decision.

❏ **Strike Price** or **Exercise Price:** The strike or exercise price is the price at which the stock is bought and sold if the option is exercised.

❏ **American Option:** An American option can be exercised at any time prior to the expiration date.

❏ **European Option:** A European option can be exercised only on the expiration date.

❏ **Contract:** Stock Options are generally defined in lots of 100 shares of the underlying stock. Contracts are standardized by strike price and expiry date. Other options such as index, interest rate, and currency options are defined by the exchange on which the option is listed.

❏ **Intrinsic Value:** The difference between the current price of the underlying stock and the exercise price. The intrinsic value is equal to the profit per share if the buyer exercised the option immediately.

The combinations of write/buy and put/call are summarized in the table below:

OPTION		CALL	PUT
LONG	The buyer buys the option thus pays the premium to the writer	Buys the right to buy shares from the writer at the strike price	Buys the right to sell shares to the writer at the strike price
SHORT	The writer sells the option thus receives the premium from the buyer	Takes on the obligation to sell shares to the buyer at the strike price	Takes on the obligation to buy shares from the buyer at the strike price
	If exercised	Writer must sell shares to the buyer	Writer must buy shares from the buyer

The following quote shows option contracts on General Electric (GE). Contracts are listed by exercise or strike prices and expiry month.

Table 24-1: Listed Option Quotations

GE	$ 40.00	Calls			Puts		
Exp	Strike	Close	Volume	Imp Vol	Close	Volume	Imp Vol
June	25.00	$ 15.10	30		$ 0.50	0	51.1%
Dec	30.00	$ 10.00	79		$ 0.05	0	
Jan	30.00	$ 10.10	16	46.8%	$ 0.05	73	48.0%
March	30.00	$ 10.20	11	31.1%	$ 0.40	0	47.4%
June	30.00	$ 10.85	30	36.2%	$ 0.75	0	40.0%
Dec	35.00	$ 5.00	192		$ 0.05	45	74.1%
Jan	35.00	$ 5.10	189	25.2%	$ 0.30	3701	40.9%
March	35.00	$ 5.80	283	32.5%	$ 0.95	194	38.5%
June	35.00	$ 6.70	198	31.8%	$ 1.85	147	37.5%
Dec	40.00	$ 0.50	10000	29.7%	$ 0.55	2679	33.2%
Jan	40.00	$ 1.45	6196	30.0%	$ 1.65	1672	35.7%
March	40.00	$ 2.50	1837	30.8%	$ 2.70	1845	35.8%
June	40.00	$ 3.80	466	31.8%	$ 3.90	234	36.3%
Dec	45.00	$ 0.05	62	65.2%	$ 5.00	164	50.2%
Jan	45.00	$ 0.15	178	29.1%	$ 5.50	26	44.5%
March	45.00	$ 0.75	553	29.3%	$ 5.80	37	33.5%
June	45.00	$ 1.75	293	29.8%	$ 6.90	35	35.4%
Dec	50.00	$ 0.05	0		$ 10.00	68	88.4%
Jan	50.00	$ 0.05	3	38.5%	$ 10.50	20	67.0%
March	50.00	$ 0.15	244	28.1%	$ 12.30		71.1%
June	50.00	$ 0.70	1259	28.7%	$ 10.90		37.2%
March	55.00	$ 0.10	0	34.6%	$ 15.50		55.0%
June	55.00	$ 0.25	25	28.1%	$ 15.40		40.2%

General Electric (GE)   *Financial Pages*

This quote shows that General Electric (GE) is trading at $40.

24.2.1 - Call Options

According to Table 24-1, you can buy a December GE $40 call option for $0.50.

You would pay $50.00 for the right to buy 100 shares of GE at $40 per share between now and the time the option expires in December. If the spot price of GE declined below $40, then you would allow the option to expire, but if the spot price of GE increased above $40, then you would exercise the option and buy 100 shares of GE at the strike price of $40.

As an alternative to exercise, you could sell the option to another investor at any time before the option expires for at least as much as the intrinsic value and leave it to the next investor to exercise.

Note that each call carries a premium equal to at least the intrinsic value.

24.2.2 - Put Options

According to Table 24-1, you can buy a December GE $40 put option for $0.55.

You would pay $55.00 for the right to sell 100 shares of GE at $40 per share between now and the time the option expires in December. If the spot price of GE rose above $40, then you would allow the option to expire but if the spot price of GE declined below $40, then you would exercise the option and sell 100 shares of GE at the strike price of $40.

As an alternative to exercise, you could sell the option to another investor at any time before the option expires for at least as much as the intrinsic value, and leave it to the next investor to exercise.

Note that each put carries a premium equal to at least the intrinsic value.

24.3 - Options Markets

The Chicago Board Options Exchange (CBOE) established April 26, 1973, listed options on 16 stocks. In many ways the establishment of the CBOE transformed the market for options as effectively as the establishment of the CBT and CME transformed the market for futures.

The Option Clearing Corporation (OCC) is jointly owned by several exchanges. The OCC acts as the guarantor of every CBOE option by taking the opposite side of every contract. It maintains computer records of all open positions by each investor. If a buyer chooses to exercise an option the OCC system randomly selects a writer with an open position and assigns the exercise notice accordingly.

The American Stock Exchange uses a specialist system. The specialists maintains a bid and ask position on his assigned options, buying and selling on his own book, and keeping the limit order book. There are also floor traders who trade on their own books, and floor brokers who trade client orders.

The Chicago Board Options Exchange (CBOE) uses market-makers, who act solely as dealers, and order book officials who keep the limit order book. Market makers are prohibited from brokering options in which they make a market, but they may broker options in which they are not market-makers.

Options are standardized as to delivery dates and strike price. The strike price is set in increments depending on the price of the underlying asset. An option expires at 10:59 pm Central Time on the Saturday following the third Friday of the designated month.

24.3.1 - Closing Transactions

As with futures, two similar contracts are canceled by the clearinghouse. If you write a May $45 call option and then want to cancel your position, you must buy a May $45 call option. The write and the buy cancel each other out.

❑ **Closing purchase transaction:** Canceling an existing short position by buying an option of the same strike price and expiry date.

❑ **Closing sale transaction:** Canceling an existing long position by writing an option of the same strike price and expiry date.

24.4 - Buying Call Options

By buying a call option contract you are paying a premium to acquire the right to buy shares at the specified exercise price.

The following table compares three option strategies: one in-the-money, one at-the-money, and one out-of-the-money, with a strategy of buying the shares directly. Note the difference in initial investment between the options strategies and the equity strategies.

Example 4:

Suppose we buy three March GE options: one at $30 (at a premium of $10.20) one at $40 (at a premium of$2.50), and one at $50 (at a premium of $0.15), all of which are quoted in Table 24-1. We examine the possible gains and losses.

Table 24-2 shows that if, on expiry in March, shares of General Electric (GE) are trading on the New York Stock Exchange at $60 per share, the $30 call option can be exercised. We would be able to buy 100 shares of GE from the person who wrote the option, paying the $30 strike price for each share. Our expenditure is $3,000. We can now sell these shares at $60 per share on the NYSE. Our revenue is $6,000. Thus the value of our option is +$3,000. To avoid transactions costs all around we can also accept $3,000 directly from the writer.

The profit on the option is the value minus the $1,020 price we initially paid for the option. So the profit is $1,980.

We calculate the rate of return as 194.1%

$$\frac{\$3,000}{\$1,020} = 2.941176 = 1 + 194.1\% \qquad \text{or} \qquad \frac{\$1,980}{\$1,020} = 1.941176 = 194.1\%$$

Table 24-2: Long Calls on GE at $30, $40, & $50 compared to a long position on GE

		Long GE Call Options			Long GE
	Strike Price:	In-the-Money $30:	At-the-Money $40:	Out-of-the-Money $50:	
Price at Expiry	Investment: Premium:	- $1,020.00	- $250.00	- $15.00	- $4,000.00
$20		option expires $0.00	option expires $0.00	option expires $0.00	$2,000.00
	VALUE:				
	π:	- $1,020.00	- $250.00	- $15.00	- $2,000.00
$30		option expires $0.00	option expires $0.00	option expires $0.00	+ $3,000.00
	VALUE:				
	π:	- $1,020.00	- $250.00	- $15.00	- $1,000.00
$40		* - $3,000.00 + $4,000.00	option expires $0.00	option expires $0.00	+ $4,000.00
	VALUE:	$1,000.00			
	π:	- $20.00	- $250.00	- $15.00	$0.00
$50		* - $3,000.00 + $5,000.00	* - $4,000.00 + $5,000.00	option expires $0.00	$5,000.00
	VALUE:	$2,000.00	$1,000.00		
	π:	+ $980.00	+ $750.00	- $15.00	+ $1,000.00
$60		* - $3,000.00 + $6,000.00	* - $4,000.00 + $6,000.00	* - $5,000.00 + $6,000.00	+ $6,000.00
	VALUE:	$3,000.00	$2,000.00	$1,000.00	
	π:	+ $1,980.00	+ $1,750.00	+ $985.00	+ $2,000.00
Rate of Return		- 100% to + 194.1%	- 100% to + 700.0%	- 100% to + 6,566.7%	- 50% to + 50%

Notice the leverage available in options. The in-the-money strategy option ($30) generates approximately the same potential profit in dollars as if we had bought 100 shares of GE outright, but the initial investment is much lower: $1,020.00 rather than $4,000.00. This means that the return on investment ranges from -100.0% to +194.1% on the in-the-money option rather than the -50.0% to +50.0% on a long position in the shares.

24.4.1 - Payout graph

The payout graph shows the value and profit for each possible price of the underlying asset.

The horizontal axis shows the spot price per share of the underlying asset at the close on the last trading day before the option expires. The vertical axis shows the value or profit. Note that the graphs kink at the exercise price. At spot prices below the exercise price the option expires worthless, and the profit line shows a loss equal to 100% of the premium. At spot prices above the exercise price the option is exercised, and the diagonal line shows an increasing profit as the price of the underlying stock increases.

The payout graph is derived from the following equations:

$$Value = \max(0, (S - X))$$
    (Eq 24-1)

$$Profit = \max(0, (S - X)) - C$$
    (Eq 24-2)

where
  S = the spot price of the underlying shares at expiry
  X = exercise price
  C = call premium per share

Figure 24-3: Long $30 Call on GE @ $10.20

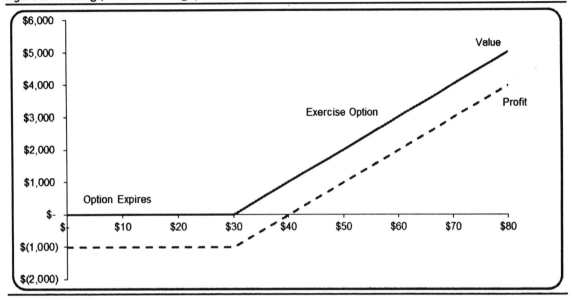

We break even on this strategy only when the option is exercised. Therefore the break-even price is given by the exercise price plus the premium, in this example $30 + $10.20 = $40.20

Call Expires	Exercise Call
$\pi = \max(0, (S_B - X)) - C = 0$	$\pi = \max(0, (S_B - X)) - C = 0$
$0 - C \neq 0$	$S_B - X - C = 0$
	$S_B = X + C$

24.5 - Writing Call Options

By writing a call option contract you are receiving a premium for granting someone else the right to acquire stock from you at the specified exercise price.

The following table compares three option strategies: one in-the-money, one at-the-money, and one out-of-the-money, with a strategy of selling the shares short.

Example 5:

> Suppose we write three March GE options: one at $30 (at a premium of $10.20), one at $40 (at a premium of $2.50), and one at $50 (at a premium of $0.15), all of which are quoted in Table 24-1. We examine the possible gains and losses.

Table 24-3 shows that if, on expiry in March, shares of General Electric (GE) are trading on the New York Stock Exchange at $60 per share, the $30 call option will be exercised. We would be obliged to sell 100 shares of GE to the person who purchased the option, accepting the $30 strike price for each share. Our revenue is $3,000. To acquire these shares to sell we must buy them at $60 per share on the NYSE. Our expenditure is $6,000. Thus the value of our option is -$3,000. To avoid transactions costs all around we can also offer $3,000 directly to the buyer.

The profit on the option is the value plus the $1,020 price we initially charged for the option. So the profit is -$1,980.

Table 24-3: Short Calls on GE at $30, $40, & $50 Compared to a Short Position on GE

Price at Expiry	Strike Price:	Short GE Call Options			Short GE
		In-the-Money $30:	At-the-Money $40:	Out-of-the-Money $50:	
	Investment:				+ $4,000.00
	Premium:	+ $1,020.00	+ $250.00	+ $15.00	
$20		option expires	option expires	option expires	
	VALUE:	$0.00	$0.00	$0.00	- $2,000.00
	π:	+ $1,020.00	+ $250.00	+ $15.00	+ $2,000.00
$30		option expires	option expires	option expires	
	VALUE:	$0.00	$0.00	$0.00	- $3,000.00
	π:	+ $1,020.00	+ $250.00	+ $15.00	+ $1,000.00
$40		* + $3,000.00			
		- $4,000.00	option expires	option expires	
	VALUE:	- $1,000.00	$0.00	$0.00	- $4,000.00
	π:	+ $20.00	+ $250.00	+ $15.00	$0.00
$50		* + $3,000.00	* + $4,000.00		
		- $5,000.00	- $5,000.00	option expires	
	VALUE:	- $2,000.00	- $1,000.00	$0.00	- $5,000.00
	π:	- $980.00	- $750.00	+ $15.00	- $1,000.00
$60		* + $3,000.00	* + $4,000.00	* + $5,000.00	
		- $6,000.00	- $6,000.00	- $6,000.00	
	VALUE:	- $3,000.00	- $2,000.00	- $1,000.00	- $6,000.00
	π:	- $1,980.00	- $1,750.00	- $985.00	- $2,000.00
Rate of Return		51.0% to - 99%	12.5% to - 87.5%	0.8% to - 49.3%	+ 100% to - 100%

The initial investment consists of a positive cash flow; the buyer of our written option pays the premium to us (or rather to our broker). If our broker did not require a margin to ensure performance, we could write as many options as we liked, collect the premiums from these options, and head for Rio. We need to deposit margin to ensure that we fulfill our obligations under the contract if exercised. We assume that our broker requires a flat $2,000 margin to write the option in each case.

$$\frac{\$2,000 + \$1,020 - \$3,000}{\$2,000} = 0.01 = 1 - 99.0\% \quad \text{or} \quad \frac{-\$1,980}{\$2,000} = -0.99 = -99.0\%$$

We placed $2,000 in our margin account and, at the end of the investment, we get the remaining $20 back: a loss of 99%. The short position in the spot market also requires a deposit of 50% of the value of the short sale, in this case also $2,000.

24.5.1 - Payout Graph

The payout graph shows the value and profit for each possible price of the underlying asset.

At spot prices below the exercise price the option expires worthless, and the profit line shows a profit equal to 100% of the premium. At spot prices higher than the exercise price the option is exercised and the diagonal line shows an increasing losses as the price of the underlying stock increases.

The payout graph is derived from the following equations:

$$Value = -\max(0, (S - X)) \qquad\qquad\qquad\qquad (Eq\ 24\text{-}3)$$

$$Profit = -\max(0, (S - X)) + C \qquad\qquad\qquad (Eq\ 24\text{-}4)$$

where
    S = the spot price of the underlying shares at expiry
    X = exercise price
    C = call premium per share

We could use $\min(0, (X - S)$ just as well; it is mathematically equivalent. But the $-\max(0, (S - X))$ emphasizes that the option is exercised when the stock price S is higher than the exercise price X.

Figure 24-4: Short $30 Call on GE @ $10.20

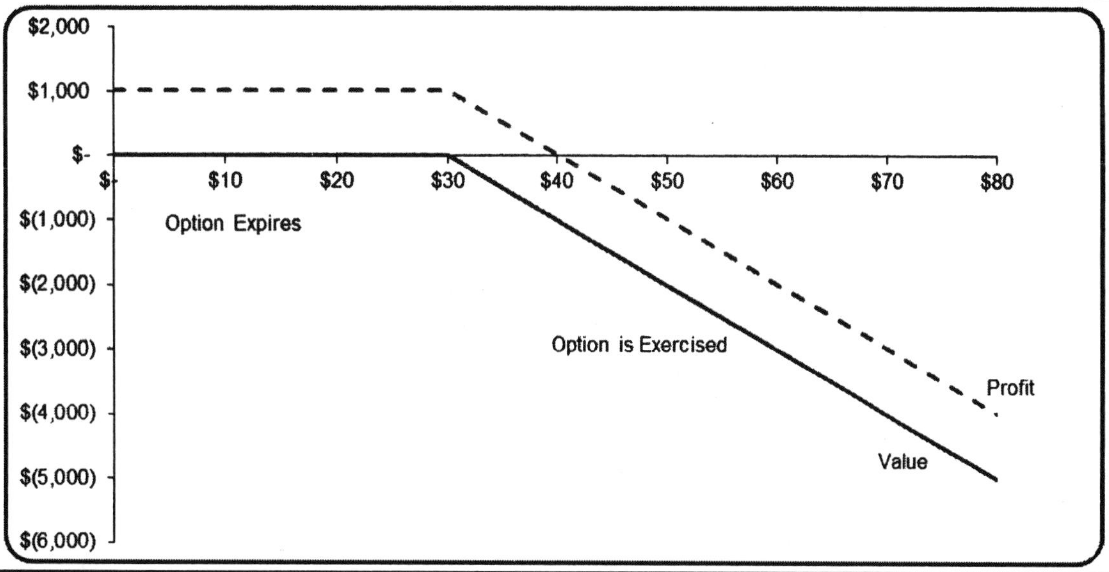

We breakeven on this strategy only when the option is exercised. Therefore the breakeven price is given by the exercise price plus the premium, in this example $30 + $10.20 = $40.20

Call Expires	Call is Exercised
$\pi = -\max(0, (S_B - X)) + C = 0$	$\pi = -\max(0, (S_B - X)) + C = 0$
$0 + C \neq 0$	$-S_B + X + C = 0$
	$S_B = X + C$

24.6 - Buying Put Options

By buying a put option contract you are paying a premium to acquire the right to sell shares at the specified exercise price.

The following table compares three option strategies: one in-the-money, one at-the-money, and one out-of-the-money, with a strategy of selling the shares short.

Example 6:

> Suppose we buy three March GE put options: one at $30 (at a premium of $0.40), one at $40 (at a premium of $2.70), and one at $50 (at a premium of $12.30), all of which are quoted in Table 24-1. We examine the possible gains and losses.

Table 24-4 shows that if, on expiry in March, shares of General Electric (GE) are trading on the New York Stock Exchange at $20 per share, the $30 put option can be exercised. We would be able to sell 100 shares of GE to the person who wrote the option, taking the $30 strike price for each share. Our revenue is $3,000. We can buy the shares we need at $20 per share on the NYSE. Our expenditure is $2,000. Thus the value of our option is +$1,000. To avoid transactions costs all around we can also accept $1,000 directly from the writer.

Table 24-4: Long Puts on GE at $30, $40 &, $50 Compared to a Short Position on GE

Price at Expiry	Strike Price:	Long GE Put Options			Short GE
		Out-of-the-Money $30:	At-the-Money $40:	In-the-Money $50:	
	Investment:				+ $4,000.00
	Premium:	- $40.00	- $270.00	- $1,230.00	
$20		* + $3,000.00	* + $4,000.00	* + $5,000.00	
		- $2,000.00	- $2,000.00	- $2,000.00	
	VALUE:	+ $1,000.00	+ $2,000.00	+ $3,000.00	- $2,000.00
	π:	+ $960.00	+ $1,730.00	+ $1,770.00	+ $2,000.00
$30			* + $4,000.00	* + $5,000.00	
		option expires	- $3,000.00	- $3,000.00	
	VALUE:	$0.00	+ $1,000.00	+ $2,000.00	- $3,000.00
	π:	- $40.00	+ $730.00	+ $770.00	+ $1,000.00
$40				* + $5,000.00	
		option expires	option expires	- $4,000.00	
	VALUE:	$0.00	$0.00	+ $1,000.00	- $4,000.00
	π:	- $40.00	- $270.00	- $230.00	+ $0.00
$50		option expires	option expires	option expires	
	VALUE:	$0.00	$0.00	$0.00	- $5,000.00
	π:	- $40.00	- $270.00	- $1,230.00	- $1,000.00
$60		option expires	option expires	option expires	
	VALUE:	$0.00	$0.00	$0.00	- $6,000.00
	π:	- $40.00	- $270.00	- $1,230.00	- $2,000.00
Rate of Return		2,400.0% to - 100%	640.7% to - 100%	143.9% to - 100%	+ 100% to - 100%

The profit on the option is the value minus the $40 price we initially paid for the option. So the profit is $960. We calculate the rate of return as 2,400.0%

$$\frac{\$1,000}{\$40} = 25 = 1 + 2,400.0\% \qquad \text{or} \qquad \frac{\$960}{\$40} = 24 = 2,400.0\%$$

Note that we generate profits when the price of the underlying stock goes down. The rate of return on the short position in the spot market is based on the assumption that our broker collected a margin of $2,000.

The at-the-money strategy option ($40) generates approximately the same potential profit in dollars as if we had short sold 100 shares of GE outright, but the initial investment is much lower: $270.00 rather than the $2,000.00 we need to pay into margin under regulation T. This means that the return on investment ranges from -100.0% to +640.7% on the at-the-money option rather than the -100.0% to +100.0% on the shares.

24.6.1 - Payout Graph

The payout graph shows the value and profit for each possible price of the underlying asset.

The horizontal axis shows the spot price per share of the underlying asset at the close on the last trading day before the option expires. The vertical axis shows the value or profit. Note that the graphs kink at the exercise price. At spot prices above the exercise price the option expires worthless, and the profit line shows a loss equal to 100% of the premium. Below the exercise price the option is exercised, and the diagonal line shows an increasing profit as the price of the underlying stock decreases.

Figure 24-5: Long $50 Put on GE @ $12.30

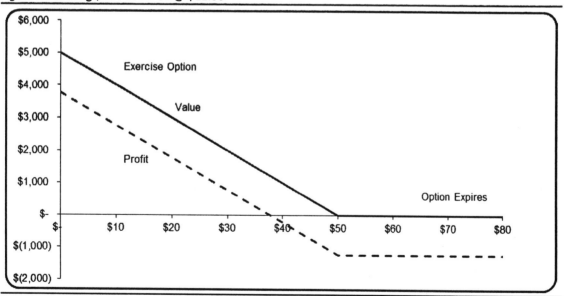

The payout graph is derived from the following equations:

$$Value = \max(0, (X - S)) \qquad\qquad \text{(Eq 24-5)}$$

$$Profit = \max(0, (X - S)) - P \qquad\qquad \text{(Eq 24-6)}$$

where
> S = the spot price of the underlying shares at expiry
> X = exercise price
> P = put premium per share

We breakeven on this strategy only when the option is exercised. Therefore the breakeven price is given by the exercise price minus the premium, in this example $50 - $12.30 = $37.70

Put Expires	Exercise Put
$\pi = max(0, (X - S_B)) - P = 0$	$\pi = max(0, (X - S_B)) - P = 0$
$0 - P \neq 0$	$X - S_B - P = 0$
	$S_B = X - P$

24.7 - Writing Put Options

By writing a put option contract you are receiving a premium for granting someone else the right to sell stock to you at the specified exercise price.

The following table compares three option strategies: one in-the-money, one at-the-money, and one out-of-the-money, with a strategy of buying the shares directly.

Example 7:

> Suppose we write three March GE options: one at $30 (at a premium of $0.40), one at $40 (at a premium of $2.70), and one at $50 (at a premium of $12.30), all of which are quoted in Table 24-1. We examine the possible gains and losses.

Table 24-5 shows that if, on expiry in March, shares of General Electric (GE) are trading on the New York Stock Exchange at $20 per share, the $30 put option will be exercised. We would be obliged to buy 100 shares of GE from the person who purchased the option, accepting the $30 strike price for each share. Our expenditure is $3,000. We can then sell them at $20 per share on the NYSE. Our revenue is $2,000. Thus the value of our option is -$1,000. To avoid transactions costs all around we can also offer $1,000 directly to the buyer.

The profit on the option is the value plus the $40 price we initially charged for the option.   Thus our profit is - $960.

The initial investment consists of a positive cash flow; the buyer of our written option pays the premium to us (or rather to our broker). If our broker did not require a margin to ensure performance we could write as many options as we liked, collect the premiums from these options, and head for Rio. We need to deposit margin to ensure that we fulfill our obligations under the contract if exercised. We assume that our broker requires a flat $2,000 margin to write the option in each case. We calculate the rate of return as -48.0%

$$\frac{\$2,000 + \$40 - \$1,000}{\$2,000} = 0.52 = 1 - 48.0\% \qquad or \qquad \frac{-\$960}{\$2,000} = -0.48 = -48.0\%$$

We placed $2,000 in our margin account and, at the end of the investment, we get the remaining $20 back: a loss of 99%.

The short position in the spot market also requires a deposit of 50% of the value of the short sale, in this case also $2,000.

Table 24-5: Short Puts on GE at $30, $40 & $50 Compared to a Long Position on GE

Price at Expiry		Short GE Put Options			Long GE
	Strike Price:	In-the-Money $30:	At-the-Money $40:	Out-of-the-Money $50:	
	Investment:				- $4,000.00
	Premium:	+ $40.00	+ $270.00	+ $1,230.00	
$20		* - $3,000.00	* - $4,000.00	* - $5,000.00	
		+ $2,000.00	+ $2,000.00	+ $2,000.00	
	VALUE:	- $1,000.00	- $2,000.00	- $3,000.00	+ $2,000.00
	π:	- $960.00	- $1,730.00	- $1,770.00	- $2,000.00
$30			* - $4,000.00	* - $5,000.00	
		option expires	+ $3,000.00	+ $3,000.00	
	VALUE:	$0.00	- $1,000.00	- $2,000.00	+ $3,000.00
	π:	+ $40.00	- $730.00	- $770.00	- $1,000.00
$40				* - $5,000.00	
		option expires	option expires	+ $4,000.00	
	VALUE:	$0.00	$0.00	- $1,000.00	+ $4,000.00
	π:	+ $40.00	+ $270.00	+ $230.00	$0.00
$50		option expires	option expires	option expires	
	VALUE:	$0.00	$0.00	$0.00	+ $5,000.00
	π:	+ $40.00	+ $270.00	+ $1,230.00	+ $1,000.00
$60		option expires	option expires	option expires	
	VALUE:	$0.00	$0.00	$0.00	+ $6,000.00
	π:	+ $40.00	+ $270.00	+ $1,230.00	+ $2,000.00
Rate of Return		-48.0% to 2.0%	-86.5% to 13.5%	-88.5% to 61.5%	- 50% to 50%

24.7.1 - Payout Graph

The payout graph shows the value and profit for each possible price of the underlying asset.

At spot prices above the exercise price the option expires worthless, and the profit line shows a profit equal to 100% of the premium. At spot prices below the exercise price the option is exercised, and the diagonal line shows an increasing losses as the price of the underlying stock decreases.

The payout graph is derived from the following equations:

$$Value = - \max(0, (X - S))$$
(Eq 24-7)

$$Profit = - \max(0, (X - S)) + P$$
(Eq 24-8)

where

     S = the spot price of the underlying shares at expiry

     X = exercise price

     P = put premium per share

Figure 24-6: Short $50 Put on GE @ $12.30

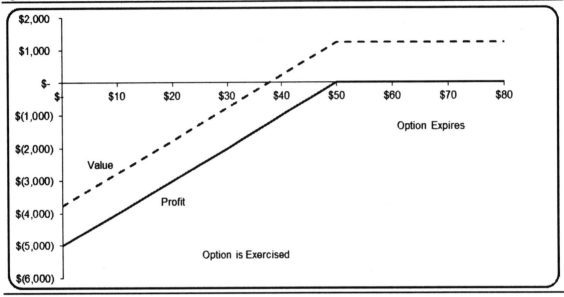

We breakeven on this strategy only when the option is exercised. Therefore the breakeven price is given by the exercise price minus the premium, in this example $50 - $12.30 = $37.70

Put Expires	Put is Exercised
$\pi = -\max(0, (X - S_B)) + P = 0$	$\pi = -\max(0, (X - S_B)) + P = 0$
$-0 + P \neq 0$	$-X + S_B + P = 0$
	$S_B = X - P$

Case Study

After learning about options three enterprising finance students thought it might be more interesting to invest in options with some real money. They pooled all their resources and in December 1994, with an initial stake of $1,825.00, began buying call options. Their strategy was to focus on companies where there was a rumor or the possibility of a takeover and buy call options. In those cases where the takeover did not materialize the options expired worthless or very nearly so. In those cases where the takeover or takeover attempt generated a price increase the options proved very profitable. By the end of April the three students had generated a portfolio of $40,570.58 ($42,775.00 before commission). This is not all return because the transactions indicate that they increased their stake

Faced with some skepticism, the students supplied the Department of Finance with Brokerage reports from which the following was compiled:

Issue	#	Expiry	Strike	Date	Price	Value	Commission	Capital Gain
Antec Corp	5	May-95	$22^1/_2$	18-Jan-95	$1^7/_8$	$937.50	$61.05	
Antec Corp	5	May-95	$22^1/_2$	19-Jan-95	$1^7/_8$	$937.50	$61.05	
Antec Corp	5	May-95	$22^1/_2$	30-Jan-95	$^7/_8$	$437.50	$44.57	
Antec Corp	5	May-95	$22^1/_2$	30-Jan-95	$^7/_8$	$437.50	$41.57	
Antec Corp	5	May-95	$22^1/_2$	1-Feb-95	$^7/_8$	$437.50	$48.85	
Antec Corp	-5	May-95	$22^1/_2$	10-Mar-95	$3^3/_4$	($1,875.00)	$89.01	
Antec Corp	-5	May-95	$22^1/_2$	10-Apr-95	3	($1,500.00)	$74.30	
Antec Corp	-5	May-95	$22^1/_2$	24-Apr-95	$3^1/_2$	($1,750.00)	$86.94	
Antec Corp	-5	May-95	$22^1/_2$	24-Apr-95	$3^3/_8$	($1,687.50)	$78.71	
Antec Corp	-5	May-95	$22^1/_2$	25-Apr-95	$3^3/_8$	($1,687.50)	$78.71	$5,312.50
Argosy Games	10	Apr-95	$12^1/_2$	14-Dec-94	$^3/_4$	$750.00	$51.92	
Argosy Games	-10	Apr-95	$12^1/_2$	29-Dec-94	$1^5/_{16}$	($1,312.50)	$105.10	$562.50
Aztar Corp	10	Mar-95	$7^1/_2$	13-Feb-95	$^3/_8$	$375.00	$48.85	
Aztar Corp	-10	Mar-95	$7^1/_2$	24-Mar-95	$1^7/_{16}$	($1,437.50)	$95.00	$1,062.50
Caesars World	10	Jan-95	50	13-Dec-94	$^7/_{16}$	$437.50	$48.85	
Caesars World	6	Jan-95	50	14-Dec-94	$^7/_{16}$	$262.50	$48.85	
Caesars World	-10	Jan-95	50	19-Dec-95	$16^1/_8$	($16,125.00)	$310.86	
Caesars World	-6	Jan-95	50	19-Dec-95	$16^1/_8$	($9,675.00)	$186.51	$25,100.00
Circus Circus	5	Mar-95	30	24-Jan-95	1	$500.00	$50.75	
Circus Circus	5	Mar-95	30	24-Jan-95	1	$500.00	$50.75	
Circus Circus	-5	Mar-95	30	18-Mar	0			
Circus Circus	-5	Mar-95	30	18-Mar	0			($1,000.00)
E Systems	7	May-95	45	19-Jan-95	$1^5/_8$	$1,137.50	$79.80	
E Systems	-7	May-95	45	3-Apr-95	$18^7/_8$	($13,212.50)	$284.30	$12,075.00
Quaker Oats	9	Jul-95	45	30-Jan-95	$1^1/_8$	$1,012.50	$105.91	
Quaker Oats	-9	Jul-95	45	6-Apr-95	$^3/_4$	($675.00)	$72.71	($337.50)
							$2,204.92	$42,775.00

24.8 - Index Options

Index options are options contracts where the underlying security is the value of a specified index. With a stock option the writer is obliged to deliver or take delivery of the specified shares whenever the buyer exercises. An index option, like an index future, settles for cash.

❑ **S&P 500:** The S&P 500 index option trades on the CBOE. One contract is defined as $100 times the index.

❑ **S&P Mini:** set at 1/10th of the S&P500 index option. All quotes are still multiplied by $100 but settlement is based on the S&P500/10

❑ **DJIA:** The Dow Jones Industrial Average option also trades on the CBOE . One contract is defined as $100 times the index/100.

❑ **DJIA Jumbo:** set at the DJIA index option * 10. All quotes are still multiplied by $100 but settlement is based on the DJIA/10

Numerous other indices provide the underlying basis for index options: the Russell, NASDAQ indices, the Nikkei, and other international indices. There are also numerous subindex options: For example Computer Technology 29 Index option, Oil 15 Index, and Institutional 75 Index options trade on AMEX; and the Defense Sector 18, Fiber Optics Sector 21; Gold/Silver 9 Index options are traded on the Philadelphia Stock Exchange.

A small sample of the index options available is included in Table 24-6.

Table 24-6: Index Options

		Call			Put		
Exp	Strike	Vol	Last	Open Int	Vol	Last	Open Int
Dow Jones Industrial Average Index Options					*DJIA: 13,260.28*		
July	132	281	2.65	1,271	185	1.65	2,524
June	133	479	0.85	21,226	241	1.20	14,228
July	133	63	2.05	1,833	72	2	1,734
July	136	88	0.65	12,657			
S&P 500 Index Options					*S&P 500: 1285.71*		
June	1100				432	0.40	173,586
June	1300	6,105	5.60	205,126	899	18.80	180,793
June	1400	6,000	0.05	108,546			
Sept	1400	278	2.20	33,935			
NASDAQ 100					*NASDAQ 100: 1616.57*		
June	1585	317	43.20	697	716	11.50	2,034
June	1600				658	14.30	9,524
Sept	1800	151	6.20	1,541			
						Financial Pages, 2012	

Example 8:

John Q. Investor buys a June DJIA put option with a strike price of 133.

The contract definition is conveniently appropriate to the Dow Jones Industrial Average, trading at 13,260.28, once we recall the contract is settled in cash using the multiplier of $100. One contract is thus defined with a strike price of $13,300: $1 per point.

The premium is quoted at 1.20. One contract is defined as $100 times the index, so JQ pays $120. [$100 * 1.20] in premium on the option contract.

_____

Suppose that at the end of June the Dow Jones stands at 12,200.

JQ exercises the option, and receives the intrinsic value of $1,100 [$100 * (133 - 12,200/100)]. This is the same as buying the index at its current level ($12,200) and then exercising the option to sell that index at the strike price of 133 ($13,300).

The holding period rate of return for the one month period is 816.7%

$$\frac{\$100 \left(133.00 - \dfrac{12,200.00}{100} \right)}{\$100 * 1.20} = \frac{\$1,100}{\$120} = 9.\overline{666} = 1 + 816.7\%$$

However, if the Dow climbs to 13,300 or higher by the third Friday of June, then the option expires worthless and JQ's rate of return will be -100%

February 1995: The Collapse of Barings Brothers Bank

Baring Brothers was Britain's oldest and most conservative bank. Known as the Queen's Bankers, Barings financed Britain's wars against the United States and France, as well as the Louisiana Purchase. The Duc de Richelieu was reputed to have said in 1791 that the six great powers of Europe were England, France, Prussia, Austria, Russia, and Baring Brothers.

Barings collapsed February 26, 1995, after a rescue package put together by the Bank of England failed. The immediate cause of the collapse was the loss of £927 million in still outstanding futures and options, attributable to the activities of one derivatives trader in Barings Futures (Singapore) Pte Ltd., Nicholas W. Leeson.

Leeson's mandate at Barings was to arbitrage the Nikkei 225 futures contract, which traded both on the Osaka Securities Exchange (OSE) and the Singapore Monetary Exchange (SIMEX). Arbitrage involves tiny profits over huge volumes, but no one seems to have noticed that Mr. Leeson had deserted the low-risk arbitrage strategy for sheer speculation: he began buying Nikkei futures in both markets. When enormous long positions accumulated in Osaka, they assumed Barings was short in Singapore, and when enormous long positions accumulated in Singapore, they assumed Barings was short in Osaka.

Leeson was also trading Nikkei options: simultaneously selling puts and calls in a straddle that paid off if the Nikkei remained fairly stable. It appears that Leeson sold some 40,000 options contracts earning Barings a profit of almost £100 million in 1994. By 1995 the premiums on his write straddles were going to pay margin on his futures contracts.

By mid-January 1995, Barings had huge positions in both futures (where they made money only if the Nikkei rose) and options (where they made money only if the Nikkei remained between 18,500 and 19,500. On January 17 the Kobe earthquake struck. On January 23 the Nikkei plunged more that 1,000 points to less than 17,800.

Whether to bolster the Nikkei, or to take advantage of a buyers market, Leeson began buying more futures. There was no control system in Barings to halt Leeson's trading; Leeson was the trader, the head of settlements, and the risk manager at Barings Futures (Singapore). Leeson fled Singapore February 23 and was arrested in Frankfurt March 2.

It was not until Leeson disappeared that Barings Brothers called someone in to unravel the situation in Singapore and not until February 26 that they figured out that Leeson had singlehandedly converted Baring Brothers from a conservative arbitrageur to a defunct speculator.

Faced with the very real possibility that the OSE and SIMEX could collapse if Barings declared bankruptcy and reneged on its positions, the Bank of England, unable to mount a rescue, organized a buyout. Barings was finally purchased by ING (Internationale Nederlanden Groep) for £1 million, although the cost, after covering trading losses, outstanding deficit, and providing working capital, was closer to £660 million. That Barings should be taken over by a Dutch Bank seems somewhat ironic since the Baring family came originally from Groningen.

Further Reading:
Stephen Fay, *The Collapse of Barings*, New York: W.W Norton & Company, Inc., 1997.

24.9 - Interest Rate Options

In addition to interest rate options, which are options on Treasury notes, bonds, and bills, there are options on interest rates themselves. Interest rate options are European options. They can be exercised only on the expiry date.

❑ **IRX:** IRX options (options on short-term interest rates) are based on the yield-to-maturity of the most recently auctioned 13-week (91-day) T-bills. The exercise price is 10 * YTM. Thus a strike price of 27½ can be interpreted as a yield of 2.75%.

❑ **LRX:** LRX Options (options on long-term interest rates) are based on the yield-to-maturity of the two most recently auctioned 7-year, 10-year, and 30-year T-bonds. The exercise price is 10 * YTM. Thus a strike price of 60 can be interpreted as a yield of 6.00%.

Table 24-7: Interest Rate Options Quote on Ten-Year Treasury Rates

Strike Price	Calls			Puts		
	July	Aug	Sept	July	Aug	Sept
20.0	0.80	1.15	1.30	1.20	0.85	0.90
22.5	0.95	0.50	0.85	1.50	1.75	2.00
25.0	0.12	0.25	1.20	4.00	3.90	3.80
27.5	0.75	0.15	0.18	6.50	6.30	6.20
30.0	0.02	0.07	0.12	9.00	8.80	8.60

Financial Pages, 2012

Example 9:

John Q. Investor buys a 27.5 September call option at a premium of $0.18. He pays $18.00. [100 * $0.18].

Suppose that by the time the option expires the yield has increased to 3.00% (a price of 30.0). JQ receives $250. [$100 * (30.0 - 27.5)].

The staggering 1,288.9% [$250/$18] holding period rate of return on this investment could well be the result of the relatively thin trading in any one contract; the last trade need not be a good indicator of the price that you could get in the next trade.

If JQ had purchased the 25.0 September call option at $1.20 instead then his profit would have been only 316% ($500/$120).

Chapter 24 - Questions & Problems

24-1:

Explain the difference between buying a call option and writing a put option.

24-2:

Construct a payout graph showing

A. The value of a $40 March call option

B. The profit of a $40 March call option purchased at a premium of $2.50

C. The value of 100 shares of GE

D. The profit on 100 shares of GE purchased at $40

24-3:

Construct a payout graph showing

A. The value of a $40 March written call option

B. The profit of a $40 March written call option sold at a premium of $2.50

C. The value of a short position of 100 shares of GE

D. The profit on a short position of 100 shares of GE sold at $40

24-4:

Construct a payout graph showing

A. The value of a $40 March put option

B. The profit of a $40 March put option purchased at a premium of $2.70

C. The value of a short position of 100 shares of GE

D. The profit on a short position of 100 shares of GE sold at $40

24-5:

Construct a payout graph showing

A.   The value of a $40 March written put option

B.   The profit of a $40 March written put option sold at a premium of $2.70

C.   The value of a long position of 100 shares of GE

D.   The profit on a long position of 100 shares of GE purchased at $40

24-6:

In each graph below

A.   Identify what option position it illustrates: buy or write; call or put.

B.   Label the value and profit lines.

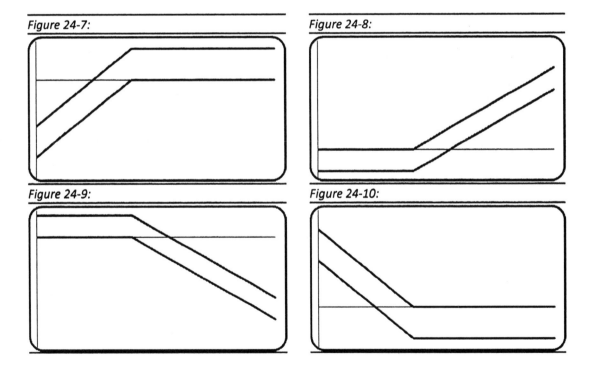

Figure 24-7:

Figure 24-8:

Figure 24-9:

Figure 24-10:

24-7:

Assume that in December you write ten March GE call options at a strike price of $30 and a premium of $10.20 John Q. Investor was the buyer. Suppose that on the last trading date before expiry GE was trading at $35.

A. Is this an in- or an out-of-the money option?

B. Will J.Q. exercise these options?

C. What is J.Q.'s profit on this transaction?

D. What would J.Q.'s profit be on this transaction if he did not exercise these options?

E. What is your profit on this transaction?

24-8:

Susan Q. Speculator buys an April call option at 70. Using the interest options quote answer the following questions.

Table 24-8: Interest Rate Options

Strike	Calls			Puts		
Price	Feb	Mar	Apr	Feb	Mar	Apr
65.0		2.125	2.70		0.625	0.750
67.5	0.300	0.450	0.450		1.875	2.000
70.0		0.375	0.450	3.250	3.750	4.000

A. How much must Susan pay for the call option?

B. Calculate the possible gains and losses if interest rates move to 6.0%, 6.5%, 7.0%, 7.5%, and 8.0%.

C. Graph the payout on Susan's call option.

Susan Q. Speculator also buys an April put options at 70.

D. How much must Susan pay for this put option?

E. Calculate the possible gains and losses if interest rates move to 6.0%, 6.5%, 7.0%, 7.5%, and 8.0%.

F. Graph the payout on Susan's put option.

Chapter 24 - Financial Models

24.1 - Option Model

Objective:

A. To graph the payout for all four primary positions: long call, short call, long put, short put.

Inputs:

B. Specify the position as long or short. Restrict the input to these two values. To do this use [Data validation] in the Finance Ribbon. In [Data Validation] allow [List] and specify the source directly. Type in the space provided: Long, Short and click on [OK]. Name cell C3 Position.

C. Specify the option as call or put. Restrict the input to these two values. To do this use [Data validation] in the Finance Ribbon. In [Data Validation] allow [List] and type: Call, Put and click on [OK]. Name cell C4 Option

D. Check the inputs by choosing Long Call from the drop-down boxes you have just created.

E. Enter $40 as the Exercise Price. Name the cell X.

F. Enter $16 as the Premium. Name the cell CP.

G. Enter 1 contract. Name the cell N.

H. Make sure that the inputs are coded finance blue. Use [Finance Fonts] in the Finance ribbon or use the shortcut Shift+Ctrl+B.

Investment

I. Calculate the investment. There are 100 shares in each contract so: C7 = N * 100 * CP.

J. The investment is negative if we are short the contracts, so we need an =IF() statement. So C7 becomes = IF(Position="Short",-1,1) * N * 100 * CP.

The way we construct the =IF() statement is much more efficient and easier to debug than the alternative = IF(Position="Short",-1* N * 100 * CP,-1* N * 100 * CP).

K. We use the same approach to calculate the breakeven price. So C8 =IF(Option="Call", X+CP, X-CP)

L. Verify the investment and breakeven price by changing the position and the option.

Calculate Value and Profit:

M. The template for model 24-1 has a column of stock prices from $0 to $100 in $10 increments. Recall equations 24-1 through 24-8:

	CALL	PUT
LONG	*Value* = max(0, (*S* − *X*)) *Profit* = max(0, (*S* − *X*)) − *C*	*Value* = max(0, (*X* − *S*)) *Profit* = max(0, (*X* − *S*)) − *P*
SHORT	*Value* = − max(0, (*S* − *X*)) *Profit* = − max(0, (*S* − *X*)) + *C*	*Value* = − max(0, (*X* − *S*)) *Profit* = − max(0, (*X* − *S*)) + *P*

N. The basic equation must be adjusted for the position (long or short) and for the option (call or put). It's always best to start simple so begin with the long call. We have named the exercise price X so all we need to adjust is the relevant stock price. Thus C11 = max(0, B11 - X) *N * 100

O. Verify the formula. Copy-drag down the column to C21.

P. If the option is a put rather than a call, we need to use a different value calculation, so build an =IF() statement. Thus B11 becomes = IF(Option="Call", max(0, B11 - X),max(0, X - B11)) * N * 100.

Q. Use Shift+Ctrl+↓ to highlight the column and Ctrl+D to copy the formula down to C21.

R. Change the option to put and verify that the value is calculating correctly.

S. If the position is short rather than long we need to adjust the value calculation, so build an =IF() statement. Thus C11 becomes
    = IF(Position="Short",-1,1) * IF(Option="Call", max(0, B11 - X),max(0, X - B11)) * N * 100.

T. Copy-drag down and verify by changing the position and the option.

Profit

U. The profit is simply the Value minus the investment. So D11 = C11 - $C$7.

V. Again, copy-drag down and verify by changing the position and the option.

Graph

W. Select the range B10:D21 and select an XY Scatter with straight lines.

X. Format the Chart to suit your own style.

Y. Create a Chart Title in cell F1. The formula = Position & " " & Option will automatically pull the inputs into the chart title.

Z. Use [Chart Tools] [Layout] [Chart Title] to create a chart title in the graph. To link to the chart title, click inside the Chart Title box and, in the formula bar enter = and select F1.

Options Model		
Position:	Long	
Option:	Call	
Exercise Price	$	40.00
Premium:	$	16.00
Contracts:		2
Investment:	$ 3,200.00	
Breakeven:	$	56.00

S	Value	Profit
$0	0.00	-3,200.00
$10	0.00	-3,200.00
$20	0.00	-3,200.00
$30	0.00	-3,200.00
$40	0.00	-3,200.00
$50	2,000.00	-1,200.00
$60	4,000.00	800.00
$70	6,000.00	2,800.00
$80	8,000.00	4,800.00
$90	10,000.00	6,800.00
$100	12,000.00	8,800.00

Long Call

Options are most frequently traded in strategies: combinations of equity and option positions that together provide a specifically engineered payout. The building blocks of these strategies are the six components: long and short positions in equity, calls, and puts.

We calculate the value and profit on the strategy by adding the value and profit of each component in the portfolio at each price level. We can do this numerically or we can add the payout graphs directly.

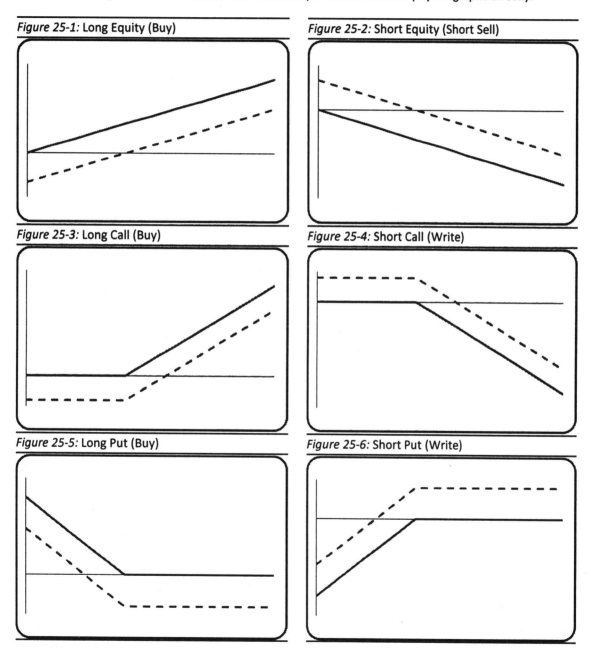

Figure 25-1: Long Equity (Buy)

Figure 25-2: Short Equity (Short Sell)

Figure 25-3: Long Call (Buy)

Figure 25-4: Short Call (Write)

Figure 25-5: Long Put (Buy)

Figure 25-6: Short Put (Write)

25.1 - Covered Call

A covered call is a written call covered by shares of the underlying security. When you write a covered call the premium paid by the buyer goes directly to the writer; there is no margin. However, the writer's stock is kept in escrow by the broker. If the option is exercised then the broker delivers the stock to the buyer. If the option expires unexercised or if the writer enters into a closing purchase, then the shares are returned to the owner.

❑ **Naked Call:** A written call not covered by the shares of the underlying security and not included as part of an overall strategy.

❑ **Covered Call:** A written call covered by shares of the underlying security.

Example 1:

> Suppose we buy 100 shares of GE at $40 and immediately write a $40 March call option at a premium of $2.50 quoted in Table 24-1. What are the possible gains and losses?

We calculate the value and profit on the strategy by adding the value and profit of each component at each price level.

Table 25-1: Construction of a $40 Covered Call on GE

Price at Expiry	Strike Price:	Write a $40 call	Buy 100 Shares of GE	Covered Call
	Investment:	+ $250.00	-$4,000.00	- $3,750.00
$20:	VALUE:	option expires $0.00	+ $2,000.00	+ $2,000.00
	π:	+ $250.00	- $2,000.00	- $1,750.00
$30:	VALUE:	option expires $0.00	+ $3,000.00	+ $3,000.00
	π:	+ $250.00	- $1,000.00	- $750.00
$40:	VALUE:	option expires $0.00	+ $4,000.00	- $4,000.00
	π:	+ $250.00	$0.00	+ $250.00
$50:	VALUE:	* + $4,000.00 - $5,000.00 - $1,000.00	+ $5,000.00	- $4,000.00
	π:	- $750.00	+ $1,000.00	+ $250.00
$60:	VALUE:	* + $4,000.00 - $6,000.00 - $2,000.00	+ $6,000.00	-$4,000.00
	π:	- $1,750.00	+ $2,000.00	+ $250.00
Rate of Return		12.5% to - 87.5%	- 50.0% to + 50.0%	-46.7% to 6.7%

We do the same thing graphically by aligning the price of the underlying stock in each graph.

Figure 25-7: Graphic Construction of a $40 Covered Call on GE

The long position on the underlying equity shows the original purchase price of $40 per share.

The short position on the call has the kink at the strike price of $40

Add value and profit vertically.

For example, at $60 $2,000 profit from the long equity plus -$1,750 from the short call gives us a profit of $250 for the strategy.

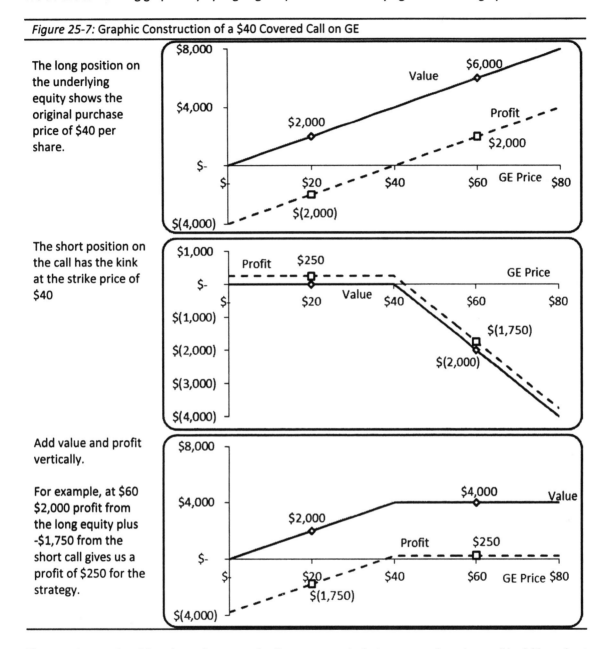

The most interesting thing about the covered call as a strategy is that we can make a short call look like a short put just by adding a long equity position. In the covered call we have just created, the profit line is indistinguishable from the profit line for a $40 put written at a premium of $2.50 per share

25.2 - Protective Put:

A protective put is a long position in the underlying equity hedged with a put option that reduced the portfolio's price risk exposure.

Example 2:

We think that the price of GE will increase, so we buy 100 shares, but hedge against the risk of loss by buying a put option. We have three possible strategies: a $30 protective put at a premium of $0.40, a $40 protective put at a premium of $2.70, or a $50 protective put at a premium of $12.30. What are the possible gains and losses?

Table 25-2: Construction of a Protective Put at $30, $40, and $50 on GE

Price at Expiry		Long Shares with Protective Put			Long GE
	Strike Price:	Out of the Money $30:	At the Money $40:	In the Money $50:	
	Shares:	-$4,000.00	-$4,000.00	-$4,000.00	-$4,000.00
	Premium:	-$40.00	-$270.00	-$1,230.00	
	Investment:	-$4,040.00	-$4,270.00	-$5,230.00	-$4,000.00
$20	VALUE:	exercise option +$3,000.00	exercise option +$4,000.00	exercise option +$5,000.00	+$2,000.00
	π:	-$1,040.00	-$270.00	-$230.00	-$2,000.00
$30	VALUE:	+$3,000.00	exercise option +$4,000.00	exercise option +$5,000.00	+$3,000.00
	π:	-$1,040.00	-$270.00	-$230.00	-$1,000.00
$40	VALUE:	+$4,000.00	+$4,000.00	exercise option +$5,000.00	+$4,000.00
	π:	-$40.00	-$270.00	-$230.00	0.00
$50	VALUE:	+$5,000.00	+$5,000.00	+$5,000.00	+$5,000.00
	π:	+$960.00	+$730.00	-$230.00	+$1,000.00
$60	VALUE:	+$6,000.00	+$6,000.00	+$6,000.00	+$6,000.00
	π:	+$1,960.00	+$1,730.00	+$770.00	+$2,000.00
Rate of Return		-25.7% to 48.5%	-6.3% to 40.5%	-4.4% to 14.7%	-50.0% to +50.0%

By looking at the comparative rates of return we can see that a $30 (out-of-the-money) protective put reduces our upside potential by 1.5% (from 50.0% to 48.5%) but provides significant downside protection (from -50.0% to -25.7%). The additional protection offered by the $40 (at-the-money) protective put reduces our upside potential to 40.5% on a 50% price move. However, the additional protection offered by the $50 (in-the-money) option comes at the price of reducing our upside potential to 14.7%.

Based on this analysis we opt for a $30 protective put.

Figure 25-8: Graphic Construction of a Protective Put

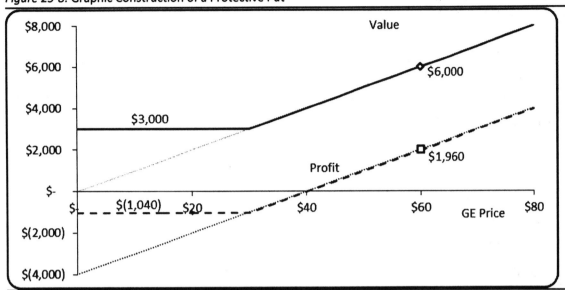

The thin dotted line represents the payout from the long equity position. The protective put limits the value to $3,000. This is like an insurance policy that provides a $3,000 payout if the stock falls below $30 per share. The profit line shows that we limit the losses on this strategy to ($1,040) but at the cost of decreasing the entire profit line by $40. This decrease reflects the cost of the put contract on 100 shares at $0.40 per share.

25.3 - Straddle

A buy or long straddle involves buying a call and a put for the same underlying stock for the same expiry date at the same exercise price. A write or short straddle involves writing a call and a put for the same underlying stock for the same expiry date at the same exercise price.

Example 3:

John Q. Investor writes a $30 March call at $10.20 and a $30 March put at $0.40.

JQ's strategy has a positive profit if the price of GE settles in the neighborhood of $30 per share. At exactly $30 both the call and the put expire, and JQ keeps the premium of $1,060. At prices below $30 the short put is exercised and the call expires; at prices above $30 the short call is exercised and the put expires. He calculates that to break even the stock price of GE must remain between $19.40 and $40.60.

Short put is exercised (S < $30)

$Profit = -100(\$30 - S) + \$1,060 = 0$
$S_{Breakeven} = \$30 - \$10.60$
$S_{Breakeven} = \$19.40$

Short call is exercised ($30 < S)

$Profit = -100(S - \$30) + \$1,060 = 0$
$S_{Breakeven} = \$30 + \$10.60$
$S_{Breakeven} = \$40.60$

Figure 25-9: $30 March Write Straddle on GE

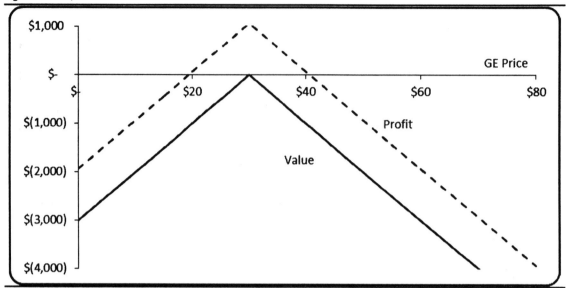

25.4 - Strangle

A strangle is similar to a straddle, but the exercise price of the call is not equal to the exercise price of the put.

Example 4:

GE is trading at $40 per share. John Q. Investor buys a $35 June put at $1.85 and a $45 June call at $1.75.

Note that both these options are $5 out-of-the-money, so buying the strangle costs JQ $360. If the price of GE increases by more than $5 then he will exercise the call; if it decreases by more than $5 then he will exercise the put. At prices between $35 and $45 JQ will allow both options to expire worthless.

JQ calculates the break-even prices as 31.40 and $48.60; if the price of GE falls below 31.40 he will make money on the put and if the price rises above $48.60 then he will make money on the call. Between $31.40 and $48.60 JQ will lose money on the strategy.

JQ exercises long put (S < $35)

$$Profit = 100\ (\$35 - S) - \$360 = 0$$
$$S_{Breakeven} = \$35 - \$3.60$$
$$S_{Breakeven} = \$31.40$$

JQ exercises long call ($45 < S)

$$Profit = 100\ (S - \$45) - \$360 = 0$$
$$S_{Breakeven} = \$45 + \$3.60$$
$$S_{Breakeven} = \$48.60$$

Figure 25-10: $35 to $45 Long Strangle on GE

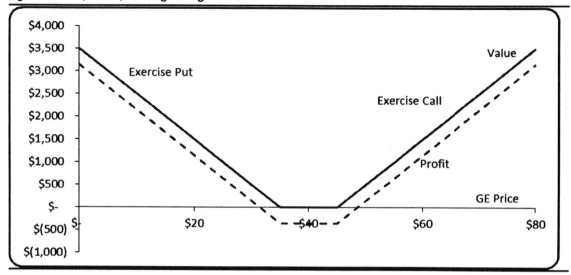

Example 5:

JQ takes another look at the buy or long strangle.

He doubts the price of GE will move above $48.60 or lower than $31.40 (a range of $17.20 is an extreme movement for a $40 stock) before the June options expire. Rather than dismiss the strategy as not being worth an investment of $360, he considers a sell or short strangle.

Selling each option at their respective premiums allows him to have a maximum profit of $360 and will not have a loss unless GE climbs higher than $48.60 or falls lower than $31.40. Graphically, we can see this very quickly by just flipping the value and profit lines with respect to the X-axis.

Figure 25-11: $35 to $45 Short Strangle on GE

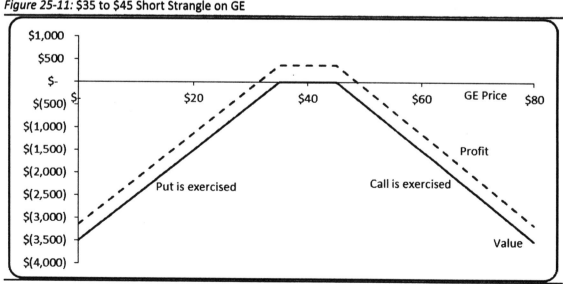

25.5 - Spreads

A spread is the simultaneous write and buy of similar but not identical options.

❏ **Time (Horizontal) Spread:** A time or horizontal spread involves writing and buying options on the same underlying security at the same strike price but for different expiration dates.

❏ **Price (Vertical) Spread:** A price or vertical spread involves writing and buying options on the same underlying security at the same expiration date but at different prices.

❏ **Bull Spread:** A price spread in which we make money when the market goes up.

❏ **Bear Spread:** A price spread in which we make money when the market goes down.

Example 6:

> JQ thinks that the price of GE will decrease so he sets up a bear spread. He writes a $30 March call option at $10.20 and buys a $40 March call option at $2.50. He collects a total premium of $770.

We know that the payout graph will have a kink at $30 and a kink at $40 and one break-even price

Both options expire	$30	$30 Short call is exercised	$40	$30 Short call is exercised & JQ exercises $40 long call
$\pi = +\$770$		$\pi = -100\,(S - \$30) + \$770$ $S_{Breakeven} = \$30 + \$7.70$ $S_{Breakeven} = \$37.70$		$\pi = -100\,(S - \$30) + 100\,(S - \$40) + \$770$ $\pi = -100S + \$3000 + 100S - \$4000 + \$770$ $\pi = -\$230$

Note that the spread protects against the large losses if the price of GE goes up. The combination of options allows us to eliminate the open-ended loss potential of a naked call.

Figure 25-12: $30 to $40 Bear Call Spread on GE

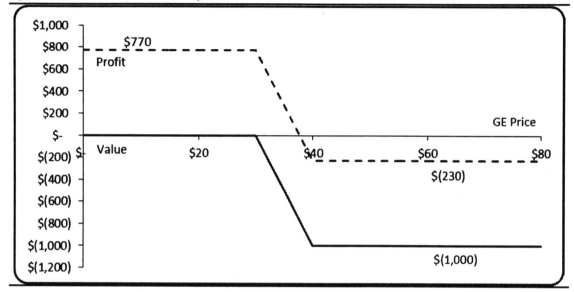

JQ summarizes the various possible outcomes of his bear spread in the following table.

Table 25-3: Construction of a $30 to $40 Bear Spread

Price at Expiry	Strike Price: Investment:	Write a $30 call + $1,020.00	Buy a $40 call -$250.00	Bear Spread + $770.00
$20:	VALUE:	option expires $0.00	option expires $0.00	$0.00
	π:	+ $1,020.00	- $250.00	+ $770.00
$30:	VALUE:	option expires $0.00	option expires $0.00	$0.00
	π:	+ $1,020.00	- $250.00	+ $770.00
$35:	VALUE:	* + $3,000.00 <u>- $3,500.00</u> - $500.00	option expires $0.00	$0.00
	π:	+ $520.00	- $250.00	+ $270.00
$40:	VALUE:	* + $3,000.00 <u>- $4,000.00</u> - $1,000.00	option expires $0.00	- $1,000.00
	π:	+ $20.00	- $250.00	- $230.00
$50:	VALUE:	* + $3,000.00 <u>- $5,000.00</u> - $2,000.00	* - $4,000.00 <u>+ $5,000.00</u> + $1,000.00	- $1,000.00
	π:	- $980.00	+ $750.00	- $230.00
$60:	VALUE:	* + $3,000.00 <u>- $6,000.00</u> - $3,000.00	* - $4,000.00 <u>+ $6,000.00</u> + $2,000.00	-$1,000.00
	π:	- $1,980.00	+ $1,750.00	- $230.00

JQ could construct a similar spread using put rather than call options.

Example 7:

> JQ writes a $30 March put option at $0.40 and buys a $40 March put option at $2.70. He pays a total premium of $230.

Again, we know that the payout graph will have a kink at $30 and a kink at $40 and one break-even price

$30 Short put is exercised & JQ exercises $40 long put	$30	$40 Long put is exercised	$40	Both options expire
$\pi = -100 (\$30 - S) + 100 (\$40 - S) - \$230$ $\pi = -\$3000 + 100S + \$4000 - 100S - \$230$ $\pi = +\$770$		$\pi = 100 (\$40 - S) - \$230$ $S_{Breakeven} = \$40 - \$2.30$ $S_{Breakeven} = \$37.70$		$\pi = -\$230$

The profit line on the bear put spread is identical to the profit line on the bear call spread. JQ hopes to find the least expensive combination depends on the prices at which he can trade each option. In this case the premia just happen to make the profit lines identical.

Even if the profit lines are identical, the value lines are not. With the call spread the both options expire when the price of GE is less than $30 at expiry, and the net premium is collected. But with the put spread both options expire when the price of GE is more than $40 at expiry and the net premium is paid.

Figure 25-13: $30 to $40 Bear Put Spread on GE

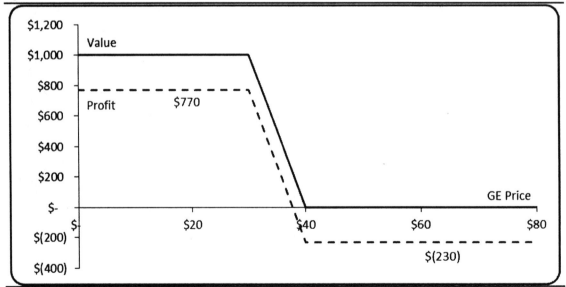

25.6 - Collar

A collar is an options strategy that protects the value of a portfolio between two bounds. The lower bound is set by a protective put. The protective put is financed by an upper bound call, which limits the portfolio's upside potential.

Example 8:

John Q. Investor holds 10,000 shares of GE. GE is currently trading at $40.

JQ can set a lower bound on the value of his holding by buying $30 June put options on his shares. The put option ensures that JQ will get at least $30 per share for his stock. At $0.75 this protective put requires an investment of $7,500.00

To generate the funds needed for the put option JQ also writes a call option on his shares. A $45 June call option is quoted at $1.75. If JQ writes $45 June calls on 4,300 shares of GE he can generate $7,525.00; enough to pay for the put options.

Figure 25-14: 10,000 Shares of GE with and without a $30 to $45 Collar

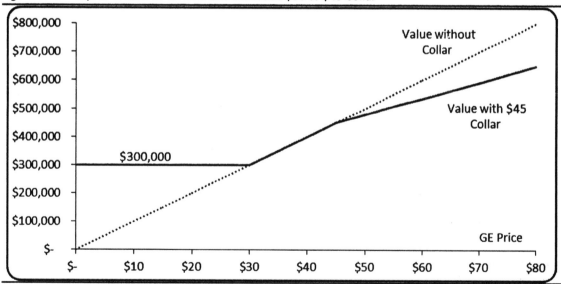

The purpose of the collar is to reduce risk exposure. Without a collar the portfolio has a payout represented by the 45° line from the origin. If the price goes up you make money; if it goes down you lose money. The collar cuts off the risk that the effective price per share goes below $30. If the price of the underlying stock decreases further we exercise the put option. This reduces the risk of loss. But you never get something for nothing (not in finance anyway). You must pay for that risk reduction somewhere. With an ordinary protective put you pay money. With a collar you pay with the risk that some of your shares will get called away. Cutting off potential losses at the bottom of the diagonal means that you must cut off some of the profits at the top of the diagonal.

Reducing risk means reducing the risk of making a profit as well as reducing the risk of making a loss.

With a collar, emphasis is placed on cutting off some of the profits at the top of the diagonal, not all. Even if the price of GE climbs to an extraordinarily high price before the expiration of the options, he can profit on the 5700 shares he continues to own.

Table 25-4: Breakdown of the Collar on 10,000 GE at $30 to $44					
Price at Expiry	Strike price:	10,000 GE	Buy 100 $30 put	Write 43 $45 call	Collar
	Investment:	- $400,000	- $7,500	+ $7,525	- $399,975
$20:	VALUE:	$200,000	* + $300,000 - $200,000 + $100,000	call expires $0	$300,000
	π:	- $200,000	+ $92,500	+ $7,525	- $99,975
$30:	VALUE:	$300,000	put expires $0	call expires $0	$300,000
	π:	- $100,000	- $7,500	+ $7,525	- $99,975
$35:	VALUE:	$350,000	put expires $0	call expires $0	$350,000
	π:	- $50,000	- $7,500	+ $7,525	- $49,975
$40:	VALUE:	$400,000	put expires $0	call expires $0	$400,000
	π:	$0	- $7,500	+ $7,525	+ $25
$45:	VALUE:	$450,000	put expires $0	call expires $0	$450,000
	π:	+ $50,000	- $7,500	+ $7,525	+ $50,025
$50:	VALUE:	$500,000	put expires $0	* - $215,000 + $193,500 - $21,500	$478,500
	π:	+ $100,000	- $7,500	- $13,975	+ $78,525
$60:	VALUE:	$600,000	put expires $0	* - $258,000 + $193,500 - $64,500	$535,500
	π:	+ $200,000	- $7,500	- $56,975	+ $135,525

JQ could also use a $60 call, but the premium is only $0.75 per share. This means that JQ needs to write 100 calls to offset the expense of his puts. Figure 25-15 shows a payout graph comparing the two strategies, illustrating the trade-off. The $60 call will not be exercised until and unless the price of GE increases to more than $60. But if it is exercised all 10,000 shares will be called away.

JQ calculates that the $60 collar dominates between $45 and $71.3158 and the $45 collar dominates at prices greater than $71.3158.

$$Value = (100 * 100 * \$60) = (43 * 100 * \$45) + (5,700 * S)$$
$$S = \$71.315789$$

Figure 25-15: 10,000 shares of GE with a $45 Collar and a $60 Collar

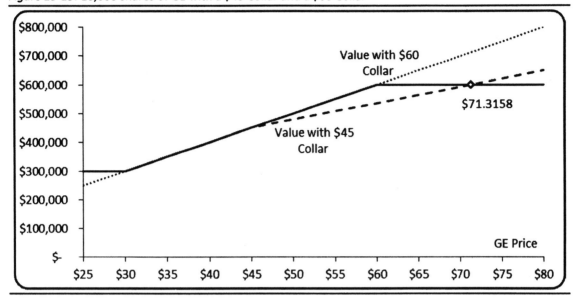

Which strategy best meets JQ's needs depends on the probability that the price of GE will rise above $71.3178 by the time the options expire.

25.7 - Synthetic Stock

Options can be traded in combinations such that the payout mimics short or long positions in the underlying stock.

Example 9:

John Q. Investor sets up two portfolios. One portfolio holds a long position in GE, the other holds a synthetic long position in GE..

❑ **Long Stock Portfolio:** JQ purchases 100 shares of GE at $40. The initial investment is $4000.

❑ **Synthetic Long Portfolio:** JQ combines a long $40 call at $3.80 with a short $40 put at $3.90. JQ's initial investment is -$10 (he collects $10 more in premium than he pays).

Figure 25-16: Synthetic Long Portfolio from a Long $40 Call and a Short $40 Put

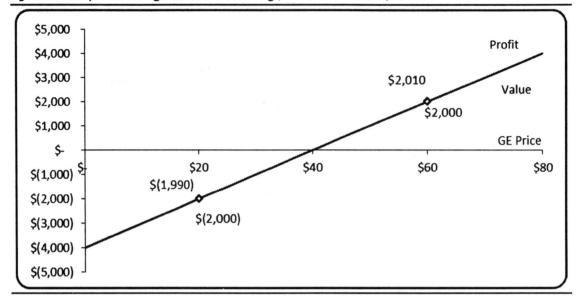

The payout on the synthetic stock is $10 more than the payout on the long position on the underlying stock, but the initial investment lends leverage. The rate of return is not ±infinity—as it would be if the initial investment were zero or negative—because JQ's broker will require margin.

Similarly, a synthetic short position is constructed from a short $40 call and a long $40 put. Synthetic shorts come in extremely handy when you would like to short-sell a stock, but for a variety of reasons, there is no stock available to borrow.

25.8 - Deconstruction

In the same way that a portfolio of options can mimic a long or a short position in the underlying stock, an existing investment instrument can be deconstructed into components, one or more of which is an option. Deconstructing an investment instrument into its component parts allows us to analyze and price these investments more easily than dealing with a complicated investment directly.

Callable Bonds

A callable corporate bond can be deconstructed into a bond and a written call option. A callable bond is essentially a covered call strategy on a bond: buy the bond and write a call option against it.

At any market yield the price on a callable bond will be lower than the price of the equivalent noncallable bond. The difference in price is the premium on the embedded call. If market yields decline, then price of the bond increases; if it increases above the call price—the strike price of the call option on the bond—then the issuer will exercise the call, forcing bond holders to sell the bonds at the call price.

Equity

Finally, think about equity—partial ownership—in the form of shares of stock in GE.

The "fully paid and non-assessable" shares are essentially a call on the value of the firm. If the firm prospers then the stock price should increase.

At the same time, the nonassessable characteristic of stock is essentially a put of the diminished value of the firm to the bondholders. If the firm falls on hard times, the value plummets, perhaps below what it owes its lenders, and through a process of bankruptcy, lenders are left with the remaining few assets hoping to recover, while the equity holders lose only the price they paid for their shares; just like losing the premium paid for a put option.

These are just a few examples of how options can be applied to better understand complex financial instruments.

Chapter 25 - Questions and Problems

25-1:

Construct a payout graph showing

A. The value and profit of a $40 March written call option sold at $2.50

B. The value and profit on a long position of 100 shares of GE purchased at $40

C. The value and profit of the covered $40 March call sold at $2.50 covered by a long position of 100 shares of GE purchased at $40

25-2:

You purchase 1000 shares of Hypothetical Resources at $50 per share. Three month $50 put options are quoted at $1 per share.

A. Show how buying put options now will hedge your position. (Hint: Show profit and loss if HR declines to $30, stays at $50, or increases to $70.)

B. Construct the payout graph. Show both value and profit.

25-3:

You have set up a strangle by buying a $30 March put on GE at $.40 and buying a $50 March call on GE at $0.15.

A. Graph the payout on this strategy. Include both the value and the profit.

B. At what prices do you break even on this strategy?

25-4:

John Q. Investor sets up a rather convoluted strangle by writing a $30 March call on GE at $10.20 and writing a $50 March put on GE at $12.30.

A. Graph the payout on this strategy. Include both the value and the profit.

B. To what prices does JQ break even on this strategy?

C. How does JQ's strategy differ from a short strangle with a $30 March put at $0.40 and a $50 March call at $0.15?

25-5:

You have set up a bear spread by buying a $40 March call on GE at $2.50 and writing a $30 March call on GE at $10.20.

A.   Graph the payout on this strategy. Include both the value and the profit.

B.   To what price must GE fall to break even on this strategy?

25-6:

Construct a bear spread using a $30 March GE put at $0.40 and a $50 March GE put at $12.30. Graph the payout.

25-7:

You have set up a bull spread by buying a $40 March call on GE at $2.50 and writing a $50 March call on GE at $0.15.

A.   Graph the payout on this strategy. Include both the value and the profit.

B.   To what price must GE rise to break even on this strategy?

25-8:

Construct a bull spread using a $30 March GE put at $0.40 and a $50 March GE put at $12.30. Graph the payout.

25-9:

John Q. Investor buys one $35 June GE call option at $6.70, writes two $40 June GE call options at $3.80, and buys one $45 GE call option at $1.75. This strategy is called a butterfly spread.

A.   Calculate the initial investment.

B.   Graph the payoff to this strategy. Include both the value and the profit.

C.   Calculate the breakeven prices.

25-10:

You set up a $40 June long straddle on GE. You buy one $40 June call option at $3.80 and one $40 June put at $3.90.

A.   Show the possible gains and losses on this strategy and calculate the rates of return.

B.   Graph the payout to this strategy. Include both the value and the profit.

C.   Calculate the breakeven prices.

25-11:

You set up a $40 June short straddle on GE. You write one $40 June call option at $3.80 and one $40 June put at $3.90.

A.   Show the possible gains and losses on this strategy and calculate the rates of return (Assume your broker requires a margin of $2,000.)

B.   Graph the payout to this strategy. Include both the value and the profit.

C.   Calculate the breakeven prices.

25-12:

John Q Investor has 10,000 shares of GE valued at $40. He would like to set up a collar using a $30 June put at $0.75, but he can't decide between a $45 June call at $1.75 and a $50 June call at $0.80.

A.   Graph the payout for each alternative. (Use the same graph.)

B.   Which strategy would you recommend?

25-13:

Consult the Hypothetical Resources option quote.

Table 25-5: Hypothetical Resources (HR)						
HR: $58.75		Call		Put		
Strike	Expiry	Vol	Last	Vol	Last	
$50	Jan	1418	9.75	2254	.75	
$50	Feb	870	12.00	615	2.45	
$60	Jan	7216	2.90	488	2.70	
$60	Feb	1273	3.15	187	4.15	
$60	Mar	837	4.40	347	5.05	
$70	Jan	223	.40	40	11.75	
$70	Feb	327	2.75	30	13.20	
$70	Mar	357	6.00	3	14.10	

A. What is the most recent closing price for Hypothetical Resources?

Kevin and Joe get into a debate on risk aversion (that gets completely out of hand). They decide to have a duel by investment. You are the unfortunate soul who gets to keep score and report the results.

B. Kevin buys ten $60 March **call** options. What is his premium?

C. Joe writes ten $70 March **put** options. What is his premium?

D. Construct payout graphs for Kevin and for Joe. Who takes the greater risk?

25-14:

A client comes to you with a portfolio that consists of 10,000 shares of Discovery Café (DVC) and nothing else. He read an article in *Business Week* about collars: he has no idea what they are but he wants one. Using the Discovery Café options quote for options expiring in July, you construct a protective put with a collar.

A. At what exercise price should you set the protective put? Why?

B. At what exercise price should you write the call? Use a payout graph to compare strategies.

Table 25-6: Discovery Café (DVC)					
DVC: $50.00		Call		Put	
Strike	Expiry	Vol	Last	Vol	Last
$40	July	1418	$10.25	554	$0.50
$45	July	2870	$6.50	615	$1.50
$50	July	7216	$3.60	988	$3.65
$55	July	1273	$1.85	98	$6.75
$60	July	83	$0.80		
$65	July	223	$0.50		

25-15:

We set up three portfolios using call options on Discovery Café (DVC). The six-month, at-the-money call options have a strike price of $100 and are currently trading at $10.

Table 25-7:   Discovery Café strategies

	Portfolio	Investment
Portfolio A	Buy 100 Discovery Café @ $100	$10,000.00
Portfolio B	Buy 10 Discovery Café call options @ $10	$10,000.00
Portfolio C	Buy 1 Discovery Café call option and a $9,000 CD paying 3% for the six-month period	$10,000.00

A. Calculate the market value and rate of return for each portfolio. (Prices from $80 to $120 in $10 increments).

B. Graph the payout for each portfolio (graph the profit on a common graph).

$\mathcal{T}$he key to options, exchange traded or real, is the ability to calculate a fair value.

26.1 - Binomial Pricing Model

The binomial pricing model seeks to derive the price of a call option through the law of one price. This is a simplified version of the binomial price model, but it illustrates the concepts.

❑ **Law of One Price:** The law of one price states that two assets with the same characteristics will, in equilibrium, have the same price. If prices differ then investors will arbitrage, buying the low price asset and selling the high price asset until prices equalize.

The binomial price model is derived from two portfolios, one containing shares and one containing call options. The two portfolios are engineered to have equal risk and equal return. Two portfolios with the same characteristics must have the same price. From this equality we can calculate the option price.

Engineer two portfolios:

❑ **Share Portfolio:** The share portfolio consists of one share of leveraged stock. In this example the price per share of the stock is $50. In one year the price will go to either $100 or to $25 with equal probability. We leverage by borrowing the net present value of the worst-case scenario. The interest rate is 3%, so we borrow $24.27 ($25/1.03). Our initial investment is $25.73 ($50 - 24.27)

At the end of one year we must pay off the debt of $25. If the price of the stock is $100 then we are left with a portfolio value of $75; if the price of the stock is $25, then we are left with a portfolio value of $0.

Figure 26-1: The Share Portfolio: a Binomial Payout on One Leveraged Share of Stock

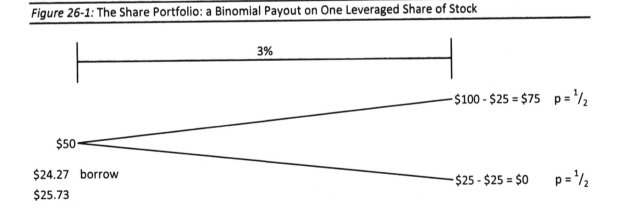

❑ **Option Portfolio:** The options portfolio consists of a call option on a share of the same stock. The exercise price (X) is $75. If the stock goes up to $100, then the value of the option will be $25; if the price of the stock goes down to $25, then the option will expire worthless.

Figure 26-2: The Option Portfolio: a Binomial Payout on One call $75 call option

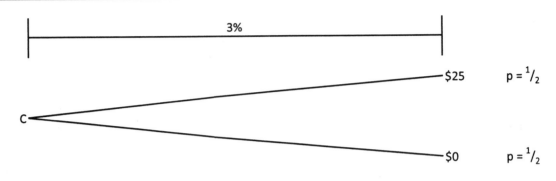

A portfolio consisting of three such options will have payout and risk characteristics exactly equal to the stock portfolio. To also have the same price three options must carry a premium of $25.73. Thus

$$C = \frac{\$25.73}{3} = \$8.577$$

Example 1:

John Q. Investor calculates that shares of Discovery Café, currently trading at $50, will either increase to $100 or decrease to $25 in one year with a 50/50 probability. The one-year $75 call option is trading at $10. He decides to take advantage of this arbitrage opportunity and constructs a fully hedged portfolio.

JQ calculates that the fair market value of the DVC option should be $8.577. The option premium, currently at $10, is too high, so JQ sells 3 options contracts at $10 per share. He generates a premium of $3,000 (3 contracts * 100 shares/contract * $10/share). Out of the $3,000 he pays $2,573 for 100 shares of Discovery Café on margin, borrowing $2,427. His initial outlay is thus -$427: he collects $427 more than he pays out.

If the price of Discovery Café goes to $100 then his portfolio consists of

100 Discovery Café (DVC)	$100.	$10,000.
3 short $75 DVC calls exercised	$25.	- $7,500.
Loan payable $2427 @ 3%		- $2,500.
		$0.

If the price of Discovery Café goes to $25 then his portfolio consists of

100 Discovery Café (DVC)	$25.	$2,500.
3 short $75 DVC calls expired	$0.	- $0.
Loan payable $2427 @ 3%		- $2,500.
		$0.

In either case JQ keeps the $427 initial premium. JQ's fully hedged portfolio is a no-risk portfolio with a positive payout.

Market forces bring prices back into equilibrium; competition to write DVC options drop the price until the price of the option is again at an equilibrium.

26.1.1 - Hedge Ratio

The Hedge Ratio on the Discovery Café is 3; JQ's fully hedged portfolio requires three written calls to offset the price movement of the shares. The hedge ratio is calculated as

$$\Delta = \frac{Price\ range\ on\ the\ stock}{Value\ range\ on\ the\ option} = \frac{S^+ - S^-}{C^+ - C^-} = \frac{S^+ - S^-}{(S^+ - X) - 0} \qquad (Eq\ 26\text{-}1)$$

Example 2:

JQ calculates the Hedge ratio on his Discovery Café portfolio as

$$\Delta = \frac{S^+ - S^-}{S^+ - X} = \frac{\$100 - \$25}{(\$100 - \$75) - \$0} = 3$$

Three options will be required to hedge one share of the underlying stock.

26.1.2 - The Multiperiod Binomial Tree

A binomial model with one time period and a 50/50 outcome mapping is entirely unrealistic. However when we break the model into multiple time periods the outcome mapping becomes more realistic.

Example 3:

Discovery Café is currently trading at $50. John Q. Investor calculates that in each calendar quarter shares can either increase by 18.9207% ($\sqrt[4]{(1+100\%)} = 1.189207$) or decrease by 15.910358% ($\sqrt[4]{(1-50\%)} = 0.84089642$). Thus at the end of one year the price of Discovery Café shows the outcomes and probabilities as shown in Figure 26-3.

Figure 26-3: Four-period Binomial tree

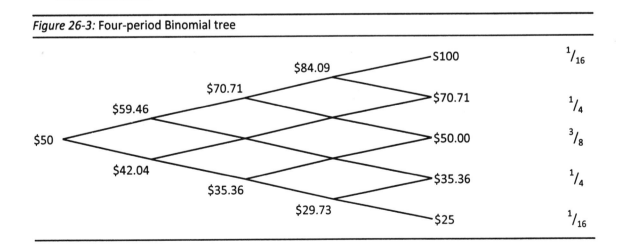

Note that the elements of the model are logarithmic. The ratio of $X : S^- : S_0 : S^+$ is 1:1:2:4 and we always borrow the NPV of S^-.

As we increase the number of intermediate time periods, the probability distribution at the end of the process looks more and more normal. The prices themselves are logarithmic, so the final distribution becomes log normal. As the number of time periods approaches infinity ∞ we approach the Black-Scholes options pricing model.

26.2 - Black-Scholes Option Pricing Model

The most widely used options valuation formula is based on the Black-Scholes option pricing model. In this model the price of a call option is given by:

$$C = S N [d_1] - X e^{-rt} N [d_2]$$

$$d_1 = \left[\frac{\ln \left(\frac{S}{X} \right) + \left(r + \frac{\sigma^2}{2} \right) t}{\sigma \sqrt{t}} \right]$$

$$d_2 = \left[d_1 - \sigma\sqrt{t} \right]$$

(Eq 26-2)

where:

C = market price of the call option,
S = current price of the underlying stock,
X = exercise or strike price of the call option,
r = current annualized rate of interest for the same period as the call option,
t = time to expiry measured in years (91 days = .25 years),
σ = standard deviation of the annual rate of return on the underlying stock, and
$N[d]$ = cumulative density function of d where $d \sim N[0,1]$

Example 4:

John Q. Investor is considering a 91 day call option on Hypothetical Resources with a strike price of $100. JQ gathers the following information.

$C = ?$
$S = \$90.$ This is the price at which the stock is currently trading.
$X = \$100$
$r = .05$ The current rate of interest on prime 90-day commercial paper is 5%
$t = .25$ 91/365 = .249315 years = .25 years
$\sigma = 0.40$ annualized standard deviation of daily returns on the underlying stock. This measures the volatility of the stock and its calculation and adjustment to reflect new information can be tricky part of the BS Model. (Review portfolio theory section.)
$N[X] =$ cumulative density function of X where $X \sim N[0,1]$

The cumulative normal distribution numbers can be taken from the tables in the back of any decent statistics book or from the tables at the back of this section.

First calculate d_1
and $N[d_1]$

$$d_1 = \left[\frac{\ln\left(\dfrac{S}{X}\right) + (r + \dfrac{\sigma^2}{2})\, t}{\sigma \sqrt{t}} \right]$$

$$d_1 = \left[\frac{\ln\left(\dfrac{90}{100}\right) + (0.05 + \dfrac{.40^2}{2})\, 0.25}{0.40 \sqrt{0.25}} \right]$$

$$d_1 = \frac{-0.105360516 + 0.0325}{0.20}$$

$$d_1 = -0.3643$$

$$N\,[\,d_1\,] = N\,[\,-0.36\,] = .35942$$

Then calculate d_2
and $N[d_2]$

$$d_2 = \left[\, d_1 - \sigma\sqrt{t}\, \right]$$

$$d_2 = -0.3643 - (0.40 \sqrt{.25})$$

$$d_2 = -0.5643$$

$$N\,[\,d_2\,] = N\,[\,-0.56\,] = 0.28774$$

Then calculate the
call premium

$$C = S\,N\,[\,d_1\,] - X\,N\,[\,d_2\,]\; e^{-rt}$$

$$= 90\,[0.35942] - 100\,[0.28774]\; e^{-(.05).25}$$

$$= 90\,[0.35942] - 100\,[0.28774]\,(0.9875778)$$

$$= 32.3487 - 28.41766$$

$$= 3.931$$

Therefore JQ should be willing to pay \$3.93 for this call option.

26.2.1 - Delta Hedge Ratio

The Hedge Ratio, Delta, the ratio of options to shares required to hedge the risk of holding the shares, is equal to $N[d_1]$

$$\Delta = \frac{\Delta\,P_{Option}}{\Delta\,P_{Underlying\ Stock}} = \frac{\Delta\,C}{\Delta\,S} = N\,[d_1] \qquad\qquad (Eq\ 26\text{-}3)$$

Example 5:

John Q. calculates a delta hedge ratio of 0.36 This means that the value of the call option increases by $0.36 whenever the price of the stock increases by $1.

It also means that if John Q. writes a call option then 0.36 shares of stock are needed to hedge each written call. Thus if JQ writes 1 contract on 100 shares, he must hold 36 shares to fully hedge his position.

Table 26-1: Discovery Café Fully Hedged Call Option

Discovery Café shares		Discovery Café $100 call options		Portfolio
Price	Long 36 shares	Premium	Short 1 contract (100 shares)	
$90.00	$3,240.00	$3.93	- $393.00	$2,847.00
+ $1.00		+ $0.36		
$91.00	$3,276.00	$4.29	- $429.00	$2,847.00
	+ $36.00		- $36.00	$0.00

If the stock price goes up by $1 then the option price will go up by $0.36. JQ gains $1 per share on 36 shares for a total gain of $36, and he loses $0.36 per share on the written call for a total loss of $36.

26.2.2 - Payout Graph

The probability that the call option will expire in the money is given by N[d_2].

Figure 26-4: Payout and Risk Profile on an Out-of-The-Money Call Option

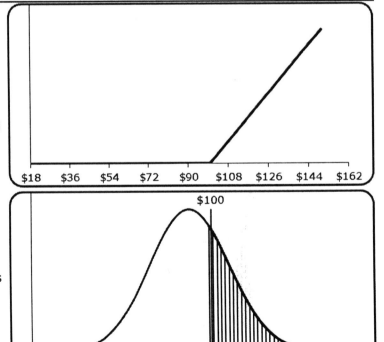

In the case of the 91-day $100 call option on HR we estimate a 29% probability that the option will expire in-the-money.

Note that the 40% volatility represents the annualized standard deviation on daily returns. To convert this to standard deviation for 91 days we use $\sigma\sqrt{t}$:

$$\sigma\sqrt{t} = 40\% \sqrt{0.25} = 20\%$$

20% of $90 is $18 so the normal distribution is with mean $90 and standard deviation $18. This means that three standard deviations out gives us a normal distribution from $90 ± 3*$18; from $36 to $144.

26.3 - Put - Call Parity Relationship

The Black-Scholes model prices a call option. We need to use the put-call parity relationship to relate the price of a put option to the price of the corresponding call. Again we use the law of one price. We engineer two portfolios with the same risk and return characteristics: one based on a call option and one based on a put option.

❑ **Put portfolio:** The put portfolio consists of:
  ❑ 100 shares of Hypothetical Resources currently trading at $90, and
  ❑ a protective put option on these shares with an exercise price of $100.

If the price of HR is less than $100 when the option expires, then exercise the option and sell the shares at $100; the portfolio has a value of $10,000. If the price of HR is greater than $100, then the portfolio has a value of 100 * price.

❑ **Call portfolio:** The call portfolio consists of:
  ❑ a call option on 100 shares of Hypothetical Resources with an exercise price of $100 and
  ❑ money held at interest to generate $10,000 on the expiry date.

If the price of HR is less than $100 when the option expires then the option expires worthless, but we still have the cash; the portfolio has a value of $10,000. If the price of HR is greater than $100, then exercise the option using the $10,000 cash to pay for the 100 shares at $100/share; the portfolio has a value of 100 * price.

Figure 26-5: Payout and Risk Profile of the Put and Call Portfolios

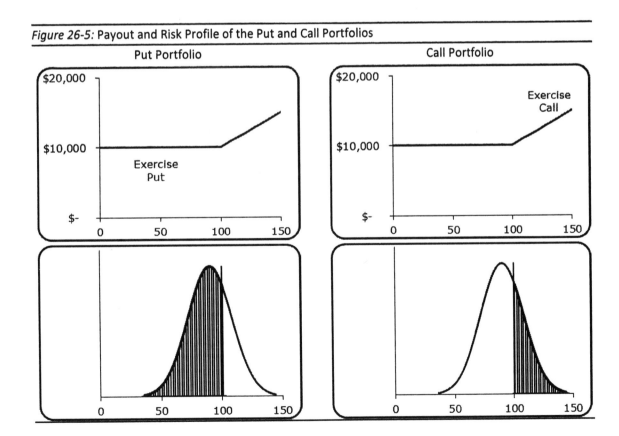

In each case the portfolio value is 100 * price of HR with a minimum value of $10,000. Because the put and call portfolios are of equal characteristics they must also be of equal cost; unequal costs would be rapidly arbitraged away. Thus

$$\text{Call Portfolio} = \text{Put Portfolio}$$

$$C + PV[X] = P + S - PV[D] \qquad \text{(Eq 26-4)}$$

$$P = C - S + [X + D]e^{-rt}$$

where
C = Price of the call option with an exercise price X
P = Price of the corresponding put option with an exercise price X
S = Price of the underlying stock
D = Dividends paid on the underlying stock during the lifetime of the put and call contracts

The last term adjusts the put call parity for dividends that are paid on the stock during the life of the option. The dividend is a cash inflow, and so the cost of the portfolio is reduced by the PV of the dividends to be received.

Example 6:

John Q. Investor is considering a 91-day $100 put option on Hypothetical Resources. HR is currently trading at $90 and is not expected to pay dividends in the interval. The interest rate is 5%, and JQ calculated a price of $3.93 for the corresponding call option. What price should JQ be willing to pay for the put option?

$$P = \$3.93 - \$90 + \$100\,e^{-(.05)(.25)}$$

$$P = \$12.69$$

The put option has an intrinsic value of $10—the $100 strike price less the $90 current stock price. So the put price consists of the $10 intrinsic value plus the $2.69 speculative value. So $12.69 seems reasonable.

26.4 - Determinants of Value

There are five determinants of an option's value. In comparative statics we analyze the effect of changing one determinant at a time holding all other determinants constant.

Table 26-2: Comparative Statics on the Price of Options

Determinant	Change	Call Value	Put Value
S = Stock Price	+	+	−
X = Exercise Price	+	−	+
r = Interest Rate	+	+	−
t = time	+	+	+
σ = volatility	+	+	+

Thus when the price of the underlying stock increases the fair market value of the call increases and the fair market value of the put decreases.

26.5 - Implied Volatility

The Black-Scholes option pricing model is a straightforward calculation from observable financial data: stock price (S), exercise price (X), interest rate (r), and time to expiry (t). The component of the model that requires judgement is the volatility of the underlying stock (σ). Thus the options pricing model can be reduced to the statement that the price of a call option is a function of the volatility of the underlying stock. In other words if you know the volatility of the underlying stock, then you can calculate the fair value of the option. And conversely, if you know the market price of the option, then you can calculate back to the volatility implied by the price.

Table 26-3: Option Pricing Model and Implied Volatility

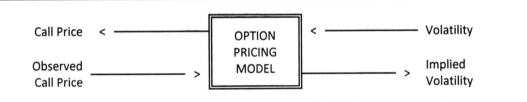

Figure 26-6 shows the put and call prices on the 91-day $100 option contracts given a stock price of $90 and an interest rate of 5%. Note that the calculated call price of $3.93 and put price of $12.69 can only result from a 40% volatility.

If we observe a call price of $6.50, then this implies that the market assumes an underlying volatility of 55%.

Figure 26-6: Put and Call Prices as a Function of Underlying Volatility

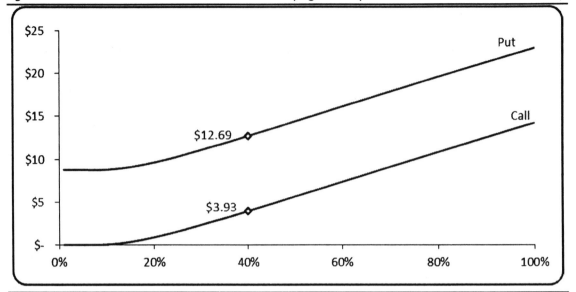

26.5.1 - *Volatility Smiles*

The entire range of options contracts has the same underlying stock, so we would expect that the underlying volatility would be the same, regardless of strike price or expiry date. After all, if the price of General Electric (GE) exhibits a standard deviation of 33%, then all options on GE should reflect this same level of volatility.

However, in practice we find that the premiums on in-the-money and out-of the money options generally reflect higher volatilities than at the money options. This pattern is described as the volatility smile.

Figure 26-7 shows the average of the implied volatility calculated on the call and put options on GE given in Table 24-1. The $40 at-the-money options reflect a fairly consistent 33% implied volatility. But volatilities are higher as the strike price increases or decreases. The exception is the June contract. June is the far away contract in this quote (which was taken in December). The pattern is more of a volatility smirk than a volatility smile.

Smirks tend to be more common with index options than stock options, but both are seen.

Figure 26-7: Implied Volatility on GE options by strike price and expiry date

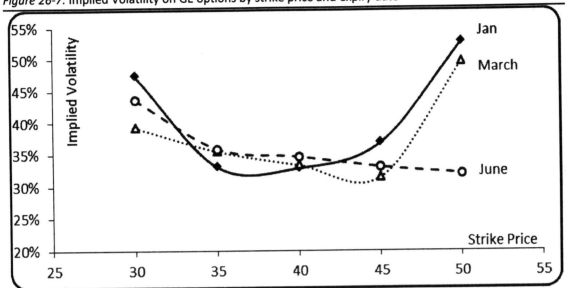

26.5.2 - Volatility Spread

Implied volatility lends itself naturally to the spread. Given the same underlying stock, and the same time to expiry, each strike price option should have the same measure of volatility. The fair market value calculated from the Black-Scholes model is very sensitive to changes in volatility, even such differences as are typically found in a volatility smile.

The volatility spread more closely resembles arbitrage than speculation in that we are trying to take advantage of different implied volatilities where they should all be the same. There is no bull or bear volatility spread because there is no need to have an opinion on the general direction of the stock.

When the options expire, we will be able to look back and calculate the actual volatility of the underlying stock, and it must, by definition, be the same for all options. So we set up the volatility spread by buying the low implied volatility options and selling the high volatility options. By exploring and setting up the spreads with all possible combinations, we should be able to choose two options that fit our risk tolerance and payoff potentials.

26.5.3 - Volatility Index

An options price index is unworkable. Even the various call prices on a single underlying stock will have different prices depending on the term to expiry and the intrinsic value. But the underlying stock is the same and thus, in theory, the various options should have the same volatility.

The Chicago Board Options Exchange publishes a volatility index (VIX) on the implied volatilities calculated on the near term options on the S&P 500 index. The volatility index, commonly called the "investor's fear gauge" is calculated on a continuous basis and provides the base for the CBOE volatility index option and the volatility index future contracts.

Figure 26-8: Volatility Index (VIX) January 1990 to May 2012

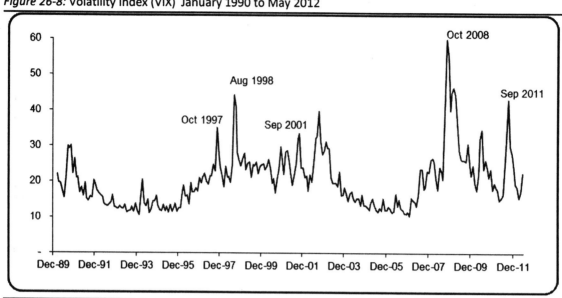

Note the increase in volatility during periods of general financial, economic, political uncertainty.

- ❑ On October 27, 1997, the Dow dropped 554 points (-7.2%)
- ❑ On August 17, 1998, Russia devalued the Ruble and defaulted on its Sovereign debt.
- ❑ September 11, 2011.
- ❑ On December 2, 2001, Enron filed for bankruptcy. At $64 billion, this was the largest bankruptcy in U.S. history.
- ❑ On July 21, 2002, WorldCom Inc. filed for bankruptcy. At $107 billion, this was the largest bankruptcy in U.S. history.
- ❑ On September 15, 2008 Lehman Brothers filed for bankruptcy. At $600 billion, this was the largest bankruptcy in U.S. history.
- ❑ In September 2011, the European debt crisis dominated the headlines.

1998: Long Term Capital Management

Long Term Capital Management (LTCM) was a hedge fund that failed in 1998. Its positions were so extensive that it was treated as too big to fail. The New York Federal Reserve organized a bailout by a consortium of investment banks and trading partners to avoid a financial meltdown.

LTCM was an elite fund. It was started in 1994 by John Meriwether. Meriwether was widely known, not only on Wall Street for his role as head of bond trading at Solomon Brothers, but by anyone who had read Michael Lewis's "Liar's Poker". The fund featured Nobel Prize winners Myron Scholes (Fischer Black died in August 1995) and Robert Merton. Scholes and Merton shared the 1997 Nobel Prize in Economics for the development of new methods of pricing derivatives.

LTCM combined fixed-income arbitrage with leverage. The arbitrage part was designed to minimize risk. For example, LTCM would arbitrage the spread between 5yr BB rated bonds and the equivalent Treasury, secure in the knowledge that the spread would return to its historical value of 200 basis points before too long. But arbitrage does not generate the kind of profits that hedge funds need. So positions were highly leveraged. By 1998 the balance sheet showed assets of $100 billion on a capital of less than $4 billion.

Leverage works both ways. In 1997 LTCM was hit by the Asian property crisis. In 1998 LTCM was hit by the default in Russian bonds. By some calculations two such "black swan" or "six sigma" events should happen every seventeen million years, not seventeen months. The fund was in trouble. As the markets fled risk—take another look at the VIX index on the previous page—spreads that should have closed, opened even further. By September 1998 LTCM owed so much money to so many key financial players that it was feared that it's failure would trigger secondary failures throughout the financial system.

The bailout was funded by financial institutions such as JP Morgan, Morgan Stanley, Goldman Sachs, Salomon Smith Barney, Merrill Lynch, UBS, Barclays, and Lehman Brothers. The collapse of LTCM has been called a dress rehearsal for 2008, so it is interesting to note that Bear Stearns, the first to fall in 2008, declined to participate in the LTCM bailout.

The fund was liquidated in 2000.

Further reading:
  Michael Lewis, *Liars' Poker: Rising Through the Wreckage on Wall Street*, New York: W.W. Norton & Company, Inc., 1989.
  Roger Lowenstein, "When Genius Failed; the Rise and Fall of Long Term Capital Management", New York: Random House, 2000.

Chapter 26 - Questions and Problems

26-1:

John Q. Investor calculates that shares of Discovery Café (DVC), currently trading at $50, will either increase to $100 or decrease to $25 in one year with a 50/50 probability. The one-year $75 call option is trading at $7. He decides to take advantage of this arbitrage opportunity and constructs a fully hedged portfolio. The interest rate is 3%

A.   Calculate the fair market value of the call option.

B.   What is the hedge ratio on this option?

C.   Set up the fully hedged portfolio. What is JQ's initial outlay?

D.   Demonstrate that the portfolio exactly breaks even whether Discovery Café increases to $100 or decreases to $25.

26-2:

John Q. Investor calculates that shares of Tardis Intertemporal (TI), currently trading at $100, will either increase to $200 or decrease to $50 in one year with a 50/50 probability. The one-year $125 call option is trading at $28. He decides to take advantage of this arbitrage opportunity and constructs a fully hedged portfolio. The interest rate is 5%

A.   Calculate the fair market value of the call option.

B.   What is the hedge ratio on this option?

C.   Set up the fully hedged portfolio. What is JQ's initial outlay?

D.   Demonstrate that the portfolio exactly breaks even whether Tardis Intertemporal increases to $200 or decreases to $50.

26-3:

You disagree with John Q. Investor. Recent developments within Hypothetical Resources lead you to believe that the stock will exhibit a volatility of σ = 0.50. Hypothetical Resources is currently trading at $90, and the applicable interest rate is 5%.

A.   What premium should you be willing to pay for the 91 day $100 call option on HR?

B.   What is the approximate probability that this option will expire in-the-money?

C.   Graph the payout and risk profile for this option and indicate the approximate probability that this option will expire worthless.

26-4:

You estimate of the volatility of Hypothetical Resources at $\sigma = 0.50$ rather than $\sigma = 0.40$ and consequently calculated a 91-day $100 call option price of $5.64 rather than $3.93. With HR trading at $90 and the interest rate of 5%, what effect does your assumption of increased volatility have on the price of the 91-day $100 put option?

26-5:

Hypothetical Resources is currently trading at $90, and you estimate the volatility at 40%. The applicable interest rate is 5%.

A. What premium should you be willing to pay for the 91 day $80 call option on HR?

B. What is the delta hedge ratio? What is the value of the call if the price of HR increases to $91?

C. What is the approximate probability that this option will expire in-the-money?

D. What premium should you be willing to pay for the 91-day $80 put option on HR?

E. What is the approximate probability that this option will expire in-the-money?

F. Graph the payout and risk profile for the put and call options, and indicate the approximate probability that each option will expire worthless.

26-6:

Hypothetical Resources is currently trading at $90. And you estimate the volatility at 40%. The applicable interest rate is 5%.

A. What premium should you be willing to pay for the 91 day $90 call option on HR?

B. What is the delta hedge ratio? What is the value of the call if the price of HR increases to $91?

C. What is the approximate probability that this option will expire in-the-money?

D. What premium should you be willing to pay for the 91 day $90 call option on HR?

E. What is the approximate probability that this option will expire in-the-money?

F. Graph the payout and risk profile for the put and call options, and indicate the approximate probability that each option will expire worthless.

Chapter 26 - Financial Modeling

26.1 - Black-Scholes Option Pricing Model

Create an options pricing calculator for the Black-Scholes option pricing formula.

$$C = S\,N\,[\,d_1\,] \; - \; X\,e^{-rt}\,N\,[\,d_2\,]$$

$$P = C - S + X\,e^{-rt}$$

$$d_1 = \left[\frac{\ln\left(\dfrac{S}{X}\right) + \left(r + \dfrac{\sigma^2}{2}\right)t}{\sigma\sqrt{t}}\right]$$

$$d_2 = \left[\,d_1 - \sigma\sqrt{t}\,\right]$$

Model Data:

A. Begin with the data needed in the Black-Scholes formula. Use the data in the Discovery Café option used in the example so that we can verify results step-by-step. The template for model 26-1 includes the relevant assumptions.

B. Format the inputs for ease of use and code them finance blue. Name the cells in column C according to the corresponding labels in column B. All the names are fairly straightforward; using them will make the formulae easier to follow. The only exception is the interest rate; we use rr because r is a reserved name in Excel.

C. Time in D5 is forced to a fraction of the format ?/365 to emphasize the unit of measurement. To force the format use Ctrl+1 to open the Format cells applet. Then use [Number] [Custom]. Under Type enter ?/365. You should see 91/365 in the sample. Click on [OK].

D. Note that 91 days is actually 0.249315 years. To make sure that we get the same numbers as in the textbook example enter .25 rather than 91/365. After the spreadsheet is built and the formulae verified we can come back and change it. The cell is formatted as a fraction, so it still shows 91/365.

Calculations:

E. Calculate the substeps in the Black-Scholes formula. This allows us to verify steps along the way and to use intermediate results like the delta hedge ratio.

F. Excel has a natural log function, so D10 = LN(S/X).

G. Use ^ as the power operator, so D11 = (rr+sigma^2/2)*t Note that Excel follows standard order of operations so that extra parentheses are not required.

H. Excel has a square root function, so D12 = sigma * SQRT(t).

I. Calculate d1 as (D10+D11)/D12.

J. Excel has a normal distribution function, so D14 = NORM.S.DIST(D13,TRUE). The True in the function returns the cumulative distribution. Use false to return the probability density function. Note that the NORM.S.DIST() function calculates the standardized normal distribution. The NORM.DIST() function requires you to specify a mean and standard deviation. Thus NORM.S.DIST(D13,TRUE) is the same as NORM.DIST(D13,0,1,TRUE).

K. Excel calculates to 16 decimal places so if you want to verify the results in the example use D14 =NORM.S.DIST(ROUND(D13,2),TRUE).

L. Calculate d_2 and $N[d_2]$ in the same way.

M. Name cells D14 and D16 Nd and Ndd, respectively. It would be easier to name them Nd1 and Nd2 but ND1 and ND2 are cell addresses, so they won't work as cell names.

N. Excel has a function EXP(x) that returns e to the x, so D17 = EXP(-rr*t). Name the cell ert.

O. Format so that the decimal places line up. Highlight D10:D17, Shift+Ctrl+1, and increase to 6 decimal places.

Options Prices:

P. Calculate the call price as = S * Nd - X * Ndd * ert.

Q. Calculate the put price as = Call - S + X * ert.

R. Format to dollars and cents (Shift+Ctrl+$) and verify that you calculate $3.93 and $12.69.

Normal Distribution:

S. In the working area of the model we construct the data that drives the graph. We need a normal distribution, so we begin by calculating the mean and standard deviation of the underlying asset—in this case shares of Discovery Café. The mean of the distribution is the current stock price S. The standard deviation over the time to expiry is the stock price $S*\sigma\sqrt{t}$.

T. The price rage we need to generate should span across three standard deviations from the mean. So we begin by setting the first Z to -3. So I3 = -3. Now increment by 0.1, so I4 = ROUND(I3 + 0.1,1). Although we should not have to round, Excel occasionally adds random millionths to numbers if you don't round, and then the mean comes out as 1.53E-15 rather than 0.

U. Copy-drag down to I63. I63 should equal +3 standard deviations from the mean.

V. Calculate the price range as = Mean + Z* standard deviation, so J3 = S + I3*S*$D$12 or equivalently, J3 = S * (1 + I3*$D$12). Verify that J3 is $36.00

W. Copy-drag down to J63. Verify that J63 is $144.

X. Calculate the value of each option at expiry. So K3 = MAX(0,J3-X) and L3 = MAX(0,X-J3).

Y. Calculate the normal distribution. So M3 = NORM.S.DIST(I3,FALSE).

Z. We want to show the probability of each option expiring in-the-money so NCall and NPut relay the normal only if the value of the option is positive. So N3 = IF(K3=0,0,M3) and O3 = IF(L3=0,0,M3).

AA. Copy-drag down to row 63.

Graph

AB. Although we generate two graphs: one for the call and one for the put, it is easiest to generate and format one chart, copy it, and delete the irrelevant series.

AC. Highlight J2:O63. From the Finance Ribbon choose [Chart] [XY Scatter][Scatter with smooth lines] Do not panic, you will get something that looks nothing like the finished product.

AD. Move the normal distribution series to the secondary Y-axis. To do this click in the chart. From [Chart Tools] [Layout] use the drop-down menu at the left end of the ribbon to choose the series Normal. [Format Selection] Under [Series Options] Plot series on Secondary Axis. You will notice that a secondary axis appears on the right hand side of the chart. The secondary axis allows you to plot prices and probabilities in the same chart.

AE. Move NCall and Nput to the secondary axis.

AF. Format the Primary Vertical Axis. Under[Axis Options] set the minimum to 0. When Excel smooths a data series it allows itself to smooth into unrealistic numbers in order to preserve an artistic curve. By setting the minimum to 0 you can prevent negative option prices from accidently creeping into your graph.

AG. Format the Secondary Vertical Axis. Under [Axis Options] set the minimum to 0 and the maximum to 0.40. The normal distribution comes from Z, so we know that the same normal will work wether the stock price is $2, $20, or $200.

AH. Format Call, Put, and Normal according to your own style.

AI. Add drop lines to NCall. To do this select the series. Under [Layout] click on [Error Bars] [More Error

Bar Options]. Under [Vertical Error Bars] select Direction: Minus, End Style: No Cap, and Percentage: 100%. Close. For some bizarre reason Excel also adds Horizontal Error Bars at the same time. So from the [Layout] drop-down list select NCall X Error Bars and hit the Delete button on your keyboard. Finally, format the series and set [Line Color] to No Line. To do this use [Chart Tools] [Format Data Series] [Line Color] [No Line]

AJ. Add drop lines to NPut the same way.

AK. When you have the chart formatted the way you want copy and paste. To do this just select the chart area, Ctrl+C to copy. Click in the spreadsheet somewhere and Ctrl+V to paste.

AL. Remove the put series from the first chart. To do this click in the chart. From the [Chart Tools] [Design] [Select Data]. Remove the series Put and NPut.

AM. Remove the call series from the second chart.

AN. In each chart use [Layout] [Chart Title] to add a chart title. Enter Put or Call.

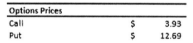

Black-Scholes Options Pricing Model		
Company		Discovery Café
Stock Price	S	$90.00
Exercise Price	X	$100.00
Time to expiry in years	t	91/365
Volatility	sigma	40%
Interest rate	rr	5%

Interim Calculations		
ln (S/X)		(0.105361)
$(r + \sigma^2/2)^*t$		0.032500
$\sigma \sqrt{t}$		0.200000
d_1		(0.364303)
$N[d_1]$	Nd	0.357816
d_2		(0.564303)
$N[d_2]$	Ndd	0.286274
e^{-rt}	ert	0.987578

Options Prices		
Call	$	3.93
Put	$	12.69

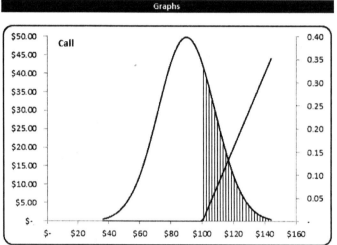

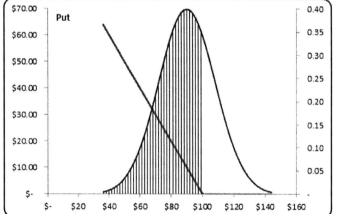

$\mathcal{U}$ p to this point, we have examined markets around the world, discovering how they are similar in more ways than they are different. We have also seen a host of securities that trade in these global markets and seen more differentiation in characteristics and implications from one security to the next.

For example, as we go from forwards and futures to options, we go from contracting obligations to do certain things, to contracting rights to do certain things. It is now time to explore instruments that have parties contracting actions that result in "what if I had done these things".

From swap agreements (that are essentially gains-from-trade economics in the realm of financial instruments) to Interest rate agreements (that combine features of swaps and options) to trading units that attempt to capture, allocate, and value intangibles, we are discovering that markets can allocate factors of production and consumption more efficiently and more effectively than dreamt of in our philosophies.

$\mathcal{A}$ swap is the financial equivalent to a gains-from-trade model in economics. Two counterparties agree to borrow where they have a comparative advantage and then trade cash flows.

Interest rate swap agreements arbitrage differential rates of interest. Plain vanilla swaps are the simplest forms of swap agreements. The agreements are engineered such that the amount of the loan is the same and payments occur on the same date. Fixed-for-floating swaps exchange a fixed rate for a rate that varies with the T-bill rate or LIBOR. Basis swaps exchange one floating rate for another.

Currency swaps exchange payments denominated in one currency for payments denominated in another.

27.1 - Interest Rate Swap Agreements

An interest rate swap is an agreement to exchange interest rate payments on a notional principal amount over a specific period of time. Generally a swap exchanges fixed rate interest payments for floating-rate payments.

❏ **Notional principal amount:** The notional principal is the principal on which payments are based but which is not exchanged.

Example 1:

The Bank of America is a large AAA rated commercial bank. Hypothetical Resources is a BBB rated industrial corporation. Each firm requires $100 million for 10 years, and each firm faces borrowing costs consistent with its credit rating:

Table 27-1: Example Interest Rate Swap: Initial Conditions

	Rating	Bond Rate	Commercial Paper Rate
Bank of America	AAA	10.00%	T-bill + .30%
Hypothetical Resources	BBB	11.90%	T-bill + .80%
Basis point difference	190	50

Note that the lower credit rating costs HR a full 190 basis points in the bond market but only 50 basis points in the commercial paper market.

The Bank of America has a comparative advantage in the bond market. However, it would prefer to stay in the short end of the market because its liabilities are short term. Hypothetical Resources has a comparative advantage in the commercial paper market. However, HR is engaged in long term R&D and would prefer long-term borrowing. The swap allows each company to borrow in the market in which it has a comparative advantage and then trade payments:

❏ Each corporation borrows in the market in which it has a comparative advantage. The Bank of America issues 10-year bonds at 10%, thus committing itself to interest payments of $5 million every six months. Hypothetical Resources issues commercial paper at T-bill plus 80; the commercial paper is running on a 182-day roll.

❑ An intermediary (generally a commercial or investment bank) sets up a swap arrangement on a notional principal amount of $100 million whereby Hypothetical Resources pays the Bank of America 11% and the Bank of America pays T-bill plus 70 basis points. Of this 20 basis points goes to the intermediary and T-bill plus 50 goes to Hypothetical Resources. (We have set up this swap so that the interest payments coincide—payment every six months—but there is no reason why they must.)

❑ **Intermediary:** Entity, generally a commercial or investment bank, that sets up the swap agreement between two counterparties.

❑ **Counterparties:** A counterparty is any legal entity that engages in an over-the-counter securities transaction.

❑ **Counterparty Risk:** Swaps that are negotiated and traded over-the-counter rather than through an exchange have counterparty risk. Because there is no clearing house, counterparty risk refers to the risk that the other party to an agreement may be unable to fulfill its obligations under the contract.

Every six months we have the following cash flows:

Table 27-2: Example Interest Rate Swap Breakdown of Semi-Annual Cash Flows

Bank of America (sells the swap or is short a swap)	
interest on bond issue	- 10.00%
interest received on swap (fixed leg)	+ 11.00%
interest payment on swap (variable leg)	- (T-bill + 0.70)%
Cost of Capital	- (T-bill - 0.30)%
Hypothetical Resources (buys the swap or is long a swap)	
interest on commercial paper	- (T-bill + 0.80)%
interest received on swap (variable leg)	+ (T-bill + 0.50)%
interest payment on swap (fixed leg)	- 11.00%
Cost of Capital	- 11.30%

On the Bank of America we have:

$$\text{Cost of Capital} = -10.00\% + 11.00\% - (\text{T-bill} + 0.70)\%$$
$$= -\text{T-bill} + 0.30\%$$
$$= -(\text{T-bill} - 0.30)\%$$

On Hypothetical resources we have:

$$\textit{Cost of Capital} = -(\text{T-bill} + 0.80)\% + (\text{T-bill} + 0.50)\% - 11.00\%$$
$$= -\text{T-bill} - 0.80\% + \text{T-bill} + 0.50\% - 11.00\%$$
$$= -11.30\%$$

As a result of the swap

❑ The Bank of America buys short-term financing at the T-bill rate less 30 basis points; 60 basis points less than it could do so in the commercial paper market.

❑ Hypothetical Resources buys long-term financing at 11.3%; 60 basis points less than it could do so in the bond market.

This is a credit arbitrage swap.

❑ **Credit Arbitrage Swap:** A credit arbitrage swap is a swap used to take advantage of differences in the credit spread in two segments of the capital market. In Example 1 this difference was between the long and the short market, but there are swaps that arbitrage credit spreads in the U.S. and Eurodollar market, or to alter the cash flow characteristics of the firm's liabilities to better match its assets.

❑ **Basis Rate Swap:** A Basis Rate Swap is a swap in which both counterparties pay floating rates. A simple example is a swap of 1-month T-bill Rate for 6-month T-bill Rate.

Example 2:

The Bank of America and the Bank of Montreal enter into a swap whereby the Bank of Montreal pays Canadian T-bill rate plus 30 basis points and receives U.S. T-bill rate plus 30 basis points.

There are variations on the plain vanilla swap. Each swap is separately negotiated, so the variations can suit the individual counterparties.

❑ **Bullet Swap:** In a bullet swap the notional principal amount is constant over the term of the swap.

❑ **Amortizing Swap:** In an amortizing swap the notional principal decreases over the term of the swap.

❑ **Accreting Swap:** In an accreting swap the notional principal increases over the term of the swap.

❑ **Roller Coaster Swap:** In an roller coaster swap the notional principal amount increases and decreases according to some predetermined formula.

27.1.1 - The Primary Market

The primary market for swap agreements exists through intermediaries, generally large commercial and investment banks, who seek out counterparties and established the terms of the swap agreement. As swaps became more common these intermediaries found themselves taking on the other side of the swap and essentially making a market in swap agreements.

27.1.2 - The Secondary Market

The secondary market for over-the-counter swaps is virtually nonexistent. If the Bank of America wishes to close out its position in the swap above, it has three alternatives:

❑ **Swap reversal:** The Bank of America would set up another swap with Fly-by-Night Industries with exactly the opposite terms of its swap agreement with Hypothetical Resources. If all goes well then the Bank of America acts as nothing more than a conduit for cash flows between Hypothetical Resources and Fly-by-Night. However, if all does not go well with Fly-by-Night then the Bank of America is still obliged to make payments on its swap agreement with HR.

❑ **Swap sale:** The Bank of America sells its side of the swap agreement to Fly-by-Night Industries. However, Hypothetical Resources might refuse to authorize the sale because it would increase the default risk.

❑ **Swap buy-back:** The Bank of America sells its side of the swap agreement back to Hypothetical Resources. Hypothetical Resources would require compensation to allow the Bank out of the swap.

27.1.3 - Exchange Traded Swaps

The CME group trades both futures and options on 5-, 7-, 10-, and 30-year interest rate swaps.

Each swap future is defined as the fixed rate side of an interest rate swap with a notional principal amount of $100,000. The fixed payment is 4% payable semi-annually. The floating side is based on the 3-month LIBOR rate.

At delivery settlement is in cash. The value of the future is the present value of the fixed payment discounted at the swap rate established at expiry by the International Swaps and Derivatives Association (ISDA)

The options contract is defined as the right, but not the obligation, to buy (or sell) a swap futures contract at expiry. Options on swap futures are European: exercisable only on the expiry date. Options are also settled in cash at the same rate as the underlying futures contract at immediate delivery.

❑ **Swaption:** A swaption is an option on a swap agreement.

Table 27-3: Swaption Breakdown of Terms

Call Swaption		If exercised
Buyer	buy a swap	pays a fixed rate an receives a floating rate
Writer	sell a swap	pays a floating rate and receives a fixed rate
Put Swaption		If exercised
Buyer	sell a swap	pays a floating rate and receives a fixed rate
Writer	buy a swap	pays a fixed rate and receives a floating rate

27.2 - Currency Swaps

A currency swap is an agreement to exchange principal and interest in one currency for principal and interest in another currency over a specific period of time.

Example 3:

Boeing is a large triple A rated military and commercial industrial manufacturer. Airlease is a triple B rated industrial leasing and service corporation. Both corporations need $9 million over 10 years.

If Boeing issued 10-year bonds in the United States it would need to promise a yield of 5%. The interest rates in Europe are higher, and if it issued 10-year bonds in Europe it would need to promise a yield of 12.60%. However inflation is higher in Europe, and real interest rates are comparable. Because the money is needed to build facilities in Europe (to compete directly with Airbus) and most of the revenue from its European division would be in euros, Boeing would prefer to borrow this money in euros.

If Airlease issued 10-year bonds in the United States it would need to promise a yield of 7%. If it issued 10 year bonds in Europe it would need to promise a yield of 13.00%. Because most of its revenues are in dollars Airlease would prefer to borrow in dollars.

Table 27-4: Example Currency Swap: Initial Conditions

Exchange Rate: €1 = $0.90	Rating	Rate in Dollars	Rate in Euros
Boeing	AAA	5.00%	12.60%
Airlease	BBB	7.00%	13.00%
Basis point difference: 160		200	40

Note that the lower credit rating costs Airlease a full 200 basis points in the U.S. but only 40 basis points in Europe. This gives us a 160 basis point driver.

27.2.1 - Engineering the Swap

Engineer the swap.

- ❑ Each corporation borrows in the market in which it has a comparative advantage.
  Boeing borrows $9 million and issues 10-year bonds at 5% in the U.S. thus committing itself to coupon payments of $225,000 every six months. Airlease borrows €10 million and issues 10 year bonds at 13.00% in Europe thus committing itself to coupon payments of €650,000 every six months
- ❑ The principal is swapped.
  Boeing swaps the $9 million to Airlease and Airlease swaps €10 million to Boeing. Note that in a currency swap the principal amount (€10 = $9) is swapped.
- ❑ Neutralize the currency risk.
  In this swap we will completely neutralize the currency risk to which the counterparties are exposed. Boeing must pay 5% on a $9 million bond issue so Boeing receives a swap payment of 5% of $9 million. Airlease must pay 13.0% on a €10 million Eurobond issue so Airlease receives a swap payment of 13% of €10 million.
- ❑ Distribute the advantage.
  We have a 160 basis point driver. We decide to give each counterparty 70 basis points and to keep 20 basis points for the intermediary.

If Boeing borrowed directly in the euro market then it would need to pay 12.6%. A 70 basis point advantage puts Boeing's payments at 11.9%. The first part of the swap must exactly neutralize Boeing's 5.0% dollar payments, so we set the Euro payments at 11.9% of €10 million.

If Airlease borrowed directly in the dollar market then it would need to pay 7.0%. A 70 basis point advantage puts Airlease's payments at 6.30%. The second part of the swap must exactly neutralized Airlease's 13.0% euro payments, so we set the dollar payments at 6.3%

The differences between the payment amounts go to the intermediary. The dollar payment is paid by Airlease. On a principal of $9 million Airlease must pay 6.3% and Boeing receives 5.0%. The remaining 1.3% goes to the intermediary. The euro payment is paid by Boeing. On a principal of €10 million Boeing must pay 11.90% and Airlease receives 13.00%. The 1.1% difference must be made up by the intermediary.

Every six months we have the following cash flows:

Table 27-5: Cash Flows under the Currency Swap Agreement in Example 3

Boeing	(borrows $9m and swaps it for €10m)		
interest on $9 bond issue	- 5.0% * $9m	-$225,000.	$ risk neutralized
interest received on swap:	+ 5.0% * $9m	+$225,000.	
interest payment on swap:	- 11.9% * €10m	- € 595,000.	
TOTAL	-11.9% * €10m	- € 595,000.	
Airlease	(borrows €10m and swaps it for $9m)		
interest on €10m bond issue	-13.0% * €10m	- €650,000.	€ risk neutralized
interest received on swap:	+13.0% * €10m	+ €650,000.	
interest payment on swap:	- 6.3% * $9m	- $283,500.	
TOTAL	- 6.3% * $9m	- $283,500.	
Intermediary			
interest received on swap:	1.3% * $9m	+ $58,500.	
interest payment on swap:	1.1% * €10m	- €55,000.	

Figure 27-1: Cash Flow Diagram of the Currency Exchange Swap Semi-Annual Payment Flow

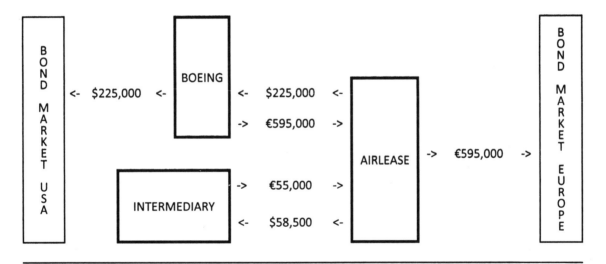

27.2.2 - Currency Risk Exposure

In this swap the two counterparties completely neutralize their currency exchange risk by passing it, in its entirety, to the intermediary. Every six months the intermediary receives $58,500 (1.3% of $9m) and must pay out €55,000 (1.1% of €10m). The rate differential is fixed at 20 basis points, but the value of the transaction in dollars depends on the euro exchange rate.

Although the euro is $0.90 when this swap is engineered, once the euro increases to more than $1.06 the intermediary starts making losses.

In July 2008, the euro approached $1.60. At that rate the intermediary must pay $88,000 for the €55,000 it must pay out to Airlease; generating a loss on the swap of $29,500 for that payment alone.

Figure 27-2: Intermediary Profit per Semi-Annual Period with respect to the Euro-Dollar Exchange Rate

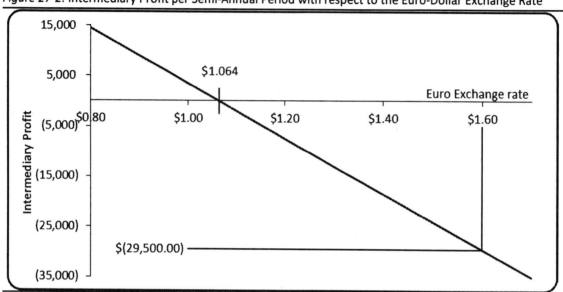

27.3 - Total Return Swaps

In a total return swap separates the credit risk on an asset from other risks by swapping payments based on the value as separate from payments based on contractual terms.

Example 4:

> John Q. Investor holds a $100,000 5-year 6% Discovery Café Bond currently trading at par. In holding the bond he faces interest rate risk and credit risk. Interest rate risk means that if interest rates increase the value of his bond will decrease. Credit risk means that Discovery Café could fail to make the payments on the bond as promised.
>
> JQ enters into a total return swap with the Speculative Hedge Fund. Under the terms of the swap, every six months, JQ pays to SHF the full amount of the coupon payment plus any change in the base value of the bond. In return SHF pays to JQ LIBOR + 0.5%.

❑ **Beneficiary:** The beneficiary of a total return swap is the counterparty seeking to insure against credit risk.

❑ **Return Leg:** The return leg of a total return swap is the interest payment plus change in the value of the reference asset made by the beneficiary.

❑ **Guarantor:** The guarantor in a total return swap takes on the credit risk.

❑ **Funding Leg:** The funding leg of the swap is the variable payment by the guarantor

Example 5:

When the first coupon is due JQ calculates the swap payments. LIBOR is at 5.5% and the Discovery Café bond is still trading at par.

Funding leg:	LIBOR + 0.5%	(5.5 + 0.5) %	$3,000.00
Return Leg:	Coupon payment	6%	($3,000.00)
	Δ Present Value		$0.00
		Net Swap Payment	$0.00

Example 6:

When the second coupon is due the Discovery Café bond is trading at 102 and LIBOR is at 5.2%. The premium on the bond means that the $100,000 bond is now valued at $102,000. JQ has an unrealized gain on the bond of $2,000. This unrealized gain is paid to the guarantor as part of the return leg. As a result JQ must pay the net swap of $2,150 to SHF.

Funding leg:	LIBOR + 0.5%	(5.2 + 0.5) %	$2,850.00
Return Leg:	Coupon payment	6%	($3,000.00)
	Δ Present Value		($2,000.00)
		Net Swap Payment	($2,150.00)

Example 7:

When the third coupon is due the Discovery Café bond is trading at 46 amid rumors of accounting irregularities. LIBOR is at 5.0%. The $100,000 Discovery Café bond is now valued at $46,000. JQ has an unrealized loss on the bond of $56,000. This unrealized loss is transferred to the guarantor as part of the return leg. As a result JQ will receive $54,750 from SHF.

Funding leg:	LIBOR + 0.5%	(5.0 + 0.5) %	$2,750.00
Return Leg:	Coupon payment	6%	($3,000.00)
	Δ Present Value		$55,000.00
		Net Swap Payment	($54,750.00)

The funding leg of the swap means that JQ still faces interest rate risk, but without facing credit risk.

27.4 - Credit Default Swaps

A credit default swap is similar to simple insurance in a market where insurance would normally not exist.

Example 8:

John Q. Investor holds a $100,000 5-year 6% Discovery Café bond currently trading at par.

JQ enters into a credit default swap with the Speculative Hedge Fund. Under the terms of the swap JQ pays a spread of 1% with quarterly payment dates on a notional principal amount of $100,000. The reference asset is the Discovery Café bond.

Every three months JQ pays $250 (¼ of 1% of $100,000) to SHF. When the Discovery Café bond declines to 46 JQ must still pay $250. Until Discovery Café misses a payment or declares bankruptcy, there is no credit event to trigger the payment from SHF to JQ to cover his losses.

Unlike the total return swap, a Credit Default Swap protects against default, not against a decline in value.

2008: AIG Bailout

American International Group (AIG) is a multinational insurance holding company based in New York. It is a federally-regulated holding company which owned 27 different state-regulated insurance companies and operated in 130 countries world wide.

AIG Financial Products, based in London, had issued credit default swaps on over $144 billion of structured securities backed by subprime mortgage loans. Issued when these securities were rated AAA the credit default swaps brought in nowhere near the funds that were required to realistically insure the securities. AIG was in trouble.

S&P placed AIG on credit watch. As a result several AIG subsidiaries were unable to roll their maturing commercial paper. The subsidiaries called on the parent company for financing.

On September 15, 2008 (the day after Lehman Brothers filed for bankruptcy), S&P downgraded AIG to A- with a warning that it was on credit watch for a possible further downgrade to somewhere in the BBB range—essentially removing it from investment grade. Moody's and Fitch followed suit. Counterparties to various swap arrangements withheld payments, and AIG was unable to borrow in the market. On the same day, insurance regulators informed AIG that it would be unable to borrow funds from its subsidiaries. The insurance companies were regulated, and the regulators did not want an insurance debacle on their hands.

As a result of the ratings downgrade, AIG was required to deposit additional collateral on swap positions outstanding. They were unable to do so. AIG shares fell to $1.25 from a high of $72.97 in December 2006.

On September 16, 2008, the Federal Reserve Bank of New York authorized a $85 loan at LIBOR + 8.5% with AIG's questionable assets as collateral. The loan also included warrants (long-term options to buy) on 79.9% of AIG. It allowed the U.S. government to stop any payments to existing shareholders. AIG needed another $27.8 billion credit facility in October. The terms and amounts were changed as AIG struggled with payments to counterparties.

In March 2009 AIG reported to Congress on where the bulk of the loan—taxpayer money—had gone. The list consists of banks and investment banks in the U.S. and Europe: $4.1 billion to Societe General, $2.6 billion to Deutsche Bank, $2.5 billion to Goldman Sachs, $1.8 billion to Merrill Lynch, and the list goes on[1].

Further reading:
  Roger Lowenstein, *The End of Wall Street*, New York: Penguin Press, 2010
  Andrew Ross Sorkin, *Too Big To Fail*, New York: New York: Viking Penguin, 2009

---

1   AIG Attachment A - Collateral Postings Under AIGFP CDS
     http://www.aig.com/aigweb/internet/en/files/CounterpartyAttachments031809_tcm385-155645.pdf

---

2012: Greek Sovereign Debt Restructuring

In 2011 Greek National Debt reached 166% of GDP. Doubts that Greece would ever be able to make full payment on the this debt triggered an increase in rates demanded on Greek Government Bonds. At the end of 2011 the rate on Greek government debt was 34.47% on the 10-year and 132.27% on the 2 year. The comparable rate on 2-year U.S. Treasuries was 0.26%[2].

Most of the Greek government debt was held in the banking system. European Banks marked these securities as "held to maturity" and valued at par. In July 2011 the Troika (the European Commission (EC), the International Monetary Fund (IMF), and the European Central bank (ECB)), agreed that Greece's bonds should be marked to market at 21% discount from book. In October 2011 this haircut was increased to 50%. On March 1, 2012, 85.8% of private sector (banks count as private sector, but the European Central bank does not) agreed to a 70% write-down of both principal and interest. Approximately €172 billion in debt was tendered for exchange.

The International Swaps and Derivative Association (ISDA) ruled that the "voluntary" haircut does not constitute a credit event. Credit default swaps on Greek debt did not trigger. Critics pointed out that the ISDA consists of representatives Bank of America, Barclays, BNP Paribas, Citibank, Credit Suisse, Deutsche Bank, Goldman Sachs, JPMorgan Chase, Morgan Stanley, and UBS: all institutions that generally sold credit default swaps. CDS positions are not publicly known so it is impossible to substantiate the accusations. Nonetheless, the failure to trigger a credit event caused much concern about the validity of credit default swap agreements.

Greece triggered a collective action clause in bonds issued under Greek law that forced the remaining bondholders to accept the restructuring. On March 9, 2012, the ISDA ruled that the collective action clause, by imposing an non-voluntary restructuring, triggered a credit event and triggered the Credit Default Swaps.

Both these rulings by the ISDA will have an effect on bondholders' willingness to allow a voluntary restructuring of debt covered by credit default swaps.

27.5 - Interest Rate Agreements

Interest rate agreements combine features of options and swaps. They look and act like a series of options but can take the place of a swap agreement in managing interest rate risk.

27.5.1 - Ceilings and Floors

An interest rate agreement is essentially interest rate insurance. The buyer pays a premium and receives in return a structured payment if and only if specific conditions are met.

---

2   E. Oltheten, T. Sougiannis, N. Travlos, & S. Zarkos, "Greece in the Eurozone: Lessons from a Decade of Experience" Working paper, SSRN id=2066125

❑ **Ceiling, Cap:** In an interest rate cap or ceiling the buyer pays a premium and, in return, is compensated by the seller if the interest rate rises above a specified strike rate.

❑ **Floor:** In an interest rate floor the buyer pays a premium and, in return, is compensated by the seller if the interest rate falls below a specified strike rate.

❑ **Strike Rate:** The strike rate is the reference rate in an interest rate agreement.

❑ **Notional Principal Amount:** The notional principal is the dollar amount on which swap and interest rate agreements are based.

Example 9:

On January 1 Tardis Intertemporal buys an interest rate cap from the Illinois Commercial Bank. The reference rate for the agreement is the 90-day T-bill rate, and the cap is set at 6%. The agreement is for quarterly settlement for one year and the notional principal amount is $1 million.

Table 27-6: Payments under a One-Year, Quarterly-Payment Interest Rate Cap at 6%

Date	T-bill Rate	Payment	
April 1	5.9%	$0.	
July 1	6.1%	$250.	= (0.1% * $1m) /4
October 1	6.8%	$2,000.	= (0.8% * $1m) /4
January 1	5.9%	$0.	

27.5.2 - Caplets

An interest rate cap can be seen as a series of options called caplets, each with the same strike rate but a different expiry date. Each caplet can be valued using the Black-Scholes option pricing model and the aggregate used to value the interest rate agreement as a whole.

Example 10:

The Interest Rate Cap purchased by Tardis Intertemporal in example 9 can be seen as four caplets. The first is call option with a strike rate of 6%, an expiry date of April 1, and a contract definition of $250,000 ($1m/4).

The second caplet is identical but with an expiry date of July 1.

27.5.3 - Collars

Interest rate floors and ceilings can be combined to form a collar.

Example 11:

> Hypothetical Resources finds itself in a position where, if the interest rate goes up over 6%, it is in deep financial trouble. However, if the interest rate goes down, its fixed income asset values increase substantially. HR can now set up a collar by buying an interest rate cap at 6% and financing the cap by selling a floor at 4%. If the interest rate goes up over 6%, the cap pays off, mitigating the firm's financial woes. If the interest rate goes down below 4% the increased value of the firm's bond holdings can be used to make payments on the floor.

2012: JP Morgan Trading Losses

On May 10, 2012, after the markets closed for the day, Jamie Dimon CEO of JP Morgan Chase announced that the firm lost $2 billion in a trading portfolio designed to hedge credit risk. The credit risk the bank assumed was in its portfolio of commercial lending to businesses that might be adversely affected by a weakening European economy. So the hedge was set to bet on a weakening Europe. But was it a hedge or a speculation?

Within days of the announcement, Ina Drew, the firm's Chief Investment Officer and head of risk management stepped down from her job, and the drama began. Specific trades were not made public, but a series of news reports and interviews with large market participants pieced together a plausible scenario as follows:

Late in 2011 the bank became bearish on the global economy, and concern for losses on business loans they had made prompted the first trade. To hedge this potential loan loss exposure, the trading/risk management office in London purchased Credit Default Swaps (CDS) on low quality bonds. These would rise in value if lower quality bonds became more stressed with a weakening economy. It was anticipated that this gain would offset rising loan losses on the bank's loan portfolio. (This strategy sounds like a hedge so far.)

However, sometime early February 2012, rising stock prices and what appeared to be positive global economic news caused a change in the outlook of the bank's management. If the economy did improve, their loans would not have the earlier feared losses, and the CDS hedge would not be needed. Worse, the value of the CDSs they purchased would fall if the economy improved. However, rather than sell the CDS contracts it had purchased earlier, the London office decided to reverse the effect through a multi-leg trade in CDS contracts on two different bond indices in a spread strategy (selling one, buying another). It is assumed they sold CDS contracts going out to the end of 2017 on an index of high quality bonds (taking in revenue by assuming the risk of high quality bonds going into default) and simultaneously, buying some CDS contracts going out to the end of 2012 on an index of low quality bonds. In essence, the view was that the spread between the two was too wide, and if the global economy was actually improving, the spread should narrow, causing an overall profit to their spread position. (This strategy sounds like the same kind of speculation that took down Long Term Capital Management in 1998.)

The size of the positions caught market participants off guard. Rumors of the "London Whale" (the nickname for one of the more well-known JPM traders in their London office) making huge bets in the credit spread markets swirled, but drew little attention outside of the trading community. By May, a quick decline in investor confidence, falling global stock prices, and worries over Greece leaving the euro caused credit spreads to widen. JP Morgan's short positions (default protection out to 2017) were hugely more expensive, but the long positions (default protection only through 2012) did not rise nearly as much. The widening of this spread resulted in the $2 billion loss the company announced on Thursday May 10, after the U.S. markets had closed. The following day JP Morgan Chase common stock lost 9% of its market value. By June estimates of the JPM 2nd quarter losses increased to $4.2 billion.

Chapter 27 - Questions and Problems

27-1:

The Bank of Champaign buys a swap arrangement from The Bank of Urbana on a notional principal of $100 million, with payments every six months for five years. The buyer pays a fixed rate of 9.05% and receives the London InterBank Offered Rate (LIBOR). The seller pays LIBOR and receives 9.0%.

A.   On the first payment date LIBOR is 6.5%. What is each party's payment and receipt on this date?

27-2:

Busey Bank can borrow money in the ten-year bond market at 10% and in the six-month corporate note market at the T-bill rate plus 0.40%. Technology Transfer Inc can borrow in the ten-year bond market at 12% and in the six-month corporate note market at the T-bill rate plus 1.0%.

A.   Busey Bank has a advantage of how many points in each market?

B.   In what market does Busey have a comparative advantage?

Set up a swap agreement such that Busey and Tech Transfer Inc. each borrow $1,000,000 in the market where they have the comparative advantage and then execute a swap whereby Tech Transfer pays 11.1% and Busey pays T-bill plus 0.5%. The Intermediary takes .1% off the fixed payment (Tech Transfer pays 11.1% and Busey receives 11.0%). Payments are made every six months.

C.   How much of a basis point advantage does each party get from the swap?

D.   What is the notional principal amount?

At the end of six months the T-bill rate is 9%.

E.   Calculate each party's payment and receipt (description, percentage, and amount) on this date. (Don't forget to include payments on corporate debt issued and that this is a semi-annual payment.)

27-3:

The Chase Manhattan Bank can borrow money in the ten-year bond market at 10% and in the six-month corporate note market at the T-bill rate plus 1.0% Tardis Intertemporal can borrow in the ten year bond market at 12% and in the six month corporate note market at the T-bill rate plus 1.8%. Each corporation anticipates a bond issue of $10 million.

A.   The Chase Manhattan has an advantage of how many basis points in each market?

B.   In what market does the Chase Manhattan have the comparative advantage?

C.   Set up a swap agreement such that the gains from trade are the same for both parties. Since you are setting up this swap as part of your graduation requirements the intermediary gets nothing. (Start by having each corporation borrow in the market where it has a competitive advantage and set the fixed payment at 11.0%.)

D.   At the end of six months the T-bill rate is 7.0%. What are the payments and receipts for each party in the swap agreement?

27-4:

Johnson & Johnson (JNJ), rated AAA, can borrow in the U.S. bond market at 5% and in the European bond market 8.6%. The Ford Motor Company (F), rated A, can borrow in the U.S. bond market at 7% and in the European bond market 9.0%. Johnson & Johnson requires €10m over ten years, and Ford requires $9m over ten years. The current rate of exchange is €1 = $0.90

A.   Set up the swap such that the intermediary takes on the entire currency exchange risk and gets 40 basis points advantage. The gains from trade are the same for both counterparties. Specify the semi-annual payments.

B.   The intermediary calculates that the exchange rate measured in the dollar price per euro has a mean of $0.90 and a standard deviation of $0.15 over the relevant period. Assuming that the exchange rate on the euro is normally distributed, graph the semi-annual payment in dollars and the risk facing the intermediary.

C.   At what exchange rate does the intermediary break even?

D.   As part of your risk analysis do a stress test: calculate the loss to the Intermediary under a five sigma event.

27-5:

On January 1, 2006, Hypothetical Resources buys an interest rate floor from the Illinois Commercial Bank paying $1,000. The reference rate for the agreement is the 90-day T-bill rate, and the floor is set at 4%. The agreement is for monthly settlement for six months, and the notional principal amount is $3 million.

Table 27-7: 90-Day T-bill Rates

Date	Rate	Payment
February 1	4.2%	
March 1	4.0%	
April 1	3.9%	
May 1	3.8%	
June 1	3.9%	
July 1	4.1%	

The T-bill rates are given in Table 27-7.

A. Calculate the payment for each month.

B. What is the present value of this interest rate agreement? Assume that the rate on the first of the month reflects the interest rate for the previous month and compound monthly.

C. Was the price Tardis Intertemporal paid for the interest rate agreement a fair one?

27-6:

On January 1 Tardis Intertemporal sets up a collar, buying an interest rate ceiling from the Illinois Commercial Bank at 7% and selling a floor to Busey Bank at 5%. Payments are made quarterly on a notional principal amount of $10,000, and the net expenditure on the floor and ceiling cancel out.

The reference rate on both agreements is the 30-day T-bill Rate. The rate on January 1 is 6%. Tardis Intertemporal's CFO expects the 30-day T-bill rate to remain at 6% but concedes that this might be wrong. He estimates a standard deviation on the 30-day T-bill rate is 10% per annum.

A. What is the standard deviation of the 30-day T-bill rate over the two-year period?

B. Graph the payout and risk profile of the collar based on the assumption that the 30-day T-bill rate is normally distributed.

$\mathcal{E}$ ven among commodities futures, less than 2% of contracts actually go to delivery. This fact, more than any other, emphasizes the role of futures and options markets in the management and allocation of price risk. Hedgers use the market to offset the price risk they face as producers and consumers. Speculators take on the risk hedgers bring to market, hoping to make a profit to compensate for the risk they agree to take. Arbitrageurs provide the means by which prices are disseminated from one market to another.

The derivatives markets opened a new chapter in market innovation with the creation of tradeable pollution rights.

Markets are efficient only when they reflect available information; markets fail when there are factors of production that have no market cost or price. So the cost of production does not incorporate the fish freely available in the ocean, the water freely flowing in the river, the air into which we freely dump our wastes, et cetera. Even the price of gasoline does not incorporate the cost of protecting sovereign rights in the part of the world where most of the oil derives.

In economics, when the marginal cost of any factor is zero, it tends to be used to the point where the marginal benefit is also zero—even to point of extinction. The true cost of these factors of production are not zero, but they are zero to the households and firms that make decisions.

There are four broad categories of response. One, markets can simply be allowed to fail. Two, governments can intervene directly. Wildlife preserves, catch limits on fish and game, and emission standards on automobiles fall into this category of response. Three, governments can impose an artificial price that may or may not be close to the actual cost to the economy. Gasoline taxes and license fees fall into this category. Four, governments can impose a cap-and-trade program whereby markets allocate these resources according to the price mechanism, essentially imposing market discipline where one does not exist by nature. Tradeable pollution rights fall into this category.

28.1 - Pollution Allowances

Pollution allowances are tradeable sulfur dioxide (SO_2) and nitrogen oxide (NO_x) emission permits. The permits were created under the Acid Rain Program in Title IV of the Clean Air Act of 1990. Under the program permits were defined and issued based on the emissions in the period 1987 to 1989 and issued for 1995. This essentially caps 1995 emissions at the 1987–1989 level.

Permits are defined by year. One 1995 permits allows the holder to emit 1 ton of SO_2 in 1995 or to bank the credit for use thereafter. Thus emissions in 2012 can thus be paid for with permits dated 2012 or banked permits from previous years; but not against 2013 permits.

The Environmental Protection Agency (EPA) reserves some 2.8% of the total annual permit allocation for auction on an annual basis. Every year the EPA auctions both spot and seven-year forward permits. Thus permits covering emissions in 2012 and in 2019 were auctioned in March 2012. Firms can hold the permits and turn them in to the EPA to cover their emissions in the designated year or sell them.

The auctions were administered by the Chicago Board of Trade (CBOT) for the 13 years ending March 2005 after which the CBOT withdrew its services.[1] The EPA now administers the auctions. Secondary trading occurs over-the-counter or over electronic markets.

Pollution rights work as follows:

Example 1:

> Tardis Intertemporal emits 1200 tons of SO_2 every year. The EPA mandates a 10% reduction to 1080 tons per year and issues 1080 to TI according to this mandate.
>
> TI estimates that installing clean air technology sufficient to reduce its emissions by the required 120 tons per year will cost $800 per ton per year, for a total cost of $96,000.
>
> SO_2 permits trade at $600. Tardis Intertemporal buys 120 permits for a total of $72,000 and continues to emit 1200 tons of SO_2

Example 2:

> Hypothetical Resources also emits 1200 tons of SO_2 every year. The EPA mandates a 10% reduction to 1080 tons per year and is also issued 1080 SO_2 permits.
>
> HR estimates that installing clean air technology sufficient to reduce its emissions by the required 120 tons per year will cost $400 per ton per year, for a total cost of $48,000.
>
> SO_2 permits trade at $600. Hypothetical Resources installs the clean air technology, incurring a cost of $96,000 and reducing its emissions to 960 tons per year. HR sells the extra 120 SO_2 permits, generating revenues of $72,000.

Without pollution allowances, if the EPA mandates a 10% across the board reduction in SO_2 emissions, and the reductions are enforceable, the emissions are reduced from a 2400 tons to 2160 tons per year, but at a total cost to the economy of $144,000.

By allowing the companies to trade pollution allowances total emissions are still reduced to 2160 tons per year, but at a total cost to the economy of $96,000. The market mechanism provides incentives for the burden of emissions reductions to fall on the firms with the lowest costs of emissions reductions. By allowing HR to sell its unused permits, it provided an incentive to spend the money necessary to reduce its emissions.

With permits trading at $600 per ton, firms able to reduce emissions for less than this amount will have the incentive to do so.

Under the "Cap and Trade" system, the right to discard production waste becomes a cost of production just like interest on capital. Firms are thus exposed to a price risk. Markets are also used to manage this risk.

---

1   The Chicago Board of Trade was not compensated by the EPA for hosting the auction, nor was it permitted to charge fees of any kind. Apparently the EPA did not fully understand the nature of the price mechanism they were seeking to use.

On April 2, 2012 the CME Group acquired the Green Exchange (GreenX). GreenX trades options and futures on U.S. and European allowances. These include emissions allowances (SO_2, NOx) and Regional Greenhouse Gas Initiative carbon allowances (RGGI), as well as EU carbon allowances (EUA) and U.N.-certified carbon offsets (CER).

SO_2 Permit Price per Ton as Determined in the Annual EPA Auction

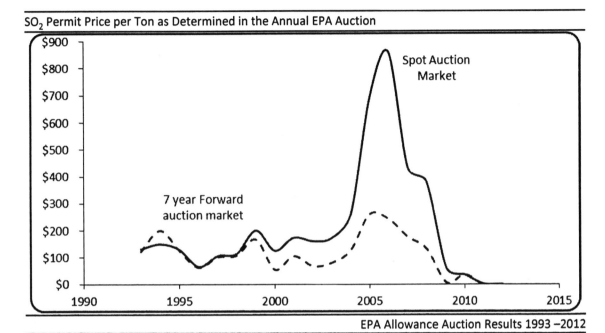

EPA Allowance Auction Results 1993 –2012

The prices have fallen dramatically, from $860.07 in 2006 to $0.56 in the March 2012 auction. This is attributed to several factors: overall demand for electricity declined, new technology made pollution control more cost effective than 2006 prices would suggest, and historically low natural gas prices prompted the conversion to cleaner technology. It was simply less expensive to convert to natural gas than to stay with coal and either install scrubbers or buy emission allowances. This left an overhang of unused emission allowances in the market, depressing prices.

In addition, there have been a number of legal challenges. In July 2008 the DC Court of Appeals struck down the Clear Air Interstate Rule (CAIR), which was designed to address the problem of pollution drifts from one state to another. On December 30, 2011 the U.S. Court of Appeals prevented the implementation of the Cross-State Air Pollution Rule (CSAPR) designed to replace CAIR. While the court battle continues, the uncertainty as to the validity of emission allowances under the original rule, CAIR, and CSAPR leaves the demand for existing allowances weak.

28.1.1 - The European Union Emission Trading Scheme (ETS)

In January 2005 the European Union launched the largest multinational, greenhouse gas emissions trading system in the world. The Emission Trading Scheme (EU ETS), involves some 11,000 power stations, factories, and refineries in all 27 countries in the EU plus Norway, Iceland, and Lichtenstein, is a cap and trade system, but there are no annual auctions, member countries frequently overallocate allowances, and markets are volatile. There is a proposal that the allowances be issued by the EU rather than by each country separately, but this proposal has not yet been implemented.

The Kyoto protocol to the United Nations Framework Convention on Climate Change (UNFCCC) commits its participating countries to a similar cap and trade system, with the UNFCCC setting caps for each nation. It provides the possibility of developing countries generating revenue from the sale of pollution credits rather than developing the industries that create the pollution.

The United States signed the Kyoto Protocol but never ratified it. Pollution rights trade in established markets, and we now have options and futures on pollution rights to manage the price risk involved. As the market for pollution rights under the Kyoto Protocol develop, the possibility exists that arbitrageurs will become active, trading rights in multiple markets, to equalize the marginal price of reducing emissions or using energy across regional and national economies.

2011: €30 million Emission Unit Fraud

On January 19, 2011 the European Union market for pollution allowances was closed after hackers stole just under €30 million of emission allowances from the accounts of Austria, the Czech Republic, Estonia, Greece, and Poland.

In March 2010, the Hungarian government was found to have sold units already used and surrendered.

Implementing computer security protocols and a common registry of allowances are simple ways to address these problems.

28.2 - Drop Options

The use of markets to allocate resources where markets fail is not limited to pollution rights, or free-access natural resources. One area where such markets might be used is in the allocation of rights to drop, or de-register for, a university course during and after registration.

In the allocation to students of scarce resources—in this case seats in class—markets fail. They fail largely because there is no cost to the student of dropping the course. There is a drop date past which, theoretically, a student can not drop. But this constraint is rarely binding. Because there is no cost to dropping a class, the right to drop is exercised to the point where the marginal benefit is zero.

To the university, however, drops are very costly. By the time the student drops a course, the seat he vacates is of no use to anyone else; registration is over, and alternate choices have been forced. There is no longer an opportunity to allocate the seat to a student who might actually have finished the class and earned a grade.

Assume the University launches a "cap and trade" system similar to that under which pollution rights are issued and traded. Every student entering the University is granted, issued to his registration account, two drop options. The drop option remains on the student's registration account until it is either used or traded.

Example 3:

Joe is a well motivated student who plans his program of study, and follows it. In the second semester of his final year he offers both his drop options on the market, and sells them for $300 each.

Example 4:

David is a less well motivated student. He goes all the way to the final week of his sophomore year and decides that engineering is not for him. He drops both his engineering courses as well as the creative writing course he took because he thought it would be an easy A. To do so, he uses both his own drop tickets and buys a third in the market for $300.

Example 5:

Anne is no more of an engineer than is David. In the same week of her sophomore year Anne comes to this realization as well. However, she finishes the courses in which she is registered, takes the grades, and transfers to liberal arts.

Example 6:

George is a senior. He uses his senior standing to register for courses that are regularly full before juniors are quite through with registration. Then, after the class has been closed to registration, he uses simultaneous drop and add technique to get his friend Mary, a sophomore, into the class. George is shocked to discover that one of his drop options has just been marked as used and cancelled.

The university monitors the trading in drop tickets as the price increases to $1200. It estimates that the cost to the university of an empty seat in class is $1000. It therefore issues 100 more drop tickets and sells them on the market. The price declines. The university then uses the revenue generated to open another section of the class in high demand.

Standardized Normal Distribution

$(Z < 0)$

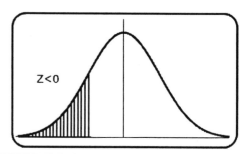

z	0.00	0.01	0.02	0.03	0.04	0.05	0.06	0.07	0.08	0.09
0.0	0.50000	0.49601	0.49202	0.48803	0.48405	0.48006	0.47608	0.47210	0.46812	0.46414
-0.1	0.46017	0.45620	0.45224	0.44828	0.44433	0.44038	0.43644	0.43251	0.42858	0.42465
-0.2	0.42074	0.41683	0.41294	0.40905	0.40517	0.40129	0.39743	0.39358	0.38974	0.38591
-0.3	0.38209	0.37828	0.37448	0.37070	0.36693	0.36317	0.35942	0.35569	0.35197	0.34827
-0.4	0.34458	0.34090	0.33724	0.33360	0.32997	0.32636	0.32276	0.31918	0.31561	0.31207
-0.5	0.30854	0.30503	0.30153	0.29806	0.29460	0.29116	0.28774	0.28434	0.28096	0.27760
-0.6	0.27425	0.27093	0.26763	0.26435	0.26109	0.25785	0.25463	0.25143	0.24825	0.24510
-0.7	0.24196	0.23885	0.23576	0.23270	0.22965	0.22663	0.22363	0.22065	0.21770	0.21476
-0.8	0.21186	0.20897	0.20611	0.20327	0.20045	0.19766	0.19489	0.19215	0.18943	0.18673
-0.9	0.18406	0.18141	0.17879	0.17619	0.17361	0.17106	0.16853	0.16602	0.16354	0.16109
-1.0	0.15866	0.15625	0.15386	0.15151	0.14917	0.14686	0.14457	0.14231	0.14007	0.13786
-1.1	0.13567	0.13350	0.13136	0.12924	0.12714	0.12507	0.12302	0.12100	0.11900	0.11702
-1.2	0.11507	0.11314	0.11123	0.10935	0.10749	0.10565	0.10383	0.10204	0.10027	0.09853
-1.3	0.09680	0.09510	0.09342	0.09176	0.09012	0.08851	0.08692	0.08534	0.08379	0.08226
-1.4	0.08076	0.07927	0.07780	0.07636	0.07493	0.07353	0.07215	0.07078	0.06944	0.06811
-1.5	0.06681	0.06552	0.06426	0.06301	0.06178	0.06057	0.05938	0.05821	0.05705	0.05592
-1.6	0.05480	0.05370	0.05262	0.05155	0.05050	0.04947	0.04846	0.04746	0.04648	0.04551
-1.7	0.04457	0.04363	0.04272	0.04182	0.04093	0.04006	0.03920	0.03836	0.03754	0.03673
-1.8	0.03593	0.03515	0.03438	0.03362	0.03288	0.03216	0.03144	0.03074	0.03005	0.02938
-1.9	0.02872	0.02807	0.02743	0.02680	0.02619	0.02559	0.02500	0.02442	0.02385	0.02330
-2.0	0.02275	0.02222	0.02169	0.02118	0.02068	0.02018	0.01970	0.01923	0.01876	0.01831
-2.1	0.01786	0.01743	0.01700	0.01659	0.01618	0.01578	0.01539	0.01500	0.01463	0.01426
-2.2	0.01390	0.01355	0.01321	0.01287	0.01255	0.01222	0.01191	0.01160	0.01130	0.01101
-2.3	0.01072	0.01044	0.01017	0.00990	0.00964	0.00939	0.00914	0.00889	0.00866	0.00842
-2.4	0.00820	0.00798	0.00776	0.00755	0.00734	0.00714	0.00695	0.00676	0.00657	0.00639
-2.5	0.00621	0.00604	0.00587	0.00570	0.00554	0.00539	0.00523	0.00508	0.00494	0.00480
-2.6	0.00466	0.00453	0.00440	0.00427	0.00415	0.00402	0.00391	0.00379	0.00368	0.00357
-2.7	0.00347	0.00336	0.00326	0.00317	0.00307	0.00298	0.00289	0.00280	0.00272	0.00264
-2.8	0.00256	0.00248	0.00240	0.00233	0.00226	0.00219	0.00212	0.00205	0.00199	0.00193
-2.9	0.00187	0.00181	0.00175	0.00169	0.00164	0.00159	0.00154	0.00149	0.00144	0.00139
-3.0	0.00135	0.00131	0.00126	0.00122	0.00118	0.00114	0.00111	0.00107	0.00104	0.00100

Standardized Normal Distribution

(Z > 0)

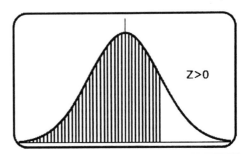

z	0.00	0.01	0.02	0.03	0.04	0.05	0.06	0.07	0.08	0.09
0.0	0.50000	0.50399	0.50798	0.51197	0.51600	0.51994	0.52392	0.52790	0.53188	0.53586
0.1	0.53983	0.54380	0.54776	0.55172	0.55600	0.55962	0.56356	0.56749	0.57142	0.57535
0.2	0.57926	0.58317	0.58706	0.59095	0.59500	0.59871	0.60257	0.60642	0.61026	0.61409
0.3	0.61791	0.62172	0.62552	0.62930	0.63300	0.63683	0.64058	0.64431	0.64803	0.65173
0.4	0.65542	0.65910	0.66276	0.66640	0.67000	0.67364	0.67724	0.68082	0.68439	0.68793
0.5	0.69146	0.69497	0.69847	0.70194	0.70500	0.70884	0.71226	0.71566	0.71904	0.72240
0.6	0.72575	0.72907	0.73237	0.73565	0.73900	0.74215	0.74537	0.74857	0.75175	0.75490
0.7	0.75804	0.76115	0.76424	0.76730	0.77000	0.77337	0.77637	0.77935	0.78230	0.78524
0.8	0.78814	0.79103	0.79389	0.79673	0.80000	0.80234	0.80511	0.80785	0.81057	0.81327
0.9	0.81594	0.81859	0.82121	0.82381	0.82600	0.82894	0.83147	0.83398	0.83646	0.83891
1.0	0.84134	0.84375	0.84614	0.84849	0.85100	0.85314	0.85543	0.85769	0.85993	0.86214
1.1	0.86433	0.86650	0.86864	0.87076	0.87300	0.87493	0.87698	0.87900	0.88100	0.88298
1.2	0.88493	0.88686	0.88877	0.89065	0.89300	0.89435	0.89617	0.89796	0.89973	0.90147
1.3	0.90320	0.90490	0.90658	0.90824	0.91000	0.91149	0.91308	0.91466	0.91621	0.91774
1.4	0.91924	0.92073	0.92220	0.92364	0.92500	0.92647	0.92785	0.92922	0.93056	0.93189
1.5	0.93319	0.93448	0.93574	0.93699	0.93800	0.93943	0.94062	0.94179	0.94295	0.94408
1.6	0.94520	0.94630	0.94738	0.94845	0.95000	0.95053	0.95154	0.95254	0.95352	0.95449
1.7	0.95543	0.95637	0.95728	0.95818	0.95900	0.95994	0.96080	0.96164	0.96246	0.96327
1.8	0.96407	0.96485	0.96562	0.96638	0.96700	0.96784	0.96856	0.96926	0.96995	0.97062
1.9	0.97128	0.97193	0.97257	0.97320	0.97400	0.97441	0.97500	0.97558	0.97615	0.97670
2.0	0.97725	0.97778	0.97831	0.97882	0.97900	0.97982	0.98030	0.98077	0.98124	0.98169
2.1	0.98214	0.98257	0.98300	0.98341	0.98400	0.98422	0.98461	0.98500	0.98537	0.98574
2.2	0.98610	0.98645	0.98679	0.98713	0.98700	0.98778	0.98809	0.98840	0.98870	0.98899
2.3	0.98928	0.98956	0.98983	0.99010	0.99000	0.99061	0.99086	0.99111	0.99134	0.99158
2.4	0.99180	0.99202	0.99224	0.99245	0.99300	0.99286	0.99305	0.99324	0.99343	0.99361
2.5	0.99379	0.99396	0.99413	0.99430	0.99400	0.99461	0.99477	0.99492	0.99506	0.99520
2.6	0.99534	0.99547	0.99560	0.99573	0.99600	0.99598	0.99609	0.99621	0.99632	0.99643
2.7	0.99653	0.99664	0.99674	0.99683	0.99700	0.99702	0.99711	0.99720	0.99728	0.99736
2.8	0.99744	0.99752	0.99760	0.99767	0.99800	0.99781	0.99788	0.99795	0.99801	0.99807
2.9	0.99813	0.99819	0.99825	0.99831	0.99800	0.99841	0.99846	0.99851	0.99856	0.99861
3.0	0.99865	0.99869	0.99874	0.99878	0.99900	0.99886	0.99889	0.99893	0.99896	0.99900

Formulae

$$R = 1 + r = \frac{V_1}{V_0}$$

$$R = 1 + r = \frac{\left[V_1 - \dfrac{date}{days} * cash\ flow \right]}{\left[V_0 + \dfrac{days - date}{days} * cash\ flow \right]}$$

Coefficient of Variation $\quad CV = \dfrac{\sigma}{E[R]}$

$$\sigma^2 = E[X^2] - E[X]^2$$

Variance $\quad \sigma^2 = E[X^2] - E[X]^2$

$$\rho_{x,y} = \frac{Cov_{x,y}}{\sigma_x\ \sigma_y}$$

Market Model $\quad R_s = \alpha + \beta\ R_{Market}$

$$\beta = \frac{n \sum xy - \sum x \sum y}{n \sum x^2 - (\sum x)^2}$$

CAPM $\quad E[R] = r_f + \beta \left(E[R_M] - r_f \right)$

$$\alpha = \frac{\sum y - \beta \sum x}{n}$$

$$Index_{Price} = \frac{\sum_{i=1}^{30} P_{it}}{D_t}$$

$$Index_{Geometric} = \left[\prod_{i=1}^{N} \frac{P_{it}}{P_{i\ t-1}} \right]^{\frac{1}{N}} * Index_{t-1}$$

$$Index_{Value} = \frac{\sum_{i=1}^{N} P_{it}\ Q_{it}}{\sum_{i=1}^{N} P_{i\ (base)}\ Q_{i\ (base)}} * 100$$

$$Index_{Arithmetic} = \frac{\sum_{i=1}^{N} \dfrac{P_{it}}{P_{i\ t-1}}}{N} * Index_{t-1}$$

$$Discount\ Paper:\ Price = Face \left(1 - rate\ \frac{days}{360} \right)$$

$$Yd_{MoneyMarket} = \frac{Interest}{Investment} * \frac{360}{days}$$

$$Money\ Market\ Interest:\ Maturity = Face \left(1 + rate\ \frac{days}{360} \right)$$

$$Yd_{Straight} = \frac{Interest}{Investment} * \frac{365}{days}$$

$$Y_{ASK} = \frac{-days \pm \sqrt{days^2 + 730(days-182.5)\dfrac{Interest}{Investment}}}{(days-182.5)}$$

$$Present\ Value = \sum_{t=1}^{T} \frac{X}{(1+r)^t}$$

$$= \frac{X}{r} \left[1 - \frac{1}{(1+r)^t} \right]$$

$$Price = \sum_{i=1}^{2n} \frac{C_t}{\left(1+\frac{Yld}{2}\right)^n} + \frac{P}{\left(1+\frac{Yld}{2}\right)^{2n}}$$

$$= \frac{C}{\left(\frac{Yld}{2}\right)}\left[1 - \frac{1}{\left(1+\frac{Yld}{2}\right)^{2n}}\right] + \left[\frac{P}{\left(1+\frac{Yld}{2}\right)^{2n}}\right]$$

$$Yd_{Income} = \frac{Coupon}{Price}$$

$$Future\ Value = C\left[\frac{(1+r)^n - 1}{r}\right]$$

$$Mortgage = principal\left[\frac{r\ (1+r)^m}{(1+r)^m - 1}\right]$$

$$\frac{\Delta P}{P} = -\frac{Duration}{\left(1 + \frac{Y}{n}\right)} * \Delta Y + \frac{1}{2}\frac{Convexity}{\left(1 + \frac{Y}{n}\right)^2} * \Delta Y^2$$

$$Hedge\ Ratio:\quad Contracts = \frac{Portfolio\ Market\ Value}{\$multiplier * futures\ value} * (\beta_P - \beta_T)$$

$$Black\ Scholes:\quad C = S\ N[\ d_1\ ] - X\ e^{-rt}\ N[\ d_2\ ]$$

$$d_1 = \left[\frac{\ln\left(\frac{S}{X}\right) + (r + \frac{\sigma^2}{2})t}{\sigma\ \sqrt{t}}\right]$$

$$d_2 = \left[\ d_1 - \sigma\ \sqrt{t}\ \right]$$

$$Put\ Call\ parity:\quad P = C - S + [\ X + Div]\ e^{-rt}$$

$$Standardized\ Normal:\ Z = \frac{X_i - \mu}{\sigma}$$